GENOCIDE

Genocide: A Comprehensive Introduction is the most wide-ranging textbook on genocide yet published. The book is designed as a text for upper-undergraduate and graduate students, as well as a primer for non-specialists and general readers interested in learning about one of humanity's enduring blights.

Over the course of sixteen chapters, genocide scholar Adam Jones:

- Provides an introduction to genocide as both a historical phenomenon and an analytical-legal concept.
- Discusses the role of imperialism, war, and social revolution in fueling genocide.
- Supplies no fewer than seven full-length case studies of genocides worldwide, each with an accompanying box-text.
- Explores perspectives on genocide from the social sciences, including psychology, sociology, anthropology, political science/international relations, and gender studies.
- Considers "The Future of Genocide," with attention to historical memory and genocide denial; initiatives for truth, justice, and redress; and strategies of intervention and prevention.

Written in clear and lively prose, liberally sprinkled with illustrations and personal testimonies from genocide survivors, *Genocide: A Comprehensive Introduction* is destined to become a core text of the new generation of genocide scholarship. An accompanying website (www.genocidetext.net) features a broad selection of supplementary materials, teaching aids, and Internet resources.

Adam Jones, Ph.D. is currently Associate Research Fellow in the Genocide Studies Program at Yale University. His recent publications include the edited volumes *Gendercide and Genocide* (2004) and *Genocide, War Crimes and the West: History and Complicity* (2004). He is co-founder and executive director of Gendercide Watch (www.gendercide.org).

GENOCIDE

A Comprehensive Introduction

Adam Jones

Routledge
Taylor & Francis Group
LONDON AND NEW YORK

First published 2006
by Routledge
2 Park Square, Milton Park, Abingdon, Oxon OX14 4RN

Simultaneously published in the USA and Canada
by Routledge
270 Madison Ave, New York, NY 10016

Reprinted 2007

Routledge is an imprint of the Taylor & Francis Group, an informa business

Typeset in Garamond by Keystroke, Jacaranda Lodge, Wolverhampton
Printed and bound in Great Britain by TJ International Ltd, Padstow, Cornwall

British Library Cataloguing in Publication Data
A catalogue record for this book is available from the British Library

Library of Congress Cataloging in Publication Data
Jones, Adam, 1963–
Genocide : a comprehensive introduction / Adam Jones.
p. cm.
Includes bibliographical references and index.
ISBN 0–415–35384–X (pbk. : alk. paper) – ISBN 0–415–35385–8 (hardback : alk. paper)
1. Genocide. 2. Genocide–Case studies. I. Title.
HV6322.7.J64 2006
304.6'63–dc22
2005030424

ISBN10: 0–415–35385–8 ISBN13: 978–0–415–35385–4 (hbk)
ISBN10: 0–415–35384–X ISBN13: 978–0–415–35384–7 (pbk)
ISBN10: 0–203–34744–7 ISBN13: 978–0–203–34744–7 (ebk)

For Jo and David Jones, givers of life,
and for Dr. Griselda Ramírez Reyes, saver of lives.

So let us not talk falsely now, the hour is getting late.
Bob Dylan, "All Along the Watchtower"

CONTENTS

ILLUSTRATIONS

MAPS

BOXES

ABOUT THE AUTHOR

Adam Jones was born in Singapore in 1963, and grew up in England and Canada. He is currently Associate Research Fellow in the Genocide Studies Program at Yale University. He holds an MA from McGill University and a Ph.D. from the University of British Columbia, both in political science. He has edited two volumes on genocide: *Gendercide and Genocide* (Vanderbilt University Press, 2004) and *Genocide, War Crimes and the West: History and Complicity* (Zed Books, 2004). He has also published two books on the media and political transition. His scholarly articles have appeared in *Review of International Studies, Ethnic and Racial Studies, Journal of Genocide Research, Journal of Human Rights*, and other publications. He is co-founder and executive director of Gendercide Watch (www.gendercide.org), a Web-based educational initiative that confronts gender-selective atrocities worldwide. Jones has lived and traveled in over sixty countries on every populated continent. His freelance journalism and travel photography, along with a selection of scholarly writings, are available at http://adamjones.freeservers.com. Email: adam@genocidetext.net.

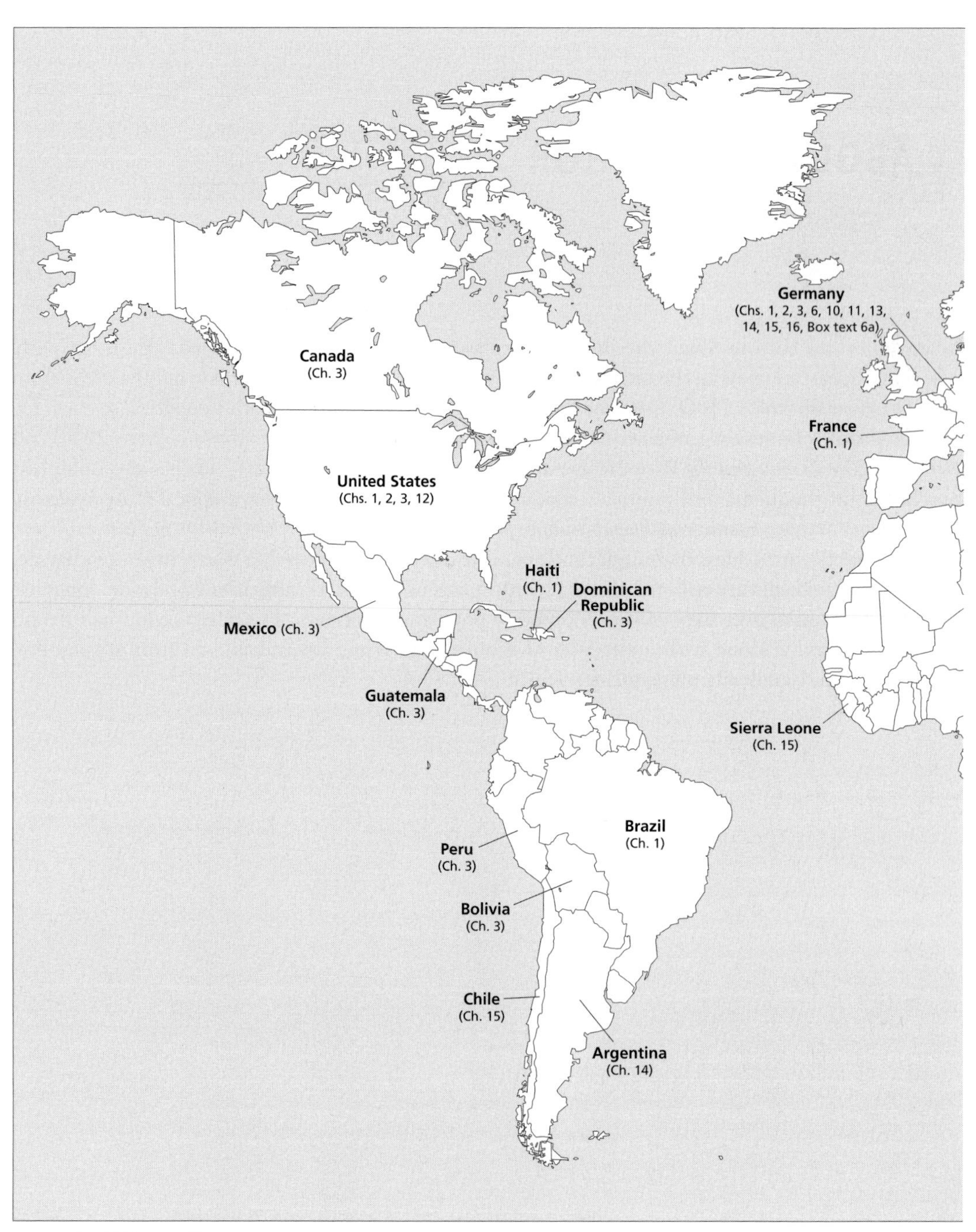

World Map Cases of genocide and mass conflict referenced in this book

Source: Chartwell Illustrators

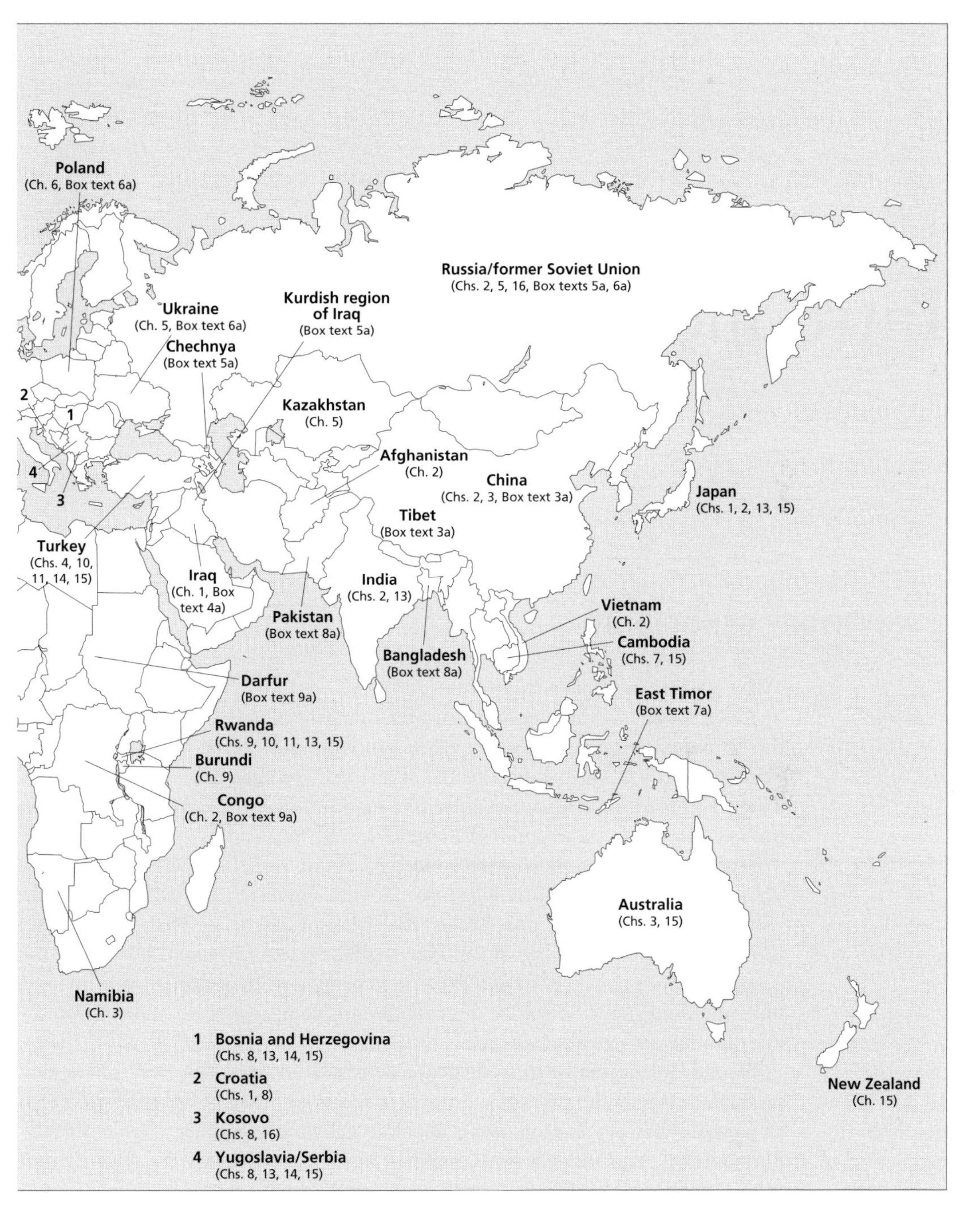

Poland
(Ch. 6, Box text 6a)
Russia/former Soviet Union
(Chs. 2, 5, 16, Box texts 5a, 6a)
Ukraine
(Ch. 5, Box text 6a)
Kurdish region of Iraq
(Box text 5a)
Chechnya
(Box text 5a)
Kazakhstan
(Ch. 5)
Afghanistan
(Ch. 2)
China
(Chs. 2, 3, Box text 3a)
Japan
(Chs. 1, 2, 13, 15)
Tibet
(Box text 3a)
Turkey
(Chs. 4, 10, 11, 14, 15)
Iraq
(Ch. 1, Box text 4a)
India
(Chs. 2, 13)
Pakistan
(Box text 8a)
Vietnam
(Ch. 2)
Cambodia
(Chs. 7, 15)
Bangladesh
(Box text 8a)
Darfur
(Box text 9a)
East Timor
(Box text 7a)
Rwanda
(Chs. 9, 10, 11, 13, 15)
Burundi
(Ch. 9)
Congo
(Ch. 2, Box text 9a)
Australia
(Chs. 3, 15)
Namibia
(Ch. 3)
New Zealand
(Ch. 15)
1 Bosnia and Herzegovina
(Chs. 8, 13, 14, 15)
2 Croatia
(Chs. 1, 8)
3 Kosovo
(Chs. 8, 16)
4 Yugoslavia/Serbia
(Chs. 8, 13, 14, 15)

Introduction

WHY STUDY GENOCIDE?

"Why would you want to study *that*?"

If you spend any time seriously investigating genocide, or even if you only leave this book lying in plain view, it is likely you will have to deal with this question. Underlying it is a tone of distaste and skepticism, perhaps tinged with suspicion. There may be a hint that you are guided by a morbid fixation on the worst of human horrors. How will you respond? Why, indeed, study genocide?

First and foremost, if you are concerned about issues such as peace, human rights, and social justice, there is a sense that with genocide you are confronting the "Big One," what Joseph Conrad called the "heart of darkness." That can be deeply intimidating and disturbing. It can even make you feel trivial and powerless. But genocide is the *opposite* of trivial. Whatever energy and commitment you invest in understanding genocide will be directed towards comprehending and confronting one of humanity's greatest scourges.

Second, intellectually, to study genocide is to study our historical inheritance. It is unfortunately the case that all stages of recorded human existence, and nearly all parts of the world, have known genocide at one time or another, often repeatedly. Furthermore, genocide may be as prevalent in the contemporary era as at any time in history. Inevitably, there is something depressing about this: Will humanity ever change? But there is also interest and personal enlightenment to be gained by delving into the historical record, for which genocide serves as a point of entry. I well remember the period, half a decade ago, that I devoted to voracious reading of the genocide studies literature, and exploring the diverse themes this opened up to me.

For the first time, events as varied as the European witch-hunts, the War of the Triple Alliance in South America (1864–70), the independence struggle in East Pakistan/Bangladesh, the global plagues of maternal mortality and forced labor – all were revealed to my bleary eyes. (I was researching case-studies for the Gendercide Watch website (www.gendercide.org), which explains the eclectic choice of subject matter.) The accounts were grim – sometimes relentlessly so. But they were also spellbinding, and they gave me a better grounding not only in world history, but also in sociology, psychology, anthropology, and a handful of other disciplines.

This raises a third reason to study genocide: it brings you into contact with some of the most interesting and exciting debates in the social sciences and humanities. To what extent should genocide be understood as reflecting epic social transformations such as modernity, the rise of the state, and globalization? How has warfare been transformed in recent times, and how are the "degenerate" and decentralized wars of the present age linked to genocidal outbreaks? How does gender shape genocidal experiences and genocidal strategies? How is history "produced," and what role do memories or denial of genocide play in that production? These are only a few of the themes to be examined in this book. I hope they will lead readers, as they have led me, towards an engagement with cutting-edge debates that have a wider, though not necessarily deeper, significance.

In writing this book, I am standing on the shoulders of giants: the genocide scholars without whose trail-blazing efforts my own work would be inconceivable. You may find their approach and humanity inspiring, as I do. One of my principal concerns is to provide an overview of the core literature in genocide studies; thus each chapter and box-text is accompanied by recommendations for further study.

Modern academic writing, particularly in the social sciences and humanities, is often riddled with impenetrable jargon and not a little pomposity. It would be pleasant to be able to report that genocide studies is free of such baggage. It isn't; but it is less burdened by it than most other fields of study. It seems this has to do with the experience of looking into the abyss, and finding that the abyss looks back. One is forced to ponder one's own human frailty and vulnerability; one is even pressed to confront one's own capacity for hating others, for marginalizing them, for supporting their oppression and annihilation. These realizations aren't pretty, but they are arguably necessary. And they can lead to a certain humility – a rare quality indeed in academia. I once described to a friend why the Danish philosopher Søren Kierkegaard (1813–55) moved me so deeply: "It's like he's grabbing you by the arm and saying, 'Look. We don't have much time. There are important things we need to talk about.'" You sense the same reading much of the genocide-studies literature: that the issues are too vital, and time too limited, to beat around the bush. George Orwell famously described political speech – he could have been referring to some academic writing – as "a mass of words [that] falls upon the facts like soft snow, blurring the outlines and covering up all the details."[1] By contrast, the majority of genocide scholars inhabit the literary equivalent of the Tropics. I hope to take up residence there too.

Finally, some good news for the reader interested in understanding and confronting genocide: your studies and actions may make a difference. To study genocide is to study processes by which *hundreds of millions* of people met brutal ends. But there are many, many people throughout history who have bravely resisted the blind rush to hatred. They are the courageous and decent souls who gave refuge to hunted Jews or desperate Tutsis. They are the religious believers of many faiths who struggled against the tide of evil, and spread instead a message of love, tolerance, and commonality. They are the non-governmental organizations that warned against incipient genocides and carefully documented those they were unable to prevent. They are the leaders and common soldiers – American, British, Soviet, Vietnamese, Indian, Tanzanian, Rwandan, and others – who vanquished genocidal regimes in modern times.[2] And yes, they are the scholars and intellectuals who have honed our understanding of genocide, while at the same time working outside the ivory tower to alleviate it. You will meet some of these individuals in this book. I hope their stories and actions will inspire you to believe that a future free of genocide and other crimes against humanity is possible.

But . . .

Studying genocide, and trying to prevent it, is not to be entered into lightly. A theme that has not been systematically addressed in the genocide studies literature is the psychological and emotional impact such studies can have on the investigator. How many genocide students, scholars, and activists suffer, as do their counterparts in the human rights and social work fields?[3] How many experience depression, insomnia, nightmares as a result of immersing themselves in the most atrocious human conduct?

The trauma is especially intense for those who have actually witnessed genocide, or its direct consequences, up close. During the Turkish genocide against Armenians (Chapter 4), the US Ambassador to Constantinople, Henry Morgenthau, received a stream of American missionaries who had managed to make their way out of the killing zone. "For hours they would sit in my office with tears streaming down their faces," Morgenthau recalled; many had been "broken in health" by the atrocities they had witnessed.[4] My friend Christian Scherrer, who works at the Hiroshima Peace Institute, arrived in Rwanda in November 1994 as part of a United Nations investigation team, only a few months after the slaughter of a million people had been terminated by forces of the Rwandan Patriotic Front (RPF) (see Chapter 9). Rotting bodies were still strewn across the landscape. "For weeks," Scherrer writes,

> following directions given by witnesses, I carefully made my way, step by step, over farmland and grassland. Under my feet, often only half covered with earth, lay the remains of hundreds, indeed thousands, of unfortunate individuals betrayed by their neighbors and slaughtered by specially enlisted bands of assassins . . . a state-sponsored mass murder . . . carried out with a level of mass participation by the majority population the like of which had never been seen before. . . . Many of those who came from outside shared the experience of hundreds of thousands of Rwandans of continuing, for months on end, or even longer, to grieve, to weep internally, and, night after night, to be unable to sleep longer than an hour or two. When they returned to Europe, many of my colleagues felt paralyzed.

He describes the experience as "one of the most painful processes I have ever been through," and the writing of his fine book, *Genocide and Crisis*, as "part of a personal process of grieving." "Investigation into genocide," he adds, "is something that remains with one for life."[5] Even as a latecomer to the Rwandan genocide – and as someone who has never visited the country – I remember being so shaken by reading a massive, agonizingly detailed human rights report on the genocide[6] that I dreamed about Rwanda for many nights, feverish visions of encountering Hutu roadblocks, of smuggling desperate Tutsis to Burundi. . . .

Now that interest in genocide is growing exponentially, and the field of comparative genocide studies along with it, this may be a good time to undertake a survey (say, of members of the International Association of Genocide Scholars) to ascertain how common such symptoms are among those who devote their lives to the theme. Meanwhile, I encourage you – especially if you are just beginning your exploration – to be attentive to signs of personal stress. Talk about it with your fellow students, your colleagues, or family and friends. Dwell on the positive examples of bravery and love for others that the study of genocide regularly provides. If that doesn't work, seek counseling through the resources available on your campus or in your community.

WHAT THIS BOOK TRIES TO DO, AND WHY

I see genocide as inseparable from the broad thrust of history, both ancient and modern – indeed, it is among history's defining features, overlapping a range of central historical processes: war, imperialism, state-building, class struggle. I perceive it as intimately linked to key institutions, in which state or broadly political authorities are often but not always principal actors: forced labor, military conscription, incarceration, female infanticide.

I adopt a comparative approach that does not elevate particular genocides over others, except to the extent that scale and intensity warrant special attention. Virtually all definable human groups – the ethnic, national, racial, and religious ones that anchor the legal definition of genocide, and others besides – have been victims of genocide in the past,[7] and are vulnerable in specific contexts today. Equally, most human collectivities – even vulnerable and oppressed ones – have proved capable of inflicting genocide. This can be a painful acknowledgment for genocide scholars to make, and for that reason it is routinely avoided. But it will be confronted head-on throughout this volume: there are no sacred cows here. Respect for taboos and tender sensibilities takes a back seat to the imperative to *get to grips with genocide* – to confront it in as clear-eyed a way as possible; to reduce the chances that mystification and wishful thinking will cloud recognition, and thereby blunt effective opposition.

The subject of genocide has never been more prominent in the public and academic debate than it is today. As one indication, consider the awarding of both the Pulitzer Prize and the National Book Award to Samantha Power for her 2002 work, *"A Problem From Hell": America and the Age of Genocide*, which criticized Western passivity in the face of genocide.[8] Power's book rapidly became a nucleus around which a mainstream interest in genocide could coalesce.

"A Problem from Hell" was as much culmination as catalyst, however. The field of comparative genocide studies has been developing for almost six decades. But it

languished between the 1940s, when Raphael Lemkin coined the term "genocide" and the UN Convention was propounded, and the early 1980s, when Leo Kuper published his field-defining contribution, *Genocide: Its Political Use in the Twentieth Century* (1981).[9] In the late 1980s and the 1990s, the field blossomed, with the formation of the International Association of Genocide Scholars (IAGS) in 1994, and the publication of dozens of monographs and comparative studies – thousands, if we include the literature focused on the Jewish catastrophe under Nazism.

Despite this proliferation, comparative genocide studies arguably has yet to find its introductory textbook. Some important edited volumes have come closest to establishing themselves as core texts (notably Frank Chalk and Kurt Jonassohn's *History and Sociology of Genocide*, and Samuel Totten *et al.*'s *Century of Genocide: Eyewitness Accounts and Critical Views*).[10] As a single-authored work, the classic in the field probably remains Kuper's *Genocide*; but it is now well over two decades old, and its author sadly deceased. Meanwhile, two fine encyclopedias and a couple of specialized bibliographies have been published, but these are costly and unwieldy for the student or general reader.

Excellent and accessible books on genocide have been published in recent years, though the large majority adopt a specific disciplinary perspective. A partial exception is probably the best of these texts, Alex Alvarez's *Governments, Citizens, and Genocide*, which approaches the subject from the angle of both political science and sociology.[11] Various scholars have explored psychological perspectives, including Roy Baumeister, Ervin Staub, and James Waller.[12] Martin Shaw has added an important volume on *War and Genocide*, from an international relations and conflict studies framework.[13] Meanwhile, highly stimulating work has begun to emanate from the discipline of anthropology. Nancy Scheper-Hughes and Beatriz Manz, among others, have done important work on genocide and crimes against humanity. Their work has been bolstered by two anthologies of anthropological studies edited by Alexander Laban Hinton.[14]

Last but not least, a rich body of case studies and comparative-theoretical material has accumulated – one this book leans on heavily, with appropriate citation. Thus it now seems an opportune moment to offer a comprehensive introductory text: one that samples the wealth of thinking and writing on genocide in an interdisciplinary way, with a broad range of case studies, and with a unified authorial voice.

The first part of *Genocide: A Comprehensive Introduction* seeks to ground readers in the basic historical and conceptual contexts of genocide. It explores the process by which the Polish-Jewish jurist Raphael Lemkin first named and defined the phenomenon, then mobilized a nascent United Nations to outlaw it. His story constitutes a vivid and inspiring portrait of an individual who had a significant, largely unsung impact on modern history. Examination of legal and scholarly definitions and debates may help readers to clarify their own thinking, and situate themselves in the discussion.

The case study section of the book (Part 2) is divided between longer case studies of genocide and capsule studies that complement the detailed treatments. I hope this structure will be conducive to discussion and comparative analysis.

The first three chapters of Part 3 explore social-scientific contributions to the study of genocide – from psychology, sociology, anthropology, and political science/

international relations. Let me indicate the ambit and limitations of this analysis. I am a political scientist by training. As well as devoting a chapter to perspectives from this discipline, I incorporate its insights elsewhere in the text (notably in Chapter 2 on "Imperialism, War, and Social Revolution," and Chapter 16 on "Strategies of Intervention and Prevention"). Likewise, Chapter 14 on "Memory, Forgetting, and Denial" touches on a significant discussion among professional historians, while the analysis of "Justice, Truth, and Redress" (Chapter 15), as well as parts of Chapter 1 on "The Origins of Genocide," explore relevant developments and debates in international law.

Even if a synoptic examination of these disciplines' insights were possible, given space limitations, I would be unable to provide it. The massive proliferation of academic production, of schools and subschools, has effectively obliterated the "renaissance" man or woman, who once moved with facility among varied fields of knowledge. Accordingly, throughout these chapters, my ambition is modest. I seek only to introduce readers to some useful scholarly framings, together with insights that I have found especially relevant and simulating.

This book at least engages with a field – genocide studies – that has been profoundly interdisciplinary from the start. The development of strict disciplinary boundaries is a modern invention, reflecting the growing scale and bureaucratization of the university. In many ways, the barriers it establishes among disciplines are artificial. Political scientists draw on insights from history, sociology, and psychology, and their own work finds readers in those disciplines. Sociology and anthropology are closely related: the former developed as a study of the societies of the industrial West, while in the latter, Westerners studied "primitive" or preindustrial societies. Other linkages and points of interpenetration could be cited. The point is that consideration of a given theme under the rubric of a particular discipline may be arbitrary. To take just one example, "ethnicity" can be approached from sociological, anthropological, psychological, and political science perspectives. I discuss it principally in its sociological context, but would not wish to see it fixed there.

Part 4, "The Future of Genocide," adopts a more forward-looking approach, seeking to familiarize readers with contemporary debates over historical memory and genocide denial, as well as mechanisms of justice and redress. The final chapter, "Strategies of Intervention and Prevention," allows readers to evaluate options for suppressing the scourge.

"How does one handle this subject?" wrote Terrence Des Pres in the preface to *The Survivor*, his study of life in the Nazi concentration camps. His answer: "One doesn't; not well, not finally. No degree of scope or care can equal the enormity of such events or suffice for the sorrow they encompass. Not to betray it is as much as I can hope for."[15] His words resonate. In my heart, I know this book is an audacious enterprise, but I have tried to expand the limits of my empathy and, through wide reading, my interdisciplinary understanding. I have also benefited from the insights and corrections of other scholars and general readers, whose names appear in the acknowledgments.

While I must depict particular genocides (and the contributions of entire academic disciplines) in very broad strokes, I have tried throughout to find room for individuals, whether as victims, perpetrators, or rescuers. I hope this serves to counter some of the abstraction and depersonalization that is inevitable in a general survey. A list of relevant internet sources, and a filmography-in-progress, may be found on the Web page for this book at http://www.genocidetext.net.[16]

ACKNOWLEDGMENTS

Genocide: A Comprehensive Introduction was born over a lively dinner in Durban, South Africa, at which I chanced to sit at the elbow of Taylor & Francis commissioning editor Craig Fowlie. I understand that one of Craig's tasks is to travel the world marshalling promising-sounding book proposals. Not bad work if you can get it. I am truly grateful for Craig's early and enduring support. Thanks also to Nadia Seemungul and Steve Thompson, and to Ann King for her sterling copy-editing.

Colleagues and administrators at the CIDE research institute in Mexico City either encouraged my study of genocide or sought to divert me from it. I gained from the positive and negative inspiration alike. For the former, thanks to Jorge Chabat, Farid Kahhat, Jean Meyer, Susan Minushkin, and Jesús Velasco. The bulk of this book was written while on contract as a project researcher at CIDE in 2004. My research assistant, Pamela Huerta, compiled comprehensive briefs for the Cambodia case study and the Tibet and Congo/Darfur box texts. Pamela, your skill and enthusiasm were greatly appreciated.

Much of *Genocide: A Comprehensive Introduction* was written during travels in late 2004 through Córdoba province in central Argentina, and in vibrant Buenos Aires. My thanks to the Argentine friends who welcomed me, especially Julieta Ayala; to the hoteliers and apartment agents who put me up along the way, notably Jorge Rodríguez; and the restaurant staff who kept me fueled with that awesome steak and *vino tinto.*

The manuscript was completed in the Mexico City home of Jessica and Esperanza Rodríguez; my warm thanks to both. In Puebla, Fabiola Martínez asked probing questions, engaged in stimulating discussions, and supplied me with tender care besides. *Gracias, mi Fabi-losa.* What one could call "post-production" took place at Yale University, where I was fortunate to obtain a two-year postdoctoral fellowship in the Genocide Studies Program for 2005–07. I will use this time to research a book on genocide and communication. I am honored by the opportunity to conduct research at one of the world's leading universities. I am especially grateful to Ben Kiernan, eminent Cambodia scholar and director of the Genocide Studies Program, for his interest in my work and support of it over the past few years. Thanks also to the Yale Center for International and Area Studies (YCIAS); its director Ian Shapiro; and associate director Richard Kane.

Kenneth J. Campbell, Jo and David Jones, René Lemarchand, Benjamin Madley, and Nicholas Robins generously read the entire manuscript. I benefited hugely from their feedback. Jo and David's meticulous proofreading of the typescript might have landed them in the dedication to this volume even if they weren't my parents. As for Ben Madley, our weekly or biweekly lunches at Yale, when we went through his insightful comments on individual chapters, were simply the most stimulating and thought-provoking discussions I have ever had about genocide. As with Jo and David, there are few pages of this book that do not bear Ben's stamp.

Other scholars, professionals, and general readers who read and commented upon various chapters include: Jennifer Archer, Peter Balakian, Donald Bloxham, Peter Burns, Thea Halo, Alex Hinton, Kal Holsti, Craig Jones, Ben Kiernan, Mark Levene, Evelin Lindner, Linda Melvern, Kathleen Morrow, A. Dirk Moses, Margaret Power, Victoria Sanford, and Christian Scherrer. I also acknowledge the insights and recommendations of two anonymous reviewers of the book proposal for Routledge. Although I have not always heeded these individuals' suggestions, their perspectives have been absolutely crucial, and have rescued me from numerous mistakes and misinterpretations. I accept full responsibility for the errors and oversights that remain.

Friends and family have always buttressed me, and stoked my passion for studying history and humanity. This book could not have been written without the nurture and guidance provided by my parents and my brother, Craig. Warmest thanks also to Atenea Acevedo, Carla Bergman, David Buchanan, Charli Carpenter, Mike Charko, Ferrel Christensen, Terry and Meghan Evenson, Jay Forster, Andrea and Steve Gunner, Henry Huttenbach, Luz María Johnson, David Liebe, John Margesson, Eric Markusen, Peter Prontzos, Hamish Telford, and Miriam Tratt.

Dr. Griselda Ramírez Reyes shares the dedication of this work. Griselda is a pediatric neurosurgeon in Mexico City. I have stood literally at her elbow as she opened the head of a three-week-old girl, and extracted a cancerous tumour seemingly half the size of the infant's brain. I hope to open a few minds myself with this work, but I would not pretend the task compares.

Adam Jones
New Haven, USA, March 2006
adam@genocidetext.net

NOTES

1 George Orwell, "Politics and the English Language" (1946), in *Inside the Whale and Other Essays* (Harmondsworth: Penguin, 1974). Available on the Web at http://www.resort.com/~prime8/Orwell/patee.html.

2 The Second World War Allies against the Nazis and Japanese; Tanzanians against Idi Amin's Uganda; Vietnamese in Cambodia in 1979; Indians in Bangladesh in 1971; soldiers of the Rwandan Patriotic Front in 1994. See also Chapter 16.

3 Writing the first in-depth study of the Soviet "terror-famine" in Ukraine in 1932–33 (see Chapter 5), Robert Conquest confronted only indirectly the "inhuman, unimaginable misery" of the famine; but he still found the task "so distressing that [I] sometimes hardly felt able to proceed." Conquest, *The Harvest of Sorrow: Soviet Collectivization and the Terror-Famine* (New York: Oxford University Press, 1986), p. 10. Donald Miller and Lorna Touryan Miller, who interviewed a hundred survivors of the Armenian genocide, wrote: "During this project our emotions have ranged from melancholy to anger, from feeling guilty about our own privileged status to being overwhelmed by the continuing suffering in our world." They described experiencing "a permanent loss of innocence about the human capacity for evil," as well as "a recognition of the need to combat such evil." Miller and Miller, *Survivors: An Oral History of the Armenian Genocide* (Berkeley,

CA: University of California Press, 1999), p. 4. After an immersion in the archive of S-21 (Tuol Sleng), the Khmer Rouge killing center in Cambodia, David Chandler found that "the terror lurking inside it has pushed me around, blunted my skills, and eroded my self-assurance. The experience at times has been akin to drowning." Chandler, *Voices from S-21: Terror and History in Pol Pot's Secret Prison* (Berkeley, CA: University of California Press, 1999), p. 145. Brandon Hamber notes that "many of the staff" working with the Truth and Reconciliation Commission in South Africa have experienced "nightmares, paranoia, emotional bluntness, physical problems (e.g. headaches, ulcers, exhaustion, etc.), high levels of anxiety, irritability and aggression, relationship difficulties and substance abuse related problems." Hamber, "The Burdens of Truth," in David E. Lorey and William H. Beezley, eds, *Genocide, Collective Violence, and Popular Memory: The Politics of Remembrance in the Twentieth Century* (Wilmington, DL: Scholarly Resources, Inc., 2002), p. 96.

4 Peter Balakian, *The Burning Tigris: The Armenian Genocide and America's Response* (New York: HarperCollins, 2003), p. 278.

5 Christian P. Scherrer, *Genocide and Crisis in Central Africa: Conflict Roots, Mass Violence, and Regional War* (Westport, CT: Praeger, 2002), pp. 1, 7.

6 African Rights, *Rwanda: Death, Despair and Defiance*, rev. edn (London: African Rights, 1995). The reader who manages to make it through the 300-page chapter titled "A Policy of Massacres" is then confronted with another 300-page chapter titled "Genocidal Frenzy."

7 "Genocide has been practiced throughout most of history in all parts of the world, although it did not attract much attention because genocide was usually accepted as the deserved fate of the vanquished." Kurt Jonassohn with Karin Solveig Björnson, *Genocide and Gross Human Rights Violations in Comparative Perspective* (New Brunswick, NJ: Transaction Publishers, 1998), p. 50.

8 Samantha Power, *"A Problem from Hell": America and the Age of Genocide* (New York: Basic Books, 2002).

9 Leo Kuper, *Genocide: Its Political Use in the Twentieth Century* (Harmondsworth: Penguin, 1981).

10 Frank Chalk and Kurt Jonassohn, *The History and Sociology of Genocide: Analyses and Case Studies* (New Haven, CT: Yale University Press, 1990); Samuel Totten, William S. Parsons and Israel Charny, eds, *Century of Genocide: Eyewitness Accounts and Critical Views* (New York: Routledge, 2004) (2nd edn).

11 Alex Alvarez, *Governments, Citizens, and Genocide: A Comparative and Interdisciplinary Approach* (Bloomington, IN: Indiana University Press, 2001).

12 Roy F. Baumeister, *Evil: Inside Human Violence and Cruelty* (New York: W.H. Freeman, 1999); James Waller, *Becoming Evil: How Ordinary People Commit Genocide and Mass Killing* (Oxford: Oxford University Press, 2002); Ervin Staub, *Roots of Evil: The Origins of Genocide and Other Group Violence* (New York: Cambridge University Press, 1989).

13 Martin Shaw, *War and Genocide: Organized Killing in Modern Society* (Cambridge: Polity Press, 2003).

14 Alexander Laban Hinton, ed., *Genocide: An Anthropological Reader* (Oxford: Blackwell Publishers, 2002); Alexander Laban Hinton, ed., *Annihilating Difference: The Anthropology of Genocide* (Berkeley, CA: University of California Press, 2002).

15 Terrence Des Pres, *The Survivor: An Anatomy of Life in the Death Camps* (Oxford: Oxford University Press, 1976), pp. v–vi.

16 Readers who are interested in the background to my engagement with genocide studies can consult the short essay, "Genocide: A Personal Journey," at http://www.genocidetext.net/personal_journey.htm.

PART ONE OVERVIEW

CHAPTER 1

The Origins of Genocide

This chapter analyzes the origins of genocide as a global-historical phenomenon, providing a sense, however fragmentary, of genocide's frequency through history. It then turns to examine the origin and evolution of the concept itself, and explore some "contested cases" that test the boundaries of the genocide framework. No chapter in the book tries to cover so much ground, and the discussion at points may seem complicated and confusing, so please fasten your seatbelts.

GENOCIDE IN PREHISTORY, ANTIQUITY, AND EARLY MODERNITY

"The word is new, the concept is ancient," wrote Leo Kuper in his seminal text of genocide studies (1981).[1*] The roots of genocide are lost in distant millennia, and will remain so unless an "archaeology of genocide" can be developed.[2] The difficulty, as Frank Chalk and Kurt Jonassohn pointed out in their early study, is that such historical records as exist are ambiguous and undependable. While history today is generally written with some fealty to "objective" facts, most previous accounts aimed rather to praise the writer's patron (normally the leader) and to emphasize the superiority of one's own gods and religious beliefs. They may also have been intended

* Throughout this book, to reduce footnoting, I gather sequential quotations and citations from the same source into an omnibus note at the end of the passage. Epigraphs for chapters and sections are not footnoted.

as rattling good stories – so that when Homer quotes King Agamemnon's quintessential pronouncement of root-and-branch genocide, one cannot know what basis it might have in fact:

> We are not going to leave a single one of them alive, down to the babies in their mothers' wombs – not even they must live. The whole people must be wiped out of existence, and none be left to think of them and shed a tear.[3]

Factually reliable or not, Agamemnon's chilling command encapsulates a fondly held fantasy of kings and commoners alike. Humanity has always nurtured conceptions of social difference that generate a primordial sense of in-group versus out-group, as well as hierarchies of good and evil, superior and inferior, desirable and undesirable. Chalk and Jonassohn again:

> Historically and anthropologically peoples have always had a name for themselves. In a great many cases, that name meant "the people" to set the owners of that name off against all other people who were considered of lesser quality in some way. If the differences between the people and some other society were particularly large in terms of religion, language, manners, customs, and so on, then such others were seen as less than fully human: pagans, savages, or even animals.[4]

The fewer the shared values and standards, the more likely members of the out-group were (and are) to find themselves beyond the "universe of obligation," in sociologist Helen Fein's evocative phrase. Hence the advent of "religious traditions of contempt and collective defamation, stereotypes, and derogatory metaphor indicating the victim is inferior, sub-human (animals, insects, germs, viruses) or super-human (Satanic, omnipotent)." If certain classes of people are "pre-defined as alien . . . subhuman or dehumanized, or the enemy," it follows that they must "be eliminated in order that we may live (Them or Us)."[5]

A vivid example of this mindset is the text that underpins the cultural tradition common to most readers of this book: the biblical Old Testament. This frequently depicts God, as one commentator put it, as "a despotic and capricious sadist,"[6] and his followers as *génocidaires* (genocidal killers). The trend starts early on, in the Book of Genesis (6: 17–19), where God decides "to destroy all flesh in which is the breath of life from under heaven," with the exception of Noah and a nucleus of human and animal life. Elsewhere, "the principal biblical rationale for genocide is the danger that God's people will be infected (by intermarriage, for example) by the religious practices of the people who surround them. They are to be a holy people – i.e., a people kept apart, separated from their idolatrous neighbors. Sometimes, the only sure means of accomplishing this is to destroy the neighbors."[7] Thus, in 1 Samuel 15: 2–3, "the LORD of hosts" declares: "I will punish the Amalekites for what they did in opposing the Israelites when they came up out of Egypt. Now go and attack Amalek, and utterly destroy all that they have; do not spare them, but kill both man and woman, child and infant, ox and sheep, camel and donkey."[8] Sometimes, as in Numbers 31, the genocide is more selective – too selective for God's tastes. As Yehuda Bauer summarizes this passage:

> All Midianite men are killed by the Israelites in accordance with God's command, but his order, transmitted by Moses, to kill all the women as well is not carried out, and God is angry. Moses berates the Israelites, whereupon they go out and kill all the women and all the male children; only virgin girls are left alive, for obvious reasons.[9]

"Obvious reasons," in that many genocides in prehistory and antiquity were designed not just to eradicate enemy ethnicities, but to incorporate and exploit some of their members. Usually, it was children (particularly girls) and women who were spared murder. They were simultaneously seen as unable to offer physical resistance, and as sources of future offspring for the dominant group (descent in patrilineal society being traced through the bloodline of the male). We see here the roots of *gendercide* against adult males and adolescent boys, discussed further in Chapter 13.

A combination of gender-selective (gendercidal) mass killing and root-and-branch genocide pervades accounts of the wars of antiquity. Chalk and Jonassohn provide a wide-ranging selection of historical events such as the Assyrian Empire's root-and-branch depredations in the first half of the first millennium BCE,* and the destruction of Melos by Athens during the Peloponnesian War (fifth century BCE), a gendercidal rampage described by Thucydides in his "Melian Dialogue."

Rome's siege and eventual razing of Carthage at the close of the Third Punic War (149–46 BCE) has been labeled "The First Genocide" by Yale scholar Ben Kiernan. The "first" designation is debatable; the label of genocide, less so. Fueled by the documented ideological zealotry of the senator Cato, Rome sought to suppress the supposed threat posed by (disarmed, mercantile) Carthage. "Of a population of 2–400,000, at least 150,000 Carthaginians perished," writes Kiernan. The "Carthaginian solution" found many echoes in the warfare of subsequent centuries.[10]

Among Rome's other victims during its imperial ascendancy were the followers of Jesus Christ. After his death at Roman hands in 33 CE, Christ's growing legions of followers were subjected to savage persecutions and mass murder. The scenes of torture and public spectacle were duplicated by Christians themselves during Europe's medieval era (approximately the ninth to fourteenth centuries CE). This period produced onslaughts such as the Crusades: religiously sanctified campaigns against "unbelievers," whether in France (the Albigensian crusade against heretic Cathars) or in the Holy Land of the Middle East.[11] Further *génocidaires* arose on the other side of the world. In the thirteenth century, a million or so Mongol horsemen under their leader, Genghis Khan, surged out of the grasslands of East Asia to lay waste to vast territories, extending to the gates of Western Europe; "entire nations were exterminated, leaving behind nothing but rubble, fallow fields, and bones."[12]

* "BCE" means "Before the Common Era," and replaces the more familiar but ethnocentric "BC" (Before Christ). "CE" replaces "AD" (*Anno Domini*, Latin for "year of the Lord"). For discussion, see ReligiousTolerance.org, "The Use of 'CE' and 'BCE' to Identify Dates," http://www.religioustolerance.org/ce.htm.

In addition to religious and cultural beliefs, what appears to have motivated these genocides was the hunger for wealth, power, and fame. These factors combined to fuel the genocides of the early modern era, dating from approximately 1492, the year of Caribbean Indians' fateful (and fatal) discovery of Christopher Columbus. The encounter between expansionist European civilization and the indigenous populations of the world is detailed in Chapter 3. The following section focuses briefly on two cases from the early modern era: a European one that presages the genocidal civil wars of the twentieth century, and an African one reminding us that genocide knows no geographical or cultural boundaries.

The Vendée uprising

In 1789, French revolutionaries, inspired by the example of their American counterparts, overthrew the despotic regime of King Louis XVI and established a new order based on the "Rights of Man." Their actions provoked immediate and intractable opposition at home and abroad. European armies massed on French borders, posing a mortal threat to the revolutionary government in Paris, and in March 1793 – following the execution of King Louis and the imposition of a *levée en masse* (mass conscription) – homegrown revolt sprouted in the Vendée. The population of this isolated and conservative region of western France declared itself unalterably opposed to the replacement of their priests by pro-revolutionary designates, and the evisceration of the male population by the *levée*. Well trained and led by royalist officers, Vendeans rose up against the central authority. That authority was itself undergoing a rapid radicalization: the notorious "Terror" of the Jacobin faction was instituted the same month as the rebellion in St.-Florent-le-Vieil. The result was a ferocious civil war that, according to French author Reynald Secher among others, constituted a genocide against the Vendean people.[13]

Early rebel victories were achieved through the involvement of all demographic sectors of the Vendée, and humiliated the central authority. Fueled by the ideological fervor of the Terror, and by foreign and domestic counter-revolution, the revolutionaries in Paris implemented a classic campaign of root-and-branch genocide. Under Generals Jean-Baptiste Carrier and Louis Marie Turreau, the Republican authorities launched a scorched-earth drive by the aptly named *colonnes infernales* ("hellish columns"). On December 11, 1793, Carrier wrote to the Committee of Public Safety in Paris, pledging to purge the Vendean peasantry "absolutely and totally."[14] Similar edicts by General Turreau in early 1794 were enthusiastically approved by the Committee, which declared that the "race of brigands" in the Vendée was to be "exterminated to the last." This included even children, who were "just as dangerous [as adults], because they were or were in the process of becoming brigands." Root-and-branch extermination was "both sound and pure," the Committee wrote, and should "show great results."[15]

The resulting slaughter targeted all inhabitants of the Vendée – even those who supported the Republicans (in today's terminology, these victims were seen as "collateral damage"). Specifically, none of the traditional gender-selective exemptions was granted to adult females, who stood accused of fomenting the rebellion through their defense of conservative religion, and their "goad[ing] . . . into martyrdom" of Vendean men.[16] In the account of a Vendean abbé, perhaps self-interested but buttressed by other testimony:

> There were poor girls, completely naked, hanging from tree branches, hands tied behind their backs, after having been raped. It was fortunate that, with the Blues [Republicans] gone, some charitable passersby delivered them from this shameful torment. Elsewhere, in a refinement of barbarism, perhaps without precedent, pregnant women were stretched out and crushed beneath wine presses. . . . Bloody limbs and nursing infants were carried in triumph on the points of bayonets.[17]

Possibly 150,000 people died in the carnage, though not all were civilians. The generalized character of the killings was conveyed by post-genocide census figures, which evidenced not the usual war-related disparity of male versus female victims, but a rough – and rare – parity. Only after this "ferocious . . . expression of ideologically charged avenging terror,"[18] and with the collapse of the Committee of Public Safety in Paris, did the genocidal impetus wane, though scattered clashes with rebels continued through 1796.

In the context of comparative genocide studies, the Vendée uprising stands as a notable example of a mass-killing campaign that has only recently been conceptualized as "genocide." This designation is not universally shared, but it seems apt in light of the large-scale murder of a designated group (the Vendean civilian population).

Zulu genocide

Between 1810 and 1828, the Zulu kingdom under its dictatorial leader, Shaka Zulu, waged one of the most ambitious campaigns of expansion and annihilation the region has ever known. Huge swathes of present-day South Africa and Zimbabwe were laid waste by Zulu armies. The European invasion of these regions, which began shortly after, was greatly assisted by the upheaval and depopulation caused by the Zulu assault.

The scale of the destruction was such, and the obliteration or dispersal of victims so intensive, that relatively little historical evidence was left to bear testimony to the terror. But it remains alive in the oral traditions of peoples of the region whose ancestors were subjugated, slaughtered, or put to flight by the Zulus.[19] "To this day, peoples in Zimbabwe, Malawi, Zambia, Tanzania, Kenya, and Uganda can trace their descent back to the refugees who fled from Shaka's warriors."[20]

At times, Shaka apparently implemented a gender-selective extermination strategy that is all but unique in the historical record. In conquering the Butelezi clan, Shaka "conceived the then [and still] quite novel idea of utterly demolishing them as a separate tribal entity by incorporating all their manhood into his own clan or following," thereby bolstering his own military; but he "usually destroyed women, infants, and old people," who were deemed useless for his expansionist purposes.[21]

However, root-and-branch strategies reminiscent of the French rampage in the Vendée seem also to have been common. According to Yale historian Michael Mahoney, Zulu armies often aimed not only at defeating enemies but at "their total destruction. Those exterminated included not only whole armies, but also prisoners of war, women, children, and even dogs."[22] Especially brutal means, including impaling, were chosen to eliminate the targets. In exterminating the helpless followers of Beje, a minor Kumalo chief, Shaka determined "not to leave alive even a child, but [to] exterminate the whole tribe," according to a foreign witness. When the foreigners protested against the slaughter of women and children, claiming they "could do no injury," Shaka responded in language that would have been familiar to the French revolutionaries: "Yes they could," he declared. "They can propagate and bring [bear] children, who may become my enemies . . . therefore I command you to kill all."[23]

Mahoney characterizes these policies as genocidal. "If genocide is defined as a state-mandated effort to annihilate whole peoples, then Shaka's actions in this regard must certainly qualify." He points out that the term adopted by the Zulus to denote their campaign of expansion and conquest, *izwekufa*, derives "from Zulu *izwe* (nation, people, polity), and *ukufa* (death, dying, to die). The term is thus identical to 'genocide' in both meaning and etymology."[24]

NAMING GENOCIDE: RAPHAEL LEMKIN

Until the Second World War, the phenomenon of genocide was a "crime without a name," in the words of British Prime Minister Winston Churchill.[25] The man who named the crime, placed it in a global-historical context, and demanded intervention and remedial action was an obscure Polish-Jewish jurist, a refugee from Nazi-occupied Europe, named Raphael Lemkin (1900–59). His personal story is one of the most remarkable of the twentieth century.

Lemkin is an exceptional example of a "norm entrepreneur" (see Chapter 12). In four short years, he succeeded in coining a term – genocide – that concisely captured an age-old historical phenomenon. He supported it with a wealth of historical documentation. He published a lengthy book (*Axis Rule in Occupied Europe*) that applied the concept to campaigns of genocide underway in Lemkin's native Poland and elsewhere in the Nazi-occupied territories. He then waged a successful campaign to persuade the new United Nations to draft a convention against genocide; another successful campaign to obtain the required number of signatures; and another to secure the necessary national ratifications. Yet Lemkin died in obscurity in 1959; his funeral drew just seven people. Only in recent years has the promise of his concept, and the UN convention that incorporated it, begun to be realized.

It is important not to romanticize Lemkin. He was an austere loner who antagonized many of those with whom he came into contact.[26] His preoccupation with genocide also drew him into bizarre opposition to other human rights initiatives, such as the Declaration of Human Rights (which became the central rights document of the contemporary age). Many have criticized the ambiguities of the genocide framework, as well as its allegedly archaic elements. We will consider these criticisms shortly. First, though, let us review the extraordinary course of Lemkin's life. This is examined at length in the first chapters of Samantha Power's *"A Problem from Hell,"* with access to Lemkin's letters and papers; the following account is based on Power's study.[27]

Growing up in a Jewish family in Wolkowysk, a town in eastern Poland, Lemkin developed a talent for languages (he would end up mastering a dozen or more), and a passionate curiosity about the national cultures that produced them. He was struck by accounts of the suffering of Christians at Roman hands, and its parallel in the pogroms then afflicting the Jews of eastern Poland. Thus began Lemkin's lifelong obsession with mass killing in history and the contemporary world. He "raced through an unusually grim reading list"[28] that familiarized him with cases from antiquity and the medieval era (including Carthage, discussed above, and the fate of the Aztec and Inca empires, described in Chapter 3). "I was appalled by the frequency of the evil," he recalled later, "and, above all, by the impunity coldly relied upon by the guilty."[29] *Why?* was the question that began to consume Lemkin. Why did states kill their own and other citizens on the basis of nationality, ethnicity, or religion? Why did onlookers ignore the killing, or applaud it? Why didn't someone intervene?

Lemkin determined to stage an intellectual and activist intervention in what he at first called "barbarity" and "vandalism." The former referred to "the premeditated destruction of national, racial, religious and social collectivities," while the latter he described as the "destruction of works of art and culture, being the expression of the particular genius of these collectivities."[30] At a conference of European legal scholars in Madrid in 1933, Lemkin's framing was first presented (though not by its author; the Polish government denied him a travel visa). Despite the post-First World War prosecutions of Turks for "crimes against humanity" (Chapter 4), governments and public opinion leaders were still wedded to the notion that state sovereignty trumped atrocities against a state's own citizens. It was this legal impunity that rankled and galvanized Lemkin more than anything else. But the Madrid delegates did not share his passionate concern. They refused to adopt a resolution against the crimes Lemkin set before them; the matter was tabled.

Undeterred, Lemkin continued his campaign. He presented his arguments in legal forums throughout Europe in the 1930s, and as far afield as Cairo, Egypt. The outbreak of the Second World War found him at the heart of the inferno – in Poland, with Nazi forces invading from the West, and Soviets from the East. As Polish resistance crumbled, Lemkin took flight. He traveled first to eastern Poland, and then to Vilnius, Lithuania. From that Baltic city he made use of connections in Sweden, and succeeded in securing refuge there.

After a spell of teaching in Stockholm, the United States beckoned. Lemkin believed the US would be both receptive to his framework, and in a position to actualize it in a way that Europe under the Nazi yoke could not. An epic 14,000-mile journey took him across the Soviet Union by train to Vladivostok, by boat to Japan, and across the Pacific. In the US, he moonlighted at Yale University's Law School before moving to Durham, North Carolina, where he had been offered a professorship at Duke University.

In his new American surroundings, Lemkin struggled with his concepts and vocabulary. "Vandalism" and "barbarity" had not struck much of a chord with his

Figure 1.1 Raphael Lemkin (1900–59)

Source: Hans Knopf/ Courtesy Jim Fussell/ preventgenocide.org.

legal audiences. Inspired by, of all things, the Kodak camera,[31] Lemkin trolled through his impressive linguistic resources for a term that was concise and memorable. He settled on a neologism with both Greek and Latin roots: the Greek "genos," meaning race or tribe, and the Latin "cide," or killing. "Genocide" was the intentional destruction of national groups on the basis of their collective identity. Physical killing was an important part of the picture, but it was only a part, as Lemkin stressed repeatedly:

> By "genocide" we mean the destruction of a nation or an ethnic group. . . . Generally speaking, genocide does not necessarily mean the immediate destruction of a nation, except when accomplished by mass killings of all members of a nation. It is intended rather to signify a coordinated plan of different actions aiming at the destruction of essential foundations of the life of national groups, with the aim of annihilating the groups themselves. The objectives of such a plan would be disintegration of the political and social institutions of culture, language, national feelings, religion, and the economic existence of national groups, and the destruction of the personal security, liberty, health, dignity, and even the lives of the individuals belonging to such groups. Genocide is directed against the national group as an entity, and the actions involved are directed against individuals, not in their individual capacity, but as members of the national group.

> . . . Genocide has two phases: one, destruction of the national pattern of the oppressed group; the other the imposition of the national pattern of the oppressor. This imposition, in turn, may be made upon the oppressed population which is allowed to remain, or upon the territory alone, after removal of the population and the colonization of the area by the oppressor's own nationals.[32]

The critical question, for Lemkin, was whether the multifaceted campaign proceeded under the rubric of policy. To the extent that it did, it could be considered genocidal, even if it did not result in the physical destruction of all (or any) members of the group.[33] The issue of whether mass killing is definitional to genocide has been debated ever since, by legal scholars, social scientists, and commentators. Equally vexing for subsequent generations was the emphasis on ethnic and national groups. These predominated as victims in the decades in which Lemkin developed his framework (and in the historical examples he studied). But by the end of the 1940s, and into the twilight of the Stalinist era in the 1950s, it was clear that political groups would play a prominent if not dominant role as targets for destruction. Moreover, the appellations applied to "communists," or by communists to "kulaks" or "class enemies" – when imposed by a totalitarian state – seemed every bit as difficult to shake as ethnic identifications, if the Nazi and Stalinist onslaughts were anything to go by. This does not even take into account the important but ambiguous areas of cross-over among ethnic, political, and social categories.

But Lemkin would hear little of this. Although he did not exclude political groups as genocide victims, he had a single-minded focus on nationality and ethnicity, for their culture-carrying capacity as he perceived it. His attachment to these core concerns was almost atavistic, and US law professor Stephen Holmes, for one, has faulted him for it:

> Lemkin himself seems to have believed that killing a hundred thousand people of a single ethnicity was very different from killing a hundred thousand people of mixed ethnicities. Like Oswald Spengler, he thought that each cultural group had its own "genius" that should be preserved. To destroy, or attempt to destroy, a culture is a special kind of crime because culture is the unit of collective memory, whereby the legacies of the dead can be kept alive. To kill a culture is to cast its individual members into individual oblivion, their memories buried with their mortal remains. The idea that killing a culture is "irreversible" in a way that killing an individual is not reveals the strangeness of Lemkin's conception from a liberal-individualist point of view.

This archaic-sounding conception has other illiberal implications as well. For one thing, it means that the murder of a poet is morally worse than the murder of a janitor, because the poet is the "brain" without which the "body" cannot function. This revival of medieval organic imagery is central to Lemkin's idea of genocide as a special crime.[34]

It is probably true that Lemkin's formulation had its archaic elements. It is certainly the case that subsequent scholarly and legal interpretations of "Lemkin's word" have tended to be more capacious in their framing. What *can* be defended, I think, is

Lemkin's emphasis on the collective as a target. One can philosophize about the relative weight ascribed to collectives over the individual, as Holmes does; but the reality of modern times is that the vast majority of those murdered *were killed on the basis of a collective identity – even if only one imputed by the killers.* The link between collective and mass, then between mass and large-scale extermination, was the defining dynamic of the twentieth century's unprecedented violence. In his historical studies, Lemkin appears to have read this correctly. Many or most of the examples he cites would be uncontroversial among a majority of genocide scholars today.[35] He saw the Nazis' assaults on Jews, Poles, and Polish Jews for what they were, and labeled the broader genre for the ages.

But for Lemkin's word to resonate today, and into the future, two further developments were required. The UN Convention on the Prevention and Punishment of Genocide (1948), adopted in remarkably short order after Lemkin's indefatigable lobbying, entrenched genocide in international and domestic law. And beginning in the 1970s, a coterie of "comparative genocide scholars," drawing upon a generation's work on the Jewish Holocaust,* began to discuss, debate, and refine Lemkin's concept – a trend that shows no sign of abating.

DEFINING GENOCIDE: THE UN CONVENTION

Lemkin's extraordinary "norm entrepreneurship" around genocide is described in Chapter 12. Suffice it to say for the present that "rarely has a neologism had such rapid success" (William Schabas). Barely a year after Lemkin coined the term, it was included in the Nuremberg indictments of Nazi war criminals (Chapter 15). To Lemkin's chagrin, genocide did not figure in the Nuremberg judgments. However, "by the time the General Assembly completed its standard sitting, with the 1948 adoption of the Convention on the Prevention and Punishment of the Crime of Genocide, 'genocide' had a detailed and quite technical definition as a crime against the law of nations."[36]

The "detailed and technical definition" is as follows:

> *Article I.* The Contracting Parties confirm that genocide, whether committed in time of peace or in time of war, is a crime under international law which they undertake to prevent and to punish.
>
> *Article II.* In the present Convention, genocide means any of the following acts committed with intent to destroy, in whole or in part, a national, ethnical, racial or religious group, as such:

* I use the word "holocaust" generically in this book to refer to especially destructive genocides, such as those against indigenous peoples in the Americas and elsewhere, Ottoman Armenians in the First World War, Jews and Roma during the Second World War, and Tutsis in Rwanda in 1994. Most scholars and commentators capitalize the "h" when referring to the Nazi genocide against the Jews, and I follow this usage when citing "the Jewish Holocaust" (see also Chapter 6, n. 1).

(a) Killing members of the group;
(b) Causing serious bodily or mental harm to members of the group;
(c) Deliberately inflicting on the group conditions of life calculated to bring about its physical destruction in whole or in part;
(d) Imposing measures intended to prevent births within the group;
(e) Forcibly transferring children of the group to another group.

Article III. The following acts shall be punishable:
(a) Genocide;
(b) Conspiracy to commit genocide;
(c) Direct and public incitement to commit genocide;
(d) Attempt to commit genocide;
(e) Complicity in genocide.[37]

Thematically, Lemkin's conviction that genocide needed to be confronted, whatever the context, was ringingly endorsed with the Convention's declaration that genocide is a crime "whether committed in time of peace or in time of war." This removed the road-block thrown up by the Nuremberg trials, which had only considered Nazi crimes committed after the invasion of Poland on September 1, 1939.

The basic thrust of Lemkin's emphasis on ethnic and national groups (at the expense of political groups and social classes) also survived the lobbying and drafting process. In the diverse genocidal strategies cited, meanwhile, we see reflected Lemkin's conception of genocide as a "coordinated plan of different actions aiming at the destruction of essential foundations of the life of national groups, with the aim of annihilating the groups themselves." However, at no point did the Convention's drafters actually define "national, ethnical, racial or religious" groups, and these have been subject to considerable subsequent interpretation. The position of the Rwanda tribunal (ICTR), that "any stable and permanent group" is in fact to be accorded protection under the Convention, is likely to become the norm in future judgments.

With regard to genocidal strategies, note the diversity of actions in Article II that qualify as genocidal – in marked contrast to the normal understanding of "genocide." One does not need to exterminate or seek to exterminate every last member of a designated group. In fact, *one does not need to kill anyone at all to commit genocide!* Inflicting "serious bodily or mental harm" qualifies, as does preventing births or transferring children between groups. It is fair to say, however, that from a legal perspective, genocide unaccompanied by mass killing is rare, and has stood little chance of being prosecuted. (I return below to the question of killing.)

Controversial and ambiguous phrases in the document include the reference to "serious bodily or mental harm" constituting a form of genocide. In practice, this has been interpreted along the lines of the Israeli trial court decision against Adolf Eichmann in 1961, convicting him of the "enslavement, starvation, deportation and persecution of . . . Jews . . . their detention in ghettos, transit camps and concentration camps in conditions which were designed to cause their degradation, deprivation of their rights as human beings, and to . . . cause them inhumane suffering and torture." The Rwanda tribunal (ICTR) adds an interpretation that this includes "bodily or mental torture, inhuman treatment, and persecution," as well as "acts of rape and mutilation." In addition, "several sources correctly take the view that mass deportations under inhumane conditions may constitute genocide if accompanied by the requisite intent."[38] "Measures to prevent births" may be held to include forced sterilization and separation of the sexes. Sexual trauma and impregnation through gang rape have received increasing attention. The destruction of groups "as such" brought complex questions of motive into play. Some drafters saw it as a means of paying lip-service to the element of motive, while others perceived it as a way to side-step the issue altogether.

Historically, it is intriguing to note how many issues of genocide definition and interpretation have their roots in contingent and improvised aspects of the drafting process. The initial draft by the UN Secretariat defined genocide's targets as "a group of human beings," adoption of which could have rendered redundant the subsequent debate over *which* groups qualified.

Responsibility for the exclusion of political groups was long laid at the door of the Soviet Union and its allies, supposedly nervous about possible application of the Convention to Soviet crimes (see Chapter 5). Schabas quashes this notion, pointing out that "rigorous examination of the *travaux* [working papers] fails to confirm a popular impression in the literature that the opposition . . . was some Soviet machination." Political collectivities "were actually included within the enumeration [of designated groups] until an eleventh-hour compromise eliminated the reference." The provision against transferring children between groups, meanwhile, "was added to the Convention almost as an afterthought, with little substantive debate or consideration."[39]

In its opening sentence, the Convention declares that the Contracting Parties "undertake to prevent and to punish" the crime of genocide. A subsequent article (VIII) states that "any Contracting Party may call upon the competent organs of the United Nations to take such action under the Charter of the United Nations as they consider appropriate for the prevention and suppression of acts of genocide or any of the other acts enumerated in Article III." But this leaves actual obligations vague.

BOUNDING GENOCIDE: COMPARATIVE GENOCIDE STUDIES

Between the 1950s and the 1980s, the term "genocide" languished almost unused by scholars. A handful of legal commentaries appeared for a specialized audience.[40] In 1975, Vahakn Dadrian's article "A Typology of Genocide" sparked renewed interest in a comparative framing. It was bolstered by Irving Louis Horowitz's *Genocide: State Power and Mass Murder* (1976), retitled *Taking Lives* in subsequent editions and, foundationally, by Leo Kuper's *Genocide: Its Political Use in the Twentieth Century* (1981). Kuper's work, including a subsequent volume on *The Prevention of Genocide* (1985), was the most significant on genocide since Lemkin's in the 1940s. It was followed by edited volumes and solo publications from Helen Fein, R.J. Rummel, Frank Chalk and Kurt Jonassohn, and Robert Melson, among others.

This early literature drew upon more than a decade of intensive research on the Jewish Holocaust, and most of the scholars were Jewish. "Holocaust Studies" has remained central to the field. But rereading this early work, one is struck by how inclusive and comparative is its framing. It tends to be global in scope, and broadly interdisciplinary at many points. The classic volumes by Chalk and Jonassohn (*The History and Sociology of Genocide*) and Totten *et al.* (*Century of Genocide*) appeared in the early 1990s, and seemed to sum up this drive for catholicity. So too, despite its heavy focus on the Jewish Holocaust, did Israel Charny's *Encyclopedia of Genocide* (1999). A rich body of case-study literature has also developed, with genocides such as those against the Armenians, Cambodians, and East Timorese – as well as indigenous peoples worldwide – receiving serious and sustained attention.

The explosion of public interest in genocide in the 1990s, and the concomitant growth of genocide studies as an academic field, has spawned a profusion of humanistic and social-scientific studies, joined by memoirs and oral histories. (The wider culture has also produced a steady stream of films on genocide and its reverberations, including *The Killing Fields, Schindler's List*, and *Hotel Rwanda.*)

To capture the richness and diversity of the genocide-studies literature in this short section would be a hopeless task. What I hope to do is, first, to use that literature constructively throughout this book; and, second, to provide suggestions for further reading, encouraging readers to explore the bounty for themselves.

With this caveat in place, let me make a few generalizations, touching on debates that will reappear at various points in these pages. Genocide scholars are concerned with two basic tasks. First, they attempt to *define* genocide and *bound* it conceptually. Second, they seek to *prevent* genocide. This implies understanding its comparative dynamics, and generating prophylactic strategies that may be applied in emergencies.

Scholarly definitions of genocide reflect the ambiguities of the Genocide Convention and its constituent debates. They can be confusing in their numerous and often opposed variants. However, surveying some of the definitions on offer, and combining them with the Lemkin and UN framings already cited, we can group them into two broad categories, and isolate some key features and variables.

BOX 1.1 GENOCIDE: SCHOLARLY DEFINITIONS (in chronological order)

Peter Drost (1959)

"Genocide is the deliberate destruction of physical life of individual human beings by reason of their membership of any human collectivity as such."

Vahakn Dadrian (1975)

"Genocide is the successful attempt by a dominant group, vested with formal authority and/or with preponderant access to the overall resources of power, to reduce by coercion or lethal violence the number of a minority group whose ultimate

continued

extermination is held desirable and useful and whose respective vulnerability is a major factor contributing to the decision for genocide."

Irving Louis Horowitz (1976)

"[Genocide is] a structural and systematic destruction of innocent people by a state bureaucratic apparatus. . . . Genocide represents a systematic effort over time to liquidate a national population, usually a minority . . . [and] functions as a fundamental political policy to assure conformity and participation of the citizenry."

Leo Kuper (1981)

"I shall follow the definition of genocide given in the [UN] Convention. This is not to say that I agree with the definition. On the contrary, I believe a major omission to be in the exclusion of political groups from the list of groups protected. In the contemporary world, political differences are at the very least as significant a basis for massacre and annihilation as racial, national, ethnic or religious differences. Then too, the genocides against racial, national, ethnic or religious groups are generally a consequence of, or intimately related to, political conflict. However, I do not think it helpful to create new definitions of genocide, when there is an internationally recognized definition and a Genocide Convention which might become the basis for some effective action, however limited the underlying conception. But since it would vitiate the analysis to exclude political groups, I shall refer freely . . . to liquidating or exterminatory actions against them."

Jack Nusan Porter (1982)

"Genocide is the deliberate destruction, in whole or in part, by a government or its agents, of a racial, sexual, religious, tribal or political minority. It can involve not only mass murder, but also starvation, forced deportation, and political, economic and biological subjugation. Genocide involves three major components: ideology, technology, and bureaucracy/organization."

Yehuda Bauer (1984)

N.B. Bauer distinguishes between "genocide" and "holocaust": "[Genocide is] the planned destruction, since the mid-nineteenth century, of a racial, national, or ethnic group as such, by the following means: (a) selective mass murder of elites or parts of the population; (b) elimination of national (racial, ethnic) culture and religious life with the intent of 'denationalization'; (c) enslavement, with the same intent;

(d) destruction of national (racial, ethnic) economic life, with the same intent; (e) biological decimation through the kidnapping of children, or the prevention of normal family life, with the same intent. . . . [Holocaust is] the planned physical annihilation, for ideological or pseudo-religious reasons, of all the members of a national, ethnic, or racial group."

John L. Thompson and Gail A. Quets (1987)

"Genocide is the extent of destruction of a social collectivity by whatever agents, with whatever intentions, by purposive actions which fall outside the recognized conventions of legitimate warfare."

Isidor Wallimann and Michael N. Dobkowski (1987)

"Genocide is the deliberate, organized destruction, in whole or in large part, of racial or ethnic groups by a government or its agents. It can involve not only mass murder, but also forced deportation (ethnic cleansing), systematic rape, and economic and biological subjugation."

Henry Huttenbach (1988)

"Genocide is any act that puts the very existence of a group in jeopardy."

Helen Fein (1988)

"Genocide is a series of purposeful actions by a perpetrator(s) to destroy a collectivity through mass or selective murders of group members and suppressing the biological and social reproduction of the collectivity. This can be accomplished through the imposed proscription or restriction of reproduction of group members, increasing infant mortality, and breaking the linkage between reproduction and socialization of children in the family or group of origin. The perpetrator may represent the state of the victim, another state, or another collectivity."

Frank Chalk and Kurt Jonassohn (1990)

"Genocide is a form of one-sided mass killing in which a state or other authority intends to destroy a group, as that group and membership in it are defined by the perpetrator."

continued

Helen Fein (1993)

"Genocide is sustained purposeful action by a perpetrator to physically destroy a collectivity directly or indirectly, through interdiction of the biological and social reproduction of group members, sustained regardless of the surrender or lack of threat offered by the victim."

Steven T. Katz (1994)

"[Genocide is] the actualization of the intent, however successfully carried out, to murder in its totality any national, ethnic, racial, religious, political, social, gender or economic group, as these groups are defined by the perpetrator, by whatever means." (*NB*. Modified by Adam Jones in 2000 to read, "murder in whole or in substantial part. . . .")

Israel Charny (1994)

"Genocide in the generic sense means the mass killing of substantial numbers of human beings, when not in the course of military action against the military forces of an avowed enemy, under conditions of the essential defencelessness of the victim."

Irving Louis Horowitz (1996)

"Genocide is herein defined as a *structural and systematic destruction of innocent people by a state bureaucratic apparatus* [emphasis in original]. . . . Genocide means the physical dismemberment and liquidation of people on large scales, an attempt by those who rule to achieve the total elimination of a subject people." (N.B. Horowitz supports "carefully distinguishing the [Jewish] Holocaust from genocide"; he also refers to "the phenomenon of mass murder, for which genocide is a synonym").

Barbara Harff (2003)

"Genocides and politicides are the promotion, execution, and/or implied consent of sustained policies by governing elites or their agents – or, in the case of civil war, either of the contending authorities – that are intended to destroy, in whole or part, a communal, political, or politicized ethnic group."

Discussion

The elements of definition may be divided into "harder" and "softer" positions, paralleling the international–legal distinction between hard and soft law. According to Christopher Rudolph,

> those who favor hard law in international legal regimes argue that it enhances deterrence and enforcement by signaling credible commitments, constraining self-serving auto-interpretation of rules, and maximizing 'compliance pull' through increased legitimacy. Those who favor soft law argue that it facilitates compromise, reduces contracting costs, and allows for learning and change in the process of institutional development.[41]

In genocide scholarship, harder positions are guided by concerns that "genocide" will be rendered banal or meaningless by careless use. Some argue that this diverts attention from the proclaimed uniqueness of the Jewish Holocaust. Softer positions reflect concerns that excessively rigid framings (for example, a focus on the total physical extermination of a group) rule out too many actions that, logically and morally, demand to be included. Their proponents may also wish to see a dynamic and evolving genocide framework, rather than a static and inflexible one.

It should be noted that these basic positions do not map perfectly onto individual authors and authorities. A given definition may even alternate between harder and softer positions – as with the UN Convention, which features a decidedly "soft" framing of genocidal strategies (including non-fatal ones), but a "hard" approach when it comes to the victim groups whose destruction qualifies as genocidal. Steven Katz's 1994 definition, by contrast, features a highly inclusive framing of victimhood, but a tightly restrictive view of genocidal outcomes: these are limited to the total physical destruction of a group. The alteration of just a few words turns it into a softer definition that happens to be my preferred one (see below).

Exploring further, the definitions address genocide's *agents, victims, goals, scale, strategies*, and *intent.*

Among ***agents***, there is a clear focus on state and official authorities – Dadrian's "dominant group, vested with formal authority"; Horowitz's "state bureaucratic apparatus"; Porter's "government or its agents" – to cite three of the first five definitions proposed. However, some scholars abjure the state-centric approach (e.g., Chalk and Jonassohn's "state or other authority"; Fein's [1993] "perpetrator"; Thompson and Quets' "whatever agents"). The UN Convention, too, cites "constitutionally responsible rulers, public officials or private individuals" among possible agents (Article IV). In practice, most genocide scholars continue to emphasize the role of the state, while accepting that in some cases – as with settler colonialism (Chapter 3) – non-state actors may play a prominent or dominant role.

Victims are standardly identified as social minorities. They exhibit deep vulnerability and/or "essential defencelessness" (Charny). This is reflected in the intensively "one-sided mass killing" inflicted upon them (see Dadrian, Horowitz, Chalk and Jonassohn, and Fein [1993]). They may be internally constituted and self-identified (that is, more closely approximating groups "as such," as required by the Genocide

Convention). From other perspectives, however, target groups may be defined by the perpetrators (e.g., Chalk and Jonassohn, Katz). The debate over political target groups is reflected in Leo Kuper's comments. Kuper grudgingly accepts the UN Convention definition, but strongly regrets the exclusion of political groups.

The ***goals*** of genocide are held to be the destruction/eradication of the victim group and/or its culture, but beyond this, the element of motive is surprisingly little stressed. Lemkin squarely designated genocidal "objectives" as the "disintegration of the political and social institutions of culture, language, national feelings, religion, and the economic existence of national groups." Bauer likewise emphasizes "denationalization." Dadrian and Horowitz go a step further, with the former's reference to a collectivity "whose ultimate extermination is held to be desirable and useful," and Horowitz's assertion of a state desire "to assure conformity and participation of the citizenry."

As for required ***scale***, this ranges from Steven Katz's targeting of a victim group "in its totality" (paralleled by Yehuda Bauer's genocide/holocaust distinction), to phrasing like "in whole or part" (Harff, the UN Convention); "in whole or in large part" (Wallimann and Dobkowski); and "in whole or in substantial part" (my modification of Katz's definition). Irving Louis Horowitz emphasizes the absolute dimension of "mass" murder "for which genocide is a synonym."[42] Some scholars maintain a respectful silence on the issue, though the element of mass or "substantial" casualties seems implicit in the cases they select and the analyses they develop.

Many people feel that lumping together a limited killing campaign, such as in Kosovo in 1999, with an overwhelmingly exterminatory one, such as the Nazis' attempted destruction of European Jews, cheapens the concept of "genocide." However, it is worth noting how another core concept of social science and public discourse is deployed: *war*. We readily use "war" to designate conflicts that kill "only" a few hundred or a few thousand people (e.g., the Soccer War of 1969 between El Salvador and Honduras; the Falklands/Malvinas War of 1982), as well as epochal descents into barbarity that kill millions or tens of millions. The gulf between minimum and maximum toll here is comparable to that between Kosovo and the Jewish Holocaust, but the use of "war" is uncontroversial. There seems to be no reason why we should not distinguish between larger and smaller, more or less exterminatory genocides in the same way.

Diverse genocidal ***strategies*** are depicted in the definitions. Lemkin referred to a "coordinated plan of different actions," and the UN Convention listed a range of such acts. For the scholars listed in our set, genocidal strategies may be direct or indirect (Fein [1993]), including "economic and biological subjugation" (Wallimann and Dobkowski). They may include killing of elites (i.e., "eliticide"); "elimination of national (racial, ethnic) culture and religious life with the intent of 'denationalization'"; and "prevention of normal family life, with the same intent" (Bauer). Helen Fein's earlier definition emphasizes "breaking the linkage between reproduction and socialization of children in the family or group of origin," which carries a step further the Convention's injunction against "preventing births within the group."

Regardless of the strategy chosen, a consensus exists that genocide is "committed with intent to destroy" (UN Convention), is "structural and systematic" (Horowitz), "deliberate [and] organized" (Wallimann and Dobkowski), "sustained" (Harff), and "a series of purposeful actions" (Fein; see also Thompson and Quets). Porter and Horowitz stress the additional role of the state bureaucracy.

Crucially, there is growing agreement that group "destruction" must involve mass killing and physical liquidation (see, e.g., Fein [1993], Charny, Horowitz, Katz/Jones). But to repeat: this is not a feature of either Raphael Lemkin's original formulations or of the UN Convention. In both of these definitions, mass killing is only one of a panoply of strategies available to *génocidaires*; the emphasis is on the destruction of the group "as such," not necessarily the physical annihilation of its members.

The question of genocidal intent

Most scholars and legal theorists agree that intent defines genocide. But what defines intent?

We begin by distinguishing *intent* from *motive.* According to Gellately and Kiernan, in criminal law, including international criminal law, the specific motive is irrelevant. Prosecutors need only to prove that the criminal act was intentional, not accidental. A conquest or a revolution that causes total or partial destruction of a group legally qualifies as intentional and therefore as genocide whatever the goal or motive, so long as the acts of destruction were pursued intentionally.[43]

Beyond this, the question of intent, as is so often true in genocide studies, centers on whether a harder or softer framing is preferred. Does one require that intent be wedded to a high degree of *purposive, coordinated action* against a target group? This would seem to be called for by the Genocide Convention's "enigmatic" phrasing, that groups must be targeted "as such." But as we have seen, this phrase was among the spontaneous formulations of the drafting process; it was inserted to satisfy delegates who sought "recognition of a motive component."[44] It was not central to the drafting of the Convention, and it need not dominate the concerns of genocide scholars.

An opposing perspective declares that, regardless of the claimed objective of the actions in question, they are intentional if they are perpetrated with the knowledge *or reasonable expectation* that they will destroy a human group in whole or in part. Legal opinion surrounding genocide has increasingly favored this more liberal interpretation (see also Chapter 15). The Rome Statute of the International Criminal Court (1998) reflects "a relatively broad understanding of intent": "a person has intent where . . . in relation to conduct, that person means to cause that consequence *or is aware that it will occur in the ordinary course of events.*"[45] Likewise, the International Criminal Tribunal for Rwanda stated in its historic Akayesu judgment (1998) that "the offender is culpable because he knew or should have known that the act committed would destroy, in whole or in part, a group."[46]

This understanding of intent combines *specific* intent, on the one hand, with *constructive* intent, on the other. As summarized elegantly by Michael Reisman and Charles Norchi, specific intent may be inferred "where actions with predictable results are taken over an extended period of time, and the consequences of these actions regularly confirm their outcome."[47] Constructive intent, meanwhile (in Alex Alvarez's words),

> includes cases in which the perpetrators did not intend to harm others but should have realized or known that the behavior made the harm likely. . . . Systematically hunting down and killing members of a group, forcibly removing other members to reservations and then withholding food and medicine, and kidnapping many of their children to raise as slaves outside of the group's culture clearly results in the destruction of that group of people, even if that result is neither intended nor desired.[48]

Personal observations

Having explored some of the commonalities and complexities of genocide frameworks, let me make clear my own preferences, since you will find them reflected in this book. I adopt a generally soft and inclusive, rather than hard and restrictive, definition of genocide. I share with Yale historian Jay Winter the conviction that "If possible, the boundaries surrounding genocide ought to be drawn liberally and not exclusively."[49] I also share the Spanish National Audience's desire, expressed in a November 1998 legal ruling, for "a dynamic or evolutive interpretation of the [Genocide] Convention."[50] Accordingly, I prefer a broader rather than narrower concept of genocidal *intent*; a fairly liberal approach to the issue of requisite numbers killed; and an acceptance of diverse genocidal *agents, strategies*, and *victim groups*.

However, my position is at the harder end of the spectrum in one sense. I adopt a narrower conception of genocidal strategy than some authorities (including Raphael Lemkin and the Genocide Convention). Specifically, I consider mass killing to be definitional to genocide. The inclusion of what some call "ethnocide" (cultural genocide) is important, valid, and entirely in keeping with Lemkin's original conception. It is also actionable under the UN Convention; but in charting my own course, I am wary of labeling as "genocide" cases where mass killing has not occurred.

The most succinct definition of genocide that I know of and agree with came out of the UN Convention – but from the initial draft as prepared by the UN Secretariat, not the one finally passed in 1948. The preamble here states that genocide is "the intentional destruction of a group of human beings."[51] "A group" is as concise a formulation as we will have, if the collective dimension of genocide is considered foundational. If a broad framing of *intent* is then adopted – for instance, if "a conscious act or acts of advertent omission may be as culpable [because intentional] as an act of commission," in Benjamin Whitaker's liberal (1985) interpretation – then this is serviceable shorthand for the approach I take in this volume.[52]

The definition of genocide that I have used most often over the past few years adjusts Steven Katz's 1994 offering. I appreciate Katz's "soft" approach to victim groups, and I think these are also worth listing, as he does. I support his emphasis on the diversity of genocidal strategies ("by whatever means") and on mass killing as a core element, but with an italicized phrase, I remove Katz's requirement of the attempted *total* extermination of a group. Genocide is thus "the actualization of the intent, however successfully carried out, to murder *in whole or in substantial part* any national, ethnic, racial, religious, political, social, gender or economic group, as these groups are defined by the perpetrator, by whatever means." I prefer to leave "substantial" imprecise; I hope its parameters will expand over time, together with our capacity for empathy. It seems clear, though, that a threshold is passed when victims mount into the tens or hundreds of thousands – although relative group size must always be factored in.

The reader should remember, however, that there is just one *legal* definition of genocide, and it is not mine. When I touch on legal aspects of genocide, I highlight the UN Convention definition, but I deploy it and other legal framings instrumentally, not dogmatically. I seek to convey an understanding of genocide in which international law is a vital but not dominant consideration.

CONTESTED CASES

With the varied academic definitions of genocide, and the ambiguities surrounding both the Genocide Convention and historical interpretation, it is not surprising that nearly every posited case of genocide will be discounted by someone else. Even the "classic" genocides of the twentieth century have found their systematic downplayers and deniers (see Chapter 14). In the case of perhaps the most enduring and destructive genocide of all time, against indigenous peoples of the Americas (Chapter 3), *most* individuals in the countries concerned would probably reject the genocide label.

With this in mind, let us consider a few controversial events and human institutions. What can the debate over the applicability of a genocide framework in these cases tell us about definitions of genocide, the ideas and interests that underlie those definitions, and the evolution in thinking about genocide? I will offer my own views in each case. Readers are also encouraged to consult the discussion of "famine crimes" in chapters 2 and 5, and of genocide against political groups in Chapter 5 on Stalin's USSR.

Atlantic slavery

Slavery is pervasive in human societies throughout history. Arguably in no context, however, did it result in such massive mortality as with Atlantic slavery between the sixteenth and nineteenth centuries.[53]

A reasonable estimate of the deaths caused by this institution is fifteen to twenty million people – by any standard, one of the worst holocausts in human history.[54] However, Atlantic slavery is rarely included in analyses or anthologies of genocide. A notable exception – Seymour Drescher's chapter in the volume *Is the Holocaust Unique?* – avoids the "genocide" label, and stresses the differences between slavery and the Jewish Holocaust.[55] (Admittedly, these are not few.) More recently, the renowned human rights scholar, Michael Ignatieff, has cited slavery-as-genocide arguments as a leading example of the tendency to "banalize" the genocide framework:

> Thus slavery is called genocide, when – whatever else it was – it was a system to exploit the living rather than to exterminate them. . . . Genocide has no meaning

> unless the crime can be connected to a clear intention to exterminate a human group in whole or in part. Something more than rhetorical exaggeration for effect is at stake here. Calling every abuse or crime a genocide makes it steadily more difficult to rouse people to action when a genuine genocide is taking place.[56]

Ignatieff's argument – that it was in slave owners' interest to keep slaves alive, not exterminate them – is probably the most common argument against slavery-as-genocide. Others point to the ubiquity of slavery through time; the large-scale collaboration of African chiefs and entrepreneurs in corraling Africans for slavery; and the supposedly cheery results of slavery for slaves' descendants, at least in North America. Even some African-American commentators have celebrated their "deliverance" from strife-torn Africa to lands of opportunity in the West.[57]

My own view is that these arguments are mostly sophistry, serving to deflect responsibility for one of history's greatest crimes. To call Atlantic slavery genocide is not to claim that "every abuse or crime" is genocide, as Ignatieff asserts; nor is it even to designate all slavery as genocidal. Rather, it seems to me an appropriate response to *particular* slavery institutions that inflicted "incalculable demographic and social losses" on West African societies,[58] as well as meeting every other requirement of the UN Genocide Convention's definition.[59] Moreover, the killing and destruction were intentional, whatever the incentives to preserve survivors of the Atlantic passage for labor exploitation. To revisit the issue of intent already touched on: If an institution is deliberately maintained and expanded by discernible agents, though all are aware of the hecatombs of casualties it is inflicting on a definable human group, then why should this not qualify as genocide?

Area bombing and nuclear warfare

Controversy has swirled around the morality both of the area bombing of German and Japanese cities by British and US air forces, and the atomic bombing of Hiroshima and Nagasaki in August 1945. The key issue in both cases is at what point legitimate military action spills over into genocide. The line is difficult to draw, in part due to the intimate relationship between war and genocide, discussed in detail in Chapter 2. In the case of strategic or "area" bombing (in which entire cities were blanketed with high explosives, after pinpoint bombing had been rejected as unworkable), the debate centers on the military utility and moral proportionality of the policy. "The effects [themselves] are clear and undisputed":

> By the end of the war in 1945, every large and medium-sized German city, as well as many smaller ones had been destroyed or badly damaged by the Allied strategic-bombing offensive. Overall, 2.7 million tons of bombs were dropped, destroying 3.6 million homes (20 per cent of the country's total), leaving 7.5 million homeless. . . . The loss of life was substantial. Estimates of deaths range from about 300,000 to 600,000, and of injuries from 600,000 to over a million. . . . Most of the civilian victims were women, infants, and elderly people. . . . About 19 per

> cent of the victims were children under the age of 16, 5 per cent of whom were babies and children below school age, and about 20 per cent of the casualties were over the age of 60.[60]

Similar destruction was inflicted on Japan, where some 900,000 civilians died. A single night's fire-bombing of Tokyo (March 9–10, 1945) killed between 90,000 and 100,000 people, more than the death-toll in the atomic bombing of Nagasaki.[61] Can this mass killing be seen as militarily necessary, or at least defensible? Did it shorten the war, for example, and thereby save the lives of large numbers of Allied soldiers? Should daylight bombing have been pursued, even though it was of dubious efficacy and led to the deaths of more Allied pilots? Or was the bombing *in*defensible, killing vastly more civilians than military requirements could possibly justify?

From a genocide-studies perspective, at issue is whether civilian populations were targeted (1) outside the boundaries of "legitimate" warfare, and (2) on the basis of their ethnic or national identity. Answers have predictably differed, with the ground-breaking genocide scholar Leo Kuper arguing that area bombing *was* genocidal (as were the atomic bombings).[62] After a nuanced consideration of the matter, Eric Markusen and David Kopf agreed.[63] Others reject the genocide framework. The Nuremberg prosecutor Telford Taylor argued that the area bombings "were certainly not 'genocides' within the meaning of the Convention . . . Berlin, London and Tokyo were not bombed because their inhabitants were German, English or Japanese, but because they were *enemy* strongholds. Accordingly, the killing ceased when the war ended and there was no longer any enemy."[64]

The genocide framing is perhaps more persuasively applied in the Japanese case, given the racist propaganda that pervaded the Pacific War, including the common depiction of Japanese as apes and vermin (see Chapter 2). As well, the bombing reached a crescendo when Japan was arguably prostrate before Allied air power. At times, the destruction (through the "thousand-bomber" raids) appears to have been inflicted to push the boundaries of the logistically possible, rather than for a coherent military purpose.

Fewer ambiguities attach to the atomic bombings at war's end. These were carried out when Japan's defeat was virtually certain; both Supreme Allied Commanders, General Dwight D. Eisenhower and General Douglas MacArthur, considered them to be "completely unnecessary."[65] Other options were also available to the US planners – including a softening of the demand for unconditional surrender, and demonstration bombing away from major population centers. There is a consensus that the destruction of Nagasaki, in particular, was gratuitous, since the power of atomic weaponry was already evident, and the Japanese government was in crisis discussions on surrender.[66]

UN sanctions against Iraq

Following Saddam Hussein's invasion and occupation of Kuwait in August 1990, the United Nations, spearheaded by the US and Great Britain, imposed sweeping economic sanctions on Iraq. These lasted beyond the 1991 Gulf War and, with modifications, were maintained through to the invasion and occupation of Iraq in 2003.

It rapidly became evident that the sanctions were exacting an enormous human toll on Iraqis, particularly children. According to a "criminal complaint" filed by former US Attorney General Ramsey Clark before a people's tribunal in Madrid, the policies were nothing short of genocidal:

> The United States and its officials[,] aided and abetted by others[,] engaged in a continuing pattern of conduct . . . to impose, maintain and enforce extreme economic sanctions and a strict military blockade on the people of Iraq for the purpose of injuring the entire population, killing its weakest members, infants, children, the elderly and the chronically ill, by depriving them of medicines, drinking water, food, and other essentials.[67]

The debate has sparked controversy and some rancor among genocide scholars. A majority reject the idea that genocide can be inflicted by "indirect" means such as sanctions, or assign the bulk of responsibility for Iraqi suffering to the corrupt and dictatorial regime of Saddam Hussein. Such arguments also emphasize the modifications to the sanctions regime in the 1990s, notably the introduction of an "Oil-for-Food" arrangement by which limited food and humanitarian purchases could be made with Iraqi oil revenues, under UN oversight.[68]

Those, including myself, who hold that the Iraq sanctions did constitute genocide acknowledge the despotic nature of the Iraqi regime (see, e.g., Box 4a). However, they point to the human damage linked by many impartial observers to the sanctions, and the awareness of that damage, reflected in comments such as those of then-Secretary of State Madeleine Albright in May 1996. Responding to figures showing 500,000 child deaths from sanctions, Albright said: "I think this is a very hard choice. But the price – we think the price is worth it."[69] Is this "infanticide masquerading as policy," as US Congressman David Bonior alleged?[70]

The reticence about the effects of sanctions may reflect the difficulty that many Western observers have in acknowledging Western-inflicted genocides. In 1998 the UN Humanitarian Coordinator for Iraq, Denis Halliday – who witnessed the impact of sanctions at first hand – resigned in protest over their allegedly genocidal character. "I was made to feel by some that I had crossed an invisible line of impropriety," he stated the following year. "Since then I have observed that the term 'genocide' offends many in our Western media and establishment circles when it is used to describe the killing of others for which we are responsible, such as in Iraq."[71]

9/11

The attacks launched on New York and Washington on the morning of September 11, 2001 constituted the worst terrorist attack in history.[72] Perhaps never outside wartime and natural disasters have so many people – well over 2,000 – been killed more or less simultaneously. But were the attacks, apparently carried out by agents of Osama bin Laden's Al-Qaeda movement, more than terroristic? Did they in fact constitute genocidal massacres by Leo Kuper's definition?[73]

In the aftermath of September 11, this question was debated on the H-Genocide academic list. Citing the UN Convention, Peter Ronayne wrote: "[It] seems at least on the surface that the argument could be made that Osama bin Laden and his ilk are intent on destroying, in whole or in part, a national group, and they're more than willing to kill members of the group." Robert Cribb, an Indonesia specialist, differed. "Surely the attacks were terrorist, rather than genocidal. At least 20% of the victims were not American, and it seems pretty likely that the destruction of human life was not for its own sake . . . but to cause terror and anguish amongst a much broader population, which it has done very effectively."[74]

Expanding on Ronayne's reasoning, if we limit ourselves to the UN Convention framing, the 9/11 attacks resulted in "killing members of the group," intentionally and (in most cases) "as such." In addition, the "destruction[,] . . . terror and anguish" they inflicted caused serious "bodily [and] mental harm to members" of the group. Moreover, it seems highly likely that the ferocity of the attack was limited only by the means available to the attackers (passenger jets used as missiles). Were nuclear bombs at hand, one suspects that they would be used against civilian populations in the US, and perhaps elsewhere. This brings us close to the Convention requirement that genocidal acts be "committed with intent to destroy, in whole or in part, a national . . . group" (i.e., US Americans).

There is thus, at least, a palpable genocidal impetus and intent in 9/11 – one that could yet result in fully fledged genocide. Only the coming decades will enable us to place the attacks in proper perspective: to decide whether they stand as isolated and discrete events and campaigns, or as opening salvos in a systematic campaign of genocide.

Structural and institutional violence

In the 1960s, peace researchers such as Johan Galtung began exploring the phenomenon of "structural violence": destructive relations embedded in social and economic systems. Some commentators argue that certain forms of structural and institutional violence are genocidal, "deliberately inflicting on [a designated] group conditions of life calculated to bring about its physical destruction in whole or in part," in the language of the UN Convention. For example, the Indian scholar and activist Vandana Shiva has described "the globalization of food and agriculture systems" under neoliberal trade regimes as "equivalent to the ethnic cleansing of the poor, the peasantry, and small farmers of the Third World. . . . Globalization of trade in agriculture implies genocide."[75] Jean Ziegler, the UN Special Rapporteur on the Right to Food, stated in October 2005: "Every child who dies of hunger in today's world is the victim of assassination," and referred to the *daily* death by starvation of 100,000 people as a "massacre of human beings through malnutrition."[76] My own work on gender and genocide (see Chapter 13) explores "gendercidal institutions" such as female infanticide and even maternal mortality, suggesting that they are forms of gender-selective mass killing, hence genocidal.

Much of structural violence is diffuse, part of the "background" of human relations. It is accordingly difficult to ascribe clear agency to phenomena such as racism, sexism, and other forms of discrimination. International relations scholar Kal Holsti rejects global-systemic visions of structural violence, like Galtung's, as "just too fuzzy," and evincing a tendency to "place all blame for the ills of the Third World on the first one." In Holsti's view, this overlooks the essential role of many Third World leaders and elites in the suffering and violence experienced by their populations. "It also fails to account for many former Third World countries that today have standards of living and welfare higher than those found in many 'industrial' countries."[77]

These points are well taken. Nonetheless, in my opinion, genocide studies should move to incorporate a nuanced portrait of structural and institutional violence as genocidal mechanisms. If our overriding concern is to prevent avoidable death and suffering, how can we shut our eyes to "the Holocaust of Neglect" that malnutrition, ill-health, and structural discrimination impose upon huge swathes of humanity?[78] Are we not in danger of "catching the small fry and letting the big fish loose," as Galtung put it?[79]

Moreover, when it comes to human institutions, it is not necessarily the case that responsibility and agency are impossible to establish. Consider the neoliberal economic policies and institutions that shape the destinies of much of the world's poor. Harvard economist Jeffrey Sachs played a key role in designing the "structural adjustment" measures imposed by the World Bank and International Monetary Fund (IMF) around the Third World and former Soviet bloc. He later turned against such prescriptions, commenting in 2002 that they had "squeezed [targeted] countries to the point where their health systems are absolutely unable to function. Education systems are broken down, and *there's a lot of death associated with the collapse of public health and the lack of access to medicine*."[80] In such cases, as Holsti points out, "distinct agents with distinct policies and identifiable consequences" may be discerned, and moral and legal responsibility may likewise be imputed.[81]

IS GENOCIDE EVER JUSTIFIED?

This question is not often posed in genocide studies; it may provoke a collective intake of breath.[82] Examining ourselves honestly, though, most people have probably experienced at least a twinge of sympathy with those who commit acts that some people consider genocidal. Others have gone much further, to outright *celebration* of genocide (see, e.g., Chapter 3). Is any of this justifiable, morally or legally?

Perhaps the most common form of genocide justification and celebration is a utilitarian one, applied most frequently in the case of indigenous peoples. These populations have standardly been accused of failing to exploit the land they inhabit, and its natural resources.[83] This latent economic potential, viewed through the lens of the Protestant work ethic and capitalist profit, is held to warrant confiscation of territories, and marginalization or annihilation of their populations.

Oppressed indigenous communities sometimes rose up in rebellion against colonial authority. While these rebellions evoke widespread sympathy, they may also be held to have taken, on occasion, a genocidal form. To the cases of Upper Peru (Bolivia) in the late eighteenth century, and the Caste War of Yucatán in the nineteenth, we might add the revolution in the French colony of Saint-Domingue that, in 1804, created Haiti as the world's first free black republic. This was a revolt not of indigenous people, but of slaves. It succeeded in expelling the whites, albeit at a devastating cost from which Haiti never really recovered. As in Bolivia and Yucatán, rebellion and counter-rebellion assumed the form of unbridled race war. Yet this war finds many sympathizers. The great scholar of the Haitian revolution, C.L.R. James, described in the 1930s "the complete massacre" of Saint-Domingue's whites: "The population, stirred to fear at the nearness of the counter-revolution, killed all [whites] with every possible brutality." But James' appraisal of the events sanctioned the race war on the grounds of past atrocities and exploitation by whites. Acknowledging that the victims were defenseless, James lamented only the damage done to the souls of the killers, and their future political culture:

> The massacre of the whites was a tragedy; *not for the whites.* For these old slave-owners, those who burnt a little powder in the arse of a Negro, who buried him alive for insects to eat . . . and who, as soon as they got the chance, began their old cruelties again; for these there is no need to waste one tear or one drop of ink. *The tragedy was for the blacks and the Mulattoes* [who did the killing]. It was not policy but revenge, and revenge has no place in politics. *The whites were no longer to be feared,* and such purposeless massacres degrade and brutalise a [perpetrator] population, especially one which was just beginning as a nation and had had so bitter a past. . . . Haiti suffered terribly from the resulting isolation. Whites were banished from Haiti for generations, and the unfortunate country, ruined economically, its population lacking in social culture, had its inevitable difficulties doubled by this massacre.[84]

Bolivia, Mexico, and Haiti are all examples of what Nicholas Robins and I call *subaltern genocide,* or "genocides by the oppressed."[85] In general, genocidal assaults that contain a morally plausible element of revenge, retribution, or revolutionary usurpation are less likely to be condemned, and are often welcomed. Allied fire-bombing and nuclear-bombing of German and Japanese cities, which Leo Kuper and other scholars considered to have been genocidal, are often justified on the grounds that "they started it" (that is, the German and Japanese governments launched mass bombings of civilians before the Allies did). The fate of ethnic-German civilians in Czechoslovakia, Poland, and other Central European countries at the end of the Second World War, and in its aftermath, likewise attracted little empathy until recent times – again because, when it came to mass expulsions of populations and attendant atrocities, the Germans too had "started it." The quarter of a million Serbs expelled from the Krajina and Eastern Slavonia regions of Croatia in 1995 (Chapter 8) now constitute the largest refugee population in Europe; but their plight evokes no great outrage, because of an assignation of collective guilt to Serbs for the Bosnian genocide. (The trend was evident again after the 1999 Kosovo war, when Serb civilians in the province were targeted for murder by ethnic Albanian extremists.)[86]

Even the September 11, 2001 terrorist attacks on the World Trade Center and Pentagon, which could be considered genocidal massacres, secured the equivocal or enthusiastic support of hundreds of millions of people worldwide. Americans were deemed to have gotten what was coming to them after decades of US imperial intervention. A similar vocabulary of justification and celebration may be found among many Arabs, and other Palestinian supporters, after massacres of Jewish civilians in Israel.

Apart from cases of subaltern genocide, the defenders and deniers of some of history's worst genocides often justify the killings on the grounds of *legitimate defensive or retributory action against traitors and subversives.* The Turkish refusal to acknowledge the Armenian genocide (Chapter 4) depicts atrocities or "excesses" as the inevitable results of an Armenian rebellion aimed at undermining the Ottoman state. Apologists for Hutu Power in Rwanda claim the genocide of 1994 was nothing more than the continuation of "civil war" or "tribal conflict"; or that Hutus were seeking to pre-empt the kind of genocide at Tutsi hands that Hutus had suffered in neighboring Burundi (Chapter 9). Sympathizers of the Nazi regime in Germany sometimes present the invasion of the USSR as a pre-emptive, defensive war against the Bolshevik threat to Western civilization (Box 6a). Even the Nazis' demonology of a Jewish "cancer" and "conspiracy" resonated deeply with millions of highly educated Germans at the time, and fuels Holocaust denial to the present, though as a fringe phenomenon.

All these cases of denial need to be rejected and confronted (see Chapter 14). *But are there instances when genocide may occur in self-defense?* The Rome Statute of the International Criminal Court abjures criminal proceedings against "the person [who] acts reasonably to defend himself or herself or another person or . . . against an imminent and unlawful use of force in a manner proportionate to the degree of danger to the person or the other person or property protected." Citing this, William Schabas notes that "reprisal and military necessity are not formally prohibited by international humanitarian law." However, "reprisal as a defense must be proportional, and on this basis its application to genocide would seem inconceivable."[87] But Schabas has a tendency, in defending a "hard" and predictably legalistic interpretation of the UN Convention, to use terms such as "inconceivable," "obviously incompatible," "totally unnecessary," "definitely inappropriate." Sometimes these may close off worthwhile discussions, such as: What is the acceptable range of responses to genocide? Can genocidal counter-assault be "proportional" in any meaningful sense?

A large part of the problem is that the plausibility we attach to reprisals and retribution frequently reflects our political identifications. We have a harder time condemning those with whom we sympathize, even when their actions are atrocious. Consciously or unconsciously, we distinguish "worthy" from "unworthy" victims.[88] And we may be less ready to label as genocidal the atrocities that our chosen "worthy" commit. We will return to this issue at the close of the book, when considering personal responsibility for genocide prevention.

FURTHER STUDY

Alex Alvarez, *Governments, Citizens, and Genocide: A Comparative and Interdisciplinary Approach*. Bloomington, IN: Indiana University Press, 2001. If I had to select one work to accompany or substitute for this one in a genocide course, it would be Alvarez's superb study.

George J. Andreopoulos, ed., *Genocide: Conceptual and Historical Dimensions*. Philadelphia, PA: University of Pennsylvania Press, 1994. Uneven but sometimes helpful compendium.

Omer Bartov, Anita Grossmann, and Mary Nolan, eds, *Crimes of War: Guilt and Denial in the Twentieth Century*. New York: New Press, 2002. Fine introduction to war crimes and genocide.

Kenneth J. Campbell, *Genocide and the Global Village*. New York: Palgrave, 2001. Brief but piquant essay.

Frank Chalk and Kurt Jonassohn, *The History and Sociology of Genocide*. New Haven, CT: Yale University Press, 1990. Early and eclectic treatment, still widely read and cited.

Israel W. Charny, ed., *The Encyclopedia of Genocide*, 2 vols. Santa Barbara, CA: ABC-CLIO, 1999. Useful reference work.

Levon Chorbajian and George Shirinian, eds, *Studies in Comparative Genocide*. New York: St. Martin's Press, 1999. First-rate collection of essays, with special attention to the Armenian genocide.

Robert Gellately and Ben Kiernan, eds, *The Specter of Genocide: Mass Murder in Historical Perspective*. Cambridge: Cambridge University Press, 2003. One of the best edited volumes on the subject; diverse and vigorously written throughout.

Jonathan Glover, *Humanity: A Moral History of the Twentieth Century*. New Haven, CT: Yale University Press, 1999. Addresses genocide but ranges far beyond it; a central work of our time.

William L. Hewitt, ed., *Defining the Horrific: Readings on Genocide and Holocaust in the Twentieth Century*. Upper Saddle River, NJ: Pearson Education, 2004. Accessible, wide-ranging readings designed for classroom use.

Kurt Jonassohn with Karin Solveig Björnson, *Genocide and Gross Human Rights Violations in Comparative Perspective*. New Brunswick, NJ: Transaction Publishers, 1998. Eclectic, open-minded volume.

Adam Jones, ed., *Genocide, War Crimes and the West: History and Complicity*. London: Zed Books, 2004. "The most comprehensive treatment of Western responsibility for mass atrocity yet published" (Richard Falk); naturally I agree.

Leo Kuper, *Genocide: Its Political Use in the Twentieth Century*. Harmondsworth: Penguin, 1981. The foundational text of comparative genocide studies, still in print.

Raphael Lemkin, *Key Writings of Raphael Lemkin on Genocide*. Compiled by PreventGenocide.org, http://www.preventgenocide.org/lemkin. Online selection of Lemkin's core work on genocide.

Michael Mann, *The Dark Side of Democracy: Explaining Ethnic Cleansing*. Cambridge: Cambridge University Press, 2005. Sprawling, frankly exhausting study of modernity and "murderous ethnic cleansing."

Nicolaus Mills and Kira Brunner, eds, *The New Killing Fields: Massacre and the Politics of Intervention.* New York: Basic Books, 2002. Exceptional essays, with a journalistic tinge.

Samantha Power, *"A Problem from Hell": America and the Age of Genocide.* New York: Basic Books, 2002. Power's multiple-award-winning work focuses on the US response to various genocides.

Alan S. Rosenbaum, ed., *Is the Holocaust Unique? Perspectives on Comparative Genocide.* Boulder, CO: Westview Press, 1998. Important, controversial essays.

Richard L. Rubenstein, *The Age of Triage: Fear and Hope in an Overcrowded World.* Boston, MA: Beacon Press, 1983. Ground-breaking study of the elimination of unwanted populations.

Dinah Shelton, ed., *Encyclopedia of Genocide and Crimes Against Humanity* (3 vols). Detroit, MI: Macmillan Reference, 2005. Massive, admirably inclusive work that supersedes Charny's edited encyclopedia (see above) as the standard reference.

Samuel Totten and Steven Leonard Jacobs, eds, *Pioneers of Genocide Studies.* New Brunswick, NJ: Transaction Publishers, 2002. Testimonial essays by leading scholars of comparative genocide studies.

Samuel Totten, William S. Parsons, and Israel W. Charny, eds, *Century of Genocide: Eyewitness Accounts and Critical Views* (2nd edn). New York: Routledge, 2004. Unparalleled collection of analyses and testimony.

Isidor Wallimann and Michael N. Dobkowski, eds, *Genocide and the Modern Age: Etiology and Case Studies of Mass Death.* Syracuse, NY: Syracuse University Press, 2000. Reissue of an early, now rather dated work.

Eric D. Weitz, *A Century of Genocide: Utopias of Race and Nation.* Princeton, NJ: Princeton University Press, 2003. Cogent overview, with case studies paralleling some in this volume.

Benjamin Whitaker, *Revised and Updated Report on the Question of the Prevention and Punishment of the Crime of Genocide* (The Whitaker Report). ECOSOC (United Nations), July 2, 1985, available in full at http://www.preventgenocide.org/prevent/UNdocs/whitaker. Significant attempt to rethink and revise the UN Genocide Convention.

NOTES

1 Leo Kuper, *Genocide: Its Political Use in the Twentieth Century* (Harmondsworth: Penguin, 1981), p. 9.

2 Frank Chalk and Kurt Jonassohn, *The History and Sociology of Genocide: Analyses and Case Studies* (New Haven, CT: Yale University Press, 1990), p. 64.

3 Quoted in Chalk and Jonassohn, *The History and Sociology of Genocide*, p. 58. Notably, when Troy did finally fall, women and girl children were spared extermination, and instead abducted as slaves (Israel Charny, ed., *The Encyclopedia of Genocide* [Santa Barbara, CA: ABC-CLIO, 1999], p. 273). See the discussion of gender and genocide in Chapter 13.

4 Chalk and Jonassohn, *The History and Sociology of Genocide*, p. 28.

5 Helen Fein, *Genocide: A Sociological Perspective* (London: Sage, 1993), p. 26.

6 K. Armstrong, *A History of God*; quoted in Roy F. Baumeister, *Evil: Inside Human Violence and Cruelty* (New York: W.H. Freeman), p. 171. "As a Jew," writes Yehuda Bauer, "I must live with the fact that the civilization I inherited . . . encompasses the call for

genocide in its canon." Bauer, *Rethinking the Holocaust* (New Haven, CT: Yale University Press, 2001), p. 41. For other examples of Old Testament genocide, see Chalk and Jonassohn, *The History and Sociology of Genocide*, pp. 62–63; Eric D. Weitz, *A Century of Genocide: Utopias of Race and Nation* (Princeton, NJ: Princeton University Press, 2003), p. 18, citing Joshua's "destruction by the edge of the sword [of] all in the city [of Jericho], both men and women, young and old, oxen, sheep, and donkeys."

7 "Genocide, God, and the Bible," http://stripe.colorado.edu/~morristo/genocide.html.

8 Cited in Louis W. Cable, "The Bloody Bible," *Freethought Today*, June/July 1997. http://www.ffrf.org/fttoday/june_july97/cable.html. See also the numerous examples of "God-ordered genocide" cited in Bill Moyers, "9/11 and the Sport of God," Commondreams.org, 9 September 2005, http://www.commondreams.org/views05/0909-36.htm.

9 Bauer, *Rethinking the Holocaust*, p. 19.

10 Ben Kiernan, "The First Genocide: Carthage, 146 BC," *Diogenes*, 203 (2004), pp. 27–39.

11 Andrew Bell-Fialkoff writes that the First Crusade (1096–99) left "a trail of blood and destruction, throughout the Rhine and the Moselle valleys, as well as in Prague and Hungary. Entire communities, perhaps tens of thousands of people in all, were wiped out. The Crusade culminated in a wholesale massacre of all non-Christians in Jerusalem." Bell-Fialkoff, *Ethnic Cleansing* (New York: St. Martin's Griffin, 1999), p. 13.

12 Eric S. Margolis, *War at the Top of the World: The Struggle for Afghanistan, Kashmir, and Tibet* (New York: Routledge, 2001), p. 155.

13 See Reynald Secher, *A French Genocide: The Vendée*, trans. George Holoch (Notre Dame, IN: University of Notre Dame Press, 2003). This section also draws on the analysis in Adam Jones, "Why Gendercide? Why Root-and-Branch? A Comparison of the Vendée Uprising of 1793–94 and the Bosnian War of the 1990s," *Journal of Genocide Research*, 8: 1 (2006), pp. 9–25.

14 Cited in Alain Gérard, *«Par principe d'humanité . . . » La Terreur et la Vendée* (Paris: Librairie Arthème Fayard, 1999), p. 295.

15 Cited in Arno J. Mayer, *The Furies: Violence and Terror in the French and Russian Revolutions* (Princeton, NJ: Princeton University Press, 2000), p. 353.

16 In the estimation of France's greatest historian, Jules Michelet; quoted in Mayer, *The Furies*, p. 325.

17 Quoted in Secher, *A French Genocide*, p. 132.

18 Mayer, *The Furies*, p. 340.

19 Michael R. Mahoney, "The Zulu Kingdom as a Genocidal and Post-genocidal Society, c. 1810 to the Present," *Journal of Genocide Research*, 5: 2 (2003), p. 263.

20 Chalk and Jonassohn, *The History and Sociology of Genocide*, p. 223.

21 Chalk and Jonassohn, *The History and Sociology of Genocide*, pp. 224–25, citing Eugene Victor Walter, *Terror and Resistance: A Study of Political Violence*.

22 Mahoney, "The Zulu Kingdom," p. 254.

23 Chalk and Jonassohn, *The History and Sociology of Genocide*, pp. 224–25. Emphasis added.

24 Mahoney, "The Zulu Kingdom," p. 255.

25 See PreventGenocide.org, "A Crime without a Name," http://www.preventgenocide.org/genocide/crimewithoutaname.htm.

26 Power herself describes Lemkin as a "wild-eyed professor with steel-rimmed glasses and a relentless appetite for rejection." Samantha Power, *"A Problem from Hell": America and the Age of Genocide* (New York: Basic Books, 2002), p. 51.

27 The only other book that purports to examine Lemkin's life and work turns out, upon naive ordering, to be a mendacious Holocaust-denial tract. Lemkin's unpublished writings, including a global history of genocide, have long been in the hands of genocide scholar Steven Jacobs, but have yet to see the light of day.

28 Power, *"A Problem from Hell,"* p. 20.

29 Lemkin quoted in Power, *"A Problem from Hell,"* p. 20.

30 Lemkin quoted in Power, *"A Problem from Hell,"* p. 21.

31 "Of particular interest to Lemkin were the reflections of George Eastman, who said he

had settled upon 'Kodak' as the name for his new camera because: 'First. It is short. Second. It is not capable of mispronunciation. Third. It does not resemble anything in the art and cannot be associated with anything in the art except the Kodak.'" Power, *"A Problem from Hell,"* pp. 42–43.

32 Lemkin cited in Steven L. Jacobs, "Indicting Henry Kissinger: The Response of Raphael Lemkin," in Adam Jones, ed., *Genocide, War Crimes and the West: History and Complicity* (London: Zed Books, 2004), p. 217.

33 On this point, see Ward S. Churchill, "Genocide by Any Other Name: North American Indian Residential Schools in Context," in Jones, ed., *Genocide, War Crimes and the West,* p. 80.

34 Stephen Holmes, "Looking Away," *London Review of Books,* November 14, 2002 (review of Power, *"A Problem from Hell"*).

35 According to Helen Fein, Lemkin's "examples of genocide or genocidal situations include: Albigensians, American Indians, Assyrians in Iraq, Belgian Congo, Christians in Japan, French in Sicily (*c.* 1282), Hereros, Huguenots, Incas, Mongols, the Soviet Union/Ukraine, [and] Tasmania." Fein, *Genocide: A Sociological Perspective,* p. 11. Lemkin's study of Tasmania has now been edited for publication: see Raphael Lemkin, "Tasmania," edited by Ann Curthoys, *Patterns of Prejudice,* 39: 2 (2005), pp. 170–96 (and Curthoys' Introduction, pp. 162–69).

36 William A. Schabas, *Genocide in International Law* (Cambridge: Cambridge University Press, 2000), p. 14.

37 As supplied in W. Michael Reisman and Chris T. Antoniou, eds, *The Laws of War: A Comprehensive Collection of Primary Documents on International Laws Governing Armed Conflict* (New York: Vintage Books, 1994), pp. 84–85.

38 Cited in Steven R. Ratner and Jason S. Abrams, *Accountability for Human Rights Atrocities: Beyond the Nuremberg Legacy* (2nd edn) (Oxford: Oxford University Press, 2001), pp. 30, 32.

39 Schabas, *Genocide in International Law,* pp. 140, 175, 178.

40 For a survey of the early legal literature, see David Kader, "Law and Genocide: A Critical Annotated Bibliography," *Hastings International and Comparative Law Review,* 11 (1988).

41 Christopher Rudolph, "Constructing an Atrocities Regime: The Politics of War Crimes Tribunals," *International Organization,* 55: 3 (summer 2001), p. 659. Rudolph cites Kenneth Abbott and Duncan Snidal, who "define 'hard' legalization as legally binding obligations characterized by high degrees of obligation, precision, and delegation, and define 'soft' legalization as a more flexible manifestation characterized by varying degrees along one or most of these same dimensions."

42 Irving Louis Horowitz, *Taking Lives: Genocide and State Power* (4th edn) (New Brunswick, NJ: Transaction Publishers, 1996), p. 265.

43 Robert Gellately and Ben Kiernan, "The Study of Mass Murder and Genocide," in Gellately and Kiernan, eds, *The Specter of Genocide: Mass Murder in Historical Perspective* (Cambridge: Cambridge University Press, 2003), p. 15.

44 Schabas, *Genocide in International Law,* p. 254.

45 Alexander K.A. Greenawalt, "Rethinking Genocidal Intent: The Case for a Knowledge-based Interpretation," *Columbia Law Review,* 99: 8 (1999), p. 2269; emphasis added.

46 *Akayesu* judgment quoted in Schabas, *Genocide in International Law,* p. 212. Schabas considers this approach "definitely inappropriate in the case of genocide."

47 Reisman and Norchi quoted in Helen Fein, "Discriminating Genocide from War Crimes: Vietnam and Afghanistan Reexamined," *Denver Journal of International Law and Policy,* 22: 1 (1993), p. 58. Gellately and Kiernan likewise write that under the prevailing international-legal understanding, "genocidal intent also applies to acts of destruction that are not the specific goal but are predictable outcomes or by-products of a policy, which could have been avoided by a change in that policy." Gellately and Kiernan, "The Study of Mass Murder and Genocide," p. 15.

48 Alex Alvarez, *Governments, Citizens, and Genocide: A Comparative and Interdisciplinary*

Approach (Bloomington and Indianapolis: Indiana University Press, 2001), p. 52. "Gradations of culpability" for genocide can be usefully mapped onto domestic law's concept of "degrees" of homicide. This is the project of Ward Churchill in his "Proposed Convention on Prevention and Punishment of the Crime of Genocide." Churchill distinguishes among "(a) *Genocide in the First Degree*, which consists of instances in which evidence of premeditated intent to commit genocide is present. (b) *Genocide in the Second Degree*, which consists of instances in which evidence of premeditation is absent, but in which it can be reasonably argued that the perpetrator(s) acted with reckless disregard for the probability that genocide would result from their actions. (c) *Genocide in the Third Degree*, which consists of instances in which genocide derives, however unintentionally, from other violations of international law engaged in by the perpetrator(s). (d) *Genocide in the Fourth Degree*, which consists of instances in which neither evidence of premeditation nor other criminal behavior is present, but in which the perpetrator(s) acted with depraved indifference to the possibility that genocide would result from their actions and therefore [failed] to effect adequate safeguards to prevent it." Churchill, *A Little Matter of Genocide: Holocaust and Denial in the Americas, 1492 to the Present* (San Francisco, CA: City Lights Books, 1997), pp. 434–35.

49 Jay Winter, "Under Cover of War: The Armenian Genocide in the Context of Total War," in Gellately and Kiernan, eds, *The Specter of Genocide*, p. 194.

50 Spanish National Audience quoted in Schabas, *Genocide in International Law*, p. 150.

51 UN Secretariat quoted in Schabas, *Genocide in International Law*, p. 53. Leo Kuper's reference to "the destruction of human groups" is even more distilled, though it eliminates intention; Leo Kuper, *The Prevention of Genocide* (New Haven, CT: Yale University Press, 1985), p. 6.

52 In 1982, the Englishman Benjamin Whitaker was appointed Special Rapporteur by the UN's Economic and Social Council (ECOSOC) to revise a previously commissioned study on reform to the Genocide Convention. Whitaker's report was submitted in 1985 and "made a number of innovative and controversial conclusions . . . Whitaker wanted to amend the Convention in order to include political groups and groups based on sexual orientation, to exclude the plea of superior orders, to extend the punishable acts to those of 'advertent omission' and to pursue consideration of cultural genocide, 'ethnocide' and 'ecocide'" (Schabas, *Genocide in International Law*, p. 467). Whitaker's proposals so divided his sponsors that his report was tabled and never acted upon – in my view, an opportunity missed to substantially advance legal and scholarly understandings of genocide.

53 For a superbly accessible introduction to the institution of Atlantic slavery, see Robert Harms, *The Diligent: A Voyage Through the Worlds of the Slave Trade* (New York: Basic Books, 2002).

54 After conducting a useful review of available sources, Matthew White concludes: "If we assume the absolute worst, a death toll as high as 60 million is at the very edge of possibility; however, the likeliest number of deaths would fall somewhere from 15 to 20 million." White, "Twentieth Century Atlas – Historical Body Count," http:// users.erols. com/mwhite28/warstatv.htm. To arrive at such a total, one can begin with the figure of eleven to fifteen million slaves "shipped between the fifteenth and the nineteenth century," cited in Hugh Thomas, *The Slave Trade: The Story of the Atlantic Slave Trade: 1440–1870* (New York: Touchstone, 1997), p. 862. (Thomas himself argues for an "approximate figure . . . [of] something like eleven million slaves, give or take 500,000.") A widely held view is that approximately 50 percent of those captured as slaves died before they were shipped from West African ports. To these eleven to fifteen million victims, one adds approximately two million more who died on the "middle passage" between Africa and the Americas, and an unknown but certainly very large number who perished after arrival, either during the brutal "seasoning" process or on the plantations.

55 Seymour Drescher, "The Atlantic Slave Trade and the Holocaust: A Comparative Analysis," in Alan S. Rosenbaum, ed., *Is the Holocaust Unique? Perspectives on Comparative Genocide* (Boulder, CO: Westview Press, 2001), pp. 97–117.

56 Michael Ignatieff, "Lemkin's Word," *The New Republic*, February 26, 2001.
57 See, e.g., the Black American journalist Keith Richburg's controversial article, "American in Africa," in *Washington Post Magazine*, March 26, 1995, available online at http://www.washingtonpost.com/wp-srv/inatl/longterm/richburg/richbrg1.htm.
58 Orlando Patterson, *Slavery and Social Death: A Comparative Study* (Cambridge, MA: Harvard University Press, 1982), p. 164.
59 The fact that slavery in the United States was far less destructive of slaves' lives, compared to the Caribbean or Portuguese America (Brazil), is an important factor in weighing the applicability of the genocide framework to different slavery institutions in the Americas. Life for slaves in the US was a calvary; in French-controlled Haiti it was a holocaust. Recall, however, that millions of slaves died *en route* to West African ports and New World plantations. These rates do not seem to have been lower for slaves shipped to US destinations.
60 Eric Langenbacher, "The Allies in World War II: The Anglo-American Bombardment of German Cities," in Jones, ed., *Genocide, War Crimes and the West*, pp. 117–19. See also Howard Zinn, "Hiroshima and Royan," in William L. Hewitt, ed., *Defining the Horrific: Readings on Genocide and Holocaust in the Twentieth Century* (Upper Saddle River, NJ: Pearson, 2004), pp. 187–99. Zinn, a renowned dissident historian, is also a US veteran of the area-bombing campaign against Germany; the chapter relates some of his personal experiences.
61 See the description of the raid in Eric Markusen and David Kopf, *The Holocaust and Strategic Bombing: Genocide and Total War in the Twentieth Century* (Boulder, CO: Westview Press, 1995), pp. 175–80.
62 "I cannot accept the view that . . . the bombing, in time of war, of such civilian enemy populations as those of Hiroshima, Nagasaki, Hamburg, and Dresden does not constitute genocide within the terms of the [UN] convention." Kuper, *Genocide*, cited in Chalk and Jonassohn, *The History and Sociology of Genocide*, p. 24. Mary Kaldor also argues that "the indiscriminate bombing of civilians . . . creat[ed] a scale of devastation of genocidal proportions." Mary Kaldor, *New and Old Wars: Organized Violence in a Global Era* (Stanford, CA: Stanford University Press, 2001), p. 25.
63 "Was strategic bombing genocidal? Put bluntly, our answer is yes." Markusen and Kopf, *The Holocaust and Strategic Bombing*, p. 255; see the extended discussion at pp. 244–58.
64 Taylor quoted in Chalk and Jonassohn, *The History and Sociology of Genocide*, p. 25.
65 Ronald Takaki, *Hiroshima: Why America Dropped the Atomic Bomb* (Boston, MA: Little, Brown, 1995), pp. 30, 153 (n.3).
66 See, e.g., Brahma Chellaney, "No Rationalization for Nagasaki Attack," *The Japan Times*, August 10, 2005, http://www.japantimes.co.jp/cgi-bin/geted.pl5?eo2005 0810bc.htm.
67 See Ramsey Clark, "Criminal Complaint against the United States and Others for Crimes against the People of Iraq (1996) and Letter to the Security Council (2001)," in Jones, ed., *Genocide, War Crimes and the West*, p. 271. The forum in question was the International Court on Crimes Against Humanity Committed by the UN Security Council on [*sic*] Iraq, held on November 16–17, 1996. For more on citizens' tribunals, see Chapter 15. Clark's phrase "for the purpose of" is not clearly supported by the evidence; an accusation of genocide founded on willful and malignant negligence is, for me, more persuasive.
68 For an argument along these lines, see John G. Heidenrich, *How to Prevent Genocide: A Guide for Policymakers, Scholars, and the Concerned Citizen* (Westport, CT: Praeger, 2001), pp. 101–3.
69 Albright on *60 Minutes*, May 12, 1996. She later disowned the comment.
70 Bonior quoted in "US Congressmen Criticise Iraqi Sanctions," BBC Online, February 17, 2000, http://news.bbc.co.uk/1/hi/world/middle_east/646783.stm.
71 Denis J. Halliday, "US Policy and Iraq: A Case of Genocide?," in Jones, ed., *Genocide, War Crimes and the West*, p. 264 (based on a November 1999 speech in Spain).
72 A useful definition of terrorism is offered by the US Congress: "any [criminal] activity that . . . appears to be intended (i) to intimidate or coerce a civilian population; (ii) to

influence the policy of a government by intimidation or coercion; or (iii) to affect the conduct of a government by assassination or kidnapping." Quoted in Noam Chomsky, *9–11* (New York: Seven Stories Press, 2001), p. 16 (note).

73 For Kuper, genocidal massacres are "expressed characteristically in the annihilation of a section of a group – men, women and children, as for example in the wiping out of whole villages." Kuper, *Genocide*, p. 10.

74 See the H-Genocide discussion logs for September 2001 at http://h-net.msu.edu/cgi-bin/logbrowse.pl?trx=lxandlist=H-Genocideanduser=andpw=andmonth=0109. The posts cited here may be found in the archives for September 16 (Ronayne) and September 20, 2001 (Cribb).

75 Vandana Shiva, "War against Nature and the Peoples of the South," in Sarah Anderson, ed., *Views from the South* (San Francisco, CA: Food First Books, 2000), pp. 93, 113. See also Paul Farmer, "On Suffering and Structural Violence: A View from Below," in Nancy Scheper-Hughes and Philippe Bourgois, eds, *Violence in War and Peace* (London: Blackwell, 2004), pp. 281–89.

76 Ziegler quoted in "UN Expert Decries 'Assassination' By Hunger of Millions of Children," UN News Center, October 28, 2005. An assistant to Ziegler confirmed that the comments were "directly translated from the French," and added that in the past Ziegler had described the "world order" as "murderous" (Sally-Anne Way, personal communication, November 3, 2005). In a similar vein, Stephen Lewis, the UN Special Envoy for HIV/AIDS in Africa, stated of the global AIDS crisis: "This pandemic cannot be allowed to continue, and those who watch it unfold with a kind of pathological equanimity must be held to account. There may yet come a day when we have peacetime tribunals to deal with this particular version of crimes against humanity." Lewis quoted in Michael Mann, *Incoherent Empire* (London: Verso, 2005), p. 61.

77 Kal Holsti, personal communication, June 29, 2005.

78 See Henry Shue, *Basic Rights: Subsistence, Affluence, and U.S. Foreign Policy* (2nd edn) (Princeton, NJ: Princeton University Press, 1996), p. 207 (n. 17). I am citing Shue somewhat out of context: his phrase refers to specific historical events during the Second World War, when "over 6 million Asians were . . . allowed to starve" under colonial (British and French) dominion. See also the discussion of imperial famines in Chapter 2. In his study of Belgian genocide in the Congo (see Chapter 2), Martin Ewans also refers to "genocide by neglect" in post-independence Africa, "with a massive, on-going loss of life . . . being treated in Europe [and elsewhere] with near total indifference." Evans, *European Atrocity, African Catastrophe: Leopold II, the Congo Free State and its Aftermath* (London: RoutledgeCurzon, 2002), p. 252.

79 Galtung quoted in Joseph Nevins, *A Not-so-distant Horror: Mass Violence in East Timor* (Ithaca, NY: Cornell University Press, 2005), p. 191.

80 Sachs quoted in J. Tyrangiel, "Bono," *Time* (Latin American edition), March 4, 2002. Princeton professor Stephen F. Cohen has argued that the death toll exacted by the "nihilistic zealotry" of proponents of "savage capitalism" was *tens of millions in Russia alone* following the collapse of the Soviet Union: to US supporters of radical free-market policies there, "the lost lives of perhaps 100 million Russians seem not to matter, only American investments, loans, and reputations." See Cohen, *Failed Crusade: America and the Tragedy of Post-communist Russia* (New York: W.W. Norton, 2000), pp. 38, 50.

81 Holsti, personal communication, June 29, 2005.

82 Ervin Staub does ask "Is mass killing ever justified?," but quickly answers in the negative, and even rejects the notion that "genocides and mass killings [are] ever 'rational' expressions of self-interest." Staub, *The Roots of Evil: The Origins of Genocide and Other Group Violence* (Cambridge: Cambridge University Press, 1989), pp. 11–12.

83 For example, this comment by "a British observer" of the genocide against Herero and Nama in German South West Africa (Chapter 3): "There can be no doubt, I think, that the war has been of an almost unmixed benefit to the German colony. Two warlike races have been exterminated, wells have been sunk, new water-holes discovered, the country mapped and covered with telegraph lines, and an enormous amount of capital has been

laid out." Quoted in Mark Levene, "Why Is the Twentieth Century the Century of Genocide?," *Journal of World History*, 11: 2 (2000), pp. 315–16.

84 C.L.R. James, *The Black Jacobins: Toussaint L'Ouverture and the San Domingo Revolution* (2nd rev. edn) (New York: Vintage Books, 1989), pp. 373–74. Emphasis added.

85 "Subaltern genocide" and "genocides by the oppressed" are terms that Nicholas Robins and I deploy in a forthcoming edited volume, *Genocides by the Oppressed: Genocides from Below in Theory and Practice.*

86 Martin Shaw writes: "Groups are always to some extent actors, participants in conflict, as well as victims of it. . . . Liberal humanitarianism often finds it easiest to represent victim groups as pure victims – innocent civilian populations attacked by state or paramilitary power. Thus the West sees Iraqi Kurds and Kosova Albanians only as helpless civilians, not as groups that have supported political movements or guerrilla struggle. . . . Armed groups may even carry out mutually genocidal war, against each others' populations. In these situations, we need to recognize the complex patterns that make groups – and often individuals – both participants and victims, at different times." Shaw, *War and Genocide: Organized Killing in Modern Society* (Cambridge: Polity Press, 2003), p. 187.

87 Schabas, *Genocide in International Law*, p. 341.

88 The terms "worthy" and "unworthy" victims are deployed by Edward S. Herman and Noam Chomsky in *Manufacturing Consent: The Political Economy of the Mass Media* (New York: Pantheon, 1988).

CHAPTER 2

Imperialism, War, and Social Revolution

IMPERIALISM AND COLONIALISM

> It was just robbery with violence, aggravated murder on a great scale, and men going at it blind. . . . The conquest of the earth, which mostly means the taking it away from those who have a different complexion or slightly flatter noses than ourselves, is not a pretty thing when you look into it too much.
>
> Marlow in Joseph Conrad's *Heart of Darkness*

Imperialism is "a policy undertaken by a state to directly control foreign economic, physical, and cultural resources."[1] Conquered territories and peoples may be incorporated into the state, as with the United Kingdom, United States, China, and the former Soviet Union; or they may be held within the economic and/or political orbit of the imperial power, while remaining nominally independent.

Imperialism is arguably as old as civilization. Contemporary usage has expanded to include indirect forms of economic, political, and cultural control – hence, for example, the popularity of the term "cultural imperialism." However, in analyzing the imperialism–genocide link, we will focus on the politico-military form of imperialism known as *colonialism.*

Colonialism is "a specific form of imperialism involving the establishment and maintenance, for an extended period of time, of rule over an alien people that is separate from and subordinate to the ruling power."[2] To understand how colonialism is interwoven with genocide throughout history, let us distinguish three basic types: settler colonialism, internal colonialism, and neo-colonialism.

In *settler colonialism*, the metropolitan power encourages or dispatches colonists to "settle" the territory. (In the British Empire, this marks the difference between settler colonies such as Canada, Australia, and New Zealand; and India, where a limited corps of 25,000 British administered a vast realm.) Settler colonialism implies displacement and occupation of the land, and is often linked to genocide against indigenous peoples (and genocidally tinged rebellions against colonialism) (see Chapter 3).

Settler colonies may also be born of genocide and other repressive processes close to the metropolitan country. The genocidal campaign against Ireland's native inhabitants from the sixteenth to nineteenth centuries, itself part of a process of settler colonization (hence Northern Ireland), prompted the migration under massive duress of millions of Irish to the British settler colonies and the United States. Likewise, the repressive drive against "asocial" lower-class elements and political dissidents resulted in the transportation of tens of thousands of prisoners to the penal colonies of Australia.[3]

The phenomenon of *internal colonialism* has received little attention in the genocide literature, but its contemporary link to genocide is perhaps the strongest of all colonial forms. A global "regime" of anti-colonialism, entrenched since the 1950s, today effectively bans interstate colonialism.[4] But internal colonialism – in which core regions of a country control and exploit peripheral regions – continues apace.[5] The greatest relevance of the concept is for genocide against indigenous peoples in countries such as Brazil, Paraguay, and Guatemala. There, native people occupy marginal positions both territorially and socially; their territories are coveted by an expanding frontier of state control and settlement from the center. Profits flow from periphery to core; the environment is ravaged. The result is the undermining and dissolution, often the destruction, of native societies, accomplished by massacres, selective killings, expulsions, coerced labor, disease, and alcoholism. Other examples of internal colonialism that have led, or threatened to lead, to genocide are the Chinese in Tibet (Box 3a); Russia in Chechnya (Box 7a); Indonesia in Aceh; and, arguably, Sudan in the Darfur region (Box 9a).

Finally there is *neo-colonialism* – an ambiguous and contested concept, but a useful one, I think. Under neo-colonialism, formal political rule is abandoned, and the colonial flag lowered. But underlying structures of control – economic, political, and cultural – remain. The resulting exploitation may have genocidal consequences, but at one remove from formal colonialism. Many commentators consider *structural violence* – that is, the violence inherent in social and economic structures – to reflect neo-colonialism: the former colonial powers have maintained their hegemony over the formerly colonized ("Third") world, and immense disparities of wealth and well-being remain as a result.

COLONIAL AND IMPERIAL GENOCIDES

The brief examination of genocide in classical and early modern times (Chapter 1) showed how frequently genocide accompanied imperial expansion and colonialism. In the modern era, the destruction of indigenous peoples has been a pervasive feature of these institutions. This is examined as a global phenomenon in Chapter 3. It remains here to provide a brief overview of other cases of genocide, or borderline genocide, under colonialism and imperialism.

Imperial famines

"Famine crimes" or "genocidal famines" have increasingly drawn the attention of genocide scholars.[6] The most extensively studied cases are Stalin's USSR (Chapter 5), Mao's China, and Ethiopia under the Dergue regime. Recently the North Korean case, in which up to two million people may have starved to death while the government remained inert, has sparked outrage.[7] The literature has focused strongly on cases of famine under dictatorial and authoritarian regimes. Influenced by Nobel Prize-winning economist Amartya Sen, who famously showed that "there has never been a famine in a functioning multiparty democracy,"[8] this has produced groundbreaking case studies such as Robert Conquest's *The Harvest of Sorrow* (USSR) and Jasper Becker's *Hungry Ghosts* (China). The millions of dead in these catastrophes, from starvation and disease, form a substantial part of the indictment of communist regimes in the compendium, *The Black Book of Communism.*[9]

However, a recent work by Mike Davis, *Late Victorian Holocausts*, reminds us that liberal orders have also been complicit in such crimes – extending far beyond the notorious example of the Great Hunger in 1840s Ireland.[10] Davis' subject is the epic famines of the later nineteenth and early twentieth centuries, linked both to nature (the El Niño phenomenon) and state policy, which devastated peasant societies from China to Brazil. He shares Sen's conviction that famines are not blows of blind fate, but "social crises that represent the failures of particular economic and political systems." Specifically, he asserts that "imperial policies towards starving 'subjects' were often the exact moral equivalents of bombs dropped from 18,000 feet."

India was largely free of famine under the Mogul emperors, but British colonial administrators refused to follow the Mogul example of laying in sufficient emergency stocks of grain. When famine struck, they imposed free-market policies that were nothing more than a "mask for colonial genocide," according to Davis. They continued ruinous collections of tax arrears, evincing greater concern for India's balance of payments than for "the holocaust in lives." When the British did set up relief camps, they took the form of work camps, which "provided less sustenance for hard labor than the infamous Buchenwald concentration camp and less than half of the modern caloric standard recommended for adult males by the Indian government." The death-toll in the famine of 1897–98 alone, including associated disease epidemics, may have exceeded eleven million. "Twelve to 16 million was the death toll commonly reported in the world press, which promptly nominated this the 'famine of the century.' This dismal title, however, was almost immediately usurped by the even greater drought and deadlier famine of 1899–1902." In 1901, the leading British medical journal the *Lancet* suggested that "a conservative estimate of excess mortality in India in the previous decade . . . was 19 million," a total that "a number of historians . . . have accepted . . . as an order-of-magnitude approximation for the combined mortality of the 1896–1902 crisis."[11]

Overall, Davis argues that market mechanisms imposed in colonial (e.g., India) and neo-colonial contexts (e.g., China and Brazil) inflicted massive excess mortality. "There is persuasive evidence that peasants and farm laborers became dramatically more pregnable to natural disaster after 1850 as their local economies were violently incorporated into the world market. . . . Commercialization went hand in hand with pauperization."[12] He explicitly links colonial and neo-colonial relations to the economic structures and policies that devastated once-thriving economies, and produced the "Third World" of the post-colonial era.

The Congo "rubber terror"

Thanks to Joseph Conrad's *Heart of Darkness*, published early in the twentieth century, the murderous exploitation of the Congo by Belgium's King Leopold has attained almost mythic status. However, not until the publication of Adam Hochschild's *King Leopold's Ghost*, at the end of the century, did contemporary audiences come to appreciate the scale of the suffering and destruction inflicted on the Congo, as well as the public outcry at the time that produced one of the first truly international campaigns for human rights.

Conrad's novella was based on a river voyage to the interior of the Congo, during which he witnessed what he called "the vilest scramble for loot that ever disfigured the history of human conscience and geographical exploration."[13] The territory that became the sorely misnamed Congo Free State was, and still is, immense (see map in Box 9a). In 1874, King Leopold commissioned British explorer Henry Stanley to secure for the monarch a place in the imperial sun. By 1885, Leopold had established the Congo as his personal fief, free of oversight from the Belgian parliament. Ivory was the prize he first hungered for, then rubber as the pneumatic tire revolutionized road travel. To muster the forced labor (*corvée*) needed to supply these goods, a reign of terror was imposed on African populations.

The result was one of the most brutal and all-encompassing *corvée* institutions the world has known. It led to "a death toll of Holocaust dimensions," in Hochschild's estimation,[14] such that "Leopold's African regime became a byword for exploitation and genocide."[15] Male rubber tappers and porters were mercilessly exploited and driven to death. A Belgian politician, Edmond Picard, encountered a caravan of conscripts:

> Incessantly, we met these porters . . . black, miserable, their only clothing a horrible dirty loincloth . . . most of them sickly, their strength sapped by exhaustion and inadequate food, which consisted of a handful of rice and stinking dried fish, pitiable walking caryatids . . . organised in a system of human transport, requisitioned by the State with its irresistible *force publique* [militia], delivered by chiefs whose slaves they are and who purloin their pay. . . . Dying on the road or, their journey ended, dying from the overwork in their villages.[16]

The population collapse during the years of Leopold's rule was astonishing. Hochschild accepts the conclusions of a Belgian government commission that "the

Figure 2.1 Imperial genocide: the wealth of the Congo, gathered by forced labor, is siphoned off by Belgian King Leopold.
Source: Reprinted from Martin Ewans, *European Atrocity, African Catastrophe*. Original source unknown.

population of the territory had 'been reduced by half'" under Belgian rule. "In 1924," he adds, "the population was reckoned at ten million, a figure confirmed by later counts. This would mean, according to the estimates, that during the Leopold period and its immediate aftermath the population of the territory dropped by approximately ten million people."[17] During this time, the region was also swept by an epidemic of sleeping sickness, "one of the most disastrous plagues recorded in human history."[18] However, as with indigenous peoples in other parts of the world, the impact of disease was exacerbated by slavery and privation, and vice versa: "The responsibility for this disaster is no less Leopold's because it was a compound one."[19]

And the demographic data presented by Hochschild shows a shocking under-representation of adult males in the Congolese population, indicating that outright genocide claimed millions of lives.[20] "Sifting such figures today is like sifting the ruins of an Auschwitz crematorium," wrote Hochschild. "They do not tell you precise death tolls, but they reek of mass murder."[21]

The only bright side to this, "one of the most appalling slaughters known to have been brought about by human agency,"[22] was the launching of an international protest movement, the Congo Reform Association, by a small handful of dedicated individuals. They included Joseph Conrad, Sir Arthur Conan Doyle – author of the Sherlock Holmes stories – and Sir Roger Casement, an Irishman who would fall before a British firing squad following the Easter Uprising of 1916. Utilizing modern means of communication, the Association spread across the European continent and to North America, dispatched observers to the Congo and published their findings.[23] All of this placed increased pressure on King Leopold to expose his territory to outside oversight. Finally, in 1908, Leopold agreed to sell his enormous fief to the Belgian government. Subsequent parliamentary monitoring appears to have substantially reduced mortality, though the "rubber terror" only truly lapsed after the First World War.

Belgium remained the colonial power in the territory until 1960, when it handed over the Congo to a despotic but pro-Western military leader, Mobutu Sese Seko. Early in the twenty-first century, the Congo is again torn apart by genocide, amidst the most destructive military conflict since the Second World War – a grim echo of the killing that rent the region under Leopold's rule (see Box 9a).

The Japanese in East and Southeast Asia

Japanese imperialism, founded on invasions of Korea and Taiwan in the late nineteenth century, grew by leaps and bounds under the military regime established during the 1930s. Domestic persecution of communists and other political opponents was combined with an aggressively expansionist agenda. In 1931, the Japanese invaded the mineral-rich Chinese region of Manchuria, setting up the puppet state of Manchukuo the following year.

In 1937, Japan effectively launched the Second World War, mounting a full-scale invasion of China's eastern seaboard and key interior points. The campaign featured air attacks that killed tens of thousands of civilians, and even more intensive atrocities at ground level. The occupation of the Chinese capital, Nanjing, in December 1937 became a global byword for war crimes. The gendercidal slaughter of as many as 200,000 Chinese men of "battle age" was accompanied by the rape of tens of thousands of children and women (see Chapter 13). Over the course of the Japanese occupation (1937–45), "nearly 2,600,000 unarmed Chinese civilians" were killed, together with half a million to one million prisoners of war.[24]

In December 1941, Japan coordinated its surprise attack on the US Pacific Fleet at Pearl Harbor with a lightning invasion of Southeast Asia. This brought the Philippines, Malaya (peninsular Malaysia), Singapore, and Indonesia under its direct rule. (Satellite control was established in Indochina, in collusion with the Vichy

French regime.) Large-scale summary killings of civilians, death marches of Asian and European populations, and atrocities against Allied prisoners-of-war all figured in the postwar war-crimes trials (Chapter 15). Also well known is the regime of *corvée* labor, one of the worst in modern history, imposed throughout the occupied territories. Not only did the notorious Burma–Thailand railroad kill 16,000 of the 46–50,000 Allied prisoners forced to work on it, but "as many as 100,000 of the 120,000 to 150,000 Asian forced laborers may have died, or 83 percent."[25] A network of trafficking of Asian women for prostitution (the so-called "comfort women") formed an integral part of this forced-labor system. Regionwide, the death-toll of *corvée* laborers probably approached, or even exceeded, one million. Both the "comfort women" and male forced laborers have in recent years petitioned the Japanese government for acknowledgment and material compensation, with some success.[26]

Like their Nazi counterparts, the Japanese believed themselves superior beings. Subject races were not considered "subhuman" in the Nazi manner, but they were clearly inferior, and were usually assigned a helot status in the "Greater Asian Co-Prosperity Sphere." Japanese fantasies of racial supremacy also led to a Nazi-style preoccupation with genocidal technology, reflected most notably in the biological warfare program and gruesome medical experiments. The notorious Unit 731 in occupied Manchuria produced chemical and biological weapons that were tested on prisoners-of-war and civilian populations, and deployed throughout the war theater. In China alone, according to Yuki Tanaka,

> In Zhejiang province, biological weapons were used six times between September 18 and October 7, 1940. . . . Around the same time 270 kilograms of typhoid, paratyphoid, cholera, and plague bacteria were sent to Nanjing and central China for use by Japanese battalions on the battlefield. . . . After the outbreak of World War II, the Japanese continued to use biological weapons against the Chinese. They sprayed cholera, typhoid, plague, and dysentery pathogens in the Jinhua area of Zhejiang province in June and July 1942. . . . It is [also] well known that Unit 731 used large numbers of Chinese people for experiments. Many Chinese who rebelled against the Japanese occupation were arrested and sent to Pingfan where they became guinea pigs for Unit 731. . . . When they were being experimented on, the [subjects] were transferred from the main prison to individual cells where they were infected with particular pathogens by such means as injections or being given contaminated food or water. . . . After succumbing to the disease, the prisoners were usually dissected, and their bodies were then cremated within the compound.[27]

In an ironic outcome from which Nazi scientists also benefited, after the Second World War the participants in Unit 731 atrocities were granted immunity from prosecution – so long as they shared their knowledge of chemical and biological warfare, and the results of their atrocious experiments, with US authorities (see Chapter 15).[28]

The US in Indochina

With the possible exception of the French war to retain Algeria (1958–62), no imperial intervention in the twentieth century provoked as much dissent and political upheaval in the colonial power as the US's long war in Vietnam. A bloody attempt by France in 1945–54 to reconquer a jewel in the colonial crown was defeated by a nationalist guerrilla movement under Ho Chi Minh and his military commander, Vo Nguyen Giap. The country was divided between the nationalist North and a US client regime in the South. Under the Geneva agreements of 1954, this was supposed to be temporary, but recognizing the inevitable victory of Ho in nationwide elections, scheduled for 1956, the South Vietnam regime under Ngo Diem refused to hold them. After 1961, the US stepped up direct military intervention. In 1965, hundreds of thousands of US troops invaded to combat the South Vietnamese guerrillas (Viet Cong), as well as regular forces infiltrating down the "Ho Chi Minh Trail" from North Vietnam.

About seven million tons of bombs and other munitions were dropped on North and (especially) South Vietnam during the course of the war. *This was more than was dropped by all countries in all theaters of the Second World War.* The bombing was combined with the creation of a network of "model villages" in the South Vietnamese countryside, kept under close US and South Vietnamese military observation. Large swathes of the countryside were then designated "free-fire zones," in which any living being could be targeted.

In 1970, US President Nixon widened the war, stepping up the "secret" bombing of neighboring Cambodia, where B-52 raids fueled the rise of the genocidal Khmer Rouge (Chapter 7). Sections of Laos, notably the Plain of Jars, were turned by saturation bombing into dead zones, the inhabitants obliterated or terrorized into flight. The bombing continued until 1973, when a peace agreement was signed and most US soldiers withdrew. Two years later, North Vietnamese forces dealt a death blow to the corrupt military regime in the South, with a final offensive that turned into a rout.

The human cost of the war to the United States was some 58,000 soldiers killed, but in Indochina, the toll was catastrophic. Somewhere between two million and five million Indochinese died, mostly at the hands of the US and its allies. In addition, "a historically unprecedented level of chemical warfare," aimed mostly at defoliating the countryside of forest cover in which guerrilla forces could hide, poisoned the soil and foodchain. "The lingering effects of chemical warfare poisoning continue to plague the health of adult Vietnamese (and ex-GIs) while causing increased birth defects. Samples of soil, water, food and body fat of Vietnamese continue to the present day to reveal dangerously elevated levels of dioxin." An estimated "3.5 million landmines and 300,000 tons of unexploded ordnance" still litter the countryside, killing "several thousand" Vietnamese every year – at least 40,000 since the war ended in 1975.[29]

The widespread international revulsion that the war evoked led to the creation, in 1966, of an International War Crimes Tribunal under the aegis of the British philosopher Bertrand Russell. The Russell Tribunal panelists were "unanimous in finding the US guilty for using illegal weapons, maltreating prisoners of war and civilians, and aggressing against Laos." Most controversially, "there was a unanimous vote of guilty on the genocide charge."[30] A leading figure in this "citizens' tribunal" (see Chapter 15) was the French philosopher Jean-Paul Sartre, who took the opportunity to write "On Genocide," a seminal essay on the theory and practice of genocide. Sartre advanced a cogent if controversial case for labeling US actions in Indochina genocidal. Those fighting the war, he alleged, were "*living out* the only possible relationship between an overindustrialized country and an underdeveloped country, that is to say, a genocidal relationship implemented through racism."[31] Pioneering genocide scholar Leo Kuper joined Sartre in calling the war genocidal, as did *prima facie* the noted theorist of human rights and international law, Richard Falk.[32]

The Soviets in Afghanistan

Soviet imperialism in Afghanistan extended the historic Russian drive for influence and control along the periphery of the empire. Severely mauled by the Nazi invasion in the Second World War, the Soviets established harshly authoritarian police states in Eastern Europe, with tentative forays beyond, notably in Asia and Africa.

Within the empire, strategies of governance varied. In Central and Eastern Europe, with the exception of postwar East Germany and the Hungarian uprising of 1956 (in which some 25,000 died), Soviet imperial power did not produce large-scale killing. Afghanistan was different. Years of growing Soviet influence culminated in the establishment of a Soviet client government in Kabul in April 1978. In 1979, a reign of terror inflicted by President Hafizullah Amin further destabilized Afghan society. Finally, in December 1979, 25,000 Soviet troops invaded to "restore stability." Amin, who had outlived his usefulness, was killed in the first hours of the invasion, and replaced by a more compliant Soviet proxy, Babrak Karmal. Occupying forces rapidly swelled to 100,000.

The occupation spawned an initially ragtag but, with US assistance, increasingly coherent Islamist-nationalist resistance, the *mujahedin*. (Ironically, they included some of the same figures who would later wage holy war against the West, including on 9/11. Osama bin Laden began his terrorist trajectory as a foreign volunteer with the *mujahedin*.) The Soviets responded ruthlessly. In "a ferocious scorched-earth campaign that combined the merciless destructiveness of Genghis Khan's Mongols with the calculated terrorism of Stalin,"[33] the Soviets inflicted massive civilian destruction, recalling the worst US actions in Indochina. "The number of dead is extremely hard to determine, but most observers agree that the war took between 1.5 million and 2 million lives, 90 percent of whom were civilians."[34] Some five million Afghans fled to Pakistan and Iran – one of the largest refugee flows in history.[35]

The Afghanistan–Vietnam comparison has often been made, sometimes with attention to alleged differences between the two. In a well-known article for the *Denver Journal of International Law and Policy*, sociologist Helen Fein undertook to examine whether either or both cases constituted genocide. Her verdict on Vietnam was that while "repeated and substantive charges of war crimes . . . appear well-founded," the charge of "genocide . . . simply [is] not supported by the acts cited." In the Soviet case, however, Fein catalogued "repeated and substantive charges of 'depopulation,' massacre, deliberate injury, forced transfer of the children of Afghanis, and occasional charges of genocide." Combined, they "sustain[ed] a prima facie charge of genocide as well as charges of war crimes."[36]

One may disagree with the gentler judgment about US conduct in Indochina (which featured bombing on a scale and of an intensity never matched in Afghanistan, for example). But it is hard to dispute the validity of the genocide framework for this instance of Soviet imperialism. It may have killed upwards of a million-and-a-half Afghanis, before Islamist resistance and internal collapse forced a withdrawal of Soviet forces in 1989.

A note on genocide and imperial dissolution

Before moving on, it is important to note the close correlation between imperial dissolution – generally accompanied and spawned by the rise of movements of national liberation – and outbreaks of mass violence, including genocide. The combination of fear, insecurity, and humiliation (see Chapter 11) that afflicts imperial powers during epochs of decline, set against a backdrop of insurgent peoples and nations seeking to hasten that decline, frequently produces violence comparable to that of empires in their insurgent and expansionist phase. A classic example is the Ottoman Empire's lashing out at Armenians and other minorities as the "sick man of Europe" stumbled towards its demise (Chapter 4). Another case analyzed in this volume is post-Soviet Russia's genocidal targeting of Chechen secessionists (Box 5a). To these instances may be added France's massively destructive war in Algeria (1958–62), Britain's brutal counter-insurgency against the Kikuyu uprising in Kenya in the early 1950s,[37] and Portugal's struggle to retain its African colonies of Mozambique, Angola, and Guinea-Bissau in the 1960s and 1970s.

GENOCIDE AND WAR

If imperialism and genocide are closely related, war and genocide are the Siamese twins of history.[38] The conjoining of the two is evident from the twentieth century alone. All three of the century's "classic" genocides – against Armenians in Turkey, Jews in Nazi-occupied Europe, and Tutsis in Rwanda – occurred in a context of civil and/or international war. The wartime context is only a necessary, not a sufficient, explanation; but as Christopher Fettweis asks of the Jewish Holocaust, "Should one be surprised that the most destructive war in history was accompanied by one of the most dramatic instances of violence against civilians?"[39] A perceptive scholar of the relationship, Martin Shaw, considers genocide to be an offshoot of "degenerate" warfare, with its large-scale targeting of civilian populations.[40]

The line between "legitimate" war and genocide is probably the hardest to draw in the entire field of genocide studies. But most scholars would now acknowledge intimate connections between the two, and many would rank war as genocide's greatest single enabling factor.

What are the points of connection between war and genocide?

- *War accustoms a society to a pervasive climate of violence.* Large portions of the male population may be drawn into institutions, the prime purpose of which is to inflict violence upon designated enemies. Much of the remaining population is cast in various productive and reproductive roles. Nearly all adults are therefore complicit in the war machine. The boundaries between legality and criminality erode. Psychological and social inhibitions diminish, often to be replaced by blood-lust.
- *War greatly increases the quotient of fear and hatred in a society.* "War creates a type of mass psychosis to which societies at peace cannot relate."[41] Both soldiers and civilians live in dread of death. Propaganda emphasizes the "traitor within." Fear fuels hatred of the one causing the fear, and dependence on the authority that pledges deliverance from the threat. The ideology of militarism inculcates "a condition of slavish docility" and "stolid passivity" throughout the militarized society.[42] Societies grow more receptive to state vigilance and violence, as well as to suspensions of legal and constitutional safeguards. Dissidence threatens unity and stability, and provokes widespread loathing and repression.
- *War eases genocidal logistics.* With the unified command of society and economy, it is easier to mobilize resources for genocide. State power is increasingly devoted to inflicting mass violence. (Indeed, the state itself, "evolving as it did within the crucible of endless rounds of combat, served initially as a more efficient apparatus to fight wars.")[43] For example, the wartime marshalling of rail and freight infrastructure was essential to the "efficient" extermination of millions of Jews, and others, in the Nazi death camps. Much of that infrastructure was built and/or maintained by forced laborers captured as spoils, another regular phenomenon in wartime.
- *War provides a smokescreen for genocide.*[44] "That's war" becomes the excuse for campaigns of extermination. Traditional sources of information, communication, and denunciation are foreclosed or rigidly controlled. "Journalism is highly restricted, and military censorship prevents the investigation of reported atrocities. The minds of nations and of the international community are on other issues in time of war."[45]
- *War fuels intracommunal solidarity and intercommunal enmity.* Many who experienced the wars of the twentieth century (if they survived) recalled them with mingled pain and pleasure. Few had ever before considered themselves citizens swept up in a common cause. Most soldiers experienced "a new kind of community held together by common danger and a common goal,"[46] which forged the most enduring friendships of their lives. In general, war "exaggerates nationalistic impulses as populations come together under outside threats. . . . During conflict group identities are strengthened as the gap between 'us' and 'them' is magnified, and individuals increasingly emphasize their solidarity with the threatened group."[47] As David Barash puts it concisely: "In enmity, there is unity"[48] (see also chapters 11, 12, 17). "What is France if not as defined against England or Germany? What is Serbia if not as defined against Germany

or Croatia?"[49] Solidarity may coalesce around a dominant ethnicity within the society, prompting the anathematizing of Other-identified minorities.

- ***War magnifies humanitarian crisis.*** Refugee flows – whether of internally or internationally displaced peoples – may destabilize the society at war, and others around it. War complicates or prevents the provision of humanitarian assistance. Millions may starve to death beyond the reach of aid agencies, as in Congo's messy and multifaceted wars (Box 9a). "New wars" (see Chapter 12) may come to feed on war-related humanitarian assistance, which can also buttress genocidally inclined state authorities, as in Rwanda in the early 1990s.[50]
- ***War stokes grievances and a desire for revenge.*** One does not need to adhere to the "ancient conflict" model of the Balkans wars to accept that manipulative politicians had plenty to manipulate. Large numbers of Serbs were spurred by the collective memory of genocide against Serbs during the Second World War to support Slobodan Milosevic's ultranationalist option. Fewer Germans would have supported Hitler or the Nazis without an abiding sense of grievance generated by the harsh Versailles Treaty imposed on Germany in 1919. The Khmer Rouge in Cambodia would have enjoyed less popular support if years of American bombing had not driven much of the country's peasant population half-mad with terror and rage.

It would be comforting to think that democratic societies are immune to these responses. Comforting, but unwise. When a liberal society is under stress, it is all too easy for it to slide towards genocide. I was reminded of this in the wake of the May 2004 execution, by slow decapitation, of an American hostage in Iraq, Nick Berg. Berg's killing was captured on video and posted to the Internet (where servers carrying it promptly crashed, overloaded by morbid demand). Lifting the Internet rug after Berg's killing exposed a brazenly genocidal discourse, as with the following statements posted by a popular right-wing blog (weblog) in the US:

> Kill them. Kill every last motherfucking one of them and anybody carrying as much as a quarter of an ounce of sympathy for them. No quarter, no prisoners, no mercy.
>
> . . . These degenerate pieces of filth must be eradicated.
>
> These subhuman slime don't deserve to live. Any second that they're granted on this planet from now on is a crime of omission on our part, as far as I'm concerned.
>
> [I] feel that this culture, this people need to be removed the way a cancer is removed from a healthy body. . . . Tell me, what do they offer humanity? What right do they have to continue to be a growing threat to the life, safety, and security of everyone else on Earth?
>
> It's time to solve this problem the way the Romans solved Carthage, from Libya to Pakistan. First, however, we should round up the leftists here in America and

> give them a choice. Stand with America or with the Islamofacists [*sic*]. Deport those who hate America and then kill every living thing.
>
> The terrorists hide behind their little rags and shout jihad ["holy war"]! I say it's time to shout CRUSADE!
>
> . . . I'd personally give the order to kill a billion Muslims tomorrow if that's what it took to insure my children's future. Sorry if that's too harsh, but shitty being them. They started it.[51]

These examples are repellent, and I apologize to Muslim readers for citing them; but it is necessary to remind ourselves of the genocidal potential that exists in all human societies. The comments are representative and generic[52] – there is nothing uniquely American about them. They are not even especially sadistic, compared to other examples that might have been chosen from the same website. Some have a timeless air, reminiscent of the proclamations of Assyrian kings or Mongol emperors as they prepared to embark on genocidal war and empire-building. (Note the passing references to classical precedents – Carthage, the Crusades.)

But if something in war's extremism is timeless, something is also distinctively modern, and this merits exploration.

The First World War and the dawn of industrial death

In July 1916, my grandfather, Alfred George Jones (1885–1949), a British volunteer soldier, arrived on the Somme farmlands of the western front in France. This terrain had just witnessed the most massive and disastrous Allied offensive of the First World War. On July 1, commemorated ever since as the "Black Day" of the British Army, an offensive by 100,000 Allied troops produced 60,000 casualties *in a single day*, including 20,000 killed. The image of British troops walking at a parade-ground pace, bayonets fixed, across the gently rolling landscapes of the Somme, and directly into withering German machine-gun fire, has become iconic in modern times: "the Somme marked the end of an age of vital optimism in British life that has never been recovered"[53] (see Figure 2.2).

My grandfather was thrown into the meat-grinder that followed, which claimed 630,000 Allied casualties and a similar number of Germans over four-and-a-half months. A sapper in the Royal Engineers, he was blown up and buried for three days by an artillery shell in "no man's land" (a term that has since become a metaphor of the cultural dislocation wrought by the First World War). He was discovered only by chance. Carried to the rear and shell-shocked, he was shipped back to England to convalesce. The experience triggered epileptic attacks that haunted him to the end of his days; but he survived to father my father. Thus, for better or worse, you hold this book in your hands because someone stumbled across my grandfather in no man's land ninety years ago, during the definitive war of modern times.[54]

The crisis caused by the "Great War," above all other conflicts in the Western experience, derived from a combination of industrial technology and physical

Figure 2.2 An iconic image of the twentieth century: soldiers go "over the top" at the Battle of the Somme, July 1916.
Source: Imperial War Museum.

paralysis. As millions of tons of munitions were unleashed, soldiers took refuge in fragile trenches that shook or collapsed from the bombardments, and that between assaults were a surreal wasteland of mud, rats, and corpses. Ten million soldiers died on all sides – a previously unimaginable figure, and one that left a gaping and traumatic hole where a generation of young European men should have been. For Martin Shaw,

> The slaughter of the trenches was in many ways the definitive experience of modern mass killing, seminal to virtually all the mass killing activities of the twentieth century. The massacre of conscripts was a starting-point for the development of each of the other strands. As the soldier-victims were mown down in their hundreds of thousands in the Somme and elsewhere, they provided a spectacle of mass death that set the tone for a century. . . . All the main paradigms of twentieth-century death were already visible in this first great phase of total war.[55]

Adolf Hitler spent four years in the trenches of the western front. He had been swept up in nationalist euphoria at the war's outbreak – there is a famous photograph of a

Berlin crowd celebrating the declaration of war, in which Hitler's face may be seen, rapt with enthusiasm. As a soldier, he fought bravely, receiving the Iron Cross Second Class. He was nearly killed in a gas attack that left him blind and hospitalized – the prone, powerless position in which he first heard of the "humiliating" armistice Germany had accepted. (For more on genocide and humiliation, see Chapter 10.) In the war's aftermath, Hitler joined millions of demobilized soldiers struggling to find a place in postwar society. His war-fueled alienation, and his nostalgic longing for the solidarity and comradeship of the trenches, marked him for life.

The Bolshevik Revolution in Russia, which spawned large-scale killing under Vladimir Lenin and epic slaughter under Joseph Stalin (Chapter 5), is inconceivable without the trauma of the war. The conflict also directly sparked the first well-known genocide of the twentieth century. The Ottoman Turks' exterminatory assault on the Armenian population of the empire killed over a million people, the vast majority of them defenseless (see Chapter 4). The genocide was carried out on the grounds of military "self-defense" against an ethnic group accused of seeking to subvert the Ottoman state, in alliance with a historic enemy (Russia). Genocidal logistics, particularly in terms of transport, were greatly facilitated by the requisites of wartime emergency.

The Second World War and the "barbarization of warfare"

The European theater of the Second World War consisted of two quite different conflicts. In the West, Nazi occupation authorities were generally more disciplined and less brutal, though this did not pertain where round-ups of Jews were concerned. In the occupied territories of the east, and in the Balkans to the south, crimes against humanity were the norm. Genocide featured prominently among them.

The heart of the eastern war was the struggle between invading German forces and the Soviet people.[56] Soviet armies were dealt a massive blow by the German *blitzkrieg* (lightning-war) of June to December 1941, which pushed all the way to the suburbs of Moscow. There ensued a titanic struggle between two totalitarian systems – the most massive and destructive military conflict in history. For Hitler, it was from the start "an ideological war of extermination and enslavement":

> its goal was to wipe out the Soviet state, to enslave the Russian people after debilitating them by famine and all other forms of deprivation, systematically to murder all "biological" and political enemies of Nazism, such as the Jews, the Gypsies [Roma], members of the Communist Party, intellectuals, and so forth, and finally to turn western Russia into a German paradise of "Aryan" colonizers served by hordes of Slav helots.[57]

Reflecting this racial animus and political extremism, the restraints that generally governed German troops in the West – the preservation of prisoners-of-war, a degree of respect for civilian lives and property – were abandoned from the outset. "This struggle must have as its aim the demolition of present Russia and must therefore be conducted with unprecedented severity," declared Panzer Group Colonel-General

Hoepner before the invasion. "Both the planning and the execution of every battle must be dictated by an iron will to bring about a merciless, total annihilation of the enemy. Particularly no mercy should be shown toward the carriers of the present Russian-Bolshevik system."[58]

The result was a "demodernization" of the eastern front from 1941 to 1945, and a concomitant "barbarization of warfare." The terms belong to Omer Bartov, who more than any other scholar has portrayed the disintegration of norms and personalities among the German *Wehrmacht* (see especially his short but provocative book, *Hitler's Army*). Amidst physical travails, primitive conditions, and endless harassment by partisans, troops turned readily to atrocity. They were granted a "license to murder disarmed soldiers and defenseless civilians," and often carried out the task with an indiscriminate enthusiasm that transported them beyond the limited controls established by the army.

The Soviet stance towards the German invader could also be blood-curdling. The poet Ilya Ehrenburg penned a leaflet for circulation among Soviet frontline troops titled simply, "Kill":

> The Germans are not human beings. From now on the word "German" is for us the worst imaginable curse. From now on the word "German" strikes us to the quick. We shall not get excited. We shall kill. If you have not killed at least one German a day, you have wasted that day. . . . If you cannot kill your German with a bullet, kill him with your bayonet. If there is calm on your part of the front, or if you are waiting for the fighting, kill a German in the meantime. . . . If you kill one German, kill another – for us there is nothing more joyful than a heap of German corpses.[59]

Thus conditioned, when Soviet troops reached German soil in East Prussia they unleashed a campaign of mass rape, murder, and terror against German civilians, who were disproportionately children and women. The campaign of gang rape, which Stalin notoriously dismissed as the Soviet soldier "having fun with a woman," is seared particularly into the German collective memory.[60] As many as two million German women were attacked: "it was not untypical for Soviet troops to rape every female over the age of twelve or thirteen in a village, killing many in the process."[61] However, whatever else may be said, Soviet ideology lacked a strong racist component. Perhaps as a result, after months of rape and killing, the regime that was finally imposed on the Soviet satellite state of East Germany was less malevolent than anything the Slavs had experienced under Nazi rule.

A trend of barbarization was also evident in the war in the Pacific, which pitted the US, UK, and China against Japanese occupation forces. In his classic *War Without Mercy*, John Dower examined the processes of mutual demonization and bestialization by the US and Japanese polities. These processes both conditioned and reflected the broader popular hostility in wartime. The American public's view of the Japanese enemy was conveyed in a poll taken in December 1944, in which, according to Gary Bass, "33 percent of Americans wanted to destroy Japan as a country after the war, 28 percent wanted to supervise and control Japan – and fully 13 percent wanted to kill *all* Japanese people."[62]

Genocide and social revolution

It is on a blank page that the most beautiful poems are written.

Mao Zedong, Chinese revolutionary leader

Revolutions are sudden, far-reaching, and generally violent transformations in the political order. Social revolutions, which go beyond a change of political regime to encompass transformations of the underlying class structure, are particularly wrenching.

Beginning with the English Civil War of 1648, the American Revolution of 1776, and the French Revolution of 1789, the modern era has witnessed an escalating series of such transformations. Revolution has been closely linked to struggles for national independence, as well as to attempts to engineer fundamental changes in the social order. The uprisings against the crumbling Ottoman Empire in the early twentieth century provided the template for the century's national liberation struggles. These coalesced as a comprehensive movement for decolonization following the Second World War.

The Soviet Revolution of 1917, which grew out of the chaos and privation of the First World War on the eastern front, epitomized the Marxist–Leninist variant of social-revolutionary strategy. This viewed "all history [as] the history of class struggle" (to cite Marx and Engels' *Communist Manifesto*). Under the influence of Soviet revolutionary V.I. Lenin, it stressed the role of a vanguard party to drag the workers and peasants to liberation, kicking and screaming if necessary (as proved to be the case).[63] Social-revolutionary struggle in the early part of the twentieth century also took a fascist form, as in Mussolini's Italy and Hitler's Germany.[64] Fascism found its shock troops among workers and the *lumpenproletariat* (lower social orders and riff-raff). Its peasant following was also considerable. But its social base resided more in the lower-middle class, and featured an alliance – or marriage of convenience – with traditional, conservative sectors.

Both communist and fascist variants of revolution are highly militarized. This reflects the clandestine organizing and cell-based struggle of revolutionary strategy, as well as the need to crush counter-revolutionary opposition before, during, and after the revolution. It also attests to the conviction of some revolutionaries that the world should share in their victory, or be subjugated by it. As Martin Shaw notes,

> *revolution itself . . . increasingly took the form of war*, particularly guerrilla war. . . . Revolutionaries pursued armed struggle not as a conclusion to political struggle, but as a central means of that struggle from the outset. Likewise, established power has used force not merely to defeat open insurrection, but to stamp out revolutionary forces and terrorize their actual or potential social supporters. As revolution became armed struggle, counter-revolution became counter-insurgency. In this sense there has been a radical change in the character of many revolutionary processes.[65]

Research into the Turkish and Nazi revolutions produced one of the key works of comparative genocide studies, Robert Melson's *Revolution and Genocide* (1996), which summarizes the linkage as follows:

1. Revolutions created the conditions for genocidal movements to come to power.
2. Revolutions made possible the imposition of radical ideologies and new orders that legitimated genocide.
3. The social mobilization of low status or despised groups [e.g., in struggles for national liberation] helped to make them targets of genocide.
4. Revolutions leading to wars facilitated the implementation of genocide as a policy of the state.[66]

But while revolution, especially social revolution, may take a genocidal form, so too may counter-revolution. This book contains numerous instances of revolutions that spawned genocides (Turkey's against the Armenians, Lenin's and Stalin's terrors, the Nazis, the Khmer Rouge in Cambodia, "Hutu Power" in Rwanda). But it includes even more cases in which colonial and contemporary state authorities sought to stamp out "revolutionary" threats through genocide. The Germans in Southwest Africa, the Chinese in Tibet, West Pakistan in East Pakistan/Bangladesh, Iraq versus the Kurds, Serbia in Kosovo, Russia in Chechnya, and Sudan in Darfur – all fit the pattern, as does the Guatemalan army's rampage against Mayan Indians in the 1970s and 1980s (see Chapter 3). In all cases, once war is unleashed, the radicalization and extremism of organized mass violence, described previously, come to dominate the equation.

The nuclear revolution and "omnicide"

> Total war is no longer only between all members of one national community and all those of another: it is also total because it will very likely set the whole world up in flames.
>
> Jean-Paul Sartre

As revolutions in the social and political sphere represent dramatic irruptions of new actors and social forces, so technological revolutions transform the world and human history. This was the case prior to the First World War, when scientific knowledge, wedded to an industrial base, facilitated the unprecedented mass slaughter of 1914–18. An even more portentous transformation was the nuclear revolution – the discovery that the splitting (and later the fusion) of atoms could unleash unprecedented energy, and could be directed towards military destruction as well as peaceful ends. Atomic bombs had the power to render conventional weapons obsolete, while "the destructive power of the hydrogen bomb was as revolutionary in comparison with the atomic bomb as was the latter to conventional weaponry."[67]

The invention of nuclear weapons, first (and fortunately last) used in war at Hiroshima and Nagasaki in August 1945, transformed civilization to its very roots. "In a real way we all lead something of a 'double life,'" wrote Robert Jay Lifton and Eric Markusen. "We are aware at some level that in a moment we and everyone and everything we have ever touched or loved could be annihilated, and yet we go about our ordinary routines as though no such threat exists."[68] In his classic cry for peace, Jonathan Schell described *The Fate of the Earth* as "poised on a hair trigger, waiting

Figure 2.3 Another iconic image: the mushroom cloud of an atomic bomb, this one dropped by the US on Nagasaki, Japan, August 9, 1945.

Source: Imperial War Museum.

for the 'button' to be 'pushed' by some misguided or deranged human being or for some faulty computer chip to send out the instruction to fire. That so much should be balanced on so fine a point . . . is a fact against which belief rebels."[69]

Lifton and Markusen compared the mindset of Nazi leaders and technocrats with those managing nuclear armories in the contemporary age. Both cultures reflected deep, sometimes hysterical preoccupations with "national security," which could be employed to depict one's own acts of aggression as pre-emptive. Both involved professionals whose specialization and distancing from the actuality of destruction helped them to inflict or prepare to inflict holocaust. A dry, euphemistic language rendered atrocity banal. Both mindsets accepted megadeath as necessary for purity and cleansing:

> With [nuclear] deterrence, there is the assumption that we must be prepared to kill hundreds of millions of people in order to prevent large-scale killing, to cure the world of genocide. With the Nazis, the assumption was that killing all Jews was a way of curing not only the Aryan race but all humankind. Involvement in a therapeutic mission helps block out feelings of the deaths one is or may be inflicting.[70]

Whatever the parallels, the immensity of modern nuclear weapons' destructive power was far beyond Hitler's wildest fantasies. Scholars coined the term "omnicide" – total killing – to describe the extinction that nuclear arms could impose: not only on humans, but on the global ecosystem and all complex life forms, with the possible exception of the hardy cockroach. Nuclearism is the one threat that can make past and present genocides seem small.

Younger readers of this book may find these comments melodramatic. They will lack direct memories of the "balance of terror" and the (il)logic of "mutually assured destruction" that pervaded the Cold War. These spawned a degree of fear and mass psychosis that marked for life many of those who lived under it, including myself. Antinuclear sentiment sparked moves towards a prohibition regime (see Chapter 12), built around arms control treaties between the superpowers and monitoring the peaceful use of nuclear energy. This left the situation still extremely volatile, as populations across the Western world recognized in the 1980s: they staged the largest protest demonstrations in postwar European and North American history.

Since that time, immediate tensions have subsided. Few today feel themselves under the perpetual shadow of the mushroom cloud; but, arguably, this reflects no diminution of the threat. Thousands of missiles remain in the armories of the major nuclear powers – enough to destroy the world many times over. While several nuclear or proto-nuclear powers have abandoned their programs (South Africa, Brazil, Argentina), other states have recently joined the nuclear club, including India, Pakistan, and probably North Korea. At least one "conflict dyad" seems capable of sparking a nuclear holocaust on short notice: that of India and Pakistan. These countries have fought four wars since 1947, and seemed poised for a fifth as recently as 2001.

In another way, too, the nuclear threat has multiplied. The Soviet collapse left thousands of missiles in varying states of decay, and often poorly guarded.[71] They made attractive targets for *mafiosi* and impoverished military officers seeking the ultimate black-market payoff. The client might be a rogue state or terrorist movement that would have little compunction about using its prize against enemies or "infidels." The next chapter of the nuclear saga thus remains to be written. It is disturbingly possible that it will be a genocidal, even omnicidal one.

FURTHER STUDY

Omer Bartov, *Hitler's Army: Soldiers, Nazis, and War in the Third Reich*. New York: Oxford University Press, 1992. Brief, seminal study; see also Bartov's *The Eastern Front*, 1941–45.

Antony Beevor, *Stalingrad: The Fateful Siege, 1942–1943*. New York: Penguin, 1999. Unforgettable depiction of the Battle of Stalingrad, a microcosm of the Soviet–German war.

Iris Chang, *The Rape of Nanking*. New York: Penguin, 1998. Account of Japan's genocidal massacres and mass rape in China in 1937–38.

John Dower, *War Without Mercy: Race and Power in the Pacific War*. New York: Pantheon, 1986. Analyzes the racism of both the US and Japanese war efforts, and its transformation into peaceful cooperation after 1945.

Barbara Ehrenreich, *Blood Rites: Origins and History of the Passions of War*. New York: Metropolitan Books, 1997. Fascinating interpretation of warfare as a vestige of human beings' prehistoric struggle against predators.

J. Glenn Gray, *The Warriors: Reflections on Men in Battle*. Omaha, NB: University of Nebraska Press, 1998. Evocation of the soldier's soul, first published in 1959.

Fred Halliday, *Revolution and World Politics: The Rise and Fall of the Sixth Great Power*. Durham, NC: Duke University Press, 1999. Global overview by a leading scholar of revolutions.

Adam Jones, "A Bibliography of War," http://adamjones.freeservers.com/bibliography_of_war.html.

Eric J. Leed, *No Man's Land: Combat and Identity in World War I*. New York: Cambridge University Press, 1979. Perhaps the most enlightening depiction of trench warfare in the First World War.

Robert Jay Lifton and Eric Markusen, *The Genocidal Mentality: Nazi Holocaust and Nuclear Threat*. New York: Basic Books, 1990. Compares the mindset of Nazi leaders and functionaries with that of their counterparts in the nuclear age.

Eric Markusen and David Kopf, *The Holocaust and Strategic Bombing: Genocide and Total War in the Twentieth Century*. Boulder, CO: Westview Press, 1995. Excellent analysis of points of sociological and psychological cross-over.

Arno J. Mayer, *The Furies: Violence and Terror in the French and Russian Revolutions*. Princeton, NJ: Princeton University Press, 2000. Epic study of two epochal revolutions.

Robert Melson, *Revolution and Genocide: On the Origins of the Armenian Genocide and the Holocaust*. Chicago, IL: University of Chicago Press, 1996. Important exploration of the interweaving of war, revolution, and genocide.

Jean-Paul Sartre and Arlette El Kaïm-Sartre, *On Genocide*. Boston, MA: Beacon Press, 1968. Sartre's controversial essay, set alongside evidence of US crimes in Vietnam.

Jonathan Schell, *The Fate of the Earth and the Abolition*. Stanford, CA: Stanford University Press, 2000. Two key works on nuclearism, now in a combined edition.

Martin Shaw, *War and Genocide: Organized Killing in Modern Society*. Cambridge: Polity Press, 2003. The best introduction to the subject.

Yukiko Tanaka, *Hidden Horrors: Japanese War Crimes in World War II.* Boulder, CO: Westview Press, 1997. Examines biological experiments, sexual enslavement, and atrocities against prisoners-of-war.

NOTES

1 Leonard Seabrooke, "Imperialism," in Martin Griffiths, ed., *Encyclopedia of International Relations and Global Politics* (London: Routledge, 2005), p. 398.

2 "Important Concepts in Global Studies," http://www.ripon.edu/academics/global/concepts.html.

3 A readable popular account is Robert Hughes, *The Fatal Shore: The Epic of Australia's Founding* (New York: Vintage, 1988).

4 Hence, I think, the recent destinies of Kuwait and East Timor.

5 The term was first deployed by leading Marxist theoreticians such as Lenin and Gramsci. The most prominent treatment of the theme is that of Michael Hechter, who built his analysis around the English conquest of the "Celtic Fringe" (Scotland, Wales, and Ireland). See Hechter, *Internal Colonialism: The Celtic Fringe in British National Development, 1536–1966* (Berkeley, CA: University of California Press, 1975).

6 For an overview of the literature and law surrounding "famine crimes," see David Marcus, "Famine Crimes in International Law," *The American Journal of International Law*, 97 (2003), pp. 245–81; and Rhoda E. Howard-Hassmann, "Genocide and State-induced Famine: Global Ethics and Western Responsibility for Mass Atrocities in Africa," *Perspectives on Global Development and Technology* (forthcoming 2006).

7 On famine crimes in North Korea, see Jasper Becker, *Rogue Regime: Kim Jong-Il and the Looming Threat of North Korea* (Oxford: Oxford University Press, 2005).

8 Amartya Sen, *Development as Freedom* (New York: Anchor, 1999), p. 168. Sen's 1977 study of the 1943–45 famine in colonial Bengal, in which some three million Indians died, prompted Henry Shue to coin his famous phrase, "the Holocaust of Neglect." Sen, "Starvation and Exchange Entitlements: A General Approach and Its Application to the Great Bengal Famine," *Cambridge Journal of Economics*, 1: 1 (1977), pp. 33–59; Shue, *Basic Rights: Subsistence, Affluence, and U.S. Foreign Policy* (2nd edn) (Princeton, NJ: Princeton University Press, 1996), p. 207 (n. 17).

9 Stéphane Courtois *et al.*, *The Black Book of Communism: Crimes, Terror, Repression* (Cambridge, MA: Harvard University Press, 1999).

10 See Cecil Woodham-Smith, *The Great Hunger: Ireland 1845–1849* (London: Hamish Hamilton, 1962).

11 Mike Davis, *Late Victorian Holocausts: El Niño Famines and the Making of the Third World* (London: Verso, 2001), pp. 158, 174.

12 Davis, *Late Victorian Holocausts*, pp. 15, 22, 37–38, 152, 287–88, 290. Eric Hobsbawm has also pointed out that colonial policy during the Indian famines occurred against a backdrop of Britain's "virtual destruction . . . of what had been a flourishing domestic and village industry which supplemented the rural incomes" across India, but which competed with British products. This "deindustrialization made the peasant village itself more dependent on the single, fluctuating fortune of the harvest," and correspondingly more vulnerable when famine struck. Hobsbawm, *The Age of Revolution, 1789–1848* (London: Abacus, 1994), p. 201.

13 Joseph Conrad, "Geography and Explorers," in Conrad, *Last Essays* (London: J.M. Dent & Sons, 1926), p. 25.

14 Adam Hochschild, *King Leopold's Ghost* (Boston, MA: Houghton Mifflin, 1998), p. 4.

15 Martin Ewans, *European Atrocity, African Catastrophe: Leopold II, the Congo Free State and its Aftermath* (London: RoutledgeCurzon, 2002), p. 3.

16 Quoted in Ewans, *European Atrocity, African Catastrophe*, pp. 112–13. Caryatids are

(female) figures in the columns of Greek architecture, "used as pillar[s]" to support friezes and other stonework (*The Concise Oxford Dictionary*).

17 Hochschild, *King Leopold's Ghost*, p. 233.

18 Neal Ascherson, *The King Incorporated: Leopold the Second and the Congo* (London: Granta, 1999), p. 251.

19 Ascherson, *The King Incorporated*, p. 9.

20 For more on the gendering of the catastrophe, see Adam Jones/Gendercide Watch, "Case Study: *Corvée* (Forced) Labour," http://www.gendercide.org/case_corvee.html.

21 Hochschild, *King Leopold's Ghost*, p. 232. Nor were the Belgians the only imperial power to inflict genocidal atrocities on Congo: according to Hochschild (p. 280), French rule in "their" part of the Congo resulted in population losses also approaching 50 percent in the most afflicted regions.

22 Ascherson, *The King Incorporated*, p. 9.

23 See also E.D. Morel's influential contribution, *Red Rubber: The Story of the Rubber Slave Trade Which Flourished on the Congo for Twenty Years, 1890–1910* (Manchester: The National Labour Press, 1920).

24 R.J. Rummel, *Death by Government* (New Brunswick, NJ: Transaction Publishers, 1997), pp. 146, 151.

25 Rummel, *Death by Government*, p. 150.

26 For in-depth treatments of Japanese forced prostitution in the occupied territories, see Yuki Tanaka, *Japan's Comfort Women: The Military and Involuntary Prostitution During War and Occupation* (London: Routledge, 2002); George L. Hicks, *The Comfort Women: Japan's Brutal Regime of Enforced Prostitution in the Second World War* (New York: W.W. Norton, 1997).

27 Yukiko Tanaka, *Hidden Horrors: Japanese War Crimes in World War II* (Boulder, CO: Westview Press, 1997), pp. 137–38. A good, brief introduction to Japanese crimes is Laurence Rees, *Horror in the East: Japan and the Atrocities of World War II* (Cambridge, MA: Da Capo Press, 2002).

28 See Sheldon H. Harris, *Factories of Death: Japanese Biological Warfare, 1932–45 and the American Cover-Up* (rev. edn) (London: Routledge, 2001).

29 S. Brian Willson, "Bob Kerrey's Atrocity, the Crime of Vietnam and the Historic Pattern of US Imperialism," in Adam Jones, ed., *Genocide, War Crimes and the West: History and Complicity* (London: Zed Books, 2004), pp. 167–69. The best single-volume history of the French and US imperial interventions in Indochina is Marilyn B. Young, *The Vietnam Wars 1945–1990* (New York: HarperPerennial, 1991).

30 Arthur Jay Klinghoffer, "International Citizens' Tribunals on Human Rights," in Jones, ed., *Genocide, War Crimes and the West*, p. 355.

31 Jean-Paul Sartre, "On Genocide," in Jean-Paul Sartre and Arlette El Kaïm-Sartre, *On Genocide* (Boston, MA: Beacon Press, 1968), p. 82.

32 "In the Vietnam War the use of bombing tactics and cruel weapons against the civilian population appears to me to establish a prima facie case of genocide against the United States." Richard Falk, writing in 1968; quoted in Arthur Jay Klinghoffer and Judith Klinghoffer, *International Citizens' Tribunals: Mobilizing Public Opinion to Advance Human Rights* (New York: Palgrave, 2002), p. 235 (n. 26).

33 Eric Margolis, *War at the Top of the World: The Struggle for Afghanistan, Kashmir, and Tibet* (New York: Routledge, 2001), p. 18.

34 Sylvain Boulouque, "Communism in Afghanistan," in Courtois *et al.*, *The Black Book of Communism*, p. 725.

35 Boulouque, "Communism in Afghanistan," p. 717.

36 Helen Fein, "Discriminating Genocide from War Crimes: Vietnam and Afghanistan Reexamined," *Denver Journal of International Law and Policy*, 22: 1 (1993), p. 61.

37 See Caroline Elkins, *Imperial Reckoning: The Untold Story of Britain's Gulag in Kenya* (New York: Henry Holt, 2005).

38 See "The Relationship Between Genocide and Total War," ch. 4 in Eric Markusen and David Kopf, *The Holocaust and Strategic Bombing: Genocide and Total War in the*

Twentieth Century (Boulder, CO: Westview Press, 1995), pp. 55–78. The Library of Social Science website (http://home.earthlink.net/~libraryofsocialscience/) has a number of Richard Koenigsberg's stimulating articles on war and genocide, including "Dying for One's Country: The Logic of War and Genocide," and "As the Soldier Dies, So Does the Nation Come Alive: The Sacrificial Meaning of Warfare."

39 Christopher J. Fettweis, "War as Catalyst: Moving World War II to the Center of Holocaust Scholarship," *Journal of Genocide Research*, 5: 2 (2003), p. 225.

40 "Genocide can be regarded as a particular form of modern warfare, and an extension of the more common form of *degenerate* war," which "involves the deliberate and systematic extension of war against an organized armed enemy to war against a largely unarmed civilian population. . . . Therefore, the best way of making sense of genocide is to see it as *a distinctive form of war*." Martin Shaw, *War and Genocide: Organized Killing in Modern Society* (Cambridge: Polity Press, 2003), p. 5.

41 Fettweis, "War as Catalyst," p. 228.

42 Barbara Ehrenreich, *Blood Rites: Origins and History of the Passions of War* (New York: Metropolitan Books, 1997), pp. 180–81.

43 Alex Alvarez, *Governments, Citizens, and Genocide: A Comparative and Interdisciplinary Approach* (Bloomington, IN: Indiana University Press, 2001), p. 68. Ehrenreich notes that "just as the elite style of warfare had called forth feudalism in settings as different as medieval Europe and Japan, mass armies everywhere led to the bureaucratic state." Ehrenreich, *Blood Rites*, p. 183.

44 I am grateful to Benjamin Madley for this insight.

45 Norman M. Naimark, *Fires of Hatred: Ethnic Cleansing in Twentieth-century Europe* (Cambridge, MA: Harvard University Press, 2001), p. 187.

46 George L. Mosse, quoted in Ehrenreich, *Blood Rites*, p. 183.

47 Alvarez, *Governments, Citizens, and Genocide*, p. 68.

48 Barash quoted in Michael Shermer and Alex Grobman, *Denying History: Who Says the Holocaust Never Happened and Why Do They Say It?* (Berkeley, CA: University of California Press, 2002), p. 93.

49 Ehrenreich, *Blood Rites*, p. 196.

50 Peter Uvin, *Aiding Violence: The Development Enterprise in Rwanda* (West Hartford, CT: Kumarian Press, 1998).

51 All quotes from comments posted to "The Anti-Idiotarian Rottweiler," May 11, 2004, http://www.nicedoggie.net/archives/004152.html.

52 The former associate editor of the *Wall Street Journal*, Paul Craig Roberts, wrote in November 2004: "Many Bush partisans send me e-mails fiercely advocating 'virtuous violence.' They do not flinch at the use of nuclear weapons against Muslims who refuse to do as we tell them. . . . Many also express their conviction that all of Bush's [domestic] critics should be rounded up and sent to the Middle East in time for the first nuke." Roberts, "There Is No One Left to Stop Them," AntiWar.com, http://www.antiwar.com/roberts/?articleid=4007.

53 John Keegan, *The First World War* (New York: Vintage, 1998), p. 299.

54 In 1989, I walked the Somme battlefields; the experience is described, with accompanying photos, in Adam Jones, "No Man's Land," *The Gazette* (Montreal), December 11, 1989 (available at http://adamjones.freeservers.com/nomans.htm).

55 Shaw, *War and Genocide*, p. 172. In a similar vein, Michael Burleigh writes that many perpetrators of the Jewish Holocaust were, like Hitler, "war veterans who, having survived the trenches, had few moral inhibitions about shooting millions into other trenches. Hitler did not pluck his wish to use poison gas against Jews from nowhere." Michael Burleigh, *Ethics and Extermination: Reflections on Nazi Genocide* (Cambridge: Cambridge University Press, 1997), p. 223.

56 A good overview of the Soviet side of the German–Soviet conflict is Richard Overy, *Russia's War* (London: Penguin, 1997). See also Alan Clark, *Barbarossa* (New York: Perennial, 1985); Antony Beevor, *Stalingrad: The Fateful Siege, 1942–1943* (London: Penguin, 1999); John Erickson's two-volume study, *The Road to Stalingrad* and *The*

Road to Berlin (New Haven, CT: Yale University Press, 1999); and British diplomat Alexander Werth's towering memoir, *Russia at War, 1941–1945* (New York: Carroll & Graf, 1999).

57 Omer Bartov, *Germany's War and the Holocaust: Disputed Histories* (Ithaca, NY: Cornell University Press, 2003), p. 7.

58 Omer Bartov, *Hitler's Army: Soldiers, Nazis, and War in the Third Reich* (New York: Oxford University Press, 1992), p. 129.

59 Ehrenburg quoted in Alfred-Maurice de Zayas, *A Terrible Revenge: The Ethnic Cleansing of the East European Germans, 1944–1950* (New York: St. Martin's Press, 1994), p. 34.

60 Stalin quoted in Milovan Djilas, *Wartime* (New York: Harvest, 1980), p. 435.

61 Norman M. Naimark, *The Russians in Germany: A History of the Soviet Zone of Occupation, 1945–1949* (Cambridge, MA: The Belknap Press, 1995), pp. 72, 133; see also pp. 235–50 on the postwar uranium mining that killed thousands of German workers.

62 Gary Paul Bass, *Stay the Hand of Vengeance: The Politics of War Crimes Tribunals* (Princeton, NJ: Princeton University Press, 2000), p. 198.

63 Karl Marx and Friedrich Engels, *The Communist Manifesto* (London: Penguin, various editions).

64 Fascism "is closely associated with imperialism, militarism and nationalism. The logic of belief in racial superiority leads to policies of conquest, domination and even elimination of lesser races." Graham Evans and Richard Newnham, *The Penguin Dictionary of International Relations* (London: Penguin, 1999), p. 168.

65 Shaw, *War and Genocide*, p. 29.

66 Robert Melson, *Revolution and Genocide: On the Origins of Armenian Genocide and the Holocaust* (Chicago, IL: University of Chicago Press, 1996), p. 18.

67 Eric Markusen and Matthias Bjørnlund, "Hiroshima: Culmination of Strategic Bombing, Beginning of the Threat of Nuclear Omnicide," paper prepared for the symposium "Terror in the Sky: Indiscriminate Bombing from Hiroshima to Today," Hiroshima Peace Institute, August 2, 2003.

68 Robert Jay Lifton and Eric Markusen, *The Genocidal Mentality: Nazi Holocaust and Nuclear Threat* (New York: Basic Books, 1990), p. 38.

69 Jonathan Schell, *The Fate of the Earth and the Abolition* (Stanford, CA: Stanford University Press, 2000), p. 182.

70 Lifton and Markusen, *The Genocidal Mentality*, p. 226.

71 See Terrence Henry, "Russia's Loose Nukes," *The Atlantic Monthly*, December 2004, pp. 74–75.

PART 2 CASES

CHAPTER 3

Genocides of Indigenous Peoples

INTRODUCTION

This chapter considers the impact of European invasion upon diverse indigenous peoples, from the Americas to Africa and Australasia. Vast geographic, temporal, and cultural differences exist among these cases, but there are also important common features in the strategies and outcomes of genocide.[1]

To grasp this phenomenon, we must first define "indigenous peoples." The task is not easy. Indeed, both in discourse and in international law, the challenge of definition remains a "complex [and] delicate" one, in Ronald Niezen's recent appraisal.[2] Nevertheless, there are "some areas of general consensus among formal attempts at definition," well captured in a 1987 UN report by José Martínez Cobo:

> Indigenous communities, peoples and nations are those which, having a historical continuity with pre-invasion and pre-colonial societies that developed on their territories, consider themselves distinct from other sectors of the society now prevailing in those territories, or parts of them. They form at present nondominant sectors of society and are determined to preserve, develop and transmit to future generations their ancestral territories and their ethnic identity, as the basis of their continued existence as peoples, in accordance with their own cultural patterns, social institutions and legal systems.[3]

By this definition, "indigenous" peoples are inseparable from processes of colonialism and imperialism which, also crucially, consigned the previously dominant population of a colonized territory to a marginal status.[4] A nexus of indigenous identity and structural subordination is generally held to persist today.

The political and activist components of the indigenist project are also clear from Martínez Cobo's definition. Indigenous peoples proclaim the validity and worth of their cultures, languages, laws, religious beliefs, and political institutions; they demand respect and political space. Increasingly, they have mobilized to denounce the genocides visited upon them in the past and demand their rights in the present. In large part thanks to the growth of international governmental and nongovernmental organizations, notably the United Nations system, these mobilizations of indigenous peoples have assumed a global character. This is analyzed further in the section on "Indigenous revival," below.

COLONIALISM AND THE DISCOURSE OF EXTINCTION

The destiny of indigenous peoples in the Americas and worldwide cannot be understood without reference to the linked institutions of imperialism and colonialism, examined in detail in the previous chapter. In general, though not overlooking the counterexample of African slavery, the destruction of indigenous peoples was less catastrophic in instances of informal empire. Correspondingly, policies of extermination and/or exploitation unto death were most pronounced in areas where Europeans sought to conquer and settle indigenous territories. The focus here will be on settler colonialism.

Three major ideological tenets stand out as justifying and facilitating the European conquests. The first, most prominent in the British realm (especially the United States, Canada, and Australasia), was a *legal-utilitarian* justification, according to which native peoples had no right to territories they inhabited, owing to their "failure" to exploit them adequately. This translated in Australasia to the fiction of *terra nullius*, i.e., that the territories in question had no original inhabitants in a legal sense; and, in America, to the similar concept of *vacuum domicilium*, "empty dwelling."[5] The second tenet, most prominent in Latin America, was a religious ideology that justified invasion and conquest as a means of saving native souls from the fires of hell. The third, more diffuse, underpinning was a *racial-eliminationist* ideology. Under the influence of the most modern scientific thinking of the age, world history was viewed as revolving around the inevitable, sometimes lamentable supplanting of primitive peoples by more advanced and "civilized" ones. This would be engineered both by human hands, through military confrontations between indigenous peoples and better-armed Europeans, and "naturally" through a gradual dying-off of the native populations. "Genocide began to be regarded as the inevitable byproduct of progress."[6]

A sophisticated study of this ideology of inevitable extinction is Patrick Brantlinger's *Dark Vanishings*. Brantlinger points to the remarkable "uniformity . . . of extinction discourse," which pervaded the speech and writings of "humanitarians, missionaries, scientists, government officials, explorers, colonists, soldiers, journalists, novelists, and poets." Extinction discourse often celebrated the destruction of native peoples, as when the otherwise humane Mark Twain, author of *Huckleberry Finn*, wrote that the North American Indian was "nothing but a poor, filthy, naked scurvy vagabond, whom to exterminate were a charity to the Creator's worthier insects and reptiles."[7] Often, though, the discourse was more complex and ambivalent, including elements of nostalgia and lament for the vanishing races. Take this passage by the English naturalist Alfred Russel Wallace, who shares credit with Charles Darwin for the theory of natural selection:

> The red Indian in North America and in Brazil; the Tasmanian, Australian, and New Zealander in the southern hemisphere, die out, not from any one special cause, but from the inevitable effects of an unequal mental and physical struggle. The intellectual and moral, as well as the physical qualities of the European are superior; the same powers and capacities which have made him rise in a few centuries from the condition of the wandering savage . . . to his present state of culture and advancement . . . enable him when in contact with the savage man, to conquer in the struggle for existence, and to increase at the expense of the less adapted varieties in the animal and vegetable kingdoms, – just as the weeds of Europe overrun North America and Australia, extinguishing native productions by the inherent vigor of their organization, and by their greater capacity for existence and multiplication.[8]

Several of the signal features of extinction discourse are apparent here, including the parallels drawn with natural processes of biological selection, and the claims of racial superiority imputed to northern peoples. But it is interesting that Wallace depicts the European conquerors as analogous to "weeds . . . overrun[ning] North America and Australia," rather than as a noble master race. Wallace was in fact an "anti-imperialist and anti-capitalist,"[9] hence the critical edge to his commentary. But like some contemporary observers (a couple of whom are cited in the section on "Celebrating genocide, denying genocide," below), Wallace found little difficulty in reconciling the extermination of native peoples with his progressive political views.

There is a close link between extinction discourse and the more virulent and systematically hateful ideologies that fueled the Nazi holocaust in Europe (Box 6a). The Nazis, writes Sven Lindqvist provocatively, "have been made sole scapegoats for ideas of extermination that are actually a common European heritage."[10] We should also note the interaction of extinction discourse with ideologies of modernization and capitalist development, which created masses of "surplus or redundant population[s]," in Richard Rubinstein's phrase. As Rubinstein explores in his *Age of Triage*, these ideologies produced destructive or genocidal outcomes in European societies as well, as with the Irish famine of 1846 to 1848 and the Jewish Holocaust of 1941–45.[11] Ironically, this modernizing ideology also resulted in the transport – as convicts or refugees from want and famine – of millions of "surplus" European peoples to the New World. Especially in Australia, these settlers became key instruments of genocide against the indigenous inhabitants of the territories to which they were consigned.

THE CONQUEST OF THE AMERICAS

> The reader may ask himself if this is not cruelty and injustice of a kind so terrible that it beggars the imagination, and whether these poor people would not fare far better if they were entrusted to the devils in Hell than they do at the hands of the devils of the New World who masquerade as Christians.
>
> Bartolomé de las Casas, Spanish friar, 1542

> I have been looking far,
> Sending my spirit north, south, east and west.
> Trying to escape death,
> But could find nothing,
> No way of escape.
>
> Song of the Luiseno Indians of California

The European holocaust against indigenous peoples in the Americas was arguably the most extensive and destructive genocide of all time. Ward Churchill calls it "unparalleled in human history, both in terms of its sheer magnitude and its duration."[12] Over nearly five centuries, and perhaps continuing to the present, an impressively wide range of genocidal measures has been imposed upon the aboriginal population of the hemisphere.[13] These include:

- genocidal massacres;
- biological warfare, using pathogens (especially smallpox and plague) to which the indigenous peoples had no resistance;[14]
- spreading of disease via the "reduction" of Indians to densely crowded and unhygienic settlements;
- slavery and forced/indentured labor, especially though not exclusively in Latin America,[15] in conditions often rivaling those of Nazi concentration camps;
- mass population removals to barren "reservations," sometimes involving death marches *en route*, and generally leading to widespread mortality and population collapse upon arrival;
- deliberate starvation and famine, exacerbated by destruction and occupation of the native land base and food resources;
- forced education of indigenous children in white-run schools, where mortality rates could reach genocidal levels.

Spanish America

The Spanish invasion, occupation, and exploitation of most of "Latin" America began in the late fifteenth century, and resulted, according to David Stannard, in "the worst series of human disease disasters, combined with the most extensive and most violent program of human eradication, that this world has ever seen."[16] The tone was set with the very first territory conquered, the densely populated Caribbean island of Hispaniola (today the Dominican Republic and Haiti). Tens of thousands of hapless Indians were exterminated outright: the Spanish "forced their way into native settlements," wrote the eyewitness Bartolomé de las Casas, "slaughtering everyone they found there, including small children, old men, [and] pregnant women."[17] Those men not killed at the outset were worked to death in gold-mines; women survivors were consigned to harsh agricultural labor and sexual servitude. Massacred, sickened, and enslaved, Hispaniola's native population collapsed, "as would any nation subjected to such appalling treatment"[18] – declining from as many as eight million people at the time of the invasion to a scant *20,000* less than three decades later.[19] African slaves were then introduced to replace the native workforce, and toiled under similarly genocidal conditions.

Rumors of great civilizations, limitless wealth, and populations to convert to Christianity in the Aztec and Inca empires lured the Spanish on to Mexico and Central America. Soon thereafter, assaults were launched against the Inca empire in present-day Peru, Bolivia, and Ecuador. At the time, the Incas constituted the largest empire anywhere in the world, but with their leader Atahuallpa captured and killed, the empire was decapitated, and quickly fell. "It is extremely difficult now to grasp the beliefs and motives of the Conquistadores [conquerors] as they cheated, tortured, burnt, maimed, murdered and massacred their way through South and Meso-America, causing such ferocious destruction that their compatriot Pedro de Ciéza de Léon complained that 'wherever Christians have passed, conquering and discovering, it seems as though a fire has gone, consuming.'"[20] A holocaust it indeed proved for the Indians enslaved on the plantations and in the silver-mines of the former Inca empire, where the Spanish instituted another genocidal regime of forced labor. Conditions in the mines – notably those in Mexico and at Potosí and Huancavelica in Upper Peru (Bolivia) – resulted in death rates matching or exceeding those of Hispaniola. According to David Stannard, Indians in the Bolivian mines had a life expectancy of three to four months, "about the same as that of someone working at slave labor in the synthetic rubber manufacturing plant at Auschwitz in the 1940s"[21] (see figure 3.1).

Only in the mid-sixteenth century did the exterminatory impact of Spanish rule begin to wane, and Indian populations to stage something of a demographic recovery. A *modus vivendi* was established between colonizers and colonized, featuring continued heavy exploitation of remaining Indian populations, but also a degree of practical autonomy for native peoples. It survived until the mid-nineteenth century, when the now-independent governments of Spanish America sought to implement the liberal economic prescriptions that were popular in Europe. This resulted in another massive assault on "uneconomic" Indian landholdings, the further erosion of the Indian land base and impoverishment of its population, and the "opening up" of both land and labor resources to capitalist transformation. Meanwhile, in South America as in North America, expansionist governments launched "Indian wars" against native nations that were seen as impediments to economic development and national progress. The extermination campaigns against Araucana Indians in Chile and the Querandí in Argentina form part of national lore in these countries; only very recently have South American scholars and others begun to examine them under the rubric of genocide.

Figure 3.1 The Cerro Rico overlooking the city of Potosí, Bolivia. Following the discovery of silver in the mid-sixteenth century, this lone mountain largely paid for the profligacy and foreign wars of the Spanish Crown for some two hundred years. Millions of native Indians and some African slaves were forced to work in horrific conditions, making the Cerro possibly the world's single biggest graveyard: anywhere from one million to eight million forced laborers perished in the mines, or from silicosis and other diseases soon after. By some estimates, the mines killed seven out of every ten people who worked there. Time for a Potosí holocaust museum, perhaps?

Source: Author's photo, 2005.

The United States and Canada

The first sustained contact between Europeans and the indigenous peoples of North America developed around the whaling industry that, in the sixteenth century, began to cross the Atlantic in search of new bounty. Whaling crews put ashore to process the catch, and were generally welcomed by the coastal peoples. Similarly, when the Pilgrims – religious refugees from England – arrived at Plymouth Rock, Massachusetts, in 1608, their survival through the first harsh winters was due solely to the generosity of Indians who opened their stores to them, and trained them in the ways of the region's agriculture. The settlers, though, responded to this amity with contempt for the "heathen" Indians. In addition, as more of them flooded into the northeastern seaboard of the future United States, they brought with them diseases that wreaked havoc on Indian communities, leading to catastrophic depopulation that paved the way for settler expansion into the devastated Indian heartlands.

Disease was "without doubt . . . the single most important factor in American Indian population decline,"[22] which in five centuries reduced the Indian population of present-day Canada and the United States from seven to ten million (though estimates range as high as eighteen million) to *237,000* by the 1890s.[23] Smallpox was the biggest killer: uncounted numbers of Indians died as did O-wapa-shaw, "the greatest man of the Sioux, with half his band . . . their bodies swollen, and covered with pustules, their eyes blinded, hideously howling their death song in utter despair."[24] Cholera, measles, plague, typhoid, and alcoholism also took an enormous toll. Other factors included "the often deliberate destructions of flora and fauna that American Indians used for food and other purposes,"[25] whether as a strategy of warfare or simply as part of the rape of the continent's resources. An example of the latter was the extermination of the great herds of bison, which were hunted into near extinction by the settlers. Perhaps sixty million of them roamed the Great Plains when Europeans arrived on the continent; "by 1895 there were fewer than *1,000* animals left," and this "had not only driven [the Indians] to starvation and defeat but had destroyed the core of their spiritual and ceremonial world."[26]

A dimension of *genocidal massacre* was also prominent throughout. According to Russell Thornton, though direct slaughter was a subsidiary cause of Native American demographic collapse, it was decisive in the trajectories of some Indian nations "brought to extinction or the brink of extinction by . . . genocide in the name of war."[27] Perhaps the first such instance in North America was the Pequot War (1636–37) in present-day Connecticut, when Puritan settlers reacted to an Indian raid by launching a campaign to exterminate hundreds of defenseless natives.[28] This "created a precedent for later genocidal wars,"[29] including another notorious mass killing more than two centuries later. In November 1864, at Sand Creek, Colorado, Colonel John Chivington commanded his state militiamen to "kill and scalp all, little and big" – including the youngest children, because "Nits make lice."[30] The ensuing massacre was so macabre that it prompted a government inquiry, at which Lieutenant James Connor testified:

> I did not see a body of man, woman or child but was scalped, and in many instances their bodies were mutilated in the most horrible manner – men, women and children's privates cut out, &c; I heard one man say that he cut out a woman's private parts and had them for exhibition on a stock . . . I also heard of numerous instances in which men had cut out the private parts of females and stretched them over their saddle-bows and wore them over their hats while riding in the ranks.[31]

Recalling this rampage decades later, US President Theodore Roosevelt would call it "as righteous and beneficial a deed as ever took place on the frontier."[32]

As noted above, killing was just one of a complex of genocidal strategies that were *intended* to result in the elimination of Indian peoples from the face of the Earth. The Yuki Indians, for example, were subjected to one of the clearest and fastest genocides of a native nation on US territory. The Yuki, numbering perhaps 20,000, inhabited territory in northern California. With the seizure of California and other

Figure 3.2 US soldiers load the corpses of Indian victims of the Wounded Knee massacre for burial in mass graves, December 1890.

Source: Smithsonian Institution National Archives.

Mexican territories in 1847, the Yuki fell under US control. The following year there began the California Gold Rush, "probably the single most destructive episode in the whole history of Native/Euro-American relations."[33] Ranchers and farmers flowed in and, among many other atrocities, murdered Yuki men and stripped the communities of children and women, taking the former for indentured servants and the latter for "wives" and concubines. The Yuki land base was expropriated and the "natives' food supply . . . severely depleted." Settler depredations received state sanction in 1859, when California governor John B. Weller "granted state commissions to companies of volunteers that excelled in the killing of Indians." The volunteers were dispatched to "Indian country," despite warnings from Army officers that they would "hunt the Indians to extermination." They proceeded to slaughter "all the Indians they encountered regardless of age or sex." The combination of "kidnapping, epidemics, starvation, vigilante justice, and state-sanctioned mass killing" virtually annihilated the Yuki, reducing their numbers from the original 20,000 to about 3,500 in 1854, and *168* by 1880.[34] An aghast eyewitness, Special Treasury Agent J. Ross Browne, subsequently wrote:

> In the history of the Indian race, I have seen nothing so cruel or relentless as the treatment of those unhappy people by the authority constituted by law for their protection. Instead of receiving aid and succor they have been starved and driven away from the Reservations and then followed into the remote hiding places where they have sought to die in peace, cruelly slaughtered until that [*sic*] a few are left and that few without hope.[35]

James Wilson likewise calls this "a sustained campaign of genocide" and argues that "more Indians probably died as a result of deliberate, cold-blooded genocide in California than anywhere else in North America."[36]

Other genocidal strategies

Forced relocations of Indian populations often took the form of genocidal death marches, most infamously the "Trails of Tears" of the Cherokee and Navajo nations,[37] which killed between 20 and 40 percent of the targeted populations *en route*. The barren "tribal reservations" to which survivors were consigned exacted their own grievous toll through malnutrition and disease.

Then there were the so-called "residential schools," in which generations of Indian children were incarcerated after being removed from their homes and families. The schools operated until very recent times; the last one in the United States was not closed until 1972. In a searing account of the residential-school experience, titled "Genocide by Any Other Name," Ward Churchill describes the program as

> the linchpin of assimilationist aspirations . . . in which it was ideally intended that every single aboriginal child would be removed from his or her home, family, community, and culture at the earliest possible age and held for years in state-sponsored "educational" facilities, systematically deculturated, and simultaneously

> indoctrinated to see her/his own heritage – and him/herself as well – in terms deemed appropriate by a society that despised both to the point of seeking as a matter of policy their utter eradication.[38]

As Churchill points out, the injunction in the UN Genocide Convention against "forcibly transferring children of the [targeted] group to another group" would be enough to qualify this policy as genocidal – and in Australia, where a similar policy was implemented, an investigative commission indeed found that it met the Convention definition of genocide. However, there was much that was genocidal in the operation of the North American residential schools apart from the "forcible transfer" of the captive native children. Crucially, "mortality rates in the schools were appalling from the outset," resulting in death rates – from starvation, disease, systematic torture, sexual predation,[39] and shattering psychological dislocation – *that matched or exceeded the death rates in Nazi concentration camps during the Second World War.* In Canada, for example, a study carried out in 1907, the so-called "Bryce Report" named after the Indian Department's chief medical officer,

> revealed that of the 1,537 children who had attended the sample group of facilities since they'd opened – a period of ten years, on average – 42 per cent had died of "consumption or tuberculosis," either at the schools or shortly after being discharged. Extrapolating, Bryce's data indicated that of the 3,755 native children then under the "care" of Canada's residential schools, 1,614 could be expected to have died a miserable death by the end of 1910. In a follow-up survey conducted in 1909, Bryce collected additional information, all of it corroborating his initial report. At the Qu'Appelle School, the principal, a Father Hugonard, informed Bryce that his facility's record was "something to be proud of" since "only" 153 of the 795 youngsters who'd attended it between 1884 and 1905 had died in school or within two years of leaving it.[40]

The experience of the residential schools reverberated through generations of native life in Canada and the US. For example, the extraordinarily high level of alcoholism among native peoples in North America was often explained in terms of an assumed genetic disposition or debility. Now, it is increasingly understood to reflect the "worlds of pain" inflicted by residential schooling, and the traumas inflicted in turn by traumatized Indians upon their own children. Churchill talks of a "Residential School Syndrome" (RSS) studied in Canada, which

> includes acutely conflicted self-concept and lowered self-esteem, emotional numbing (often described as "inability to trust or form lasting bonds"), somatic disorder, chronic depression and anxiety (often phobic), insomnia and nightmares, dislocation, paranoia, sexual dysfunction, heightened irritability and tendency to fly into rages, strong tendencies towards alcoholism and drug addiction, and suicidal behavior.[41]

A contemporary case: The Maya of Guatemala

Modern Guatemala is riven by some of the greatest economic disparities in the world, with the Mayan highlands exposed to severe exploitation and abuse on the coffee and sugar plantations of the mountains and coastal plains. In 1944, what is still known as the "Ten Years' Spring" began under two reformist presidents, Juan José Arévalo and Jacobo Arbenz. Arbenz, in particular, introduced significant labor and land reforms. These were aimed at promoting successful capitalist modernization in Guatemala, not socialist revolution. But a communist aim was imputed to the reformers by key players in the United States – particularly the owners and shareholders of the United Fruit Company, furious at the expropriation of unused lands with compensation offered on the basis of the land's declared tax value, which was predictably low. With intimate access to the Eisenhower administration, and exploiting the atmosphere of anti-communism that pervaded the US in the 1950s, United Fruit and other opponents of Arbenz depicted him as a Soviet stooge. The result was a CIA-sponsored military coup in 1954 that overthrew Arbenz and installed a series of brutal military rulers.[42]

Popular mobilizations against military rule, and in defense of native rights, mounted in the 1970s, and also spawned a rebel movement headed by the Guerrilla Army of the Poor (EGP). The Guatemalan regime's response to the guerrilla threat was massive and annihilatory. A holocaust descended upon the Mayan highlands. In just six years, some 440 Indian villages were obliterated and some 200,000 Indians massacred, often after torture, in scenes fully comparable to the early phase of Spanish colonization half a millennium earlier. The genocide proceeded with the enthusiastic support of the Reagan administration in the US, which reinstated aid to the Guatemalan military and security forces when it took power in 1981.[43]

In 1992, the quincentenary of Columbus' invasion of Hispaniola, Rigoberta Menchú, a Guatemalan Mayan, was awarded the Nobel Peace Prize. Menchú lost most of her immediate family in the genocide, and subsequently became a symbol and spokesperson for indigenous peoples worldwide.[44] In 1996, the war was brought formally to an end by a UN-mediated peace accord, and a "Historical Clarification Commission" was established to investigate the atrocities of the 1970s and 1980s. The Commission's final report, released in February 1999, pointed to acts of "extreme cruelty . . . such as the killing of defenseless children, often by beating them against walls or throwing them alive into pits where the corpses of adults were later thrown; the amputation of limbs; the impaling of victims; the killings of persons by covering them in petrol and burning them alive," all part of "military operations directed towards the physical annihilation" of opposition forces. It ascribed to the government and its paramilitary allies responsibility for 93 percent of the human rights violations it investigated and reported; most of these "occurred with the knowledge or by the order of the highest authorities of the State."[45] Finally, the Commission's report took the important step of labeling the Guatemalan government's campaign as *genocidal.* All Maya had been designated as supporters of communism and terrorism, the report noted, leading to "aggressive, racist and extremely cruel . . . violations that resulted in the massive extermination of defenseless Mayan communities."[46]

AUSTRALIA'S ABORIGINES AND THE NAMIBIAN HERERO

The cases of the aboriginal populations of British-colonized Australia and German-colonized Namibia further illuminate the fate of indigenous peoples worldwide. In both instances, decades of denial gave way, at the twentieth century's close, to a greater readiness to acknowledge the genocidal character of colonial actions.

Genocide in Australia

In 1788, the "First Fleet" of British convicts was dumped on Australian soil. Over the ensuing century-and-a-half, the aboriginal population of the island continent – estimated at about 750,000 when the colonists arrived – was reduced to just 31,000 in 1911. The destruction was so immense that it was often claimed that one aboriginal population, that of the island of Tasmania off Australia's southern coast, had been exterminated down to the very last person. This claim has now been decisively challenged, as we will review shortly.

As in North America, the colonists did not arrive in Australia with the explicit intention of exterminating the Aborigines. The massive destruction inflicted on Australian Aborigines instead reflected a concatenation of ideologies, pressures, and circumstances. Arriving whites were aghast at the primitive state of the Aborigines, and quickly determined that they were (1) barely, if at all, human[47] and (2) utterly useless to the colonial enterprise. Aboriginal lands, however, were coveted, particularly as convicts began to be freed (but not allowed to return to England) and as new waves of free settlers arrived during the nineteenth century. As the Australian colonial economy came to center on vast landholdings for sheep-raising and cattle-grazing, the standard trend of expansion into the interior brought colonists into ever-wider and more conflictive contact with the Aborigines. Through the expedient of direct massacre – "at least 20,000 aborigines, perhaps many more, were killed by the settlers in sporadic frontier skirmishes throughout the nineteenth century and lasting into the late 1920s"[48] – Aborigines were driven away from areas of white settlement and from their own sources of sustenance. When they responded with desperate raids on the settlers' cattle stocks, settlers "retaliated" by "surround[ing] an aborigine camp at night, attack[ing] at dawn, and massacr[ing] men, women, and children alike."[49]

Formal colonial policy did not generally favor genocidal measures. Indeed, the original instructions to colonial Governor Arthur Phillip were that he "endeavour by every means in his power to open an intercourse with the natives and to conciliate their goodwill, requiring all persons under his Government to live in amity and kindness with them." But these "benign utterances of far-away governments" contrasted markedly with "the hard clashes of interest on the spot."[50] Colonial officials often turned a blind eye to atrocities against the Aborigines, and failed to intervene effectively to suppress them. It is important to note as well that until the late nineteenth century, no Aborigine was allowed to give testimony in a white man's court, rendering effective legal redress for dispossession and atrocity a practical impossibility. Moreover, extinction discourse took full flight, with the British novelist Anthony Trollope, for example, writing in the 1870s that the Aborigines' "doom is to be exterminated; and the sooner that their doom is accomplished, – so that there can be no cruelty [!], – the better will it be for civilization."[51]

The combination of clashes between frontier settlers and natives, epidemic disease, and extermination campaigns was strikingly similar to the North American experience. The destruction of the aboriginal population of Tasmania, an island off Australia's southern coast, is often cited as a paradigmatic case of colonial genocide. The 3–4,000 native inhabitants were broken down by the usual traumas of contact, and the handful of survivors of massacre and disease were dispatched (in a supposedly noble gesture) to barren Flinders Island. There, they were prey to further bouts of disease and chronic malnutrition, to which the Europeans and their leaders responded with indifference.[52]

The destruction was so extensive that, as noted, many observers contended that the island's aboriginals had been completely annihilated by the end of the nineteenth century. This appears to have been true for full-blooded aboriginals, the last of whom, a woman named Truganini, died in 1876. It ignored, however, aboriginals of mixed blood – perhaps numbering in the thousands – whose descendants live on today. Brantlinger argues that this was convenient for the colonizers, since "it meant that the government could ignore the claims to recognition, land rights, schools, and so forth, of the mixed-race Tasmanians – officially they did not exist as a separate or unique population and culture."[53]

As was true for indigenous peoples elsewhere, the twentieth century witnessed not only a demographic revival of the Australian Aborigines but – in the latter half of the century – the emergence of a powerful movement for land rights and restitution. Subsequently, this movement's members worked to publicize the trauma caused by the kidnapping of aboriginal children and their placement in white-run institutional "homes." These were strikingly similar, in their underlying (assimilationist) ideology, rampant brutality, and sexual predation, to the "residential schools" imposed upon North American Indians during the same period. In response to growing protest about these "stolen generations" of aboriginal children (the title of a landmark 1982 book by Peter Read),[54] a national commission of inquiry was struck in 1995. Two years later it issued its report, *Bringing Them Home*, which stated that Australia's policy of transferring aboriginal children constituted genocide by the UN Convention definition. This claim provoked immense and still-unresolved controversy. The Australian Prime Minister at the time (and still), John Howard, denounced the "black armband" view of his country's history (that is, an "excessive" emphasis on negative elements of the Australian and aboriginal experience). However, although many voices were raised in public fora and the mass media supporting Howard's rejectionist stance, there was also widespread public sympathy for Aborigines, as Colin Tatz points out:

> The Australian public has responded to this National Inquiry in a quite unprecedented way: hundreds of thousands sign "sorry books," thousands stand in queues to listen to removed [aboriginal] people telling their stories, many more thousands plant small wooden hands, signifying their hands up to guilt or sorrow,

> on lawns and beaches across the country. The Australian Labor Party has pledged apology on return to office. State governments, churches, mission societies, city and shire councils proclaim both sorrow and apology.[55]

Moreover, Tatz reports, "the dreaded 'g' word is firmly with us. . . . Genocide is now in the vocabulary of Australian politics, albeit grudgingly, or even hostilely."[56]

The Herero genocide

For many years, the Ottoman campaign against the Armenians (Chapter 4) was considered the first genocide of the twentieth century. Now, it is acknowledged that the designation is more accurately applied to German colonial forces' near-extermination of the Herero nation in present-day Namibia, which took place in the century's first decade.[57]

Although the Germans were late arrivals on the colonial scene, the pattern of colonial invasion and occupation that provoked the Herero uprising was a familiar one. Drawn by the opportunities for cattle ranching, some 5,000 Germans had flooded into the territory by 1903. Colonists' deception, suasion, and violent coercion pushed the native population into an ever-narrower portion of its traditional land-holdings. In 1904, the Hereros rose up against the Germans. Herero chief Samuel Maherero led his fighters against military outposts, killing about 120 Germans. This resistance to colonial domination infuriated the German leader Kaiser Wilhelm II, who responded by dispatching a hardliner, Lt.-Gen. Lothar von Trotha, to "German South-West Africa." Von Trotha was firmly convinced that Africans "are all alike. They only respond to force. It was and is my policy to use force with terrorism and even brutality. I shall annihilate the revolting tribes with rivers of blood and rivers of gold. Only after a complete uprooting will something emerge."[58]

After defeating the Hereros at the Battle of Hamakari in August 1904, the German Army chased survivors into the bone-dry wastes of the Kalahari desert. Von Trotha then issued his notorious "annihilation order" (*Vernichtungsbefehl*). In it, he pledged that "within the German borders every Herero, with or without a gun, with or without cattle, will be shot. I will no longer accept women and children [as prisoners], I will drive them back to their people or I will let them be shot at."[59] The order remained in place for several months, until a domestic outcry led the German Chancellor to rescind it. A contemporary account describes Hereros emerging from the Kalahari "starved to skeletons with hollow eyes, powerless and hopeless."[60] They were then allowed to move from the frying-pan to the fire: concentration camps. "A continuing desire to destroy the Hereros played a part in the German maintenance of such lethal camp conditions," writes Benjamin Madley; he notes elsewhere that "according to official German figures, of 15,000 Hereros and 2,200 Namas incarcerated in camps, some 7,700 or 45 percent perished."[61] (Following the cessation of the Herero war, another tribal nation, the Nama, also rose up in revolt against German rule and was similarly crushed, with approximately half the population killed. Many scholars accordingly refer to the Namibian events as the genocide of the Hereros and Namas.)

An advantage of a comparative and global-historical approach to genocide is that it allows us to perceive important connections between campaigns of mass killing and group destruction that are widely separated in time and space. Scholarship on the genocide against the Hereros provides an excellent example. It is increasingly acknowledged not only that this was the first genocide of the twentieth century, but that it paved the way, in important respects, for the prototypical mass slaughter of that century – the Jewish Holocaust (Chapter 6). As summarized by Madley:

> The Herero genocide was a crucial antecedent to Nazi mass murder. It created the German word *Konzentrationslager* [concentration camp] and the twentieth century's first death camp. Like Nazi mass murder, the Namibian genocides were premised upon ideas like *Lebensraum* [living space], annihilation war [*Vernichtungskrieg*], and German racial supremacy. Individual Nazis were also linked to colonial Namibia. Hermann Goering, who built the first Nazi concentration camps, was the son of the first governor of colonial Namibia. Eugen Fischer, who influenced Hitler and ran the institute that supported Joseph Mengele's medical "research" at Auschwitz, conducted racial studies in the colony. And Ritter von Epp, godfather of the Nazi party and Nazi governor of Bavaria from 1933–1945, led German troops against the Herero during the genocide.[62]

Following the independence of Namibia in 1990 (from South Africa, which had conquered the territory during the First World War), survivors' descendants called on Germany to apologize for the Herero genocide, and provide reparations. Why, asked Herero leaders, was Germany willing to pay tens of billions of dollars to Jewish survivors of Nazi genocide, but not even to acknowledge crimes against the Hereros? Following strategies developed by Jewish advocates, the Hereros filed suit in the United States for US$4 billion in compensation – half from the German government, half from German companies that were alleged to have profited from the occupation of Herero lands. In August 2004 – the centenary of the Herero uprising – the German development-aid minister, Heidemarie Wieczorek-Zeul, attended a ceremony at Okakarara in the region of Otjozondjupa, where the conflict had formally ended back in 1906. The minister issued a formal apology that included the "G-word": "We Germans accept our historic and moral responsibility and the guilt incurred by Germans at that time. . . . The atrocities committed at that time would have been termed genocide."[63] She also promised German development aid as an oblique form of recompense.

DENYING GENOCIDE, CELEBRATING GENOCIDE

Denial is regularly condemned as the final stage of genocide (see Chapter 14). How, then, are we to class the mocking or even *celebrating* of genocide? These are sadly not uncommon responses, and they are nowhere more prominent than with regard to genocides of indigenous peoples.

Among most sectors of informed opinion in the Americas – from Alaska to Tierra del Fuego – the notion that indigenous peoples experienced a "genocide" at the hands of their white conquerors is not only dismissed, but openly *derided*.[64] In a September 2001 post to the H-Genocide academic mailing list, Professor Alexander Bielakowski of the University of Findlay engaged in what seemed outright genocidal denial, writing that "if [it] was the plan" to "wipe out the American Indians . . . the US did a damn poor job following through with it."[65] This is a curious way to describe the annihilation of up to 98 percent of the indigenous population of the United States over three centuries. The fine British historian Michael Burleigh takes a similarly flippant jab in his book *Ethics and Extermination*, scoffing at notions of "the 'disappearance' of the [Australian] Aboriginals or Native Americans, some of whose descendants mysteriously seem to be running multi-million dollar casinos."[66] How can a tiny Indian elite be considered representative of the poorest, shortest-lived ethnic minority in the US and Canada?

Celebrations of indigenous genocide also have no clear parallel in mainstream discourse. Thus one finds prominent essayist Christopher Hitchens describing protests over the Columbus quincentenary as "an ignorant celebration of stasis and backwardness, with an unpleasant tinge of self-hatred." For Hitchens, the destruction of Native American civilization was simply "the way that history is made, and to complain about it is as empty as complaint about climatic, geological or tectonic shift." He justified the conquest on classic utilitarian grounds:

> It is sometimes unambiguously the case that a certain coincidence of ideas, technologies, population movements and politico-military victories leaves humanity on a slightly higher plane than it knew before. The transformation of part of the northern part of this continent into "America" inaugurated a nearly boundless epoch of opportunity and innovation, and thus *deserves to be celebrated with great vim and gusto*, with or without the participation of those who wish they had never been born.[67]

The arrogance and contempt on display in these comments is echoed in the pervasive appropriation of Indian culture and nomenclature by North American white culture. Note, for example, the practice of adopting ersatz Indian names and motifs for professional sports teams. James Wilson argues that calling a Washington, DC football franchise the "Redskins" is "roughly the equivalent of calling a team 'the Buck Niggers' or 'the Jewboys.'"[68] Other acts of appropriation include naming gas-guzzling vehicles (the Winnebago, the Jeep Cherokee) after Indian nations, so that peoples famous for their respectful custodianship of the environment are instead associated with technologies that damage it. This is carried to sinister extremes with the grafting of Indian names onto US military weaponry, as with the Apache attack helicopter and the Tomahawk cruise missile. In Madley's opinion, such nomenclature "casts Indians as threatening and dangerous," subtly providing "a post-facto justification for the violence committed against them."[69]

COMPLEXITIES AND CAVEATS

Several of the complicating factors in evaluating the genocide of indigenous peoples have been noted. Prime among them is the question of intent. (Before proceeding, recall that some genocide scholars reject the Genocide Convention's emphasis on intentionality, and argue that the emphasis should be on *outcomes*. If this standard is adopted, there is nothing in recorded human experience to set alongside the genocide of the indigenous peoples in the Americas. It lasted longer, and destroyed a greater percentage and possibly a greater total number of victims, than any genocide in history.)

Specific intent is easy enough to adduce in the consistent tendency towards massacre and physical extermination, evident from the earliest days of European conquest of the Americas, Africa, Australasia, and other parts of the world. But in most or perhaps all cases, this accounted for a minority of deaths among the colonized peoples.

The forced-labor institutions of Spanish America also demonstrated a high degree of conscious intent. When slaves are dying like flies before your eyes, after only a few months down the mines or on the plantations, and your response is not to alter conditions but to feed more human lives into the inferno, this is "first-degree" genocide (in Ward Churchill's conceptualizing; see Chapter 1, note 48). The mechanisms of death were not appreciably different from those of many Nazi slave-labor camps.

Disease was the greatest killer. Here, a lesser – but by no means insignificant – degree of intent obtained. There is little doubt about the genocidal intent underlying conscious biological warfare against Indian nations. A lesser but still substantial degree of intent also featured in the numerous cases where disease was exacerbated by malnutrition, overwork, and outright enslavement.[70] In some cases, though, entire Indian nations were virtually wiped out by pathogens before they had ever set eyes on a European. In addition, many of the connections between hygiene, overcrowding, and the spread of disease were poorly understood for much of the period of the attack on indigenous peoples. Concepts of second- and third-degree genocide would seem to apply here.

Further complexity arises in the agents of the killing. Genocide studies emphasizes the role of the state as the central agent of genocide, and one certainly finds a great deal of state-planned, state-sponsored, and state-directed killing of indigenous peoples. In many and perhaps most cases, however, the direct perpetrators of genocide were colonial *settlers* rather than those in authority. Indeed, as in Australia, settlers often protested the alleged lack of state support and assistance in confronting the "savages" on the frontier. To the extent that policies were proposed to halt the destruction of native peoples, it was often those in authority who proposed them, though effective measures were rarely implemented. Measures were taken, as at Flinders Island, to "protect" and "preserve" aboriginal groups, but often these actually contributed to the genocidal process. As Colin Tatz has pointed out, "nowhere does the [Genocide] Convention implicitly or explicitly rule out intent with *bona fides*, good faith, 'for their own good' or 'in their best interests.'"[71]

Helpful here might be Tony Barta's concept of the "genocidal *society* – as distinct from a genocidal state." This is defined as a society "in which the whole bureaucratic apparatus might officially be directed to protect innocent people but in which a whole race is nevertheless subject to remorseless pressures of destruction inherent in the very nature of the society."[72] The nature of settler colonialism, in other words, made conflict with native peoples, and their eventual large-scale destruction, almost inevitable. State authorities, though they might occasionally have decried more wanton acts of violence against natives, were above all concerned with ensuring that the colonial or post-colonial endeavor succeeded. If the near-annihilation of the indigenous population was the result, this was sometimes lamented (perhaps with romantic and nostalgic overtones, as described in Brantlinger's *Dark Vanishings*), but it was never remotely sufficient to warrant the cancellation or serious revision of the enterprise.[73]

A few other ambiguous features of genocides against indigenous peoples may be cited. First, the prevailing elite view of history has tended to underestimate the role of the millions of people who migrated from the colonial metropole to the "New World." These settlers and/or administrators were critical to the unfolding of the genocides, not only through the diseases they carried, but (notably in Australasia) through the massacres they authorized and implemented.[74] It should not be forgotten, however, that many of them were fleeing religious persecution or desperate material want. Think of the millions of Irish who abandoned their homeland during the Great Hunger of 1846–48, or the English convicts shipped off for minor crimes to penal colonies and barren, disease-ridden settlements in the Antipodes. Settlers and administrators often suffered dreadful mortality rates. As with the indigenous population, death usually resulted from exposure to pathogens to which they had no resistance. To cite an extreme example, "it is said that 6,040 died out of the total of 7,289 immigrants who had come to Virginia by February, 1625, or around 83 percent."[75] Elsewhere, "tropical maladies turn[ed] assignments to military stations, missions, or government posts into death watches."[76]

Finally, we should be careful not to romanticize indigenous peoples and their societies prior to the European invasion. To limit the discussion to the Americas: it was broadly true that genocide, and war unto genocide, featured only rarely. War among North American Indian communities (excluding present-day Mexico) was generally "farre lesse bloudy and devouring than the cruell Warres of Europe," as a European observer put it.[77] The Iroquois expansion into Huron territories in the seventeenth century is an exception, but mass violence was far more pervasive in Central America and Mexico, at least during certain periods. In the classic era of Mayan civilization (600–900 CE), war seems to have been waged with frequency and sometimes incessantly; many scholars now link endemic conflict to the collapse of the great Mayan cities, and the classical civilization along with it. The Aztecs of Mexico, meanwhile, warred to capture prisoners for religious sacrifice, sometimes thousands at a time, at their great temple in Tenochtitlán (now Mexico City). The Aztecs so ravaged and alienated surrounding nations that these subjects enthusiastically joined with invading Spanish forces to destroy them.

This pattern of collaboration with the conquering force, often arising from and exacerbating the tensions of indigenous international relations, was quite common throughout the hemisphere. Soon Indians, too, became willing participants in genocidal wars against other Indian nations – and sometimes against members of the colonizing society as well. Reference has already been made (Chapter 1) to *subaltern genocide*, in which oppressed peoples adopt genocidal strategies against their oppressors. Latin America offers several notable examples, studied in detail by Nicholas Robins in his book *Native Insurgencies and the Genocidal Impulse in the Americas.*[78] The millenarian "Great Rebellion" in Upper Peru (Bolivia) in the 1780s aimed explicitly to slaughter or expel all white people from the former Inca realm. In Mexico's Yucatán peninsula in the mid-nineteenth century, Mayan Indians rose in revolt to extirpate the territory's whites or drive them into the sea.[79] In both cases, the genocidal project advanced some distance before the whites launched a successful (and genocidal) counter-attack. I believe we can sympathize with the enormous and often mortal pressure placed upon indigenous peoples, while still recognizing that a genocidal counter-strategy sometimes resulted.

INDIGENOUS REVIVAL

As the case study of Guatemala demonstrated, assaults on indigenous peoples – including outright genocide – are by no means confined to distant epochs. According to Ken Coates, "the era from the start of World War II through to the 1960s . . . [was] an era of unprecedented aggression in the occupation of indigenous lands and, backed by the equally unprecedented wealth and power of the industrial world, the systematic dislocation of thousands of indigenous peoples around the world."[80] In many regions, invasions and occupations by settlers and multinational corporations, seeking to exploit indigenous lands and resources, continue to the present.

No less than in past periods, however, invasion and attempted domination have fueled indigenous resistance. In recent decades, for the first time, this has assumed the form of a *global* mobilization of indigenous peoples. The "indigenous revival" is closely linked to movements for decolonization that transformed world politics in the twentieth century. It also reflects the development of human-rights philosophies and legislation – particularly in the fertile period following the Second World War, when numerous rights instruments were developed (including the UN Genocide Convention). Decolonization brought to fruition the pledges of self-determination that had featured in the charter of the League of Nations, but had withered in the face of opposition from colonial powers such as Britain, France, and the Netherlands. But this was liberation from domination by external colonial forces. What of societies that were or had become formally independent as nation-states, but where a "pigmentocracy" of (usually) white people ruled over masses of displaced, exploited, and marginalized indigenous peoples? As Ronald Niezen points out, the horrors of the Nazi era in Europe "contributed to a greater receptiveness at the international level to measures for the protection of minorities," given the increasing recognition "that states could not always be relied upon to protect their own citizens, that states could even pass laws to promote domestic policies of genocide."[81] At the same time as this realization was gaining ground, so was an acceptance among the diverse colonized peoples that they were members of a global indigenous class. The United Nations, which in 1960 declared self-determination to be a human right, became a powerful forum for the expression of indigenous aspirations, particularly with the creation in

1982 of a Working Group on Indigenous Populations in the UN Economic and Social Council (ECOSOC). Attending a session of the working group, Mick Dodson, an Australian aboriginal representative, described his dawning recognition that "We were all part of a world community of Indigenous peoples spanning the planet; experiencing the same problems and struggling against the same alienation, marginalisation and sense of powerlessness."[82]

An event of great significance in the Western hemisphere was the first Continental Indigenous International Convention, held in Quito, Ecuador in July 1990, and "attended by four hundred representatives from 120 indigenous nations and organizations."[83] Simultaneously, the number of non-governmental organizations (NGOs) grew exponentially, so that by 2000 the UN High Commissioner for Human Rights could cite some 441 organizations of indigenous peoples worldwide. And indigenous peoples in many parts of the world strove to use the "master's tools" – the educational and legal systems of the dominant society – to reclaim the lands, political rights, and cultural autonomy stripped from them by their colonial conquerors.

At the national level, the impact of these movements is increasingly far-reaching. In the United States, an ever-greater number of individuals are choosing to self-identify as Native Americans,[84] and more and more native nations are petitioning for federal recognition; an "Indigenous Peoples' Day" has supplanted Columbus Day in some US cities. In Latin America, the impact has been more dramatic still. Indigenous peoples in Ecuador and Bolivia have "converged in mass mobilizations, breathtaking in their scale and determination," that overthrew governments and ushered in "a new revolutionary moment in which indigenous actors have acquired the leading role."[85] In Mexico on January 1, 1994, indigenous peoples in the poverty-stricken southern state of Chiapas rose up in revolt against central authorities – the so-called Zapatista rebellion – protesting the disastrous impact on the native economy of cheap, subsidized corn exports from the US under the recently signed North American Free Trade Agreement (NAFTA). The Zapatistas have since established substantial local autonomy in their zone of control. "Even on the outskirts of Mexico City, about 100,000 Nahuatl Indians, descended from the Aztecs, have set up 12 indigenous communities and are demanding that the government recognize their autonomy."[86]

Finally, in Guatemala – the country that witnessed the Western hemisphere's worst twentieth-century genocide – the Mayan Indian movement emerged from the genocide of the late 1970s and early 1980s with renewed vigor and conviction.[87] The country's Mayan populations won the right to be educated in their own languages, and filed high-profile legal cases against racist discrimination; in 2000 a Mayan woman, Otilia Lux de Cotí, became the first Indian cabinet minister (for culture and sports) in the country's history. "There has been a very heartening change in the public's sense of what is right," stated Tani Adams of the CIRMA think-tank in Guatemala City. "Things are changing very fast in Guatemala. Churches, the state, the media, everyone knows this issue has to be dealt with."[88] However, the changes took place against a backdrop of continued dire poverty and social marginalization for the majority of Guatemalan Maya, and the pernicious racism of the dominant society. This is a combination familiar to indigenous peoples worldwide, and a basis for the claim, advanced by some, that genocide continues today.[89]

Figure 3.3 "The Maya Zone is not an ethnographic museum, it is a people on the march." A mural celebrating the indigenous revival in Yucatán, Mexico. It adorns a museum wall in Puerto Felipe Carrillo, formerly Chan Santa Cruz, capital of the semi-independent Mayan kingdom established after the genocidal Caste War of 1847–48 (see pp. 29, 85).

Source: Author's photo, 2002.

FURTHER STUDY

Patrick Brantlinger, *Dark Vanishings: Discourse on the Extinction of Primitive Races, 1800–1930.* Ithaca, NY: Cornell University Press, 2003. Examines European attitudes towards "primitive" races and their extinction.

Dee Brown, *Bury My Heart at Wounded Knee: An Indian History of the American West.* New York: Owl Books, 2001. First published in 1971, and still the classic introduction to the native North American experience.

Bartolomé de las Casas, *A Short Account of the Destruction of the Indies*. London: Penguin, 1992. First published in 1552: a Spanish friar's unrelenting description of colonial depredations in the Americas.

Alfred A. Cave, *The Pequot War*. Amherst, MA: University of Massachusetts Press, 1996. Definitive work on the Pequot genocide.

Ward Churchill, *A Little Matter of Genocide: Holocaust and Denial in the Americas, 1492 to the Present*. San Francisco, CA: City Lights Books, 1997. Forceful polemic, with attention to genocide as a legal and academic concept.

Ken S. Coates, *A Global History of Indigenous Peoples: Struggle and Survival*. Basingstoke: Palgrave Macmillan, 2004. A solid introduction, especially good on the Second World War and the postwar era.

Mark Cocker, *Rivers of Blood, Rivers of Gold: Europe's Conquest of Indigenous Peoples*. New York: Grove Press, 2001. Comprehensive survey, ranging from the Americas to Africa and Australasia.

Mary Crow Dog with Richard Erdoes, *Lakota Woman*. New York: HarperPerennial, 1991. Rich memoir by a Native American activist.

Richard Drinnon, *Facing West: The Metaphysics of Indian Hating and Empire Building*. New York: Schocken Books, 1990. The racist ideology underlying US wars against American Indians, Filipinos, and Indochinese.

Jan-Bart Gewald, *Herero Heroes: A Socio-political History of the Herero of Namibia, 1890–1923*. Athens, OH: Ohio University Press, 2001. Study of the Herero genocide and its aftermath.

Francis Jennings, *The Invasion of America: Indians, Colonialism, and the Cant of Conquest*. New York: W.W. Norton, 1975. Early, widely cited account of the formative period of white–Indian interaction in North America.

Sven Lindqvist, *"Exterminate All the Brutes": One Man's Odyssey into the Heart of Darkness and the Origins of European Genocide*. New York: The New Press, 1996. Epigrammatic meditation on the links between colonialism and Nazi genocide.

Rigoberta Menchú with Elisabeth Burgos-Débray, *I, Rigoberta Menchú: An Indian Woman in Guatemala*. New York: Verso, 1987. Memoir, by the Nobel Peace Prize-winner, of her family's experience in the genocide against Mayan Indians.

MariJo Moore, ed., *Genocide of the Mind: New Native American Writing*. New York: Thunder's Mouth Press/Nation Books, 2003. Soul-searching reflections by native writers.

Alan Moorehead, *The Fatal Impact: The Invasion of the South Pacific, 1767–1840*. New York: HarperCollins, 1990. First published in 1966, this remains a moving introduction to the devastation of Pacific indigenous peoples.

A. Dirk Moses, ed., *Genocide and Settler Society: Frontier Violence and Stolen Indigenous Children in Australian History*. New York: Berghahn Books, 2004. Seminal collection of essays.

Ronald Niezen, *The Origins of Indigenism: Human Rights and the Politics of Identity*. Berkeley, CA: University of California Press, 2003. The growth of contemporary indigenous identities and movements.

Nicholas Robins, *Native Insurgencies and the Genocidal Impulse in the Americas*. Bloomington, IN: Indiana University Press, 2005. Ground-breaking study of

Indian millenarian movements that adopted genocidal strategies against the European invader.

David E. Stannard, *American Holocaust: The Conquest of the New World.* New York: Oxford University Press, 1992. Perhaps the most enduring of the works published for the Columbus quincentenary.

Russell Thornton, *American Indian Holocaust and Survival: A Population History since 1492.* Norman, OK: University of Oklahoma Press, 1990. Foundational text on the demographic impact of European conquest and colonization.

Daniel Wilkinson, *Silence on the Mountain: Stories of Terror, Betrayal, and Forgetting in Guatemala.* Boston, MA: Houghton Mifflin, 2002. Intimate glimpse of upheaval in Mayan Indian communities during the genocide; usefully read alongside Menchú (see above).

James Wilson, *The Earth Shall Weep: A History of Native America.* New York: Atlantic Monthly Press, 1998. Fine overview of the native experience in North America.

Ronald Wright, *Stolen Continents: The "New World" Through Indian Eyes.* Boston, MA: Houghton Mifflin, 1993. Examines the conquest throughout the Western hemisphere from the perspective of its victims.

Geoffrey York, *The Dispossessed: Life and Death in Native Canada.* London: Vintage UK, 1990. Harrowing journalistic account of poverty and cultural dislocation among Canada's native peoples.

NOTES

1 For concise overviews, see Robert K. Hitchcock and Tara M. Twedt, "Physical and Cultural Genocide of Various Indigenous Peoples," in Samuel Totten *et al.*, eds, *Century of Genocide: Eyewitness Accounts and Critical Views* (New York: Garland Publishing, 1997), pp. 372–407; and Elazar Barkan, "Genocides of Indigenous Peoples: Rhetoric of Human Rights," in Robert Gellately and Ben Kiernan, eds, *The Specter of Genocide: Mass Murder in Historical Perspective* (Cambridge: Cambridge University Press, 2003), pp. 117–40.

2 Ronald Niezen, *The Origins of Indigenism: Human Rights and the Politics of Identity* (Berkeley, CA: University of California Press, 2003), p. 18.

3 Quoted in Niezen, *The Origins of Indigenism*, p. 20.

4 However, some have criticized definitions that emphasize colonialism as being too Eurocentric, denying agency to indigenous peoples, and overlooking imperial conquests by non-Western societies. See, e.g., Ken S. Coates, *A Global History of Indigenous Peoples: Struggle and Survival* (Basingstoke: Palgrave Macmillan, 2004), pp. 8–9.

5 See Benjamin Madley, "Patterns of Frontier Genocide, 1803–1910: The Aboriginal Tasmanians, the Yuki of California, and the Herero of Namibia," *Journal of Genocide Research*, 4: 2 (2004), p. 168.

6 Sven Lindqvist, *"Exterminate All the Brutes": One Man's Odyssey into the Heart of Darkness and the Origins of European Genocide* (New York: The New Press, 1996), p. 123.

7 Twain quoted in Patrick Brantlinger, *Dark Vanishings: Discourse on the Extinction of Primitive Races, 1800–1930* (Ithaca, NY: Cornell University Press, 2001), p. 10. Twain's complete essay on "The Noble Red Man," originally published in *The Galaxy* in 1870, is available on the Web at http://www.twainquotes.com/Galaxy/187009c.html.

8 Wallace quoted in Brantlinger, *Dark Vanishings*, pp. 185–86.

9 Brantlinger, *Dark Vanishings*, p. 186.

10 Lindqvist, *"Exterminate All the Brutes,"* p. 9.

11 Richard L. Rubenstein, *The Age of Triage: Fear and Hope in an Overcrowded World* (Boston, MA: Beacon Press, 1983), p. 1.
12 Ward Churchill, *A Little Matter of Genocide: Holocaust and Denial in the Americas, 1492 to the Present* (San Francisco, CA: City Lights Books, 1997), p. 97.
13 Russel Lawrence Barsh points to the concentration of Indians on "reservations" (a system that "undoubtedly brought chronic malnutrition to a great proportion of North America's indigenous population"), destruction of forests, and denial of access to clean water as additional factors promoting high Indian mortality (his analysis concentrates on the later nineteenth century). See Barsh, "Ecocide, Nutrition, and the 'Vanishing Indian,'" in Pierre L. van den Berghe, ed., *State Violence and Ethnicity* (Niwot, CO: University Press of Colorado, 1990), pp. 224, 231, 239.
14 See Elizabeth A. Fenn, "Biological Warfare in Eighteenth-century North America: Beyond Jeffery Amherst," *The Journal of American History*, 86: 4 (March 2000), pp. 1552–80.
15 On the North American variant, see Tony Seybert, "Slavery and Native Americans in British North America and the United States: 1600 to 1865," http://www.slaveryinamerica.org/history/hs_es_indians_slavery.htm.
16 David E. Stannard, *American Holocaust: The Conquest of the New World* (New York: Oxford University Press, 1992), p. 54.
17 Bartolomé de las Casas, *A Short Account of the Destruction of the Indies* (London: Penguin, 1992), p. 15.
18 De las Casas, *A Short Account*, p. 24.
19 James Wilson, *The Earth Shall Weep: A History of Native America* (New York: Atlantic Monthly Press, 1998), p. 34.
20 Wilson, *The Earth Shall Weep*, p. 35.
21 Stannard, *American Holocaust*, p. 89.
22 Russell Thornton, *American Indian Holocaust and Survival: A Population History since 1492* (Norman, OK: University of Oklahoma Press, 1987), p. 44.
23 Churchill, *A Little Matter of Genocide*, p. 97.
24 Testimony cited in Thornton, *American Indian Holocaust and Survival*, p. 95.
25 Thornton, *American Indian Holocaust and Survival*, p. 51.
26 Wilson, *The Earth Shall Weep*, p. 283; see also Coates, *A Global History*, p. 128.
27 Thornton, *American Indian Holocaust and Survival*, p. 47.
28 For a summary of the Pequot War, see "'We Must Burn Them,'" ch. 13 in Francis Jennings, *The Invasion of America: Indians, Colonialism, and the Cant of Conquest* (New York: W.W. Norton, 1975), pp. 202–27.
29 Wilson, *The Earth Shall Weep*, p. 94.
30 Chivington quoted in Michael Mann, *The Dark Side of Democracy: Explaining Ethnic Cleansing* (Cambridge: Cambridge University Press, 2005), p. 98.
31 Connor quoted in Wilson, *The Earth Shall Weep*, p. 274.
32 Roosevelt quoted in Paul R. Bartrop, "Punitive Expeditions and Massacres: Gippsland, Colorado, and the Question of Genocide," in A. Dirk Moses, ed., *Genocide and Settler Society: Frontier Violence and Stolen Indigenous Children in Australian History* (New York: Berghahn Books, 2004), p. 209.
33 Wilson, *The Earth Shall Weep*, p. 228.
34 These figures were provided by Benjamin Madley, a leading authority on the Yuki genocide.
35 Frank Chalk and Kurt Jonassohn, *The History and Sociology of Genocide* (New Haven, CT: Yale University Press, 1990), pp. 197–99.
36 Wilson, *The Earth Shall Weep*, pp. 228, 231.
37 "The Trail Where They Cried," in the Cherokee translation (Coates, *A Global History*, p. 185). For a detailed account, see John Ehle, *Trail of Tears: The Rise and Fall of the Cherokee Nation* (New York: Doubleday, 1988).
38 Ward Churchill, "Genocide by Any Other Name: North American Indian Residential Schools in Context," in Adam Jones, ed., *Genocide, War Crimes and the West: History and Complicity* (London: Zed Books, 2004), p. 87.

39 Canada's Ministry of National Health and Welfare cited evidence in 1993 that "100% of the children at some [residential] schools were sexually abused between 1950 and 1980" (*The Globe and Mail*); in the United States a "wall of silence" still surrounds this subject. Churchill, "Genocide by Any Other Name," pp. 104–5.
40 Churchill, "Genocide by Any Other Name," p. 97.
41 Churchill, "Genocide by Any Other Name," pp. 105–6.
42 The coup, and its prelude and aftermath, have been well studied as a paradigmatic case of US interventionism. The classic account is Stephen C. Schlesinger and Stephen Kinzer, *Bitter Fruit: The Story of the American Coup in Guatemala*, expanded edn (Cambridge, MA: Harvard University Press, 1999). See also Richard H. Immerman, *The CIA in Guatemala: The Foreign Policy of Intervention* (Austin, TX: University of Texas Press, 1982), and, on the aftermath, Stephen M. Streeter, *Managing the Counterrevolution: The United States and Guatemala, 1954–1961* (Athens, OH: Ohio University Press, 2000).
43 "Despite his aw-shucks style, Reagan found virtually every anti-communist action justified, no matter how brutal. From his eight years in the White House, there is no historical indication that he was troubled by the bloodbath and even genocide that occurred in Central America during his presidency, while he was shipping hundreds of millions of dollars in military aid to the implicated forces." Robert Parry, "Reagan and Guatemala's Death Files," in William L. Hewitt, ed., *Defining the Horrific: Readings on Genocide and Holocaust in the Twentieth Century* (Upper Saddle River, NJ: Pearson Education, 2004), p. 247. Very little of this surfaced in the nauseating encomiums to Reagan following his death in 2004.
44 Menchú's autobiography (Rigoberta Menchú with Elisabeth Burgos-Débray, *I, Rigoberta Menchú: An Indian Woman in Guatemala* [New York: Verso, 1987]) is a classic of indigenous literature, though controversy has attended some of the personal history that Menchú recounts – a notable case of the struggle over history and memory examined in Chapter 14. For an overview, see Arturo Arias, ed., *The Rigoberta Menchú Controversy* (Bloomington, MN: Minnesota University Press, 2001).
45 *Guatemala: Memory of Silence: Report of the Commission for Historical Clarification*, February 1999, http://shr.aaas.org/guatemala/ceh/report/english/conc2.html.
46 Quoted in Mireysa Navarro, "Guatemalan Army Waged 'Genocide,' New Report Finds," *New York Times*, February 26, 1999; reprinted in Hewitt, ed., *Defining the Horrific*, pp. 255–58 (quoted passage from p. 256).
47 "Whites spoke of Aborigines as 'horribly disgusting,' lacking 'any traces of civilization,' 'constituting in a measure the link between the man and the monkey tribe,' or 'undoubtedly in the lowest possible scale of human nature, both in form and intellect.'" Madley, "Patterns of Frontier Genocide," p. 169.
48 Mann, *The Dark Side of Democracy*, p. 80.
49 Mann, *The Dark Side of Democracy*, p. 81.
50 Colin Tatz, "Genocide in Australia," AIATSIS Research Discussion Papers No. 8, 1999, http://www.aiatsis.gov.au/rsrch/rsrch_dp/genocide.htm.
51 Trollope quoted in Mark Cocker, *Rivers of Blood, Rivers of Gold: Europe's Conquest of Indigenous Peoples* (New York: Grove Press, 2001), p. 178.
52 The exterminatory character of the Flinders system was acknowledged in 1999 by the Tasmanian Premier, Jim Bacon, who referred to the Wybalenna concentration camp as "a site of genocide." Quoted in Madley, "Patterns of Frontier Genocide," p. 175. Madley adds (p. 176): "From the outset, British authorities knew that conditions on Flinders Island were lethal. Inaction despite clear warnings and high mortality rates suggests that population decline was government policy, or was considered preferable to returning the survivors to their homes. . . . In 1836 the commander of Launceston visited Flinders Island and warned that if conditions were not improved, 'the race of Tasmania . . . will . . . be extinct in a quarter of a century.' . . . Still, the government did not address the issues contributing to mortalities. In fact, they operated Flinders Island with virtually no policy amendments for over a decade, until closing the reserve in 1847. The colonial

government may not have planned to kill large numbers of Aborigines on Flinders Island, but they did little to stop mass death when they were clearly responsible for it."

53 Brantlinger, *Dark Vanishings*, pp. 129–30, citing the work of Lyndall Ryan. See also Cocker, *Rivers of Blood, Rivers of Gold*, pp. 181–84.

54 Peter Read, *The Stolen Generations: The Removal of Aboriginal Children in NSW, 1883–1969* (Sydney: Government Printer, 1982); revised edition available on the Web at http://www.daa.nsw.gov.au/publications/25.html.

55 Tatz, "Genocide in Australia." A quite extraordinary role in alerting white Australians to the aboriginal plight was played by the rock group Midnight Oil. The group's signature hit, "Beds Are Burning" (from *Diesel and Dust*, 1987), helped define the land-rights issue for the white majority. They also sang about aboriginal territories irradiated by UK nuclear testing in the 1950s ("Maralinga," 1984) and the fate of the Tasmanian aboriginals ("Truganini," from *Earth and Sun and Moon*, 1993). On their first North American tour, an aboriginal band, Yothu Yindi, memorably opened the show. The lead singer of "The Oils," Peter Garrett (a lawyer by training), was elected a Labor Member of Parliament in the 2004 federal election.

56 Colin Tatz, *With Intent to Destroy: Reflecting on Genocide* (London: Verso, 2003), p. xvi.

57 For a solid overview, see Jon Bridgman and Leslie J. Worley, "Genocide of the Hereros," ch. 1 in Totten *et al.*, eds, *Century of Genocide*, pp. 3–40.

58 Von Trotha quoted in Cocker, *Rivers of Blood, Rivers of Gold*, p. 328.

59 Von Trotha quoted in Jan-Bart Gewald, "Imperial Germany and the Herero of Southern Africa: Genocide and the Quest for Recompense," in Jones, ed., *Genocide, War Crimes and the West*, p. 61.

60 Quoted in Gewald, "Imperial Germany and the Herero," p. 62.

61 Madley, "Patterns of Frontier Genocide," p. 188; Benjamin Madley, "From Africa to Auschwitz: How German South West Africa Incubated Ideas and Methods Adopted and Developed by the Nazis in Eastern Europe," *European History Quarterly*, 35: 3 (2005), p. 181.

62 Benjamin Madley, personal communication, September 30, 2005. pp. 429–64.

63 Andrew Meldrum, "German Minister Says Sorry for Genocide in Namibia," *Guardian*, August 16, 2004, http://www.guardian.co.uk/print/0,3858,4993918-103532,00.html.

64 In academia, the denialist position is associated with scholars such as Steven Katz, Guenter Lewy, William Rubinstein, and (in Australia) Keith Windschuttle.

65 Alexander Bielakowski, post to H-Genocide, September 26, 2001; see my response of the same date in the H-Genocide archives, http://h-net.msu.edu/cgi-bin/logbrowse.pl?trx=lmandlist=H-Genocide.

66 Michael Burleigh, *Ethics and Extermination: Reflections on Nazi Genocide* (Cambridge: Cambridge University Press, 1997), p. 181.

67 Christopher Hitchens, "Minority Report," *The Nation*, October 19, 1992, emphasis added. Hitchens' "vulgar social Darwinism, with its quasi-Hitlerian view of the proper role of power in history" is effectively pilloried in David E. Stannard's essay, "Uniqueness as Denial: The Politics of Genocide Scholarship," in Alan S. Rosenbaum, ed., *Is the Holocaust Unique? Perspectives on Comparative Genocide* (2nd edn) (Boulder, CO: Westview Press, 2001), pp. 245–90 (on Hitchens, p. 248).

A personal confession: I identified with such viewpoints until a little over a decade ago, when I was slapped rudely awake by Geoffrey York's book *The Dispossessed: Life and Death in Native Canada* (London: Vintage UK, 1990). I now believe that this outlook represented a deep failure of moral imagination on my part. Probably, it was grounded in the same factors that seem to inform the comments of Hitchens and others: ignorance; cultural hubris; and discomfort at acknowledging genocide perpetrated by one's "own" people.

68 Wilson, *The Earth Shall Weep*, p. xx.

69 Benjamin Madley, personal conversation, August 16, 2005.

70 See Tzvetan Todorov, *The Conquest of America: The Question of the Other* (New York: Harper Perennial, 1992), pp. 135–38.

71 Tatz, *With Intent to Destroy*, p. 99.
72 Tony Barta, "Relations of Genocide: Land and Lives in the Colonization of Australia," in Isidor Wallimann and Michael N. Dobkowski, eds, *Genocide and the Modern Age: Etiology and Case Studies of Mass Death* (Westport, CT: Syracuse University Press, 2000), p. 240.
73 Another sophisticated analysis of the issues of agency and intent is A. Dirk Moses, "An Antipodean Genocide? The Origins of the Genocidal Moment in the Colonization of Australia," *Journal of Genocide Research*, 2: 1 (2000), pp. 89–106.
74 For example – to cite a case where colonial administrators have often been credited with seeking to prevent or impede genocide against indigenous peoples – the Lieutenant Governor of Tasmania, Sir George Arthur, imposed martial law in the territory in 1828. He called for "the most energetic measures on the part of the settlers themselves," though adding that "the use of arms is in no case to be resorted to until other measures for driving them off have failed." As Benjamin Madley notes, "Martial law made killing Aborigines legal until they had all been 'driven off,' resulting, within a year of the issuing of the decree, in the slaughter of over two-thirds of Tasmania's Aboriginal population." Madley, "Patterns of Frontier Genocide," p. 174.
75 Thornton, *American Indian Holocaust and Survival*, p. 69.
76 Coates, *A Global History*, p. 132.
77 Roger Williams, quoted in Wilson, *The Earth Shall Weep*, p. 55. Writes G.B. Nash: "The nature of pre-contact Indian war was far different than the wars known in Europe, both in duration and in scale of operations. Unlike the Europeans, Native Americans could not conceive of total war that was fought for months or even years, that did not spare non-combatants, and that involved the systematic destruction of towns and food supplies. Wars among Indians were conducted more in the manner of short forays, with small numbers of warriors engaging the enemy and one or the other side withdrawing after a few casualties had been inflicted." Quoted in Jeffrey P. Blick, "Genocidal Warfare in Tribal Societies as a Result of European-induced Culture Conflict," *Man*, New Series, 23: 4 (1988), p. 658. See also "Savage War," ch. 9 in Jennings, *The Invasion of America*, pp. 146–70, pointing (among other things) to the extent to which Europeans themselves imported methods of warfare that were subsequently depicted as "savage" customs.
78 Nicholas Robins, *Native Insurgencies and the Genocidal Impulse in the Americas* (Bloomington, IN: Indiana University Press, 2005).
79 See Nelson Reed, *The Caste War of Yucatan* (Stanford, CA: Stanford University Press, 1964).
80 Coates, *A Global History*, pp. 226–27. See also the case of the Aché Indians of Paraguay, described in one of the early treatises of genocide studies: Richard Arens, *Genocide in Paraguay* (Philadelphia, PA: Temple University Press, 1976), perhaps most cited today for the epilogue by Jewish Holocaust survivor Elie Wiesel.
81 Niezen, *The Origins of Indigenism*, p. 40.
82 Quoted in Niezen, *The Origins of Indigenism*, p. 47.
83 Elazar Barkan, *The Guilt of Nations: Restitution and Negotiating Historical Injustices* (New York: W.W. Norton, 2000), p. 161.
84 For a survey of the trend, see Jack Hitt, "The Newest Indians," *New York Times Magazine*, August 21, 2005.
85 "Bolivia Fights Back: An Introduction," and Forrest Hylton and Sinclair Thomson, "Insurgent Bolivia," both in *NACLA Report on the Americas*, November to December 2004, pp. 14–15.
86 Hector Tobar, "Across the Americas, Indigenous Peoples Make Themselves Heard," *Los Angeles Times*, October 19, 2003.
87 For a synoptic treatment of the Mayan resurgence, see Edward F. Fischer and R. McKenna Brown, eds, *Maya Cultural Activism in Guatemala* (Austin, TX: University of Texas Press, 1996).
88 Quoted in Catherine Elton, "Guatemala Faces Its Racist Issues," *The Herald*

(International Edition), October 28, 2004. Niezen's *The Origins of Indigenism* provides a broad, up-to-date overview of the strategies and accomplishments of indigenous movements worldwide.

89 For example, Ward Churchill notes that US Indians in the contemporary era "incur by far the lowest annual and lifetime incomes of any group . . . and the highest rates of infant mortality, death by malnutrition, exposure, and plague disease. Such conditions produce the sort of endemic despair that generates chronic alcoholism and other forms of substance abuse among more than half the native population – factors contributing not only to further erosion in physical health but to very high accident rates – as well as rates of teen suicide up to 14.5 times the national average. . . . 'Genocidal' is the only reasonable manner in which to describe the imposition, as a matter of policy, of such physiocultural effects upon any target group." Churchill, *A Little Matter of Genocide*, pp. 247–48. Conditions among Australian aboriginals are strikingly similar: this group "ended the twentieth century at the very top, or bottom, of every social indicator available." See the statistics cited in Tatz, *With Intent to Destroy*, pp. 104–5.

BOX 3A TIBET UNDER CHINESE RULE

Imperialism and colonialism have been inflicted on indigenous peoples throughout the "Third World." However, countries in the developing world are themselves often the product of imperial expansion and domination. In both pre-modern and contemporary incarnations, these states have proved willing to use imperial and colonial strategies against indigenous peoples within their reach. As with Western imperialism, the enterprise has regularly spawned genocidal atrocities. Chinese rule over Tibet is a case in point.

We should distinguish at the outset between two versions of Tibet that are often confused. Ethnic Tibet – the area in which self-identified Tibetans reside – covers more or less the area of the Tibetan plateau, a zone dominated by grassland that is also "the source of the world's ten greatest river systems,"[1] but this includes the areas of Amdo and Kham (often referred to as "eastern Tibet"). These were traditionally under the control of warlords more beholden to the Han Chinese center than to the Tibetan authorities in *U-tsang*, central Tibet – with its capital at Lhasa, home to the supreme religious authority, the Dalai Lama. "Tibet" today is generally taken – except by Tibetans – to refer to the Tibet Autonomous Region (TAR) declared by China in 1965. This constitutes barely half the territory of ethnic Tibet, while the more populous territories of "Outer Tibet" (including Amdo and Kham) are mostly divided between the Chinese provinces of Sichuan and Qinghai. Although home to about half of all ethnic Tibetans, these provinces are populated by a Han Chinese majority, and the demographic disproportion is increasing.[2]

Historically, Tibet was itself the product of empire-building, and for 300 years (seventh to tenth centuries CE) was one of the most powerful states in Asia. Although Tibet's Buddhist lamas were pressured into an enduring tribute relationship with the Mongol and Manchu emperors of China from the thirteenth to the twentieth century, not until after the Manchu collapse in 1911 was Tibet actually declared part of the Chinese state, but the Nationalist regime that made the declaration was never in a position to enforce it. From 1911 to 1950, "the Tibetan Government exercised internal and external freedom, which clearly demonstrated the country's independence."[3]

To justify their invasion of eastern Tibet in 1950, the communist Chinese government depicted pre-occupation Tibet as "a hell on earth ravaged by feudal exploitation," with rapacious monks oppressing a cowed and impoverished peasant population.[4] The real picture was more complex. Tibet was authoritarian, with a powerful monastic class that exacted high taxes from the laboring population. Supporters of Tibetan nationalism acknowledge that "traditional Tibetan society – like most of its Asian contemporaries – was backward and badly in need of reforms." But there was no hereditary rule. The supreme authority, the Dalai Lama, was chosen from the ordinary population as the reincarnation of his predecessor – an egalitarian strategy mirroring the upward mobility that life as a monk could provide. In addition, the system was not truly feudal: peasants "had a legal identity, often with documents stating their rights, and also had access to courts of law," including "the right to sue their masters."[5] Peasant holdings appear to have provided adequate subsistence, with crop failures and other agricultural emergencies offset by efficiently administered state reserves.

During the Nationalist era, as noted above, Tibet was claimed but not administered by China. That changed dramatically in 1949–50, after Mao Zedong's Communist Party took power in Beijing. With rationales that ranged from bringing civilization to the natives, to the need to counter moves by American "hegemonists," the Chinese government invaded and partially occupied Tibet in October 1950. "Tibet's frantic appeals for help to the United Nations, India, Britain, and the United States were ignored, or rebuffed with diplomatic evasions. No nation was about to challenge the new People's Republic of China, which had some ten million men under arms, over the fate of an obscure mountain kingdom lost in the Himalayas."[6] The logistical challenge of doing so would also have been nightmarish.

In May 1951, China imposed a punitive treaty for the "peaceful liberation" of the entire country. The so-called 17-Point Agreement guaranteed Tibetan political, religious, and educational rights, but allowed troops of the People's Liberation Army (PLA) to enter the territory, and gave the Chinese control over foreign affairs.[7] The Chinese also enjoyed a free hand in the eastern Tibetan territories. They used it to impose communist measures such as collectivization of agriculture. Rebellion against the measures was swift and violent among the Tibetans of the east. The Chinese responded with much greater violence, killing thousands of Tibetans and incarcerating tens of thousands under brutal and torturous conditions.

When the spark of rebellion reached central Tibet, in 1959, it launched a general uprising that the Chinese rapidly moved to suppress. The Dalai Lama fled across the border into India, where he still resides in Dharamsala, presiding over a Tibetan exile community.[8] In the aftermath of the rebellion, the Chinese government instituted a regime of "struggle" against supposedly reactionary elements. In scenes that evoke the proceedings in Cambodia under the Khmer Rouge (see Chapter 7), communist cadres denounced, tortured, and frequently executed "enemies of the people." "These struggle sessions resulted in more than 92,000 deaths" out of a total Tibetan population of about six million people.[9] The killings may be seen as part of a genocidal strategy against Tibetans as a whole, but also as an "eliticide," targeting the better-educated and leadership-oriented elements among the Tibetan population.

The Tibetan insurgency was a direct response to the Great Leap Forward and the Cultural Revolution, two communist campaigns that turned China upside down and killed millions or *tens* of millions. In 1958, Mao announced the Great Leap, designed to accomplish in China what Stalin achieved in the Soviet Union: industrialize a peasant nation in short order. At unfathomable cost, Stalin succeeded in his goal (Chapter 5). But China's Great Leap was an unmitigated failure, as well as a human catastrophe. Deluded by fantasies of agricultural "science" and peasant industrial potential, the communist authorities announced massive grain surpluses. The surpluses were a fiction; local authorities told the central authority what it wanted to hear. But as in Stalin's USSR, they served as the basis for grain seizures that provoked mass famine – the worst in China's long and famine-plagued history, "result[ing] in the deaths of an estimated 40 million people in the three years between 1959 and 1962."[10] No group suffered more than ethnic Tibetans; "perhaps one in five died" between 1959 and 1963.[11]

After the 1959 uprising, an equally catastrophic toll was inflicted by the forced-labor camps of Qinghai and Sichuan, which swept up hundreds of thousands of Tibetans, mostly adult males.[12] They were set to work extracting Tibet's precious minerals and building its military infrastructure, especially roads and railways. Toiling at high, frozen altitudes and with minimal food rations, tens of thousands of Tibetans died in the first half of the 1960s, in conditions that rivaled the worst outposts of the Soviet Gulag. According to Jean-Louis Margolin, "it appears that very few people (perhaps as few as 2 percent) ever returned alive from the 166 known camps, most of which were in Tibet or the neighboring provinces."[13] As during the Second World War in the USSR, the death rate in the camps was exacerbated by the famine raging outside their gates.

The second Chinese campaign to devastate Tibet was the "Great Proletarian Cultural Revolution," unleashed in 1966. Another decisive break with the Chinese past was ordered. In Tibet, the epitome of "reaction" and "feudalism," persecution and destruction occurred on a vast scale:

> From July 1966 onwards, Red Guards [communist militants] began the systematic destruction of Tibetan civilization. Monasteries, temples and other

> holy sites such as Jokhang, Ramoche and Norbulingka were condemned as breeding-grounds for counter-revolutionary notions and shut down, looted, destroyed and even air-bombed. The historic monastery-towns of Drepung, once the largest such Tibetan town with 10,000 monks, and Ganden, with 3000 monks, were obliterated. Statues, scriptures and ritual objects were smashed, taken away or thrown into bonfires that burned for days. Religious and cultural practices including folk fairs, festivals and traditional songs were banned. Religious leaders were branded as "reactionary demons" and the Dalai Lama as a "bandit and a traitor." In the process, thousands of monks were slaughtered.[14]

The violence of the Cultural Revolution waned by 1969. Mao Zedong died in 1976, and the extremist phase of the Chinese revolution passed with him. The 1980s were marked by an opening up to the West which launched a remarkable transformation of China's economy and society, continuing today. This phase has been characterized by a softening of China's position towards Tibetan national and cultural rights.[15] However, with increasing Han Chinese migration, Tibetans have become a minority in their capital of Lhasa. Renewed ideological campaigns, such as the "Strike Hard" and "Spiritual Civilization" initiatives, have been aimed at the so-called "Dalai Clique" – notably representatives of those Tibetan religious institutions that were allowed to revive after the Cultural Revolution. Hundreds of monks and nuns have been arrested, and thousands more expelled from their institutions.

Tibetan resistance continued beneath the surface, occasionally breaking out into open revolt. In March 1989 there occurred "the largest anti-Chinese demonstration in [Lhasa] since 1959."[16] It was met by instant crack-downs, mass round-ups, and the routine use of torture on Tibetan detainees. Shakya describes the atmosphere in the wake of this outbreak as one of "general malaise" characterized by "a near-universal enmity towards the Chinese" on the part of ethnic Tibetans.[17]

Overall, it seems likely that hundreds of thousands of Tibetans have died as the direct result of Chinese actions since 1950, overwhelmingly in the decade following the 1959 invasion. The Tibetan government-in-exile estimates 1.2 million deaths, but Jean-Louis Margolin, writing in *The Black Book of Communism*, finds this "difficult to believe." He calculates instead a death-toll "as high as 800,000 – a scale of population loss comparable to that in Cambodia under the Khmer Rouge" (see Chapter 7).[18]

As early as 1960, the International Commission of Jurists declared that there existed "a *prima facie* case that on the part of the Chinese, there has been an attempt to destroy the national, ethnical, racial and religious group of Tibetans by killing members of the group and causing serious bodily harm to members of the group. . . . These acts constitute the crime of genocide under the Genocide Convention of the United Nations of 1948."[19] Since then, supporters of Tibetan self-determination have regularly deployed a genocide discourse –

for example, Maura Moynihan of Refugees International. Writing in *The Washington Post* in 1998, Moynihan argued that Tibet was the victim of "a grimly familiar, 20th-century, state-sponsored genocide, justified by a new, scientific-materialist ideology of 'reform' and 'progress,' swiftly and efficiently enacted with modern weaponry and just as swiftly and efficiently denied and concealed."[20] These claims are hotly disputed, however, by the Chinese government and its supporters.

The response of Tibet's government-in-exile to Chinese occupation has been realistic and moderate. A five-point plan that the Dalai Lama presented in a 1987 speech to the US Congress included the following proposals:

1 Transformation of the whole of Tibet into a zone of peace.
2 Abandonment of China's population transfer policy which threatens the very existence of the Tibetan people.
3 Respect for the Tibetan people's fundamental human rights and democratic freedoms.
4 Restoration and protection of Tibet's natural environment and the abandonment of China's use of Tibet for the production of nuclear weapons and dumping of nuclear waste.
5 Commencement of earnest negotiations on the future status of Tibet and of relations between the Tibetan and Chinese people.[21]

The Dalai Lama has made it clear that Tibetans are willing to accept autonomy within China, rather than full independence. Such an arrangement seems remote, however, given China's economic ambitions for Tibet, and its growing military presence there.

FURTHER STUDY

Jasper Becker, *Hungry Ghosts: Mao's Secret Famine.* New York: Henry Holt, 1998. Describes the catastrophe of Mao's "Great Leap Forward," with particular attention to ethnic Tibetan suffering.

Central Tibetan Administration, *Tibet Under Communist China – Fifty Years.* Available at http://www.tibet.net/publication/50yrs/report.html. A detailed report by the Tibetan government-in-exile; partisan but well-researched, and reflecting the government's political moderation.

Mary Craig, *Tears of Blood: A Cry for Tibet.* Washington, DC: Counterpoint Press, 2000. Impassioned overview of Tibet under Chinese rule.

Tsering Shakya, *The Dragon in the Land of Snows: A History of Modern Tibet Since 1947.* New York: Penguin Compass, 2000. "The first scholarly history of Tibet under Chinese occupation" (*Time*); objective and fair-minded.

NOTES

1 Central Tibetan Administration (hereafter, CTA), *Tibet under Communist China – Fifty Years* (2001), http://www.tibet.net/eng/diir/pubs/rail_report.pdf, p. 54.
2 The distinction between "Outer Tibet" and "Inner Tibet" was first made in the 1913 to 1914 Simla Conference and Convention, in which Tibet, China, and Britain participated. "Chinese suzerainty over the whole of Tibet was recognized but China engaged not to convert Tibet into a Chinese province. The autonomy of Outer Tibet was recognised and China agreed to abstain from interference in its internal administration which was to rest with Tibetans themselves. In Inner Tibet the central Tibetan Government at Lhasa was to retain its existing rights." George N. Patterson, "China and Tibet: Background to the Revolt," *The China Quarterly*, 1 (January–March 1960), p. 90.
3 Tsering Shakya, *The Dragon in the Land of Snows: A History of Modern Tibet since 1947* (New York: Penguin Compass, 2000), p. xxx.
4 Shakya, *The Dragon in the Land of Snows*, p. xxviii.
5 CTA, *Tibet under Communist China*, p. 130.
6 Eric S. Margolis, *War at the Top of the World: The Struggle for Afghanistan, Kashmir, and Tibet* (New York: Routledge, 2001), p. 195.
7 See the full text of the "Agreement of the Central People's Government and the Local Government of Tibet on Measures for the Peaceful Liberation of Tibet" at http://www.tibetinfo.net/publications/docs/spa.htm.
8 See Frank Morales, *The Revolt in Tibet* (New York: Macmillan, 1960).
9 CTA, *Tibet under Communist China*, p. 9.
10 Shakya, *The Dragon in the Land of Snows*, p. 262.
11 Jasper Becker, *Hungry Ghosts: Mao's Secret Famine* (New York: Henry Holt, 1998), p. 166.
12 Shakya refers to "areas where all able young men had been arrested and imprisoned, leaving the villages inhabited only by old people and women." *The Dragon in the Land of Snows*, p. 271.
13 Jean-Louis Margolin, "China: A Long March into Night," in Stéphane Courtois *et al.*, *The Black Book of Communism: Crimes, Terror, Repression*, trans. Jonathan Murphy and Mark Kramer (Cambridge, MA: Harvard University Press, 1999), p. 545.
14 "The Cultural Revolution and Its Legacy in Tibet," http://www.columbia.edu/cu/ccba/cear/issues/spring98/text-only/hennsidebar2.htm.
15 For an overview of this period, see Solomon M. Karmel, "Ethnic Tension and the Struggle for Order: China's Policies in Tibet," *Pacific Affairs*, 68 (Winter 1995–96), pp. 485–505.
16 Shakya, *The Dragon in the Land of Snows*, p. 430.
17 Shakya, *The Dragon in the Land of Snows*, p. 421.
18 Margolin, "China," p. 546.
19 Quoted in Shakya, *The Dragon in the Land of Snows*, p. 223; see the "ICJ Report on Tibet 1960," http://www.tibet.com/Resolution/icj60.html.
20 Maura Moynihan, "Genocide in Tibet," *The Washington Post*, January 25, 1998. Tibetan nationalists have often alleged that China is guilty of another strategy of genocide under the terms of the UN Convention: preventing Tibetan births through forcible sterilization of Tibetan women. However, the evidence does not support this. See Melvyn C. Goldstein and Cynthia M. Beall, "China's Birth Control Policy in the Tibet Autonomous Region: Myths and Realities," *Asian Survey*, 31: 3 (March 1991), pp. 285–303.

21 See "The Five Point Peace Plan for Tibet, by His Holiness the Dalai Lama, Washington, DC, 21 September 1987," http://www.freetibet.org/info/file/file3.html. The proposals were "further clarified" but "also developed . . . further" in the Dalai Lama's speech to European Parliament representatives in June 1988; for details, see Shakya, *The Dragon in the Land of Snows*, p. 423.

CHAPTER 4

The Armenian Genocide

> Sir: I have the honor to report to the Embassy about one of the severest measures ever taken by a government and one of the greatest tragedies in all history.
>
> American Consul Leslie Davis, writing to Henry Morgenthau, US Ambassador in Constantinople, June 30, 1915

INTRODUCTION

The murder of over a million Armenians in Turkey between 1915 and 1923 presaged Adolf Hitler's even more gargantuan assault on European Jews in the 1940s. However, for decades, the events were almost forgotten. War crimes trials – the first in history – were held after the Allied occupation of Turkey, but were abandoned in the face of Turkish resistance. In August 1939, as he prepared to invade western Poland, Hitler mused to his generals that Mongol leader "Genghis Khan had millions of women and men killed by his own will and with a gay heart. History sees in him only a great state builder." And in noting his instructions to the Death's Head killing units "to kill without mercy men, women and children of Polish race or language," Hitler uttered some of the most resonant words in the history of genocide: *"Who, after all, talks nowadays of the annihilation of the Armenians?"*[1]

Fortunately, Hitler's rhetorical question could not sensibly be asked today – except in Turkey. Over the past four decades, a growing movement for consciousness-raising, apology, and restitution has entrenched the Armenian catastrophe as one of the three "classic" genocides of the twentieth century. It was not the century's *first* genocide, as is often alleged. The Congo "rubber terror" (Chapter 2) was ongoing as the century dawned, and the German destruction of the Herero (Chapter 3) preceded the Turkish assault on Armenians by over a decade. Yet in its scale, central coordination, and systematic implementation, the Armenian holocaust may perhaps be considered the first truly "modern" genocide.

If Hitler's derisive comment would be out of place today, neither could it have been made at the time of the Armenian genocide itself. The fate of the "starving Armenians" in 1915–17 was the subject of outrage and mass mobilization around the Western world. In the United States, it spawned "the first international human rights movement in American history," resuscitated for contemporary audiences by Peter Balakian. "It seems that no other international human rights issue has ever preoccupied the United States for such a duration," Balakian noted in his account of the genocide and US response, *The Burning Tigris.*[2]

The term "holocaust," which most people associate with the Jewish genocide at Nazi hands, seems to have been used first in a human-rights context to describe Armenian suffering – by the *New York Times* in 1895, during a major round of massacres that preceded the full-scale genocide of 1915–17. Moreover, both US and German representatives in Turkey – ranging from Ambassador Henry Morgenthau and his network of consuls, to missionaries and Germans employed on the Berlin–Baghdad railway – compiled reams of eyewitness testimony and photographic images that still sear the conscience nearly a century later (see Figures 4.1 and 4.2). In the outrage felt by these observers, and their multifaceted strategies to spread the news to the outside world, we see the dawn of the modern age of human-rights activism.

ORIGINS OF THE GENOCIDE

Three key factors shaped the Armenian tragedy: (1) the decline of the Ottoman Empire, which provoked desperation and humiliation among Turkey's would-be revolutionary modernizers, and eventually violent reaction;[3] (2) the vulnerable position of the Armenians in the Ottoman realm; and (3) the outbreak of the First World War, history's most cataclysmic war to that point, which confronted Turkey with invasion from the west (at Gallipoli) and from the Russians in the northeast.

Armenians are an ancient people, having inhabited the southern Caucasus region for perhaps 3,000 years. Christianized early in the first millennium, they took pride in having preserved their faith through centuries of imperial domination, following the crushing of the independent Armenian state by Muslim Mamluks in 1375. By the late nineteenth century, they constituted the largest non-Muslim population in the Anatolian heartland of the Ottoman Empire.[4] In many respects their position under Ottoman rule may be, and has been, likened to that of European Jews prior to their emancipation (Chapter 6). Isolated from the mainstream by their religious beliefs, marginalized politically and economically, both urban Armenians and Jews nonetheless found niches in the economy and halls of power. Armenian culture, like its Jewish counterpart, placed great emphasis on learning; accordingly, representatives of both groups rose to positions of influence in politics and the professions even when formally disenfranchised. But both groups correspondingly came to be viewed with envy and distaste by many in the wider society.[5] In the modern era of liberal nationalism, both Armenians and Jews secured political and cultural guarantees. In the Armenian case, though, these were more rhetorical than substantive; and even such lip-service was too much for the more reactionary Ottoman elements, who eventually united behind an exclusivist and ultra-nationalist agenda.

In Chapter 10, I argue that humiliation is one of the greatest psychological spurs to violence, including mass violence and genocide. The final decades of the Ottoman Empire constituted an almost unbroken string of humiliations for its rulers and Muslim populations. Indeed, the empire had been in decline since its armies were repulsed from the gates of Western Europe, at Vienna in 1688. "As well as the loss of Greece and effectively Egypt, in the first twenty-nine years of the nineteenth century alone the empire had lost control of Bessarabia, Serbia, Abaza, and Mingrelia." In 1878, the empire "cede[d] ownership of or genuine sovereignty over . . . Bosnia, Herzegovina, Bulgaria, Kars, Ardahan, and Cyprus," with "the losses of that year alone comprising one-third of Ottoman territory and 20 per cent of the empire's inhabitants."[6]

In the first few years of the twentieth century, outright collapse loomed. In 1908, Bulgaria declared full independence, and Crete was also lost. A day later, Austria annexed Bosnia and Herzegovina. Italy seized Libya in 1912. The following year, Albania and Macedonia seceded. Summarizing these disasters, Robert Melson noted that "out of a total area of approximately 1,153,000 square miles and from a population of about 24 million, by 1911 the Turks had lost about 424,000 square miles and 5 million people";[7] and by 1913, only a narrow strip of European territory remained in their grasp. These multiple blows to Ottoman power and pride have been well captured by Turkish author Taner Akçam, who writes of

> the slow but continuous disintegration of the great empire, the military defeats in wars that continued over the years, the loss of tens of thousands of people, a society whose dignity was scorned along with the constant loss of self-worth, overwhelmed by the imagery of a great history, fantasies about recreating the past, the terminal bursting of these dreams, and the inability to absorb and integrate these numerous contradictions.[8]

Amidst the disasters, Ottoman rulers were predictably hypersensitive to outside "interference" in imperial affairs. Such involvement had begun with the imperial campaign in Ottoman-ruled Bulgaria in 1875–76, when British politician (later prime minister) William Gladstone had protested atrocities against the (mostly Christian) Bulgars. The co-religionist theme continued when both Britain and Russia sought to increase their influence in the Ottoman realm by advocating on behalf of the empire's Armenian population.[9] As a result, and fatefully, the Armenians – who had previously enjoyed the status of "millet" (recognized minority community) within the empire, despite the discrimination directed against them[10] – came to be viewed as a subversive population aligned with the Ottomans' mortal enemies. Suspicions were heightened by the advent, in the 1870s and 1880s, of a small number of Armenian revolutionary societies – part of a broader "'Armenian Renaissance'

(*Zartonk*) that gained momentum from the middle of the nineteenth century on," marked "by the return from European universities of hundreds of Ottoman Armenian students inspired by romantic and liberal ideas, the use of the vernacular as the written language, the development of the Armenian press in major cities, and the establishment of numerous schools in provincial towns and even villages."[11] These societies, like the small number of Armenian political parties that mobilized subsequently, demanded full equality within the empire, and occasionally appealed to outside powers for protection and support. These actions aroused the hostility of Muslim nationalist elements, and eventually prompted a violent backlash.

With the Ottomans' hold over their empire faltering, and Armenian nationalists newly insurgent, a wave of large-scale massacres swept across Armenian-populated territories. Between 1894 and 1896, "the map of Armenia in Turkey went up in flames. From Constantinople to Trebizond to Van to Diyarbekir, and across the whole central and eastern plain of Anatolia, where historic Armenia was lodged, the killing and plunder unfolded."[12] Vahakn Dadrian, the leading historian of the Armenian genocide, considers the 1894–96 massacres "a test case for the political feasibility, if not acceptability by the rest of the world, of the enactment by central authorities of the organized mass murder of a discordant nationality."[13] The killings were, however, more selective than would be the case in the 1915–17 conflagration. Among other things, they displayed a pronounced gendercidal character (see Chapter 13), with Armenian males of "battle age" overwhelmingly the targets.[14] Children and women were generally spared outright murder – though many did die, and a great many women suffered grievously from wanton sexual attacks. As well, central state direction was more difficult to discern than it would be in 1915–17. According to Donald Bloxham, the main role was played by "Muslim religious leaders, students, and brotherhoods," though many ordinary Muslims, especially Kurds, also participated.[15] Nonetheless, between 80,000 and 200,000 Armenians were killed in the great pogrom.[16]

The killings provoked widespread international opprobrium; Armenian representatives petitioned the Ottoman Court for protection and civil guarantees. "The list of Armenian demands was broad and basic," according to Balakian. It included "fair taxation; guarantees of freedom of conscience; the right of public meetings; equality before the law; protection of life, property, and honor (this meant the protection of women)."[17] Rhetorical assurances were issued, but the daringly direct petition increased perceptions of the Armenians as a restive and "uppity" minority.

In 1908, the tottering Ottoman sultanate was overthrown in the Young Turk revolution, led by a group of modernization-minded military officers. Armenians joined with many other peoples of the realm in welcoming the transformations. In the first blush of post-revolutionary enthusiasm, "a wave of fraternal effusions between Ottoman Christians and Muslims swept the empire."[18] It seemed there was a place for all, now that despotism had been overturned. Indeed, Christians (together with Jews and other religious minorities) were now granted full constitutional rights.[19]

Unfortunately, as is usually the case with revolutionary movements, the new Ottoman rulers (grouped under the Committee of Union and Progress, CUP) were split into liberal-democratic and authoritarian factions. The latter was guided by a "burgeoning ethnic nationalism (still informed by Islam) blended with a late-imperial paranoid chauvinism";[20] its leading ideologist was Ziya Gökalp, whose "pan-Turkism was bound up in grandiose romantic nationalism and a 'mystical vision of blood and race.'"[21] Within the CUP, amidst "economic and structural collapse, the vision of a renewed empire was born – an empire that would unite all Turkic peoples and stretch from Constantinople to central Asia. This vision, however, excluded non-Muslim minorities, such as the Armenians."[22]

In January 1913, in the wake of the shattering Balkan defeats of the previous year, the extremist CUP faction launched a coup against the moderates and took power. The new ruling triumvirate – Minister of Internal Affairs Talat Pasha; Minister of War Enver Pasha; and Minister of the Navy Jemal Pasha – quickly established a *de facto* dictatorship. Under the rubric of the so-called Special Organization of the CUP that they directed, this trio would plan and oversee the Armenian genocide, with the Special Organization's affiliates in the Anatolia region serving as ground-level organizers.[23]

WAR, MASSACRE, AND DEPORTATION

> It appears that a campaign of race extermination is in progress under a pretext of reprisal against rebellion.
>
> Ambassador Morgenthau to the US Secretary of State, July 16, 1915

In Chapter 2, we saw that a situation of all-out war is often integral to the perpetration of genocide. The slaughter of the Armenians is a paradigmatic example. The extreme-nationalist ideology of the dominant CUP faction under Talat, Enver, and Jemal spread nationwide, as Turkey confronted twin emergencies: an Allied invasion of the Dardanelles peninsula (aimed at forcing a way through the Straits to the Black Sea and conquering Constantinople), and a mobilization of Russian forces on the northeast frontier. Ever since, Turkish governments have justified their denial of the Armenian genocide by reference to the atmosphere of emergency and chaos. There is no reason to accept these explanations at face value, but also no reason to discount the war's role in facilitating the extermination of two-thirds of Ottoman Armenians.[24]

In April 1915, just as the Allies were about to mount their invasion of the Dardanelles, the Turkish army launched an assault on Armenians in the city of Van, who were depicted as traitorous supporters of the Russian enemy. In scenes that have become central to Armenian national identity, the Armenians of Van organized a desperate resistance that succeeded in fending off the Turkish attack for weeks. Eventually, the resistance was crushed, but it provided the "excuse" for the infliction of full-scale holocaust against the Armenians, with the stated justification of removing a population sympathetic to the Russian army then battling the Ottomans in eastern Anatolia. As one young Turk, Behaeddin Shakir, wrote to a party delegate early in April: "It is the duty of all of us to effect on the broadest lines the realization of the noble project of wiping out of existence the Armenians who have for centuries been constituting a barrier to the Empire's progress in civilization."[25]

The genocide was accompanied, and to some extent presaged, by atrocities against other Christian populations of the empire, particularly Greeks and Assyrians. A strong case may be made that these campaigns were part-and-parcel of a broader Turkish genocide against all "indigenous Christians" of the Ottoman realm, as Talat Pasha described the target group. Historian Donald Bloxham refers to "a general anti-Christian chauvinism" in which "Christian and Entente nationals were cast as collective targets."[26] Thea Halo has also drawn attention to the suffering of Greek and Assyrian Christians;[27] but only now are these events beginning to attract meaningful scholarly interest.

The course of the Armenian genocide

On April 24, 1915, in a classic act of "eliticide" in Constantinople and other major cities, hundreds of Armenian notables were rounded up and imprisoned. The great majority were subsequently murdered outright, or tortured and worked to death in isolated locales. (To the present, April 24 is commemorated by Armenians around the world as "Genocide Memorial Day.") This was followed by a coordinated assault on Armenians throughout most of the Armenian-populated zone; a few coastal populations were spared, but would be targeted later.

The opening phase of the assault consisted of a clear-cut gendercide against Armenian males. Like the opening eliticide, this was aimed at stripping the Armenian community of those who might mobilize to defend it. Throughout the Armenian territories, males of "battle age" not already in the Ottoman Army were conscripted. In US Ambassador Henry Morgenthau's imperishable account, the Armenians "were stripped of all their arms and transformed into workmen," then worked to death. In other cases, more direct measures were applied: "it now became almost the general practice to shoot them in cold blood."[28] By July 1915, some 200,000 Armenian men had been exterminated by these methods,[29] reducing the remaining community "to a condition of near-total helplessness, thus an easy prey for destruction."[30]

The CUP authorities turned next to destroying the remainder of the Armenian population. A "Temporary Law of Deportation" and "Temporary Law of Confiscation and Expropriation" were passed by the executive.[31] Surviving Armenians were told that they were to be transferred to safe havens. However, as Morgenthau wrote, "The real purpose of the deportation was robbery and destruction; it really represented a new method of massacre. When the Turkish authorities gave the orders for these deportations, they were merely giving the death warrant to a whole race; they understood this well, and, in their conversations with me, they made no particular attempt to conceal the fact."[32] Modern bureaucratic structures and communications technologies, especially the railroad and telegraph, were critical to the enterprise.

The pattern of deportation was consistent throughout the realm, attesting to its central coordination. Armenian populations were called by town criers to assemble in a central location, where they were informed that they would shortly be deported – a day to a week being the time allotted to frantically gather belongings for the journey, and to sell at bargain-basement prices whatever they could. In scenes reminiscent of the Nazi deportation of Jews to concentration camps, local populations

Figure 4.1 A Danish missionary, Maria Jacobsen, took this photo of Armenian men in the city of Harput being led away for mass murder on the outskirts of town, May 1915.

Source: Courtesy Karekin Dickran's Danish-Armenian archive collection.

were depressingly eager to exploit Armenians' misery and dispossession. "The scene reminded me of vultures swooping down on their prey," wrote US Consul Leslie Davis. "It was a veritable Turkish holiday and all the Turks went out in their gala attire to feast and to make merry over the misfortunes of others. . . . [It was] the opportunity of a lifetime to get-rich-quick."[33]

Looting and pillaging were accompanied by a concerted campaign to destroy the Armenian cultural heritage. "Armenian monuments and churches were dynamited, graveyards were plowed under and turned into fields of corn and wheat, and the Armenian quarters of cities were torn down and used for firewood and scrap, or occupied and renamed."[34] Then the Armenian population was led away on foot – or in some cases dispatched by train to the wastelands of the Deir el-Zor desert in distant Syria, in conditions which ensured that tens of thousands died *en route*.

Kurdish tribespeople swooped down to pillage and kill, but the main strike force mobilized for mass killing was the so-called *chétés*, bands of violent convicts originally released from prison to fight against the Russians, and subsequently deployed by the tens of thousands to exterminate Armenians. As with the Serb paramilitary units unleashed in the Bosnian war of the 1990s (see Chapter 8), the genocide's organizers believed that using such forces "would enable the government to deflect responsibility. For as the death tolls rose, they could always say that 'things got out of control,' and it was the result of 'groups of brigands.'"[35]

Figure 4.2 Armenian children and women suffered horrific atrocities during the deportations; the minority that reached refuge were often on the verge of death from starvation, wounds, and exhaustion.

Source: Maria Jacobsen/Courtesy Karekin Dickran's Danish-Armenian archive collection.

The attacks on the remaining children, women, and elderly of the deportation caravans gave rise to hellish scenes. Armenians were forced to run a gauntlet of soldiers, *chétés*, and marauding Turkish and Kurdish peasants. "The whole course of the journey became a perpetual struggle with the Moslem inhabitants," wrote Morgenthau:

> Such as escaped . . . attacks in the open would find new terrors awaiting them in the Moslem villages. Here the Turkish roughs would fall upon the women, leaving them sometimes dead from their experiences or sometimes ravingly insane. . . .

> Frequently any one who dropped on the road was bayoneted on the spot. The Armenians began to die by hundreds from hunger and thirst. Even when they came to rivers, the gendarmes [guards], merely to torment them, would sometimes not let them drink."[36]

"In a few days," according to Morgenthau,

> what had been a procession of normal human beings became a stumbling horde of dust-covered skeletons, ravenously looking for scraps of food, eating any offal that came their way, crazed by the hideous sights that filled every hour of their existence, sick with all the diseases that accompany such hardships and privations, but still prodded on and on by the whips and clubs and bayonets of their executioners.[37]

In thousands of cases, children and women were kidnapped and seized by villagers; the women were kept as servants and sex-slaves, the children converted to Islam and raised as "Turks." One young male survivor described his group being gathered together in a field while word went out to the local population: "Whoever wants a woman or child, come and get them." "Albert said that people came and took whomever they wanted, comparing the scene to sheep being sold at an auction."[38]

BOX 4.1 ONE WOMAN'S STORY: VERGEEN

In 1975, an Armenian-American named Virginia (Vergeen) Meghrouni died at the age of 73. Before her death, she placed a copy of her memoir of the Armenian genocide with Mae Derdarian, the daughter of a woman she had met in Syrian exile, and remained friends with thereafter. Derdarian published Meghrouni's memoir as a book, *Vergeen: A Survivor of the Armenian Genocide*, in 1996.[39]

Vergeen grew up in Kayseri, a medium-sized city in central Turkey. Christians – both Armenians and Greeks – made up one-third of the population. Armenians in the town experienced restrictions on the use of their language, but nonetheless were "the town's leaders in industry, business and cultural activities." In childhood, Vergeen lost both her father and a sister, but her father left generous life insurance, and she and her mother lived comfortably. Vergeen attended a French-run school. At the age of 8, she was betrothed per tradition to a much older Armenian boy, Armen, who emigrated to the United States before the outbreak of the First World War.

When war came, Vergeen's beloved French teachers were repatriated to France, now Turkey's enemy. All the able-bodied Armenian males of Kayseri were drafted into army labor brigades, "usually without food and in extremely unsanitary

continued

conditions." With potential defenders of the community out of the way, the government mounted brutal searches for hidden arms and ammunition in Armenian homes, executing anyone caught with a weapon. All Armenian schools were closed. Rumors circulated that the government was planning to deport all Armenians from Turkey.

The rumours quickly became fact. On June 15, 1915, notices appeared around Kayseri commanding Armenians to "leave all your belongings. . . . Close your shops and businesses. . . . You have ten days to comply with this ultimatum." Vergeen's mother briefly considered converting to Islam in order to avoid deportation, but young Vergeen demanded her mother stay the course and accept expulsion rather than conversion. "During the following, excruciating months of exile, my insistence about leaving Kayseri tormented me. Why didn't I listen to Mama? Why didn't we stay with some of the others who pretended to accept Islam?"

Joining the Armenian caravan out of the city, Vergeen found herself "exhilarated at first by all the excitement." Her excitement rapidly evaporated. The caravan passed a refugee camp where "we could see that dysentery was rampant; many of the young and elderly were stooped or lying outside their tents, moaning in painful agony. Further on, we saw unattended infants crawling in and out of a tent, their faces covered with insects . . . screaming for mothers long gone."

The caravan proceeded, driven on by vicious guards, harassed and attacked by Turkish and Kurdish civilians. As elsewhere, remaining men had been separated at the outset and taken away for mass killing. The children, women, and elderly were all but defenseless in the face of the attacks by guards and civilians, both of whom numbered rape and slaughter among their genocidal repertoire. "Week after week, our caravan moved on. . . . Even though I was becoming numb and hardened, I could not bear looking at the ghastly sights, thinking that could be Mama and me one day. Decaying corpses were often scattered all over the terrain, some half-eaten by dogs and wolves, some with gaping stomachs slashed by scavenging soldiers looking for ingested lira [Turkish money]. The pitiful sounds of the dying and the stench of those long dead assailed the air for miles."

They passed through "wretched" Katma in Turkey, then Aleppo in Syria, and finally arrived in "godforsaken" Ras-al-Ayn, a site that would become synonymous with Armenian suffering. For a time, though, Ras-al-Ayn seemed a genuine refuge. Vergeen's mother had managed to secrete some money that allowed them to buy adequate food for the first time in weeks. They were fortunate to survive a raging typhus epidemic that struck the camp in Autumn 1915.

It was too good to last. After four months, Turkish soldiers invaded the camp and rounded up its remaining inhabitants, apparently for extermination. But a Bedouin Arab present at the camp had spotted Vergeen. He expressed his wish to take her as a servant in his home. An Armenian woman implored Vergeen to accept the offer – on the condition that the woman, Vergeen's mother, and several other Armenians also accompany her. The deal was struck. Vergeen, renamed Noura, began her life as a servant in the Bedouin household of Yousuf and his wife Aneche.[40] Her face was tattooed in the manner of Bedouin women – markings that she would have surgically removed much later in life.

At first, things seemed tolerable – and then, tragedy struck. Yousuf, irritated by the extra mouths he had to feed, arranged for the murder of Vergeen's mother outside the Bedouin camp. "Days later, I found out the details . . . Oh! MAMA! An explosive rage surged through my gut . . . I wanted revenge! . . . [But] all I could do was weep." Further trauma followed. Though he had usually treated her well, Yousuf still considered Vergeen his property. One day he summoned her away from camp and raped her, "damn[ing] me . . . with an indelible stain in the dawn of my life."

After one failed attempt at escape, Vergeen finally managed to sneak away from the camp while Yousuf's wife was in labor. Alighting first at a foreign-run railroad station, Vergeen passed the rest of the war at a hospital in Aleppo, where the Syrian authorities had at last been persuaded to grant refugee status to deported Armenians.

After the war, Vergeen was able to establish contact with Armen, her betrothed from many years earlier, in the United States. She traveled by train to Port Said, Egypt, and in November 1920 by British cargo ship to New York. In January 1921, she and Armen were married. The family eventually moved to southern California, where Vergeen lived out her days, and wrote her memoirs of the horrors and upheavals now receding into the past.

For those not abducted, the death marches usually meant extermination, as was intended. Morgenthau cited one convoy that began with 18,000 people and arrived at its destination with 150 survivors, all children and women. The state of the survivors, moreover, was such that they often died within days of reaching refuge. J.B. Jackson, the US consul in Aleppo, Syria, recounted eyewitness descriptions of:

> over 300 women [who] arrived at Ras-el-Ain, at that time the most easterly station to which the German–Baghdad railway was completed, entirely naked, their hair flowing in the air like wild beasts, and after travelling six days afoot in the burning sun. Most of these persons arrived in Aleppo a few days afterwards, and some of them personally came to the Consulate and exhibited their bodies to me, burned to the color of a green olive, the skin peeling off in great blotches, and many of them carrying gashes on the head and wounds on the body as a result of the terrible beatings inflicted by the Kurds.[41]

By 1917, between half and two-thirds of Ottoman Armenians had been exterminated in the ways described. But this was not the end. Large-scale massacres continued. In the final months of the First World War, Turkey crossed the Russian frontier and occupied sizable parts of Russian Armenia. There, according to historian Vahakn Dadrian, "the genocidal engine of destruction unleashed by the Young Turk Ittihadists was once more activated to decimate and destroy the other half of the Armenian population living beyond the established frontiers of Turkey. . . . According to Soviet and Armenian sources, in five months of Turkish conquest and occupation about 200,000 Armenians of the region perished."[42] By this point, the killing was not all one-sided. "Reciprocally, Armenians attacked civilian populations in Turkish towns and villages, massacring civilians and doing as much damage as they could. Having survived genocide, some of the Armenian irregulars were attempting to avenge the atrocities of 1915."[43]

THE AFTERMATH

Turkey's defeat in the First World War, and the subsequent collapse and occupation of the Ottoman Empire, offered surviving Armenians an opportunity for national self-determination. In 1918, an independent Republic of Armenia was declared in the southwestern portion of Transcaucasia, a historically Armenian territory that had been under Russian sovereignty since the early nineteenth century. US President Woodrow Wilson was granted the right to delimit a new Armenian nation, formalized at the Treaty of Sèvres in 1920. Later that year, Wilson supervised the drawing of boundaries for independent Armenia that included parts of historic Ottoman Armenia in eastern Turkey.

Turkey, however, staged a rapid political recovery following its abject military defeat. The new leader, Mustafa Kemal (known as Ataturk, "father of the Turks"), quickly renounced the Sèvres Treaty, and declared in a secret communication that it was "indispensable that Armenia be annihilated politically and physically."[44] The regime invaded, and quickly reconquered six of the former Ottoman provinces that had been granted to independent Armenia under Sèvres. What remained of Armenia was swallowed up by the new Soviet Union. Following a brief period of cooperation with Armenian nationalists, the Soviets took complete control in 1921, and Armenia was incorporated into the Transcaucasian Soviet Federated Socialist Republic (TSFSR) in 1922. A separate Armenian Soviet Socialist Republic was created in 1936.

In the interim (1918–20) between the Ottoman collapse and the ascendancy of the nationalist Ataturk regime, and at the insistence of the Allies (who, as early as 1915, with an eye on the postwar dismemberment of the Turkish heartland, had accused the Young Turk rulers of "crimes against humanity"), the Turkish government – at British insistence – held a remarkable series of trials of those accused of directing and implementing the Armenian genocide. In April 1919, the Court pronounced that "the disaster visiting the Armenians was not a local or isolated event. It was the result of a premeditated decision taken by a central body . . . and the immolations and excesses which took place were based on oral and written orders issued by that central body."[45] Over a hundred former government officials were indicted, with most being transferred to British custody on the island of Malta. A number were convicted, and Talat, Enver, and a pair of other leadership figures were sentenced to death. They were not in Allied custody, however, and in the end, only three relatively minor figures were executed. The nationalist sentiment that spawned Ataturk's revolution staunchly opposed the trials – and in the face of that opposition and Allied pandering, the impetus for justice began to waver. "Correspondingly the sentences grew weaker, as the court refrained from handing down death sentences, finding most of the defendants only 'guilty of robbery, plunder, and self-enrichment at the expense of the victims.'"[46]

Eventually, in a tactic to be duplicated by Serbs in Bosnia-Herzegovina decades afterwards, Ataturk took dozens of British hostages from among the occupying forces. For Britain, which had decided some time earlier that the best policy was "cutting its losses," this was the final straw.[47] Anxious to secure the release of their hostages, and more generally to placate the new Turkish regime, the British freed many of the Turks in its custody. In July 1923, the Allies signed the Treaty of Lausanne with the Turks, which made no mention of the independent Armenia pledged at Sèvres. It was an "abject, cowardly and infamous surrender," in the estimation of British politician Lloyd George.[48]

Denied formal justice, a number of Armenian militants settled on a vigilante version. All three of the main organizers of the genocide were killed in the postwar period: Talat Pasha in Berlin in 1921, at the hands of Soghomon Tehlirian, who had lost most members of his family in the genocide; Enver Pasha while leading an anti-Bolshevik revolt in Turkestan in 1922 (in an ambush "led by an Armenian Bolshevik officer");[49] and Jemal Pasha, by Armenians in Tiflis in 1922.

THE DENIAL

In the summer of 2003, I made a pilgrimage to Gallipoli, at the southern end of Turkey's Dardanelles peninsula.[50] There, in April 1915, Allied forces staged an invasion aimed at breaking through the Dardanelles Straits, occupying Constantinople, and knocking Turkey out of the First World War. Over nine months of attacks launched from the narrow ribbon of beach they occupied, up precipitous cliffs and through thorny gulleys, the Allies sought fruitlessly to reach the Straits. Fierce Turkish resistance stopped every thrust. In the end the Allies withdrew, having suffered tens of thousands of casualties, mostly from disease. Today, their carefully tended cemeteries dot the landscape, as do those where a similar number of Turkish casualties are buried.

It is likely that if the Gallipoli campaign had succeeded, the genocide against the Armenians would not have occurred. But it did – unless, that is, you shared the views of the author of a guidebook to the battlefields, available at souvenir shops in Çannakale across the Straits. According to this text, the Armenians were "privileged subjects of the Ottoman Empire [who] had been disloyal during the war, having crossed the [Russian] border, joined the Russian Army, and fought against the Turks":

> Furthermore, they were hoarding arms for a movement to set up an independent Armenian state in Turkey. They had staked their future on the victory of the Allies and, like the Greeks, gloated over every Turkish reverse in the war. They were rich, and many of them handled commerce throughout the empire. In effect, they were a fifth column inside the country. . . . The leaders were punished with death and the rest put on the road to the south of the empire, to Syria and Mesopotamia [Iraq], in order to reduce the Armenian population near the Russian border. This event would later be introduced to the world as the so-called "Turkish massacre" and be turned into negative propaganda against the modern Republic of Turkey by the Armenian diaspora.[51]

In the author's mind, the death and destruction inflicted on the Armenians did not constitute genocide or even "massacre," but was a necessary and morally justifiable response to the insidious machinations of Armenian rebels. The "rich," "gloat[ing] . . . fifth column" got what was coming to it. In espousing these viewpoints, moreover, the author was simply reflecting the general Turkish attitude towards the Armenian events.

This is classic genocide denial, force-fed to an international community by a sustained Turkish government campaign. As Donald Bloxham summarizes, Turkey has "written the Armenians out of its history books, and systematically destroyed Armenian architecture and monuments to erase any physical traces of an Armenian presence." Moreover, "Armenian genocide denial is backed by the full force of a Turkish state machinery that has pumped substantial funding into public-relations firms and American university endowments to provide a slick and superficially plausible defence of its position."[52] In these efforts (analyzed in comparative context in Chapter 14), Turkey has been greatly assisted by its close alliance with the US, its membership in NATO, and its mutually supportive arrangement with Israel.[53] For the US, Turkey was critically important in the "containment" of the Soviet Union during the Cold War. Today, it serves as a secular bulwark against Muslim-fundamentalist ferment in the Middle East. Accordingly, US military leaders, as well as "security"-minded politicians, have played a key role in denial of the genocide.[54] The close US–Turkish relationship means that Turkish studies in the United States is well-funded, not only through Turkish government sources, but thanks to the large number of contractors (mainly arms manufacturers) who do business with Turkey.

In recent years, however, the denial efforts of the Turkish government and its supporters have met with decreasing success. "Today, twenty countries, most of them in Europe, acknowledge the Armenian Genocide, as do the European Parliament, the United Nations, and the International Association of Genocide Scholars."[55] The most prominent national-level action was a 1998 resolution by the French National Assembly: a single sentence reading, "France recognizes the Armenian genocide of 1915."[56] This was passed over strong Turkish objections and threats of economic reprisals against French companies doing business with Turkey. In April 2004, the Canadian House of Commons voted to recognize "the death of 1.5 million Armenians between 1915 and 1923 as a genocide . . . and condemn this act as a crime against humanity."[57]

The United States still held out. After numerous abortive initiatives, the House of Representatives seemed poised in October 2000 to acknowledge the Armenian tragedy as genocide, and condemn its perpetrators. However, "minutes before the House was due to vote" on the measure, "J. Dennis Hastert, the speaker, withdrew the resolution . . . citing President Clinton's warnings that a vote could harm national security and hurt relations with Turkey, a NATO ally." National Security Council spokesman P.J. Crowley expressed the relief of many in government: "We applaud the speaker's decision. It was the right thing to do for America's national interests, the right thing to do for stability in a volatile region, and the right thing to do for both Turkey and Armenia."[58] The setback nonetheless seemed likely to be surmounted eventually. "In time – it will pass," said Aram Sarafian, a spokesperson for the National Organization of Republican Armenians. "Every year it gets closer."[59]

Even in Turkey, cracks are beginning to appear in the façade of denial. This was evident in the brave work of Taner Akçam and other scholars, and relatedly in the move towards rapprochement with the country's Kurdish minority. In the 1970s and 1980s, the Kurds had been exposed to ghastly persecutions and violence reminiscent, at times, of the Armenian genocide. The opening to the Kurds was dictated, in large part, by Turkey's desire to join the European Union (EU). As democratization measures took hold, aimed at smoothing the country's path into Europe, it seemed possible that recognition of the holocaust against Armenians would follow. "History," declared Turkish writer Sechuk Tezgul, "is waiting for that honest Turkish leader who will acknowledge his ancestors' biggest crime ever, who will apologize to the Armenian people, and who will do his best to indemnify them, materially and morally, in the eyes of the world."[60]

FURTHER STUDY

Taner Akçam, *From Empire to Republic: Turkish Nationalism and the Armenian Genocide.* London: Zed Books, 2004. The first book in English by the dissident Turkish scholar.

Peter Balakian, *The Burning Tigris: The Armenian Genocide and America's Response.* New York: HarperCollins, 2003. The best overview of the genocide and the US humanitarian response; see also *Black Dog of Fate* (memoir).

Donald Bloxham, *The Great Game of Genocide: Imperialism, Nationalism, and the Destruction of the Ottoman Armenians.* Cambridge: Cambridge University Press, 2005. Excellent on the international machinations surrounding the "Armenian question."

Vahakn N. Dadrian, *The History of the Armenian Genocide: Ethnic Conflict from the Balkans to Anatolia to the Caucasus.* Providence, RI: Berghahn Books, 1995. Background to the genocide.

Mae Derdarian, *Vergeen: A Survivor of the Armenian Genocide.* Los Angeles, CA: Atmus Press Publications, 1998. Survivor's testimony, sampled in this chapter.

G. S. Graber, *Caravans to Oblivion: The Armenian Genocide, 1915.* New York: John Wiley & Sons, 1996. Readable popular account.

Richard G. Hovannisian, ed., *The Armenian Genocide in Perspective.* New Brunswick,

NJ: Transaction Publishers, 1986. Early collection, still in print and still a lucid introduction.

Robert Melson, *Revolution and Genocide: On the Origins of the Armenian Genocide and the Holocaust.* Chicago, IL: University of Chicago Press, 1992. Theoretically rich study.

Donald E. Miller and Lorna Touryan Miller, *Survivors: An Oral History of the Armenian Genocide.* Berkeley, CA: University of California Press, 1999. Oral history focusing on the experiences of Armenian children.

Henry Morgenthau, *Ambassador Morgenthau's Story.* http://www.cilicia.com/morgenthau/MorgenTC.htm. Memoirs of the US Ambassador to Constantinople.

Ronald Grigor Suny, *Looking Toward Ararat: Armenia in Modern History.* Bloomington, IN: Indiana University Press, 1993. Examines the rise of Armenian nationalism, the genocide, and the subsequent politics of Soviet Armenia and the diaspora.

The Treatment of Armenians in the Ottoman Empire, 1915–16. http://www.cilicia.com/bryce/a00tc.htm. Text of the British "Blue Book" (published in 1916) on atrocities against the Armenians.

NOTES

1 In German, *"Wer redet heute noch von der Vernichtung der Armenier?"* Hitler quoted in Ronnie S. Landau, *The Nazi Holocaust* (Chicago, IL: Ivan R. Dee, 1994), p. 15. On the documentary evidence for Hitler's statement, see Vahakn N. Dadrian, *The History of the Armenian Genocide: Ethnic Conflict from the Balkans to Anatolia to the Caucasus* (6th rev. edn) (New York: Berghahn Books, 2003), pp. 403–9.

2 Peter Balakian, *The Burning Tigris: The Armenian Genocide and America's Response* (New York: HarperCollins, 2003), p. xiii.

3 Throughout this chapter, for convenience, I refer to "Turkey" and "the Ottoman Empire" interchangeably.

4 The shrinking of the empire meant that the Ottoman realm became more homogeneous, and the minority Christians of the realm (the Armenians, Assyrians, and Pontic Greeks) stood out more prominently. Whereas the Ottoman Empire had once been unusually diverse, cosmopolitan, and tolerant, its dissolution spurred those who yearned for an ethnically "pure" Turkish homeland. I am indebted to Benjamin Madley for this point.

5 It should be noted that "only parts of the Armenian population fall into the prosperous middleman category – much of this is an Ottoman/Turkish stereotype. Probably 80 percent of the Armenian population was rural, much of that number living in the same grinding poverty as ordinary Kurds and Turks." Donald Bloxham, personal communication, August 31, 2005.

6 Donald Bloxham, *The Great Game of Genocide: Imperialism, Nationalism, and the Destruction of the Ottoman Armenians* (Oxford: Oxford University Press, 2005), pp. 30–31.

7 Melson quoted in Donald E. Miller and Lorna Touryan Miller, *Survivors: An Oral History of the Armenian Genocide* (Berkeley, CA: University of California Press, 1999), p. 47. The death-toll associated with these upheavals was also immense, though its precise parameters are unclear. See Justin McCarthy's revisionist study, *Death and Exile: The Ethnic Cleansing of Ottoman Muslims, 1821–1922* (Princeton, NJ: The Darwin Press, 1995). McCarthy claims that during the period under consideration, "Five and one-half million Muslims died, some of them killed in wars, others perishing as refugees from starvation and disease" (p. 1).

8 Taner Akçam, "The Genocide of the Armenians and the Silence of the Turks," in Levon Chorbajian and George Shirinian, eds, *Studies in Comparative Genocide* (New York: St. Martin's Press, 1999), p. 137.

9 For an overview of the actions and motivations of the foreign powers, see Bloxham, *The Great Game of Genocide*; and Manoug Somakian, *Empires in Conflict: Armenia and the Great Powers, 1895–1920* (London: I.B. Tauris, 1995).

10 Among the discriminatory measures was the so-called "boy collection or *devshirme*, which meant that Ottoman officials would take children from their Christian families, convert them to Islam, and put them to work in the Ottoman military and civil service." Balakian, *The Burning Tigris*, p. 41.

11 Stephan Astourian, "The Armenian Genocide: An Interpretation," *The History Teacher*, 23: 2 (February 1990), p. 123.

12 Balakian, *The Burning Tigris*, p. 59.

13 Dadrian, *The History of the Armenian Genocide*, p. 151.

14 For more on the gendercidal character of the Armenian holocaust, targeting both men and women, see Adam Jones/Gendercide Watch, "Case Study: The Armenian Genocide," http://www.gendercide.org/case_armenia.html, from which some passages in this chapter are adapted.

15 Bloxham, *The Great Game of Genocide*, p. 55.

16 For analysis of the death-toll, see Dadrian, *The History of the Armenian Genocide*, pp. 153–57.

17 Balakian, *The Burning Tigris*, p. 58.

18 Astourian, "The Armenian Genocide," p. 129.

19 In April 1909, another massacre of Armenians occurred in the city of Adana, with similar killing campaigns occurring "all across Cilicia and around the Gulf of Alexandretta." However, "this time the new revolutionary government decided to act and prosecuted 34 Turks and 6 Armenians for their part in the communal strife." Andrew Bell-Fialkoff, *Ethnic Cleansing* (New York: St. Martin's Griffin, 1999), p. 150.

20 Bloxham, personal communication, August 31, 2005.

21 Balakian, *The Burning Tigris*, p. 164.

22 Miller and Miller, *Survivors*, p. 39.

23 For example, Bahaeddin Şakir, who headed the Special Organization in the eastern Ottoman provinces, wrote in February 1915 of the CUP's decision that "the Armenians living in Turkey will be destroyed to the last. The government has been given ample authority. As to the organization of the mass murder, the government will provide the necessary explanations to the governors, and to the army commanders. The delegates of [the CUP] in their own regions will be in charge of this task." Cited in Astourian, "The Armenian Genocide," p. 139.

24 In conversations with a top official of the German Embassy in Constantinople, Talat Pasha, the Ottoman Minister of the Interior, stated (in the official's summary) that he "wanted to take advantage of the world war to thoroughly get rid of its internal enemies, the indigenous Christians." Cited in Astourian, "The Armenian Genocide," p. 116.

25 Shakir quoted in Ronald Grigor Suny, *Looking Toward Ararat: Armenia in Modern History* (Bloomington, IN: Indiana University Press, 1993), p. 112.

26 Bloxham, *The Great Game of Genocide*, p. 71.

27 Thea Halo, "The Exclusivity of Suffering: When Tribal Concerns Take Precedence over Historical Accuracy," unpublished research paper, 2004 (see also the discussion of genocide denial in Chapter 14). Bloxham describes the policy adopted towards Ottoman Greeks from 1913 to 1916 as "a combination of population engineering and economic appropriation, using boycotts, murders, terrorization, and then deportation" (*The Great Game of Genocide*, p. 64). However, he argues that generalized killing of Greeks did not occur until 1921–22, following the Greek invasion and occupation of large parts of Turkey; and then it took place in the context of a "war of extermination" featuring comparably widespread atrocities against civilians by both Greek and Turkish forces. See Bloxham, *The Great Game of Genocide*, pp. 64, 164.

28 Henry J. Morgenthau, *Murder of a Nation*, http://www.cilicia.com/morgenthau/MorgenTC.htm.
29 Michael Mann, *The Dark Side of Democracy: Explaining Ethnic Cleansing* (Cambridge: Cambridge University Press, 2005), p. 148.
30 Dadrian, *The History of the Armenian Genocide*, p. 226.
31 See Dadrian, *The History of the Armenian Genocide*, pp. 221–22.
32 Morgenthau, *Murder of a Nation.*
33 Davis quoted in Balakian, *The Burning Tigris*, p. 234.
34 Norman M. Naimark, *Fires of Hatred: Ethnic Cleansing in Twentieth-century Europe* (Cambridge, MA: Harvard University Press, 2001), p. 41.
35 Balakian, *The Burning Tigris*, pp. 182–83.
36 Morgenthau, *Murder of a Nation.*
37 Morgenthau, *Murder of a Nation.*
38 Miller and Miller, *Survivors*, p. 110.
39 Mae M. Derdarian, *Vergeen: A Survivor of the Armenian Genocide*, based on a memoir by Virginia Meghrouni (Los Angeles, CA: Atmus Press Publications, 1996). The quoted material in this section is drawn from pp. 26, 33, 38, 41–42, 45–48, 93, and 107.
40 For an overview of this practice, see Ara Sarafian, "The Absorption of Armenian Women and Children into Muslim Households As a Structural Component of the Armenian Genocide," ch. 9 in Omer Bartov and Phyllis Mack, *In God's Name: Genocide and Religion in the Twentieth Century* (New York: Berghahn Books, 2001), pp. 209–21.
41 Miller and Miller, *Survivors*, p. 119.
42 Vahakn N. Dadrian, "The Comparative Aspects of the Armenian and Jewish Cases of Genocide: A Sociohistorical Perspective," in Alan S. Rosenbaum, ed., *Is the Holocaust Unique? Perspectives on Comparative Genocide* (Boulder, CO: Westview Press, 1998), pp. 127–28.
43 Balakian, *The Burning Tigris*, p. 320.
44 Cited in Balakian, *The Burning Tigris*, p. 328. In a precursor to subsequent Turkish campaigns of genocide denial, Ataturk claimed that the Armenians killed were "victims of foreign intrigues" and guilty of abusing "the privileges granted them."
45 Quoted in Gary Jonathan Bass, *Stay the Hand of Vengeance: The Politics of War Crimes Tribunals* (Princeton, NJ: Princeton University Press, 2000), p. 127.
46 Balakian, *The Burning Tigris*, p. 341. For more on the trials, see Vahakn Dadrian, "The Turkish Military Tribunal's Prosecution of the Authors of the Armenian Genocide," *Holocaust and Genocide Studies*, 11: 1 (spring 1997).
47 Bass, *Stay the Hand of Vengeance*, p. 136.
48 Lloyd George quoted in Bass, *Stay the Hand of Vengeance*, p. 144.
49 Balakian, *The Burning Tigris*, p. 345.
50 See the photo galleries of the (beautiful) battlefield sites at http://adamjones.freeservers.com/turkey2003.htm. Peter Weir's film, *Gallipoli*, is a fair depiction of events from the viewpoint of Australian soldiers.
51 Mustafa Aşkin, *Gallipoli: A Turning Point* (Çanakkale: Mustafa Aşkin, n.d.), p. 40.
52 Bloxham, *The Great Game of Genocide*, pp. 211, 228. See also Amy Magaro Rubin, "Critics Accuse Turkish Government of Manipulating Scholarship," *Chronicle of Higher Education*, October 27, 1995.
53 On the Turkish–Israeli relationship, see Yair Auron, *The Banality of Denial: Israel and the Armenian Genocide* (New Brunswick, NJ: Transaction Publishers, 2003). It should be stressed that many Jewish scholars in Israel and the US have worked diligently to acknowledge and explore the Armenian genocide, and its parallels with the Nazi holocaust against the Jews.
54 The trend began early on. Colby Chester, a retired US admiral, wrote in 1922 in the *New York Times Current History*: "The Armenians were moved from the inhospitable regions where they were not welcome and could not actually prosper but to the most delightful

and fertile parts of Syria . . . where the climate is as benign as in Florida and California whither New York millionaires journey each year for health and recreation. . . . And all this was done at great expense of money and effort." Quoted in Balakian, *The Burning Tigris*, p. 376.

55 Peter Balakian, personal communication, September 11, 2005.

56 "French Parliament Recognises 1915 Armenian Genocide," Reuters dispatch, May 29, 1998. However, "the wording of the resolution was deliberately designed to remove any suggestion of the responsibility of the modern Turkish state for the genocide; indeed no perpetrator agency of any sort was recalled in the brief statement of recognition." Bloxham, *The Great Game of Genocide*, p. 224.

57 "Turkey Denounces Armenian Genocide Vote in Commons," CBC News, April 22, 2004, http://www.cbc.ca/stories/print/2004/04/22/turkeyreaxn040422.

58 Eric Schmitt, "House Backs Off on Turkish Condemnation," *New York Times*, October 20, 2000.

59 Marinka Peschmann, "A Position John Kerry Has Held for 20 Years," Canada Free Press, September 17, 2004.

60 Tezgul quoted in Balakian, *The Burning Tigris*, p. 391.

BOX 4A THE ANFAL CAMPAIGN AGAINST IRAQI KURDS, 1988

Twenty to twenty-five million Kurds are spread across Iran, Iraq, Turkey, and Syria, constituting by most estimates the world's largest nation without a state of its own. In March 1987, Saddam Hussein's cousin from his hometown of Tikrit, Ali Hassan al-Majid, was appointed Secretary-General of the ruling Ba'ath Party's Northern Region. This included Iraqi Kurdistan, a Kurdish-dominated area that had long chafed under Ba'athist rule.

In the wake of the First World War, with US President Woodrow Wilson's call for national self-determination still resounding, Kurds were promised a homeland of their own – Kurdistan. However, the victorious Allies backed away from this pledge, made in the Treaty of Sèvres (1920). In an attempt to court the new Turkish regime of Kemal Ataturk, and fearful of destabilizing Iraq and Syria (then under British and French mandates, respectively), the Allies reneged on their commitment to Kurdish independence. The Kurds instead were divided among Turkey, Iraq, and Syria. The ascent to power of Saddam Hussein in 1968 (he became president in 1979) at first seemed to augur well for the Kurds; an autonomy agreement was reached in 1970. But it rapidly broke down, and in March 1974 the Kurdish Democratic Party (KDP) rose up against the central regime, sparking a full-scale war the following year and the flight of 130,000 Kurds to Iran.

In 1980, war erupted between Iraq and neighboring Iran. The Kurds were now viewed as a "fifth column," draining military resources from the struggle with Iran. Once Iraq and Iran had reached a ceasefire, the full venom of the Iraqi regime – judged by the scholar and activist Noam Chomsky to be "perhaps the most violent and repressive . . . in the world"[1] – could be directed against the Kurds. Al-Majid, whose genocidal exploits with poison gas would earn him the moniker "Chemical Ali" in the West, was Saddam Hussein's chosen agent for solving the "Kurdish problem."

By the time the Anfal Campaign was unleashed in 1988,* the Kurds had already suffered grievously at Iraqi hands. The most notable instance was one of the largest gendercidal massacres of modern times (for more on gendercide, see Chapter 13). A particularly restive Kurdish clan was the Barzani; its members had been forcibly relocated south to desert wastes, where they lived under the watchful eyes and ready guns of Iraqi security forces. The onset of the Iran–Iraq war in 1980 heightened the sense of threat among the Ba'ath leadership. Although the displaced populations were not involved in subversive activities, two of the clan leader's sons were leading guerrilla forces in the north. That was enough. All 8,000 men among the displaced Barzanis were rounded up and transported to southern Iraq, where they disappeared. Saddam Hussein left little doubt about what had happened to them: "They betrayed the country and they betrayed the covenant, and we meted out a stern punishment to them, and they went to hell."[2]

In February–March 1988, the regime moved to full-fledged genocide against Iraqi Kurds, featuring an offensive that stunned the world. On March 16, an aerial attack with chemical weapons was launched on the Kurdish town of Halabji, near the Iranian border. Thousands of civilians died from bombardments with mustard gas and sarin, a nerve agent. After the raid, journalists and photographers reached the scene from Iranian territory; photographs and video footage of Kurdish corpses were flashed around the world. It was not enough to arouse sustained international opposition, however. Governments, both Western and non-Western, were too committed to the Iraqi side in the Iran–Iraq war, too covetous of Iraqi oil, and too anxious to sell Iraq weapons and chemical ingredients, to care much about the fate of a dispossessed minority.[3]

The Anfal campaign consisted of eight distinct operations lasting until September 1988. Throughout this period, the standard Iraqi strategy was to attack Kurdish settlements with artillery and airstrikes, conduct mass killings on the spot, and cart off the remainder of the population for "processing" further south. Hundreds of thousands of Kurds were trucked to concentration camps, most notoriously the Topzawa camp near the northern Iraqi city of Kirkuk. There, the standard gendercidal selection procedure was implemented, with adult and teenage males separated for execution. The operations of the killers were "uncannily reminiscent of . . . the activities of the *Einsatzkommandos*, or mobile killing units, in the Nazi-occupied lands of Eastern Europe" (Chapter 6):

* The name chosen for the campaign, Anfal ("the spoils"), referred to the eighth *sura* of the Qur'an, which pledges to "cast into the unbelievers' hearts terror . . . smite above the necks, and smite every finger of them," delivering "the chastisement of the Fire."

> Some groups of prisoners were lined up, shot from the front, and dragged into predug mass graves; others were made to lie down in pairs, sardine-style, next to mounds of fresh corpses, before being killed; still others were tied together, made to stand on the lip of the pit, and shot in the back so that they would fall forward into it – a method that was presumably more efficient from the point of view of the killers. Bulldozers then pushed earth or sand loosely over the heaps of corpses. Some of the grave sites contained dozens of separate pits and obviously contained the bodies of thousands of victims.[4]

Children, women, and the elderly were also swept up in the mass executions, killed in bombardments and gassings, or selectively targeted after the "battle-age" males had been destroyed. Others perished from starvation or disease in the concentration camps. While gendercidal slaughter was ubiquitous and systematic,[5] the targeting of the wider Kurdish population was "subject to extreme regional variations," with the majority of indiscriminate murder occurring in "two distinct 'clusters' that were affected by the third and fourth Anfals [i.e., stages of the campaign]." The area targeted most systematically for root-and-branch genocide appears to have been southern Germian, which abutted the Arab heartland of Iraq and was targeted during the third Anfal (April 7–20, 1988). The region was considered a hotbed of rebels from the Patriotic Union of Kurdistan (PUK), the Kurdish group that was the principal military target of the Anfal campaign. While "males aged fifteen to fifty routinely vanished from all parts of Germian," in this southern region "the disappeared include[d] significant numbers of women and children." Mass executions involving "an estimated two thousand women and children" took place at a site on Hamrion Mountain, between the cities of Tikrit and Kirkuk.[6] Although the mass killing phase had concluded by the end of 1988, large areas of Kurdish territory were left devastated and either totally depopulated or stripped of their men.[7]

At the end of the 1991 Gulf War, Kurdish aspirations for autonomy were finally realized. When Kurds rose up in renewed rebellion, Hussein – a ceasefire with Allied forces freshly signed – turned his army against them. Hundreds of thousands fled to Iran and Turkey, prompting the Allies to create a safe area and no-fly zone. This provided the Kurds with a territorial autonomy that has lasted, in effect, until the present.

As a result of the uprising, Kurdish forces seized some four million documents from Iraqi archives in the country's northern regions, and transported them to safe areas. The documents became the foundation of Human Rights Watch's investigation of Anfal. Examination of the documents left little doubt in the investigators' minds that Iraq had committed genocide against the Kurds: "concerning the crucial 1987–1989 period . . . the evidence is sufficiently strong to prove a case of genocidal intent on the part of the Iraqi Government." About 100,000 Kurds – Kurdish estimates range up to 180,000 – perished in Anfal, "systematically put to death in large numbers by order of the central Iraqi government."[8]

In December 2003, nine months after their controversial invasion of Iraq, US forces discovered a dishevelled Saddam Hussein on a farm along the Tigris River. At the time of writing (September 2005), the interim Iraqi government was preparing to place Hussein and a number of other Ba'ath leaders, including Ali Hassan al-Majid, on trial for genocide and crimes against humanity. Reflecting US opposition to the International Criminal Court (ICC – see Chapter 15), the accused would not face an international tribunal, leading many to wonder whether the proceedings would be merely a kangaroo court. Nonetheless, there was at last the possibility that justice would be administered to Hussein and his henchmen for their many crimes, including the genocidal rampage against Iraqi Kurds.

FURTHER STUDY

Human Rights Watch-Middle East, *Iraq's Crime of Genocide: The Anfal Campaign Against the Kurds*. New Haven, CT: Human Rights Watch/Yale University Press, 1995. The most intensive investigation of the Anfal events; see also *The Anfal Campaign in Iraqi Kurdistan: The Destruction of Koreme*.

Kanan Makiya, *Republic of Fear: The Politics of Modern Iraq*. Berkeley: University of California Press, 1998. A good overview of the terroristic Saddam Hussein regime; see also *Cruelty and Silence*.

Jonathan C. Randal, *After Such Knowledge, What Forgiveness? My Encounters with Kurdistan*. Boulder, CO: Westview Press, 1999. Taut journalistic account of Iraq's war against the Kurds, with detailed attention to the historical context.

NOTES

1 Chomsky quoted in Kanan Makiya, *Cruelty and Silence: War, Tyranny, Uprising, and the Arab World* (New York: W.W. Norton, 1994), p. 273.

2 See Martin van Bruinessen, "Genocide in Kurdistan?," in George J. Andreopoulos, ed., *Genocide: Conceptual and Historical Dimensions* (Pittsburgh, PA: University of Pennsylvania Press, 1994), pp. 156–57.

3 As indicated, this followed an extended pattern of undermining and betrayal of Kurdish aspirations by the "international community." A solid overview of the machinations surrounding the Kurds in the 1970s is given by Jonathan C. Randal, *After Such Knowledge, What Forgiveness?* (Boulder, CO: Westview Press, 1999). Of the US and Western attitude during Anfal, Samantha Power writes: "US policy-makers and Western journalists treated Iraqi violence [during Anfal] as if it were an understandable attempt to suppress rebellion or a grisly consequence of the Iran–Iraq war. Since the United States had chosen to back Iraq in that war, it refrained from protest, denied it had conclusive proof of Iraqi chemical weapons use, and insisted that Saddam Hussein would eventually come around. . . . The Washington establishment deemed Hussein's broader campaign of destruction, like

Pol Pot's a decade before and Turkey's back in 1915, an 'internal affair.'" Power, *"A Problem from Hell": America and the Age of Genocide* (New York: Basic Books, 2002), pp. 171–72.

4 Human Rights Watch-Middle East (hereafter, HRW-ME), *Iraq's Crime of Genocide: The Anfal Campaign Against the Kurds* (New Haven, CT: Human Rights Watch/Yale University Press, 1995), p. 12.

5 For a more detailed analysis of the gendercidal aspects of the slaughter, and the visible evidence of it following the campaign, see Adam Jones/Gendercide Watch, "Case Study: The Anfal Campaign (Iraqi Kurdistan), 1988," http://www.gendercide.org/case_anfal.html, from which this boxed text is adapted.

6 See HRW-ME, *Iraq's Crime of Genocide*, pp. 13, 96, 115, 171. One small boy, Taimour Abdullah Ahmad, witnessed and survived a massacre of children and women; his story received wide international attention. See "An Interview with the Anfal Survivor, Taimour," http://www.fas.harvard.edu/~irdp/taimour.html.

7 For a vivid description of the "almost total economic stagnation," "deserted" factories, and "villages . . . populated by only women and children" in the Kurdish zone, see Jeffrey Pilkington, "Beyond Humanitarian Relief: Economic Development Efforts in Northern Iraq," *Forced Migration Review*, http://www.fmreview.org/rpn236.htm.

8 HRW-ME, *Iraq's Crime of Genocide*, pp. xvii, x.

CHAPTER 5

Stalin's Terror

Enemies are not people. We're allowed to do what we like with them. People indeed!
Soviet secret police interrogator to Eugenia Ginzburg, in *Journey into the Whirlwind*

"No other state in history," writes genocide scholar Richard Rubenstein, "has ever initiated policies designed to eliminate so many of its own citizens as has the Soviet Union."[1] The judgment must be moderated both in relative and absolute terms: the proportion of the Cambodian population killed as a direct result of Khmer Rouge policies (Chapter 7) approached one-quarter, while in absolute terms Mao Zedong has been accused of inflicting a death-toll, mostly through famine, that may have dwarfed even the Soviet Union's. Nonetheless, there is very little in the record of human experience to match the violence unleashed between 1917, when the Bolsheviks took power, and 1953, when Joseph Stalin died and the Soviet Union moved to adopt a more restrained and largely non-murderous domestic policy.

The Soviet "Gulag" system has become synonymous with Soviet repression. The Gulag (an acronym) was a "vast network of labour camps . . . scattered across the length and breadth of the Soviet Union, from the islands of the White Sea to the shores of the Black Sea, from the Arctic Circle to the plains of central Asia, from Murmansk to Vorkuta to Kazakhstan, from central Moscow to the Leningrad [St. Petersburg] suburbs."[2] However, emphasis on the Gulag tends to detract from the other means of Soviet genocide: the "terror-famine" imposed on Ukraine and other regions; the mass executions; the deportations to isolated and barren regions that condemned numerous exile groups to starvation and death by exposure, if they did not perish during the deportations themselves.

Likewise, overemphasis on the figure of Stalin may lead the analyst to understate the role of the legions of satraps who did Stalin's bidding, as well as the precedent for Stalin's "maelstrom of murder"[3] in the system of terror that his predecessor, Vladimir Lenin, imposed. This chapter will attempt to do justice to these diverse themes and factors.

THE BOLSHEVIKS SEIZE POWER

The Bolshevik Revolution took place against a backdrop of centuries of dictatorship and underdevelopment in Russia, as well as the most destructive war up until that point in European history (see Chapter 2). By 1917, Russian armies facing German and Austro-Hungarian forces had been pushed to the brink of collapse, and the Russian population confronted famine. Bread riots broke out in the capital, Petrograd (St. Petersburg). In the face of growing popular and elite opposition, Tsar Nicholas II abdicated, turning over power to a liberal-dominated provisional government under Alexander Kerensky. Fatefully, Kerensky's regime chose to continue the war. Russian forces crumbled in a poorly conceived military offensive. Hundreds of thousands of soldiers deserted. Across Russia's fertile regions, spontaneous seizures of land added to the chaos.

Poised to exploit the turmoil was Lenin's Bolshevik party. Lenin was a Russian of noble birth who had discovered Marxist socialism and agitated from exile for the overthrow of the tsarist regime. Spirited back to Russia on a sealed train by the German government, which saw Lenin (presciently) as a means of removing Russia from the war, Lenin and the Bolsheviks found themselves in a minority position *vis-à-vis* the leading socialist faction, the Mensheviks. Lenin improved Bolshevik fortunes with the promise of "Bread, Peace, Land." But the party was still a marginal force, almost non-existent outside the major cities, when Lenin made the decision to launch a coup against the weakened Kerensky regime.

After storming the Winter Palace in Petrograd and seizing key infrastructure, the Bolsheviks found themselves in power – but with many predicting that their regime would last only weeks or months. To bolster their position and popular base, they quickly sued for peace with Germany and, in the Treaty of Brest-Litovsk (March 1918), gave up some of Russia's most fertile, resource-rich territories.

"There can be no revolution without counterrevolution," writes historian Arno Mayer.[4] A potent counterrevolution now confronted the new "Soviet Union" (the "soviets" were workers' councils taken over by the Bolsheviks as a means of controlling Russia's working classes). "White" political forces sought to overthrow the Bolshevik "Reds." Russia's former allies, notably Britain and the United States, were furious at Lenin's retreat from the First World War, and terrified at the prospect of socialist revolution spreading across Europe. With funding, arms, and tens of thousands of troops on the ground, they backed the Whites in a three-year struggle to the death with the Bolshevik regime.

This civil war, one of the most destructive of the twentieth century, lasted until 1921 and claimed an estimated nine million lives on all sides. Its "influence . . . on the whole course of subsequent history, and on Stalinism, cannot possibly be overestimated. It was in the civil war that Stalin and men like Stalin emerged as leaders, while others became accustomed to harshness, cruelty, terror."[5] Red forces imposed "War Communism," an economic policy that repealed peasants' land seizures, forcibly stripped the countryside of grain to feed city dwellers, and suppressed private commerce. All who opposed these policies were "enemies of the people." "This is the hour of truth," Lenin wrote in a letter to a comrade in mid-1918. "It is of supreme importance that we encourage and make use of the energy of mass terror directed against the counterrevolutionaries."[6] The Cheka, the first incarnation of the Soviet secret police (later the NKVD and finally the KGB), responded with gusto. Lenin and other Bolshevik leaders may have viewed mass terror as a short-term measure;[7] but its widespread use belies claims that it was Stalin's invention.

The civil war left the Reds victorious but the Soviet Union shattered. Famine had struck large areas of the country, and millions in rural areas were being kept alive only through foreign, especially US, generosity.[8] Acknowledging reality – a capacity not yet extinguished among Bolsheviks – Lenin repealed the War Communism measures. He allowed peasants to return to the land, and instituted the so-called New Economic Policy (NEP). Under the NEP, market mechanisms were revived, and the economy was regenerated.

Weakened by an assassination attempt and a series of strokes, Lenin died in 1924, leaving the field open for an up-and-coming Bolshevik leader to launch his drive for absolute power.

Joseph Stalin was born Joseph Dzhugashvili in Gori, Georgia, in 1879. His Caucasian background, his abusive upbringing, and the years he spent in Russian Orthodox seminaries have all been linked to his personality and subsequent policies: "There has been too much cod-psychology about Stalin's childhood," cautions Simon Sebag Montefiore in his biography of Stalin, "but this much is certain: raised in a poor priest-ridden household, he was damaged by violence, insecurity and suspicion but inspired by the local traditions of religious dogmatism, blood-feuding and romantic brigandry."[9]

In the pre-revolutionary period, the brigand led a series of daring bank robberies that brought him to the attention of high officials. It was at this time that Dzhugashvili adopted his party moniker, Stalin, meaning "Man of Steel." Captured by the tsarist authorities, he endured two spells of exile in Siberia.

After the Bolsheviks seized power, Stalin was appointed General Secretary of the Communist Party in 1922. In itself, the post was an undistinguished administrative one. But Stalin used it to build a power base and establish control over the party bureaucracy, while also earning a reputation as "a dynamic leader who had a hand in nearly all the principal discussions on politics, military strategy, economics, security and international relations."[10] When Lenin died in 1924, a struggle for supremacy pitted Stalin against his nemesis, Leon Trotsky, and a host of lesser party figures. Stalin's victory was slow and hard-won, but by 1927 he and his allies had succeeded in expelling Trotsky from the party and, in 1929, from the country.[11]

By 1928, Stalin was entrenched as supreme Soviet leader. With world revolution seemingly a distant prospect, Stalin chose the course of "socialism in one country," which for him meant "a new programme of extremely – almost hysterically – rapid industrialization."[12] In this decision lay the seeds of two principal genocidal policies under Stalin: the massive expansion of the Gulag system, which killed millions; and the campaign against the peasantry, whose grain was needed to feed cities swelled by the crash industrialization.

The two strategies intersected. By fomenting a spurious "class war" in the countryside, Stalin could expropriate the holdings of the wealthier (or less poor) peasants; conscript millions of them into forced labor on industrial projects; and also use the new bounty of prisoners to extract natural resources (especially gold and timber) that could be sold abroad for the hard currency needed to purchase industrial machinery and pay foreign advisors.

COLLECTIVIZATION AND FAMINE

Whatever the rhetoric of their claims to represent the working people of the land and the factories, the Soviet attitude towards the peasants was one of thinly disguised contempt. "On the one hand they were the People incarnate, the soul of the country, suffering, patient, the hope of the future," writes Robert Conquest, a leading historian of the Stalinist era. "On the other, they appeared as the 'dark people,' backward, mulish, deaf to argument, an oafish impediment to all progress."[13]

Of this group, it was the so-called "kulaks" who aroused the greatest Bolshevik hatred. The definition of "kulak" was subject to terrifyingly random variations, but in general the kulaks were better-off peasants, perhaps only slightly better-off. Owning a cow or hiring a helper could be enough to label one as a kulak, with consequences that were often fatal, even in the earliest phase of Bolshevik rule. "Merciless mass terror against the kulaks. . . . Death to them!" pronounced Lenin, before death took him as well.[14]

Stalin, as was his habit, carried things to extremes. In January 1930, his regime "chillingly approved the liquidation of kulaks as a class."[15] Over the next two years, the Soviet dictatorship forced millions onto collective (state-controlled) farms.[16] Resisters and "class enemies," mostly male heads of family, were shot by the tens of thousands. Hundreds of thousands more, perhaps over a million, were sent to concentration camps, often under conditions that killed them before they arrived. Official statistics show the camp system swelling from 212,000 inmates in 1931 to more than 500,000 in 1934 and nearly a million by 1935.[17] Nearly two million other "kulaks" were sent into internal exile, either to distant corners of the Soviet Union or to marginal lands closer to home.[18]

After the "kulaks" were destroyed or banished, the regime's agents scoured the newly collectivized countryside for grain to feed the cities. Often the tax imposed on peasants exceeded the total amount that could be harvested. The inexorable result was widespread famine, not only in Ukraine, but in the Volga region, Kazakhstan, and other territories afflicted by the twin evils of forced collectivization and grain seizures. Stalin and his associates cared little. If famine was the price of collectivization, it was the price of progress. Countless people would die, but to utilitarian ends: the Soviet Union would "develop," and buttress itself against a hostile world.

In addition, wreaking havoc on Ukraine had the effect of weakening Ukrainian nationalist aspirations for a generation, perhaps permanently. Whether Stalin deliberately inflicted the famine as a means to this end is debatable.[19] Regardless, and predominantly as the result of Stalin's strategy of collectivization through mass terror, "a veritable crescendo of terror by hunger" descended on Ukraine, along with the Caucasus and Soviet Central Asia.[20] "A former activist" in Ukraine described the consequences:

> The most terrifying sights were the little children with skeleton limbs dangling from balloon-like abdomens. Starvation had wiped every trace of youth from their faces, turning them into tortured gargoyles; only in their eyes still lingered the reminder of childhood. Everywhere we found men and women lying prone, their faces and bellies bloated, their eyes utterly expressionless.[21]

A recent and credible estimate of excess deaths in the famine, across all regions of the USSR from 1930 to 1933, is 5.7 million[22] – approximately the number of European Jews killed by the Nazis, including those murdered indirectly by starvation and disease.

THE GULAG

As noted, hundreds of thousands of the "kulaks" deported during the collectivization drive landed in the Gulag system. They toiled in a "system of unofficial slavery,"[23] overworked and malnourished, on industrial projects and infrastructure, though much of their labor was diverted to hare-brained schemes such as the White Sea Canal, which claimed thousands of lives but fell into near-disuse after its completion.[24] Far from atypical was the fate of "scores of thousands of prisoners, almost entirely peasants . . . thrown ashore at Magadan [in Siberia] in an ill-considered crash programme to exploit the newly discovered gold seams in the area." Robert Conquest wrote that "whole camps perished to a man, even including guards and guard dogs"; "not more than one in fifty of the prisoners, if that, survived" their first year of incarceration in such conditions.[25]

It was these Siberian camps, devoted either to gold-mining or timber harvesting, that inflicted the greatest toll throughout the Gulag's existence. Such camps "can only be described as extermination centres," according to Leo Kuper.[26] The camp network that came to symbolize the horrors of the Gulag was that of the Kolyma gold-fields, where "outside work for prisoners was compulsory until the temperature reached –50C and the death rate among miners in the goldfields was estimated at about 30 per cent per annum."[27] Apart from death by starvation, disease, accidents, and overwork, NKVD execution squads pronounced death sentences on a whim. In just one camp, Serpantinka, "more prisoners were executed . . . in the one year 1938, than the total executions throughout the Russian Empire for the whole of the last century of Tsarist rule."[28] The number of victims claimed by the Kolyma camps alone was between a quarter of a million and over one million; in the lightly populated region today, "skeletons in frozen, shallow mass graves far outnumber the living."[29] Other names engraved on Russians' historical memory include Norilsk, "the centre of a group of camps more deadly than Kolyma"; and Vorkuta, with a regime characterized by "extravagant cold," "exhaustion," and a "starvation diet" reminiscent of the Nazi camps.[30]

Were the imprisoned multitudes in the Soviet Union *meant* to die? Can we, in other words, speak of genocidal intent? The answer may vary according to geographical location and historical-political context. The deaths in the northern camps of the Arctic Circle appear to have exhibited a high degree of intentionality. The predominantly peasant and political prisoners were regularly depicted as subhuman or (in the case of "politicals") as the most dangerous of enemies. At best, they were viewed as expendable fodder for the mines and quarries and frozen forests. Since the most dangerous conditions imaginable were inflicted, tolerated, and perpetuated; since life expectancy in the camps was often measured in weeks and months; and since almost no measures were proposed or implemented to preserve prisoners alive, their fate seems no less genocidal than that of the American Indians worked and starved to death in the Spanish silver-mines (Chapter 3).

However, unlike the Spanish mines or the Nazi death camps, conditions varied substantially across the vast Gulag system (apart from the worst of the war years, when privation reigned not only in the camps, but across the USSR). Outside the Arctic camps, work regimes were less harsh and death rates far lower. Here, indeed – and even in Siberia after the years of true holocaust, 1938–39 – high mortality rates could be viewed as impeding socialist production. While work regimes in the Nazi death camps were simply intended to inflict mass murder, the function of the Soviet camps was primarily economic and political. Camp commanders who impeded these functions by imposing an overly destructive regime could be sanctioned, even dismissed. Finally, at no point did the Soviets institute a "selection" process analogous to the Nazi ritual of dispatching older or weaker prisoners (along with children and pregnant women) for immediate slaughter. In fact, Soviet practice differed sharply.[31]

THE GREAT PURGE OF 1937–38

> I am shot! – lightly clad. They judged me;
> The dull, featureless gun barrels carried out the sentence.
>
> Anatoly Potyekin

In 1934, the "kulaks" – at least, those who had survived incarceration in the Gulag – were joined by new waves of enemies of the people: the "terrorists," "saboteurs," and "provocateurs" arrested by the hundreds of thousands after the assassination of Leningrad party chief Sergei Kirov. The Kirov murder "laid the foundation for a random terror without even the pretence of a rule of law."[32] Stalin used it as a launching pad for the great purge of 1937–38, in which 1,575,000 people were arrested, 1,345,000 sentenced, and over 681,000 executed ("more than 85 percent of all the death sentences handed down during the entire Stalinist period").[33]

It is the purge of the Communist Party that many view as the zenith of Stalinist terror. (Stalin's "one true novelty," according to Martin Amis, "was the discovery of another stratum of society in need of purgation: Bolsheviks.")[34] However, as the Gulag's chronicler, Anne Applebaum, points out, this is misleading. Millions had already died – in famines, while undergoing deportation, in exile, and in camps – before Stalin turned against the "Old Bolsheviks" and their alleged legions of co-conspirators. Moreover, the apex of the Gulag was actually much later, following the Second World War.

However, the purge does display better than any other event the ruthless megalomania and intense paranoia of the dictator. In brief, "those without blind faith were to die,"[35] and eventually hundreds of thousands of the blindly faithful were obliterated as well. The campaign began with incremental moves against the "Right opposition," led by Nikolai Bukharin, which had questioned the crash-collectivization and crash-industrialization campaigns, and was now calling for a return to the New Economic Policy and reconciliation with the shattered peasantry. The opposition was targeted in three separate "show trials" between 1936 and 1938, in which Bukharin and other leaders were accused of conspiring with Trotskyite and foreign elements to sabotage communism in the Soviet Union. The evidence presented was almost non-existent, convictions relying on absurd confessions extracted through torture, threats against family members, and (bizarrely) appeals to revolutionary solidarity.[36]

The old guard was convicted *en bloc*, and usually sentenced to execution. But the net was cast far and wide. Everyone who confessed named names (and more names, and still more names). Investigations and arrests snowballed. Meanwhile, the prevailing paranoia meant that sabotage lurked around every corner, in every seemingly innocuous situation. According to Soviet dissident Alexander Solzhenitsyn, "any adult inhabitant of this country, from a collective farmer up to a member of the Politburo, always knew that it would take only one careless word or gesture and he would fly off irrevocably into the abyss."[37] "Most of us didn't live in any real sense," wrote Nadezhda Mandelstam in her autobiography *Hope Against Hope*, "but existed from day to day, waiting anxiously for something until the time came to die. . . . In the years of the terror, there was not a home in the country where people did not sit trembling at night, their ears straining to catch the murmur of passing cars or the sound of the elevator."[38]

Like careerists and *génocidaires* everywhere, NKVD officials and others in "the exterminating profession" were anxious to match, and if possible exceed, the expectations of those in command. If "enemies of the people" could not be found in sufficient numbers, individuals – overwhelmingly adult men – were simply rounded up, shot outright, or charged under Article 58 and shipped off to the camps.[39]

The Great Purge ended only when it became clear that "at the rate arrests were going, practically all the urban population would have been implicated within a few months."[40] As usual, Stalin's underlings took the fall. The NKVD was purged, and its leader, Nikolai Yezhov, arrested and executed.[41] Stalin went on to preside over the eighteenth Party Congress in March 1939, proclaiming the great accomplishments of the purge. Only thirty-five of the nearly 2,000 delegates who had attended the previous Party Congress were still around to celebrate with him.[42]

THE WAR YEARS

The Soviet invasion of Poland in 1939, following the signing of a non-aggression pact with Nazi Germany, brought with it mass atrocities that are still relatively little known. The exception is the murder, on Stalin's orders, of 20,000 Polish officers who were then buried in the Katyn forest.[43] Although horrific, this was only a small part of a wider campaign against the Polish nation. Apart from the officer class of the military, the campaign concentrated on the destruction of political leaders, members of the professional and intellectual classes, and businesspeople. The war against the Ukrainian people was thus duplicated in Poland and, subsequently, in the Baltic states, which the Soviets invaded and occupied in 1940.

The "eliticidal" character of the campaign is conveyed by a list of those officially designated for arrest and deportation from Lithuania. According to Anne Applebaum, the targets included members of "political parties; former members of the police or the prison service; important capitalists and bourgeoisie; former officers of the national armies; family members of all of the above; anyone repatriated from Germany; refugees from 'former Poland'; as well as thieves and prostitutes." However, this was not sufficient for one Soviet commissar, who added (in his words): "Esperantists [those speaking the 'universal language' of Esperanto]; philatelists; those working with the Red Cross; refugees; smugglers; those expelled from the Communist Party; priests and active members of religious congregations; the nobility, landowners, wealthy merchants, bankers, industrialists, hotel and restaurant owners."[44]

BOX 5.1 ONE MAN'S STORY: JANUSZ BARDACH

One of the millions of foreign victims of Stalinist terror was Janusz Bardach, a Jew whose family hailed from Odessa in Russia, but who grew to maturity in the Polish town of Wlodzimierz-Wolynski. There, Bardach experienced some of the discrimination meted out to Jews in Poland. (It would explode into murderous frenzy during the period of the German occupation, when many Poles proved eager to lend the Nazis a hand in their genocidal designs against Jews.)[45] "In school I sensed that my classmates didn't truly accept me; I felt I was a stranger among them. Some called me names and made me feel that I couldn't live happily among Poles because I was Jewish."[46] But the family held fast amidst the anti-Jewish racism, which included commercial boycotts and harassment by government bureaucrats.

continued

When the Nazis invaded Poland in September 1939, Bardach was dealt a "stinging reminder" of his outsider status: the Polish army declined Jews' offers to help defend the nation. Bardach joined the flight of military-age males to the east of the country. Having imbibed left-socialist influences in his adolescence, he was happy to meet Soviet troops storming into eastern Poland (they were occupying the eastern half of the country, as agreed in the previous month's Nazi–Soviet pact). The heroic Soviets would protect Jews like him from Nazi depredations, Bardach was convinced. "I believed that the Soviet Union was a paradise for the oppressed, ruled by workers and peasants, and that the Red Army was the enforcer of social justice. I couldn't imagine them as my enemies." His joy only increased when he learned that his home town of Wlodzimierz-Wolynski would be just inside the Soviet occupation zone.

Bardach's faith in the Soviet revolution began to waver when he was forced to serve as a civilian witness accompanying a unit of the NKVD, the Soviet secret police, on a night-time raid of numerous local homes. His brother, Jurek, was caught up in the dragnet and badly beaten during interrogation; so when, in summer 1940, the Red Army announced a military draft of men of Bardach's age, he was dismayed, and sought to flunk the medical. To his further chagrin, he was pronounced fully fit. He chose assignment to a tank corps, since it offered a term of four years' service instead of the usual five.

In June 1941, the Germans broke the Nazi–Soviet pact and launched their invasion of eastern Poland and the USSR. Bardach's thoughts turned to his family on the front lines. He himself was soon in mortal danger, however. Exhausted, with Soviet forces in pell-mell retreat, Bardach lost concentration at the helm of his T-34 tank. While traversing a river, he inadvertently left a hatch open, and the tank capsized.

For this, Bardach was sentenced to death. "I sat with my face in my hand, stunned by how quickly and easily the death sentence was pronounced." Then the first of several events, so fortuitous as to be almost miraculous, came to his salvation. An NKVD officer recognized his surname – the officer had grown up next to the Bardachs in Odessa! Bardach's sentence was commuted to ten years' hard labor.

He was sent to a way-station, Burepolom, in northwest Russia. *En route*, in a crowded and unsanitary cattle-car, he took to socializing with the *urkas* – the common criminals, with their own enduring subculture. Most memoirs by Soviet intellectuals in the Gulag exude horror of the *urka*. Many inmates reported savage treatment at their hands. But Bardach somehow established a rapport that lasted through his incarceration, and made of the *urkas* valued allies, sometimes friends.

The *urkas* told him about his ultimate destination, Kolyma. "There, it was said, the guards shot prisoners for sport or sent them to work without coats or boots and placed bets on how long it would take them to freeze to death." Bardach was terrified. "I had never done hard physical work, and the thought of spending ten years at it was terrifying . . . I had little chance of surviving."

At Burepolom, Bardach was set to tree-felling. "Starvation was routine," he recounted. "We weren't given enough food to sustain us throughout one day of hard work, let alone weeks and months. Starving prisoners hunted for mice and rats with sticks and stones. They cooked them on the wood-burning stove and peeled off the fur before engulfing them. It made me sick to watch, despite the emptiness in my own stomach. At times I felt I could eat anything. . . . Gradually I learned that anything I could chew – even a leaf or fresh twig – gave the illusion of eating."

Bardach was then launched on an epic journey across the length of the Soviet Union, by railway car and "slave ship," to Kolyma – the very harshest outpost of the Gulag. On arrival, he was "assigned to clear a new area of boulders, stones, roots, and shrubs." He learned crucial survival skills, especially the fine art of faking work by "creat[ing] the illusion of activity" and thereby marshaling his energy. Still, "the oppressive work regimen was a form of torture in itself. Sometimes I thought hacking the cement-hard soil with a wrought-iron crowbar was unbearable. I felt the limits of my endurance approaching . . . hunger made me weak and defenseless . . . I still wanted to live, but I thought about injuring myself as so many other prisoners had done, hoping to win several days in the hospital, to be assigned to a lighter job, to be transferred to another camp."

The work proceeded even in the intense cold of the coldest populated region on the planet: "Touching a metal tool with a bare hand could tear off the skin, and going to the bathroom was extremely dangerous. A bout of diarrhea could land you in the snow forever." Disease was rife amid the hard labor, minimal nutrition, and squalid living conditions. Bardach came down with scurvy, and was sent to the hospital zone. There, another semi-miracle occurred. After successfully inflating his medical credentials (he had a year of medical training in prewar Poland), Bardach was granted a post as an orderly. He was released after the war, and returned home – only to discover that virtually his entire family had perished at Nazi hands.

Tens of thousands of people were executed, and hundreds of thousands more consigned to the Gulag, which now expanded to include camps in occupied territories. When the Nazi–Soviet Pact collapsed and Germany invaded Soviet-occupied Poland in June 1941, fresh catastrophe descended. Forced into pell-mell retreat, NKVD killing squads massacred many of those whom they had imprisoned on Polish territory. Legions of others were deported on foot, in scenes "hauntingly similar to the marches undertaken by the prisoners of the Nazi concentration camps four years later"[47] (see Chapter 6).

The tide turned in 1943, with the critical Soviet victories at Stalingrad and Kursk. By 1944, the Soviets were moving back into Poland and then on to German territory in East Prussia. Some of the destruction wreaked upon German civilians by vengeful Soviet armies is discussed in Box 6a on "The Nazis' Other Victims." Notable here is the Gulag's relentless expansion into Germany and other newly occupied lands (Romania, Bulgaria). In Germany, the so-called *spetslagerya* were sometimes established in former Nazi concentration camps. Once again, Soviet policy aimed to undermine any national resistance to the new Soviet order. The inmates were predominantly "judges, lawyers, entrepreneurs, businessmen, doctors and journalists." Of the 240,000 incarcerated, over one-third – 95,000 people – perished in the *spetslagerya,* while camps in Romania were more deadly still.[48] In addition, 600,000 Japanese prisoners were taken during the few days that the two countries were at war in August 1945. The camp system in fact reached its apogee well after the Second World War had ended, in 1950.

Finally, in one of modern history's most tragic ironies, Soviet prisoners-of-war who survived the Nazis' genocidal treatment (see Box 6a) to be repatriated were arrested *en masse* in the USSR on suspicion of collaboration with the Germans. Most were sentenced to long terms in the Gulag, with hundreds of thousands consigned to mine uranium for the Soviet atomic bomb; "few survived the experience."[49] As Solzhenitsyn noted sardonically: "In Russian captivity, as in German captivity, the worst lot of all was reserved for the Russians."[50]

THE DESTRUCTION OF NATIONAL MINORITIES

We have already seen that Soviet skepticism towards nationalist forces led to genocidal mass repression and man-made famine in Ukraine, whose people were the most powerful and resource-rich of those inclined towards autonomy or independence.[51] During the Second World War, this mindset unleashed a campaign of similar viciousness against an array of national minorities across the southern territories of the Soviet empire. The Soviet Germans living in the Volga region, numbering well over a million, were a predictable target once Hitler's Germany launched its invasion of the Soviet Union in 1941. Depicted as saboteurs and "fifth columnists," they were rounded up and deported from territories they had settled for centuries – some 1.2 million in all.[52]

The Nazi drive into the Caucasus and Crimea in 1942 spelled doom for a host of other minorities there and in Soviet Central Asia. Accused of collaborating with the German invader, polyglot groups were rounded up by the NKVD and expelled from their homelands – generally under terrible conditions, and to desolate territories where agriculture was difficult and infrastructure non-existent. "The seven peoples deported during the war were: Balkars, Chechens, Crimean Tatars,[53] Ingushi, Karachai, Kalmyks, and Meskhetians. The deportations began with the Karachai and the Kalmyks near the end of 1943, continued in the first half of 1944 with Chechens, Ingushi, and Balkars, and culminated in the removal of the Crimean Tatars in the middle of that year."[54] With the translocation went a systematic assault on the foundations of these minorities' cultures:

> For the first time, Stalin had decided to eliminate not just members of particular, suspect nationalities, or categories of political "enemies," but entire nations – men,

> women, children, grandparents. . . . After they had gone, the names of all of the deported peoples were eliminated from official documents – even from the *Great Soviet Encyclopædia.* The authorities wiped their homelands off the map, abolishing the Chechen-Ingush Autonomous Republic, the Volga-German Autonomous Republic, the Kabardino-Balkar Autonomous Republic, and the Karachai Autonomous Province. The Crimean Autonomous Republic was also liquidated, and Crimea simply became another Soviet province.[55]

The devastation of the Chechen nation was only one of many, but it had especially fateful consequences. The Chechen genocide – Applebaum estimates that 78,000 Chechens died on transport trains alone[56] – resonates to the present. The fierce Chechen struggle for independence in the 1990s (see Box 5a) reflects memories of the genocide during the Second World War. The response of the post-Soviet Russian government has been a new round of genocide, with tens of thousands of Chechens killed and hundreds of thousands more displaced as refugees.[57]

In the final months of his life, Stalin directed his paranoid zeal against a minority that so far had largely escaped targeting as such: Soviet Jews. Those arrested in the so-called "Doctors' Plot" in January 1953 were mostly Jewish, and fear reigned that the arrests presaged a repeat of the Great Purge. But in March, the dictator died. Rapidly, a "thaw" spread through Soviet life. Over the course of the next decade, the vast majority of Gulag prisoners were released, the "camp-industrial complex" was shut down, and many of the dead and still living were formally rehabilitated. Limited criticisms were aired of Stalin and the cult of personality, "the most grandiose in history,"[58] that surrounded him.

The height of the thaw came under Stalin's eventual successor, Nikita Khrushchev. A Ukrainian who had helped consign millions of his fellow Ukrainians to death or the Gulag, Khrushchev nonetheless permitted the first real blast of truth about life in the camps to be published in the USSR: Alexander Solzhenitsyn's novella *One Day in the Life of Ivan Denisovich.* But in 1964, Khrushchev was ousted for his failed brinkmanship during the Cuban Missile Crisis, and his disastrous domestic agricultural policies. A new chill descended. When Solzhenitsyn completed his massive three-volume study of *The Gulag Archipelago,* he could publish it only abroad; and though the work won its author the Nobel Prize for literature, it led to his house arrest and forced exile. Only with a new and deeper thaw under Mikhail Gorbachev did a genuine reckoning with the Stalinist and Gulag legacies begin – although post-Soviet citizens have proven notably reluctant to revisit this aspect of the national past.[59]

STALIN AND GENOCIDE

The misery and violence inflicted on the Soviet Union during Stalin's reign would seem, on its face, to constitute genocide. Certainly in the case of the destruction of the national minorities, the term seems unavoidable. Not only were hundreds of thousands of minority members killed – through execution, lethal deportation, disease, privation – but a systematic assault was mounted on the foundations of their

Figure 5.1 A diehard supporter of Joseph Stalin (larger photo) and Vladimir Lenin carries their portraits in Moscow's Red Square on the fiftieth anniversary of Stalin's death, March 5, 2003. Many Russians who survived Stalin's reign remember it as a time of economic development, national unity, and patriotic pride. They yearn for the return of a "strong hand" amidst the social dislocation of the post-communist period.

Source: Alexander Natruskin – Reuters/Corbis.

national cultures. A similar approach was adopted in the case of Ukraine and occupied Poland.

The application of a genocide framework to the human havoc of the Ukrainian famine (1931–32) is more controversial. But the famine killed millions; it took place against a backdrop of persecution, mass execution, and incarceration clearly aimed at undermining Ukrainians as a national group. Moreover, we know from the documentary record that a clear picture of what was occurring in Ukraine was available to the Soviet leadership throughout the famine. The expulsion of vast numbers of "kulaks" to marginal territories; the continuation of grain seizures at the height of the famine; the refusal to distribute reserve stores of grain to starving peasants while preventing them from fleeing the famished countryside – these actions, it seems to me and to most genocide scholars, should be considered genocidal.

As for the mass political repressions, particularly those against the "kulaks" and the Communist Party itself, we confront again perhaps the deepest deficiency of the UN Genocide Convention – its failure to include political and socioeconomic groups among the categories of genocide's victims. Not surprisingly, Stalin's USSR played a significant role in forestalling efforts to include these groups. However, most scholars believe today that this exclusion is outmoded, founded on *realpolitik* and on the relative novelty of "politicides" at the time the Convention was drafted. By contrast, in the contemporary period, political and socioeconomic groups are probably *most* likely to be targeted in campaigns of mass killing. In this sordid aspect of twentieth-century history, Stalin was the trail-blazer.

FURTHER STUDY

Note: The Stalinist period in the USSR has become a classic study of dictatorship and political terror, generating a literature second only to studies of Nazism and the Jewish Holocaust (Chapter 6). The following is a small sample of works in English.

Martin Amis, *Koba the Dread: Laughter and the Twenty Million*. New York: Hyperion, 2002. British novelist's uneven but evocative study of Stalin's era and personality.

Anne Applebaum, *Gulag: A History*. London: Penguin, 2003. Winner of the Pulitzer Prize; an epic single-volume history of the Soviet forced-labor camps.

Janusz Bardach, *Man is Wolf to Man: Surviving the Gulag*, trans. Kathleen Gleeson. Berkeley, CA: University of California Press, 1999. Vivid memoir, sampled in this chapter.

Robert Conquest, *The Harvest of Sorrow: Soviet Collectivization and the Terror-Famine*. New York: Oxford University Press, 1986. Conveys the single-minded sadism and human destruction of the Ukrainian famine of 1929–33.

Robert Conquest, *The Great Terror: A Reassessment*. New York: Oxford University Press, 1990. Updated version of Conquest's seminal 1960s study.

Stéphane Courtois *et al.*, *The Black Book of Communism: Crimes, Terror, Repression*, trans. Jonathan Murphy and Mark Kramer. Cambridge, MA: Harvard University Press, 1999. Massive indictment of communist regimes; includes Nicolas Werth's study of the USSR, "A State Against Its People."

R.W. Davies and Stephen G. Wheatcroft, *The Years of Hunger: Soviet Agriculture, 1931–1933*. Basingstoke: Palgrave Macmillan, 2004. Volume in the series "The Industrialisation of Soviet Russia"; usefully consulted alongside Conquest's *Harvest of Sorrow*.

Miron Dolot, *Execution by Hunger: The Hidden Holocaust*. New York: W.W. Norton, 1985. Memoir of the Ukrainian famine.

Orlando Figes, *A People's Tragedy: A History of the Russian Revolution*. New York: Viking, 1996. Peerless study of the wars and crises that brought Lenin and Stalin to power.

Sheila Fitzpatrick, *Everyday Stalinism: Ordinary Life in Extraordinary Times: Soviet*

Russia in the 1930s. Oxford: Oxford University Press, 1999. Individual perspectives on broad social transformations; see also *The Russian Revolution, 1917–1932*, a concise account.

Eugenia Ginzburg, *Journey into the Whirlwind*. New York: Harvest, 2002. Account of arrest and the Gulag; see also its sequel, *Within the Whirlwind*.

Adam Hochschild, *The Unquiet Ghost: Russians Remember Stalin*. New York: Viking, 1994. Taut work on history and memory.

Nadezhda Mandelstam, *Hope Against Hope*, trans. Max Hayward. New York: The Modern Library, 1999. Powerful, poetic recollections of Stalinist terror.

Simon Sebag Montefiore, *Stalin: The Court of the Red Tsar*. London: Phoenix, 2004. Montefiore's description of life in Stalin's "court" is gossipy but galvanizing.

Robert Service, *Stalin: A Biography*. Cambridge, MA: The Belknap Press, 2005. A very serviceable biography, though brisk with the human consequences of Stalin's rule.

Varlam Shalamov, *Kolyma Tales*. London: Penguin, 1994. Documentary-style short stories about the Kolyma camps, by a former inmate.

Alexander Solzhenitsyn, *The Gulag Archipelago, 1918–1956*. New York: HarperPerennial, 2002. Abridged one-volume version of Solzhenitsyn's classic three-volume study of the camp system.

Robert W. Thurston, *Life and Terror in Stalin's Russia, 1934–1941*. New Haven, CT: Yale University Press, 1996. Fine social history.

Chris Ward, ed., *The Stalinist Dictatorship* (2nd edn). London: Arnold, 1998. Comprehensive survey of the roots and functioning of the Stalinist system.

NOTES

1 Richard Rubenstein, *The Age of Triage: Fear and Hope in an Overcrowded World* (Boston, MA: Beacon Press, 1983), p. 19.

2 Anne Applebaum, *Gulag: A History* (London: Penguin, 2004), p. 3. "Gulag" was an acronym for the Russian term *Glavnoe upravlenie lagerei*, meaning "Main Camp Administration" (ibid.).

3 Robert Service, *Stalin: A Biography* (Cambridge, MA: The Belknap Press, 2005), p. 602.

4 Arno J. Mayer, *The Furies: Violence and Terror in the French and Russian Revolutions* (Princeton, NJ: Princeton University Press, 2000), p. 45.

5 Alec Nove, *Stalinism and After* (London: George Allen & Unwin, 1975), p. 23.

6 Lenin quoted in Nicolas Werth, "A State Against Its People: Violence, Repression, and Terror in the Soviet Union," in Stéphane Courtois *et al.*, *The Black Book of Communism: Crimes, Terror, Repression*, trans. Jonathan Murphy and Mark Kramer (Cambridge, MA: Harvard University Press, 1999), p. 70.

7 Werth, no friend of Leninism, argues that "the use of terror as a key instrument in the Leninist political project had been foreseen during the outbreak of the civil war, and was intended to be of limited duration" ("A State Against Its People," p. 265).

8 "At the maximum, the American Relief Administration and its associated organizations were feeding over 10,400,000 mouths, and various other organizations nearly two million more, for a total of more than 12,300,000" (Robert Conquest, *The Harvest of Sorrow: Collectivization and the Terror-Famine* (New York: Oxford University Press, 1986), p. 56). This must qualify as one of the most extraordinary and successful "humanitarian interventions" in history, saving millions of lives.

9 Simon Sebag Montefiore, *Stalin: The Court of the Red Tsar* (London: Phoenix, 2004), p. 27.
10 Service, *Stalin: A Biography*, p. 174.
11 In exile, Trotsky founded the "Fourth International" of the socialist movement, and became the most outspoken opponent of Stalin's policies. A Stalinist agent tracked him down and killed him in Mexico City in 1940.
12 Applebaum, *Gulag*, p. 62.
13 Conquest, *The Harvest of Sorrow*, p. 19.
14 Lenin quoted in Montefiore, *Stalin: The Court of the Red Tsar*, p. 45.
15 Service, *Stalin: A Biography*, p. 267.
16 This was in one respect ironic, since in the pre-revolutionary era Stalin had been one of the strongest proponents of "let[ting] the peasants grab the land and do with it whatever they wanted"; he considered Lenin's plans for full state ownership to be "naïve and unrealisable." Also ironically, in the light of his subsequent genocides against Ukrainians and Caucasians, in the 1920s Stalin was the Communist Party's leading exponent of "the principle that each people in the Soviet state should have scope for national and ethnic self-expression." Service, *Stalin: A Biography*, pp. 94, 202.
17 Applebaum, *Gulag*, p. 515.
18 See Werth, "A State Against Its People," p. 155, with an "estimate that approximately 300,000 deportees died during the process of deportation."
19 This is Robert Conquest's assertion (*The Harvest of Sorrow*, p. 196), but is contested by R.W. Davies and Stephen G. Wheatcroft in *The Years of Hunger: Soviet Agriculture, 1931–1933* (Basingstoke: Palgrave Macmillan, 2004), pp. 440–41.
20 Conquest, *The Harvest of Sorrow*, p. 224. Two critical policy decisions were the January 1933 order to prevent peasants from fleeing the famine-stricken countryside, which "effectively decreed the death of millions who were starving," and the continued export of grain "'in the interests of industrialization.'" See Werth, "A State Against Its People," p. 167.
21 Testimony quoted in Conquest, *The Harvest of Sorrow*, p. 245.
22 Davies and Wheatcroft, *The Years of Hunger*, p. 415. According to Werth, about four million of the victims were Ukrainian ("A State Against Its People," p. 167).
23 Service, *Stalin: A Biography*, p. 495.
24 See Applebaum, *Gulag*, Ch. 4.
25 Conquest, *The Harvest of Sorrow*, pp. 127–28.
26 Leo Kuper, *Genocide: Its Political Use in the Twentieth Century* (Harmondsworth: Penguin, 1981), p. 150.
27 Kuper, *Genocide*, p. 150.
28 Robert Conquest, *Kolyma: The Arctic Death Camps* (London: Methuen, 1978), p. 229.
29 Adam Hochschild, *The Unquiet Ghost: Russians Remember Stalin* (New York: Viking, 1994), p. xxv. "I asked four . . . researchers, who between them have written or edited more than half a dozen books on the *gulag*, what was the total Kolyma death toll. One estimated it at 250,000, one at 300,000, one at 800,000, and one at 'more than 1,000,000.' . . . We will probably never know the answer" (p. 237).
30 Kuper, *Genocide*, p. 150.
31 "I have not, it must be noted, found any memoirs describing 'selections' of the sort that took place in German death camps. That is, I have not read of regular selections which ended in weak prisoners being taken aside and shot. . . . Weak prisoners were not murdered upon arrival in some of the further-flung camps, but rather given a period of 'quarantine,' both to ensure that any illnesses they were carrying would not spread, and to allow them to 'fatten up,' to recover their health after long months in prison and terrible journeys." Applebaum, *Gulag*, p. 175.
32 Montefiore, *Stalin: The Court of the Red Tsar*, p. 151. Robert Conquest calls the Kirov killing "the crime of the century" because it became "the keystone of the entire edifice of terror and suffering by which Stalin secured his grip on the Soviet peoples." Conquest, *The Great Terror: A Reassessment*, p. 37.

33 Werth, "A State Against Its People," pp. 190, 264.
34 Martin Amis, *Koba the Dread: Laughter and the Twenty Million* (New York: Hyperion, 2002), p. 32.
35 Montefiore, *Stalin: The Court of the Red Tsar*, p. 214.
36 The strength of appeals to solidarity and party unity in extracting confessions from the "Old Bolsheviks" was memorably captured in Arthur Koestler's 1940 novel, *Darkness at Noon* (New York: Bantam, 1984).
37 Alexander Solzhenitsyn, *The Gulag Archipelago Two* (New York: Harper & Row, 1975), p. 633.
38 Nadezhda Mandelstam, *Hope Against Hope* (New York: Modern Library, 1999), pp. 322–23, 352.
39 See, e.g., Robert W. Thurston, *Life and Terror in Stalin's Russia, 1934–1941* (New Haven, CT: Yale University Press, 1996), pp. 79–80.
40 Conquest, *The Great Terror: A Reassessment*, p. 433.
41 In part to shift blame from Stalin, the purge became known subsequently as the *Yezhovshchina*, or "The Reign of Yezhov," in Werth's translation ("A State Against Its People," p. 184).
42 Conquest, *The Great Terror: A Reassessment*, p. 438.
43 The Nazis uncovered some 4,000 of the corpses during Operation Barbarossa in 1941. The Soviet regime accused them of spreading libels, and blamed the Nazis for the crime at the Nuremberg tribunal.
44 Applebaum, *Gulag*, pp. 382–83.
45 See Jan Gross, *Neighbors: The Destruction of the Jewish Community in Jedwabne, Poland* (Princeton, NJ: Princeton University Press, 2002).
46 Janusz Bardach, *Man is Wolf to Man: Surviving the Gulag* (Berkeley, CA: University of California Press, 1999). The quoted passages in this section are drawn from pp. xiii, 11, 19, 88, 106, 114, 133–34, 192, 204, 220, 231, and 233.
47 Applebaum, *Gulag*, pp. 378–79.
48 Applebaum, *Gulag*, p. 410.
49 Service, *Stalin: A Biography*, p. 508.
50 Alexander Solzhenitsyn, *The Gulag Archipelago One* (New York: Harper & Row, 1974), p. 240.
51 An earlier precedent, important for understanding Leninist–Stalinist continuity, is the genocide against the Don and Kuban Cossacks during the civil war of 1919 to 1920. According to Eric Weitz, "'Cossack' came to mean anti-Soviet, a synonym for 'enemy' that carried an implicit racialization of a group defined not even by ethnicity but by its special service relationship to the czarist state." The death-toll was 300,000 to 500,000 out of a population of three million. Eric D. Weitz, *A Century of Genocide: Utopias of Race and Nation* (Princeton, NJ: Princeton University Press, 2003), p. 69; see also Werth, "A State Against Its People," pp. 98–102.
52 Finnish speakers in the Karelia region of northwest Russia also suffered after the Finns, seeking to regain territories lost to Stalin in the winter war of 1939–40, joined the Nazi thrust into the Soviet Union.
53 On the Crimean Tatars, see Brian Glyn Williams, "Hidden Ethnocide in the Soviet Muslim Borderlands: The Ethnic Cleansing of the Crimean Tatars," *Journal of Genocide Research*, 4: 3 (2002), pp. 357–73.
54 Lyman H. Legters, "Soviet Deportation of Whole Nations: A Genocidal Process," ch. 4 in Samuel Totten *et al.*, *Century of Genocide: Eyewitness Accounts and Critical Views* (New York: Garland Publishing, 1997), pp. 112–35. See also Institute for the Study of the USSR, *Genocide in the USSR: Studies in Group Destruction* (New York: The Scarecrow Press, 1958); J. Otto Pohl, "Stalin's Genocide against the 'Repressed Peoples,'" *Journal of Genocide Research*, 2: 2 (June 2000), pp. 267–93.
55 Applebaum, *Gulag*, p. 388.
56 Ibid. According to Nicolas Werth, "Of the 608,749 people deported from the Caucasus, 146,892, or nearly 1 in 4, had died by 1 October 1948. . . . Of the 228,392 people

deported from the Crimea, 44,887 had died after four years." Werth, "A State Against Its People," p. 223.

57 After Stalin's death, the remnants of some deported nationalities were allowed to return to their former territories, but the extinguished political units were not always revived.

58 Service, *Stalin: A Biography*, p. 592.

59 The epilogue of Applebaum's *Gulag* explores this phenomenon.

BOX 5A CHECHNYA

As discussed in Chapter 5, the people of Chechnya were among a number of nationalities accused of complicity with the Nazis during the Second World War, rounded up, and deported under murderous conditions to distant and barren lands. At least 390,000 Chechens – perhaps many more – were uprooted in this way. Fully a quarter of them died *en route* to their exile, and survivors faced a constant struggle against the elements and thin soils.[1] After Stalin's death, most of these populations were returned to their homelands; but bitter memories lingered, and explain something of the extraordinary persistence of Chechen rebel forces in their war for independence.[2]

One must dig deeper, however, for the roots of Chechen nationalism and its conflict with "Greater Russia." Chechens were at the forefront of efforts to resist Russian expansion during the mid-nineteenth century. When the North Caucasus was finally overwhelmed by tsarist forces and incorporated into the empire, some 600,000 Caucasians – 100,000 of them Chechens – "were sent to the Ottoman Empire, where tens of thousands perished from starvation and disease."[3]

The Chechens rallied after the Bolshevik Revolution of 1917, but their declaration of independence was doomed by renewed Russian (now Soviet) expansionism. The Bolsheviks occupied Chechnya, and in 1924 established the Chechen-Ingush Autonomous Region that Stalin would cancel in the 1940s.

The great liberalizing wave that struck the Soviet Union and Eastern Europe in the late 1980s resulted in the breakup of the Soviet empire; but Chechnya was a federal unit of Russia, not a Soviet union republic. When Russian leader Boris Yeltsin took over from Soviet leader Mikhail Gorbachev, he decided that no secession from Russia itself would be allowed. In the Chechen case, there were also material considerations: a major oil pipeline ran through Chechnya, which was home to rich petroleum resources of its own. Whoever controlled them was guaranteed a strategic presence in the region as a whole.

Russian policy also reflected an ingrained racism towards Chechens. Chechnya had long been an "obsession" for the Russians, writes journalist David Remnick: "an image of Islamic defiance, an embodiment of the primitive, the devious, the elusive." Chechens were seen as bumpkins and "black asses." "Yeltsin knew well that for many Russians the Chechens were nothing more than a tribe of 'thieving niggers.'"[4]

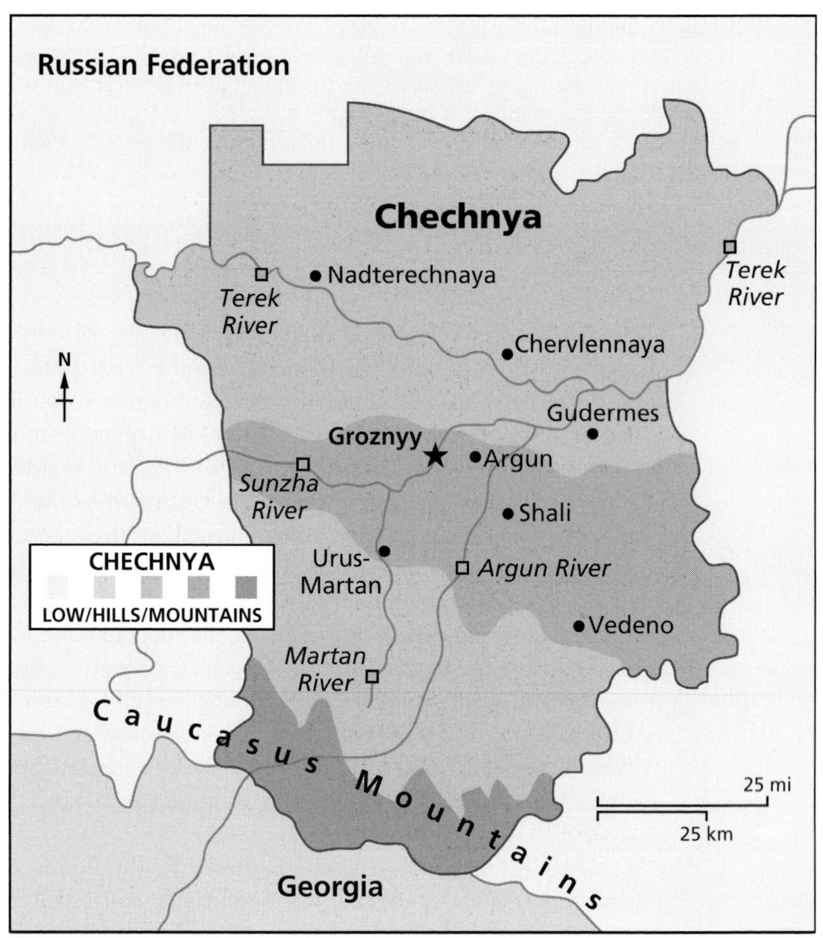

Map 5a.1 Chechnya

Source: Map provided by WorldAtlas.com

In 1991, the mercurial Chechen leader, Dzhokar Dudayev – previously a general in the Soviet air force – rebelled against Moscow and declared Chechnya independent. Under his rule, "Chechnya became an epicenter of financial scams and illegal trade in oil and contraband, and a safe haven for criminals from all over Russia," while violence against ethnic Russians in the territory rose alarmingly.[5]

The bombastic, alcoholic Yeltsin countered by seeking to undermine the Chechen regime from within.[6] When a Russian-led assault on Grozny, using Chechen forces opposed to Dudayev, ended in shambles, the Russians reacted with fury. In December 1994, 40,000 Russian troops – mostly ill-trained conscripts – were sent into Chechnya. Yeltsin apparently believed the declaration of his defense minister, Pavel Grachev, that the territory could be conquered "in two hours by a single paratrooper regiment."[7] Two years later, Russian forces were still there.

The first assault on Grozny was disastrous. Russian tank columns and troop concentrations were torn apart by hit-and-run rebel attacks. The humiliated Russians responded with mass atrocity against civilians. The bombing and shelling of Grozny was "the heaviest artillery bombardment that anyone had seen since the Second World War."[8] Numerous other towns and villages where rebels were allegedly present were also targeted. Tens of thousands of Chechens were killed, overwhelmingly civilians. In a grim irony, many of the victims were ethnic Russians who lacked the contacts in the countryside that allowed many Chechens to flee to refuge in the Caucasus foothills. When the Russians finally claimed control of Grozny in March, visiting journalists marveled at "the sheer scale of the destruction," with the city "not only in ruins but . . . destroyed [to] its very foundations." Even years later, the heart of the city remained "a desert scene of rubble and burnt-out buildings."[9]

To the extent that Russians discriminated in their killing, the strategy was predominantly gendercidal (see Chapter 13). "I killed a lot," a Russian soldier returned from Chechnya told Maura Reynolds of the *Los Angeles Times*:

> I wouldn't touch women or children, as long as they didn't fire at me. But I would kill all the men I met during mopping-up operations. I didn't feel sorry for them one bit. They deserved it. I wouldn't even listen to the pleas or see the tears of their women when they asked me to spare their men. I simply took them aside and killed them.[10]

In keeping with such strategies, mass round-ups and detentions of Chechen men were staged, with detainees passed through "filtration camps" run by the Russian military and FSB (formerly the KGB). Torture was frequent in the camps, and "disappearances" rampant.

All of this occurred in Europe; yet few Europeans, or others, raised their voices in protest. Russia, even in its post-Soviet incarnation, is a great power, and a nuclear one. European governments have been more interested in courting it and profiting from its immense resources than in criticizing "internal" practices, even genocidal ones. The response of the Clinton and Bush administrations was likewise "woefully late and pitifully restrained."[11]

Terrifying and destructive as the war was, it was just the first round. In 1996, astonishingly, rebel forces penetrated and reoccupied Grozny, holding it for weeks against a sustained, and again indiscriminate, Russian counter-attack. For the Russian public, this was the final straw. Public opposition to the slaughter (albeit mainly to the deaths of Russian conscripts) drove Yeltsin's approval ratings to dismally low levels. The Russian media enjoyed their most brilliant moment since 1917, with press reports and TV investigations relentlessly documenting the Chechen chaos. Finally, Russian forces pulled out in defeat, leaving the territory still nominally part of Russia, but effectively in the hands of Chechen rebels and warlords.

With the economy and infrastructure virtually destroyed, Chechnya again lapsed into lawlessness. In September 1999, Yeltsin, now a lame duck, sent the troops back in. His policy was energetically continued and expanded by his successor, Vladimir Putin, who pledged pungently to "corner the bandits in the shithouse and wipe them out."[12] Putin believed that a hard line on Chechnya would help him consolidate his power and appeal to voters in future elections.[13]

Under Putin, the murderous Russian tactics of the previous conflict were revived, from indiscriminate bombardment to filtration camps. Again adult males were special targets. Human Rights Watch stated that "every adult Chechen male" was being treated "as if he were a rebel fighter."[14] Chechen women were also assaulted and raped on an increasing scale.[15]

None of it worked. Once again, Russian forces became mired in an intractable guerrilla war. As the quagmire deepened, Putin sought to indigenize the war. "Chechenization" became the new buzzword; but as fast as the Russians could come up with new satraps, the rebels assassinated them. "Who but a masochist would want to run Chechnya now?" wondered *The Economist*, after President Akhmad Kadyrov was blown up by a rebel bomb in May 2004.[16]

As for the rebels, their own actions, within Chechnya and beyond, were becoming ever more atrocious and unrestrained. In 2004 alone, hundreds of schoolchildren died in the town of Beslan in neighbouring Ingushetia, when Russian forces stormed a school seized by rebels. Two civilian passenger planes downed by female Chechen rebels – the so-called "Black Widows"[17] – added to the casualty count.

The toll among Chechen civilians, though, was vastly greater – probably approaching 100,000 as of early 2005. Matthew Evangelista wrote in *Current History* that "a plausible case" could be made that Russia has "violated the Genocide Convention for 'acts committed with intent to destroy, in whole or in part, a national, ethnical, racial, or religious group.'"[18]

If Russian violence has remained constant, so has the "mixture of eager complicity and mute acquiescence" displayed by the outside world.[19] After September 11, 2001, Putin's regime positioned itself as a valuable ally in the "war on terror." This provided an ideal camouflage and justification for Russia's continuing genocidal campaign against Chechen Muslims. Lindsey Hilsum writes: "Chechnya is a shameful example of western leaders refusing to confront another government on human rights abuses and war crimes because, in the end, strategic and political issues matter more. Chechnya is complex and dangerous and miserable, and we just don't care enough to try to make a difference."[20]

FURTHER STUDY

Matthew Evangelista, *The Chechen Wars: Will Russia Go the Way of the Soviet Union?* Washington, DC: Brookings Institution Press, 2002. Astute political analysis, with a chapter on "War Crimes and Russia's International Standing."

Carlotta Gall and Thomas de Waal, *Chechnya: Calamity in the Caucasus.* New York: New York University Press, 1998. Well-informed journalistic account of the first Chechen war.

Human Rights Watch, *Swept Under: Torture, Forced Disappearances, and Extrajudicial Killings during Sweep Operations in Chechnya.* February 2002. Available at http://www.hrw.org/reports/2002/russchech. Major HRW report on atrocities in the renewed war against Chechens.

Anna Politkovskaya, *A Small Corner of Hell: Dispatches from Chechnya.* Chicago, IL: University of Chicago Press, 2003. Brave account by a Russian reporter on the scene.

NOTES

1 On the struggle to survive after deportation, see Michela Pohl, "'It Cannot Be That Our Graves Will Be Here': The Survival of Chechen and Ingush Deportees in Kazakhstan, 1944–1957," *Journal of Genocide Research*, 4: 3 (2002), pp. 401–30.

2 See Birgit Brauer, "Chechens and the Survival of Their Cultural Identity in Exile," *Journal of Genocide Research*, 4: 3 (2002), pp. 387–400. Brauer writes (p. 399): "One of the side effects of the deportation was that the surviving Chechens became much closer and stronger as a people. Their families and villages may have been torn apart, but their defiance against these circumstances led to the development of a national identity."

3 Tony Wood, "The Case for Chechnya," *New Left Review*, 30 (November–December 2004), p. 10.

4 David Remnick, *Resurrection: The Struggle for a New Russia* (New York: Vintage, 1998), pp. 266, 271.

5 Nabi Abdullaev, "Chechnya Ten Years Later," *Current History* (October 2004), p. 332.

6 President Dudayev was assassinated by a Russian missile in April 1996; his successor, Aslan Maskhadov, was killed in March 2005.

7 Grachev quoted in Remnick, *Resurrection*, p. 278.

8 Carlotta Gall and Thomas de Waal, *Chechnya: Calamity in the Caucasus* (New York: New York University Press, 1998), p. 219.

9 Gall and de Waal, *Chechnya*, p. 227.

10 Maura Reynolds, "War Has No Rules for Russian Forces Battling Chechen Rebels," *Los Angeles Times*, September 17, 2000.

11 Remnick, *Resurrection*, p. 284.

12 Sebastian Smith, "Grozny Gangsters Hold Sway in a Wasteland Created by Russia," *The Times*, December 11, 2004.

13 See the trenchant analysis of Putin's policies, and their underlying motivations, in Wood, "The Case for Chechnya," pp. 27–31.

14 Human Rights Watch cited in Geoffrey York, "Russians Accused of Executing Chechens," *Globe and Mail*, February 14, 2000.
15 See "Serious Violations of Women's Human Rights in Chechnya," Human Rights Watch backgrounder, January 2002, http://www.hrw.org/backgrounder/eca/chechnya_women.htm.
16 "A Gaping Hole," *The Economist*, May 15, 2004.
17 See Chris Stephen, "The Black Widows of Chechnya," *The Scotsman*, September 17, 2004, http://news.scotsman.com/topics.cfm?tid=610andid=1090202004.
18 Matthew Evangelista, *The Chechen Wars: Will Russia Go the Way of the Soviet Union?* (Washington, DC: Brookings Institution Press, 2002), p. 142; see also p. 177.
19 Wood, "The Case for Chechnya," p. 36.
20 Lindsey Hilsum, "The Conflict the West Always Ignores," *New Statesman*, January 26, 2004.

CHAPTER 6

The Jewish Holocaust

INTRODUCTION

The genocide of European Jews – which many scholars and others call simply "the Holocaust"[1] – "is perhaps the one genocide of which every educated person has heard."[2] Between 1941 and 1945, five to six million Jews were systematically murdered by the Nazi regime, its allies, and its surrogates in the Nazi-occupied territories.[3] Yet despite the extraordinary scale and intensity of the genocide, its prominence in recent decades was far from preordained. The Second World War killed upwards of fifty million people, and attitudes in the two decades following the Nazi defeat tended to mirror those of European countries and leaders during the war, who generally refused to ascribe special significance or urgency to the Jewish catastrophe. Only with the Israeli capture of Adolf Eichmann, the epitome of the "banality of evil" in Hannah Arendt's famous phrase, and his trial in Jerusalem in 1961 did the Jewish catastrophe begin truly to entrench itself in the Western consciousness, and become the paradigmatic genocide of human history. Even today, in the evaluation of genocide scholar Yehuda Bauer, "the impact of the Holocaust is growing, not diminishing."[4]

This impact is expressed in the diverse debates about the Holocaust. Among the searching questions asked are: How could the systematic murder of millions of helpless individuals have sprung from one of the most developed and "civilized" of Western states? What are the links to European anti-semitism? How central a figure was Hitler in the genesis and unfolding of the slaughter? What part did "ordinary men" and "ordinary Germans" play in the extermination campaign? How extensive was Jewish resistance? What was the role of the Allies (notably Britain, France, the

USSR, and the United States), both before and during the Second World War, in abandoning Jews to destruction at Nazi hands? And what is the relationship between the Jewish Holocaust and the postwar state of Israel? This chapter addresses these controversies in its latter sections, while also touching on the debate over the alleged "uniqueness" of the Jewish tragedy.

ORIGINS

Until the later nineteenth century, Jews were uniquely stigmatized within the European social hierarchy. Medieval Christianity "held the Jews to violate the moral order of the world. By rejecting Jesus, by allegedly having killed him, the Jews stood in defiant opposition to the otherwise universally accepted conception of God and Man, denigrating and defiling, by their very existence, all that is sacred. As such, Jews came to represent symbolically and discursively much of the evil in the world."[5] Jews – especially male Jews (see Chapter 13) – were reviled as "uprooted, troublesome, malevolent, shiftless."[6]

The Catholic church, and later the Protestant offshoot founded by the virulently anti-semitic Martin Luther, assailed Jews as "thirsty bloodhounds and murderers of all Christendom."[7] The most primitive and powerful myth was the so-called "blood libel": the claim that Jews seized and murdered Gentile children in order to use their blood in the baking of ceremonial bread for the Passover celebration.[8] Fueled by this and other fantasies, regular pogroms – localized campaigns of violence, killing, and repression – scarred European Jewish history. At various points, Jews who refused to convert to Christianity were also rounded up and expelled, most notoriously from Spain and Portugal in 1492.

The rise of modernity and the nation-state recast traditional anti-semitism in new and contradictory guises. (The term "anti-semitism" is a product of this era, coined by the German Wilhelm Marr in 1879.) On one hand, Jews were viewed as *enemies* of modernity. Cloistered in the cultural isolation of ghettos (to which previous generations had consigned them), they could never be truly part of the nation-state, which was rapidly emerging as the fulcrum of modern identity.[9] On the other hand, for sectors suspicious of or threatened by modernity, Jews were seen as dangerous *agents* of modernity: as key players in oppressive economic institutions; as urban, cosmopolitan, transcultural elements who threatened the unity and identity of the *Völk* (people).

It would be erroneous, however, to present European history as one long campaign of discrimination and repression against Jews. For several centuries Jews in Eastern Europe "enjoyed a period of comparative peace, tranquillity and the flowering of Jewish religious life."[10] They were even more prominent, and valued, in Muslim Spain. Moreover, modern ideologies of nationalism sometimes followed the liberal "melting-pot" motif exemplified by the United States. Those Jews who sought integration with their wider societies could be accepted. The late nineteenth and early twentieth centuries are seen as something of a golden age for Jews in France, Britain, and Germany, even while some two-and-a-half million Jews were fleeing tsarist Russia in the face of brutal pogroms.

Germany was widely viewed as one of the more tolerant European societies; Prussia, the first German state to grant citizenship to its Jews, had done so as early as 1812. How, then, could Germany turn first to persecuting, then to slaughtering, nearly two-thirds of the Jews of Europe? Part of the answer lies in the fact that, although German society was in many ways tolerant and progressive, German politics was never liberal or democratic, in the manner of both Britain and France.[11] Moreover, German society was deeply destabilized by defeat in the First World War, and by the imposition of a ruinous and humiliating peace settlement at Versailles in 1919. Germany was forced to shoulder full blame for the outbreak of the "Great War." It lost its overseas colonies, along with some of its European territories; its armed forces were reduced to a fraction of their former size; and onerous reparations were demanded. "A tidal wave of shame and resentment, experienced even by younger men who had not seen military service, swept the nation," writes Richard Plant. "Many people tried to digest the bitter defeat by searching furiously for scapegoats."[12] Such dark currents ran beneath the political order, the Weimar Republic, that prevailed after the war. Democratic but fragile, it presided over economic chaos – first the hyperinflation of 1923, which saw the German mark slip to 4.2 trillion to the dollar, and then the widespread unemployment of the global Great Depression beginning in 1929.

The result was political extremism. Its prime architect and beneficiary was the NSDAP (abbreviated to "Nazi") party, founded by Adolf Hitler and sundry alienated colleagues. Hitler, a highly decorated First World War veteran and failed artist from Vienna, assumed the task of resurrecting Germany and imposing its hegemony on all Europe. This vision would lead to the deaths of tens of millions of people. But it was underpinned in Hitler's mind by an epic hatred of Jews – "these black parasites of the nation," as he called them in his prison-penned tirade, *Mein Kampf* (My Struggle).[13]

Hitler's path to power was far from direct. By 1932, Hitler seemed to many to have passed his peak. The Nazis won only a minority of parliamentary seats in that year's elections; more Germans voted for parties of the Left than of the Right. But divisions between the Socialists and Communists made the Nazis the largest single party in the Reichstag, and allowed Hitler to become Chancellor in January 1933.

Once installed in power, the Nazis proved unstoppable. Within three months, they had seized "total control of [the] German state, abolishing its federalist structure, dismantling democratic government and outlawing political parties and trade unions." The Enabling Act of March 23, 1933 gave Hitler "*carte blanche* to terrorize and neutralise all effective political opposition."[14] Immediately thereafter, the Nazis' persecutory stance towards Jews became plain. Within a few months, Jews saw their businesses placed under Nazi boycott; their mass dismissal from hospitals, the schools, and the civil service, and public book-burnings of Jewish and other "degenerate" works. The Nuremberg Laws of 1935 stripped Jews of citizenship and gave legal shape to the Nazis' race-based theories: intermarriage or sexual intercourse between non-Jews and Jews was prohibited.

With the Nuremberg edicts, and the threat of worse measures looming, increasing numbers of Jews fled abroad. The abandonment of homes and capital in Germany meant penury abroad – the Nazis would allow only a fraction of one's wealth to be exported. The general unwillingness of the outside world to accept Jewish refugees meant that many more Jews longed to leave than actually could. Hundreds of those who remained behind committed suicide as the humiliation of Nazi rule imposed upon them a "social death."[15]

The persecution mounted further with the *Kristallnacht* (Night of Broken Glass) on November 9–10, 1938, "a proto-genocidal assault"[16] that targeted Jewish properties, residences, and persons. Several dozen Jews were killed outright, billions of deutschmarks in damage was inflicted, and some 30,000 male Jews were rounded up and imprisoned in concentration camps.[17] Now applications to flee increased dramatically, but this occurred just as Hitler was driving Europe towards crisis and world war, and as Western countries all but closed their frontiers to Jewish would-be emigrants.

"Ordinary Germans" and the Nazis

In recent years a great deal of scholarly energy has been devoted to Hitler's and the Nazis' evolving relationship with the German public. Two broad conclusions may be drawn from the work of Robert Gellately and David Bankier – and also from one of the most revelatory personal documents of the Nazi era, the diaries of Victor Klemperer (1881–1960). (Klemperer was a Jew from the German city of Dresden who survived the entire Nazi era, albeit under conditions of privation and persecution, thanks to his marriage to an "Aryan" woman.)

The first insight is that Nazi rule, and the isolation of the Jews for eventual expulsion and extermination, counted on a broad well-spring of popular support. This was based on Hitler's pledge to return Germany to social order, economic stability, and world-power status. The basic thesis of Gellately's book, *Backing Hitler: Consent and Coercion in Nazi Germany*, is that "Hitler was largely successful in getting the backing, one way or another, of the great majority of citizens." Moreover, this was based on the anathematizing of whole classes of citizens: "the Germans generally turned out to be proud and pleased that Hitler and his henchmen were putting away certain kinds of people who did not fit in, or who were regarded as 'outsiders,' 'asocials,' 'useless eaters,' or 'criminals.'"[18]

Victor Klemperer's diaries provide an "extraordinarily acute analysis of the day-to-day workings of German life under Hitler" and "a singular chronicle of German society's progressive Nazification."[19] Klemperer oscillated between a conviction that German society had become thoroughly Nazified, and the ironic conviction (given his expulsion from the body politic) that the soul of the Germany he loved would triumph. "I certainly no longer believe that [the Nazi regime] has enemies inside Germany," he wrote in May 1936. "The majority of the people is content, a small group accepts Hitler as the lesser evil, no one really wants to be rid of him. . . . And all are afraid for their livelihood, their life, all are such terrible cowards." But as late as March 1940, with the Second World War well underway, "I often ask myself where all the wild anti-Semitism is. For my part I encounter much sympathy, people help me out, but fearfully of course." He noted numerous examples of verbal contempt, but also a surprising number of cases where colleagues and acquaintances went out of their way to greet him warmly, and even police officers who accorded him treatment that was "very courteous, almost comically courteous." "Every Jew has his Aryan angel," one of his fellow inmates in an overcrowded communal house told him in 1941. But by then Klemperer had been stripped of his job, pension, house, and typewriter; he would shortly lose his right to indulge even in his cherished cigarettes. In September 1941, he was forced to put on a yellow Star of David identifying him as a Jew. It left him feeling "shattered": nearly a year later, he would describe the star as "torture – I can resolve a hundred times to pay no attention, it remains torture."[20] Hundreds of miles to the East, the program of mass killing was gearing up, as Klemperer was increasingly aware.

If Klemperer and other Jews were the prime target of this demonization and marginalization of social groups, they were not the *only* focus, and for some years they were not necessarily the principal one. Communists (depicted as closely linked to Jewry) and other political opponents, handicapped and senile Germans, homosexuals, Roma (Gypsies), Polish intellectuals, vagrants, and other "asocial" elements all occupied the attention of the Nazi authorities during this period, and were often the victims of "notorious achievements in human destruction" that exceeded the persecution of the Jews until 1941.[21] Of these groups, political opponents (especially communists) and the handicapped and senile were most at risk of extreme physical violence, torture, and murder. "The political and syndical [trade union] left," wrote Arno Mayer, "remained the principal target of brutal repression well past the time of the definitive consolidation of the new regime in July–August 1934."[22] In the slaughter of the handicapped, meanwhile, the Nazis first "discovered that it was possible to murder multitudes," and that "they could easily recruit men and women to do the killings."[23] (See Box 6a for more on the fate of political oppositionists and the handicapped under Nazi rule.)

THE TURN TO MASS MURDER

> Here I am, then, on the bottom. One learns quickly enough to wipe out the past and the future when one is forced to. A fortnight after my arrival [at Auschwitz] I already had the prescribed hunger, that chronic hunger unknown to free men, which makes one dream at night, and settles in all the limbs of one's body. . . . I push wagons, I work with a shovel, I turn rotten in the rain, I shiver in the wind; already my own body is no longer mine: my belly is swollen, my limbs emaciated, my face is thick in the morning, hollow in the evening; some of us have yellow skin, others grey. When we do not meet for a few days we hardly recognize each other.
>
> Primo Levi, Auschwitz survivor

Between the outbreak of the Second World War in September 1939 and the onset of full-scale extermination in mid-1941, the Nazis were busy consolidating and confining the Jews under their control. The core policy in the occupied territories of the East was *ghettoization*: confinement of Jews in festering, overcrowded zones of major cities. One can make a solid argument that with ghettoization came clear genocidal intent: "The Nazis sought to create inhuman conditions in the ghettos, where a combination of obscene overcrowding, deliberate starvation . . . and outbreaks of typhus and cholera would reduce Jewish numbers through 'natural wastage.'"[24] Certainly, the hundreds of thousands of Jews who died in the ghettos are counted as victims of the Holocaust.

In the months following the German invasion of the Soviet Union on June 22, 1941, some *1.2 million* Jews were rounded up and murdered, mostly by point-blank rifle fire. The direct genocidal agents were the so-called *Einsatzgruppen*, four death-squad battalions – some 3,000 men in all – who followed behind the regular German army.[25] They were joined by other formations, such as the notorious Reserve Police Battalion 101 studied by historian Christopher Browning and political scientist Daniel Goldhagen.

The role of the regular German army, or *Wehrmacht*, in this eruption of full-scale genocide received attention at the Nuremberg trials of 1945–46 (see Chapter 15). However, in part because the Western allies preferred to see the *Wehrmacht* as gentlemanly opponents, and subsequently because the German army was being reconstructed as an ally by both sides in the Cold War, a myth was cultivated that the *Wehrmacht* had acted "honorably" in the occupied territories. Scholarly inquiry has now demonstrated that this is "a wholly false picture of the historical reality."[26] Permeated to the core by the Nazis' racist ideology, the *Wehrmacht* was key to engineering the mass murder of 3.3 million Soviets seized as prisoners-of-war (see Box 6a).[27] The *Wehrmacht* was also central to the perpetration of the Jewish Holocaust. The *Einsatzgruppen*, writes Hannah Arendt, "needed and got the close cooperation of the Armed Forces; indeed, relations between them were usually 'excellent' and in some instances 'affectionate' (*herzlich*, literally 'heartfelt'). The generals . . . often lent their own men, ordinary soldiers, to assist in the massacres."[28] A great many ordinary soldiers "delighted in death as spectators or as perpetrators."[29] As SS Lieutenant-Colonel Karl Kretschmer wrote home in September 1942: "Here in Russia, wherever the German soldier is, no Jew remains."[30]

Even such massive slaughter could not hope to eliminate European Jewry in a "reasonable" time. Moreover, the intensely intimate character of murder by gunfire, with human tissue and brain matter spattering onto the clothes and faces of the German killers, began to take a psychological toll. The difficulty was especially pronounced in the case of mass murders of children and women. While it was relatively easy for the executioners to persuade themselves that adult male victims, even unarmed civilians, were dangerous and deserved their cruel fate, the argument was harder to make for people traditionally viewed as passive, dependent, or helpless.[31]

To reduce this stress, and to increase the logistical efficiency of the killing, the industrialized "death camp" with its gas chambers came to the fore. Both were refinements of existing institutions and technologies. The death camps grew out of the concentration-camp system the Nazis had established upon first taking power in 1933, while killings by gas had first been employed in 1939 as part of the "euthanasia" campaign that was such a vital forerunner of genocide against the Jews. (It was wound down, in fact, at the precise point that the campaign against European Jews turned to root-and-branch extermination.) Gas chambers allowed for the desired psychological distance between the killers and their victims.

Principally by this means, one-and-a-quarter million Jews were killed at Auschwitz – actually a complex of three camps, of which Auschwitz II (Birkenau) operated as the killing center. Zyklon B (cyanide gas in crystal form) was overwhelmingly the means of murder at Auschwitz. Nearly two million more Jews died by varied means including gas, shootings, beatings, and starvation at the other "death camps" in occupied Poland, distinguished from the vastly larger Nazi network of concentration camps by their core function of extermination. These were Chelmno (where 200,000 Jews were slaughtered); Sobibor (260,000); Belzec (500,000); Treblinka (800,000, mostly from the Polish capital Warsaw); and Majdanek (130,000).[32]

Figure 6.1 The ruins of the undressing room adjacent to the gas chamber and crematorium complex known as Krema II, at the Auschwitz-Birkenau death camp in western Poland, dynamited by the Nazis in the closing stages of the Second World War. Jews and other victims were told they would be taking showers; instead, they were asphyxiated with cyanide gas, and their bodies incinerated in the crematorium complex at the rear of the photo.

Source: Courtesy Dr. Michael Shermer.

Figure 6.2 Mass burial of prisoners' corpses in the Bergen-Belsen concentration camp following liberation, May 1945.
Source: United States Holocaust Memorial Museum.

It would be misleading to distinguish too sharply between the "death camps" where gas was the normal means of extermination, and the broader network of camps in which killings of Jews also reached exterminatory levels. As Daniel Goldhagen has argued, "after the beginning of 1942, the camp system in general was lethal for Jews," and well over a million died outside the death camps, killed by starvation, disease, and overwork.[33] Perhaps 500,000 more, in Raul Hilberg's estimate, succumbed in the Jewish ghettos, themselves a kind of concentration camp. Finally, tens of thousands died on the brutal and nonsensical forced marches of camp inmates as Allied forces closed in.[34]

Notoriously, the extermination system continued to function even when it impeded the war effort. In March 1944, the Nazis intervened to occupy Hungary as a bulwark against advancing Soviet forces. Adolf Eichmann promptly arrived to supervise the rounding up for slaughter of the country's Jews. Thousands were saved by the imaginative intervention of Swedish diplomat Raoul Wallenberg (see Chapter 10). But some 400,000 were packed off to be gassed at Auschwitz-Birkenau and other death camps – despite the enormous strain this imposed on the rail system and the Nazis' dwindling human and material resources. It often seemed that the single-minded devotion to genocidal destruction outweighed even the Nazis' desire for self-preservation.

BOX 6.1 ONE WOMAN'S STORY: NECHAMA EPSTEIN

Nechama Epstein was a Polish Jew from Warsaw who was just 18 years old when she "and her family were herded into the city's ghetto together with 350,000 other Jews."[35] One of the few survivors of the Auschwitz death camp, she was interviewed after the war by David P. Boder, an American psychologist who published a book titled *I Did Not Interview the Dead*. However, Boder chose not to include his conversation with Epstein; her testimony did not see the light of day until it was excerpted in Donald Niewyk's chapter for the powerful anthology, *Century of Genocide*. Her account, Niewyk noted, "reveals a remarkable breadth of experiences, including survival in ghettos, slave labor camps, and extermination centers."[36]

Epstein described the grim privations of life in the Warsaw ghetto – the very ghetto that would rise up so heroically against the Germans in mid-1944, and be crushed. "It was very bad," she remembered. "We had nothing to sell any more. Eight people were living on a kilo of beets a day. . . . We did not have any more strength to walk. . . . Every day there were other dead, small children, bigger children, older people. All died of a hunger death."

Epstein was caught up in the mass round-up of Jews to be shipped to the extermination center at Treblinka in September 1942. Packed into a single cattle-car with 200 other Jews, she passed an entire night before the train began to move: "We lay one on top of the other. . . . One lay suffocating on top of another. . . . We could do nothing to help ourselves. And then real death began." Tormented by thirst and near-asphyxiation, Jews struggled with each other for a snatch of air or any moisture. "Mothers were giving the children urine to drink."

Some enterprising prisoners managed to saw a hole in the cattle-car, and Epstein, among others, leapt out. With the help of a Polish militia member, she found her way to the Miedryrzec ghetto, where she passed the next eight months. "Every four weeks there were new deportations." The first of these she survived by hiding in an attic and eating raw beets. "I did not have anything to drink. The first snow fell then, so I made a hole in the roof and pulled in the hand a little snow. And this I licked. And this I lived on."

Her luck ran out at the time of the last deportation. She was led away, to a transport and apparently her doom, on "a beautiful summer day" in 1943. This time the destination was Majdanek, another of the extermination centers in occupied Poland. There, "We were all lined up. There were many who were shot [outright]. . . . The mothers were put separately, the children separately, the men separately, the women separately. . . . The children and the mothers were led to the crematory. All were burned. . . . We never laid eyes on them again."

continued

She spent two months at Majdanek. "I lived through many terrible things. We had nothing to eat. We were so starved. . . . The food consisted of two hundred grams of bread a day, and a little soup of water with nettles." A German SS woman entered the barracks every day "at six in the morning . . . beating everybody."

In July 1943, Epstein was shipped off to Auschwitz. By good fortune, she was consigned to a work camp rather than to immediate extermination in the Birkenau gas chambers. "We worked carrying stones on barrows, large stones. To eat they did not give us. We were beaten terribly" by German women guards: "They said that every day they must kill three, four Jews." She fell sick, and survived her time in the hospital only by hiding from the regular round-ups that carted off ill inmates to the crematoria. "Christian women were lying there, so I climbed over to the Christians, into their beds, and there I always had the good fortune to hide."

In October, the entire sick-ward was emptied. "There was a girl eighteen years old, and she was crying terribly. She said that she is still so young, she wants to live. . . . [But] nothing helped. They were all taken away." When she emerged from the ward, she saw the Auschwitz crematory burning in the night: "We saw the entire sky red [from] the glow of the fire. Blood was pouring on the sky." But Epstein again survived the selection for the Birkenau extermination center. She was sent back to Majdanek, where she witnessed SS and Gestapo killers forcing male inmates to dig mass graves, then lining up hundreds of female inmates to be shot. Over the course of a further eight months at Majdanek, she remained among the handful of inmates – several hundred only – who were spared gassing and cremation.

Epstein was eventually sent to a forced-labor center: Plaszow, near Krakow (the same camp featured in Steven Spielberg's film *Schindler's List*). By late 1944, the Soviets were approaching Plaszow. "We were again dragged away. I was the second time taken to Auschwitz." After that, she was dispatched to Bergen-Belsen; then to Aschersleben in Germany proper, where she labored alongside Dutch, Yugoslav, and French prisoners-of-war.

American forces were now closing in from the West. Epstein was conscripted into a death march alongside 500 other inmates. "Only women. Two hundred fell en route." At last, after a march of more than 250 kilometres, she reached Theresienstadt in Czechoslovakia. This had long served as a "model" detention facility for the Nazis – the only one to which Red Cross representatives were admitted. "We were completely in tatters. . . . We were very dirty. . . . We were badly treated. We were beaten. They screamed at us. 'Accursed swine! You are filthy. What sort of people are you?'" Epstein and her fellow inmates now looked like the "subhumans" the Germans had been indoctrinated to expect.

On the very last day of the European war, May 8, 1945, Theresienstadt was liberated by Russian forces. "We didn't believe it. . . . We went out, whoever was able. . . . We went out with great joy, with much crying. . . .

"But now there began a real death. People who had been starved for so many years. . . . The Russians had opened all the German storehouses, all the German stores, and they said, 'Take whatever you want.' People who had been badly starved, they shouldn't have eaten. . . . And the people began to eat, to eat too much, greedily. . . . Hundreds of people fell a day. . . . People crawled over the dead." Typhus broke out. But Epstein survived. She returned to Warsaw, married, and emigrated to Palestine.

DEBATING THE HOLOCAUST

Many of the central themes of the Nazis' attempted destruction of European Jews have served as touchstones for the broader field of comparative genocide studies. No other genocide has generated remotely as much literature as the Jewish Holocaust, including thousands of books and essays. It is important, therefore, to explore some major points of debate, not only for the insights they give into the events described in this chapter, but for their relevance to genocide studies as a whole.

Intentionalists vs. functionalists

The core of the debate over the past two decades has revolved around a scholarly tendency generally termed "intentionalist," and a contrasting "functionalist" interpretation. Intentionalists, as the tag suggests, place primary emphasis on the *intention* of the Nazis, from the outset, to eliminate European Jews by means that eventually included mass slaughter. Such an approach tends to emphasize the figure of Adolf Hitler and his monomaniacal zeal to eliminate the Jewish "cancer" from Germany and Europe. ("Once I really am in power," Hitler had told a journalist as far back as 1922, "my first and foremost task will be the annihilation of the Jews.")[37] Necessary as well was the anti-semitic dimension of both Nazi ideology and European history. This fueled the Nazis' animus against the Jews, and also ensured there would be no shortage of "willing executioners" to do the dirty work.

The functionalist critique, on the other hand, downplays the significance of Hitler as an individual. It "depicts the fragmentation of decision-making and the blurring of political responsibility," and emphasizes "the disintegration of traditional bureaucracy into a crooked maze of ill-conceived and uncoordinated task forces," in Colin Tatz's summary.[38] Also stressed is the evolutionary and contingent character of the campaign against the Jews: from legal discrimination, to concentration, to mass murder. In this view, "what happened in Nazi Germany [was] an unplanned 'cumulative radicalization' produced by the chaotic decision-making process of a polycratic regime and the 'negative selection' of destructive elements from the Nazis' ideological arsenal as the only ones that could perpetually mobilize the disparate and otherwise incompatible elements of the Nazi coalition."[39]

This sometimes acrimonious debate gave way, in the 1990s, to a growing recognition that the intentionalist and functionalist strands are not irreconcilable. "Both positions in the debate have a number of merits and demerits; both ultimately reflect different forms of historical explanation; and the ground between them is steadily narrowing in favour of a consensus which borrows elements from both lines of argument."[40] The raw material for Nazi genocide was present from the start, but required a host of historically contingent features to actualize and maximize it. Michael Shermer and Alex Grobman propose the term "intentional functionalism" to capture this interplay of actors and variables.[41]

Jewish resistance

The depiction of Jews as having gone meekly to their deaths was first advanced by Raul Hilberg in his massive 1961 treatise *The Destruction of the European Jews*, and then enshrined by Hannah Arendt in her controversial account of *Eichmann in Jerusalem*. Both Hilberg and Arendt noted the close pre-war coordination between the Jewish Agency (which sought to promote Jewish immigration to Palestine) and the Nazi authorities.[42] They also stressed the role of the Jewish councils (*Judenräte*), bodies of Jews delegated by the Nazis to oversee the ghettos, and the round-ups for "transport" of Jewish civilians. "The whole truth," as Arendt summarized it, was that without Jewish leadership and organization, the Jewish people would have suffered "chaos and plenty of misery" at Nazi hands, "but the total number of victims would hardly have been between four and a half and six million people."[43]

While it may be true that "the salient characteristic of the Jewish community in Europe during 1933–1945 was its step-by-step adjustment to step-by-step destruction,"[44] research has starkly undermined this depiction of Jewish passivity and complicity. Scholars have described how, under horrific circumstances, Jews found ways to resist: going into hiding; struggling to preserve Jewish culture and creativity; and even launching armed uprisings. (The mass escape from the Sobibor death camp in October 1943, and the Warsaw ghetto uprising of April 1944, are the most famous of these rebellions against the Nazis.)[45] Large numbers of Jews also joined the armed forces of the Allies, or fought as partisans behind German lines. On balance, "it is pure myth that the Jews were merely 'passive,'" writes Alexander Donat in his memoir *The Holocaust Kingdom*:

> The Jews fought back against their enemies to a degree no other community anywhere in the world would have been capable of were it to find itself similarly beleaguered. They fought against hunger and starvation, against disease, against a deadly Nazi economic blockade. They fought against murderers and against traitors within their own ranks, and they were utterly alone in their fight. They were forsaken by God and by man, surrounded by hatred or indifference. Ours was not a romantic war. Although there was much heroism, there was little beauty – much toil and suffering, but no glamour. We fought back on every front where the enemy attacked – the biological front, the economic front, the propaganda front, the cultural front – with every weapon we possessed.[46]

The Allies and the churches: Could the Jews have been saved?

The genocide against European Jews *could* have been avoided, argues the historian Yehuda Bauer, just as the Second World War itself might never have occurred – "had the Great Powers stopped Nazi Germany when it was still weak." But at this point, "nobody knew that a Holocaust was even possible, because nobody knew what a Holocaust was; the Germans had not decided on anything like it in the 1930s."[47] The Allies, haunted by the carnage of the First World War, sought accommodation ("appeasement") rather than confrontation.

The Evian Conference of July 1938, held in a French town on Lake Geneva, brought together representatives of Western countries to address the Jewish plight. In retrospect, and even at the time, it offered the best chance to alleviate the plight of German Jews, through the simple expedient of opening up Western borders to Jewish refugees. But instead, the West ducked its responsibility. In Germany, Hitler could barely conceal his delight. The rejection of the Jews not only further humiliated Jews themselves, but pointed out the hypocrisy of the outside world's humanitarian rhetoric.

Turning to the period of full-scale genocide against the Jews, it seems clear that details of the killing operations were known to the Allies early on. For example, radio communications of the Nazi Order Police, alluding to mass murder, were intercepted. But the Allies were observing from an insuperable distance, with Germany at the height of its powers on the European continent. The sheer speed of the slaughter also militated against meaningful intervention. "From mid-March 1942 to mid-February 1943," that is, in less than a year, "over one-half the victims of the Jewish Holocaust . . . lost their lives at the hands of Nazi killers."[48]

It may be argued that the inclusion of targets such as Auschwitz's gas chambers and crematoria in the Allied bombing campaign, along with key transport points for Jews, could have disrupted the smooth functioning of the Nazi killing machine. The case is especially cogent for the latter stages of the war, as with the genocide of the Hungarian Jews in 1944–45 (when the USSR might also have been able to intervene). But on pre-war evidence, it is hard to believe that, if more effective military measures could have been found, the Allies would have placed saving Jews higher on the list of military priorities – or that doing so would have made much of a difference.

The role of the Christian churches has also been scrutinized and criticized. Pope Pius XII's placating of the Nazi regime in Germany, and his silence on the persecution of the Jews – which included the rounding up and deportation of Roman Jews under his very nose – are notorious.[49] Within Germany, the churches did virtually nothing to impede the genocide and a great deal to overlook it, effectively facilitating it. The Nazis demonstrated at numerous points their keen sensitivity to public opinion, including religious opinion – protests from German churches were partly responsible for driving the "euthanasia" campaign underground after 1941 – but these were not forthcoming from more than a handful of principled religious voices. When it came to defending co-parishioners whom the Nazis deemed of Jewish origin, "both Church and Church members drove away from their community, from their churches, people with whom they were united in worship, as one drives away mangy dogs from one's door."[50]

The most successful examples of resistance to Hitler's genocidal designs for European Jewry came from a handful of Western and Northern European countries that were either neutral or under relatively less oppressive occupation regimes. Here, sometimes, extension of the killing campaign could impose political costs that the Nazis were not willing to pay. The most vivid display of public opposition swept up virtually the entire adult population of Denmark, led by the royal family. When the Nazis decreed the imposition of the Jewish yellow star, *everyone* adopted it, and the regulation was rescinded. Subsequently, Danes arranged for the evacuation of the majority of the country's Jews to neutral Sweden, where they lived through the rest of the war (see Chapter 10). Sweden, meanwhile, saved "about half of Norwegian Jewry and almost all of the Danish Jews," and in 1944:

> involved herself more heavily in the heart of Europe, particularly in Budapest, where, along with Switzerland, Portugal, and the Vatican, the Swedish legation issued "protective passports," established safe houses, and generally attempted to restrain the German occupants and their Hungarian puppets from killing more Jews on Hungarian soil in the final hours of the war. Upon the liberation of Jews in concentration camps in the spring of 1945, Sweden accepted thousands of victims for medical treatment and rehabilitation.[51]

Willing executioners?

Just as scholars have demonstrated increased interest in "micro-histories" of public opinion under the Nazis, and the role of ordinary German citizens in accepting and sustaining the regime, so have searching questions been asked about the role of different sectors of the German population in the genocide. As a result of decades of research by Raul Hilberg and many others, it is now a truism that not only German social and economic elites, but all the professions (up to and including the clergy, as we have seen), were deeply corrupted or compromised by the Nazi state. In Michael Burleigh's words, an "understanding of the process of persecution [on racial grounds] now includes greater awareness of the culpable involvement of various sections of the professional intelligentsia, such as anthropologists, doctors, economists, historians, lawyers and psychiatrists, in the formation and implementation of Nazi policies."[52] For such figures, "the advent of the Nazi regime was coterminous with the onset of 'boom' conditions. No one asked or compelled these academics and scientists actively to work on the regime's behalf. Most of them could have said no. In fact, the files of the regime's many agencies bulge with their unsolicited recommendations."[53]

What of the genocidal participation of ordinary Germans? This subject has spawned the most vigorous debate in Holocaust studies over the past decade, though illumination has not always matched the heat generated.

At the heart of the controversy was the publication, in 1992 and 1996 respectively, of Christopher Browning's *Ordinary Men: Reserve Police Battalion 101 and the Final Solution in Poland*, and Daniel Goldhagen's *Hitler's Willing Executioners: Ordinary Germans and the Holocaust*. Both of these scholars examined the same archives on

Reserve Police Battalion 101, which consisted overwhelmingly of Germans drafted from civilian police units (often too old for regular military service). The archival records described in detail the battalion's killings of helpless, naked Jewish civilians in occupied Poland during 1941–42, and the range of reactions among group members.

In interpreting the archival record, Browning acknowledged the importance of "the incessant proclamation of German superiority and incitement of contempt and hatred for the Jewish enemy." But he also stressed other factors: "conformity to the group," that is, peer pressure; the desire for praise, prestige, and advancement; and the threat of marginalization and anathematization in highly dangerous wartime circumstances. He referred to "the mutually intensifying effects of war and racism. . . . Nothing helped the Nazis to wage a race war so much as the war itself."[54]

Goldhagen, dismissing Browning's work, advanced instead a monocausal thesis. The Jewish Holocaust was the direct outgrowth of "eliminationist" anti-semitism, which by the twentieth century had become "common sense" for Germans. By 1941, "ordinary Germans easily became genocidal killers . . . [and] did so even though they did not have to." They "kill[ed] Jews willingly and often eagerly."[55]

With the controversy now cooled, it is easier to appreciate the significance of "the Goldhagen debate." Goldhagen did counter a trend towards bloodless analysis and abstract theorizing in studies of the Jewish catastrophe. In addition, by achieving mass popularity, Goldhagen's book, like Samantha Power's *"A Problem From Hell"* (2001), broke down the usual wall between scholarship and public discussion. However, the core elements of Goldhagen's thesis – that there was something unique about German anti-semitism that spawned the Holocaust; that Germans were only too ready to leap to bloodthirsty murder of Jews – have been undermined. Not only was anti-semitism historically stronger in countries other than Germany, but the virulence of its expression during the Second World War in countries such as Lithuania and Romania exceeded that of Germany. The Nazis, as noted above, were reluctant to confront "ordinary Germans" with bloody atrocity. Nor could they rely on a widespread popular desire to inflict cruelty on Jews as the foundational strategy for implementing their genocide.

Israel and the Jewish Holocaust

It has occasionally happened that an experience of great suffering warrants the creation or validation of a homeland for the afflicted group, in the form of a nation-state or quasi-state. Such was the case with East Timor (Box 7a), the world's newest nation, born from Indonesian occupation and genocide. The Kurdish protected zone and *de facto* state in northern Iraq may also qualify (see Box 4a); but no case is as dramatic as that of Israel in the wake of the Second World War. The dream of the decades-old Zionist movement, namely to establish a Jewish homeland in Palestine through political mobilization and mass immigration, became a reality with extraordinary rapidity in the postwar period, as Britain abandoned its territorial mandate over Palestine, and Arabs and Jews fought over the territory. "Anti-Zionism in the Jewish community collapsed, and a consensus that Jewry, abandoned during the war, had to have a home of its own crystallized overnight."[56] Jewish survivors of Nazi genocide provided Palestine with a critical mass of Jewish immigrants and, in the decades following the declaration of the Israeli state on May 15, 1948, Israel received tens of billions of dollars from the Federal Republic of Germany as reparations for the mass murder and expropriation inflicted on the Jews.

To a significant degree, successive Israeli governments have relied on the Holocaust as a touchstone of Jewish experience and national identity. Palestinians and their supporters, for their part, have tended to adopt the genocide framework as well, but in order to draw attention to the Palestinian plight at Israeli hands. They have sought to draw parallels between Israeli repressive policies and those of their Nazi forebears. Often such comparisons seem hysterical and/or counterproductive; but sometimes they have resonated. Notable was the free passage granted by Israeli forces to Christian Phalangist militia in the Palestinian refugee camps of Sabra and Shatila, during the Israelis' 1982 invasion of Lebanon. This led predictably to the genocidal massacre of thousands of defenseless Palestinians, as Israeli troops stood passively by.

Is the Jewish Holocaust "uniquely unique"?

Few historical and philosophical questions have generated such intense scholarly debate in genocide studies as this one. On one level, it is clearly facile. As Alex Alvarez puts it: "All genocides are simultaneously unique and analogous."[57] The question is whether the Jewish Holocaust is *sui generis* – that is, "uniquely unique."[58]

In genocide studies, a well-known exponent of the uniqueness thesis is Steven Katz, who devoted his immense tome *The Holocaust in Historical Context, Vol. 1* to arguing that the Jewish Holocaust was "phenomenologically unique by virtue of the fact that never before has a state set out, as a matter of intentional principle and actualized policy, to annihilate physically every man, woman, and child belonging to a specific people."[59] The Nazi campaign against the Jews was the only true genocide, as Katz defined the term (see p. 18; recall that my own preferred definition of genocide reworks Katz's).

Many other scholars have argued against the uniqueness hypothesis. "I object very strongly," wrote Israel Charny, "to the efforts to name the genocide of any one people as the single, ultimate event, or as the most important event against which all other tragedies of genocidal mass death are to be tested and found wanting."[60] Phillip Lopate has likewise argued that claims of uniqueness tend to bestow "a sort of privileged nation status in the moral honor roll."[61] This claim of privilege then carries over to "the Jewish state," Israel, helping to blunt criticism of its treatment of the Palestinians.[62]

My own view should be clearly stated: the Jewish Holocaust was *not* "uniquely unique." On no analytical dimension – speed, scale, scope, intensity, efficiency, cruelty, ideology – does it stand alone and apart. If it is unique in its mix of these ingredients, so too are most of the other major instances of mass killing in their own way. I also believe that uniqueness proponents, like the rest of us, were severely shaken by the holocaust in Rwanda in 1994 (see Chapter 9). The killing there proceeded much faster than the slaughter of the Jews; killed a higher proportion of the designated victim group (some 80 percent of Rwandan Tutsis versus two-thirds of European Jews); was carried out by "a chillingly effective organizational structure that would implement the political plan of genocide more efficiently than was achieved by the industrialized death camps in Nazi Germany";[63] and – unlike the Jewish catastrophe – featured intensive participation in killing duties by the mass of the general population. Was Rwanda, then, "uniquely unique"? The claim seems at least as tenable as in the case of the Jewish Holocaust – but in both cases, a nuanced comparative framework is preferable.[64]

The Jews *were* unique as a target of the Nazis. "In the end," writes Raul Hilberg, ". . . the Jews retained their special place."[65] According to Omer Bartov,

> It was *only* in the case of the Jews that there was a determination to seek out every baby hidden in a haystack, every family living in a bunker in the forest, every woman trying to pass herself off as a Gentile. It was only in the case of the Jews that vast factories were constructed and managed with the sole purpose of killing trainload after trainload of people. It was only in the case of the Jews that huge, open-air, public massacres of tens of thousands of people were conducted on a daily basis throughout Eastern Europe.[66]

Lastly, the Jewish Holocaust holds a unique place in genocide studies. Among all the world's genocides, it alone produced a scholarly literature that spawned, in turn, a comparative discipline. Specialists on the subject were also central in constituting the field and its core institutions, such as the International Association of Genocide Scholars (IAGS) and the *Journal of Genocide Research*: "Genocide studies is really the outgrowth of the study of the Holocaust," as Thomas Cushman has noted.[67]

FURTHER STUDY

Note: No genocide has generated remotely as much scholarly attention as the Nazis' against the Jews. The following is a bare sampling of core works in English; others are cited in subsequent chapters.

Götz Aly, *"Final Solution": Nazi Population Policy and the Murder of the European Jews.* London: Arnold, 1999. Aly's "functionalist" argument emphasizes the role of Nazi bureaucrats confronted with problems of population management in the occupied territories.

Omer Bartov, ed., *The Holocaust: Origins, Implementation, Aftermath: Rewriting Histories.* London: Routledge, 2000. Excellent anthology of writings by many leading scholars.

Omer Bartov, *Germany's War and the Holocaust: Disputed Histories.* Ithaca, NY: Cornell University Press, 2003. Powerful essays by the principal scholar of the *Wehrmacht*'s war on the eastern front; see also *Hitler's Army.*

Christopher Browning, *Ordinary Men: Reserve Police Battalion 101 and the Final Solution in Poland.* New York: Perennial, 1993. Based on some of the same archival sources as Goldhagen's *Hitler's Willing Executioners* (see below), but emphasizes group dynamics in addition to anti-semitism.

Michael Burleigh and Wolfgang Wippermann, *The Racial State: Germany 1933–1945*. Cambridge: Cambridge University Press, 1991. How Nazi racial ideology inspired genocidal policy.

Alexander Donat, *The Holocaust Kingdom*. New York: Holocaust Library, 1978. Classic memoir of ghetto and death camp, sensitively told and translated.

Henry Friedlander, *The Origins of Nazi Genocide: From Euthanasia to the Final Solution*. Chapel Hill, NC: University of North Carolina Press, 1995. Traces the evolution of the Nazi killing machine from the initial targeting of disabled and handicapped Germans to the mass slaughter of Jews and Roma.

Saul Friedländer, *Nazi Germany and the Jews, Volume I: The Years of Persecution, 1933–1939*. New York: HarperCollins, 1997. Innovative, highly readable account of the years preceding the onset of full-fledged genocide.

Robert Gellately, *Backing Hitler: Consent and Coercion in Nazi Germany*. Oxford: Oxford University Press, 2001. Argues that ordinary Germans generally supported Nazi policies, often exhibiting enthusiasm beyond the call of duty.

Daniel J. Goldhagen, *Hitler's Willing Executioners: Ordinary Germans and the Holocaust*. New York: Vintage, 1997. Controversial book ascribing a monocausal explanation for the genocide, rooted in Germans' visceral hatred of the Jews.

Richard Grunberger, *A Social History of the Third Reich*. London: Penguin, 1974. Encyclopedic overview of Nazism's social impact.

Raul Hilberg, *The Destruction of the European Jews* (3rd edn), 3 vols. New Haven, CT: Yale University Press, 2003. Massive, meticulous study of the bureaucracy of death.

Adolf Hitler, *Mein Kampf* (My Struggle), trans. Ralph Mannheim. Boston, MA: Houghton Mifflin, 1943. First published in 1925–26; lays out Hitler's vision of German destiny, as well as his virulent hatred of the Jews.

Ian Kershaw, *The Nazi Dictatorship: Problems and Perspectives of Interpretation* (4th edn). London: Arnold, 2000. Classic overview of, and contribution to, scholarly debates about the nature of the Nazi regime.

Victor Klemperer, *I Will Bear Witness: A Diary of the Nazi Years*, 2 vols. New York: Modern Library, 1999, 2001. One of the essential documents of the twentieth century: the testimony of a German Jew who lived through the entire Nazi era.

Ronnie S. Landau, *The Nazi Holocaust*. Chicago, IL: Ivan R. Dee, 1994. A good overview of the origins and course of the Jewish catastrophe.

Primo Levi, *Survival in Auschwitz*. New York: Touchstone, 1996. Haunting account of a year and a half in the Nazi death camp; see also *The Drowned and the Saved*.

Alan S. Rosenbaum, ed., *Is the Holocaust Unique? Perspectives on Comparative Genocide* (2nd edn). Boulder, CO: Westview Press, 2000. Wide-ranging and controversial examination of the "uniqueness" thesis.

Ron Rosenbaum, *Explaining Hitler: The Search for the Origins of His Evil*. New York: Perennial, 1999. Quest for the essence of the malignancy that was Hitler.

John Weiss, *Ideology of Death: Why the Holocaust Happened in Germany*. Chicago, IL: Ivan R. Dee, 1996. Why did only Germany, among anti-semitic European societies, produce a full-scale genocide against the Jews?

NOTES

1 In religious usage, a "holocaust" is "a sacrificial offering wholly consumed by fire in exaltation of God" (Arno J. Mayer, *Why Did the Heavens Not Darken? The "Final Solution" in History* [New York: Pantheon, 1988], p. 16). However, in the twentieth century, this was supplanted by a secular usage, in which "holocaust" designates "a wide variety of conflagrations, massacres, wars, and disasters." See Jon Petrie's fascinating etymological study, "The Secular Word HOLOCAUST: Scholarly Myths, History, and 20th Century Meanings," *Journal of Genocide Research*, 2: 1 (2000), pp. 31–64.

2 Donald L. Niewyk, "Holocaust: The Jews," in Samuel L. Totten *et al.*, eds, *Century of Genocide: Eyewitness Accounts and Critical Views* (New York: Garland Publishing, 1997), p. 136. The figure of 5.1 to 5.4 million killed is used by the US Holocaust Museum; see Peter Balakian, *The Burning Tigris: The Armenian Genocide and America's Response* (New York: HarperCollins, 2003), p. 195.

3 Statistics cited in Michael Shermer and Alex Grobman, *Denying History: Who Says the Holocaust Never Happened and Why Do They Say It?* (Berkeley, CA: University of California Press, 2002), p. 174.

4 Yehuda Bauer, *Rethinking the Holocaust* (New Haven, CT: Yale University Press, 2001), p. xi.

5 Daniel Jonah Goldhagen, *Hitler's Willing Executioners: Ordinary Germans and the Holocaust* (New York: Vintage, 1997), pp. 37–38. For a detailed study of the progressive demonization of the Jews, see Steven T. Katz, "Medieval Antisemitism: The Process of Mythification," ch. 6 in Katz, *The Holocaust in Historical Context, Vol. 1: The Holocaust and Mass Death before the Modern Age* (Oxford: Oxford University Press, 1994), pp. 225–316. However, as Mark Levene has pointed out to me, there was also a sense in which medieval Christianity *needed* the Jews – "for its own Christological endtime" and teleological myth. It may thus have been constrained from launching a full-scale genocidal assault on them. Levene, personal communication, August 26, 2005.

6 Colin Tatz, *With Intent to Destroy: Reflecting on Genocide* (London: Verso, 2003), p. 44.

7 Luther quoted in Raul Hilberg, *The Destruction of the European Jews* (3rd edn), Vol. 1 (New Haven, CT: Yale University Press, 2003), p. 13.

8 The most infamous anti-semitic tract of modern times is the *Protocols of the Elders of Zion* (1903), a pamphlet that is now generally held to have been devised by the Tsar's secret police in pre-revolutionary Russia, but which purported to represent the ambitions and deliberations of a global Jewish conspiracy against Christian civilization. For the complete text of the *Protocols*, and a point-by-point refutation, see Steven Leonard Jacobs and Mark Weitzman, *Dismantling the Big Lie: the Protocols of the Elders of Zion* (Jersey City, NJ: Ktav Publishing House, 2003 – nb: the centenary of the *Protocols*).

9 In addition, for exponents of biological anti-semitism (a nineteenth-century invention), Jews came to be viewed as *innately* at odds with Western-Christian civilization. Religious conversion could no longer expunge their Jewishness – which helps explain why this option was denied to Jews under Nazi rule. My thanks to Benjamin Madley for this point.

10 Ronnie S. Landau, *The Nazi Holocaust* (Chicago, IL: Ivan R. Dee, 1994), p. 44.

11 In the case of France, strong arguments have been made that anti-semitism was far more widespread and virulent, in elite and popular opinion, than was true in Germany. But "in France – unlike Germany – whatever the strength of antisemitic feeling on the streets, in the bars and in the universities, political power always remained in the hands of the liberal republicans, a government which never endorsed political antisemitism" (Landau, *The Nazi Holocaust*, p. 63). However, when dictatorial government and "eliminationist anti-semitism" (Goldhagen's term) *were* imposed in France from 1940 to 1944 – under direct Nazi occupation and under the Vichy puppet regime – the authorities and a key section of the population cooperated enthusiastically in the transport for mass execution of the Jews.

12 Richard Plant, *The Pink Triangle: The Nazi War against Homosexuals* (New York: Owl Books, 1988), p. 23.

13 Adolf Hitler, *Mein Kampf* (My Struggle), trans. Ralph Mannheim (Boston: Houghton Mifflin, 1943), p. 562.

14 Landau, *The Nazi Holocaust*, pp. 317, 122.

15 See Orlando Patterson, *Slavery and Social Death: A Comparative Study* (Cambridge, MA: Harvard University Press, 1982), and the discussion in Goldhagen, *Hitler's Willing Executioners*, pp. 168–70.

16 Goldhagen, *Hitler's Willing Executioners*, p. 141.

17 For an excellent short analysis of the *Kristallnacht*, see Leonidas E. Hill, "The Pogrom of November 9–10, 1938 in Germany," in Paul R. Brass, ed., *Riots and Pogroms* (Washington Square, NY: New York University Press, 1996), pp. 89–113.

18 Robert Gellately, *Backing Hitler: Consent and Coercion in Nazi Germany* (Oxford: Oxford University Press, 2001), p. vii.

19 Omer Bartov, *Germany's War and the Holocaust: Disputed Histories* (Ithaca, NY: Cornell University Press, 2003), p. 197.

20 Victor Klemperer, *I Will Bear Witness 1933–1941* (New York: The Modern Library, 1999), pp. 165, 329–30, 393, 422, 429; Klemperer, *I Will Bear Witness 1942–1945* (New York: The Modern Library, 2001), pp. 66, 71.

21 Christopher R. Browning, *The Path to Genocide: Essays on Launching the Final Solution* (Cambridge, MA: Cambridge University Press, 1992), p. ix.

22 Mayer, *Why Did the Heavens Not Darken?*, pp. 114, 116–17.

23 Michael Burleigh, "Psychiatry, German Society and the Nazi 'Euthanasia' Programme," in Omer Bartov, ed., *The Holocaust: Origins, Implementation, Aftermath* (London: Routledge, 2000), p. 70.

24 Landau, *The Nazi Holocaust*, pp. 154–55. In his memoir of the Warsaw ghetto, Alexander Donat gives a figure for half a million ghetto internees as "27,000 apartments in an area of 750 acres, with six or seven persons to a room" (Donat, *The Holocaust Kingdom* [Washington, DC: Holocaust Library, 1999], p. 24). A famous portrait of life in the Warsaw ghetto in 1941, conveying the hardship and horror of ghetto life, is provided by the photographs taken by a German army officer, Heinrich Jost. See Gunther Schwarberg, *In the Ghetto of Warsaw: Photographs by Heinrich Jost* (Göttingen: Steidl Publishing, 2001).

25 See Richard Rhodes, *Masters of Death: The SS-Einsatzgruppen and the Invention of the Holocaust* (New York: Alfred A. Knopf, 2002).

26 Bartov, *Germany's War and the Holocaust*, p. 14. See also the excellent two-part essay by Wolfgang Weber, "The Debate in Germany over the Crimes of Hitler's *Wehrmacht*," World Socialist Web Site, September 19–20, 2001, http://www.wsws.org/articles/2001/sep2001/wehr-s19.shtml and http://www.wsws.org/articles/2001/sep2001/wehr-s20.shtml.

27 A key "tipping point" for the Wehrmacht's "indiscriminate, systematic and wholesale resort to carnage" was the Commissar Order issued on June 6, 1941, which called for "Communist Party functionaries . . . to be identified . . . and murdered by the army either on the spot or in rear areas." "Effectively," notes Michael Burleigh, "the army was assuming the functions hitherto performed by the Einsatzgruppen, namely the killing of an entire group of people solely by virtue of their membership of that group and without formal process." Burleigh, *Ethics and Extermination: Reflections on Nazi Genocide* (Cambridge: Cambridge University Press, 1997), p. 67.

28 Hannah Arendt, *Eichmann in Jerusalem: A Report on the Banality of Evil* (New York: The Viking Press, 1965), p. 107.

29 Hilberg, *The Destruction of the European Jews*, (3rd edn), Vol. 1 (New Haven, CT: Yale University Press, 2003), p. 337.

30 Kretschmer quoted in Shermer and Grobman, *Denying History*, p. 185.

31 This gendered element of the slaughter is discussed further in Chapter 13.

32 The statistics are drawn from Landau, *The Nazi Holocaust*.

33 "Whether the Germans were killing [Jews] immediately and directly in the gas chambers of an extermination camp or working and starving them to death in camps that they had not constructed for the express purpose of extermination (namely in concentration or 'work' camps), the mortality rates of Jews in camps was at exterminatory, genocidal levels and typically far exceeded the mortality rates of other groups living side by side with them. . . . The monthly death rate for Jews in Mauthausen [camp] was, from the end of 1942 to 1943, 100 percent. Mauthausen was not formally an extermination camp and, indeed, it was not for non-Jews, who at the end of 1943 all had a mortality rate below 2 percent." Goldhagen, *Hitler's Willing Executioners*, p. 173.
34 On the forced marches of Jews and other camp inmates, see ch. 14, "Marching to What End?," in Goldhagen, *Hitler's Willing Executioners*, pp. 355–71.
35 Niewyk, "Holocaust: The Jews," p. 150.
36 Ibid; for Epstein's testimony, see pp. 150–70.
37 Hitler quoted in Gerald Fleming, *Hitler and the Final Solution* (Berkeley, CA: University of California Press, 1984), p. 17.
38 Tatz, *With Intent to Destroy*, p. 22.
39 Browning, *The Path to Genocide*, p. 86.
40 Michael Burleigh and Wolfgang Wippermann, *The Racial State: Germany 1933–1945* (Cambridge: Cambridge University Press, 1991), p. 96.
41 Shermer and Grobman, *Denying History*, p. 213.
42 Hilberg, *The Destruction of the European Jews*, Vol. 1, pp. 139–40; Arendt, *Eichmann in Jerusalem*, pp. 59–60.
43 Arendt, *Eichmann in Jerusalem*, pp. 117–18, 125. See also the discussion in Hilberg, *The Destruction of the European Jews*, Vol. 1, pp. 218–22. "With the growth of the destructive function of the Judenräte, many Jewish leaders felt an almost irresistible urge to look like their German masters" (p. 219).
44 Raul Hilberg, *Perpetrators, Victims, Bystanders: The Jewish Catastrophe 1933–1945* (New York: Perennial, 1993), p. 170. In *The Destruction of the European Jews* (Vol. 2, p. 901), Hilberg refers to "masses of Jewish deportees, numb, fantasy-ridden, and filled with illusions, [who] reacted with mechanical cooperation to every German command" (the specific reference is to the Hungarian deportations of 1944).
45 See Richard Rashke, *Escape from Sobibor* (Champaign, IL: University of Illinois Press, 1995); Israel Gutman, *Resistance: The Warsaw Ghetto Uprising* (Boston, MA: Houghton Mifflin, 1998).
46 Donat, *The Holocaust Kingdom*, p. 7.
47 Bauer, *Rethinking the Holocaust*, p. 213.
48 Browning, *The Path to Genocide*, p. ix.
49 See Daniel Jonah Goldhagen, *A Moral Reckoning: The Role of the Catholic Church in the Holocaust and Its Unfulfilled Duty of Repair* (New York: Alfred A. Knopf, 2002).
50 Reginald H. Phelps, quoted in Goldhagen, *Hitler's Willing Executioners*, p. 443.
51 Hilberg, *Perpetrators, Victims, Bystanders*, p. 258.
52 Burleigh, *Ethics and Extermination*, pp. 155, 164.
53 Burleigh and Wippermann, *The Racial State*, p. 51.
54 Christopher Browning, *Ordinary Men: Reserve Police Battalion 101 and the Final Solution in Poland* (New York: HarperPerennial, 1998), pp. 184, 186.
55 Goldhagen, *Hitler's Willing Executioners*, pp. 277, 446.
56 Hilberg, *Perpetrators, Victims, Bystanders*, p. 191. As Martha Minow comments, "The creation of Israel could be viewed as a kind of international reparation effort." Minow, *Between Vengeance and Forgiveness: Facing History after Genocide and Mass Violence* (Boston, MA: Beacon Press, 1998), p. 133.
57 Alex Alvarez, *Governments, Citizens, and Genocide: A Comparative and Interdisciplinary Approach* (Bloomington, IN: Indiana University Press, 2001), p. 14.
58 The phrase "uniquely unique" was first used by Alice L. Eckhardt and Roy Eckhardt; see Gunnar Heinsohn, "What Makes the Holocaust A Uniquely Unique Genocide?", *Journal of Genocide Research*, 2: 3 (2000), p. 430 (n. 95).

59 Katz, *The Holocaust in Historical Context*, p. 28.
60 Charny quoted in David Stannard, "Uniqueness as Denial: The Politics of Genocide Scholarship," in Alan S. Rosenbaum, ed., *Is the Holocaust Unique? Perspectives on Comparative Genocide* (Boulder, CO: Westview Press, 1998), p. 198.
61 Lopate cited in Helen Fein, *Genocide: A Sociological Perspective* (London: Sage Publications, 1993), p. 52.
62 A recent polemic charges that a "Holocaust industry" has been created to win financial concessions from banks, industrial enterprises, and others who profited from the Jewish catastrophe. See Norman G. Finkelstein, *The Holocaust Industry: Reflections on the Exploitation of Jewish Suffering* (new edn) (New York: Verso, 2003).
63 Nicholas Wheeler, *Saving Strangers: Humanitarian Intervention in International Society* (Oxford: Oxford University Press, 2000), p. 212.
64 Interestingly, Vol. 2 of Steven Katz's *The Holocaust in Historical Context*, which was supposed to apply his uniqueness thesis to twentieth-century cases of mass killing, was scheduled for publication some years ago, but has yet to appear. I have often wondered whether Katz hit an insuperable roadblock in applying his thesis to the Rwandan genocide.
65 Hilberg, *The Destruction of the European Jews*, Vol. 3, p. 1075.
66 Bartov, *Germany's War and the Holocaust*, p. 106.
67 Thomas Cushman, "Is Genocide Preventable? Some Theoretical Considerations," *Journal of Genocide Research*, 5: 4 (2003), p. 528.

BOX 6A THE NAZIS' OTHER VICTIMS

While most people associate Nazi genocide with the Jewish Holocaust, a plethora of other victim groups actually accounted for the majority of those killed by the Nazis. Only in 1942 did the mass murder of Jews come to predominate, as historian Christopher Browning points out:

> If the Nazi regime had suddenly ceased to exist in the first half of 1941, its most notorious achievements in human destruction would have been the so-called euthanasia killing of seventy to eighty thousand German mentally ill and the systematic murder of the Polish intelligentsia. If the regime had disappeared in the spring of 1942, its historical infamy would have rested on the "war of destruction" against the Soviet Union. The mass death of some two million prisoners of war in the first nine months of that conflict would have stood out even more prominently than the killing of approximately one-half million Jews in that same period.

"Ever since," writes Browning, the Jewish Holocaust "has overshadowed National Socialism's other all-too-numerous atrocities."[1] It does so in this book as well. However, it is important to devote attention, however inadequate, to Nazism's other victims.

PRE-WAR PERSECUTIONS AND THE "EUTHANASIA" CAMPAIGN

Communists and socialists

The first Nazi concentration camp was at Dachau, near Munich. Opened in March 1933, two months after the Nazis took power – its stated purpose was "to concentrate, in one place, not only all Communist officials but also, if necessary, the officials of . . . other Marxist formations who threaten the security of the state."[2] Bolshevism was as central to Hitler's *Weltanschauung* (worldview) as anti-semitism, embodying the decadent, modernist tendencies that he loathed with a vengeance. In fact, Hitler's ideology and geopolitical strategy is best seen as motivated by a hatred of "Judeobolshevism," and a conviction that the Nazis' territorial ambitions in Central and Eastern Europe were obtainable only through a decisive and victorious confrontation with "the Marxist-cum-Bolshevik 'octopus' and the Jewish world conspiracy."[3]

One can distinguish between pre-war and wartime phases of the campaign against communists and socialists. In the pre-war stage, these sectors dominated the security policies of the Reich. They were the major targets of state violence and incarceration in camps; Jews-as-Jews were not targeted for substantial physical violence or imprisonment until *Kristallnacht* in 1938, by which time the German Left had been crushed. Communists, socialists, and other Left-oppositionists were also purged from public institutions in a manner very similar to the Jews.[4]

After the occupation of western Poland in September–October 1939, and especially with the invasion of eastern Poland and the Soviet Union in June 1941, the struggle against Bolshevism became intimately bound up with the Nazis' ambition to subdue, enslave, and exterminate the Slavic "subhuman." From this point on, the Nazis' ideological struggle against communists and socialists became intertwined with the national and military struggle with the USSR; the threat of ethnic swamping by "barbarians from the East"; and the assault on European Jewry.

Asocials and undesirables

The Nazis' quest for racial purity and social homogeneity meant that "asocial" elements were to be annihilated or, in some cases, reformed. An effective study of this phenomenon is Robert Gellately's book on Nazism and German public opinion, *Backing Hitler*. Considered asocial was "anyone who did not participate as a good citizen and accept their social responsibilities." Among the groups harassed and punished were men[5] seen as "shirking" paid work, or otherwise congenitally prone to unemployment or vagabondage. Gellately describes a "special action" organized by Nazi police chief Heinrich Himmler in March 1937 "to arrest 2,000 people out of work":

> The instruction was to send to concentration camps, those who "*in the opinion of the Criminal Police*" were professional criminals, repeat offenders, or habitual sex offenders. The enthusiasm of the police was such that they arrested not 2,000, but 2,752 people, only 171 of whom had broken their probation. Police used the event as a pretext to get rid of "problem cases." Those arrested were described as break-in specialists (938), thieves (741), sex offenders (495), swindlers (436), robbers (56), and dealers in stolen goods (86). Only 85 of them [3 percent] were women.[6]

According to Gellately, "A recurrent theme in Hitler's thinking was that in the event of war, the home front would not fall prey to saboteurs, that is, anyone vaguely considered to be 'criminals,' 'pimps,' or 'deserters'." The result was that "asocial" men, along with some women accused of involvement in the sex trade or common crimes, were confined in "camps [that] were presented as educative institutions . . . places for 'race defilers, rapists, sexual degenerates and habitual criminals'" (quoting an article in *Das Schwarze Korps* newspaper). Although "these camps were nothing like the death camps in the eastern occupied territories, the suffering, death, and outright murder in them was staggering."[7]

Just as Jews and Bolshevism blurred in the Nazis' ideology, it is important to recognize the overlap among asocials, Jews, and Roma (Gypsies). It was a cornerstone of the Nazi demonization of Jews that they were essentially a parasitic class, incapable of "honest" work and thus driven to usury, lazy cosmopolitanism, and criminality. Likewise, perhaps the *core* of the Nazi racial hatred of Roma lay in their stereotypical depiction as shiftless and inclined to criminal behavior. The genocidal consequences of these stereotypes are examined in the "Other Holocausts" section, below.

Homosexual men

For all the promiscuous hatreds of Adolf Hitler, "homophobia was not one of his major obsessions,"[8] and Hitler does not seem to have been the moving force behind the brutal Nazi campaign against gay men. (Lesbian women were never systematically targeted or arrested.)[9] Rather, that dubious honor goes to the owlish Heinrich Himmler, supreme commander of the SS paramilitary force, "whose loathing of homosexuals knew no bounds."[10] As early as 1937, in a speech to the SS academy at Bad Toelz, Himmler pledged: "Like stinging nettles we will rip them [homosexuals] out, throw them on a heap, and burn them. Otherwise . . . we'll see the end of Germany, the end of the Germanic world." Later he would proclaim to his Finnish physiotherapist, Dr. Felix Kersten:

> We must exterminate these people root and branch. Just think how many children will never be born because of this, and how a people can be broken in nerve and spirit when such a plague gets hold of it. . . . The homosexual is a traitor to his own people and must be rooted out.[11]

As these comments suggest, the reviling of gays was intimately linked to Nazi beliefs surrounding asocial and "useless" groups, who not only contributed nothing productive to the body politic, but actively subverted it. Gay males – because they chose to have sex with men – "were self-evidently failing in their duty to contribute to the demographic expansion of the 'Aryan-Germanic race,' at a time when millions of young men had perished in the First World War."[12] Just as Roma and (especially) Jews were deemed parasites on German society and the national economy, so were gays labeled "as useless as hens which don't lay eggs" and "sociosexual propagation misfits."[13] (They did, however, have their uses: among some conquered peoples, homosexuality was to be encouraged, since it "would hasten their degeneracy, and thus their demise.")[14]

Richard Plant's study of the Nazi persecution of gays, *The Pink Triangle*, estimated the number of men convicted for homosexual "crimes" from 1933 to 1944 to be "between 50,000 and 63,000, of which nearly 4,000 were juveniles."[15] In the concentration camps that were the destiny of thousands of them, their "fate . . . can only be described as ghastly."[16] Like the Jews, they were forced to wear a special badge (the pink triangle of Plant's title), were referred to contemptuously as *Mannweiber* ("manwives"), and were segregated from their fellow prisoners, who often joined in the contempt and brutalization. An inmate at Dachau reported that "the prisoners with the pink triangle did not live very long; they were quickly and systematically exterminated by the SS."[17] According to Konnilyn Feig, they found themselves "tormented from all sides as they struggle[d] to avoid being assaulted, raped, worked, and beaten to death."[18] Gay men were also among the likeliest candidates for grotesque medical experiments. At no point was support and solace likely from relatives or friends, because of the shame and stigma attaching to their "crimes." Plant estimates that the large majority of homosexuals consigned to concentration camps perished there – some 5,000 to 15,000 men.[19]

Jehovah's Witnesses and religious dissidents

If gays were dragged into the Nazi holocaust by their "traitorous" reluctance to contribute to Germany's demographic revival, Jehovah's Witnesses – already anathematized as a religious cult by the dominant Protestant and Catholic religious communities – were condemned for refusing to swear loyalty to the Nazi regime and to serve in the German military. In April 1935, the faith was formally outlawed, and later that year the first 400 Jehovah's Witnesses were consigned to the Sachsenhausen concentration camp. By 1939 the number incarcerated there and in other prisons and camps had ballooned to 6,000.

When war broke out in September 1939, the Witnesses' rejection of military service aroused still greater malevolence. Only a few days after the German invasion of Poland, a believer who refused to swear loyalty to the regime, August Dickmann, was executed by the Gestapo "in order to set an example."[20] In all, "Over the course of the dictatorship, as many as 10,000 members of the community were arrested, with 2,000 sent to concentration camps, where they were treated dreadfully and as many as 1,200 died or were murdered."[21]

In a curious twist, however, a positive stereotype also arose around the Witnesses. They came to be viewed in the camps as "industrious, neat, and tidy, and uncompromising in [their] religious principles." Accordingly,

> the SS ultimately switched to a policy of trying to exploit [the Witnesses'] devotion to duty and their reliability. . . . They were used as general servants in SS households or put to work in small Kommandos [work teams] when there was a threat that prisoners might escape. In Ravensbrück [women's concentration camp], they were showcased as "exemplary prisoners," while in Niederhagen, the only camp where they constituted the core population, they were put to work on renovations.[22]

As for mainstream religion, in general the Nazis deeply distrusted it, preferring their own brand of mysticism and *Völk*-worship. Their desire not to provoke unrest among the general population, or (prior to 1939) international opposition, limited their campaign against the main Protestant dominations and the large Catholic minority in Germany. No such restraint obtained in occupied Poland, however, where leading Catholic figures were swept up in the broad campaign of eliticide against the Polish intelligentsia. At home, as the war turned against Germany, religious dissidents of all stripes came to be hounded mercilessly, and were often imprisoned and killed. The best-known case is that of the Protestant pastor Dietrich Bonhoeffer, who declaimed against the Nazi regime from his pulpit, and was hanged in Flossenburg concentration camp shortly before the war ended. His *Letters and Papers from Prison* has become a classic of devotional literature.[23]

The handicapped and infirm

As with every other group the Nazis targeted, the campaign against the handicapped and infirm exploited a popular receptiveness based on long-standing patterns of discrimination and anathematization in European and Western culture. An offshoot of the Western drive for modernity was the development of a science of eugenics, taking both positive and negative forms: "Positive eugenics was the attempt to encourage increased breeding by those who were considered particularly fit; negative eugenics aimed at eliminating the unfit."[24] The foci of this international movement were Germany, Great Britain, and the United States (the US pioneered the use of forced sterilization against those considered "abnormal").[25] In Germany, the privations of the post-First World War period fueled similar philosophies and prescriptions. Treatises by noted legal and medical authorities in the 1920s railed against those "unworthy of life" and demanded the "destruction" of disabled persons in institutions. This was not murder but "mercy death."[26] Such views initially found strong public backing, even among many relatives of institutionalized patients.[27]

Once installed in power, the Nazis worked to deepen the trend. Within a few months, they had promulgated the Law for the Prevention of Hereditarily Diseased Progeny, beginning a policy that by 1945 had led to the forced sterilization of some 300,000 people. The Marriage Health Law followed in 1935, under which Germans seeking to wed were forced to provide medical documentation proving that they did not carry hereditary conditions or afflictions. If they could not so demonstrate, the application was rejected.[28]

In the two years prior to the outbreak of the Second World War, Hitler and other Nazi planners began paving the way for the collective killing of disabled infants and children, then of adults. Hitler used the "fog of war" to cover the implementation of the campaign (the authorization, personally signed by Hitler on September 8, 1939, was symbolically backdated to September 1 to coincide with the invasion of Poland). "An elaborate covert bureaucracy"[29] was established in a confiscated Jewish property at Tiergartenstrasse 4 in Berlin, and "Aktion T-4" – as the extermination program was dubbed – moved into high gear. The program's "task was to organise the registration, selection, transfer and murder of a previously calculated target group of 70,000 people, including chronic schizophrenics, epileptics and long-stay patients."[30] All were deemed *unnutze Esser*, "useless eaters" – surely one of the most macabre phrases in the Nazi vocabulary. In the end, the plan was overfulfilled. Among the victims were an estimated 6,000 to 7,000 children, who were starved to death or administered fatal medication. Many adults were dispatched to a prototype gas chamber.[31]

At every point in the chain of death, the complicity of nurses, doctors, and professionals of all stripes was overwhelmingly enthusiastic but, as the scope of the killing widened, the general population, and Germany's churches, proved more ambivalent, to the point of open protest. Eventually, in August 1941, "Aktion T-4" was closed down in Germany. But a decentralized version continued in operation until the last days of the war, and even beyond (the last victim died on May 29, 1945, under the noses of Allied occupiers). Meanwhile, the heart of the program – its eager supervisors and technicians – was bundled east, to manage the extermination of Jews and others in the death camps of Treblinka, Belzec, and Sobibor in Poland. Thus, "the euthanasia program was the direct precursor of the death factories – ideologically, organizationally, and in terms of personnel."[32]

Predictably, then, mass murder in the eastern occupied territories also targeted the handicapped. "In Poland the Germans killed almost all disabled

Poles . . . The same applied in the occupied Soviet Union."[33] With the assistance of the same *Einsatzgruppen* death squads who murdered hundreds of thousands of Jews in the first year of the war, some 100,000 people deemed "unworthy of life" were murdered at one institution alone, the Kiev Pathological Institute in Ukraine. In all, perhaps a quarter of a million handicapped and disabled individuals died to further the Nazis' fanatical social-engineering scheme.

OTHER HOLOCAUSTS

The Slavs

The ethnic designation "Slav" derives from the same root as "slave," and that is the destiny to which Nazi policies sought to consign Poles, Russians, Ukrainians, White Russians (Belorussians), and other Slavic nations. "The Slav is born a slave crying for a master," Hitler told his inner circle.[34] In his mind, the Slavs were not just bestial but dangerous and expansionist, at least when dominated and directed by Jews. It may be argued that the confrontation with the Slavs was inseparable from, and as central as, the campaign against the Jews. Consider the words of Colonel-General Hoepner, commander of Panzer Group 4 in the invasion of the Soviet Union, on sending his troops into battle:

> The war against the Soviet Union is an essential component of the German people's struggle for existence. It is the old struggle of the Germans against the Slavs, the defense of European culture against the Muscovite-Asiatic flood, the warding off of Jewish Bolshevism. This struggle must have as its aim the demolition of present Russia and must therefore be conducted with unprecedented severity. Both the planning and the execution of every battle must be dictated by an iron will to bring about a merciless, total annihilation of the enemy.[35]

The first victims of the anti-Slav genocide were, however, Polish. There, Slavic ethnicity combined with a nation-state that Hitler designated for genocide from the outset. Hitler's famous comment, "Who, after all, talks nowadays of the annihilation of the Armenians?" (see Chapter 4) is often mistaken as referring to the impending fate of Jews in Nazi-occupied territories. In fact, Hitler was speaking just before the invasion of Poland on September 1, 1939, referring to commands he had issued to "kill without pity or mercy all men, women, and children of Polish descent or language. Only in this way can we obtain the living space we need."[36] Richard Lukas is left in little doubt of Nazi plans:

> While the Germans intended to eliminate the Jews before the end of the war, most Poles would work as helots until they too shared the fate of the Jews. . . . The conclusion is inescapable that had the war continued, the Poles

> would have been ultimately obliterated either by outright slaughter in gas chambers, as most Jews had perished, or by a continuation of the policies the Nazis had inaugurated in occupied Poland during the war – genocide by execution, forced labor, starvation, reduction of biological propagation, and Germanization.

Others dispute the claim that non-Jewish Poles were destined for annihilation. Nonetheless, as Lukas notes, "during almost six years of war, Poland lost 6,028,000 of its citizens, or 22 percent of its total population, the highest ratio of losses to population of any country in Europe." Nearly three million of the murdered Poles were Jews, but "over 50 percent . . . were Polish Christians, victims of prison, death camps, raids, executions, epidemics, starvation, excessive work, and ill treatment."[37] Six million Poles were also dispatched to Germany to toil as slave-laborers. Soviet depredations during the relatively brief period of the USSR's occupation of eastern Poland (September 1939 to June 1941), and again after the war, also contributed significantly to the death-toll (see Chapter 5).

As for the Slavs of Ukraine, Russia, and other parts of the Soviet Union, their suffering is legendary. A commonly cited estimate is that *more than twenty-seven million* Soviet citizens died, about eighteen million of them civilians.[38] Titanic Russian sacrifices and, eventually, crushing military force were the key to Nazi Germany's defeat, with the other Allies playing an important supporting role. Between the German invasion of the USSR in June 1941 and the D-Day invasion of France in June 1944, some 80 percent of German forces were deployed in the East, and the overwhelming majority of German military casualties occurred there. As Yugoslav partisan leader Arso Jovanovic put it at the time: "Over there on the Eastern front – that's the real war, where whole divisions burn up like matchsticks" – and millions of civilians along with them.[39]

Soviet prisoners-of-war

"Next to the Jews in Europe," wrote Alexander Werth, "the biggest single German crime was undoubtedly the extermination by hunger, exposure and in other ways of . . . Russian war prisoners."[40] Yet the murder of at least 3.3 million Soviet POWs is one of the least-known of modern genocides; there is still no full-length book on the subject in English.[41] It also stands as one of the most intensive genocides of all time. The large majority of POWs, some 2.8 million, were killed in just eight months of 1941–42, a rate of slaughter matched (to my knowledge) only by the 1994 Rwanda genocide.[42]

The Soviet men were captured in massive encirclement operations in the early months of the German invasion, and in gender-selective round-ups that occurred in the newly occupied territories. All men between the ages of 15 and 65 were deemed to be prisoners-of-war, and liable to be "sent to the rear." Given that the Germans, though predicting victory by such epic encirclements, had deliberately avoided making provisions for sheltering and feeding millions of prisoners, "sent to the rear" became a euphemism for mass murder.

"Testimony is eloquent and prolific on the abandonment of entire divisions under the open sky," writes Alexander Dallin:

> Epidemics and epidemic diseases decimated the camps. Beatings and abuse by the guards were commonplace. Millions spent weeks without food or shelter. Carloads of prisoners were dead when they arrived at their destination. Casualty figures varied considerably but almost nowhere amounted to less than 30 percent in the winter of 1941–42, and sometimes went as high as 95 percent.[43]

Figure 6.a1 A wounded Soviet prisoner-of-war is dispatched "to the rear;" near Novgorod, Russia (fall/winter 1941–42?).

Source: Corbis.

A Hungarian tank officer who visited one POW enclosure described "tens of thousands of Russian prisoners. Many were on the point of expiring. Few could stand on their feet. Their faces were dried up and their eyes sunk deep into their sockets. Hundreds were dying every day, and those who had any strength left dumped them in a vast pit."[44] Cannibalism was common. Nazi leader Hermann Goering joked that "in the camps for Russian prisoners of war, after having eaten everything possible, including the soles of their boots, they have begun to eat each other, and what is more serious, have also eaten a German sentry."[45]

Hundreds of thousands of Soviet prisoners were sent to Nazi concentration camps, including Auschwitz, which was originally built to house and exploit them. Thousands died in the first tests of the gas chamber complex at Birkenau. Like the handicapped and Roma, then, Soviet POWs were guinea-pigs and stepping-stones in the evolution of genocide against the Jews. The overall estimate for POW fatalities – 3.3 million – is probably low. An important additional group of victims comprises Soviet soldiers, probably hundreds of thousands of them, who were killed shortly after surrendering.

In one of the twentieth century's most tragic ironies, the two million or so POWs who survived German incarceration were arrested upon repatriation to the USSR, on suspicion of collaboration with the Germans. Most were sentenced to long terms in the Soviet concentration camps, where tens of thousands died in the final years of the Gulag (see Chapter 5).

The Romani genocide (*Porrajmos*)

Perhaps more than any other group, the Nazi genocide against Romani (Gypsy) peoples* parallels the attempted extermination of European Jews. Roma were subjected to virulent racism in the centuries prior to the Holocaust – denounced as dirty, alien, and outside the bonds of social obligation. (Ironically, the Roma "were originally from North India and belonged to the Indo-Germanic speaking, or as Nazi racial anthropologists would have it, 'Aryan' people.")[46]

The grim phrase "lives undeserving of life," which most people associate with Nazi policy towards the handicapped and the Jews, was coined with reference to the Roma in a law passed only a few months following Hitler's ascent to power. Mixed marriages between Germans and Roma, as between "Aryan" Germans and Jews, were outlawed in 1935. The 1935 legislation against "hereditarily diseased progeny," the cornerstone of the campaign against the handicapped, specifically included Roma among its targets.

In July 1936, more than two years prior to the first mass round-up of Jewish men, Romani men were dispatched in their hundreds to the Dachau

* The term "Gypsy" has derogatory connotations, and is now often substituted by Roma/Romani, a practice followed in this book.

concentration camp outside Munich. (The measures were popular: Michael Burleigh noted "the obvious glee with which unwilling neighbours and local authorities regarded the removal of Sinti and Roma from their streets and neighbourhoods.")[47] While Hitler decreed a brief moratorium on anti-Jewish measures prior to the 1936 Berlin Olympics, raids were conducted in the vicinity of Berlin to capture and incarcerate Roma.

"On Combating the Gypsy Plague" was the title of a 1937 polemic by Heinrich Himmler, taking a break from his fulminations on homosexuals and Jews. It "marked the definitive transition from a Gypsy policy that was understood as a component of the extirpation of 'aliens to the community' . . . to a persecution *sui generis*."[48] The following year, the first reference to an *endgültige Lösung der Zigeunerfrage*, a "total solution" to the Romani "question," appeared in a Nazi pronouncement.[49] A thousand more Roma were condemned to concentration camps in 1938.

A few months after the outbreak of the Second World War, some 250 Romani children at Buchenwald became test subjects for the infamous Zyklon-B cyanide crystals later used to exterminate Jews *en masse*. In late 1941 and early 1942, some 5,000 Roma were deported from Austria to the death camp at Chelmno, where they were murdered in the mobile gas vans then being deployed against Jews in eastern Poland and the Soviet Union. Up to a quarter of a million more perished in *Einsatzgruppen* executions, "legitimised with the old prejudice that the victims were 'spies.'"[50]

In December 1942, Himmler decreed that Roma be deported to the most notorious of the death camps, Auschwitz-Birkenau. There they lived in a "family camp" (so named because Romani families, unlike Jewish ones, were not broken up), while the Nazi authorities decided what to do with them. A camp doctor who spoke with psychologist Robert Jay Lifton described conditions in the Romani barracks as "extraordinarily filthy and unhygienic even for Auschwitz, a place of starving babies, children and adults."[51] Those who did not die from privation, disease, or horrific medical experiments were finally consigned to the gas chambers in August 1944. In all, "about 20,000 of the 23,000 German and Austrian Roma and Sinti deported to Auschwitz were killed there."[52]

When the toll of the camps is combined with *Einsatzgruppen* operations, the outcome in terms of Romani mortality rates was not that different from the Jewish Holocaust. From a much smaller population, the Roma lost between 500,000 and 1.5 million of their members in the catastrophe that they call the *Porrajmos* ("Devouring"). While the lower figure is standard, Romani scholar Ian Hancock argues that it is "grossly underestimated," failing to recognize the extent to which Romani victims of (for example) the *Einsatzgruppen* death squads were designated as "partisans," "asocials," and other labels that disguised the ethnic element.[53]

Until recent years, however, the *Porrajmos* has been little more than a footnote in histories of Nazi mass violence. In part, this reflects the fact that Roma constituted a much smaller proportion of the German and European population than did Jews – about 0.05 percent. In addition, most Roma before and after the Second World War were illiterate, and thus unable to match the outpouring of victims' testimonies and academic analyses by Jewish survivors and scholars. Finally, and relatedly, while anti-semitism subsided dramatically after the war, Roma continued to be marginalized and stigmatized by European societies, as they are today.

The result, in Sybil Milton's words, has been "a tacit conspiracy of silence about the isolation, exclusion, and systematic killing of the Roma, rendering much of current Holocaust scholarship deficient and obsolete."[54] Even in contemporary Europe, Roma are the subject of regular violence and persecution. Only since the late 1970s has a civil-rights movement, along with a body of scholarly literature, arisen to confront discrimination and memorialize Romani suffering during the Nazi era.

Germans as victims

For decades after the end of the Second World War, it was difficult to give voice to German suffering in the war. Sixty years after the war's end, it is easier to accept claims that the Germans, too, should be numbered among the victims of Nazism – and victims of Nazism's victims.

Predictably, the discussion is most piquant within Germany (its role in shaping German historical memory is discussed further in Chapter 14). Two books published in 2003 symbolized the new visibility of the issue. A novel by Nobel Prize-winning author Günter Grass, *Im Krebsgang* (*Crabwalk*), centers on the twentieth century's worst maritime disaster: the torpedoing of the *Wilhelm Gustloff* by a Soviet submarine, as the converted luxury liner attempted to carry refugees (and some soldiers) from East Prussia to the German heartland, ahead of advancing Soviet armies. Nine thousand people died. In addition, a revisionist historian, Jörg Friedrich, published *Brandstätten* (*Fire Sites*), a compendium of grisly, never-before-seen archival photographs of German victims of Allied fire-bombing (see Chapter 14).[55]

Estimates of the death-toll in the area bombing of German cities "range from about 300,000 to 600,000, and of injuries from 600,000 to over a million." The most destructive raids were those on Hamburg (July 27–28, 1943) and Dresden, "the German Hiroshima" (February 13, 1945).[56] Both strikes resulted in raging fire-storms that suffocated or incinerated almost all life within their radius. As discussed in Chapter 1, various genocide scholars have described these and other aerial bombardments as genocidal.

Included among the estimated eight million German soldiers killed on all fronts during the war are those who died as prisoners-of-war in the Soviet Union. Many German POWs were simply executed; most were sent to concentration camps where, like their Soviet counterparts, they died of exposure, starvation, and additionally overwork. "In all, at least one million German prisoners died out of the 3,150,000 [captured] by the Red Army," and this does not reflect those summarily shot before they could be taken prisoner.[57] In one of the most egregious cases, of 91,000 Sixth Army POWs seized following the German surrender at Stalingrad in 1943, only 6,000 survived to be repatriated to Germany in the 1950s.[58]

A final horror inflicted on German populations was the reprisal killings and mass expulsions of ethnic Germans from the Soviet Union and Eastern Europe, often from territories their families had inhabited for centuries. As early as September 1939, in the opening weeks of the Nazi invasion of Poland, an estimated 60,000 ethnic Germans were allegedly murdered by Poles.[59] With the German army in retreat across the eastern front in 1944–45, large numbers of Germans fell prey to the vengeful atrocities of Soviet troops (notably in East Prussia) and local populations (especially in Poland and Czechoslovakia). Some twelve to fourteen million ethnic Germans were uprooted, of whom about two million perished. Much of this occurred after the war had ended, under the aegis of Allied occupation authorities, as the philosopher Bertrand Russell noted in an October 1945 protest letter:

> In Eastern Europe now mass deportations are being carried out by our allies on an unprecedented scale, and an apparently deliberate attempt is being made to exterminate millions of Germans, not by gas, but by depriving them of their homes and of food, leaving them to die by slow and agonizing starvation. This is not done as an act of war, but as a part of a deliberate policy of "peace."[60]

Moreover, an agreement reached among the Allies at the Yalta Conference (February 1945) "granted war reparations to the Soviet Union in the form of labor services. According to German Red Cross documents, it is estimated that 874,000 German civilians were abducted to the Soviet Union." They suffered a higher casualty rate even than German prisoners-of-war, with some 45 percent dying in captivity.[61]

FURTHER STUDY

Michael Berenbaum, ed., *A Mosaic of Victims: Non-Jews Persecuted and Murdered by the Nazis.* New York: New York University Press, 1990. Wide-ranging collection of essays.

Michael Burleigh, *Ethics and Extermination: Reflections on Nazi Genocide.* Cambridge: Cambridge University Press, 1997. Essays on themes including "euthanasia," the German–Soviet war, and the racial state.

Henry Friedlander, *The Origins of Nazi Genocide: From Euthanasia to the Final Solution.* Chapel Hill, NC: University of North Carolina Press, 1995. The evolution of Nazi mass murder.

Robert Gellately and Nathan Stoltzfus, eds, *Social Outsiders in Nazi Germany*. Princeton, NJ: Princeton University Press, 2001. Examines the Nazi campaign against "unwanted populations."

Gerhard Hirschfeld, ed., *The Policies of Genocide: Jews and Soviet Prisoners of War in Nazi Germany*. Boston, MA: Allan & Unwin, 1986. The links between the fate of the Jews and the Soviet prisoners.

Guenter Lewy, *The Nazi Persecution of the Gypsies*. Oxford: Oxford University Press, 2000. The first major work in English on the Roma holocaust, though with a disturbing denialist slant.

Norman M. Naimark, *The Russians in Germany: A History of the Soviet Zone of Occupation, 1945–1949*. Cambridge, MA: The Belknap Press, 1995. Strong on atrocities against German women and workers under Soviet occupation.

Richard Plant, *The Pink Triangle: The Nazi War against Homosexuals*. New York: Owl, 1986. The persecution and killing of homosexuals, described by a refugee of the Nazi regime.

Martin K. Sorge, *The Other Price of Hitler's War: German Military and Civilian Losses Resulting from World War II*. Westport, CT: Greenwood Press, 1986. Concise account of German suffering in the war.

Frederick Taylor, *Dresden: Tuesday, February 13, 1945*. New York: HarperCollins, 2004. In-depth study of the Allied fire-bombing of the historic German city.

Alfred-Maurice de Zayas, *A Terrible Revenge: The Ethnic Cleansing of the East European Germans, 1944–1950*. New York: St. Martin's Press, 1994. The atrocities against ethnic Germans, ably cataloged.

NOTES

1 Christopher R. Browning, *The Path to Genocide: Essays on Launching the Final Solution* (Cambridge: Cambridge University Press, 1992), p. ix.
2 Heinrich Himmler's announcement of Dachau's opening, quoted in Arno J. Mayer, *Why Did the Heavens Not Darken? The Final Solution in History* (New York: Pantheon, 1988), p. 125.
3 Mayer, *Why Did the Heavens Not Darken?*, pp. 107–8.
4 According to Dominique Vidal, approximately 150,000 communists and left-leaning social democrats were incarcerated in concentration camps between 1933 and 1939. Vidal, "From 'Mein Kampf' to Auschwitz," *Le Monde diplomatique*, October 1998.
5 "The 'work-shy' were [defined as] males medically fit to work, but who (without good reason) refused jobs on two occasions, or quit after a short time." Robert Gellately, *Backing Hitler: Consent and Coercion in Nazi Germany* (Oxford: Oxford University Press, 2001), p. 98.
6 Gellately, *Backing Hitler*, p. 96.
7 Gellately, *Backing Hitler*, pp. 60, 63, 68, 70.
8 Geoffrey J. Giles, "The Institutionalization of Homosexual Panic in the Third Reich," in Gellately and Stoltzfus, eds, *Social Outsiders in Nazi Germany* (Princeton, NJ: Princeton University Press, 2001), p. 233.

9 "Lesbians were not subjected to formal persecution in the Third Reich, despite the fact that some zealous legal experts demanded this. . . . In a state which extolled manly, martial roughness, lesbians were less of a threat to the regime than men who subverted its crude stereotypes of 'normal' male behaviour." Michael Burleigh and Wolfgang Wippermann, *The Racial State: Germany 1933–1945* (Cambridge: Cambridge University Press, 1991), p. 268.
10 Richard Plant, *The Pink Triangle: The Nazi War against Homosexuals* (New York: Owl Books, 1988), p. 62.
11 Himmler quoted in Plant, *The Pink Triangle*, pp. 89, 99.
12 Michael Burleigh, *Ethics and Extermination: Reflections on Nazi Genocide* (Cambridge: Cambridge University Press, 1997), p. 162.
13 Quoted in Plant, *The Pink Triangle*, p. 102.
14 Plant, *The Pink Triangle*, p. 99.
15 Plant, *The Pink Triangle*, p. 149.
16 Quoted in Plant, *The Pink Triangle*, p. 166.
17 Saul Friedländer, *Nazi Germany and the Jews, Volume 1: The Years of Persecution, 1933–1939* (New York: HarperCollins, 1997), p. 206.
18 Konnilyn Feig, "Non-Jewish Victims in the Concentration Camps," in Michael Berenbaum, ed., *A Mosaic of Victims: Non-Jews Persecuted and Murdered by the Nazis* (New York: New York University Press, 1990), p. 163.
19 Plant, *The Pink Triangle*, p. 154.
20 Gellately, *Backing Hitler*, p. 75.
21 Ibid. For Web links and a bibliography on the persecution and killings of Jehovah's Witnesses, see "A Teacher's Guide to the Holocaust: Jehovah's Witnesses," http://fcit.coedu.usf.edu/holocaust/people/VictJeho.htm.
22 Wolfgang Sofsky, *The Order of Terror: The Concentration Camp*, trans. William Templer (Princeton, NJ: Princeton University Press, 1999), pp. 122–23.
23 Dietrich Bonhoeffer, *Letters and Papers from Prison* (New York: Touchstone, 1997). See also the United States Holocaust Memorial Museum page on Bonhoeffer's life and work at http://www.ushmm.org/bonhoeffer/.
24 Henry Friedlander, "The Exclusion and Murder of the Disabled," in Gellately and Stolzfus, eds, *Social Outsiders in Nazi Germany*, p. 146.
25 "Between 1907 and 1939, more than 30,000 people in twenty-nine [US] states were sterilized, many of them unknowingly or against their will, while they were incarcerated in prisons or institutions for the mentally ill." See "Handicapped: Victims of the Nazi Era, 1933–1945," *A Teacher's Guide to the Holocaust*, http://fcit.coedu.usf.edu/holocaust/people/USHMMHAN.HTM.
26 Friedlander, "The Exclusion and Murder of the Disabled," p. 147.
27 An opponent of such views, Ewald Meltzer, the director of Katherinenhof juvenile asylum in Saxony, decided in 1925 "to carry out a poll of the views on 'euthanasia' held by the parents of his charges. To his obvious surprise, some 73 per cent of the 162 respondents said that they would approve 'the painless curtailment of the life of [their] child if experts had established that it is suffering from incurable idiocy.' Many of the 'yes' respondents said that they wished to offload the burden represented by an 'idiotic' child, with some of them expressing the wish that this be done surreptitiously, in a manner which anticipated later National Socialist practice." Burleigh, *Ethics and Extermination*, p. 121.
28 Recall that under the UN Convention definition of genocide, preventing births within a group may be considered genocidal.
29 Burleigh, *Ethics and Extermination*, p. 123.
30 Ibid.
31 See "'Wheels Must Roll for Victory!' Children's 'Euthanasia' and 'Aktion T-4,'"

ch. 3 in Michael Burleigh, *Death and Deliverance: 'Euthanasia' in Germany c. 1900–1945* (London: Pan Books, 1994), pp. 97–127.

32 Sofsky, *The Order of Terror*, p. 243.

33 Friedlander, "The Exclusion and Murder of the Disabled," p. 157.

34 Hitler quoted in Jürgen Zimmerer, "Colonialism and the Holocaust: Towards an Archaeology of Genocide," in Dirk Moses, ed., *Genocide and Settler Society: Frontier Violence and Stolen Indigenous Children in Australian History* (New York: Berghahn Books, 2004), p. 55.

35 Quoted in Omer Bartov, *Hitler's Army: Soldiers, Nazis, and War in the Third Reich* (New York: Oxford University Press, 1992), p. 129.

36 Heinrich Himmler, tasked with engineering the destruction of the Polish people, parroted Hitler in proclaiming that "all Poles will disappear from the world. . . . It is essential that the great German people should consider it as its major task to destroy all Poles." Hitler and Himmler quoted in Lukas, "The Polish Experience during the Holocaust," p. 89.

37 Lukas, "The Polish Experience," p. 90.

38 Anthony Beevor, *Stalingrad* (New York: Viking Press, 1998), p. 428.

39 Quoted in Milovan Djilas, *Wartime* (New York: Harvest, 1980), p. 73. Omer Bartov writes: "It was in the Soviet Union that the Wehrmacht's back was broken long before the Western Allies landed in France, and even after June 1944 it was in the East that the Germans continued to commit and lose far more men. . . . By the end of March 1945 the *Ostheer*'s [German eastern front] casualties mounted to 6,172,373 men, or double its original manpower on 22 June 1941, a figure which constituted fully four-fifths of the [Germans'] total losses . . . on all fronts since the invasion of the Soviet Union." Bartov, *Hitler's Army*, pp. 29, 45. Alec Nove points out that more Russians died in the German siege of Leningrad (1941–43) "than the total of British and Americans killed from all causes throughout the war." Nove, *Stalinism and After* (London: George Allen & Unwin, 1975), p. 93.

40 Alexander Werth, *Russia at War, 1941–45* (New York: Carroll & Graf, 1999), p. 634.

41 Interestingly, a photo of the Soviet prisoners features on the cover of a recent and prominent volume: Robert Gellately and Ben Kiernan, eds, *The Specter of Genocide: Mass Murder in Historical Perspective* (Cambridge: Cambridge University Press, 2003). There is, however, only a passing mention of the genocide in the text itself (p. 260).

42 If the upper-end estimates for those killed in Bangladesh genocide of 1971 are accurate (three million; see Box 8a), this might also match the intensiveness of Rwanda and the genocide against Soviet POWs.

43 Alexander Dallin, *German Rule in Russia, 1941–45: A Study of Occupation Policies* (2nd edn) (London: Macmillan, 1981), pp. 414–15; Omer Bartov, *The Eastern Front, 1941–45: German Troops and the Barbarization of Warfare* (Basingstoke: Macmillan, 1985), p. 110.

44 Quoted in Werth, *Russia At War*, pp. 635–36.

45 Quoted in Dallin, *German Rule in Russia*, p. 415.

46 Burleigh and Wippermann, *The Racial State*, p. 116.

47 Burleigh, *Ethics and Extermination*, p. 167.

48 Michael Zimmermann, "The National Socialist 'Solution of the Gypsy Question,'" ch. 7 in Ulrich Herbert, ed., *National Socialist Extermination Policies: Contemporary German Perspectives and Controversies* (New York: Berghahn Books, 2000), p. 194.

49 Sybil H. Milton, "'Gypsies' as Social Outsiders in Nazi Germany," in Gellately and Stoltzfus, eds, *Social Outsiders in Nazi Germany*, p. 222.

50 Burleigh and Wippermann, *The Racial State*, p. 125.

51 Robert Jay Lifton, *The Nazi Doctors: Medical Killing and the Psychology of Genocide* (New York: Basic Books, 1986), p. 161 (the quoted passage is Lifton's paraphrase).
52 Milton, "'Gypsies' as Social Outsiders," p. 226.
53 Ian Hancock, "O Baro Porrajmos: The Romani Holocaust", in William L. Hewitt, ed., *Defining the Horrific: Readings on Genocide and Holocaust in the 20th Century* (Upper Saddle River, NJ: Pearson Education, 2004), p. 164. See also the discussion of *Einsatzgruppen* and *Sonderkommando* killings of Roma in the USSR and Poland, in Zimmermann, "The National Socialist 'Solution of the Gypsy Question,'" pp. 197–98.
54 Sybil Milton, "Holocaust: The Gypsies," in Samuel Totten *et al.*, eds, *Century of Genocide* (New York: Garland Publishing, 1997), p. 188.
55 Günter Grass, *Crabwalk*, trans. Krishna Winston (New York: Harvest, 2004); Jörg Friedrich, *Brandstätten* (Berlin: Propylaen, 2003).
56 Eric Langenbacher, "The Allies in World War II: The Anglo-American Bombardment of German Cities," in Adam Jones, ed., *Genocide, War Crimes and the West: History and Complicity* (London: Zed Books, 2004), p. 118. See also Hermann Knell's study of the lesser-known attack on Würzburg in March 1945, *To Destroy a City: Strategic Bombing and Its Human Consequences in World War II* (Cambridge, MA: Da Capo Press, 2003).
57 S.P. MacKenzie, "The Treatment of Prisoners in World War II," *Journal of Modern History*, 66: 3 (September 1994), p. 511.
58 Beevor, *Stalingrad*, p. 430.
59 Martin K. Sorge, *The Other Price of Hitler's War: German Military and Civilian Losses Resulting from World War II* (Westport, CT: Greenwood Press, 1996), p. 89.
60 Russell cited in Alfred-Maurice de Zayas, *A Terrible Revenge: The Ethnic Cleansing of the East European Germans, 1944–1950* (New York: St. Martin's Press, 1994), p. 111.
61 De Zayas, *A Terrible Revenge*, p. 116.

CHAPTER 7

Cambodia and the Khmer Rouge

ORIGINS OF THE KHMER ROUGE

One view of Cambodia prior to the upheavals of the late 1960s and 1970s depicted it as a "gentle land." Peaceful Buddhists presided over one of the rice bowls of Southeast Asia, where peasants owned the soil they tilled. This picture is far from false. Indeed, Cambodia was abundant in rice, and peasant landownership was comparatively high. But the stereotype overlooks a darker side of Cambodian history and society: absolutism, a politics of vengeance, a ready recourse to torture. "Patterns of extreme violence against people defined as enemies, however arbitrarily, have very long roots in Cambodia," wrote historian Michael Vickery.[1] Journalist Elizabeth Becker likewise pointed to "a tradition of violence," adding: "The Cambodian communist movement was an expression of these conflicting, desperate impulses."[2]

This is not to say that "a tradition of violence" determined that the Khmer Rouge (KR) would come to power. In fact, until relatively late in the process, it was a marginal presence. However, neither was the Khmer Rouge an outright aberration. Certainly, the KR's emphasis on concentrating power and wielding it in tyrannical fashion was entirely in keeping with Cambodian tradition. "Absolutism . . . is a core element of authority and legitimacy in Cambodia," writes David Roberts.[3] As for the supposedly pacific nature of Buddhism, the religion that overwhelmingly predominated in Cambodia, Vickery denounces it as "arrant nonsense." "That Buddhists may torture and massacre is no more astonishing than that the Inquisition burned people or that practicing Catholics and Protestants joined the Nazi SS."[4]

Another element of Cambodian history and politics is an aggressive nostalgia for past glories. Cambodia under the Angkor Empire, which peaked from the twelfth to the fourteenth centuries, was a powerful nation, incorporating vast territories that today belong to its neighbors. It extended to the South China Sea, and included southern regions of Vietnam as well as regions of present-day Laos, Thailand, and Burma. At the height of its power, forced laborers built the great temples of Angkor Wat, the world's largest religious complex. Ever since, including for the Khmer Rouge, Angkor Wat has served as Cambodia's national symbol.

Cambodian nationalists harked back constantly to these halcyon days, and advanced irredentist territorial claims with varying degrees of seriousness. Most significantly, the rich lands of today's southern Vietnam were designated Kampuchea Krom, "Lower Cambodia" in nationalist discourse, though they have been part of Vietnam since at least 1840. This rivalry with Vietnam, and a messianic desire to reclaim "lost" Cambodian territories, fed Khmer Rouge fanaticism. The government led by the avowedly anti-imperialist Communist Party of Cambodia (the official name of the KR) was as xenophobic and expansionist as any regime in Asia.

By the nineteenth century, Cambodia's imperial prowess was long dissipated, and the country easily fell under the sway of the French. On the pretext of creating a buffer between their Vietnamese territories, British-influenced Burma, and independent Siam (Thailand), the French established influence over the Court of King Norodom. The king, grandfather of Prince Norodom Sihanouk who would rule during the KR's early years, accepted protectorate status. He eventually became little more than a French vassal.

As elsewhere in their empire, France fueled nationalist aspirations in Cambodia – by economic exploitation and political subordination, but also by the efforts of French scholars, who worked to "'recover' a history for Cambodia." This bolstered "Khmer pride in their country's heritage," providing "the ideological foundation of the modern drive for an expression of an independent Khmer nation."[5]

Another crucial French contribution to Khmer nationalism was the awarding of academic scholarships to Cambodians for study in Paris. In the 1950s, the French capital was perhaps the richest environment for revolutionary ferment anywhere in the world. The French Communist Party, which had led the resistance to Nazi occupation, emerged from the war as a powerful presence in mainstream politics. Pre-war Paris had nurtured nationalists from the French colonies, including Vietnam's Ho Chi Minh. The postwar period likewise provided a persecution-free environment in which Third World revolution could gestate. The Algerian Frantz Fanon, author of *The Wretched of the Earth*, was a beneficiary. Others included the leadership core of the future Khmer Rouge.[6] Those who studied in Paris in the 1950s included:

- Saloth Sar, who subsequently took the name Pol Pot, "Brother Number One" in the party hierarchy and Prime Minister of Democratic Kampuchea during the KR's period in power;
- Khieu Samphan, later President of Democratic Kampuchea (DK);
- Son Sen, DK's deputy Prime Minister and Minister of Defense and Security;
- Ieng Sary, deputy Prime Minister in charge of foreign affairs during the DK period;
- his wife, Ieng (Khieu) Thirith, Minister of Social Action for the DK regime.[7]

In retrospect, Khmer Rouge fanaticism was fueled by some of the ideological currents of the time. The French Communist Party was in its high-Stalinist phase, supporting campaigns against "enemies of the people." Intellectuals like Fanon, meanwhile, were drawn to the thesis "that only violence and armed revolt could cleanse the minds of Third World peoples and rid them of their colonial mentalities."[8]

Cambodian nationalism remained quiescent during the years of the Second World War, which Cambodia spent under Vichy French administration,[9] but the 1950s and 1960s were a period of nationalist ferment throughout the Third World. The government of Prince Norodom Sihanouk was positioning itself as an anti-colonialist, politically neutral force in Southeast Asia. Sihanouk was a leader of the Non-Aligned Movement that burst onto the world stage at the Bandung Conference in 1955.

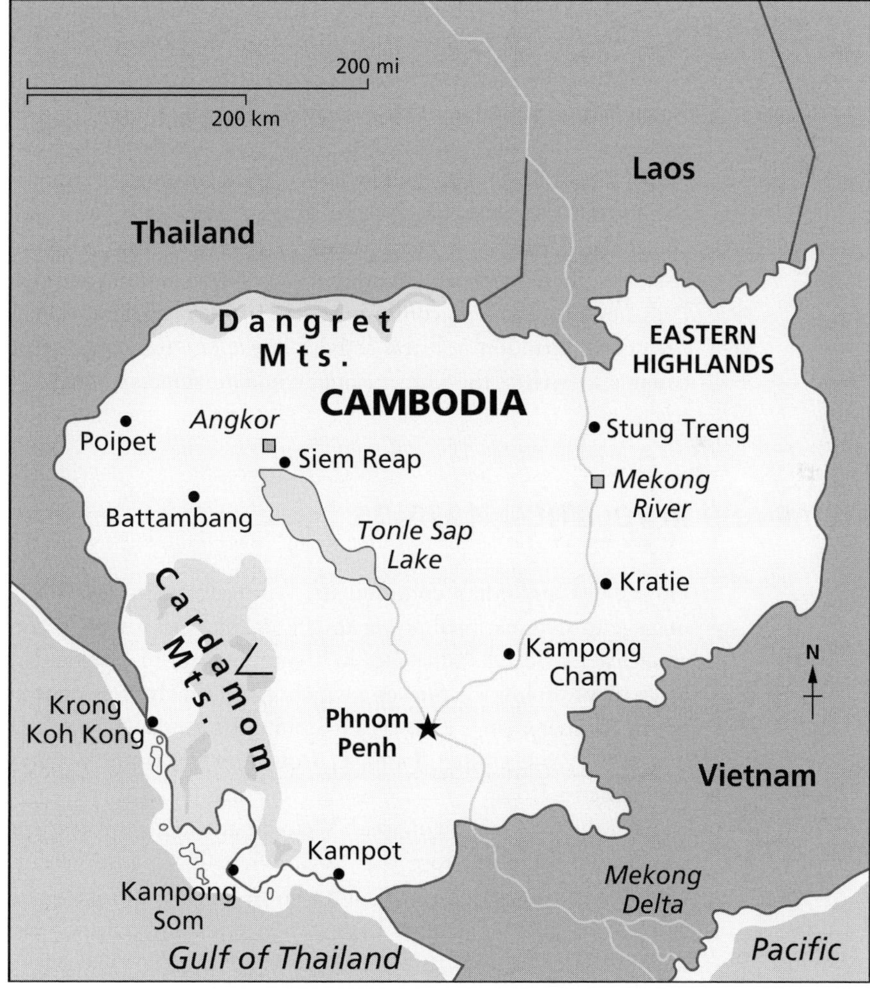

Map 7.1 Cambodia

Source: Map provided by WorldAtlas.com

Many returning students flocked to the Indochinese Communist Party, which united communist movements in Vietnam and Cambodia. Tensions soon developed between the two wings, however. Cambodians like Pol Pot felt they "had to carry excrement for the Vietnamese," according to Khieu Thirith.[10] Following the 1954 Vietnamese victory over the French at Dien Bien Phu, and the signing of the Geneva Accords, the Vietnamese withdrew from Cambodia, but split the Cambodian membership by transferring some 1,000 of its cadres to Vietnam, leaving another 1,000 behind in Cambodia – including Pol Pot and the future core leadership of the Khmer Rouge. This would have fateful consequences when returning communist cadres who had spent their formative period in Vietnam were targeted by the KR for extermination, together with all ethnic Vietnamese in Cambodia (or within reach on the other side of the border). In the case of Vietnamese remaining in Cambodia, the destruction was *total.*

In 1966, Sihanouk, whose police had been quietly implementing a campaign of "government murder and repression" against communists in the countryside,[11] launched a crackdown on members of the urban left whom he had not fully co-opted. Khieu Samphan and Hou Youn were forced underground in 1967. Not least of the problems of the Cambodian Communist Party was its estrangement from Hanoi. The North Vietnamese regime of Ho Chi Minh determined to support the neutralist and anti-imperialist Sihanouk, and not to aid a rebellion by its Cambodian communist "brothers." Hanoi valued Sihanouk as a bulwark against US domination of Southeast Asia, and therefore as an ally in the Vietnamese national struggle. By contrast, Pol Pot's new Cambodian communist leadership considered Sihanouk a US ally. It decided to abandon political activity in the city for armed struggle in the remote countryside, where the Khmer Rouge could nurture its revolution beyond Sihanouk's reach.

WAR AND REVOLUTION, 1970–75

How did Cambodia's communists, politically marginal throughout the 1960s, manage to seize national power in 1975? The explanation, according to Cambodia specialist David Chandler, lies in a combination of "accidents, outside help, and external pressures. . . . Success, which came slowly, was contingent on events in South Vietnam, on Vietnamese Communist guidance, on the disastrous policies followed by the United States, and on blunders made by successive Cambodian governments."[12]

After the US invasion of South Vietnam in 1965, conflict spilled increasingly into Cambodia. Supplies from the North Vietnamese government, destined for the guerrillas of the National Liberation Front in the south, moved down the "Ho Chi Minh Trail" cutting through Laos and eastern Cambodia. US bombing of the trail, including areas inside Cambodia from 1969, pushed Vietnamese forces deeper into Cambodia, until they came to control significant border areas. The Vietnamese, giving priority to their own liberation struggle, urged restraint on their Cambodian communist allies, but in 1970, as war spread across Cambodia, the extension of

Vietnamese power provided a powerful boost for the Khmer Rouge, including vital training. In the early 1970s, the Vietnamese forces were inflicting far more damage on Cambodian government forces than was the KR.

The Vietnamese occupation of Cambodian border areas provoked two major responses from the United States, both central to the horrors that followed. First, in 1970, came US support for a coup against Prince Sihanouk, whom the US saw as a dangerous socialist and neutralist. He was replaced by Lon Nol, Sihanouk's former right-hand man and head of the armed forces, a general with fanatical religious commitments who believed that "Buddhist teaching, racial virtues, and modern science made the Khmers invincible."[13] (Clearly, extreme chauvinism in Cambodia was not an invention of Democratic Kampuchea.) Lon Nol duly repaid his benefactors by inviting the US and South Vietnam to launch an invasion of Cambodian territory, which lasted for three months.[14]

The significance of this action was outweighed by a second US response: the escalation from 1970 of the campaign of saturation bombing first launched against Vietnamese border sanctuaries in Cambodia in 1969. The campaign climaxed in 1973, a year that saw *a quarter of a million tons* of bombs dropped on Cambodia in just six months. This was one-and-a-half times as much high explosive as the US had unleashed on Japan during the whole of the Second World War – a country with which it was at least formally at war. In total, between 1969 and 1973, more than half a million tons of munitions descended on rural Cambodia.

The impact was devastating. Tens or hundreds of thousands of Cambodians were killed.[15] After bombing raids, "villagers who happened to be away from home returned to find nothing but dust and mud mixed with seared and bloody body parts."[16] Moreover, the assault effectively destroyed the agricultural base of an agricultural nation – more effectively, in fact, than had Stalin with his collectivization campaign against the Soviet peasantry (Chapter 5). "The amount of acreage cultivated for rice dropped from six million at the beginning of the war to little more than one million at the end of the bombing campaign," writes Elizabeth Becker.[17] Malnutrition was rampant, and mass starvation was only avoided by food aid from US charitable organizations. (This should be borne in mind when the aftermath of the Khmer Rouge victory is considered, below.)[18]

Probably genocidal in itself, unquestionably "one of the worst aggressive onslaughts in modern warfare,"[19] the US bombing of a defenseless population was also the most important factor in bringing the genocidal Khmer Rouge to power. One KR leader who defected, Chhit Do, eloquently captured the political impact of the bombardment:

> Every time after there had been bombing, [the Khmer Rouge guerrillas] would take the people to see the craters, to see how big and deep the craters were, to see how the earth had been gouged out and scorched. . . . The ordinary people . . . sometimes literally shit in their pants when the big bombs and shells came. . . . Their minds just froze up and they would wander around mute for three or four days. Terrified and half-crazy, the people were ready to believe what they were told. . . . That was what made it so easy for the Khmer Rouge to win the people over.

> . . . It was because of their dissatisfaction with the bombing that they kept on cooperating with the Khmer Rouge, joining up with the Khmer Rouge, sending their children off to go with them.[20]

"This is not to say that the Americans are responsible for the genocide in Cambodia," as Michael Ignatieff notes. "It is to say that a society that has been pulverised by war is a society that is very susceptible to genocide."[21]

Under the Paris Peace Accords of 1973, Vietnamese forces evacuated Cambodia, but the focus of military opposition to the Lon Nol regime had already shifted to the Khmer Rouge. Buoyed by Vietnamese arms and training, they were now a hardened and effective force – at least a match for poorly motivated and half-starved government conscripts. The KR moved rapidly to besiege Phnom Penh and other cities. Meanwhile, in the areas of the countryside already under their control, they implemented the first stage of their distinctive – and phenomenally destructive – revolutionary ideology.

A GENOCIDAL IDEOLOGY

In their jungle camps, the Khmer Rouge developed the philosophy that would guide their genocidal program. Let us consider the basic elements of this world view, and its consequences from 1975 to 1979:

- ***Hatred of "enemies of the people."*** Like many communist revolutionaries of the twentieth century – notably those in the USSR and China – the KR exhibited a visceral hatred of the revolution's enemies, and targeted them mercilessly. As with Lenin-Stalin and Mao Zedong, too, "enemies" were loosely defined. They could be members of socioeconomic classes. The Khmer Rouge targeted the rich/bourgeoisie; professionals (including those who returned from abroad to help the new regime); "imperialist stooges" (collaborators with the US and its client regime in Phnom Penh); and the educated class. In effect, this swept up most urbanites. Enemies could also be designated on ethnic grounds. Just as Stalin waged genocide against the people of Ukraine and the Caucasus, so the Khmer Rouge exterminated ethnic Vietnamese, Chinese, Muslim Chams – in fact, almost every ethnic minority in Cambodia. (Even geographically defined Khmers were targeted for annihilation, such as those from southern Vietnam or the "traitorous" Eastern Zone in 1978.) The enemy could also be religious believers seen to be out of step with the KR pseudo-religion that now ruled the roost.

  Lastly, enemies could be purged on the basis of supposed subversion or betrayal of the revolution from within. Stalin's purges of the Soviet Communist Party (Chapter 5) would be matched and exceeded, relative to population and party membership, by the Khmer Rouge's hysterical attacks on internal enemies.
- ***Xenophobia and messianic nationalism.*** As noted, the KR – in tandem with other Cambodian nationalists – harked back to the Angkor Empire. As is standard with nationalism, territorial claims reflected the zenith of power in the nation's past. Pol Pot and his regime apparently believed in their ability to reclaim the "lost"

Cambodian territories of Kampuchea Krom in southern Vietnam. Territorial ambitions were combined with a broader fear and hatred of ethnic Vietnamese, seen both as Cambodia's historical enemy and the betrayer of Cambodian communism. A desire was imputed to the Vietnamese to conquer Cambodia and destroy its revolution – a paranoid vision that harmonized with the Khmer Rouge's messianic sense of Cambodia as "the prize other powers covet."[22]

Racism and xenophobia produced an annihilationist ideology that depicted Cambodia's ethnic Vietnamese minority as a deadly internal threat to the survival of the Khmer nation. Khmer Krom from the historically Cambodian territories of southern Vietnam were targeted with similar venom. Finally, the xenophobia led to repeated Cambodian invasions of Vietnamese territory in 1977 and 1978. These eventually sparked the Vietnamese invasion that overthrew the regime.

- ***Peasantism, anti-urbanism, and primitivism.*** Like the Chinese communists, but unlike the Soviets, the Khmer Rouge gleaned support from rural rather than urban populations. Peasants were the guardians of the true and pure Cambodia against alien, cosmopolitan city-dwellers. However, the Khmer Rouge vision of the peasantry was misguided from the first. As Ben Kiernan pointed out, the DK regime attacked the three foundations of peasant life: religion, land, and family. The KR rejected the peasants' attachment to Buddhist religion; imputed to peasants a desire for agricultural collectivization that was alien to Cambodia; revived the hated *corvée* (forced labor); and sought to destabilize and dismantle the family unit.

The primitivist dimension of Khmer Rouge ideology seems to have been influenced by the tribal peoples among whom KR leaders lived in Cambodia's eastern jungles. These people, in particular the Khmer Loeu (highland Khmer), often welcomed the KR presence at first. They provided indispensable refuge and sustenance for the party in its nascent period. "Pol Pot and Ieng Sary . . . claimed later to have been inspired by the spirit of people who had no private property, no markets, and no money. Their way of life and their means of production corresponded to the primitive communist phase of social evolution in Marxist thinking," and likely influenced the KR decision to abandon the market and the money economy.[23] Soldiers from the highland tribes played an important role in the KR's final campaign to crush the Lon Nol regime, but increasingly fell victim to the genocide against ethnic minorities under DK (see below).[24]

A bizarre aspect of KR primitivism was the conviction that no natural challenge was insuperable, no scientific accomplishment unattainable, if peasant energies and know-how were tapped. "The young are learning their science from the workers and peasants, who are the sources of all knowledge," declared Radio Phnom Penh.[25] "Formerly to be a pilot required a high school education – twelve to fourteen years," declared another classic piece of propaganda. "Nowadays, it's clear that political consciousness is the decisive factor. . . . As for radar, we can learn how to handle it after studying for a couple of months."[26] Not surprisingly, the Khmer Rouge air force never amounted to much.

In Mao Zedong's "Great Leap Forward," an almost identical mentality had produced outcomes in China that were both absurd and catastrophic. Agriculture reeled from *faux*-scientific attempts to boost crop yields. Backyard furnaces churned out unusable steel. Vast conscript forces toiled on dams that collapsed with the first river swell. In addition, the diversion of resources, combined with willful misreporting of production figures, produced history's worst famine.[27] Undeterred, the DK regime announced that an even more impressive "*Super* Great Leap Forward" would be initiated in Cambodia. Like Mao's experiment, the Super Great Leap would be about self-sufficiency. Foreign help was neither desirable nor required, and even the Chinese model was dismissed. Indeed, the country would be all but sealed off from the outside world.[28]

- ***Purity, discipline, militarism.*** Like the Nazis, the Khmer Rouge expressed their racism through an obsessive emphasis on racial purity. Like the Soviets and Chinese, purity was also defined by class origin, and as an unswerving fealty to revolutionary principle and practice. Self-discipline was a critical component. It demonstrated revolutionary ardor and self-sacrifice. In most revolutions of Left and Right, rigorous discipline has spawned an ideology of chaste sexuality – though this has not necessarily been matched in practice. There is little question that the Khmer Rouge presided over a regime of "totalitarian puritanism,"[29] perhaps without equal in the twentieth century. Among other things, "any sex before marriage was punishable by death in many cooperatives and zones."[30]

  Discipline among revolutionaries also buttresses the inevitable military confrontation with the counter-revolution. Kiernan and Boua consider militarism to be *the* defining feature of Khmer Rouge rule, reflected in "the forced evacuation of the cities, the coercion of the population into economic programmes organized with military discipline, the heavy reliance on the armed forces rather than civilian cadres for administration, and the almost total absence of political education or attempts to explain administrative decisions in a way that would win the psychological acceptance of the people affected by them."[31]

  Some of the ironies and contradictions of Khmer Rouge ideology should be stressed. Despite their idealization of the peasants, no senior Khmer Rouge leader was of peasant origin. Virtually all were city-bred intellectuals. Pol Pot came from the countryside, but from a prosperous family with ties to the Royal Court in Phnom Penh. As noted above, the core group of leaders belonged to the small, privileged intellectual class able to study overseas on government scholarships. These racist chauvinists, opposed to any foreign "interference" including assistance, were by background among the most "cosmopolitan" Cambodians in history. The genocide they inflicted on intellectuals and urban populations in general, as well as on hundreds of thousands of peasants, was thus profoundly hypocritical as well as indelibly brutal.

A POLICY OF "URBICIDE," 1975

Throughout world history, human civilization has meant urbanization (the Latin *civitas* is the etymological root of both "city" and "civilization"). Accordingly, forces that aim to undermine a civilization or destroy a human group often attack the urban foundations of group identity. "Deliberate attempts at the annihilation of cities as mixed physical, social, and cultural spaces"[32] constitute *urbicide*.[33] The term was originally coined in the Serbo-Croatian language, by Bosnian architects, to describe the Serb assault on Sarajevo and the Croat attack on Mostar during the Balkan wars of the 1990s, but there are numerous historical precedents. A classical example, one of many, is the Roman siege and obliteration of Carthage (see Chapter 1). Significantly, this was preceded by an ultimatum that the Carthaginians abandon their city for the countryside. When the ultimatum failed to produce the desired results, the Romans made plain their opposition to Carthage *as a city*. They razed it to rubble, and consigned the surviving population to dispersal as slaves across the known world.

Apart from the Balkans case, contemporary examples of urbicide include the Nazi assaults on Leningrad and Stalingrad during the Second World War; the Syrian assault on the rebellious city of Hama in 1982; and the Russian obliteration of Grozny in Chechnya (1994–95). There are few more vivid instances, however, than the policy imposed by the Khmer Rouge on Phnom Penh and other cities in March 1975. "For most of the people in Cambodia's towns what happened during those few days literally overturned their lives."[34]

Within hours of arriving in the capital, the Khmer Rouge was rounding up its two million residents for deportation to the countryside. Bedraggled caravans of deportees headed back to their old life (in the case of refugees from rural zones) or to a new one of repression and privation (for the urbanites). Similar scenes occurred in other population centers nationwide. Without damage to a single building, whole cities were destroyed.

To residents, the Khmer Rouge justified the deportations on the grounds that the Americans were planning an aerial attack on Cambodian cities. (Given recent history, this was not an inconceivable prospect.) To an international audience – on the rare occasions when KR leaders bothered to provide rationales – the urbicide was depicted as a humanitarian act. With the end of the US aid that had fed swollen city populations, albeit inadequately, "the population had to go where the food was," in the words of Ieng Sary.[35] But this excuse faltered in light of the KR's obstinate emphasis on self-sufficiency. Most revealingly, foreign donations of food and other aid went unsolicited, and were rejected when offered.

Instead, as Frank Chalk and Kurt Jonassohn have contended, the reason for the evacuations was found in Khmer Rouge ideology: *"the deportations were nothing less than an attack on the very idea of a city."*[36] The urban environment was associated with corruption, exploitation, and Western decadence. These ran counter to the revolutionary cadre's purity, self-discipline, and respect for Cambodian tradition. One might also speculate that the personal experience of the Khmer Rouge leaders was mirrored in the deportations. The few urban communists had been banned, persecuted, and killed under Sihanouk. In the end, the leaders were forced to flee to remote rural areas. Why should not the urban population, "unproductive" and politically suspect as it was, be forced to do the same in 1975?

After the urbicide, and for the remainder of the DK period, Phnom Penh and other cities remained ghost towns. They were inhabited by only a skeleton crew of KR leaders, cadres, and support staff. The countryside thus served as the backdrop for the Khmer Rouge assault on Cambodia's culture and people.

"BASE PEOPLE" VS. "NEW PEOPLE"

The peasantry, the base of Khmer Rouge support, were depicted as "base" people (*neak moultanh*). Deported city-folk were "new" people (*neak thmey*), late arrivals to the revolution. In a sense, though, all of Cambodia was new and revolutionary in the Khmer Rouge conception. The year 1975 was declared "Year Zero" – a term that evokes the nihilistic core of KR policies.

The reception that awaited new people varied significantly, in ways that decisively affected their chances of survival. Some reports attest to a reasonably friendly welcome from peasants. In other cases, the peasants – who had suffered through the savage US bombing campaign and the violence and upheaval of civil war – felt the newcomers had received a just comeuppance. This was bolstered by the preferential treatment the base people received from most KR authorities. Srey Pich Chnay, a Cambodian former urbanite, described his experiences to Ben Kiernan and Chanthou Boua in 1979:

> The Khmer Rouge treated the peasants as a separate group, distributing more food to them than to the city people, and assigning them easier tasks (usually around the village), whereas the city people almost always worked in the fields. Sometimes the peasants, as well as the Khmer Rouge themselves, would say to the newcomers, "You used to be happy and prosperous. Now it's our turn."[37]

Loung Ung's memoir conveys the tension of this confrontation between different worlds, and the experience, unfamiliar to a privileged urbanite, of finding herself suddenly despised:

> The new people are considered the lowest in the village structure. They have no freedom of speech, and must obey the other classes. The new people . . . cannot farm like the rural people. They are suspected of having no allegiance to the Angkar [i.e., the KR leadership] and must be kept under an ever-watchful eye for signs of rebellion. They have led corrupt lives and must be trained to be productive workers. To instill a sense of loyalty . . . and break what the Khmer Rouge views as an inadequate urban work ethic, the new people are given the hardest work and the longest hours.[38]

There is a flavor here of *subaltern genocide*, a "genocide by the oppressed" against those seen as oppressors (see Chapter 1). Michael Vickery has argued that the DK period was characterized *above all* by the revolutionary terror of the peasantry against urbanites and the intellectual/professional classes: "It is certainly safe to assume that [KR leaders] did not foresee, let alone plan, the unsavory developments of 1975–79. *They were petty-bourgeois radicals overcome by peasant romanticism.*"[39]

Elizabeth Becker likewise suggests that peasants "formed the visceral basis of the revolution and the totalitarianism it produced."[40] However, there are difficulties with this framing. One is that, as Kiernan has pointed out, Vickery's informants were predominantly *non*-peasants, poorly placed to describe the dynamics of a peasant revolution. Another is that, as we have seen, power was centralized in a leadership that was overwhelmingly urban and intellectual. Even at the regional and local level, where KR cadres with a peasant background were more likely to hold sway, there is little evidence that their policies *responded* to a groundswell of peasant resentment. Rather, they reflected instructions and frameworks supplied by the center. "By 1977," writes Kiernan, "the DK system was so tightly organized and controlled that little spontaneous peasant activity was possible."[41]

CAMBODIA'S HOLOCAUST, 1975–79

> Our brothers and sisters of all categories, including workers, peasants, soldiers, and revolutionary cadres have worked around the clock with soaring enthusiasm, paying no attention to the time or to their fatigue; they have worked in a cheerful atmosphere of revolutionary optimism.
>
> Radio Phnom Penh broadcast under the KR

> There were no laws. If they wanted us to walk, we walked; to sit, we sat; to eat, we ate. And still they killed us. It was just that if they wanted to kill us, they would take us off and kill us.
>
> Cham villager interviewed by Ben Kiernan

In Cambodia between 1975 and 1978, the KR's genocidal ideology found full expression. The result was one of the worst genocides, relative to population, in recorded history. In less than four years, mostly in the final two, mass death descended on the Cambodian population. In substantial part, this was the result of direct KR murders of anyone perceived as an enemy. Internal purges reached a crescendo in 1977–78, claiming hundreds of thousands of lives. Even more significant were the privation, disease, and ultimately famine that rent rural Cambodia. This swelled the death-toll to an estimated 1.7 to 1.9 million, out of a population estimated at just under eight million in April 1975. Between 21 and 24 percent of the entire Cambodian population died in the short period under discussion.[42]

Most scholars, however, accept that "complex regional and temporal variations" were evident under the KR.[43] Temporally, life in many regions appears to have been spartan but tolerable for most of the first two years of KR rule. State terror had yet to descend with full force. Thousands of executions certainly accompanied the forced evacuations of Phnom Penh and other cities, and more took place in the countryside, but there are also accounts of moderate and reasonable Khmer Rouge cadres.

Then things changed. "Most survivors of DK agree that living conditions (that is, rations, working hours, disruptions to family life, and the use of terror) deteriorated sharply in 1977." David Chandler points to three reasons for the shift: "the regime's insistence on meeting impossible agricultural goals at a breakneck pace"; growing leadership paranoia about "plots"; and, further fueling that paranoia, the mounting conflict with Vietnam.[44] The most exterminatory period was probably the final one: in 1978, prior to Vietnam's successful invasion in December. The repression visited upon the Eastern Zone over the preceding months had turned it into a graveyard, with up to a quarter of a million people killed.[45]

The extent of regional variation in Democratic Kampuchea is one of the most hotly debated aspects of the KR regime. Michael Vickery has argued that "almost no two regions were alike with respect to conditions of life":

> The Southwestern and Eastern Zones, the most important centers of pre-1970 communist activity, were the best organized and most consistently administered, with the East, until its destruction in 1978, also providing the more favorable conditions of life, in particular for "new" people. In contrast, the West, the Northwest, except for [the region of] Damban 3, and most of the North-Center, were considered "bad" areas, where food was often short, cadres arbitrary and murderous, and policy rationales entirely beyond the ken of the general populace.[46]

Other scholars, however, emphasize the "unchanging character" and "highly centralized control" that marked KR rule.[47] Central direction was certainly evident in the establishment and operation of three key genocidal institutions: the forced-labor system, the mass executions, and the internal purge.

BOX 7.1 ONE GIRL'S STORY: LOUNG UNG

"We are very modern – our bathroom is equipped with amenities such as a flushing toilet, an iron bathtub, and running water. I know we are middle-class because of our apartment and the possessions we have." So wrote Loung Ung at the outset of her memoir, *First They Killed My Father: A Daughter of Cambodia Remembers*.[48]

Loung indeed belonged to a privileged minority. She was a Chinese Cambodian whose father, Ung, was a fairly successful businessman. As for his rank of major in the Cambodian army, he said it was forced on him by the Lon Nol dictatorship. Nonetheless, it branded him as an "imperialist stooge" in the eyes of the communist revolutionaries in the countryside.

For some years, the family lived in comfortable isolation in the capital, Phnom Penh. Loung attended a private school, and studied French and Chinese as well as Khmer. But apocalyptic changes were looming.

Loung was not quite 5 years old in April 1975 when strange men in black pajamas paraded menacingly through the streets of Phnom Penh. They were the Khmer Rouge guerrillas, who had crushed Lon Nol's army and seized power. Within hours, along with two million other residents of refugee-swollen Phnom Penh, Loung and her family were forcibly deported to the Cambodian countryside. It was "Year Zero," and one of the most far-reaching revolutions of the twentieth century was underway.

After days of exhausting walking, the family arrived at the village of Krang Truop, located in the Western Zone of the newly declared country of Democratic

Kampuchea. The transition from city to countryside shocked Loung's childish sensibilities. "Here, instead of concrete city buildings and houses, people live in huts made out of straw that squat on four stilts above elephant grass in the middle of rice paddies. . . . 'The village is so poor,' I say to Pa."

"*So are we*," cautioned her father. "From now on we are as poor as all these people here." If anyone were to discover his affiliation with the former government, it might mean death for all of them. Loung learned: "Not only am I never to talk to anyone about our former lives, but I'm never to trust anyone either."

When dangerously familiar faces appeared in the village a few months after the revolution, the family fled to a new location. Food supplies, adequate in the first months, began to dry up, and there was no market – or money – to buy more. "To survive, my older siblings shake the trees at night, hoping to find June bugs. The younger kids, because we are closer to the ground, catch frogs and grasshoppers for food."

The family stayed on the move, hoping to keep a step ahead of the Khmer Rouge's security apparatus. Its murderous ways were already becoming widely known through stories related in hushed voices late at night – the only time that people could gather, after exhausting days of work in the paddies and forests. "We live and are treated like slaves," Loung related. "Hunger, always there is hunger." Religious worship was banned. The new religion was the Khmer Rouge's genocidal blend of Khmer racism, totalitarianism, and peasant communism.

The family alighted in the Northwestern Zone, probably the harshest in the entire country. There, Loung's sister died of food poisoning. Soon after, her father was led away by Khmer Rouge soldiers, never to return. "I cannot stop thinking of Pa and whether or not he died with dignity. . . . Some prisoners are not dead when they are buried."

With the family decimated, the true reign of terror began. "Entire families disappear overnight. . . . We all pretend not to notice their disappearance." Combined with the mass murder of suspected traitors and "enemies of the people," there was the relentless work, the constantly gnawing hunger. Deliverance came only with the Vietnamese invasion that expelled the Khmer Rouge from power. Loung made her way first to Vietnam, then to a refugee camp in Thailand. In 1980, she began a new life in the United States.

- ***Forced labor*** imposed a work regime that was unprecedented in modern Cambodia. Both base people and new people arose before dawn and were allowed to rest only after dark.[49] Food was distributed exclusively in communal kitchens, and after the 1975–76 interlude there was almost never enough. What good harvests occurred were confiscated in large part by KR cadres. The population could not buy extra supplies: money and markets were outlawed. They could not supplement rations with produce from their own plots, since all private property was banned. They could not engage – legally, at least – in traditional peasant foraging for alternative food sources. Any attempt to do so was seen as distracting from work, and was severely punished. They could not even draw upon networks of family solidarity and sharing. Although the KR never banned the family per se, they invigilated and eroded it by various means.[50]

Those who fell sick from overwork and malnutrition, or from the malaria that spread across Cambodia when the KR decided to refuse imports of pesticide, had little hope of treatment. Medicine was scarce, and usually reserved for the KR faithful. In addition, former urban residents from the Southwestern Zone, one of six main administrative zones in the DK, were again relocated *en masse* to the Northwestern Zone. Some 800,000 people were dumped in the northwest with desperately inadequate provisions. Perhaps 200,000 died of starvation, or in the mass killings that descended in 1978, when imported cadres from the Southwestern Zone imposed a new round of purges (described below).

- ***Mass executions.*** These were generally conducted against "class enemies," on the one hand, and ethnic minorities on the other. Suspect from the start, "new people" were the most likely Khmer victims of such atrocities. Frequently, entire families would be targeted. "The Khmer Rouge actually had a saying . . . which encouraged such slaughter: 'To dig up grass, one must also dig up the roots' (*chik smav trauv chik teang reus*). . . . This phrase meant that cadres 'were supposed to "dig up" the entire family of an enemy – husband, wife, kids, sometimes from the grandparents down – so that none remained . . . to kill off the entire line at once so that none of them would be left to seek revenge later, in turn.'"[51] A witness to one mass execution, Bunhaeng Ung, provided a ghastly account:

> Loudspeakers blared revolutionary songs and music at full volume. A young girl was seized and raped. Others were led to the pits where they were slaughtered like animals by striking the backs of their skulls with hoes or lengths of bamboo. Young children and babies were held by the legs, their heads smashed against palm trees and their broken bodies flung beside their dying mothers in the death pits. Some children were thrown in the air and bayoneted while music drowned their screams. . . . At the place of execution nothing was hidden. The bodies lay in open pits, rotting under the sun and monsoon rains.[52]

These were the "killing fields" made infamous by the 1985 film of the same name.[53] How many died in such executions is uncertain, but it was in the hundreds of thousands.

- ***Violent internal purges*** became a feature of KR insurgent politics well before the revolutionary victory, but after Democratic Kampuchea was established, the paranoia of the KR leaders increased, and their zeal for purges along with it. Pol Pot declared before a party audience in 1976 that "a sickness [exists] inside the party": "As our socialist revolution advances . . . seeping more strongly into every corner of the party, the army and among the people, we can locate the ugly microbes."[54] The language was strikingly similar to that employed by Stalin's henchmen against "enemies of the people" in the 1930s.

During the DK period, two major regional purges occurred. Both were carried out by Ta Mok, nicknamed "The Butcher" for his efforts. The first, as noted above, occurred in 1977–78 in the Northwestern Zone. The second, more of a "conventional military suppression campaign,"[55] was launched in May 1978 against the sensitive Eastern Zone bordering Vietnam. The east, "the heartland of Khmer communism," was the best-administered zone in the country; but the Phnom Penh authorities viewed its residents and cadres as "Khmer bodies with Vietnamese minds."[56] The campaign pushed the Eastern Zone into open rebellion against the center, and finally into the arms of Vietnam. Eastern Zone rebels would give a "Cambodian face" to the Vietnamese invasion at the end of the year, and to the the People's Republic of Kampuchea which it established.

Tens of thousands of victims of these and other purges passed through KR centers designed for interrogation, torture, and execution. The most notorious was Tuol Sleng in the capital, codenamed "S-21," where an estimated 14,000 prisoners were incarcerated during the KR's reign. Only *ten* are known to have survived.[57] Now a Museum of Genocide in Phnom Penh, it was one of many such centers across Democratic Kampuchea (see Figure 7.1).

As in Mao's China and Stalin's USSR, the purges fed on themselves, and eventually undermined the capacity of the revolution to resist its enemies. Just as Stalin's purges of the Soviet military and bureaucracy left the USSR exposed to Nazi invasion, the Khmer Rouge killing sprees paved the way for Vietnam's rapid conquest of Cambodia in 1978.

GENOCIDE AGAINST BUDDHISTS AND ETHNIC MINORITIES

Early commentaries on Khmer Rouge atrocities emphasized the targeting of class and political enemies. Subsequent scholarship, especially by Ben Kiernan, has revealed the extent to which the KR also engaged in genocidal targeting of religious groups and ethnic minorities.

Cambodian Buddhism suffered immensely under the genocide: "the destruction was nearly complete, with more devastating consequences for Cambodia than the Chinese attack on Buddhism had had for Tibet" (Box 3a).[58] Religious institutions were emptied, and often obliterated. Monks were sent to the countryside or executed. "Of the sixty thousand Buddhist monks only three thousand were found alive after the Khmer Rouge reign; the rest had either been massacred or succumbed to hard labor, disease, or torture."[59]

A patchwork of ethnic minorities, together constituting about 15 percent of the population, was exposed to atrocities and extermination. Local Vietnamese were targeted most virulently. Kiernan offers the stunning estimate that *fully 100 percent of ethnic Vietnamese perished under the Khmer Rouge.*[60] The Muslim Chams were despised for their religion as well as their ethnicity. "Their religion was banned, their schools closed, their leaders massacred, their villages razed and dispersed."[61] Over one-third of the 250,000 Chams alive in April 1975 perished under DK.[62]

Figure 7.1 Some of the haunting photos of victims of "S-21," the Tuol Sleng torture and execution center in Phnom Penh, today a Museum of Genocide. Only ten inmates out of 14,000 survived their incarceration at Tuol Sleng. The Khmer Rouge carefully registered and photographed the prisoners; this provides valuable evidence of the Cambodian genocide.

Source: Courtesy Ben Kiernan.

As for Cambodia's Chinese population, it was concentrated in the cities, and it is sometimes hard to distinguish repressive action based on racial hatred from repression against the urbanite "new people." Regardless, in DK this group "suffered the worst disaster ever to befall any ethnic Chinese community in Southeast Asia."[63] Only half the Chinese population of 430,000 at the outset of Khmer Rouge rule survived to see its end.

The grim tale of minority suffering under the Khmer Rouge does not end there. "The Thai minority of 20,000 was reportedly reduced to about 8,000. Only 800 families survived of the 1,800 families of the Lao ethnic minority. Of the 2,000 members of the Kola minority, 'no trace . . . has been found.'"[64]

AFTERMATH: POLITICS AND THE QUEST FOR JUSTICE

On December 25, 1978, 150,000 Vietnamese soldiers, accompanied by 15,000 Cambodian rebels and air support, crossed the border of Democratic Kampuchea and seized Phnom Penh in two weeks. The Khmer Rouge leadership fled to sanctuaries in western Cambodia and across the border in Thailand.[65] The KR would use these for the ensuing decade-and-a-half as it fought to return to power through a tripartite coalition of forces opposed to Vietnamese occupation. (Prince Sihanouk, who had spent most of the DK years under *de facto* house arrest in Phnom Penh, served as figurehead for the coalition from 1982.) Meanwhile, former KR leaders, the rebels from the Eastern Zone, were appointed as Vietnamese surrogates to run the new People's Republic of Kampuchea (PRK). While Heng Samrin was appointed president, real power eventually fell into the hands of his former subordinate in the Eastern Zone, Hun Sen.

Throughout the 1980s, in one of the twentieth century's "more depressing episodes of diplomacy,"[66] the Western world moved from branding the Khmer Rouge as communist monsters to embracing them as Cambodia's legitimate representatives. The US led a push to grant Cambodia's General Assembly seat to the anti-Vietnamese coalition dominated by the Khmer Rouge.

Why this Orwellian flip-flop? US hostility to Vietnam was still pronounced after the US defeat of 1975. An enemy of Vietnam was America's friend, regardless of its sanguinary past. Thus one witnessed the anomalous sight, throughout the 1980s, of genocidal communists receiving some of their firmest backing from Washington, DC. China was also an important player – as it had been throughout the Khmer Rouge years in power, despite KR pledges to make Cambodia "self-sufficient."

In October 1991, with the Cold War at an end, the Comprehensive Political Settlement of the Cambodian Conflict was signed in Paris. Vietnamese forces had left the country in 1989. The United Nations stepped in to supervise the peace process. It launched UNTAC, the UN Transitional Authority in Cambodia, "the single most ambitious field operation in [UN] history."[67] However, the path to national elections in 1993 was fraught with difficulties. The Khmer Rouge boycotted the vote, and stepped up military attacks.

Ultimately, in May 1993, relatively peaceful elections were held, but they did not produce the results Hun Sen desired. Voters gave a plurality of votes to Prince Ranariddh, son of Norodom Sihanouk. Hun Sen, the "great survivor of Cambodian politics,"[68] then used his control over Cambodia's key institutions to strong-arm Ranariddh into accepting a coalition government. By 1997, Hun Sen had tired of the arrangement. He launched what was in essence a *coup d'état*, re-establishing himself as the unquestioned supreme authority. The absolutist strain in Cambodian politics was proving difficult to shake, especially against a backdrop of economic and social breakdown.

Amidst all this, the campaign to bring surviving Khmer Rouge leaders to justice proceeded, albeit haltingly.[69] The project was marginalized throughout the 1980s by US and communist Chinese opposition. The 1998 death of Pol Pot in his jungle exile, apparently from natural causes, further blunted the impetus, as did messy wrangling between the United Nations and the Cambodian government over the nature and composition of any tribunal. In June 2003, however, the two parties came to an agreement. The Cambodian tribunal was to include "international jurists, lawyers and judges [who] will occupy key roles as the co-prosecutor, co-investigating judge and two out of five trial court judges, and must be a party to conviction or exoneration of any accused."[70] This "mixed tribunal" adds an interesting variant to the quest for legal justice in cases of genocide (see Chapter 15).

FURTHER STUDY

Elizabeth Becker, *When the War Was Over: Cambodia and the Khmer Rouge Revolution*. New York: Public Affairs, 1998. The most accessible overview of the Khmer Rouge years.

David P. Chandler, *The Tragedy of Cambodian History: Politics, War and Revolution since 1945*. New Haven, CT: Yale University Press, 1991. Fine short history.

Tom Fawthrop and Helen Jarvis, *Getting Away with Genocide? Cambodia's Long Struggle against the Khmer Rouge*. London: Pluto Press, 2004. Justice in post-genocide Cambodia.

Evan R. Gottesman, *Cambodia after the Khmer Rouge: Inside the Politics of Nation Building*. New Haven, CT: Yale University Press, 2003. Political change and continuity after the genocide.

Alexander Laban Hinton, *Why Did They Kill? Cambodia in the Shadow of Genocide*. Berkeley, CA: University of California Press, 2005. Original and insightful anthropological analysis, also drawing on social and existential psychology.

Ben Kiernan, *The Pol Pot Regime: Race, Power and Genocide in Cambodia under the Khmer Rouge*. New Haven, CT: Yale University Press, 1996. Detailed study of the Khmer Rouge years; a sequel to *How Pol Pot Came to Power*.

Haing Ngor with Roger Warner, *A Cambodian Odyssey*. New York: Macmillan, 1987. Lengthy memoir by the Cambodian doctor and genocide survivor who won an Oscar for playing Dith Pran in *The Killing Fields*.

William Shawcross, *Sideshow: Kissinger, Nixon and the Destruction of Cambodia* (rev. edn). New York: Cooper Square Press, 2002. The US air war against Cambodia and its role in bringing the Khmer Rouge to power.

Loung Ung, *First They Killed My Father: A Daughter of Cambodia Remembers*. New York: HarperCollins, 2000. Memoir of a Chinese-Cambodian girl who lived through the genocide, sampled in this chapter.

Michael Vickery, *Cambodia 1975–1982*. Boston, MA: South End Press, 1984. Revisionist study, arguing for an emphasis on local/regional dynamics.

NOTES

1 Michael Vickery, *Cambodia 1975–1982* (Boston, MA: South End Press, 1984), p. 7.

2 Elizabeth Becker, *When the War Was Over: Cambodia and the Khmer Rouge Revolution* (New York: Public Affairs, 1998), p. xv. See also Alexander Laban Hinton's discussion of a "Cambodian model of disproportionate revenge" in "A Head for an Eye: Revenge in the Cambodian Genocide," in Hinton, ed., *Genocide: An Anthropological Reader* (Malden, MA: Blackwell, 2002); and Ervin Staub, *The Roots of Evil: The Origins of Genocide and Other Group Violence* (Cambridge: Cambridge University Press, 1989), pp. 200–1.

3 David W. Roberts, *Political Transition in Cambodia, 1991–1999: Power, Elitism and Democracy* (New York: St. Martin's Press, 2001), p. 205.

4 Vickery, *Cambodia 1975–1982*, p. 9.

5 Becker, *When the War Was Over*, p. 37.
6 "Khmer Rouge" (Red Khmers) is actually a label applied derisively to the CPK by Cambodian President Norodom Sihanouk.
7 Two other members of the core KR group would hold important regional posts under DK. These were Mok, who would serve as party secretary in the DK's Southwest Zone, and carry out a vicious purge of the Northwest Zone in 1977; and Ke Pauk, a key military leader who directed the Kampuchean army to genocidal ends. A more independent member of the Paris group, Hou Youn, was purged and killed in 1975, at the dawn of the DK era, apparently for his opposition to the forced evacuation of Phnom Penh. Ke Pauk died of natural causes in February 2002. The seminal study of the origins of Cambodian communism is Ben Kiernan, *How Pol Pot Came to Power: Colonialism, Nationalism, and Communism in Cambodia, 1930–1975* (2nd edn) (New Haven, CT: Yale University Press, 2004).
8 Frank Chalk and Kurt Jonassohn, *The History and Sociology of Genocide* (New Haven, CT: Yale University Press, 1990), p. 400.
9 The Japanese, who invaded and occupied Phnom Penh in 1941, left day-to-day administration to the local French authority. This was run by the French puppet government established at Vichy in 1940, following France's defeat by Nazi Germany.
10 Khieu Thirith quoted in Becker, *When the War Was Over*, p. 75.
11 Becker, *When the War Was Over*, p. 87.
12 David P. Chandler, *The Tragedy of Cambodian History: Politics, War, and Revolution since 1945* (New Haven, CT: Yale University Press, 1991), p. 108.
13 Chandler, *The Tragedy of Cambodian History*, p. 205.
14 The coup, invasion, and subsequent bombing campaign are memorably described in William Shawcross, *Sideshow: Kissinger, Nixon, and the Destruction of Cambodia* (rev. edn) (New York: Cooper Square Press, 2002).
15 Tom Fawthrop and Helen Jarvis, *Getting Away with Genocide? Elusive Justice and the Khmer Rouge Tribunal* (London: Pluto Press, 2004), p. 245. Estimates range from 50–150,000 (Ben Kiernan in *The Pol Pot Regime: Race, Power and Genocide in Cambodia under the Khmer Rouge* (New Haven, CT: Yale University Press, 1996)) to 600,000 or more (Christopher Hitchens in *The Trial of Henry Kissinger*).
16 Samantha Power, *"A Problem from Hell": America and the Age of Genocide* (New York: Basic Books, 2002), p. 94.
17 Becker, *When the War Was Over*, p. 17.
18 In the view of Leo Kuper, "the [Khmer Rouge] government of Kampuchea had every justification for its indictment of American imperialists. . . . They had left the new rulers with a most desperate food crisis and the overwhelming task of immediately restoring the cultivation of rice in a war-shattered country. They bear a heavy responsibility for many of the subsequent developments under the revolutionary government." Leo S. Kuper, *Genocide: Its Political Use in the Twentieth Century* (Harmondsworth: Penguin, 1981), p. 159.
19 Vickery, *Cambodia 1975–1982*, p. 15. Kiernan cites "one peasant youth [who] recalled B-52s bombing his village three to six times per day for three months. Over one thousand people were killed, nearly a third of the population. Afterwards, 'there were few people left . . . and it was quiet.'" Ben Kiernan, *The Pol Pot Regime: Race, Power and Genocide in Cambodia under the Khmer Rouge.* (New Haven, CT: Yale University Press, 1998), p. 23.
20 Chhit Do quoted in Power, *"A Problem from Hell,"* pp. 94–95.
21 Ignatieff quoted in *Crimes against Humanity*, documentary produced by the Imperial War Museum, London, December 2002 (from the official transcript supplied by the IWM).
22 Becker, *When the War Was Over*, p. 304. According to Pol Pot, speaking in July 1975: "In the whole world, since the advent of the revolutionary war and since the birth of US imperialism, no country, no people, and no army has been able to drive the imperialists out to the last man and score total victory over them [as we have]." This was "a precious model for the world's people." Quoted in Kiernan, *The Pol Pot Regime*, p. 94.

23 Chandler, *The Tragedy of Cambodian History*, p. 175.
24 On the fate of the tribal peoples, see Kiernan, *The Pol Pot Regime*, pp. 302–9.
25 Cited in Chalk and Jonassohn, *The History and Sociology of Genocide*, p. 405.
26 Cited in Eric D. Weitz, *A Century of Genocide: Utopias of Race and Nation* (Princeton, NJ: Princeton University Press, 2003), p. 152.
27 "Officials produce statistics; statistics produce officials," as the Chinese saying has it (cited in "No Sign of a Landing," *The Economist*, January 29, 2005). On the Great Leap Forward and the famine of 1959–61, see Jasper Becker, *Hungry Ghosts: Mao's Secret Famine* (New York: Henry Holt, 1998); for a concise account, see Jean-Louis Margolin, "The Greatest Famine in History (1959–1961)," in William L. Hewitt, ed., *Defining the Horrific: Readings on Genocide and Holocaust in the Twentieth Century* (Upper Saddle River, NJ: Pearson, 2004), pp. 211–18.
28 "The borders were closed, foreign embassies and press agencies expelled, newspapers and television stations shut down, radios confiscated, mail and telephone use suppressed, the speaking of foreign languages punished." Kiernan, *The Pol Pot Regime*, p. 9.
29 Fawthrop and Jarvis, *Getting Away with Genocide?*, p. 94.
30 Becker, *When the War Was Over*, p. 224.
31 Ben Kiernan and Chanthou Boua, *Peasants and Politics in Kampuchea, 1942–1981* (London: Zed Press, 1982), p. 239.
32 The quoted passage is drawn from a posted announcement of "an international and interdisciplinary academic workshop" titled "Urbicide: The Killing of Cities," at the University of Durham, November 24–25, 2005.
33 The first book in English to address the phenomenon of urbicide is Stephen Graham, ed., *Cities, War, and Terrorism: Towards an Urban Geopolitics* (Oxford: Blackwell, 2004). See especially ch. 7, Martin Shaw, "New Wars of the City: Relationships of 'Urbicide' and 'Genocide'" (an earlier version of which is available at http://www.sussex.ac.uk/Users/hafa3/city.htm); and ch. 8, Martin Coward, "Urbicide in Bosnia," also available at http://www.sussex.ac.uk/Users/mpc20/pubs/urbicide.html.
34 Chandler, *The Tragedy of Cambodian History*, p. 250.
35 Quoted in Chalk and Jonassohn, *The History and Sociology of Genocide*, p. 403.
36 Chalk and Jonassohn, *The History and Sociology of Genocide*, p. 404, emphasis added. The functions of association and social communication were also targeted in the urbicide. "Without towns . . . there would be . . . no human agglomeration facilitating private communication between individuals. Nowhere that the exchange of news and ideas could escape tight monitoring that reduced it to a minimum. No venue for a large crowd to assemble." Kiernan, *The Pol Pot Regime*, p. 64.
37 Kiernan and Boua, *Peasants and Politics in Kampuchea*, pp. 345–46. Urban folk, for their part, "often found it impossible to accept that they had become the servants of dark, uneducated people." Chandler, *The Tragedy of Cambodian History*, p. 243.
38 Loung Ung, *First They Killed My Father: A Daughter of Cambodia Remembers* (New York: HarperCollins, 2000), p. 62.
39 Vickery, *Cambodia 1975–1982*, pp. 66, 286–87, emphasis added. Curiously, Vickery echoes these prejudices, describing Cambodian urbanites as "spoiled, pretentious, contentious, status-conscious at worst, or at best simply soft, intriguing, addicted to city comforts and despising peasant life" (p. 26).
40 Becker, *When the War Was Over*, p. 137.
41 Kiernan, *The Pol Pot Regime*, p. 212.
42 The statistics are of course subject to dispute. For calculations, see Ben Kiernan, "The Demography of Genocide in Southeast Asia: The Death Tolls in Cambodia, 1975–79, and East Timor, 1975–80," *Critical Asian Studies*, 35: 4 (2003), pp. 586–87.
43 Chandler, *The Tragedy of Cambodian History*, p. 265.
44 Chandler, *The Tragedy of Cambodian History*, pp. 270–71.
45 Hinton, *Why Did They Kill?*, p. 167.
46 Vickery, *Cambodia 1975–1982*, pp. 68–69, 86.
47 Chandler, *The Tragedy of Cambodian History*, p. 265.

48 Ung, *First They Killed My Father*, p. 7. The other quotes in this section are drawn from pp. 12, 18, 38–39, 47, 53, 66, 81, 105, 121.
49 "1978 was the year of hardest work, night and day. We planted from 4 a.m. to 10 a.m., then ate a meal. At 1 p.m. we started again, and worked until 5 p.m., and then from 7 to 10 p.m. . . . There was not enough food, and foraging was not allowed." Testimony cited in Ben Kiernan, "The Cambodian Genocide – 1975–1979," in Samuel Totten *et al.*, eds, *Century of Genocide: Eyewitness Accounts and Critical Views* (New York: Garland Publishing, 1997), p. 359.
50 These included valuing children over parents (the young were the "blank slates" of the revolution); encouraging children to spy on their elders and report "suspicious activities" to KR cadres; and, in later stages, the outright seizure and sequestering of children to be raised and indoctrinated by party representatives.
51 Hinton, "A Head for an Eye," p. 273.
52 Ung quoted in Alexander Laban Hinton, *Why Did They Kill? Cambodia in the Shadow of Genocide* (Berkeley, CA: University of California Press, 2005), p. 168.
53 The film is an interesting example of popular culture as consciousness-raising (see also Chapter 16). "In a matter of months *The Killing Fields* catapulted Cambodia from Cold War politics to mass culture. Black-pajamaed Khmer Rouge joined the brown-shirted Nazis as recognizable villains of the twentieth century. The term killing fields became part of the American vocabulary." Becker, *When the War Was Over*, p. 459. Haing Ngor, who won an Academy Award for playing Dith Pran, wrote in his memoir that until the movie was released, "relatively few people knew what had happened in Cambodia during the Khmer Rouge years – intellectuals and Asia experts had, maybe, but not the general public. The film put the story of those years in terms that everybody could understand." Haing Ngor with Roger Warner, *A Cambodian Odyssey* (New York: Macmillan, 1987), p. 455. Tragically, Ngor, who had survived four years under the Khmer Rouge, was killed in a street hold-up in Los Angeles.
54 Pol Pot quoted in Kiernan, *The Pol Pot Regime*, p. 336.
55 Kiernan, "The Cambodian Genocide," pp. 338–39.
56 Ben Kiernan, "Genocidal Targeting: Two Groups of Victims in Pol Pot's Cambodia," in P. Timothy Bushnell *et al.*, eds, *State Organized Terror: The Case of Violent Internal Repression* (Boulder, CO: Westview Press, 1991), pp. 209, 212. In an echo of Nazi Germany's labeling of Jews with the Star of David, inhabitants of the Eastern Zone were outfitted with blue scarves (*kromar*) that allowed them to be easily identified and eliminated once deported from the zone (see pp. 213–18).
57 Statistics cited in Fawthrop and Jarvis, *Getting Away with Genocide?*, p. 245. On Tuol Sleng, see David Chandler, *Voices from S-21: Terror and History in Pol Pot's Secret Prison* (Berkeley, CA: University of California Press, 1999).
58 Becker, *When the War Was Over*, p. 254.
59 Sydney Schanberg, "Cambodia," in Hewitt, ed., *Defining the Horrific*, p. 261. Ironically, as Alexander Hinton notes, "the DK regime's glorification of asceticism, detachment, the elimination of attachment and desire, renunciation (of material goods and personal behaviors, sentiments, and attitudes), and purity paralleled prominent Buddhist themes that were geared toward helping a person attain greater mindfulness." Hinton, *Why Did They Kill?*, p. 197.
60 Kiernan, *The Pol Pot Regime*, p. 458.
61 Kiernan, "Genocidal Targeting," p. 218.
62 Kiernan, *The Pol Pot Regime*, p. 461.
63 Kiernan, "The Cambodian Genocide," p. 341.
64 Kiernan, "The Cambodian Genocide," p. 342.
65 The best account of the Vietnam–Cambodia relationship during the Khmer Rouge era, and the Vietnamese invasion of 1978–79, is Nayan Chanda, *Brother Enemy: The War after the War* (New York: Collier, 1986).
66 Eric Hobsbawm, *The Age of Extremes: A History of the World, 1914–1991* (New York: Vintage Books, 1994), p. 451.

67 Mats Berdal and Michael Leifer, "Cambodia," in James Mayall, ed., *The New Interventionism, 1991–1994: United Nations Experience in Cambodia, Former Yugoslavia and Somalia* (Cambridge: Cambridge University Press, 1996), p. 36.
68 Nicholas Wheeler, *Saving Strangers: Humanitarian Intervention in International Society* (Oxford: Oxford University Press, 2000), p. 84.
69 For a fine overview of the twisted course of justice in Cambodia, see "A Case Study: The Atrocities of the Khmer Rouge," Part III in Steven R. Ratner and Jason S. Abrams, *Accountability for Human Rights Atrocities in International Law: Beyond the Nuremberg Legacy* (2nd edn) (Oxford: Oxford University Press, 2001), pp. 267–328.
70 Fawthrop and Jarvis, *Getting Away with Genocide?*, p. 240.

BOX 7A EAST TIMOR

East Timor's tragic road to independence began the same year – 1975 – that the Khmer Rouge took power in Cambodia. For four years thereafter, events in these two Southeast Asian lands moved in grim tandem. Both witnessed genocides as severe, in terms of proportion of population killed, as any since the Jewish Holocaust. The Khmer Rouge regime in Cambodia became a byword for ideological fanaticism and the brutal exercise of power, sparking international condemnation. In contrast, the genocide in East Timor was protested and publicized only by a small group of Timorese exiles, human rights activists, and concerned scholars.[1] Unlike the Cambodian genocide, it continued until 1999, when both cases finally drew the attention of international prosecutors.

In the 1990s, as Indonesian atrocities continued, the Timor solidarity movement grew. The global network it established was the key ingredient in confronting the final blast of Indonesian genocide, in 1999, aiming to overturn a pro-independence referendum result. East Timor thus offers an inspiring example of a genocide ended, in large part, by popular mobilization and protest.

East Timor owes its distinctiveness from the rest of the island of Timor, and the Indonesian archipelago as a whole, to its colonization by the Portuguese in the mid-seventeenth century. The division of the island between the Portuguese and Dutch was formalized in 1915. During the Second World War, the colonial regime gave way to Japanese occupation. This spawned the first large-scale resistance movement in East Timor, assisted by Australian troops. When Australia abandoned the territory, the Timorese were left at the mercy of the Japanese, who slaughtered an estimated 60,000 of them – 13 percent of the entire population. (Notably, some of the most powerful calls in the 1975–99 period for solidarity with East Timor came from Australian Second World War veterans, who recalled the solidarity the Timorese had shown them.)

After the war, the Dutch East Indies became the independent Republic of Indonesia. Portugal, meanwhile, re-established control over East Timor. But in April 1974, a left-wing military coup against the fascist government in Lisbon

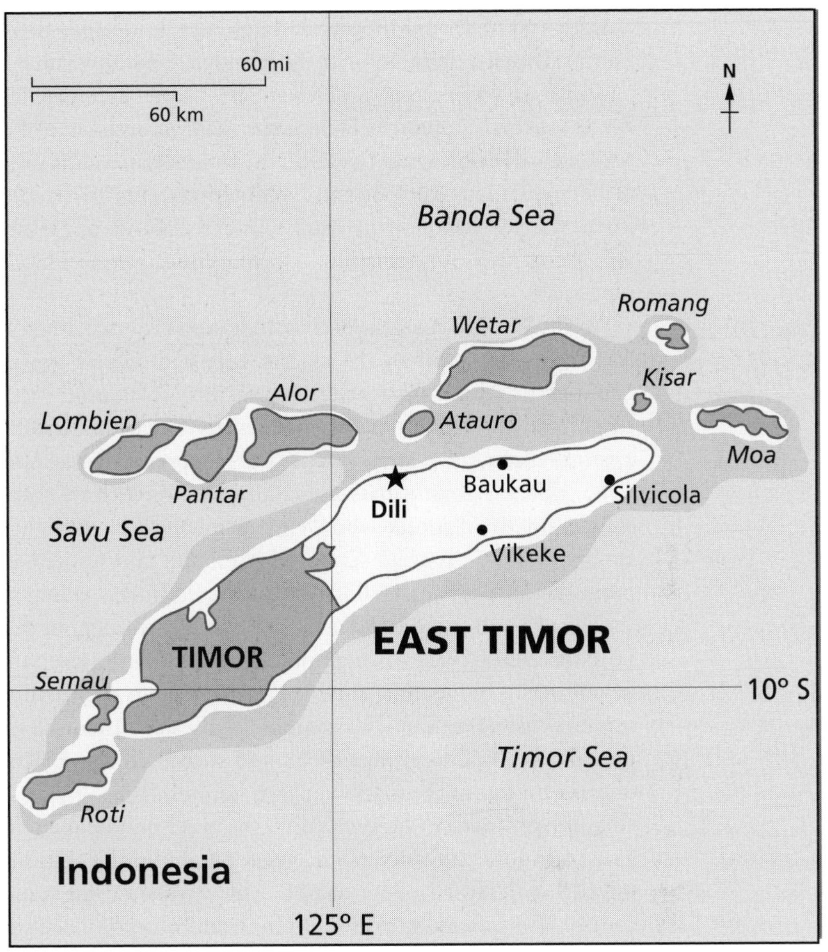

Map 7a.1 East Timor

Source: Map provided by WorldAtlas.com

established a democratic government, leading Portugal rapidly to retreat from its overseas empire (including Angola and Mozambique). Indigenous political parties sprang up in East Timor, and elections for a National Constituent Assembly were set for 1976, with full independence anticipated three years later.

By 1975, the leading political force in the territory was Fretilin (the Revolutionary Front of Independent East Timor), which had established strong grass-roots support throughout the countryside. In 1975, Fretilin won village-level elections over its main competitor, the Timorese Democratic Union (UDT). Disaffected UDT members, responding to Indonesian machinations, refused to accept the result. Their abortive coup was quickly crushed, with a death-toll of several thousand. The UDT leadership fled to Indonesia, and Fretilin issued a declaration of independence on November 28, 1975.

Just over a week later, on December 7 – after receiving the green light from the US – the Indonesians launched a massive invasion of East Timor by land, sea, and air. In the largest city, Dili, the Indonesian military murdered thousands of Timorese in mass executions. Fretilin forces were driven into the mountainous interior. Over the following years, tens of thousands of Timorese civilians would join them, preferring isolation in dismal conditions to Indonesian violence and repression.

With Dili and secondary towns under their control, Indonesian forces fanned out across the territory. Massacres occurred almost everywhere they went. Families of suspected Fretilin supporters were annihilated along with the suspects themselves. In many cases, entire village populations were targeted for extermination. This strategy reached its apogee in the Aitana region in July 1981, where "a ghastly massacre . . . murdered everyone, from tiny babies to the elderly, unarmed people who were not involved in the fighting but were there simply because they had stayed with Fretilin and wanted to live freely in the mountains."[2] Perhaps 10,000 Timorese died in this killing spree alone.

The atrocities continued on a smaller scale throughout the 1980s. At Malim Luro in August 1983, for example, "after plundering the population of all their belongings, [Indonesian troops] firmly tied up men, women and children, numbering more than sixty people. They made them lie on the ground and then drove a bulldozer over them, and then used it to place a few centimetres of earth on top of the totally crushed corpses."[3]

Survivors of the various rampages were imprisoned under the vigilant gaze of Indonesian soldiers and local paramilitaries. Disease, starvation, and forced labor caused many deaths. The territories not under full Indonesian control also suffered genocide. Indonesian forces launched repeated scorched-earth sorties; rained bombs on civilian populations; and imposed a strict blockade on Fretilin-held areas that led, as designed, to starvation. According to Timor specialist John Taylor, tens of thousands of Timorese died as a result of this war of "encirclements, bombing, uprooting of the population, malnutrition and generalized brutalities."[4] In total, an estimated 170,000 Timorese – "24 to 26 percent of East Timor's 1975 population" – died between 1975 and 1999.[5]

With the international community's acceptance of Indonesia's "new order,"[6] it seemed unlikely that the independence movement could survive, let alone emerge victorious. In the 1990s, however, Indonesia's hold weakened. On November 12, 1991, some 270 civilians were slaughtered by Indonesian troops in Dili's Santa Cruz cemetery. Witnessed by several foreign observers, who managed to escape with film footage, the Dili Massacre provoked the first substantial international outcry against genocide in East Timor. The territory's profile was raised further in 1996, when the Nobel Peace Prize was awarded to the leader of the East Timor Catholic Church, Bishop Belo, and Fretilin's leader in exile, José Ramos Horta. Meanwhile, taking advantage of new Internet technologies, the international Timorese solidarity movement – now led by the East Timor Action Network (ETAN) – organized demonstrations and lobbied governments to condemn Indonesian repression.

A dramatic transformation within Indonesia catalyzed the final drive for independence. In 1998, with Indonesia suffering an economic crisis, General Suharto, the long-time military dictator, resigned and handed power to his vice-president, B.J. Habibie. Habibie stunned the world by announcing, in January 1999, that Indonesia was willing to "let East Timor go" if its people chose independence in a referendum. The United Nations, with Portugal taking the lead, rapidly announced a plebiscite, eventually scheduled for August 30.

Behind the scenes, the Indonesian military – which had amassed huge economic holdings in East Timor over the previous twenty-five years – prepared to sabotage the independence process. It relied on locally raised paramilitary forces (the so-called *ninjas*), overseen by the elite Kopassus army unit, to terrorize the population into voting to stay with Indonesia. In the prelude to the plebiscite, hundreds of Timorese, especially activist youth, were murdered by death squads or in local-level massacres.[7] Despite these atrocities, the UN fatefully chose to leave "security" for the referendum in the hands of the Indonesian army.

The stage was thus set for the violence and destruction unleashed at the end of August 1999. Voting peacefully and in overwhelming numbers, 78.5 percent of Timorese opted for independence. The Indonesian military and its local allies swung immediately into action. As international observers looked on in horror, and the UN hunkered down in its headquarters, militia killed unknown numbers of Timorese. (A regularly cited figure is 1,500, but this may be a substantial undercount.)[8] Indonesian troops and their local militia forces burned swathes of territory and entire city neighborhoods to the ground, in a campaign aimed at "the virtual demolition of the physical basis for survival in the territory."[9]

The UN then decided to evacuate staff from its Dili compound, and leave the terrified Timorese gathered there to their fate. This craven action was only avoided by an unprecedented staff rebellion against the edict.[10] Meanwhile, hundreds of thousands of demonstrators took to the streets in North America, Europe, and Australia, bringing sustained pressure to bear on their governments.[11] With memories of Rwanda and Bosnia (see chapters 8–9) doubtless reverberating in his mind, UN Secretary-General Kofi Annan issued a strongly worded warning to Indonesia. The Clinton administration in the US also announced that it was prepared to suspend the military aid on which the Indonesian armed forces depended. The Australian government, for its part, offered to lead a stabilization force to occupy and patrol the territory. Faced with this concerted opposition, the Indonesian government backed down. Australian forces deployed in Dili on September 20; a week later, Indonesia ceded control to the international contingent.

East Timor became the world's newest nation two years later, in August 2001. The happy ending, however, was undermined by material and human devastation, spiralling unemployment, and social dislocation.[12] Meanwhile, only the most cursory investigation was launched into atrocities during the plebiscite period and its aftermath. By contrast with the hundreds of forensic investigators dispatched to Kosovo after the 1999 war there (Chapter 8), fewer than a dozen were allotted to East Timor, and only for a short period. As a result, no clear picture of the scale of the Indonesian-directed killing has yet emerged. As for military commander General Wiranto and his cohorts, who oversaw "Operation Clean Sweep," punishment proved elusive. Newly democratic Indonesia pledged to administer it, but *The Economist* reported in August 2004 that "of the 16 members of the Indonesian security forces and two East Timorese civilians who were indicted [by Indonesian courts], all the Indonesians have either been acquitted or freed on appeal," while the Timorese received light punishments. Impunity ruled, but the East Timorese government was reluctant to press the matter with "its vast and powerful neighbour."[13] Controversially, it opposed the creation of an international tribunal to prosecute those responsible for the atrocities.

FURTHER STUDY

Peter Carey and G. Carter Bentley, eds, *East Timor at the Crossroads: The Forging of a Nation.* Honolulu, HI: University of Hawaii Press, 1995. Essays on the Timorese independence struggle.

Tim Fischer, *Seven Days in East Timor: Ballots and Bullets.* London: Allen & Unwin, 2000. Eyewitness account of the 1999 independence plebiscite.

Matthew Jardine, *East Timor: Genocide in Paradise.* Berkeley, CA: Odonian Press, 1999. A succinct introduction.

Joseph Nevins, *A Not-so-distant Horror: Mass Violence in East Timor.* Ithaca, NY: Cornell University Press, 2005. A recent and decent work, good on the post-1999 quest for justice.

John G. Taylor, *East Timor: The Price of Freedom.* London: Zed Books, 2000. The best all-round study, with a chronology.

NOTES

1 Among the academic voices were Noam Chomsky and Edward S. Herman. In a classic 1979 study, they compared the outraged news coverage devoted to Cambodia with the near-total media blackout on East Timor. Victims of the communist Khmer Rouge were "worthy victims," they wrote ironically, while the East Timorese – whose tormentor, Indonesia, was a valued Western ally – were deemed "unworthy," and thus consigned to oblivion. Chomsky and Herman, *The American Connection and Third World Fascism,* Vol. 1 of *The Political Economy of Human Rights* (Boston, MA: South End Press, 1979).

2 Source cited in John G. Taylor, *East Timor: The Price of Freedom* (London: Zed Books, 2000), p. 118. See also Taylor's fine chapter, "'Encirclement and Annihilation': The Indonesian Occupation of East Timor," in Robert Gellately and Ben Kiernan, eds, *The Specter of Genocide: Mass Murder in Historical Perspective* (Cambridge: Cambridge University Press, 2003), pp. 163–85.

3 Source cited in Taylor, *East Timor*, p. 103. Together with indiscriminate, "root-and-branch" massacres of this type, a pattern of gendercidal killings of males was also evident, as it would be after the independence referendum in 1999. For a detailed investigation, see Adam Jones/Gendercide Watch, "Case Study: East Timor, 1975–99," http://www.gendercide.org/case_timor.html, from which part of this box text is adapted.

4 Taylor, *East Timor*, p. 151.

5 Ben Kiernan, "The Demography of Genocide in Southeast Asia: The Death Tolls in Cambodia, 1975–79, and East Timor, 1975–80," *Critical Asian Studies*, 35: 4 (2003), p. 594, citing research by Gabriel Defert.

6 According to Joseph Nevins, "Although there were numerous and diverse reasons for the various countries' support for Jakarta, the principal rationale was simple: Indonesia was a populous country with great market potential and a very wealthy resource base and occupied a strategic location." Nevins, *A Not-so-distant Horror: Mass Violence in East Timor* (Ithaca, NY: Cornell University Press, 2005), p. 77.

7 Nevins, *A Not-so-distant Horror*, p. 83.

8 See, e.g., Ellen Nakashima, "For Survivors of E. Timor Massacres, Justice Still Elusive," *Washington Post*, September 16, 2005. For an examination of the physical, eyewitness, and circumstantial evidence pertaining to the Timorese death-toll in 1999, see Jones/Gendercide Watch, "Case Study: East Timor."

9 Noam Chomsky, "East Timor Is Not Yesterday's Story," *ZNet*, October 23, 1999.

10 A heart-stopping depiction of these events, by someone who lived through the tension-racked days in the UN compound, is Geoffrey Robinson, "'If You Leave Us Here, We Will Die,'" ch. 10 in Nicolaus Mills and Kira Brunner, eds, *The New Killing Fields: Massacre and the Politics of Intervention* (New York: Basic Books, 2002), pp. 159–83.

11 The fact that the Timor events followed closely on the war in Kosovo (March–June 1999), which *had* prompted Western intervention, added to the pressure on governments – an interesting case of "norm grafting" (see Chapter 12).

12 "More than five years [after the Indonesian withdrawal] many public facilities still lie in ruins, much of the country's social infrastructure is below pre-September 1999 levels, and unemployment and underemployment are massive as a result of the very low levels of economic development." Nevins, *A Not-so-distant Horror*, p. 206.

13 "Above the Law," *The Economist*, August 14, 2004. Progress has, however, been made by the Serious Crimes Unit within East Timor, established with UN help. "This body has indicted some 375 people and secured more than 50 convictions. Most of those convicted are militiamen who say they were acting under the orders of the Indonesian armed forces. About 280 indictees remain at large in Indonesia. They include the Indonesian commander at the time, General Wiranto, for whom the unit has issued an arrest warrant," though the Timorese government (!) refused to forward it to Interpol (ibid.). It is notable that all of the accusations and legal initiatives pertain to the 1999 atrocities; even leading human rights organizations such as Amnesty International have declined to recommend prosecutions for the genocide committed against Timorese over the previous quarter-century. See Nevins, *A Not-so-distant Horror*, p. 165.

CHAPTER 8

Bosnia and Kosovo

The dissolution of Yugoslavia in the early 1990s brought genocide back to Europe after nearly half a century. During those years the world looked on, shocked but ineffectual, as the multiethnic state of Bosnia-Herzegovina collapsed into genocidal war. The most extensive and systematic atrocities were committed by Serbs against Muslims, but clashes between Croatians and Serbs, and between Muslims and Croatians, claimed thousands of lives. The restive Serb province of Kosovo, with its ethnic-Albanian majority, was another tinder-box, though mass violence did not erupt there until spring 1999.

ORIGINS AND ONSET

Yugoslavia, the federation of "Southern Slavs," was cobbled together from the disintegrated Ottoman Empire after the First World War. Fragile federations everywhere are prone to violence in times of crisis, as a glance around the contemporary world confirms (Russia, Indonesia, Iraq). For Yugoslavia, the crisis came in the Second World War, when the federation was riven by combined Nazi invasion and genocidal intercommunal conflict. Yugoslavia in fact became one of the most destructive theaters of history's most destructive war. Under the German occupation regime in Serbia and the fascist Ustashe government installed by the Nazis in Croatia, most of Yugoslavia's Jewish population was wiped out. Hundreds of thousands of Croatian Serbs were rounded up by the Ustashe and slaughtered, most notoriously at the Jasenovac death camp.

Muslims in Bosnia mostly collaborated with the Nazis, earning them the enduring enmity of the Serb population. The Serbs themselves were divided between the Chetniks, who supported the deposed royalist regime, and a partisan movement led by Josip Broz, known then and after as Tito. Chetnik massacres and widespread atrocities prompted an equally murderous response from Tito's forces. After the partisans seized power in the Yugoslav capital, Belgrade, in the late stages of the war, thousands of Chetniks fled to neighboring countries. The majority were returned to Yugoslavia to face extrajudicial punishment. Throughout 1945–46, Tito's forces killed tens of thousands of Chetniks and other political opponents.

The socialist state that Tito instituted, however, was comparatively liberal by the standards of Central and Eastern Europe. Yugoslavs enjoyed extensive freedom of movement and travel. Millions worked overseas, especially in Germany. The country gained a reputation not only for comparative openness, but also for successful ethnic pluralism. Tito, a Croatian, worked to ensure that no ethnic group dominated the federation. Political mobilization along ethnic lines was banned (resulting in a wave of detention and imprisonment in the 1970s, when Croatian leaders within the Yugoslav Socialist Party sought greater autonomy for Croatia). State authorities worked hard to defuse ethnic tensions and generate an overarching Yugoslav identity, with some success.

But Tito died in May 1980, and his multinational federation began rapidly to unravel amidst pervasive economic strife. A weak collective leadership faltered when confronted by an emergent generation of ethnonationalist politicians, most prominently Slobodan Milosevic in Serbia and Franjo Tudjman in Croatia. Tudjman, "a small-minded, right-wing autocrat,"[1] led a political movement – the HDZ – that explicitly revived Ustashe symbolism and rhetoric. He also allowed, and probably supervised, a campaign of harassment and violence against the large Serbian population of the Krajina region. Serbs were dismissed from their jobs, allegedly to redress preferential treatment granted to them in the past. Worse would follow.

In Milosevic of Serbia, meanwhile, we see one of the most influential European politicians of the second half the twentieth century – albeit a malign influence. Milosevic, though, was not especially talented or charismatic. Rather, he was a classic *apparatchik* (child of the system) who realized sooner than most that rousing nationalist passions was the best way to exploit the Yugoslav upheavals.[2]

Milosevic sowed the seeds for genocide in April 1987, on a visit to the restive Albanian-dominated province of Kosovo. (Ironically, it was over Kosovo that the term "genocide" was first deployed in a contemporary Balkans context – by Serbs, to describe their people's supposed destiny there at the hands of the Albanian majority.)[3] Dispatched by Serb President Ivan Stambolic, his mentor, to undertake talks with the local Communist Party leadership, Milosevic was greeted by a rowdy outpouring of Serbs barely kept in check by police. Rocks were thrown, apparently as a provocation. The police reacted with batons. Milosevic was urged to calm the crowd. Instead, he told them: "No one should dare to beat you," "unwittingly coining a modern Serb rallying call."[4]

Transformed by the ecstatic reaction to his speech, Milosevic forged ahead with his nationalist agenda. A few months later, in September 1987, he shunted aside his mentor, Ivan Stambolic, and took over the presidency. In 1989, Serbs initiated a

Map 8.1 Bosnia

Source: Map provided by WorldAtlas.com

repressive drive in Kosovo that ended the province's autonomy within Serbia, threw tens of thousands of ethnic Albanians out of their jobs, and made of Kosovo "one large militia camp . . . a squalid outpost of putrefying colonialism."[5] In retrospect, this was the key event that unraveled Yugoslavia. After the Kosovo crackdown, no ethnic group could feel entirely safe in a Serb-dominated federation.

In 1991–92, Yugoslavia exploded into open war. On June 25, 1991, Croatia and Slovenia declared themselves independent. A surreal ten-day war for Slovenia resulted in the withdrawal of the Yugoslav Army (JNA) and the abandonment of Yugoslav claims to the territory. Croatia, though, was a different matter. It included sizable Serb populations in Krajina (the narrow strip of territory running adjacent to the Dalmatian coast and bordering Serb-dominated areas of Bosnia-Herzegovina) and Eastern Slavonia.

Milosevic recognized the inevitability of Croatia's secession, but sought to secure territories in which Serbs were strongly represented for his "Greater Serbia." In December 1991, after several months of fighting, the Krajina Serbs declared their independence from Croatia. Meanwhile, the world's attention was captured by the artillery bombardment of the historic port of Dubrovnik; less so by the far more severe JNA assault on Vukovar, which reduced the city to rubble and was followed by the genocidal slaughter of some 200 wounded Croatian soldiers in their hospital beds.

The independence declarations by Slovenia and Croatia left multiethnic Bosnia-Herzegovina in an impossible position. As epitomized by its major city, Sarajevo – hitherto a model of ethnic tolerance – Bosnia was divided among Muslims, Serbs, and Croatians. Attempting to leave Yugoslavia would surely mean war by Bosnian Serbs to integrate "their" zone of Bosnia into Milosevic's Greater Serbia, while remaining within the federation meant enduring Serb domination. In February 1992, Bosnia-Herzegovina declared independence from Yugoslavia. Bosnian Serbs immediately declared independence from Bosnia-Herzegovina.

Bosnia then became the most brutal battlefield of the Balkan wars. Serb gunners began an artillery assault on Sarajevo that evoked outrage around the world, conveniently distracting international attention from much greater atrocities elsewhere in Bosnia, especially in the industrialized east.[6] The Yugoslav army was ordered out, but left most of its weapons in the hands of Bosnian Serbs, who now constituted a formidable 80,000-man army. Bosnian Muslims, hampered by their land-locked territory and limited resources, were in many places simply crushed by Serb forces. Then – from early 1993 – they found themselves fighting their former Croatian allies as well, in a war nearly as vicious as the Serb–Muslim confrontation. Not surprisingly, the Muslims responded by generating "a strident, xenophobic Muslim nationalism" mirroring that of their tormentors.[7] However, neither it nor its Croatian counterpart ever matched Serb nationalism in destructiveness. An in-depth United Nations report subsequently ascribed 90 percent of atrocities in Bosnia-Herzegovina to Serbs, and just 10 percent to Croatians and Muslims combined.[8]

In August 1992, Western reporters broke the story of Serb-run concentration camps in Bosnia where Muslim males, and some females, were detained.[9] At Omarska, the grimmest of the camps, "there were routine and constant beatings; in the dormitories, on the way to and from the canteen or the latrines, all the time. The guards used clubs, thick electrical cable, rifle butts, fists, boots, brass knuckle-dusters, iron rods. . . . Every night, after midnight, the guards called out the names of one or more prisoners. These prisoners were taken out and beaten bloody, their bones often broken and their skin punctured."[10] Thousands died; of the survivors, Penny Marshall of ITN wrote that they were reduced to "various stages of human decay and affliction; the bones of their elbows and wrists protrude like pieces of jagged stone from the pencil thin stalks to which their arms have been reduced."[11] Such images, reminiscent of Nazi concentration camps, sparked an international uproar. Combined with revelations of mass executions and the rape of Bosnian-Muslim women, the camps spawned the first widespread use of the term "genocide" in a Balkans context.

GENDERCIDE AND GENOCIDE IN BOSNIA

The strategy of "ethnic cleansing," as it rapidly came to be known in Western media and public discussion, was meant to ensure not only military victory and the expulsion of target populations, but also a permanent post-genocide arrangement. As Laura Silber and Alan Little argue, "the technique . . . was designed to render the territory ethnically pure, and to make certain, by instilling a hatred and fear that would endure, that Muslims and Serbs could never again live together."[12]

Central to this policy was killing civilians, overwhelmingly men of "battle age." The war in Bosnia-Herzegovina offers one of the most vivid modern instances of gendercide, or gender-selective mass killing, discussed in comparative context in Chapter 13. As with most cases of gendercide, the gender variable interacted with those of *age* and *community prominence* to produce a genocidal outcome in Bosnia (and again in Kosovo in 1999). Journalist Mark Danner described the *modus operandi* of Serb forces as follows:

> 1. *Concentration.* Surround the area to be cleansed and after warning the resident Serbs – often they are urged to leave or are at least told to mark their houses with white flags – intimidate the target population with artillery fire and arbitrary executions and then bring them out into the streets.
> 2. *Decapitation.* Execute political leaders and those capable of taking their places: lawyers, judges, public officials, writers, professors.
> 3. *Separation.* Divide women, children, and old men from men of "fighting age" – sixteen years to sixty years old.
> 4. *Evacuation.* Transport women, children, and old men to the border, expelling them into a neighboring territory or country.
> 5. *Liquidation.* Execute "fighting age" men, dispose of bodies.[13]

Throughout the Bosnian war, this strategy was implemented in systematic fashion – primarily, but not only, by Serb military and paramilitary forces. The Srebrenica slaughter of July 1995 is by far the most destructive instance of gendercidal killing in the Balkans; but there are dozens of more quotidian examples. Some are cited in a short section of the Helsinki Watch report, *War Crimes in Bosnia-Hercegovina*, covering the first and most murderous phase of the war:

> In my village, about 180 men were killed. The army put all men in the center of the village. After the killing, the women took care of the bodies and identified them. The older men buried the bodies. (Trnopolje)

> The army came to the village that day. They took us from our houses. The men were beaten. The army came in on trucks and started shooting at the men and killing them. (Prnovo)

> The army took most of the men and killed them. There were bodies everywhere. (Rizvanovici)

Figure 8.1 Gendercide in Bosnia: a mass grave of Srebrenica victims from the Branjevo farm near Pilica village, unearthed by forensic investigators. A member of the forensic team, Fernando Moscoso, said: "Constantly seeing their faces, their arms and legs contorted and twisted over one another, that's what really gets to you. At night, when I close my eyes I still see them."

Source: Magnum Photos/Gilles Peress.

> Our men had to hide. My husband was with us, but hiding. I saw my uncle being beaten on July 25 when there was a kind of massacre. The Serbs were searching for arms. Three hundred men were killed that day. (Carakovo)[14]

Six years after the war ended, "of the approximately 18,000 persons registered by the ICRC in Bosnia-Herzegovina as still missing in connection with the armed conflict . . . 92% are men and 8% are women."[15]

As in Armenia in 1915, with community males murdered or incarcerated, Serb soldiers and paramilitaries were better able to inflict atrocities on remaining community members. Women, especially younger ones, were special targets. They were subject to rape, often repeatedly, often by gangs, and often in the presence of a father or husband. Typical was the testimony offered by "E.," just 16 years old:

> Several Chetniks arrived. One, a man around 30, ordered me to follow him into the house. I had to go. He started looking for money, jewelry and other valuables. He wanted to know where the men were. I didn't answer. Then he ordered me to undress. I was terribly afraid. I took off my clothes, feeling that I was falling apart. The feeling seemed under my skin; I was dying, my entire being was murdered.

> I closed my eyes, I couldn't look at him. He hit me. I fell. Then he lay on me. He did it to me. I cried, twisted my body convulsively, bled. I had been a virgin.
>
> He went out and invited two Chetniks to come in. I cried. The two repeated what the first one had done to me. I felt lost. I didn't even know when they left. I don't know how long I stayed there, lying on the floor alone, in a pool of blood.
>
> My mother found me. I couldn't imagine anything worse. I had been raped, destroyed and terribly hurt. But for my mother this was the greatest sorrow of our lives. We both cried and screamed. She dressed me.
>
> I would like to be a mother some day. But how? In my world, men represent terrible violence and pain. I cannot control that feeling.[16]

It was in the Bosnian context that the term "genocidal rape" was minted, stressing the centrality of sexual assaults of women to the broader campaign of "cleansing." It should be noted that men and adolescent boys were also sexually assaulted and tortured on a large scale in detention facilities such as Omarska and Trnopolje.[17]

BOX 8.1 ONE MAN'S STORY: NEZAD AVDIC

July 1995. For three years, the city of Srebrenica, with its majority Bosnian-Muslim population, had been one of the major conflict points of the war in Bosnia-Herzegovina. In April 1993, with Srebrenica on the verge of falling to Bosnian Serb forces, the United Nations oversaw the evacuation of children, women, and the elderly, while abiding by Serb demands that no males of "battle age" be permitted to leave. It then declared Srebrenica a UN-protected "safe haven." This status held for a little over two years, under the watchful gaze of first Canadian, then Dutch peacekeepers. The population experienced ever-greater hunger and material deprivation. It also fell under the sway of Naser Oric, a Muslim paramilitary leader who organized murderous raids out of the enclave against Serb civilians in surrounding villages.[18]

Finally, on July 6 1995, the Bosnian Serbs decided to implement their "endgame."[19] Serb General Ratko Mladic promised his men a "feast": "There will be blood up to your knees."[20] The peacekeepers watched without firing a shot as the Serbs overcame light Bosnian-Muslim resistance and rounded up most of the population.

Understanding immediately that they were at mortal risk, thousands of "battle-age" men sought to flee through the surrounding hills to Muslim-controlled territory. Most were killed in the hills, or massacred *en masse* after capture. The men who remained behind, including elderly and adolescent males, were systematically separated from the children and women, who – as in 1993 – were allowed to flee in buses to safety. The captured males were trucked off to be slaughtered.

Nezad Avdic, a 17-year-old Bosnian Muslim, was among the intended victims. "When the truck stopped, we immediately heard shooting outside," he recalled. "The Chetniks [Serb paramilitaries] told us to get out, five at a time. I was in the middle of the group, and the men in front didn't want to get out. They were terrified, they started pulling back. But we had no choice, and when it was my turn to get out with five others, I saw dead bodies everywhere."

Avdic was lined up in front of a mass grave. "We stood in front of the Chetniks with our backs turned to them. They ordered us to lie down, and as I threw myself on the ground, I heard gunfire. I was hit in my right arm and three bullets went through the right side of my torso. I don't recall whether or not I fell on the ground unconscious. But I remember being frightened, thinking I would soon be dead or another bullet would hit. I thought it would soon be all over."

Lying among wounded men, "hear[ing] others screaming and moaning," Avdic maintained his deathlike pose. "One of the Chetniks ordered the others to check and see what bodies were still warm. 'Put a bullet through all the heads, even if they're cold.'" But his partner replied: "Fuck their mothers! They're all dead."[21]

They weren't. "I heard a truck leave," Avdic said. "I didn't know what to do. . . . I saw someone moving about ten metres away from me and asked, 'Friend, are you alive?'"

With his companion, Avdic managed to flee the scene after Serb forces departed. He was one of a tiny handful of survivors of a connected series of genocidal massacres that claimed more than 7,000 lives. This made Srebrenica the worst slaughter in Europe since the killings of political opponents by Yugoslav partisan forces after the Second World War. Srebrenica was also the crowning genocidal massacre of the Balkan wars of the 1990s – but not, unfortunately, the final one. The Serb assault on Kosovo, with its ethnic-Albanian majority, would follow in 1999, with scenes that echoed Srebrenica, though on a smaller scale.

THE INTERNATIONAL DIMENSION

If the caliber of the political leadership on all sides of the Balkan wars left much to be desired, the same may be said of international policy-making, beginning with Germany's machinations over Croatian and Slovenian independence. Animated by a vision of expanding economic and political influence, Germany – led by its foreign minister, Hans-Dietrich Genscher – pressed the rest of the European Union to support the dissolution of Yugoslavia. The campaign was fiercely opposed by British representative Lord Carrington, whose plan to safeguard peace in the Balkans depended upon a carrot of recognition being extended to the nascent states in return for guarantees of safeguards for minorities. Bosnian Muslim leader Alija

Izetbegovic desperately tried to head off a German/EU declaration of support, while UN Secretary-General Perez de Cuellar warned Genscher that recognizing Croatia would unleash "the most terrible war" in Bosnia-Herzegovina.[22] The efforts were to no avail, and German/EU recognition was duly granted in May 1992. Many see this as an important spur to the genocide unleashed across Bosnia in ensuing months.

The pivotal role of the United States was characterized by vacillation on the independence issue, guided by a conviction that "we don't have a dog in this fight" (George Bush Sr.'s Secretary of State, James Baker, speaking in 1992). The besieging of Srebrenica and other Muslim-majority cities in Bosnia in spring 1993 forced a US-led response to establish six "safe areas" under UN protection, but these were never effectively defended. When Srebrenica fell to the Serbs, it was "protected" by fewer than 400 Dutch peacekeepers, mostly lightly armed and under orders not to fire their weapons except in self-defense. Genocidal massacres were the predictable result. Suspicion has swirled that, mass atrocities aside, the US and EU were not unhappy to see the "safe areas" fall to the Serbs. (An unnamed US official stated at the time that "While losing the enclaves has been unfortunate for Bosnia, it's been great for us.")[23]

The Americans and Europeans turned a blind eye to Croatia's rearmament, which violated the arms embargo formally imposed on all sides. The US also forged a "tacit agreement to allow Iran and other Moslem countries to expand covert arms supplies to the Bosnians."[24] A month after Srebrenica fell, the Croatians combined with Muslim forces to launch Operation Storm, a dramatic offensive against the Serb-held Krajina region.[25] Milosevic, once the Bosnian Serbs' ardent champion, now abandoned them, the better to present himself as a Balkans peacemaker, and secure the lifting of economic sanctions.

In a matter of days, the Croatian-Muslim offensive overran Krajina, resulting in "another biblical movement of people" as up to 200,000 Serbs fled to Serb-populated regions of Bosnia.[26] Croatian President Tudjman celebrated the expulsions, declaring that the country's Serbs had "disappeared ignominiously, as if they had never populated this land."[27] The Krajina *fait accompli* left in its wake Europe's largest refugee population, but it was welcomed in the West, especially by the US.[28] In the aftermath, the Clinton government invited the warring parties to talks at Wright-Patterson Air Force Base in Dayton, Ohio. They resulted in the signing of a comprehensive peace agreement (the Dayton Accords) in November 1995, and the introduction of 60,000 NATO peacekeepers to police it.

However, there was still a final genocidal act to be played out in Milosevic's campaign for a Greater Serbia – in Kosovo, the Serb province where his nationalist drive had begun.

KOSOVO, 1998–99

To counter the Serb police state imposed in 1989, a parallel political structure arose in Kosovar Albanian communities, built around the non-violent resistance movement led by Ibrahim Rugova. Remarkably, this parallel authority managed to preserve

Albanian-language education and a semblance of social services for otherwise dispossessed ethnic Albanians.

Eventually, after nearly a decade of "a system of apartheid that excluded the province's majority Albanian population from virtually every phase of political, economic, social, and cultural life,"[29] an armed guerrilla movement – the Kosovo Liberation Army (KLA) – launched attacks in 1997. Many KLA leaders desired the political union of Kosovo's Albanians with their "compatriots" across the border in Albania proper. Guerrilla war through 1998 and into 1999 resulted in the Serb killing of hundreds of ethnic-Albanian civilians, and the internal displacement of 200,000 more. Milosevic now began to plan a decisive resolution of the Kosovo quandary. "In a long career, this would be his masterpiece, cleansing the Serb homeland of its Albanian interlopers in a matter of weeks."[30]

European countries sought to head off full-scale war, dispatching an observer team (the Kosovo Verification Commission) to monitor a ceasefire between the Serbs and the KLA. Both sides were guilty of violations, but the mass murder by Serb paramilitaries of dozens of Kosovar men at the village of Racak (January 16, 1999) sparked the greatest outrage. Abortive negotiations under Western auspices at Rambouillet, France, ended in impasse and acrimony. Pro-Serb commentators have accused Western countries, in league with the KLA, of stage-managing a crisis at Rambouillet in order to discipline Milosevic with a quick military defeat.[31]

It did not turn out that way. On March 19, 1999, the Serbs launched "a massive campaign of ethnic cleansing, aimed not only at tipping the demographic balance [of Kosovo] in Belgrade's favor but also – by driving hundreds of thousands of desperate Albanians over the border into the fragile neighboring states of Macedonia and Albania – at threatening the Western allies with the destabilization of the entire Balkan peninsula."[32] The campaign reached full ferocity after March 24, when NATO began high-altitude bombing of Serb positions in Kosovo and other targets throughout Yugoslavia. This would remain the exclusive NATO military tactic. The Allies seemed terrified of taking casualties, on the ground or in the air, and jeopardizing popular support for the war. They also assumed that Milosevic would quickly crumble in the face of Allied aerial assault. This proved "a colossal miscalculation," and there are in fact grounds for arguing that the bombing prompted an escalation and intensification of the Serbs' genocidal strategies. "NATO leaders, then, stand accused of exacerbating the very humanitarian disaster that their actions were justified as averting."[33]

The Serb campaign against Kosovar Albanians bore many of the hallmarks of earlier Serb campaigns. Army units and paramilitary forces worked in close coordination to empty the territory of ethnic Albanians through selective acts of terror and mass murder. Gendercidal killing again predominated, as in the largest massacre of the war, at the village of Meja:

> Shortly before dawn on April 27, according to locals, a large contingent of Yugoslav army troops garrisoned in Junik started moving eastward through the valley, dragging men from their houses and pushing them into trucks. "Go to Albania!" they screamed at the women before driving on to the next town with their prisoners. By the time they got to Meja they had collected as many as 300 men.

> The regular army took up positions around the town while the militia and paramilitaries went through the houses grabbing the last few villagers and shoving them out into the road. The men were surrounded by fields most of them had worked in their whole lives, and they could look up and see mountains they'd admired since they were children. Around noon the first group was led to the compost heap, gunned down, and burned under piles of cornhusks. A few minutes later a group of about 70 were forced to lie down in three neat rows and were machine-gunned in the back. The rest – about 35 men – were taken to a farmhouse along the Gjakove road, pushed into one of the rooms, and then shot through the windows at point-blank range. The militiamen who did this then stepped inside, finished them off with shots to the head, and burned the house down. They walked away singing.[34]

About 10,000 ethnic Albanians died during the war, along with some Serbs and Roma (Gypsies).[35] The killings were accompanied by the largest mass deportation of a civilian population in decades. Some 800,000 Kosovar Albanians were rounded up and expelled to Albania and Macedonia. Pictures of the exodus bolstered Western resolve, and the Allies began to talk about putting boots on the ground.

In response to Russian pressure, and perhaps chastened by his indictment on war-crimes charges (on May 27, 1999), Milosevic agreed to a ceasefire. The arrangement allowed for the withdrawal of Serb forces from Kosovo, and the introduction of 18,000 NATO troops along with 3,500 UN police. These outside forces arrived quickly, but not rapidly – or resolutely – enough to prevent a round of revenge attacks launched by ethnic Albanians against Serb civilians in northern Kosovo. These prompted 150,000 Serbs to flee as refugees to the Serbian heartland, where they joined the 200,000 still stranded by Operation Storm in 1995.

AFTERMATHS

The Dayton Accords brought peace to Bosnia-Herzegovina, and between Croatia and what was left of Yugoslavia. They also froze in place the genocidal "ethnic cleansing" of preceding years. The peace was the peace of the grave: a quarter of a million people had died in Bosnia-Herzegovina, while an astonishing 1,282,000 were registered as internally displaced.[36] Despite formal declarations that all displaced persons should be allowed to return to their homes, in Bosnia the "ground reality . . . in many ways resembles *de facto* nationalist partition rather than a single, sovereign state. . . . The overwhelming majority of Bosnians, well over 90%, now live in areas that are largely homogeneous in the national sense."[37]

The new state of Bosnia-Herzegovina was administered by the Organization for Security and Cooperation in Europe (OSCE), under an arrangement that gave its High Representative "far-reaching powers . . . extend[ing] well beyond military matters to cover the most basic aspects of government and state."[38] Over US$5 billion was pledged to "the largest per capita reconstruction plan in history,"[39] and tens of thousands of NATO troops arrived to police the peace. (In December 2004, NATO was replaced by a 7,000-strong European Union force, though most of the troops simply switched badges.) This "experiment in externally imposed democratisation" preserved a tenuous stability across the territory, but it was unclear, as of 2005, whether it could generate anything like an organic nation-state.

An important test of the post-Dayton era was the peace agreement between Croatia and rump Yugoslavia. In 2004, with Croatia pushing for membership in the European Union, the new Prime Minister Ivo Sanader shifted decisively away from the extreme nationalism of Franjo Tudjman, who had died in 2001. After years of "insurmountable impediments" (according to Human Rights Watch) being placed in the way of Serbs attempting to return to their homes, Sanader promised greater receptiveness. As the British newspaper the *Guardian* pointed out, however, he ran "little political risk" for doing so, "simply because so few Serbs are returning." While some 70,000 mostly elderly Serbs had returned, over 200,000 remained refugees in Bosnia-Herzegovina and Serbia and Montenegro.[40]

What of those who had supervised and committed the atrocities? Many lived in comfort, protected by their ethnic communities and by the lackadaisical approach of NATO forces to rounding them up. But the course of international justice registered successes. The International Criminal Tribunal for the Former Yugoslavia (ICTY), established by the UN Security Council in May 1993, began its proceedings at the Hague on May 16, 1996. Many greeted the tribunal with derision, viewing it as too little, too late. Nonetheless, by late 2004 the Tribunal had conducted fifty-two prosecutions and sentenced thirty individuals. Its greatest coup came on June 28, 2001, when former Yugoslav president Slobodan Milosevic was transported to the Hague to stand trial. (Milosevic had been toppled by a popular uprising in September 2000, after refusing to recognize adverse election results.) The successor government under Vojislav Kostunica saw surrendering Milosevic as the price of rejoining the international community. Milosevic, charged with genocide for crimes in Bosnia-Herzegovina,[41] waged a protracted and spirited defense before the tribunal, but died in March 2006 before a verdict was reached.

Milosevic's partners in crime during the war in Bosnia-Herzegovina – former Bosnian Serb president Radovan Karadzic and General Ratko Mladic, the butcher of Srebrenica – remained at large. But at least one prominent Bosnian Serb commander, General Radislav Krstic, was captured and turned over to the Hague, where he was found guilty in August 2001 of the crime of genocide for his leading role in the carnage at Srebrenica. Croatian, Bosnian Muslim, and Kosovar Albanian suspects also faced the tribunal – as with the 2001 indictment of Croatian General Ante Gotovina for atrocities committed in Krajina, and Kosovo Prime Minister Ranush Haradinaj, indicted by the tribunal in March 2005 on charges of "murder, rape and deportation of civilians."[42] (For more on the ICTY, see Chapter 15.)

Whatever precarious stability obtained in Bosnia, it was not matched in Kosovo, which remained under Serb sovereignty but international control. Ethnic-Albanian extremists sought to provoke panic and flight among the territory's beleaguered Serbs (and Roma, whom Kosovar Albanians perceived as Serb allies and henchmen). In March 2004, the largest anti-Serb pogrom to date killed nineteen people and destroyed hundreds of Serb homes. Human Rights Watch criticized international forces for doing little to stop the violence: "In many cases, minorities under attack were left entirely unprotected and at the mercy of the rioters. . . . In too many cases,

Nato peacekeepers locked the gates to their bases and watched as Serb homes burned."[43] Both the political status of Kosovo and the future of the Serb population in the north were in doubt as this book went to press.

FURTHER STUDY

Fred Abrahams, Gilles Peress, and Eric Stover, *A Village Destroyed, May 14, 1999: War Crimes in Kosovo.* Berkeley, CA: University of California Press, 2001. Vivid photographic record and text.

David Chandler, *Bosnia: Faking Democracy after Dayton* (2nd edn). London: Pluto Press, 1999. Overview of Bosnia's early postwar years.

Misha Glenny, *The Fall of Yugoslavia: The Third Balkan War* (3rd rev. edn). London: Penguin, 1996. Solid journalistic overview, best read alongside Silber and Little (see below).

Helsinki Watch, *War Crimes in Bosnia-Hercegovina, Vol. 2.* New York: Human Rights Watch, 1993. Detailed investigation of atrocities in the early phase of the Bosnian war.

Michael Ignatieff, *Virtual War: Kosovo and Beyond.* New York: Viking, 2000. Examines Kosovo in the context of modern media and military technologies.

Robert D. Kaplan, *Balkan Ghosts: A Journey Through History.* New York: St. Martin's Press, 1993. Clichéd but influential survey of recent Balkans history.

Organization for Security and Cooperation in Europe (OSCE), *Kosovo/Kosova: As Seen, As Told.* Available at http://www.osce.org/kosovo/documents/reports/hr/part1/. The most detailed report on atrocities in Kosovo.

David Rohde, *Endgame: The Betrayal and Fall of Srebrenica, Europe's Worst Massacre Since World War II.* Boulder, CO: Westview Press, 1998. Heart-stopping account of the 1995 catastrophe.

Michael P. Scharf and William A. Schabas, *Slobodan Milosevic on Trial: A Companion.* New York: Continuum, 2002. Background to, and evaluation of, the case against the former Serbian dictator.

Louis Sell, *Slobodan Milosevic and the Destruction of Yugoslavia.* Durham, NC: Duke University Press, 2002. Excellent study of Milosevic's rise and fall.

Laura Silber and Allan Little, *The Death of Yugoslavia* (rev. edn). London: BBC Books, 1996. The best introduction to the breakup of Yugoslavia.

Chuck Sudetic, *Blood and Vengeance: One Family's Story of the War in Bosnia.* London: Penguin, 1998. Intimate portrait of Bosnia in upheaval.

Ed Vulliamy, *Seasons in Hell: Understanding Bosnia's War.* New York: St. Martin's Press, 1994. Seminal reportage from the war zone.

NOTES

1 Misha Glenny, *The Fall of Yugoslavia* (3rd rev. edn) (London: Penguin, 1996), p. 86.

2 Of Milosevic, Louis Sell writes, "Nationalism for him was just a tool. Milosevic dropped nationalism just as quickly when it became inconvenient to his efforts to cultivate the image of a peacemaker." Louis Sell, *Slobodan Milosevic and the Destruction of Yugoslavia*

(Durham, NC: Duke University Press, 2002), p. 170. For insights into the roots of Serb nationalism, see Branimir Anzulovic, *Heavenly Serbia: From Myth to Genocide* (New York: New York University Press, 1999).

3 On the early deployment of the rhetoric of "genocide" in the Balkan wars, see Bette Denich, "Dismembering Yugoslavia: Nationalist Ideologies and the Symbolic Revival of Genocide," *American Ethnologist*, 21 (1994), pp. 367–90. In 1986, a declaration by the Serbian Academy of Sciences and Arts referred to "the physical, political, legal, and cultural genocide of the Serbian population of Kosovo" (quoted in Peter Ronayne, "Genocide in Kosovo," *Human Rights Review*, 5: 4 [July 2004], p. 59). Kosovo had additional symbolic importance to Serbs as the site of "the Serbian Golgotha," a famous 1389 battle with the Ottoman armies that Serbs viewed as a heroic defeat, though most historians regard its outcome as inconclusive. See Michael Sells, "Kosovo Mythology and the Bosnian Genocide," ch. 8 in Omer Bartov and Phyllis Mack, *In God's Name: Genocide and Religion in the Twentieth Century* (New York: Berghahn Books, 2001), pp. 180–205.

4 Laura Silber and Allan Little, *The Death of Yugoslavia* (rev. edn) (London: BBC Books, 1996), p. 37.

5 Glenny, *The Fall of Yugoslavia*, pp. 46, 67.

6 "Though Sarajevo grabbed the headlines, it was clear from the first day of the war that eastern Bosnia, with its hydroelectric dams, highways, and Muslim-majority population, was the key to the Serb leaders' plans to partition Bosnia." Chuck Sudetic, *Blood and Vengeance: One Family's Story of the War in Bosnia* (London: Penguin, 1998), p. 100. Silber and Little also note that "during the summer months of 1992 . . . the world's media concentrated almost exclusively on the siege and bombardment of [Sarajevo], even though much more decisive battles and campaigns were being waged elsewhere. . . . [This] suited Serb leaders very well." Silber and Little, *The Death of Yugoslavia*, p. 253.

7 Aside from the thousands of human casualties, the Muslim–Croatian conflict claimed the famous bridge at Mostar, which mirrored Sarajevo with its Catholic, Greek Orthodox, and Muslim populations. The bridge was totally destroyed by Croatian shelling, and reopened only in 2004.

8 Cited in James Waller, *Becoming Evil: How Ordinary People Commit Genocide and Mass Killing* (Oxford: Oxford University Press, 2002), p. 262.

9 Among the reporters was Ed Vulliamy, who has given a detailed descriptions of the camps and their discovery in his book *Seasons in Hell* (New York: St Martin's Press, 1994).

10 David Hirsh, *Law against Genocide: Cosmopolitan Trials* (London: Glasshouse Press, 2003), pp. 66–67.

11 Marshall quoted in Silber and Little, *The Death of Yugoslavia*, p. 250.

12 Silber and Little, *The Death of Yugoslavia*, p. 245.

13 Mark Danner, "Endgame in Kosovo," *New York Review of Books*, May 6, 1999, p. 8

14 Helsinki Watch, *War Crimes in Bosnia-Hercegovina*, Vol. 2 (New York: Human Rights Watch, 1993), pp. 82–83.

15 International Committee of the Red Cross, "The Impact of Armed Conflict on Women," March 6, 2001, available at http://www.reliefweb.int/library/documents/2001/icrc-women-17oct.pdf.

16 Slavenka Draculic, "Rape After Rape After Rape," *New York Times*, December 13, 1992.

17 For example, the most bestial of the camps, Omarska, held some 2,000 men and thirty-three to thirty-eight women (Helsinki Watch, *War Crimes in Bosnia-Hercegovina*, p. 87). For analysis, in global-historical context, of the sexual torture and rape of Bosnian males, see Augusta Del Zotto and Adam Jones, "Male-on-male Sexual Violence in Wartime: Human Rights' Last Taboo?," paper presented to the Annual Convention of the International Studies Association (ISA), New Orleans, LA, March 23–27, 2002. Available online at http://adamjones.freeservers.com/malerape.htm.

18 The raids were accompanied by "a horde of Muslim refugees, men and women, young and old, who were driven by hunger and, in many cases, a thirst for revenge. Thousands strong, these people would lurk behind the first wave of attacking soldiers and run amok

when the defenses around Serb villages collapsed. Some of the refugees used pistols to do the killing; others used knives, bats, and hatchets. But most of them had nothing but their bare hands and the empty rucksacks and suitcases they strapped onto their backs. They came to be known as *torbari*, the bag people. And they were beyond [Naser] Oric's control." Sudetic, *Blood and Vengeance*, p. 157.

19 See David Rohde, *Endgame: The Betrayal and Fall of Srebrenica, Europe's Worst Massacre since World War II* (New York: Farrar, Straus and Giroux, 1997).

20 Quoted in Mark Danner, "The Killing Fields of Bosnia," *New York Review of Books*, September 24, 1998 (citing reporting by Roy Gutman of *Newsday*).

21 Avdic's testimony is recounted in Jan Willem Honig and Norbert Both, *Srebrenica: Record of a War Crime* (London: Penguin, 1996), p. 62.

22 Perez de Cuellar quoted in Glenny, *The Fall of Yugoslavia*, p. 164.

23 Quoted in Sell, *Slobodan Milosevic*, p. 234.

24 Sell, *Slobodan Milosevic*, p. 215.

25 See Mark Danner, "Operation Storm," *New York Review of Books*, October 22, 1998.

26 Glenny, *The Fall of Yugoslavia*, p. 284.

27 Tudjman quoted in "Stormy Memories," *The Economist*, July 30, 2005.

28 Stated one European diplomat: "Until now at least the international community has been united in its condemnation of ethnic cleansing. Now it seems one of its members is openly supporting the mass movement of population by the most terrible force." Quoted in Glenny, *The Fall of Yugoslavia*, p. 285.

29 Sell, *Slobodan Milosevic*, p. 93.

30 Danner, "Endgame in Kosovo," p. 11.

31 This is a common theme of the literature cited in Chapter 16, n. 26.

32 Sell, *Slobodan Milosevic*, p. 304.

33 Nicholas Wheeler, *Saving Strangers: Humanitarian Intervention in International Society* (Oxford: Oxford University Press, 2000), p. 269.

34 Sebastian Junger, "The Forensics of War," in Junger, *Fire* (New York: W.W. Norton, 2001), p. 158. Another reporter estimates that 500 men were killed in the Meja massacre: see Joshua Hammer, "On the Trail of Hard Truth," *Newsweek*, July 9, 2000.

35 The debate over the alleged "exaggeration" of Kosovar Albanian deaths was spirited after the war, and reflects, in Samantha Power's estimation, "the inescapable difficulty of accurately gauging the scale of atrocities while they are being committed." Power, *"A Problem from Hell": America and the Age of Genocide* (New York: Basic Books, 2002), p. 467. Power notes that the ICTY "has received reports that some 11,334 Albanians are buried in 529 sites in Kosovo alone"; moreover, "In 2001 some 427 dead Albanians from Kosovo were exhumed in five mass graves that had been hidden in Serbia proper. An additional three mass grave sites, containing more than 1,000 bodies, were found in a Belgrade suburb and awaited exhumation. Each of the newly discovered sites lies near Yugoslav army or police barracks" (pp. 471–72). For a critique of attempts to downplay genocide in Kosovo, see Adam Jones, "Kosovo: Orders of Magnitude," *IDEA: A Journal of Social Issues*, 5: 1 (July 2000), available at http://www.ideajournal.com/articles.php?id=24.

36 Figures on dead and displaced from Rory Keane, *Reconstituting Sovereignty: Post-Dayton Bosnia Uncovered* (Burlington, VT: Ashgate, 2002), p. 69.

37 Sumantra Bose, *Bosnia after Dayton: Nationalist Partition and International Intervention* (London: Horst & Co., 2002), pp. 22, 34.

38 David Chandler, *Bosnia: Faking Democracy after Dayton* (2nd edn) (London: Pluto Press, 1999), p. 43.

39 Bose, *Bosnia after Dayton*, p. 6.

40 Ian Traynor, "Croatia Builds Goodwill in Serb Villages," *Guardian*, June 19, 2004.

41 Genocide was "curiously absent" from the charge-sheet for Milosevic's actions in Kosovo, "despite the fact that the arc of crime and atrocity in Kosovo seems to fit the Convention's legal definition quite neatly." Peter Ronayne, "Genocide in Kosovo," *Human Rights Review*, 5: 4 (2004), p. 66.

42 "Ex-Kosovo PM Pleads Not Guilty to War Crimes," Reuters dispatch, March 14, 2005.
43 "UN and Nato Slammed over Kosovo," *BBC Online*, July 26, 2004. http://news.bbc.co.uk/1/hi/world/europe/3928153.stm.

BOX 8A GENOCIDE IN BANGLADESH, 1971

By some estimates, the mass killings in Bangladesh – at the time, East Pakistan – are on a par with the twentieth century's most destructive genocides. At least one million Bengalis, perhaps as many as three million,[1] were massacred by the security forces of West Pakistan, assisted by local allies. Yet the genocide remains almost unknown in the West. Only recently has its prominence slightly increased, as a result of a handful of education and memorialization projects.[2]

Although it preceded events in the Balkans by two decades, the Bangladeshi genocide is usefully placed alongside the Bosnia and Kosovo case study. Both conflicts had at their core a militarized security threat; a crisis surrounding secession of federal units; and ethnic conflict. On a strategic and tactical level, both genocides featured strong elements of "eliticide" (the destruction of the socioeconomic and intellectual elites of a target group), as well as the gendercidal targeting of adult and adolescent males (see Chapter 13).

The federation of East and West Pakistan was forged in the crucible of Indian independence in 1947–48. Most of India had been under British rule for two centuries. As independence loomed after the Second World War, two distinct political projects arose. One, associated with the century's leading proponent of non-violence, Mohandas (Mahatma) Gandhi, sought to keep India whole and prevent division along religious and ethnic lines. However, strong Hindu and Muslim nationalist movements, together with the departing British, pushed for the creation of two states – one Hindu-dominated (India), the other Muslim-dominated (Pakistan). This project emerged triumphant, but not without enormous bloodshed. The partition of India in 1947 witnessed one of the greatest movements of peoples in modern times, as millions of Muslims fled India for Pakistan, and millions of Hindus moved in the other direction. Hundreds of thousands of people were slaughtered on both sides.[3]

Not the least of Pakistan's post-independence difficulties was its division into two wings, separated by 1,200 miles of Indian territory and an ethnolinguistic gulf. West Pakistan, home to some fifty-five million people in 1971, was predominantly Urdu-speaking. The Bengali speakers of East Pakistan occupied only one-third of total Pakistani territory, but were the demographic majority – some seventy-five million people. Most were Muslim, but there was also a large Bengali Hindu minority (the Biharis) who suffered especially savage treatment during the genocide. Even Bengali Muslims were viewed as second-class citizens by the inhabitants of wealthier West Pakistan. Pakistani Lieutenant-General A.A.K. Niazi referred to the Ganges river plain – home to the majority of

Map 8a.1 Bangladesh

Source: Map provided by WorldAtlas.com

Bengalis and the largest city, Dhaka – as a "low-lying land of low, lying people." According to R.J. Rummel, "Bengalis were often compared with monkeys and chickens. . . . The [minority] Hindus among the Bengalis were as Jews to the Nazis: scum and vermin that [had] best be exterminated."[4]

Reacting to West Pakistan's persistent discrimination and economic exploitation,[5] a strong autonomy movement arose in the East, centered on the Awami League of Sheikh Mujibur Rahman. The spark for the conflagration came in December 1970, in national elections held to pave the way for a transition from military rule. The Awami League won a crushing victory – 167 out of East Pakistan's 169 parliamentary seats. This gave the League a majority in the Pakistani Parliament as a whole, and the right to form the next government.

West Pakistani rulers, led by General Yahya Khan, saw this as a direct threat to their power and interests. After negotiations failed to resolve the impasse, Khan met with four senior generals on February 22, 1971, and issued orders to annihilate the Awami League and its popular base. From the outset, they planned a campaign of genocide. "Kill three million [Bengalis]," said Khan, "and the rest will eat out of our hands."[6]

On March 25, the genocide was launched. In an attempt to decapitate East Pakistan's political and intellectual leadership, Dhaka University – a center of nationalist agitation – was attacked. Hundreds of students were killed in what was dubbed "Operation Searchlight." Working from prepared lists, death squads roamed the streets. Perhaps 7,000 people died in a single night, 30,000 over the course of a week. The terror sparked an epic flight by Bengalis: "it was estimated that in April some thirty million people [!] were wandering helplessly across East Pakistan to escape the grasp of the military."[7] The ten to twelve million-strong Hindu community of East Pakistan was also targeted *en bloc*; Hindus comprised most of the ten million souls who fled to India as refugees. This spurred increasing calls for Indian military intervention, which would have the added advantage – from India's perspective – of dismembering Pakistan. (The countries had already fought two full-scale wars by 1971; they were, and remain, poised for another one.) The surviving Awami League leadership moved quickly to declare a fully independent Bangladesh, and to organize a guerrilla resistance.

With the opening eliticide accomplished, the West Pakistani leadership moved to eradicate the nationalist base. As the election results suggested, this comprised the vast majority of Bengalis. Genocidal killing, however, followed a gendercidal pattern, with all males beyond childhood viewed as actual or potential guerrilla fighters. To produce the desired number of corpses, the West Pakistanis set up "extermination camps"[8] and launched a massive round of gendercidal killing:

> The place of execution was the river edge [here, the Buriganga River outside Dhaka], or the shallows near the shore, and the bodies were disposed of by the simple means of permitting them to flow downstream. The killing took place night after night. Usually the prisoners were roped together and made to wade out into the river. They were in batches of six or eight, and in the light of a powerful electric arc lamp, they were easy targets, black against the silvery water. The executioners stood on the pier, shooting down at the compact bunches of prisoners wading in the water. There were screams in the hot night air, and then silence. The prisoners fell on their sides and their bodies lapped against the shore. Then a new bunch of prisoners was brought out, and the process was repeated. In the morning the village boatmen hauled the bodies into midstream and the ropes binding the bodies were cut so that each body drifted separately downstream.[9]

The West Pakistani campaign extended to mass rape, aimed at "dishonoring" Bengali women and undermining Bengali society. Between 200,000 and 400,000 women were victimized. "Girls of eight and grandmothers of seventy-five had been sexually assaulted," wrote feminist author Susan Brownmiller in her book, *Against Our Will: Men, Women and Rape.*[10] An unknown number of women were gang-raped to death, or executed after repeated violations.

The slaughter and other atrocities were ended by one of the rare instances of successful outside intervention in genocide.[11] Indian troops invaded in December 1971, vanquishing West Pakistani forces in a couple of weeks. The independence of Bangladesh was sealed, though at a staggering human cost.

In blood-letting following the expulsion of the West Pakistani army, perhaps 150,000 people were murdered by independence forces and local vigilantes. Biharis who had collaborated with West Pakistani authorities were dealt with especially harshly.[12] Themes of the post-genocide era include the continued suffering and social marginalization of hundreds of thousands of Bengali rape victims, and the enduring impunity of the *génocidaires.* None of the leaders of the genocide has ever been brought to trial; all remain comfortably ensconced in Pakistan (the former West Pakistan) and other countries. In recent years, activists have worked to try those leaders before an international tribunal, so far without success.[13]

FURTHER STUDY

Rounaq Jahan, "Genocide in Bangladesh," in Samuel Totten *et al.*, eds, *Century of Genocide: Eyewitness Accounts and Critical Views.* New York: Garland Publishing, 1997. A rare treatment in the genocide-studies literature.

Anthony Mascarenhas, *The Rape of Bangla Desh.* Delhi: Vikas Publications, 1971. A decent overview; one takes what one can get in English on this little-studied subject.

Robert Payne, *Massacre.* London: Macmillan, 1973. Journalistic account of the genocide.

Richard Sisson and Leo Rose, *War and Secession: Pakistan, India, and the Creation of Bangladesh.* Berkeley, CA: University of California Press, 1990. Focuses on policy-making by leaders during the crisis.

NOTES

1 R.J. Rummel observes: "The human death toll over only 267 days was incredible. Just to give for five out of the eighteen districts some incomplete statistics published in Bangladesh newspapers or by an Inquiry Committee, the Pakistani army killed 100,000 Bengalis in Dacca, 150,000 in Khulna, 75,000 in Jessore, 95,000 in Comilla, and 100,000 in Chittagong. For eighteen districts the total is 1,247,000 killed. This was an incomplete toll, and to this day no one really knows the final

toll . . .," which Rummel estimates may have reached three million. Rummel, *Death By Government* (New Brunswick, NJ: Transaction Publishers, 1994), p. 331.

2 See in particular the Liberation War Museum Online at http://www.liberationmuseum.org/.

3 On partition, see Paul R. Brass, "The Partition of India and Retributive Genocide in the Punjab, 1946–47: Means, Methods, and Purposes," *Journal of Genocide Research*, 5: 1 (March 2003), pp. 71–101; Urvashi Butalia, *The Other Side of Silence: Voices from the Partition of India* (Durham, NC: Duke University Press, 2000).

4 Rummel, *Death by Government*, p. 335.

5 "The Bangladesh nationalist movement was also fueled by a sense of economic exploitation. Though jute, the major export earning commodity, was produced in Bengal, most of the economic investments took place in Pakistan. A systematic transfer of resources took place from East to West Pakistan creating a growing economic disparity and a feeling among the Bengalis that they were being treated as a colony by Pakistan." Rounaq Jahan, "Genocide in Bangladesh," ch. 10 in Samuel Totten *et al.*, eds, *Century of Genocide: Eyewitness Accounts and Critical Views* (New York: Garland Publishing, 1997), p. 292.

6 Quoted in Robert Payne, *Massacre* (London: Macmillan, 1973), p. 50.

7 Payne, *Massacre*, p. 48.

8 Leo Kuper, *The Prevention of Genocide* (New Haven, CT: Yale University Press, 1985), p. 47.

9 Payne, *Massacre*, p. 55. For more on the gendercidal character of the large majority of killings during the genocide, see Adam Jones/Gendercide Watch, "Case Study: Genocide in Bangladesh, 1971," http://www.gendercide.org/case_bangladesh.html, from which Box 8a is adapted.

10 Susan Brownmiller, *Against Our Will: Men, Women and Rape* (New York: Bantam, 1975), p. 83.

11 For a concise overview of the Indian intervention, see Nicholas J. Wheeler, "India as Rescuer? Order versus Justice in the Bangladesh War of 1971," ch. 2 in Wheeler, *Saving Strangers: Humanitarian Intervention in International Society* (Oxford: Oxford University Press, 2000), pp. 55–77. For a discussion of the role of the United States and then-secretary of state Henry Kissinger, see Suhail Islam and Syed Hassan, "The Wretched of the Nations: The West's Role in Human Rights Violations in the Bangladesh War of Independence," in Adam Jones, ed., *Genocide, War Crimes and the West: History and Complicity* (London: Zed Books, 2004), pp. 201–13.

12 During the genocide, Urdu-speaking Biharis in East Pakistan "joined the West Pakistanis in killing the Bengalis." This exposed them to retaliation from "Awami League supporters [who] also engaged in killing the West Pakistanis and Biharis in East Pakistan. A white paper issued by the Pakistani government shows that the Awami League had massacred at least 30,000 Biharis and West Pakistanis," atrocious behavior that nonetheless does not match the systematic slaughter of Bengalis by the West Pakistanis and their Bihari allies. See Wardatul Akman, "Atrocities against Humanity during the Liberation War in Bangladesh: A Case of Genocide," *Journal of Genocide Research*, 4: 4 (2002), p. 549; also "The Right to Self Determination: The Secession of Bangladesh," ch. 4 in Kuper, *The Prevention of Genocide*, pp. 44–61.

13 See, e.g., the website of the evocatively named "Bangla Nuremberg" project, http://www.shobak.org/bangla_nuremberg/.

CHAPTER 9

Holocaust in Rwanda

INTRODUCTION: HORROR AND SHAME

The genocide that consumed the tiny Central African country of Rwanda from April to July 1994 was in some ways without precedent. In just twelve weeks, at least one million people – overwhelmingly Tutsis, but also tens of thousands of Hutus opposed to the genocidal government – were murdered, primarily by machetes, clubs, and small arms. About 80 percent of victims died in a "hurricane of death . . . between the second week of April and the third week of May," noted Gérard Prunier. "If we consider that probably around 800,000 people were slaughtered during that short period . . . the daily killing rate was at least five times that of the Nazi death camps."[1]

While debate has raged over the extent of the complicity of "ordinary Germans" in the genocide against the Jews and others, the German killers were in uniform, and strict measures were taken to ensure that the civilian population did not witness the mass slaughter. In Rwanda, by contrast, the civilian Hutu population – men, women, and even children – was actively conscripted and comprised the bulk of *génocidaires*: "For the first time in modern history, a state succeeded in transforming the mass of its population into murderers."[2]

Despite noble pledges of "Never Again" following the Jewish Holocaust, the international community stood by while a million defenseless victims died. Numerous warnings of impending genocide were transmitted, and an armed United Nations "assistance mission" (UNAMIR), under the command of Canadian Major-General Roméo Dallaire, had been in place in the capital, Kigali, since October 1993.

In what one UNAMIR officer would later refer to as an "act of total cowardice,"[3] well-armed foreign forces were flown in when the genocide broke out – but only to evacuate whites. In one notorious instance captured on video, at the Caraes Psychiatric Hospital in Ndera, Kigali prefecture, a few sobbing whites were evacuated while rapacious militia members cruised just outside the gates, and some hundreds of terrified Tutsi refugees begged the foreign troops for protection. "Solve your problems yourselves," shouted one soldier to the crowd. The Tutsis were massacred within hours of the troops' departure.[4]

With the expatriates safely removed, the UN Security Council turned its attention to withdrawing UNAMIR forces. A US State Department memorandum of April 14, 1994 instructed the US mission to the UN to "give highest priority to full, orderly withdrawal of all UNAMIR personnel as soon as possible."[5] On April 21, the Council voted to withdraw all but 270 of the 2,500-strong UNAMIR contingent. "In a clearly illegal act," General Dallaire and Brigadier General Henry Kwami Anyidoho, who commanded the Ghanaian contingent of the UN force, managed to defy the Council order and hold on to about 470 peacekeepers. Even these few were enough to save thousands of lives over the course of the genocide.[6]

On May 17, the UN Security Council would finally vote to despatch 5,500 troops to Rwanda, "but authorizing a higher troop figure is not the same as actually finding the troops' contributors."[7] The troops did not arrive until after the genocide had ended. The United States spent long weeks bickering with the UN over the lease of ancient armored-personnel carriers. They, too, would not arrive until "after the genocide was over and they were stripped of machine guns, radio[s], tools, spare parts and training manuals. General Dallaire described them as tons of rusting metal."[8]

For all the lofty rhetoric of universal human rights, it seemed, "Rwanda was simply too remote, too far, too poor, too little, and probably too black to be worthwhile," in the scathing assessment of human rights investigator Alison Des Forges.[9] General Dallaire, for his part, issued a blistering denunciation at the end of his tenure in 1994: "Although Rwanda and UNAMIR have been at the centre of a terrible human tragedy, that is not to say Holocaust, and although many fine words had been pronounced by all, including members of the Security Council, the tangible effort . . . has been totally, completely ineffective."[10]

In March 2004, UN Secretary-General Kofi Annan offered a qualified apology for member states' unwillingness to confront the Rwandan catastrophe. "The international community failed Rwanda, and that must leave us always with a sense of bitter regret and abiding sorrow." Ten years after the slaughter, Annan asked: "Are we confident that, confronted by a new Rwanda today, we can respond effectively, in good time?" His response was sobering: "We can by no means be certain we would."[11]

BACKGROUND TO GENOCIDE

Understanding the human catastrophe that consumed Rwanda in 1994 requires attention to a host of complex factors. They include:

- the colonial and post-colonial history of the country, notably the politicization of Hutu and Tutsi ethnicities under Belgian rule and into the independence era that began in 1959;
- the authoritarian and tightly regulated character of the political system installed by the nation's post-independence rulers, including the second-class political status it assigned to Tutsis, fueling a Tutsi-led rebel movement based in Uganda;
- the role of outside actors, especially France, in financing and fueling Hutu extremism;
- the pervasive economic crisis in Rwanda, one of the world's poorest and most densely populated countries;
- the international factors that inhibited and occasionally encouraged humanitarian interventions in the first half of the 1990s.

As with the Balkans genocide (Chapter 8), foreign observers tended to view the Rwandan conflict as an expression of "ancient tribal hatreds." Until the twentieth century, however, "Hutus" and "Tutsis" did not constitute separate nations. It is hard even to describe them as distinct ethnicities, since they share the same language, territory, and religion. Rather, the two groups in the pre-colonial period may be viewed as *social castes*, based on material wealth. Broadly speaking, Tutsis were those who owned cattle; Hutus tilled the land and provided labor to the Tutsis. The designations were hardly arbitrary, and they indeed had a basis in physiognomic differences (see below). But they were fluid and permeable, as Professor of Government Mahmood Mamdani notes: "The rare Hutu who was able to accumulate cattle and rise through the socioeconomic hierarchy could *kwihutura* – shed Hutuness – and achieve the political status of a Tutsi. Conversely, the loss of property could also lead to the loss of status, summed up in the Kinyarwanda word *gucupira*." These processes were "of little significance statistically," but "their social and political significance cannot be overstated."[12] Thus, "although Rwanda was definitely not a land of peace and bucolic harmony before the arrival of the Europeans, there is no trace in its precolonial history of systematic violence between Tutsi and Hutu as such."[13]

From its beginnings around the seventeenth century, the political organization of Rwandan society featured "centralised forms of political authority and . . . a high degree of social control," reflecting "the fact that the land is small, the population density is (and has always been) high and social interactions are constant, intense and value-laden."[14] This authoritarianism reached its apogee under the rule of Mwami Kigeri Rwabugiri (1860-1895), at which point traditional obligations of *corvée* labor came to be imposed on Hutus alone, "thereby polarizing the social difference between Hutu and Tutsi."[15]

In 1894, Germany established indirect suzerainty over Rwanda, coopting and taking over the pyramidal structure of political rule. The Germans gave way, after their defeat in the First World War, to Belgian colonial administration. The Belgians were the first to rigidly codify Hutu and Tutsi designations. In the divide-and-rule tradition, Tutsis became colonial favorites and protégés.[16] In part, this reflected the Tutsis' minority status – it is often easier for colonizers to secure the allegiance of a minority, which recognizes that its survival may depend on bonds with the imperial authority (see Chapter 12). It also derived from an egregious nineteenth-century

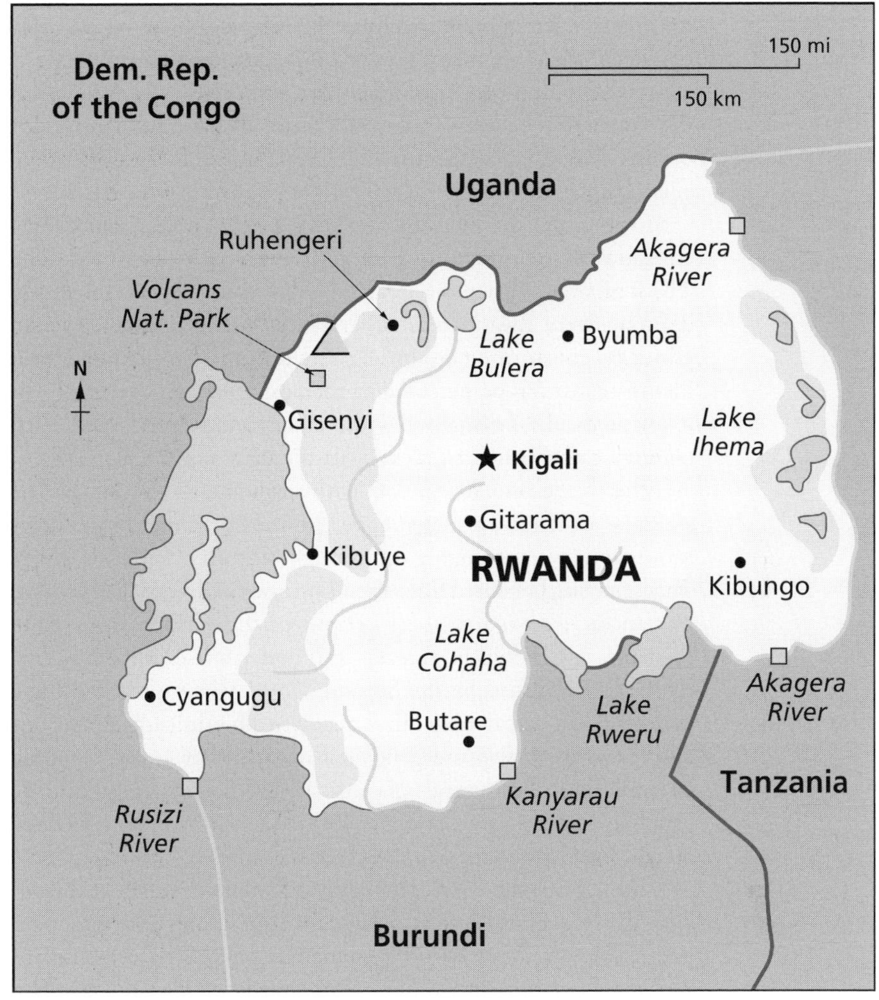

Map 9.1 Rwanda

Source: Map provided by WorldAtlas.com

contribution of the nascent discipline of anthropology. Early explorers of Central Africa, notably the Englishman John Hanning Speke, propounded the "Hamitic hypothesis." This depicted the Hutu as offspring of Ham, the black son of Noah, cursed by God and destined forever to serve as "hewers of wood and drawers of water"; and, by noble contrast, the Tutsi caste, descended from the Nilotic civilization of classical Egypt. As was typical of imperial racial theorizing, the mark of civilization was grafted on to physiognomic difference, with the generally taller, supposedly more refined Tutsis destined to rule, and shorter, allegedly less refined Hutus to serve.[17]

Under Belgian rule and afterwards, Tutsis and Hutus were indoctrinated with this Hamitic hypothesis. The *caste* character of the designations was gradually transformed into a *racial* distinction that shaped ethnic identity and fueled Hutu resentment, which erupted first in post-independence massacres in 1959–60 and then, in 1994, in genocide. In 1994, taller Hutus died at roadblocks because they were assumed to be Tutsis, whatever their identity cards said. And the corpses of thousands of Tutsi victims were dumped into the Nyabarongo river, which flowed into Lake Victoria, the source of the Nile – thus symbolically dispatching Tutsis back to their "Nilotic" origins (see Chapter 12 for more on the symbolic dimension of the Rwandan genocide).[18]

It was under the Belgians, too, that a new, racially segregated state, church, and education system was constructed. Tutsis were assigned a dominant role in each.[19] The symbol of the newly bureaucratized system was the distribution of identity cards defining every Rwandan as either Hutu, Tutsi, or Twa – the last of these a Pygmy ethnicity, constituting around 2 percent of the population. The institution of these identity cards was perpetuated by the post-colonial government, and in 1994 proved a key genocidal facilitator. At the thousands of roadblocks established across the country, carrying a Tutsi identity card meant a death sentence.

After the Second World War, with anti-colonial national liberation movements in ascendance, Belgian authorities performed a dramatic about-face. Pro-independence movements were springing up throughout the colonized world, and in Rwanda the Tutsis, having benefited from their positions of dominance in education and the state bureaucracy, moved to the forefront of the various anti-colonial initiatives. The Belgians, perceiving the threat – and perhaps also influenced by the democratizing tendency unleashed by the Second World War – switched their favor to the less-educated, less-threatening Hutu majority. This unleashed pent-up Hutu frustrations, and led to the first proto-genocidal massacres of Tutsis, claiming several thousand victims. Tens of thousands of Tutsis fled to neighboring Zaire, Tanzania, and especially Uganda, where the exiles formed an armed rebel movement and launched attacks into Rwanda.

Throughout the 1960s, remaining Rwandan Tutsis established a *modus vivendi* with the new Hutu-dominated order. Although almost totally frozen out of formal political power, they were not systematically expelled from other institutional spheres, such as schools and the Catholic Church; and under the rule of Hutu dictator Juvénal Habyarimana, who seized the presidency in a 1973 coup, their conditions improved.

But trouble was brewing just beneath the surface. Although Habyarimana projected a liberal image, to attract foreign aid, his regime was dominated by the *akazu*, or "little house": "a tightly knit mafia" of Hutus from the north of Rwanda that coalesced around the figure of Habyarimana's wife, Agathe.[20] It was the *akazu* that, operating as "the 'invisible government' of Rwanda during Habyarimana's reign,"[21] gradually increased ethnic hatred against the Tutsis, encouraging a climate of fear and panic to forestall demands for democracy.

In 1987, Rwandan exiles in Uganda formed the Rwandan Patriotic Front, and in 1990 the RPF launched a military invasion of Rwanda.[22] This offensive had three crucial results. First, it brought immediate outside assistance to prop up the Habyarimana regime – from France, a country that had constructed its post-colonial role in Africa around support for *La Francophonie*, the network of French-speaking countries that Paris viewed as a bulwark against the "Anglo" influence typified by Uganda. French forces succeeded in stalling the RPF invasion, and they remained to train and advise the Hutu military and militias that would implement the 1994 genocide. Second, military conflict exacerbated the economic crisis in Rwanda. "Fragile at the start, the Rwandan economy . . . crumbled under the burden of the costs of war," wrote Alison Des Forges. "Living conditions worsened dramatically as per capita income that stood at US $320 in 1989 (nineteenth poorest in the world) fell to US $200 in 1993."[23] Third, the invasion, with its abuses and atrocities against Hutu civilians, contributed to a growing climate of fear among ordinary Hutus, already deeply anxious after genocidal massacres of Hutus in next-door Burundi by the Tutsi-dominated armed forces there.[24]

Invasion from without; economic crisis; growing domestic and international support for extremists – it is hard to imagine more propitious circumstances for genocide. Between 1990 and 1993, "a series of minipogroms against Tutsi [took place] in different parts of the country," which in retrospect appear to be "rehearsals for the conflagration of 1994."[25] Perhaps 2,000 people were murdered. A UN Special Rapporteur, Bacre Waly Ndiaye, visited Rwanda in April 1993 and "decided that the word genocide was appropriate and that the Convention on the Prevention and Punishment of the Crime of Genocide of 1948 was applicable" to these killings. His superiors in Geneva warned him to avoid the term, but he used it nonetheless in his report, which was quickly buried ("Ndiaye said later that he might just as well have put the report in a bottle and thrown it into the sea").[26]

Exterminationist propaganda against Tutsis became commonplace in Rwanda. As early as December 1990, the infamous "Hutu Ten Commandments" were issued by the Hutu extremist paper *Kangura*; "The Hutu must be firm and vigilant against their common Tutsi enemy," read one of the commandments. In August 1993, the radio station RTLM (Radio-Télévision Libre des Mille Collines) began broadcasting, with funding from the Christian Democratic International.[27] RTLM transformed the staid Rwandan media, and fueled a hysterical fear of the threat posed by RPF forces and their "fifth column" inside Rwanda – the Tutsi minority, designated by RTLM as *inyenzi*, or "cockroaches." "The cruelty of the *inyenzi* is incurable," declared one broadcast; "the[ir] cruelty . . . can only be cured by their total extermination."[28]

Propaganda and militia killings reached a peak precisely when the Habyarimana regime was being pressured to respect its 1990 pledge to implement multiparty democracy and seek peace with the RPF. The Arusha Peace Accords of August 1993 guaranteed free elections in less than two years, to include the RPF, which had been allowed to install several hundred troops in Kigali. Some 2,500 foreign peacekeepers arrived to constitute the United Nations Assistance Mission for Rwanda (UNAMIR); their task was to monitor the ceasefire and the prelude to elections.

The Arusha Accords and the UNAMIR intervention proved to be the last straw for "Hutu Power" extremists. Genocide against the Tutsi minority would simultaneously eliminate the perceived constituency for the RPF; resolve the economic crisis through distribution of Tutsi land, wealth, and jobs; and bind the Hutu majority in genocidal complicity. The extremists imported hundreds of thousands of machetes in 1993–94; this weapon would become the symbol of the Rwanda genocide.

GENOCIDAL FRENZY[29]

At 8:30 p.m. on April 6, 1994, the plane carrying President Habyarimana back from talks in Tanzania was shot down as it neared Kigali airport. By 9:18, the Presidential Guard had begun to erect roadblocks around Kigali.

The following day, working from carefully prepared lists, soldiers and militias began murdering thousands of Tutsis and oppositionist Hutus. Crucially, ten Belgian peacekeepers protecting the moderate Prime Minister, Agathe Uwimiliyana, were seized, tortured, and murdered, along with Uwimiliyana herself. The murders prompted Belgium to withdraw its remaining forces from Rwanda. Over the heated protests of UNAMIR commander Dallaire, other countries followed suit. Foreign journalists also departed *en bloc*.

From the start, the extremist government capitalized on several factors that they appear to have known would limit outside opposition to the genocide. First, they played upon stereotypes of African "tribal conflict," depicting the killings as reciprocal excesses. Second, they seem to have realized that killing some foreign troops would scare away the remainder, with memories still fresh of the 1993 Battle of Mogadishu, when two dozen Pakistani troops and eighteen US Rangers died at the hands of Somali militias.[30] Third, the extremists benefited from the "blind commitment" of the French government to its Rwandan counterpart: "the Rwandese leadership kept believing that *no matter what it did*, French support would always be forthcoming. And it had no valid reasons for believing otherwise."[31] Lastly, the "Hutu Power" regime exploited the limited energy and resources of international media and public opinion where Africa was concerned, and the fact that media attention was overwhelmingly directed towards the inaugural free elections in South Africa.

Army and militia forces went street to street, block by block, and house to house, in Kigali and every other major city save Butare in the south (which resisted the genocidal impetus for two weeks before its prefect was deposed and killed, and replaced by a compliant *génocidaire*). Tutsis were dragged out of homes and hiding places and murdered, often after torture and rape. At the infamous roadblocks, those carrying Tutsi identity cards – along with some Hutus who were deemed to "look" Tutsi – were shot or hacked to death. Often the killers, whether drunk and willing or conscripted and reluctant, severed the Achilles' tendon of their victims to immobilize them. They would be left for hours in agony, until the murderers mustered the energy to return and finish them off. Numerous accounts exist of Tutsis paying to be killed by rifle bullets, rather than slowly and agonizingly with machetes and hoes.

In what can only be called "an incomprehensible scandal,"[32] the killings took place literally before the eyes of UNAMIR and other foreign forces, whose mandate and orders forbade them to intervene. As early as April 9, in the church at Gikondo in Kigali, a slaughter occurred that presaged the strategies to be followed in coming weeks – one that was witnessed by Polish nuns, priests, and UN military observers:

> A Presidential Guard officer arrived and told the soldiers not to waste their bullets because the Interahamwe [Hutu Power militia] would soon come with machetes. Then the militia came in, one hundred of them, and threatening the [Polish]

> priests they began to kill people, slashing with their machetes and clubs, hacking arms, legs, genitals and the faces of the terrified people who tried to protect the children under the pews. Some people were dragged outside the church and attacked in the courtyard. The killing continued for two hours as the whole compound was searched. Only two people are believed to have survived the killing at the church. Not even babies were spared. That day in Gikondo there was a street littered with corpses the length of a kilometre. . . . The killing in Gikondo was done in broad daylight with no attempt to disguise the identity of the killers, who were convinced that there would be no punishment for their actions.[33]

The following day, April 10, the UN established contact with military observers in Gisenyi, the heartland of Hutu extremism, where mass killing had erupted three days earlier. The stunned observers described "total chaos" with "massacres everywhere," leaving tens of thousands of Tutsi corpses.[34] With such reports to hand, and the eyewitness testimony of observers in Gikondo, the UN and the international community was fully aware, within a few days of Habyarimana's death on April 6, that killing on a genocidal scale was occurring in Rwanda. They did nothing, though there were more than enough troops on hand to stop the killings in Kigali at the very least.[35] Indeed, Security Council members – notably France and the US – both cautioned against and actually ridiculed the use of the word "genocide." It seems evident, in retrospect, that the *génocidaires* were not only hoping for such a response, but were awaiting it before launching a full-scale slaughter. Linda Melvern's fine book *Conspiracy to Murder* conveys the sense of suspended animation in the first week of the genocide, while Hutu Power gauged international reactions to the opening wave of killing. When it became clear there would be no outside impediment, murder spread like a virus across the territories under extremist control. By April 23, Roméo Dallaire, on a journey north from the capital, was "pass[ing] over bridges in swamps that had been lifted by the force of the bodies piling up on the struts. We had inched our way through villages of dead humans. . . . We had created paths amongst the dead and half-dead with our hands. And we had thrown up even when there was nothing in our stomachs."[36]

Tens of thousands of Tutsis sought sanctuary in schools, stadiums, and especially places of worship. But there was no sanctuary to be had. In fact, those encouraging them to seek it were usually *génocidaires* working to concentrate their victims for mass killing. Astonishingly, church figures across Rwanda played a leading role in legitimizing and even inflicting genocidal killing (although "many priests, pastors and nuns" also displayed "courage and compassion," hiding and protecting potential victims).[37]

Parish churches, along with schools and similar facilities, were soon piled thigh-high with the shot, hacked, and savaged corpses of the victims.[38] One such massacre, in fact, may stand as the most concentrated ground-level slaughter of the twentieth century (by which is meant a mass killing inflicted in hours or days rather than months or years, and by means other than aerial bombing). On April 20, at the parish of Karama in Butare prefecture, "between thirty-five and forty-three thousand people died *in less than six hours*."[39] This was more than were killed in the Nazis' two-day slaughters of Jews outside Odessa and Kiev (at Babi Yar) in 1941, or in the largest single-day extermination spree in the gas chambers of Auschwitz-Birkenau.[40]

Figure 9.1 Tutsi women murdered in the Rwandan genocide of 1994.

Source: Panos Pictures/Martin Adler.

BOX 9.1 ONE WOMAN'S STORY: GLORIOSE MUKAKANIMBA

A Tutsi woman and mother of three, Gloriose Mukakanimba lived in the Rwandan capital of Kigali, where she ran a tailoring shop. On April 7, 1994, she witnessed the outbreak of the most intensive mass-killing spree in human history. Hutu militias –

the so-called *interahamwe* ("those who fight together") – went door-to-door. They first targeted "prominent and rich people," Gloriose said, but quickly moved on to attack ordinary citizens: "They shot you just because you were a Tutsi. When they started using machetes, they didn't even bother to ask for ID cards. It was as if they had carried out a census; they knew you were a Tutsi."

Gloriose's home was one of those invaded. "Around 11:00 a.m. on Sunday [April 10] a large group of interahamwe came to our house. They tried to break the gate. They had difficulties with the gate so they cut through the hedge. They came in and started searching the house." After a while, they prepared to leave – but their leader arrived and ordered them "to go back in and kill." Her family was ordered outside. There, her husband, Déo Rutayisire, and her brother, Maurice Niyoyita, were hacked to death with machetes. Gloriose tried to flee with her 2-year-old daughter in her arms, but the child slipped from her grasp, "and I saw them cutting her up. I ran with all the strength I had."

While she desperately sought a place to hide, Gloriose was stunned to hear her neighbors calling out to the militia members: "Here she is, here she is!" "These were neighbors I had already considered friends, people I felt had been kind to me." Finally she found sanctuary in an abandoned house with an old vehicle parked adjacent. "The bonnet was open and it did not have an engine. I jumped right inside the bonnet and stayed there for about a day and a half." Militia scoured the house, coming close to the car where she was hiding. "I could feel them so near to me. I was terrified to death. I stopped myself from breathing."

When the interahamwe moved on, Gloriose begged for refuge from a neighbor who had been friendly with her sister. But the neighbor demanded that she leave. She decided to return to her house, only to run into an "ambush [that] had been set up for me." She was detained for a few hours, until the militia decided to execute her. An interahamwe "hit me with the machete. Fortunately it was dark and he could not see very well. He kept trying to aim for my neck but I instinctively put my hands over my neck. He kept hitting my hands, thinking it was my neck. After a while, I decided to let him think I was dead." Finally "they left, thinking they had finished their job."

Gloriose ran to hide in a water-filled ditch. But "some other militia saw me and went to tell my killers that they had not completed their job. The next morning, my killers came back, this time with guns and grenades." They shot and tossed grenades into the trench, but Gloriose was able to evade them. "It was a very long trench. This made it difficult for them to know my exact location because of course I kept moving."

Apparently believing she must have been killed by the fusillade, the militia again moved on. "I spent the night in the trench. The wounds in my arms were not only extremely painful but had come to smell. I decided to come out of the trench for fear that I would die there." She fled to the nearby residence of one of the few surviving Tutsi families in the area: "I found out that the husband had been an invalid for a long time; maybe that's why the killers let them live." Together with her rescuers, she joined a flood of Tutsis heading towards the lines of the rebel Rwandan Patriotic Front in Gitarama district.

On the verge of starvation, she and her companions finally stumbled on an RPF patrol. She was taken to a health center in the city of Rutare. There, her wounds were treated, and she was interviewed by researchers from African Rights, a London-based organization that would go on to publish the most detailed and harrowing account of the Rwandan genocide.[41]

In Kibuye prefecture, some 20,000 Tutsis had congregated at Gatwaro stadium. The stadium was surrounded by soldiers and militia, who began firing into the stadium and at anyone who sought to flee. Twelve thousand people died in a single day. Elsewhere in the prefecture, perhaps the most exterminatory killing of the genocide took place. "Entire Tutsi communities were wiped out with no witnesses left to tell what happened. From a population of 252,000 Tutsi in a 1991 census, by the end of June there were an estimated 8,000 left alive."[42]

Many Tutsis fled to high ground, such as Bisesero mountain in southwestern Rwanda. The "mountain of death" was the scene of unforgettable acts of resistance, as Tutsis sought desperately to fend off the attacks. A survivor, Claver Mbugufe, recalled:

> There were constant attempts to kill the refugees at Bisesero. But we were always able to defend ourselves. Towards mid-May, when we were still in the grip of the interahamwe militia and their allies, they received enormous reinforcements. . . . Soldiers also came and set up a camp near Bisesero for three days, during which they killed many refugees. We spent the entire day running up and down. We tried to concentrate our defence in one area in order to break their stranglehold. We did everything possible to kill any one of them who stood in our way. Sometimes, we even managed to wrest guns from soldiers and policemen. We killed many of these aggressors.[43]

Despite such heroism, some 50,000 people died at Bisesero in April and May. A series of other massacres, notably in Cyahindu prefecture, claimed over 10,000 victims at one time. Then there were the "death camps" such as those in the Kabgayi archbishopric, where "over thirty thousand terrified Tutsis" congregated.[44] Militia roamed freely through Kabgayi, selecting Tutsi men and boys for execution, and women and girls for rape. (The gendering of the Rwandan catastrophe is discussed further in Chapter 13.) This horror ended only when the Rwandan Patriotic Front captured Kabgayi on June 2.

Throughout, a remarkable feature of the genocide was its routinized character. The killings were "marked not by the fury of combat or paroxysms of mob violence, but by a well-ordered sanity that mirrored the rhythms of ordinary collective life."[45] Killers arrived for their duties at a designated hour, and broke off their murderous activities at five in the afternoon, as though clocking off.

Another signal feature, as noted above, was the involvement of ordinary Hutus in the slaughter. "Had the killing been the work of state functionaries and those bribed by them," writes Mamdani, "it would have translated into no more than a string of massacres perpetrated by death squads. Without massacres by machete-wielding civilian mobs, in the hundreds and thousands, there would have been no genocide."[46] In a development perhaps unprecedented in the history of genocide, Hutu women flocked or were conscripted by the tens of thousands to participate in the killing of Tutsis and the stripping of corpses. To the extent that their violence was directed against Tutsi women,

> there appears to have been a kind of gendered jubilation at the "comeuppance" of Tutsi females, who had for so long been depicted in Hutu propaganda as Rwanda's sexual elite. Otherwise, the motivations for women's involvement as genocidal killers frequently paralleled those of Hutu men: bonds of ethnic solidarity . . . suasion and coercion by those in authority (including other women); the lure of material gain; and the intoxicating pleasure of untrammelled sadism.[47]

It is impossible to know how many of the killers, male and female, would have avoided their role if they could. It is clear, however, that hundreds of thousands of Hutus participated eagerly. "It was as if all the men, women and children had come to kill us," recalled one survivor.[48] Many were motivated by greed – the chance to loot Tutsi belongings and seize Tutsi land (see Chapter 10). And for those at the bottom of the social ladder, there was the unprecedented opportunity to exercise life-and-death power over others. Gérard Prunier captures this element vividly, noting that "social envy came together with political hatred to fire the . . . bloodlust":

> In Kigali the [militias] . . . had tended to recruit mostly among the poor. As soon as they went into action, they drew around them a cloud of even poorer people, a lumpenproletariat of street boys, rag-pickers, car-washers and homeless unemployed. For these people the genocide was the best thing that could ever happen to them. They had the blessings of a form of authority to take revenge on socially powerful people as long as these [victims] were on the wrong side of the political fence. They could steal, they could kill with minimum justification, they could rape and they could get drunk for free. This was wonderful. The political aims pursued by the masters of this dark carnival were quite beyond their scope. They just went along, knowing it would not last.[49]

It did not last – in part because the killers were running out of victims, but in larger part because the genocide distracted the Hutu Power regime from confronting RPF forces. Immediately following the outbreak of the genocide on April 6–7, the RPF contingent in Kigali had moved out of its barracks to establish control over several neighborhoods of the capital, thereby protecting thousands of Tutsis who would otherwise have faced certain death. Rwanda thus witnessed the surreal phenomenon of street battles in the heart of the capital, while the government was extending the holocaust to every corner of the countryside under its control. That control rapidly ebbed, however, as the RPF renewed its offensive. By mid-June, they had decisively defeated Rwandan government forces, which were pushed into a limited zone in the southwest of the country. The offensive was accompanied by large-scale revenge killings of Hutus in territory that RPF soldiers had overrun. Estimates of those killed range as high as 50,000, with many summary executions, particularly of "battle-age" Hutu men who were automatically assumed to have participated in the genocide.[50]

At this point, foreign forces finally staged a decisive intervention – but one that primarily benefited the *génocidaires*. On June 17, France proposed to the UN Security Council that French troops be sent to Rwanda under UN auspices. Four days later, thousands of French troops began assembling on the Rwandan border with Zaire – an indication of how rapidly a substantial intervention can be mounted when the political will exists.[51] On July 4, the RPF gained full control of the capital, Kigali; the following day, France, with UN approval in hand, established a "safe zone" in the southwest.

The French intervention succeeded in saving the lives of thousands of Tutsis, but that was not its main motivation. Rather, the intervention was a continuation of the long-standing French support for the Hutu Power government. It permitted the orderly evacuation of nearly *two million* Hutus, including tens of thousands of *génocidaires*, to refugee camps in neighboring Zaire. As Gérard Prunier writes, "the refugees moved to the camps in perfect order, with their *bourgmestres* and communal counsellors at their head. Inside the camps they remained grouped according to their *communes* of origin and under the control of the very political structure which had just been responsible for the genocide."[52]

This mass flow of refugees was highly visible to international media that gained access to the camps. The humanitarian crisis – especially outbreaks of cholera and other diseases that killed thousands of refugees – was something the international community could address with minimum risk. The Clinton government in the US, which had spent the period of the mass slaughter instructing its representatives to avoid using the word "genocide" and placing obstacle after obstacle in the path of intervention, now leapt into action. US troops arrived within days to begin distribution of water, supplies, and medical aid to the camps.

"Like a monstrous cancer, the camps coalesced, solidified and implanted themselves in the flesh of east Zaire."[53] Hutu extremists inflicted genocidal atrocities against Tutsis living in eastern Zaire and staged cross-border raids into Rwanda, prompting the newly installed RPF regime in Rwanda to launch operations in the region that themselves led to the deaths of thousands of civilians, together with hard-core *génocidaires*.[54] According to Rwanda expert Christian Scherrer, "The export of genocide from Rwanda is the main cause in the spread of conflict to the whole of the Central African region, and the chief reason for the unprecedented violence, intensity, and destructiveness of that conflict" – possibly the most murderous since the Second World War.[55] The complex war in the Democratic Republic of Congo is examined in Box 10a.

AFTERMATH

Early estimates of the death-toll in the Rwandan genocide were between 500,000 and 800,000, overwhelmingly Tutsis. Subsequent investigations have revised these mind-boggling figures upward. A detailed census in July 2000 cited 951,018 victims, but estimated the total death-toll at over a million. According to a subsequent report, "93.7% of the victims were killed because they were identified as Tutsi; 1% because they were related to, married to or friends with Tutsi; 0.8% because they looked like Tutsi; and 0.8% because they were opponents of the Hutu regime at the time or were hiding people from the killers."[56]

Since Hutu Power was crushed in Rwanda in July 1994, the country has faced a staggering task of material reconstruction, human recovery, restitution, and political reconciliation. Fleeing Hutus had stripped the country almost bare, down to the zinc roofing on houses. Nonetheless, the Tutsi-dominated regime scored notable successes. Economic production was restored to pre-1994 levels. Approximately 1.3 million Hutu refugees were repatriated from camps in Zaire (now the Democratic Republic of Congo). At least a façade of pluralism was maintained in government and state ranks: the victorious RPF established a "government of national unity" that featured a few Hutus in prominent positions. Meanwhile, "All young Rwandans are [now] obliged to attend 'solidarity camps' where they are taught to love one another," an experience that "some find . . . useful," and "others less so."[57]

The basic orientation of the post-genocide government is clear: it is guided by "the conviction that power is the condition of Tutsi survival."[58] Its "Never Again" rallying cry can be interpreted as a pledge that never again will Hutus achieve dominance in Rwandan politics. "The reality," wrote Gérard Prunier in 1997, "is that the government is perceived by the average Hutu peasant as a foreign government."[59] It is uncertain whether subsequent years warrant an alteration of that assessment.

The quest for justice has taken both national and international forms. In November 1994, the United Nations established the International Criminal Tribunal for Rwanda in Arusha, Tanzania. However, despite an impressive budget of US$1.8 billion, the tribunal proceeded excruciatingly slowly. It did not hear its first case until 1997, and as of May 2004 it had "convicted just 18 defendants of genocide and crimes against humanity and . . . delivered 15 judgments against 21 defendants."[60] One of these convictions, however – that of Jean-Paul Akayesu – broke important legal ground with its "historic determination that systematic rape was a crime against humanity and that sexual violence constituted genocide in the same way as any other act."[61] In another case, two former media officials of Rwandan "hate radio" were convicted of using media as genocidal instruments (see Chapter 15).[62]

In Rwanda itself, some 120,000 accused *génocidaires* languished in grim conditions in jail, while the country's shattered legal system sought to bring at least some of them to trial. Finally, in 2003, it was recognized that formal proceedings could never cope with the massive number of accused. Over 20,000 prisoners were released, and others were promised a reduction of sentences in return for confessions. The most interesting – and controversial – form of attempted justice is *gacaca*, or "on the grass," a traditional form of tribunal that sacrifices formal legal procedures and protections for speedy results that are widely viewed as acceptable to ordinary Rwandans. The *gacaca* experiment, launched in January 2001, is discussed further in Chapter 15.

While reconstruction and attempted reconciliation proceeded, thousands of Tutsis continued to die from genocidal assaults – not only in cross-border attacks launched by diehard *génocidaires* in Congo, but also from the effects of rape-induced AIDS. One rape survivor, Eugenie Muhayimana, described how she had been kidnapped by a Hutu militia member, held throughout the period of the genocide, and then taken to Zaire when her captor fled in the mass exodus of July 1994. "He would torture and harass me daily. . . . He would rape me and go off to fight. He would come back. He would rape me again. I came to hate my whole life. The only thing I could feel each day was death." Interviewed by the *Los Angeles Times* in 2004, Muhayimana was HIV-positive and living in the "Village of Hope" in Kigali, a sanctuary for widows of the genocide established by the Rwandan Women's Network. Asked what were her hopes for the future, she responded: "My first wish is to see my children grow, to see them well-fed, to see them go to school and to university. My second wish is to get access to antiretroviral drugs. If I have got two years to live, that might push it out to four. If I have four left, that could push it to eight more years or even to 10, so I could see them as adults. Then I can die. I don't want to leave them when they're young."[63] But with only 2 percent of the estimated 100,000 Rwandans in need of the antiretrovirals actually receiving them, Eugenie's dream seemed unlikely to be realized.

FURTHER STUDY

African Rights, *Rwanda: Death, Despair and Defiance* (rev. edn). London: African Rights, 1995. Immense and harrowing depiction of the Rwandan holocaust.

Roméo Dallaire, *Shake Hands with the Devil: The Failure of Humanity in Rwanda.* New York: Carroll & Graf, 2004. Autobiography of the leader of the UN mission in Rwanda in 1993–94.

Alison Des Forges, *Leave None to Tell the Story: Genocide in Rwanda.* New York: Human Rights Watch, 1999. An indispensable human-rights report on the genocide.

Nigel Eltringham, *Accounting for Horror: Post-genocide Debates in Rwanda.* London: Pluto Press, 2004. The aftermath.

Ghosts of Rwanda. http://www.pbs.org/wgbh/pages/frontline/shows/ghosts/. Webpage for the PBS *Frontline* documentary, including interviews, video, and useful links.

Philip Gourevitch, *We Wish to Inform You That Tomorrow We Will be Killed With Our Families: Stories from Rwanda.* New York: Farrar, Straus & Giroux, 1998. Gourevitch's bestselling work is energetic but overrated.

Jean Hatzfeld, *Machete Season: The Killers in Rwanda Speak*, trans. Linda Coverdale. New York: Farrar, Straus & Giroux, 2005. Chilling testimony from imprisoned *génocidaires.*

Mahmood Mamdani, *When Victims Become Killers: Colonialism, Nativism, and the*

Genocide in Rwanda. Princeton, NJ: Princeton University Press, 2001. How political identity was constructed for Hutus and Tutsis.

Linda Melvern, *Conspiracy to Murder: The Rwanda Genocide and the International Community*. London: Verso, 2004. Follow-up to the author's hard-hitting critique, *A People Betrayed: The Role of the West in Rwanda's Genocide*.

Gérard Prunier, *The Rwanda Crisis: History of a Genocide*. New York: Columbia University Press, 1997. The standard source on the origins of the genocide.

Carol Rittner, John K. Roth and Wendy Whitworth, eds, *Genocide in Rwanda: Complicity of the Churches?* St. Paul, MN: Paragon House, 2004. Insights into the church's role.

Christian P. Scherrer, *Genocide and Crisis in Central Africa: Conflict Roots, Mass Violence, and Regional War*. Westport, CT: Praeger Publishers, 2002. The most complete account of the politics of the genocide and its regional repercussions.

NOTES

1 Gérard Prunier, *The Rwanda Crisis: History of a Genocide* (New York: Columbia University Press, 1997), p. 261.

2 Christian P. Scherrer, *Genocide and Crisis: Conflict Roots, Mass Violence, and Regional War* (Westport, CT: Praeger, 2002), p. 109.

3 Colonel Luc Marchal, UNAMIR commander in Kigali; quoted in *Chronicle of a Genocide Foretold: Part 2, "We Were Cowards"* (Ottawa: National Film Board of Canada [hereafter, NFB], 1997).

4 International Panel of Eminent Personalities (IPEP) report, quoted in Kenneth J. Campbell, *Genocide and the Global Village* (New York: Palgrave, 2001), p. 78. The scenes at the psychiatric hospital, and the Belgian soldier's comment, are available in the NFB documentary *Chronicle of a Genocide Foretold: Part 2.*

5 Quoted in Maxim Kniazkov, "US 'Ran from Rwanda Responsibility,'" Agence France-Presse dispatch, August 22, 2001.

6 Linda Melvern, *A People Betrayed: The Role of the West in Rwanda's Genocide* (London: Zed Books, 2000), p. 174. See also Roméo Dallaire, *Shake Hands with the Devil: The Failure of Humanity in Rwanda* (New York: Carroll & Graf, 2004). The International Committee of the Red Cross (ICRC) also refused to abandon the field, performing extraordinarily dangerous and heroic work throughout the genocide (see Melvern, *A People Betrayed*, p. 215).

7 John Heidenrich, *How to Prevent Genocide: A Guide for Policymakers, Scholars, and the Concerned Citizen* (Westport, CT: Praeger, 2001), p. 199.

8 Linda Melvern, *Conspiracy to Murder: The Rwanda Genocide* (London: Verso, 2004), p. 240.

9 Quoted in NFB, *Chronicle of a Genocide Foretold*. Samantha Power writes: "It is shocking to note that during the entire three months of the genocide, [President] Clinton never assembled his top policy advisers to discuss the killings. . . . Rwanda was never thought to warrant its own top-level meeting." Power, *"A Problem From Hell": America and the Age of Genocide* (New York: Basic Books, 2002), p. 366.

10 Quoted in Power, *"A Problem from Hell,"* p. 382.

11 Annan speaking at Memorial Conference on Rwanda Genocide, New York; United Nations Press Release, SG/SM/9223, AFR/870, HQ/631, 26 March 2004. http://www.un.org/News/Press/docs/2004/sgsm9223.doc.htm.

12 Mahmood Mamdani, *When Victims Become Killers: Colonialism, Nativism, and the Genocide in Rwanda* (Princeton, NJ: Princeton University Press, 2001), pp. 51, 70.

13 Prunier, *The Rwanda Crisis*, p. 39.
14 Prunier, *The Rwanda Crisis*, p. 3.
15 Mamdani, *When Victims Become Killers*, p. 66.
16 Prunier notes that "by the end of the Belgian presence in Rwanda in 1959, forty-three [prefectural] chiefs out of forty-five were Tutsi as well as 549 sub-chiefs out of 559." Prunier, *The Rwanda Crisis*, p. 27.
17 The myth still occasionally surfaces, as when Andrew Bell-Fialkoff refers to "the Hamitic Tutsi." Bell-Fialkoff, *Ethnic Cleansing* (New York: St. Martin's Griffin, 1999), p. 182.
18 Christopher Taylor, *Sacrifice as Terror: The Rwandan Genocide of 1994* (Oxford: Berg, 1999), pp. 128–30.
19 See Mamdani, *When Victims Become Killers*, p. 88.
20 Melvern, *A People Betrayed*, p. 42.
21 Scherrer, *Genocide and Crisis*, p. 105.
22 Many commentators have accused the RPF, under then-General, now-President Paul Kagame, of "recklessness" for launching this invasion. Bill Berkeley, for example, contends that "No rational person could have looked at the history of repeated mass slaughters in Rwanda and Burundi since 1959 and doubted for a moment that at least one likely outcome of such an invasion would be massive violence against defenseless Tutsi civilians." Berkeley, "Road to a Genocide," in Nicolaus Mills and Kira Brunner, eds, *The New Killing Fields: Massacre and the Politics of Intervention* (New York: Basic Books, 2002), p. 114. See also Alan J. Kuperman, "Provoking Genocide: A Revised History of the Rwandan Patriotic Front," *Journal of Genocide Research*, 6: 1 (March 2004), pp. 61–84.
23 Alison Des Forges, *Leave None to Tell the Story: Genocide in Rwanda* (New York, Human Rights Watch, 1999), p. 122.
24 Burundi, like Rwanda, has a large Hutu majority and a small but traditionally dominant Tutsi minority. In 1972, some 200,000 Hutus were slaughtered by the Tutsi-dominated army, in what has been termed an "eliticide": the primary targets were educated and/or wealthy Hutu males. The 1972 genocide was echoed by further outbreaks of mass killing of Hutu in 1988 (20,000 killed) and 1991 (a further 3,000 deaths). In October 1993 the Hutu president of the country was killed, leading to an outburst of genocidal violence against both Tutsis and Hutus that established a "basic pattern" for the events in Rwanda the following year (Scherrer, *Genocide and Crisis*, p. 3). Bill Berkeley estimates that "another hundred and fifty thousand have died in Burundi's continuing bloodshed" since 1993 (Berkeley, "Road to a Genocide," p. 110).
25 Catharine Newbury, "Ethnicity and the Politics of History in Rwanda," in David E. Lorey and William H. Beezley, eds, *Genocide, Collective Violence, and Popular Memory: The Politics of Remembrance in the Twentieth Century* (Wilmington, DL: Scholarly Resources, Inc., 2002), p. 76.
26 Melvern, *Conspiracy to Murder*, pp. 62–64.
27 Scherrer, *Genocide and Crisis*, p. 122.
28 Quoted in Melvern, *A People Betrayed*, p. 155.
29 This phrase is drawn from the title of ch. 8 of African Rights, *Rwanda: Death, Despair and Defiance* (rev. edn) (London: African Rights, 1995).
30 The deaths of the US troops in Somalia were recounted in the book and film *Black Hawk Down.*
31 Prunier, *The Rwanda Crisis*, p. 107.
32 Scherrer, *Genocide and Crisis*, p. 364.
33 Melvern, *Conspiracy to Murder*, p. 182.
34 Melvern, *Conspiracy to Murder*, p. 168.
35 "The officers of UNAMIR believe to this day that had the European troops that came to rescue the expats stayed on in Rwanda, the killing could have been stopped there and then. . . . Together with the moderates in the Rwandan army and with the peacekeepers there would have been ample troops to restore calm. There were already 2,500 peacekeepers with UNAMIR, there were 500 Belgian para-commandos, part of the evacuation

force, together with 450 French and 80 Italian soldiers from parachute regiments. In neighbouring Kenya there were 500 Belgian para-commandos, also a part of the evacuation operation. In Burundi there were 250 US Rangers, elite troops, who had come to evacuate the US nationals. There were 800 more French troops on standby." Melvern, *Conspiracy to Murder*, p. 188.

36 Dallaire, *Shake Hands with the Devil*, p. 325.

37 African Rights, *Death, Despair and Defiance*, p. 922. As one *génocidaire* recalled: "The white priests took off at the first skirmishes. The black priests joined the killers or the killed. God kept silent, and the churches stank from abandoned bodies." Quoted in Jean Hatzfeld (trans. Linda Coverdale), *Machete Season: The Killers in Rwanda Speak* (New York: Farrar, Straus & Giroux, 2005), p. 142. On the churches' role more generally, see Hugh McCullum, *The Angels Have Left Us: The Rwanda Tragedy and the Churches* (Geneva: WCC Publications, 2004); and Carol Rittner, John K. Roth and Wendy Whitworth, eds, *Genocide in Rwanda: Complicity of the Churches?* (St. Paul, MN: Paragon House, 2005).

38 According to Christian Scherrer, "The map showing the places where the largest massacres occurred was almost identical with that of the religious centers in the various dioceses and parishes of Rwanda." Scherrer, *Genocide and Crisis*, p. 113.

39 African Rights, *Rwanda: Not So Innocent: When Women Become Killers* (London: African Rights, 1995), p. 26, emphasis added.

40 The death-tolls usually cited for these cases are 36,000 (Odessa) and 33,000 (Kiev); according to Eugen Kogon, the highest number of killings in a single day at Auschwitz-Birkenau was 34,000 (Kogon, *The Theory and Practice of Hell* [New York: The Berkley Publishing Company, 1980], p. 241).

41 African Rights, *Rwanda: Death, Despair and Defiance*, pp. 590–95.

42 Melvern, *Conspiracy to Murder*, p. 224.

43 African Rights, *Rwanda: Death, Despair and Defiance*, p. 665.

44 African Rights, *Rwanda: Death, Despair and Defiance*, p. 708.

45 Darryl Li, "Echoes of Violence," in Mills and Brunner, eds, *The New Killing Fields*, p. 125.

46 Mamdani, *When Victims Become Killers*, p. 225.

47 Adam Jones, "Gender and Genocide in Rwanda," in Jones, ed., *Gendercide and Genocide* (Nashville, TN: Vanderbilt University Press, 2004), p. 123.

48 African Rights, *Rwanda: Not So Innocent*, p. 88.

49 Prunier, *The Rwanda Crisis*, pp. 231–32.

50 See Des Forges, *Leave None to Tell the Story*, p. 734.

51 Linda Melvern wrote that "the French operation included everything UNAMIR needed. There were more than 2,500 elite soldiers from the French Foreign Legion, paratroopers, marines and special forces, all equipped with state-of-the-art weaponry, communications, one hundred armoured vehicles, heavy mortars, helicopters, and even jet aircraft. There was an armada of cargo aircraft." Melvern, *Conspiracy to Murder*, p. 243.

52 Prunier, *The Rwanda Crisis*, p. 267.

53 Michela Wrong, *In the Footsteps of Mr. Kurtz: Living on the Brink of Disaster in Mobutu's Congo* (New York: HarperCollins, 2001), p. 245.

54 See Marie Béatrice Umutesi, *Surviving the Slaughter: The Ordeal of a Rwandan Refugee in Zaire*, trans. Julia Emerson (Madison, WI: University of Wisconsin Press, 2004).

55 Scherrer, *Genocide and Crisis*, p. 198.

56 Melvern, *Conspiracy to Murder*, pp. 250–51.

57 "The Road out of Hell," *The Economist*, March 27, 2004.

58 Mamdani, *When Victims Become Killers*, p. 261.

59 Prunier, *The Rwanda Crisis*, p. 370.

60 Joanne O'Connor, "Quest for Justice in Rwanda Moves Slowly But Surely," TheLawyer.com, 1 June 2004. http://www.thelawyer.com/cgi-bin/item.cgi?id=109910andd=11andh = 24andf=46.

61 Melvern, *Conspiracy to Murder*, p. 251.

62 On the so-called "media trials," see Dina Temple-Raston, *Justice on the Grass: Three Rwandan Journalists, Their Trial for War Crimes and a Nation's Quest for Redemption* (New York: The Free Press, 2005).

63 Robyn Dixon, "AIDS a Cruel Echo of '94 Rwanda Genocide," *Los Angeles Times*, May 2, 2004.

BOX 9A CONGO AND DARFUR

In 2005, as this book was being prepared for publication, genocide again stalked Africa. A brutal counter-insurgency war in Darfur – a western region of Sudan, Africa's largest country – had sparked international condemnation and application of the "genocide" label, but only limited international intervention. Probably over 100,000 people had died – perhaps as many as 350,000.

To the southwest, Congo was again threatening to descend into full-scale war, as Rwanda's army staged another invasion, supposedly to suppress remnants of the Hutu forces that had murdered a million Tutsis in 1994 (Chapter 9). The complex and excruciatingly destructive conflict(s) in Congo had killed between 3.8 million and 4.7 million people over six years, according to the International Rescue Committee (IRC).[1] Even the lower estimate represented the destruction of "far more lives than any other conflict since the Second World War."[2]

CONGO AND "AFRICA'S WORLD WAR"

Congo was the backdrop for one of the greatest but least-known genocides in modern history – the Belgian "rubber terror" (see Chapter 2). After independence from Belgium in 1960, Congo fell under the sway of an army colonel, Mobutu Sese Seko. Mobutu proved to be corrupt and megalomaniacal, "a ruthless crook who fitted his palace with a nuclear shelter, hired [the] Concorde for shopping trips and so gutted the treasury that inflation between October 1990 and December 1995 totalled 6.3 billion per cent."[3]

The catalyst for Mobutu's downfall came from the eastern boundary of Congo's vast territory, thousands of kilometers from Kinshasa, the capital. In the final stages of the 1994 genocide in Rwanda, as Tutsi rebel forces closed in from the north and east, Hutu *génocidaires* staged a mass evacuation of populations under their control, across the Congolese border to the city of Goma (see Chapter 9). Ironically, it was *this* humanitarian crisis that galvanized the world, not the genocide against Tutsis. Ironically, too, the outside aid that flooded in was instrumental in permitting the *génocidaires* to reconstitute themselves as a terrorist force, brutally controlling the refugee population and launching attacks against Tutsis in both Congo and Rwanda.

In the face of this threat, in 1997 Rwanda assisted the overthrow of the Mobutu regime by Laurent Désiré Kabila, viewed as an effective Rwandan proxy

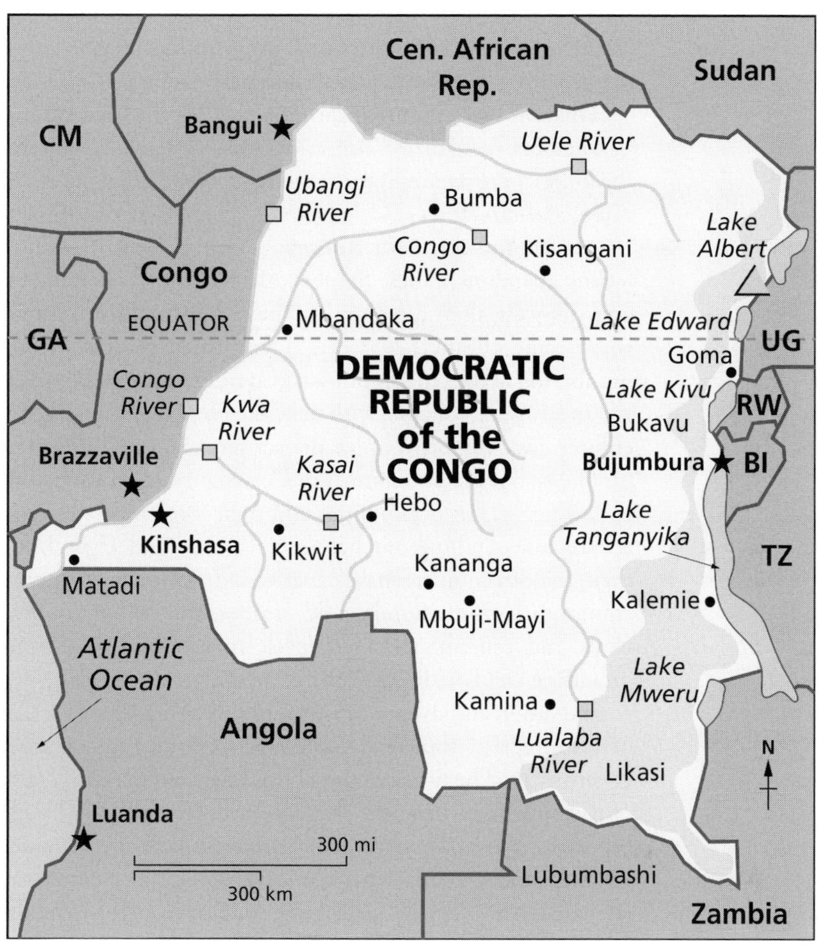

Map 9a.1 Congo

Source: Map provided by WorldAtlas.com

and partner in the struggle against Hutu killers. *En route* to Kinshasa, Kabila's force and the Rwandan army rampaged against Hutu populations in eastern Congo. By one estimate, some 200,000 people died.[4]

Once in power, Kabila fell under the sway of Hutu representatives in Kinshasa, supporting renewed cross-border killing operations in Rwanda.[5] Rwanda soon began planning a *coup d'état* against its former protégé. An attempted drive on Kinshasa by Rwandan forces and anti-Kabila Congolese was halted only by the military intervention of Angola and Zimbabwe. Together with Namibia and Chad, these represented the coalition that maintained Kabila in power until his 2001 assassination. (He was succeeded by his son Joseph.) Meanwhile, Rwanda, Uganda, and Burundi lined up with the anti-Kabila rebels who dominated the eastern half of the country. Congo had become "Africa's world war." It was a continental struggle that "reached almost without interruption from the Red Sea to the Atlantic Ocean."[6]

This was also a prototypical "new war," of the kind examined in Chapter 12. Clashes between major concentrations of armed forces were rare. Many of the killers were paramilitaries and freebooters, often cut adrift from more traditional military forces. Others were government troops who felt abandoned by central authorities in Kinshasa: "Paid poorly, if at all, undisciplined and feeling abandoned, these fighters calculate they have more to gain from looting and shooting than maintaining the fiction of an integrated national army."[7] Internecine conflicts between these armed groups provoked refugee flows numbering in the tens of thousands as recently as January 2005. Warlordism was rife amidst state collapse, with the Congolese government unable to "make [and] enforce laws, maintain order, deliver services, or ensure security."[8]

The rich mineral resources of Congo proved an irresistible lure – "literally a goldmine"[9] – for local militias and their foreign patrons. The spoils were such as to cause a falling-out between Rwanda and Uganda over how to divide them.[10] Both countries have experienced miraculous leaps in their export of key commodities – diamonds, gold, timber, and coltan (an ore used in computer chips and cell phones) – at levels that exceed total domestic production, providing vivid evidence of the pillaging.[11]

Starvation and disease caused millions of deaths in the Congo wars, but tens or hundreds of thousands also died at the hands of rebel militias and the government. The forces of the FDLR (the Democratic Forces for the Liberation of Rwanda, born from the fleeing *génocidaires* of 1994) staged many attacks;[12] but it was the RCD rebels (the Congolese Rally for Democracy, supported by Rwanda and Uganda) that committed the most extensive atrocities against civilians. In 1999, UN Special Investigator Robert Garreton accused the rebels of running torture centers that amounted to "extermination" sites. Garreton declared: "The rebel forces must understand that they do not have any popular support and that they are seen as aggressors who have placed the people under a climate of terror."[13]

DARFUR

For half a century, Sudan has been racked by a civil war that many observers have characterized as genocidal – between the Muslim Arab-dominated north (home to the capital, Khartoum) and the predominantly Christian and animist south. In recent decades, northern imposition of Arabic and *shariah*, or Islamic law, have fueled southern rebellion. The conflict has exacted "a huge and terrible human toll," with possibly two million killed. Brookings Institution scholar Francis Deng characterized it in 2001 as "the worst humanitarian disaster in the world today."[14]

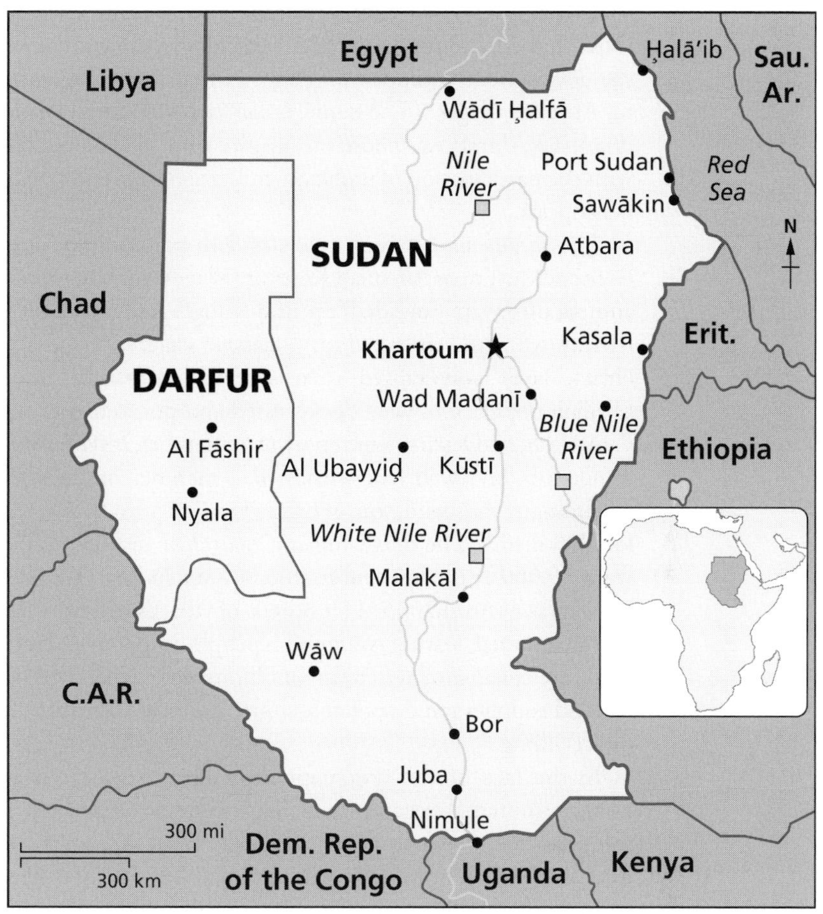

Map 9a.2 Darfur

Source: Reproduced with the permission of the Minister of Public Works and Government Services, 2005

Curiously, though, it was a smaller-scale tragedy elsewhere in Sudan – in the remote region of Darfur, bordering Chad – that captured world attention in 2004. Darfur also provoked the most voluble debate over application of the "genocide" label since Rwanda in 1994.

For decades, sporadic conflict flickered in Darfur between Arab pastoralists and African agriculturalists. The onset of recurring drought exacerbated tensions, pushing Arab northerners further into the African heartland. Feelings of marginalization, invasion, and exploitation provided a constituency for the rebellion that first erupted in June 2003, led by a still-shadowy group called the Sudan Liberation Army (SLA).

SLA attacks on Sudanese government offices and police provoked a violent reaction from the military government in Khartoum, led by General Omar al-Bashir. Employing time-honored counter-insurgency strategies (precisely those that Khartoum had used for decades in the conflict with South Sudan), the government equipped an Arab militia, the *Janjaweed*, to mount attacks on African villages. (The name *Janjaweed* "translates roughly as 'evil men on horseback,' [and] was chosen to inspire fear.")[15] The assaults were carried out with the participation of Sudanese military forces, equipped with bombers and helicopters.

The *Janjaweed* behaved much as Serb paramilitary units did in invading Bosnian Muslim or Albanian Kosovar villages (see Chapter 8). Adult male non-combatants were rounded up and slaughtered in gendercidal massacres.[16] African women were raped on a massive scale, by assailants who called them "black slaves" and "rap[ed] them so that they [would] bear Arab children."[17] Civilian populations were dispossessed and put to flight.

A US State Department report of September 2004 found that 61 percent of refugees interviewed had witnessed a member of their family killed (overwhelmingly a husband, son, or brother); 67 percent had seen others outside their family killed.[18] The death-toll is a matter of dispute, with estimates ranging from 70,000 at the low end to 400,000, including those killed by disease and hunger, as of April 2005.[19] Hundreds of villages had been destroyed, damaged, and abandoned, leaving two million people uprooted and too terrified to return. With the collapse of agriculture, millions were dependent on outside food aid. As food supplies ran desperately short, "genocide by attrition" began to replace direct killing.[20]

In the face of the systematic atrocities, a consensus was forged among nongovernmental organizations, and some governments, that the campaign was genocidal.[21] According to the Aegis Trust in Britain, this conclusion was unavoidable. "Was the killing intentional? Yes. Was it systematically organised by the al-Bashir regime using government-armed Janjaweed militias, bombers and helicopter gunships? Yes. Were the victims chosen because of their ethnic and racial identity? Yes. This, in short is genocide. The genocide continues."[22] Famously, in September 2004, US Secretary of State Colin Powell agreed. "We concluded – I concluded – that genocide has been committed in Darfur, and that the government of Sudan and the Janjaweed bear responsibility and that genocide may still be occurring."[23] However, as the *New York Times* pointed out, Powell's statement came "with the quick assurance that this didn't mean the United States was prepared to take any further action."[24] Powell's declaration was followed by the virtual disappearance of Darfur from the US political agenda – though in this respect, America was hardly alone.

CONCLUSION

Positive steps were taken in Congo in 2004–05. Congolese President Joseph Kabila had struck agreements to draw most rebel forces into a national government. A 16,000-strong UN intervention force, MONUC, which deployed to eastern Congo in 1999, gained notoriety in the first years of its mandate for standing by ineffectually while civilians were oppressed and even massacred before its eyes. By 2005 it was finally adopting a firmer stance against the rampaging militias, and had succeeded in quelling some of their violence. Its resources and ambit were limited, however.[25] As for the Rwandan Hutu *génocidaires*, they seemed to be tiring of the struggle. In March 2005, the dominant faction announced that it was prepared to return to Rwanda and join the mainstream political process.

After the noisy international debate over the "genocide" label, Darfur again slipped to the margins of diplomacy and public concern. "For the world at large Darfur was and remained the quintessential 'African crisis': distant, esoteric, extremely violent, rooted in complex ethnic and historical factors which few understood, and devoid of any identifiable practical interest for the rich countries."[26] An African Union peacekeeping force, just 6,700-strong in a territory as large as France, lacked a mandate to protect civilians and was instead reduced to "watching the tragedy unfold."[27] The UN Security Council, "despite threatening sanctions . . . has done nothing, preferring to allow the African Union to take the lead in a hopelessly under-equipped mission."[28] Both China and Russia, among Council veto-wielders, were deeply opposed to any intervention not approved by the Sudanese government. Meanwhile, some 10,000 people a month were dying "as the bombing, slaughter and rape continue[d]."[29]

FURTHER STUDY

John F. Clark, ed., *The African Stakes of the Congo War*. London: Palgrave Macmillan, 2004. Wide-ranging edited collection on the regional implications of war and genocide in Congo.

Alex De Waal, *Famine That Kills: Darfur, Sudan* (rev. edn). Oxford: Oxford University Press, 2004. Updated edition of an important study.

Gérard Prunier, *Darfur: The Ambiguous Genocide*. Ithaca, NY: Cornell University Press, 2005. Concise introduction by the author of *The Rwanda Crisis* (see Chapter 9).

Michela Wrong, *In the Footsteps of Mr. Kurtz: Living on the Brink of Disaster in Mobutu's Congo*. New York: Perennial, 2002. Insightful journalistic account of life in Congo (then Zaire) under the Mobutu dictatorship.

NOTES

1 International Rescue Committee statistics cited in "An Almost Hopeless Case," *The Economist*, January 22, 2005 ("at least 3.8 million people"); James Astill, "Conflict in Congo Has Killed 4.7m, Charity Says," *Guardian*, April 8, 2003,

http://www.guardian.co.uk/Print/0,3858,4643138,00.html ("a total of 4.7 million people have died").

2 Astill, "Conflict in Congo."

3 "Africa's Unmended Heart," *The Economist*, June 11, 2005.

4 Kisangani Emizer, cited in Ola Olsson and Heather Congdon Fors, "Congo: The Prize of Predation," *Journal of Peace Research*, 41: 3 (2004), p. 325.

5 Christian P. Scherrer, *Genocide and Crisis in Central Africa: Conflict Roots, Mass Violence, and Regional War* (Westport, CT: Praeger, 2002), p. 267.

6 International Crisis Group (hereafter ICG), "How Kabila Lost His Way: The Performance of Laurent Désiré Kabila's Government," background paper, May 21, 1999. See also Jeremy M. Weinstein, "Africa's 'Scramble for Africa': Lessons of a Continental War," *World Policy Journal*, 17: 2 (summer 2000), pp. 11–20; Thomas M. Callaghy, "Life and Death in the Congo: Understanding a Nation's Collapse," *Foreign Affairs*, 80: 5 (2001), pp. 143–49.

7 Rory Carroll, "Violence Threatens to Engulf Congo," *Guardian*, November 26, 2004. http://www.guardian.co.uk/print/0,3858,5072001-110889,00.html.

8 Weinstein, "Africa's 'Scramble for Africa.'"

9 Pro-RPF newspaper reporting on alleged corruption and "shameful degeneration" among Ugandan forces in Congo; cited in ICG, "Africa's Seven-nation War," report, May 21, 1999, p. 19.

10 See Lara Santoro, "False Dawn," *The New Republic*, July 3, 2000.

11 See Olsson and Fors, "Congo: The Prize of Predation." For an overview of the smuggling networks in Rwanda and Uganda, see Francoise Misser, "Looking for Scapegoats," *African Business*, 259 (November 2000).

12 See, e.g., Craig Timberg, "Rwanda's Tormentors Emerge from the Forest to Haunt Congo: Hutu Guerrillas Find New Victims," *Washington Post*, February 10, 2005. Throughout the war, Rwanda exploited the 1994 genocide to justify invading its giant neighbor as and when it chose. "We know that there is an argument that the FDLR does not constitute a threat to the Rwandan government," stated Rwandan special envoy Richard Sezibera in December 2004. "Fine! But for us we start counting the dead from the 1 million plus in the 1994 genocide. In our view, even one death today caused by the FDLR is a continuation of the genocide." ICG, "Back to the Brink in Congo," Africa Briefing, December 17, 2004, p. 2.

13 ICG, "Africa's Seven-nation War," p. 18.

14 Francis M. Deng, "Sudan – Civil War and Genocide," in William L. Hewitt, *Defining the Horrific: Readings on Genocide and Holocaust in the Twentieth Century* (Upper Saddle River, NJ: Pearson, 2004), pp. 223–24.

15 Scott Straus, "Darfur and the Genocide Debate," *Foreign Affairs*, 84: 1 (2004), p. 126. According to Gérard Prunier, "Sociologically the *Janjaweed* seem to have been of six main origins: former bandits and highwaymen who had been 'in the trade' since the 1980s; demobilized soldiers from the regular army; young members of Arab tribes having a running land conflict with a neighbouring 'African' group . . . common criminals who were pardoned and released from gaol if they joined the militia; fanatical members of the Tajammu al-Arabi ['(Arab Union), a militantly racist and pan-Arabist organization which stressed the "Arab" character of the province']; and young unemployed 'Arab' men, quite similar to those who joined the rebels on the 'African' side." Gérard Prunier, *Darfur: The Ambiguous Genocide* (Ithaca, NY: Cornell University Press, 2005), pp. 45, 97–98.

16 For a compendium of reportage on gender-selective massacres and other atrocities, see Adam Jones/Gendercide Watch, "Gendercide in Darfur," http://www.gendercide.org/darfur01.htm.

17 Public International Law and Policy Group (PILPG), "Genocide in Darfur: A Legal Analysis," September 2004, http://www.africafiles.org/printableversion.asp?id=6727.
18 State Department statistics cited in PILPG, "Genocide in Darfur."
19 The lower death-toll, based on rough UN computations, is dismissed by Prunier as "obsolete" and unverified. He cites a figure of 310,000 killed by the *beginning* of 2005 (see Prunier, *Darfur: The Ambiguous Genocide*, pp. 151–52). For calculations of the 400,000 figure, see "Darfur's Real Death Toll," *Washington Post* (editorial), April 24, 2005, http://www.washingtonpost.com/wp-dyn/articles/A12485-2005Apr23.html.
20 Prunier, *Darfur: The Ambiguous Genocide*, p. 117.
21 "Organizations arguing that the massacres in Darfur fulfil the international legal definition of genocide include Physicians for Human Rights and the UK-based campaigning group Justice Africa. Human Rights Watch and the International Crisis Group have not employed the term 'genocide,' but both say Sudanese government forces and Janjawid militias are responsible for crimes against humanity, war crimes, and 'ethnic cleansing.' Amnesty International has called for the setting up of an international inquiry to examine charges of war crimes and 'allegations of genocide.'" John Ryle, "Disaster in Darfur," *The New York Review of Books*, 51: 13 (August 12, 2004), http://www.nybooks.com/articles/17326.
22 Aegis Trust report quoted in Anne Penketh, "Darfur: Never Again?," *The Independent*, January 26, 2005.
23 Terence Neilan, "Powell Says Sudan Abuses Qualify as Genocide," *The New York Times*, September 9, 2004.
24 Scott Anderson, "How Did Darfur Happen?," *New York Times*, October 17, 2004.
25 See Edmund Sanders, "UN Stretched Thin in Congo," *Los Angeles Times*, September 12, 2005.
26 Prunier, *Darfur: The Ambiguous Genocide*, p. 124.
27 Prunier, *Darfur: The Ambiguous Genocide*, p. 145.
28 Penketh, "Darfur: Never Again?" Rwanda is second only to Nigeria among contributors of troops for the peacekeeping mission. The Rwandan government has used its participation in the Darfur protection force to gain "leverage with which to pursue its interests more assertively in its immediate neighbourhood without risking serious censure." In other words, as a quid pro quo for its intervention in Darfur, Rwanda is able to evade criticism of its "reckless" and often atrocious policies in Congo. ICG, "Back to the Brink," p. 5.
29 "Justice in Darfur," *The Economist*, February 5, 2005.

PART 3 SOCIAL SCIENCE PERSPECTIVES

CHAPTER 10

Psychological Perspectives

It is too late to stop the technology. It is to the psychology that we should now turn.
Jonathan Glover

Understanding genocide requires getting inside the minds of those who commit it, and those who seek to prevent or limit it. This is the province of psychology. Not surprisingly, many of the more prominent scholars and analysts of genocide are psychologists and psychiatrists, including Israel Charny, Ervin Staub, Roy Baumeister, Robert Jay Lifton, and James Waller.

In approaching psychological contributions in this chapter, I will put aside one fruitful line of inquiry, focusing on the "authoritarian personality" and the mass psychology of fascism. Associated with central twentieth-century figures such as Theodor Adorno, Wilhelm Reich, and Erich Fromm, these investigations located fascism's psychological roots in childhood experiences of parental authoritarianism and repression. They also emphasized mechanisms of psychological projection, displacing onto others the violence derived from a lack of personal self-esteem (or, alternatively, hysterical narcissism), as well as various sexual neuroses. I do not plumb this literature here, partly because space is limited, and partly because it is well covered by James Waller in his outstanding book *Becoming Evil*.[1] However, elements of this framework seep into the following discussion, which considers in detail mechanisms of narcissism, greed, fear, and humiliation in fueling and explaining genocide. Some of the earlier Reichian attention to familial and social-psychological dynamics is paralleled in the closing discussion of genocidal perpetrators and rescuers.

NARCISSISM, GREED, AND FEAR

What motivates *génocidaires*? I see four psychological elements as essential: narcissism, greed, fear, and humiliation. The first three are addressed here, with a separate section reserved for genocide and humiliation.

Narcissism

The Greek god Narcissus became so enraptured with his own reflection in a pool that he "fell in love with himself, and not being able to find consolation, he died of sorrow by the same pool."[2] The myth speaks to our propensity for hubristic self-love, a phenomenon first studied in a psychological and psychiatric context by Sigmund Freud (1856–1939). Freud described narcissism as a formative and necessary stage of ego development, but also sketched notes on a *narcissism of minor differences*. This refers, in Anton Blok's summary, to "the fact that the fiercest struggles often take place between individuals, groups and communities that differ very little – or between which the differences have greatly diminished."[3] Scholars of genocide are often struck by how groups that seem close linguistically, geographically, and/or religiously can succumb to bitter intercommunal conflict: Hutus and Tutsis, Serbs and Croatians, Catholics and Protestants. At a deeper level, Freud observed that "the communal feeling of groups requires, in order to complete it, hostility towards some extraneous minority."[4] The psychological dynamic by which the "Self" and the "We" are defined against the "Other" is fundamental to genocide.

Of equal significance is *malignant* or *pathological* narcissism, in which others exist only to fortify, magnify, and idolize the self.[5] Profound insecurity, anxiety, and unease often accompany this form of narcissism – a fear that without validation by others, the self will be undermined or annihilated.[6] But this seems to vanish at the extremes of malignant narcissism, where true *psychopathy* lies. This is a murderous egotism, incapable of empathy with others, that considers human destruction inconsequential if it serves to increase personal power and glory.

Malignant narcissism and psychopathy are common among *génocidaires* in modern history. Consider Adolf Hitler, whose stunted, injured ego found transcendence in holocaust. (How Hitler, the failed artist and rootless ex-soldier, must have reveled in the version of the Lord's Prayer devised by the League of German Girls: "Adolf Hitler, you are our great Leader. Thy name makes the enemy tremble. Thy Third Reich comes, thy will alone is law upon earth . . ."!)[7] Consider as well Joseph Stalin and Mao Zedong, "fanatics, poets, paranoiacs, peasants risen to rule empires whose history obsessed them, careless killers of millions";[8] or the Hutu Power extremists of Rwanda, convinced that their crushing of Tutsi "cockroaches" would enshrine their version of manifest destiny.

Collective pathological narcissism is also a factor in genocide. Shifting the level of analysis and diagnosis from the individual to the collective is a controversial move. But it seems apt when a majority or dominant minority of a nation's citizens hold that their country is somehow innately superior, gifted by God or destiny, the bearers of a sole truth, or limitlessly capable. The philosopher Sam Vaknin has summarized the criteria for collective pathological narcissism:

> The group as a whole, *or members of the group* . . . feel grandiose and self-important. . . . [They are] obsessed with group fantasies of unlimited success, fame, fearsome power or omnipotence, unequalled brilliance, bodily beauty or performance, or ideal, everlasting, all-conquering ideals or political theories. . . . [They] are firmly convinced that the group is unique. . . . [They] require excessive admiration, adulation, attention and affirmation – or, failing that, wish to be feared and to be notorious. . . . [They] feel entitled. They expect unreasonable or special and favorable priority treatment. They demand automatic and full compliance with expectations. . . . They rarely accept responsibility for their actions . . . [They] are devoid of empathy. They are unable or unwilling to identify with or acknowledge the feelings and needs of other groups. . . . [They] are arrogant and sport haughty behaviors or attitudes coupled with rage when frustrated, contradicted, punished, limited, or confronted. . . . [All of] this often leads to anti-social behavior, cover-ups, and criminal activities on a mass scale.[9]

One of the countries of which I am a citizen, Great Britain, was probably the world leader in collective pathological narcissism during the nineteenth and early twentieth centuries. Generations of schoolchildren grew up imbibing their elders' conviction that Britain was God's gift to humankind, particularly to the darker races it was destined to rule. British culture and civilization were supreme, and British men and women were uniquely noble, brave, virtuous, and incorruptible. Traces of this mentality persist even in the post-colonial era, and can resurge with virulent passion in times of crisis, as I observed firsthand on a visit to Britain during the Falklands/Malvinas War of 1982.[10]

In the past century, the societies that have most dramatically evinced a tendency towards collective pathological narcissism are three totalitarian states – Nazi Germany (1933–45), Stalinist Russia (1928–53), and Maoist China (1949–76) – and, since 1945, a democratic one, the United States.[11] The presence of the US in this list, like its British predecessor, suggests that collective pathological narcissism is not tied to a particular political system or ideology. Psychological theorist Robert Jay Lifton has analyzed the contemporary US variant in his book *Superpower Syndrome*, pointing to:

> a bizarre American collective mind-set that extends our very real military power into a fantasy of cosmic control, a mind-set all too readily tempted by an apocalyptic mission. The symptoms are of a piece, each consistent with the larger syndrome: unilateralism in all-important decisions, including war-making ones; the use of high technology to secure the ownership of death and history; a sense of entitlement concerning the right to identify and destroy all those considered to be terrorists or friends of terrorists, while spreading "freedom" and virtues seen as preeminently ours throughout the world; the right to decide who may possess weapons of mass destruction and who may not, and to take military action using nuclear weapons if necessary against any nation that has them or is thought to be

> manufacturing them; and underneath all of these symptoms, a righteous vision of ridding the world of evil and purifying it spiritually and politically.[12]

This mindset has been intensified and fortified by the events of September 11, 2001, but it is not a product of them. Rather, distinctively American ideologies of unlimited space and power, combined with the country's unchallenged superpower status since the Second World War, have generated a consensus (though very far from a universal view) that the US is destined to dominate the world and prevent any challenge to its hegemony. In past epochs, the mentality has spawned genocidal or proto-genocidal atrocities against Native Americans, Filipinos, Indochinese, and others. Will it one day produce nuclear war and "omnicide" (Chapter 2)? In light of the most recent framing of American "national security" doctrine (post-9/11),[13] and the explicit envisioning of nuclear strikes against countries alleged to be harboring terrorists or developing weapons of mass destruction,[14] the prospect is not far-fetched.

Greed

"These people are like vultures swarming down, their eyes bleary, their tongues hanging out with greed, to feed upon the Jewish carcass." So wrote an appalled German businessman, observing the Nazi "Aryanization" of Jewish properties.[15] But few Germans shared his scruples. Most viewed the dispossession of the Jews of Germany as a once-in-a-lifetime opportunity, and made the most of it: "Looted Jewish property was a magnet which attracted millions brought up to believe in the myth of the Jewish wealth."[16]

Not only did the Nazis encourage "Aryan" Germans to exploit the Jewish plight, but they took full advantage themselves. Even as the Holocaust was reaching its peak in 1941–42, "Hitler himself was not above sanctioning opportunities to extort foreign currency in return for ransoming very rich Jews."[17] In the Nazi death camps, Jews were robbed not only of their few remaining possessions, but of their hair, which was sold for mattress stuffing – and (after death) of the gold fillings in their teeth, melted down for bullion.

Greed is "an overriding theme in human affairs,"[18] and a principal motive of genocidal perpetrators and bystanders alike. The opportunity to strip victims of their wealth and property – either by looting it outright, or purchasing it at desperation prices – and to occupy their forcibly vacated dwellings appears again and again in accounts of genocide. As Armenians were rounded up and massacred or driven off on death marches (Chapter 4), the US consul in Trebizond, Oscar Heizer, reported: "A crowd of Turkish women and children follow the police about like a lot of vultures and seize anything they can lay their hands on and when the more valuable things are carried out of the house by the police they rush in and take the balance. I see this performance every day with my own eyes."[19] At the height of Stalin's purges in the Soviet Union (Chapter 5), there was "frequent house-moving because every execution created a vacant apartment and dacha which were eagerly occupied by survivors and their aspirational Party housewives, ambitious for grander accommodation."[20] In Rwanda in 1994 (Chapter 9), Tutsi rural victims "had land and at times cows. . . .

Somebody had to get these lands and those cows after their owners were dead," a significant incentive "in a poor and increasingly overpopulated country."[21] "[We] had tasted comfort and overflowing plenty," one Hutu killer recalled. "Greed had corrupted us."[22]

Greed is more than a desire for material goods beyond those necessary for survival. It is intimately connected to the hunger for power, domination, and prestige. "Man does not strive for power only in order to enrich himself economically," noted the sociologist Max Weber. "Power, including economic power, may be valued 'for its own sake.' Very frequently the striving for power is also conditioned by the social 'honor' it entails."[23] "Functionalist" analysts of the Jewish Holocaust emphasize the eagerness with which underlings sought to implement Hitler's grand plans, generating a dynamic that was to a considerable degree independent of direct orders.[24] Simon Sebag Montefiore notes that in Stalinist Russia, a "Terror entrepreneurialism" reigned, with a "succession of ambitious torturers who were only too willing to please and encourage Stalin by finding Enemies and killing them for him."[25] Often these individuals were designated next for execution; but there were always upwardly mobile men and women waiting to take their place.[26]

Even a brief moment in the sun may be enough to motivate the *génocidaires*, as with the "street boys, rag-pickers, [and] car-washers" whom Gérard Prunier described as vengefully targeting Tutsis in Rwanda's genocide (see p. 243).[27] Greed reflects objective material circumstances, but also, like narcissism, the core strivings of ego. Greed is never satiated; but when it is fed, one feels validated, successful – even omnipotent. Perhaps the only force that can truly match it as a motivator for genocide is *fear*.

Fear

"No power so effectively robs the mind of all its powers of acting and reasoning as fear," wrote British statesman Edmund Burke.[28] To grasp the central role of fear in genocide, it is worth distinguishing between *mortal terror* and *existential dread*. Mortal terror is fear of a threat to physical being and integrity. Existential dread revolves around our sense of personal identity, destiny, and social place; it evokes, or threatens to evoke, feelings of shame, dishonor, and humiliation.

Mortal terror is "animal fear," perhaps in a double sense. In a form that is often hard to distinguish from mere reflex, it is common across species, but it attains a particular pitch of intensity in the human animal, apparently the only one capable of foreseeing its own death.[29] In the eyes of some scholars and philosophers, this "death anxiety" is the worm in humanity's psychic apple – and a key factor in genocide. "Driven by nameless, overwhelming fears," wrote Israel Charny, "men turn to the primitive tools of self-protection, including the belief that they may spare themselves the terrible fate of death by sacrificing another instead of themselves."[30]

We may first have gleaned a more immediate form of animal fear from predatory animals themselves. In her book *Blood Rites*, Barbara Ehrenreich traces phenomena as disparate as separation anxiety in infants, religious rituals including human sacrifice, and intercommunal warfare to the terrifying encounter of prehumans and primitive humans with predatory beasts. "Nothing gets our attention like the prospect of being ripped apart, sucked dry, and transformed into another creature's meal," she writes.[31] The predator may have been the original "Other," transformed – as humans gained the upper hand over the animal kingdom – into the predatory out-group. The human "Other" in turn bounded and delineated the in-group (clan, tribe, ethnic group) where one finds sustenance and support, including in communal self-defense.[32] Evolutionary psychologists – those who apply evolutionary biology to psychology – deploy such connections to argue that "human behavior in the *present* is generated by universal reasoning circuits that exist because they solved adaptive problems in the past."[33] But social psychologists – studying people in situations of group interaction – have also found that subjects "who believe others will attack them respond with more aggression than they direct against targets who do not elicit such a belief." These phenomena are inextricably tied to intercommunal violence and genocide:

> Fear of the immediate or more distant future is a pivotal element in a number of approaches to ethnic warfare. . . . Fear induces people to support even very costly violence, because the choice seems to be between becoming a victim or becoming a participant. . . . According to this approach, a high degree of affect is expressed when the stakes are large (genocide involves large stakes), and so emotion follows a rational assessment by ordinary people of their situation. The improbability of genocide is not decisive, for the stakes are too high to chance it.[34]

Mortal terror, heightened and manipulated by genocide's architects, is a common – though not ubiquitous – feature of genocidal killing. Two vivid examples are the Balkan wars and Rwandan genocide of the 1990s (see Chapters 8–9). Prominent among Serbs' historical memories were the genocidal atrocities inflicted against them by the fascist Ustasha regime in Croatia during the Second World War. The revival of Ustasha-style symbolism and rhetoric by Franjo Tudjman's Croatian nationalist regime provoked deep anxieties, heightened when discrimination began against Serb professionals and officials within Croatia. In these varied ways "the Croats signaled the reasonableness of Serb fears," which was then "manipulated by Slobodan Milosevic, who needed the Croat issue to secure his power."[35]

The Rwandan holocaust of 1994 occurred in the aftermath of a massive blood-letting in neighboring Burundi, where between 50,000 and 100,000 civilians, overwhelmingly Hutus, had been massacred by the Tutsi-dominated military following a failed coup. Some 350,000 Hutus fled to Rwanda, bringing firsthand accounts of atrocities; among these refugees were some of the most unrestrained genocidal killers of Tutsis in 1994. The slaughter revived memories of an even greater killing of Hutus in 1972, when an "eliticidal" attempt was made to exterminate virtually all Hutus who had education or professional status (mainly adult males). Combined with the Tutsi-led rebel invasion of Rwanda in 1990, an "image of the Tutsi as the embodiment of a mortal danger . . . [was] hauntingly evident," according to René Lemarchand.[36] A final element added to the mix, at least for Rwanda's Hutu males, was the threat of mortal retribution from their leaders if they did *not* participate in mass murder: "Many Hutu were driven to kill their Tutsi neighbors because they knew they had no other option; refusal to comply meant that they themselves would be killed the next day."[37]

Even in the prototypical case of genocide against a completely defenseless and objectively non-threatening population – the Jewish Holocaust – mortal terror may have figured, though in heavily hystericized form. As Raul Hilberg notes, "the Germans drew a picture of an international Jewry ruling the world and plotting the destruction of Germany and German life."[38] It may appear preposterous to depict Jewish children, women, and elderly as in any sense a "threat" to the German population. It was, however, easier to present adult Jewish males (in fact, any adult males) in this fashion. This helps explain why, both within Germany and in the Nazi-occupied territories of Eastern Europe, this demographic group was demonized in the propaganda generated to guide the genocidal enterprise (see Chapter 13); and why incarceration and physical extermination were first directed against this group. Moreover, the intimate twinning of Jew and Bolshevik/communist in the Nazi mindset brought a fear-evoking dimension that was *not* just hysterical, in that Soviet Russia and Slavic civilization could be presented as a logical threat to the German heartland. These ingredients were stirred together in a propaganda leaflet distributed to German troops on the eastern front:

> Anyone who has ever looked at the face of a red commissar knows what the Bolsheviks are like. Here there is no need for theoretical expressions. We would insult the animals if we described these mostly Jewish men as beasts. They are the embodiment of the Satanic and insane hatred against the whole of noble humanity. . . . The masses, whom they have sent to their deaths by making use of all means at their disposal such as ice-cold terror and insane incitement, would have brought an end to all meaningful life, had this eruption not been dammed at the last moment.[39]

Mortal terror also contains a strong element of psychological *projection.* One justifies genocidal designs by imputing such designs to perceived opponents. The Tutsis/Croatians/Jews/Bolsheviks must be killed because they harbor intentions to kill us, and will do so if they are not stopped/prevented/annihilated. Before they are killed, they are brutalized, debased, and dehumanized – turning them into something resembling "subhumans" or "animals" and, by a circular logic, justifying their extermination. Projection may also assist in displacing guilt and blame from genocidal perpetrators to their victims.[40] Wolfgang Sofsky notes that the Nazis designated Jews as the principal guards and hands-on oppressors of fellow Jews in the concentration camps, as well as those (the *Sonderkommandos*) who carried out much of the industrial processing of corpses in the death camps. It is "as though [the Nazi regime] wished to prove that the members of the subrace accepted any degradation and even killed one another: as though it wished to shift the burden of guilt onto the victims themselves."[41]

The possibility of physical/psychological displacement and dispossession is foundational to existential dread. "Desperation is a theme that runs through a great deal of ethnic violence," writes Donald Horowitz. "A good many groups are convinced that they are or soon will be swamped, dominated, and dispossessed by their neighbors, perhaps even rendered extinct."[42] Since the physical annihilation of the individual is not impending, existential dread may seem to be subordinate to mortal terror. To view it as such would be a serious error. Group identity is so supreme a value that many individuals will choose to sacrifice their own lives to defend it. Likewise, people will often choose physical death over existential shame, dishonor, or loss of status and "respect" before one's peers.[43] Time-honored codes of warriorhood, masculine honor, and female virginity/sexual fidelity provide examples. Underlying much existential dread is the fear of *humiliation* – a phenomenon that merits extended treatment.

GENOCIDE AND HUMILIATION

> If I've learned one thing covering world affairs, it's this: The single most under-appreciated force in international relations is humiliation.
>
> Thomas Friedman, *New York Times* columnist

What Friedman perceived in global affairs, psychologists and others have explored at the level of the individual. Humiliation has been defined by Evelin Lindner as "the enforced lowering of a person or group, a process of subjugation that damages or strips away their pride, honor or dignity."[44] It is increasingly recognized as a primary motivating force in human behavior, particularly violent behavior. Lindner cited Suzanne Retzinger and Thomas Scheff's finding that "humiliated fury" plays a major role "in escalating conflict between individuals and nations."[45] Robert Jay Lifton wrote that "Humiliation involves feelings of shame and disgrace, as well as helplessness in the face of abuse at the hands of a stronger party. These are among the most painful and indelible of human emotions. He who has known extreme shame and humiliation may forever struggle to recover a sense of agency and self-respect."[46] Psychologist James Gilligan, who conducted research among hardened convicts in US prisons, went so far as to argue that "the basic psychological motive, or cause, of violent behavior is the wish to ward off or eliminate the feeling of shame and humiliation – a feeling that is painful and can even be intolerable and overwhelming – and replace it with its opposite, the feeling of pride."[47]

Humiliation thus figures prominently in the most extreme manifestations of human aggression: murder, war, genocide. Indeed, it is difficult to find a historical or contemporary case of genocide in which humiliation is not a central motivating force.[48] It suffices to consider the three best-known genocides of the twentieth century:

- In the case of the Armenian genocide, the Young Turk authorities in Constantinople were humiliated by military defeats in the Balkans and northern Africa (1909–13), and by the secession of imperial territories including Serbia, Bulgaria, and Albania. They were humiliated by the presence of a religious and ethnic minority in their midst (Christian Armenians) that included a prosperous "middleman" sector, and was supposedly assisting Russian designs on Turkey at a time of imperial vulnerability (the First World War). Moreover, it appears that

Turkish authorities and commentators today would experience a sense of humiliation if they acknowledged and apologized for the Armenian genocide. Humiliation is thus a key underpinning of genocide denial.[49]

- The Nazis rose to national prominence by exploiting national humiliation, which they translated into vengefulness and hatred against Germany's supposed tormentors. After four years of fighting in the First World War, the Germans were stunned by their army's collapse on the western front late in 1918. The defeated forces flooding back across the Rhine formed the core of the extreme right-wing groups that proliferated in the early 1920s – including one around Adolf Hitler, whose writings and declarations are replete with horror at Germany's humiliation.[50] Outrage and humiliation greeted the imposition of the punitive Versailles Treaty in 1919, further fueling extremist and revanchist movements. Humiliation sought an outlet in scapegoating; the Nazis argued that it was the Jews who had delivered Germany a treacherous "stab in the back" to prostrate the country before the Western Allies, Bolshevism, and capitalism. As Germany moved from hyperinflation in the 1920s to the Great Depression at decade's end, economic pressures and privation added to feelings of humiliation, especially among men whose self-image was intimately bound up with their "provider" status.[51]
- In Rwanda under Belgian colonialism, Tutsis were taught that they were descended from the "civilized" peoples of the Nile region, while Hutus were unrefined bumpkins. Tutsis were depicted (and came to view themselves) as tall, powerful, educated, attractive; Hutus were presented as the humiliating antithesis. The 1959 revolution establishing Hutu political dominance was represented as a vanquishing of humiliation for the Hutu masses; now Tutsis would be put "in their place." But when a Tutsi exile movement invaded from Rwanda in 1990, Hutu dominance was threatened. The descent into economic crisis around the same time meant humiliating unemployment for hundreds of thousands of Hutus – again especially poignant for adult men, who would be conscripted in vast numbers as agents of the genocide.

It is not surprising, given the intense humiliation of the *génocidaires*, that gratuitous and humiliating cruelties are routinely inflicted upon victims. Many students of the Armenian, Jewish, and Rwandan holocausts are stunned by the care taken not only to exterminate members of the target groups, but to strip them of dignity and inflict maximum suffering before death. In part, as genocide scholar Jacques Semelin argues, this reflects a desire to render victims "worthy" of genocide – that is, to reduce them to the dirty/cowering/impotent status that the genocidal ideology sees as their nature.[52] But it may also speak to feelings of humiliation, and a desire to transfer that humiliation to the hated Other.

Humiliation also figures strongly in subaltern genocide, the "genocides by the oppressed" mentioned in Chapter 1. There are, of course, both fantasies and realities of oppression. Nearly every *génocidaire* considers himself or herself oppressed by the target of genocide: Turks by Armenians, Germans by Jews, Khmers by Vietnamese. In many cases, these framings are the spawn of myth and paranoia. In other instances, there may be a more objective character to the convictions. Hutus in Rwanda *had* experienced social subordination and humiliation at Tutsi hands. The Kosovar extremists who waged a low-level campaign of persecution and – arguably – genocide against Serbs in Kosovo were motivated by years of Serb brutalization and suppression. Islamist terrorism also carries a tinge of subaltern genocide: its exponents keenly feel the humiliation of centuries of conquest and domination by Western "Crusaders." "What America is tasting now is only a copy of what we have tasted," declaims Osama bin Laden. "Our Islamic nation has been tasting the same for more than 80 years, of humiliation and disgrace."[53] Commentators have often wondered how it is that relatively privileged Arabs – even those directly exposed to and benefiting from the prosperity and cosmopolitanism of the West – can plan and conduct terrorist attacks that may descend to the level of genocidal massacre. Humiliation is key to understanding this phenomenon; the educated and privileged may feel it even more strongly than the masses.[54]

"The cruelest result of human bondage," writes the political scientist James C. Scott, "is that it transforms the assertion of personal dignity into a mortal risk."[55] A further problem is that revolt against such bondage, aimed at vanquishing humiliation and re-establishing dignity and self-respect, can take murderous and genocidal forms. To anticipate the discussion of genocide prevention in Chapter 16, subordinate groups, while struggling legitimately for their rights and dignity, should be extremely wary of the vengefulness that is often born of humiliation.

THE PSYCHOLOGY OF PERPETRATORS

> From our findings, we must conclude not only that such personalities are not unique or insane, but also that they could be duplicated in any country of the world today.
>
> Douglas Kelley, investigating psychiatrist at the Nuremberg Tribunal for Nazi war criminals

> *Q.* How do you shoot babies?
> *A.* I don't know. It's just one of those things.
>
> US soldier, participant in the genocidal massacre of hundreds of Vietnamese civilians at My Lai (1968); interviewed by Mike Wallace of CBS

In 1992, Christopher Browning published his ground-breaking book *Ordinary Men*, about a battalion of German police reservists and conscripts – mostly middle-aged men too old for active military service – who functioned as a killing squad on the eastern front in 1941–42. "The men of Reserve Police Battalion 101 were the unlikeliest of mass murderers. They did not represent special selection or even random selection. . . . They were simply ordinary people who went about completing the murderous tasks assigned them with considerable indifference."[56] As Daniel Goldhagen demonstrated in *Hitler's Willing Executioners*, these tasks included corraling and executing Jews and "saboteurs," including children and women, with rifle shots to the back of the head. Often the men emerged spattered with blood and brain matter. The sheer gruesomeness of the task led some to accept their commanding officer's offer to absent themselves from the slaughter without penalty.

But surprisingly few bowed out: Browning estimates that 80 to 90 percent of the battalion eventually participated in close-up mass killings of Jews. Others began by feeling queasy, but accustomed themselves to the killing, even coming to enjoy it. Some excused themselves initially, but subsequently returned. Most numbed themselves with alcohol.

How to explain this routinized participation in acts of unimaginable horror? Although criticized by Goldhagen for downplaying the role of Jew-hatred in the murders, Browning *did* acknowledge that the "deluge of racist and anti-Semitic propaganda" played a key role.[57] But he placed additional emphasis on "the mutually intensifying effects of war and racism"; obedience to authority; peer pressure and the "threat of isolation" from the group (with possibly mortal consequences in wartime); machismo; and feelings of obligation, duty, and honor.

Among the research that Browning cited to support his thesis was the twentieth century's most famous series of psychological studies, conducted by Stanley Milgram beginning in the early 1960s, and known ever since as "the Milgram experiments."[58] The basic design was elegantly simple, yet open to complex variations. A mild-mannered and agreeable middle-aged man, an accountant by profession, was contracted and trained to serve as the "learner" of the experiments (Figure 10.1). He was placed on one side of a wall, and a designated subject (the "teacher") was seated on the other, in front of a generator supposedly capable of administering shocks of increasing voltage to the learner. "The generator had thirty different switches running in fifteen-volt increments from 15 to 450 volts," writes James Waller. "The higher levels of shock were labeled in big letters as 'Intense Shock,' 'Extreme Intensity Shock,' 'Danger: Severe Shock,' and, ominously, 'XXX.'" To give the subject a taste of the treatment he would supposedly be meting out to the learner, he or she was administered a shock of 45 volts – "a level strong enough to be distinctly unpleasant." As the subject asked questions of the learner, incorrect answers were met with commands from a white-coated authority figure (the "experimenter") for the subject to administer "shocks" of ever-greater intensity to the learner. "At 300 volts, the learner vigorously pounded on the laboratory walls in protest. . . . The learner's pounding was repeated after 315 volts. Afterward, he was not heard from again," but the subject was instructed to disregard this, and to continue to turn the dial.[59]

The greatest shock of all was the experiment's results, which have echoed through the disciplines of psychology and sociology. An absolute majority of subjects – twenty-six out of forty – "*obeyed the orders of the experimenter to the end*, proceeding to punish the victim until they reached the most potent shock available on the generator."[60] Sometimes they did so stoically and dispassionately: the face of one subject is described as "hard, impassive . . . showing total indifference as he subdues the screaming learner and gives him shocks. He seems to derive no pleasure from the act itself, only quiet satisfaction at doing his job properly."[61] Most subjects, however, displayed tension, stress, concern, confusion, shame. When the experimental design was altered to make the learner dimly visible, some subjects sought to avoid the consequences of their actions by "avert[ing] their eyes from the person they were shocking, often turning their heads in an awkward and conspicuous manner."[62] But the experimenter assured them that he took full responsibility for the consequences of the subject's actions. Moreover, the subject was told he or she had "no other choice";

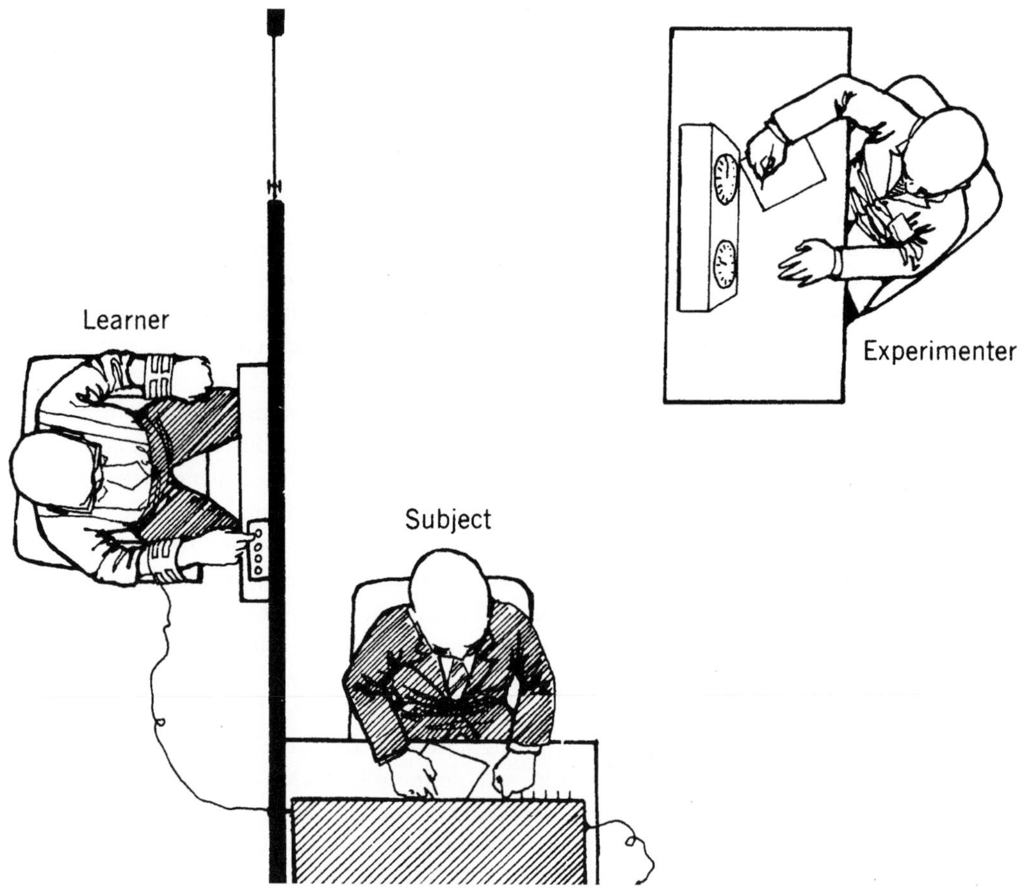

Figure 10.1 The core of the Milgram experiments: an authority figure (the experimenter, top right) commands a subject to administer supposed shocks when a learner answers a question incorrectly. The subject is instructed to increase the voltage as the actor conveys first pain, then ominous silence. How far will an ordinary person turn the dial?

Source: From Stanley Milgram, *Obedience to Authority* (New York: Random House, 1995)

his or her continued participation was "essential." Despite clear misgivings, as noted above, the majority of subjects not only administered the "shocks" but stayed the course to the end.[63] A fair number projected their own stress and shame on to the learner, blaming him "for having volunteered for the experiment, and more viciously, for his stupidity and obstinacy." Interestingly, the obedience displayed by women "was virtually identical to the performance of men," though "the level of conflict experienced by the women was on the whole higher than that felt by our male [subjects]."[64]

Variations on the core experiment helped Milgram to zero in on some of the factors affecting obedience. Subjects placed in greater physical proximity to the learner, sometimes even touching him, were less likely to proceed than those more remotely positioned: "the changing set of spatial relations leads to a potentially shifting set of alliances over the several experimental conditions." Christopher Browning noted that "when not under the direct surveillance of the scientist, many of the subjects 'cheated' by giving lower shocks than prescribed."[65] When an ordinary-seeming person was substituted for the white-coated experimenter, "only a third as many [subjects] followed the common man as followed the experimenter." Furthermore, when other "subjects" were added and secretly instructed to rebel against the authority figure, "the effects of [such] peer rebellion [were] very impressive in undercutting the experimenter's authority." This led Milgram to conclude that "the mutual support provided by men for each other is the strongest bulwark we have against the excesses of authority." In a point relevant to our discussion of gender and genocide (Chapter 13), Milgram noted that selecting an adult male for the "learner" role probably affected the outcome. "As victims, [women] would most likely generate more disobedience, for cultural norms militate against hurting women even more strongly than hurting men. . . . Similarly, if a child were placed in the victim's role, disobedience would be much greater."[66]

Milgram summarized his results, which have been confirmed by dozens of subsequent studies:[67]

> What is surprising is how far ordinary individuals will go in complying with the experimenter's instructions. . . . It is the extreme willingness of adults to go to almost any lengths on the command of an authority that constitutes the chief finding of the study and the fact most urgently demanding explanation. . . . Ordinary people, simply doing their jobs, and without any particular hostility on their part, can become agents in a terrible destructive process. Moreover, even when the destructive effects of their work become patently clear, and they are asked to carry out actions incompatible with fundamental standards of morality, relatively few people have the resources needed to resist authority.[68]

Milgram emphasized that "every sign of tension" among the subjects was "evidence of the failure of authority to transform the [subject] to an unalloyed state of agency."[69] There was at least a latent capacity and desire to resist. In this context, it is worth examining the comportment of the minority of subjects who refused to "shock" the learner. One was a professor of Old Testament studies, who may have drawn on his religious convictions to resist:

> EXPERIMENTER: It's absolutely essential to the experiment that we continue.
> SUBJECT: I understand that statement, but I don't understand why the experiment is placed above this person's life.
> EXPERIMENTER: There is no permanent tissue damage.
> SUBJECT: Well, that's your opinion. If he [the learner] doesn't want to continue, I'm taking orders from him.
> EXPERIMENTER: You have no other choice sir, you must go on.
> SUBJECT: If this were Russia maybe, but not in America.[70]

Another subject, an industrial engineer, grew "incredulous and indignant" when ordered to continue administering the shocks:

> EXPERIMENTER: You have no other choice.
> MR. RENSALEER: I *do* have a choice. . . . Why don't I have a choice? I came here on my own free will. I thought I could help in a research project. But if I have to hurt somebody to do that, or if I was in his place, too, I wouldn't stay there. I can't continue. I'm very sorry. I think I've gone too far already, probably.[71]

To anticipate our discussion of the psychology of "rescuers," below, the resisters demonstrated a high degree of empathy for the learner – and of ego independence, symbolized by their refusal to submit blindly to an authority figure.[72] It is intriguing that one participant in the experiments, a young man named Ron Ridenhour who "refused to give even the first shock," went on to serve in the US military in Vietnam; it was he who "blew the whistle on the massacre at My Lai" (see the epigraph to this section).[73] But the resisters were, to repeat, a minority. Milgram voiced his expectation that outside of the laboratory environment – and especially in conditions of all-consuming dictatorship or totalitarianism – they would be far fewer.

In his account of the experiments, Milgram moved beyond psychology to the sociology of modernity and bureaucratic complexity, which granted individuals a large measure of physical and psychological distance from the consequences of their actions. It is not surprising, therefore, to find the sociologist Zygmunt Bauman drawing on Milgram's work to support his contention that "the process of rationalization facilitates behaviour that is inhuman and cruel."[74] This theme is explored further in the discussion in Chapter 11 about sociological perspectives on genocide.

The Zimbardo experiments

Other insights into the psychology of genocide and group violence may be drawn from a second classic set of experiments, conducted by a Stanford University team under the social psychologist Philip Zimbardo in 1971. (These inspired the 2001 German film *The Experiment.*) As Zygmunt Bauman summarizes:

> In Zimbardo's experiment (planned for a fortnight, but stopped after one week for fear of irreparable damage to the body and mind of the subjects) volunteers had been divided at random into prisoners and prison guards. Both sides were given the symbolic trappings of their position. Prisoners, for example, wore tight caps which simulated shaven heads, and gowns which made them appear ridiculous. Their guards were put in uniforms and given dark glasses which hid their eyes from being looked into by the prisoners. No side was allowed to address the other by name; strict impersonality was the rule. There was [a] long list of petty regulations invariably humiliating for the prisoners and stripping them of human dignity. This was the starting point. What followed surpassed and left far behind the designers' ingenuity. The initiative of the guards (randomly selected males of college age, carefully screened against any sign of abnormality) knew no bounds. . . . The construed superiority of the guards rebounded in the submissiveness of the prisoners, which in its turn tempted the guards into further displays of their powers, which were then duly reflected in more self-humiliation on the part of

> the prisoners. . . . The guards forced the prisoners to chant filthy songs, to defecate in buckets which they did not allow them to empty, to clean toilets with bare hands; the more they did it, the more they acted as if they were convinced of the non-human nature of the prisoners, and the less they felt constrained in inventing and administering measures of an ever-more appalling degree of inhumanity.[75]

This slightly overstates the case. In fact, the guards divided into three factions, with about one-third assuming "cruel, callous, sadistic, dominating, authoritarian, tyrannical, coercive, and aggressive roles." James Waller describes a middle group as "tough but fair," while a final segment "emerged as 'good guards' and tried to help the prisoners when they could."[76] Christopher Browning points out that the behavior of Zimbardo's guards was strikingly similar to that of the "ordinary men" he studied for his eponymous book – from the "nucleus of increasingly enthusiastic killers who volunteered," through those who "performed . . . when assigned but who did not seek opportunities to kill," through "a small group (less than 20 percent) of refusers and evaders."[77] However, it must be remembered that Zimbardo's experiment was terminated after only a few days; it is impossible to say how many of the "tough but fair" group and the hold-outs would eventually have behaved sadistically, had it continued.

To the public, Zimbardo's results were as shocking as Milgram's. They depicted "the sudden transmogrification of likeable and decent American boys into near monsters of the kind allegedly to be found only in places like Auschwitz or Treblinka."[78] Contemporary readers are likely to think of the American men and women who inflicted sadistic and humiliating abuses on inmates at Abu Ghraib prison near Baghdad, along with many other sites in occupied Iraq and at the US-run prison at Guantánamo Bay, Cuba.[79] Indeed, in the wake of the Abu Ghraib revelations, many commentators cited the Zimbardo experiments as evidence that (in the words of criminologist David Wilson) "If you give a person power over someone who is powerless, someone who has been demonised or made to seem less human, then that absolute power corrupts absolutely."[80]

THE PSYCHOLOGY OF RESCUERS

Just when immersion in the genocidal actions of "ordinary" men and women leaves you wallowing in pessimism, the rescuers come again to the rescue. The historical record is replete with accounts of brutal perpetrators, and bystanders whose "neutrality . . . helps the stronger party in an unequal struggle."[81] But it is also filled with testimonials to the brave souls who interceded to save total strangers (as well as friends and acquaintances) from genocide.

The most famous of these figures are associated with the Jewish Holocaust, in part because that campaign of mass murder is better known than all the rest put together. Many readers will be familiar with the extraordinary collective opposition mounted by the people of Nazi-occupied Denmark, which, it should be conceded, had been "awarded a degree of autonomy that was unusual for a region under German occupation." In 1943, Nazi officials encountered "a local population unanimous in its resolve" to preserve Danish Jews from round-up and extermination. Virtually the entire Jewish population, several thousand strong, was successfully transferred by the operators of small boats to safety in neutral Sweden. According to Raul Hilberg, "help came from every quarter. The Danish police shielded the operators by warning them of danger, individuals helped to sell Jewish belongings, taxi drivers transported the Jews to the ports, house and apartment owners offered the victims shelter, Pastor Krohn [an advocate for the Jews] handed out blank baptismal certificates, druggists supplied free stimulants to keep people awake, and so on." It was, writes Hilberg, "one of the most remarkable rescue operations in history."[82]

Among individual rescuers of Jews, at least before the release of Steven Spielberg's film *Schindler's List* – about the exploits of a German industrialist who saved hundreds of Jews from the gas chambers of Auschwitz-Birkenau – the most renowned was probably a Swedish representative in Budapest, Raoul Wallenberg:

> In 1944 the United States belatedly established the War Refugee Board (WRB) to aid and rescue the victims of Nazism. Fearing the imminent deportation of Hungarian Jewry, the WRB solicited the help of a number of neutral countries to protect this endangered community. Sweden embraced the American proposal and appointed Wallenberg as a special envoy to Hungary whose sole mission was to avert the deportation of Jews. Taking advantage of his diplomatic immunity and money contributed by private organizations like the American Jewish Joint Distribution Committee, Wallenberg issued bogus Swedish "protective passports," rented apartment buildings to serve as Jewish sanctuaries under Swedish protection, and personally whisked hundreds of Hungarian Jews off German transports on the pretext that they were wards of Sweden. Wallenberg's example inspired other neutral embassies and the International Red Cross office in Budapest to protect Jews too. According to some estimates, the rescue campaign launched by Wallenberg may have saved as many as 100,000 Jews.[83]

Wallenberg's story has overshadowed those who facilitated his rescue, such as the Swedish diplomat Per Anger. According to historian Henry Huttenbach, it was Anger who first "hit on the idea of issuing Jews temporary Swedish passports and identity cards. . . . Anger's undivided cooperation allowed Wallenberg to succeed. . . . It is safe to say that Wallenberg's mission to save Hungarian Jews from deportation would not have got off the ground had Wallenberg not had the total support from the Swedish Embassy, that is, from Per Anger."[84]

In the grimmest of ironies, Wallenberg the rescuer survived the Nazis, only to disappear into the custody of Soviet forces occupying Hungary. For reasons unknown, he appears to have spent years in detention before finally dying in the camps sometime in the 1950s.[85]

An equally striking rescuer was Chiune Sugihara, the Japanese consul in Lithuania, who received a flood of Jews fleeing the Nazi-Soviet invasion of Poland in 1939. Sugihara:

> willingly issued them transit visas by considerably stretching his own government's official rules, allowing the Polish Jews to cross Soviet territory en route to Japan

Figure 10.2 Per Anger, the Swedish diplomat who worked with Raoul Wallenberg to save 100,000 Hungarian Jews from the Nazis, poses with a portrait of Wallenberg in 1985. Wallenberg probably died in a Soviet camp after the Second World War; Anger died in 2001.

Source: US Holocaust Memorial Museum/Courtesy Per and Ellena Anger.

SCHUTZ-PASS Nr. 28/69.

Name: Lili Katz
Név:

Wohnort: Budapest
Lakás:

Geburtsdatum: 13.Sept.1913.
Születési ideje:

Geburtsort: Budapest
Születési helye:

Körperlänge: 164 cm.
Magasság:

Haarfarbe: blond Augenfarbe: grau
Hajszín: Szemszín:

Unterschrift:
Aláírás:

SCHWEDEN SVÉDORSZÁG

Die Kgl. Schwedische Gesandtschaft in Budapest bestätigt, dass der Obengenannte im Rahmen der — von dem Kgl. Schwedischen Aussenministerium autorisierten — Repatriierung nach Schweden reisen wird. Der Betreffende ist auch in einen Kollektivpass eingetragen.

Bis Abreise steht der Obengenannte und seine Wohnung unter dem Schutz der Kgl. Schwedischen Gesandtschaft in Budapest.

Gültigkeit: erlischt 14 Tage nach Einreise nach Schweden.

A budapesti Svéd Kir. Követség igazolja, hogy fentnevezett — a Svéd Kir. Külügyminisztérium által jóváhagyott — repatriálás keretében Svédországba utazik.

Nevezett a kollektív útlevélben is szerepel.

Elutazásáig fentnevezett és lakása a budapesti Svéd Kir. Követség oltalma alatt áll.

Érvényét veszti a Svédországba való megérkezéstől számított tizennegyedik napon.

Reiseberechtigung nur gemeinsam mit dem Kollektivpass. Einreisevisum wird nur in dem Kollektivpass eingetragen.

Figure 10.3 Wallenberg and Anger issued letters of protection (Schutz-pass), similar to this one for Lili Katz, through the Swedish legation in Budapest. The documents had no legal force, but, combined with a healthy measure of bluff, they saved tens of thousands of lives. In the bottom left of the pass is the letter "W," standing for Wallenberg. Budapest, 1944.

Source: US Holocaust Memorial Museum, courtesy of Lena Kurtz Deutsch.

> and, from there, to anywhere they wished. Before the Japanese government reassigned him, Sugihara issued some 4,500 visas, many of them handwritten, and he did not stop issuing visas until literally the moment before his train carried him out. . . . His visas were also easy to counterfeit. Combined with those forgeries, Sugihara's efforts may well have saved some 10,000 Jews.[86]

Famous rescuers such as these took advantage of their professional positions to undertake their missions; but, of course, millions of people in the twentieth century alone utilized their occupational and bureaucratic positions to kill rather than save. What distinguishes individuals who choose to shelter and assist those at mortal risk of genocide, often at mortal risk to themselves?

In many cases, religious motivations have played an important role. At its best and most humane, religion embodies universal values of compassion and mercy (for more on this, see Chapter 16). And so we find the Catholic cleric Dompropst Bernard Lichtenberg of Berlin, rejecting the passivity and anti-semitism of the church hierarchy, and daring "to pray publicly for all Jews, baptized [as Christians] or not." When his efforts failed to save Jews from transportation to the death camps, he "*demanded that he be allowed to join [them] on their journey to the East.*" He was imprisoned, and picked up by the Gestapo upon his release; he died *en route* to Dachau.[87] Less demonstrative but no less religiously imbued were the actions of the "kind and gentle" Muslim notable recalled by a survivor of the Armenian holocaust, who took refuge in his home:

> The bey followed Islamic law to the letter and was a devout believer. He prayed five times a day and fasted one month out of the year. I used to join him in these [observances]. He had also made a pilgrimage to Mecca and was thus called "Haji." He was a principled and just man. He felt genuine sorrow for the Armenian massacre and considered it a sin to bring any confiscated Armenian possessions into his home. He used to condemn the Turkish government, saying, "The Armenians are a hardy, intelligent, and industrious people. If there are any guilty among them, the government can arrest and punish them instead of slaughtering a helpless and innocent people."[88]

However, it is also the case that "more intense religiosity is frequently associated with greater prejudice";[89] and in any case, religious belief is by no means necessary to rescuers *tout court.* Often it matters only that one be "so overcome by the human tragedy of the genocide" that she or he feels impelled to intercede. During the Rwanda catastrophe of 1994, Paul Rusesabagina, Hutu proprietor of the Hotel Mille Collines in Kigali, saved nearly 1,300 refugees – mostly Tutsi, as was his wife – from slaughter at the hands of rampaging Hutu militia, preserving them for the full two-and-a-half months of the genocide. (The 2004 film of his exploits, *Hotel Rwanda*, brought international attention to this rescuer.) Rusesabagina "rationed water from the swimming pool, had checkpoints removed, bribed killers with money and Scotch whisky and kept a secret telephone line open to the outside world." "I wanted to keep my people, the refugees, safe," he told a suddenly interested world. "That was my main objective and I tried to keep that up to the end . . . I rather take myself as someone who did his duties and responsibilities, someone who remained until the end when others changed completely their professions, and most of them became killers and others were killed."[90]

With the guidance of Samuel and Pearl Oliner, let us dig a little deeper into the psychology of rescuers. In 1988 the Oliners published a volume on "Rescuers of Jews in Nazi Europe," based on hundreds of interviews with those identified as such by the staff of the Yad Vashem museum. *The Altruistic Personality* has since become a classic, not only of Jewish Holocaust literature but of the social sciences.

What did the Oliners and their researchers discover about the motivations of those who aided, sheltered, and protected defenseless Jews, when most around them were turning their backs or actively assisting with the slaughter? Consider some of the testimonies of these otherwise ordinary individuals:

> I had contact all the time with people who were against Hitler. They told me the most horrible things – transports, gas chambers, drownings, gassing in trains – I knew that a huge injustice was taking place. I felt tense, I couldn't sleep.
>
> I could smell the smoke from Majdanek [death camp] . . .
>
> He had nobody else to help him. [The Jews] could not survive on their rations.
>
> . . . When [the Germans] started taking the Jewish people, that really lit my fire. They took them like sheep, throwing them into trains. I couldn't stand it anymore. . . . They took innocent people and I wanted to help.
>
> Somebody had to do it.
>
> . . . Unless we helped, they would be killed. I could not stand that thought. I never would have forgiven myself.
>
> Can you see it? Two young girls come, one sixteen or seventeen, and they tell you a story that their parents were killed and they were pulled in and raped. What are you supposed to tell them – "Sorry, we are full already?"
>
> . . . I was so ashamed of what other so-called Christians did that I felt I wanted to do the contrary.
>
> If you can save somebody's life, that's your duty.
>
> We helped people who were in need. Who they were was absolutely immaterial to us. It wasn't that we were especially fond of Jewish people. We felt we wanted to help everybody who was in trouble.[91]

The personal values and psychological orientations cited again and again by the Oliners revolve around these core themes: *altruism* (from the Latin: literally, "otherism"), *universalism, care* ("the obligation to help the needy"), *compassion* (literally, "together feeling"), *empathy, equity/egalitarianism, justice* (defined as "the right of innocent people to be free from persecution"), *respect, fairness*, and *patriotism* (understood as "encompass[ing] national acceptance of pluralistic and diverse groups in relationships of equality rather than mere tolerance").[92] It is clear from the Oliners' account that these orientations have an abiding basis in the family upbringings of the rescuers. Rescuers were significantly more likely than non-rescuers to describe their parents as *benevolent, loving, kind, tolerant, compassionate, non-abusive*, prone to *explain* rather than punish, *extensive* rather than restrictive in their orientation towards others. The result, more commonly among rescuers than among bystanders, was an "ego orientation" that emphasized not only these traits, but a basic *strength, autonomy, independence.* As the authors eloquently put it:

> Already attuned to conferring meaning on events through their particular moral sensibilities, [rescuers] depended on familiar patterns to discern the significance of the unprecedented events at hand. To a large extent, then, helping Jews was less a decision made at a critical juncture than a choice prefigured by an established character and way of life. As Iris Murdoch observes, the moral life is not something that is switched on at a particular crisis but is rather something that goes on continually in the small piecemeal habits of living. Hence, "at crucial moments of choice most of the business of choosing is already over." Many rescuers themselves reflected this view, saying that they "had no choice" and that their behavior deserved no special attention, for it was simply an "ordinary" thing to do.[93]

Even with these strong familial buttresses, the psychology of the rescuer did not necessarily arise "out of the blue" or in purely disinterested fashion. Geographical proximity, particularly in urban settings, facilitated matters. Nationalist sentiment was not absent: French rescuers were more likely to help Jews who were French citizens than stateless refugees. Frequently, rescuers had had previous positive relationships with Jews: as childhood friends, co-workers, neighbors. Sometimes Christian rescuers had a perception of Jews as a "chosen people," intimately related through the shared religious tradition. "Several rescuers acknowledged that they became dependent on the Jews they helped," for household chores, assistance with repairs and maintenance, and so on.[94] In some cases, rescuers had little idea what they were getting themselves into; small and low-risk acts of kindness would lead inexorably to dramatic acts of long-term and high-risk helping. Sometimes the rescued promised the rescuer a material reward after the war was over. More attractive and more traditionally "innocent" Jews (particularly children) were especially likely to receive aid. Sometimes sexually intimate relationships developed, as they frequently do in situations of stress and shared danger.

At times, rescuers felt disappointed or disillusioned by the response of the rescued after the danger was over. This serves as a reminder that rescuer psychology is not to be romanticized. I do believe, however, that it is to be *idealized*, in the profoundest sense of the word. These people, who usually considered themselves to be utterly ordinary, point us to the human motivations that may one day bring an end to genocide in our world. Let us hope they are indeed ordinary – or at least more common than is commonly realized. Because "if humankind is dependent on only a few autonomously principled people, then the future is bleak indeed."[95]

FURTHER STUDY

Roy F. Baumeister, *Evil: Inside Human Violence and Cruelty.* New York: W.H. Freeman, 1999. Involving inquiry into the nature of evil.

Christopher Browning, *Ordinary Men: Reserve Police Battalion 101 and the Final Solution in Poland.* New York: HarperPerennial, 1998. How a group of middle-aged German reservists was conscripted into genocidal killing.

Thomas Kenneally, *Schindler's List.* New York: Touchstone, 1993. Fact-based novel about the famous rescuer of Jews; basis for the film.

Neil J. Kressel, *Mass Hate: The Global Rise of Genocide and Terror.* New York: Plenum Press, 1996. Focuses on the psychology of genocidal perpetrators; usefully read alongside Waller (see below).

Robert J. Lifton, *The Nazi Doctors: Medical Killing and the Psychology of Genocide.* New York: Basic Books, 1986. Analyzes the complex psychology of medical workers/murderers at Auschwitz.

Stanley Milgram, *Obedience to Authority: An Experimental View.* New York: HarperPerennial, 1995. "The Milgram Experiments": a classic of social-scientific investigation.

Leonard S. Newman and Ralph Erber, eds, *Understanding Genocide: The Social Psychology of the Holocaust.* Oxford: Oxford University Press, 2002. Essays on perpetrators and bystanders in the Jewish and other genocides.

Samuel P. Oliner and Pearl M. Oliner, *The Altruistic Personality: Rescuers of Jews in Nazi Europe.* New York: The Free Press, 1988. Intensely moving large-sample study.

Irene Gut Opdyke with Jennifer Armstrong, *In My Hands: Memories of a Holocaust Rescuer.* New York: Anchor Books, 2001. Brief, potent memoir.

Ervin Staub, *The Roots of Evil: The Origins of Genocide and Other Group Violence.* Cambridge: Cambridge University Press, 1989. Early study of the psychology of genocide.

Samuel Vaknin, *Malignant Self-love: Narcissism Revisited* (5th rev. edn). Skopje: Narcissus Publications, 2003. Lengthy work by an authority on narcissism.

James Waller, *Becoming Evil: How Ordinary People Commit Genocide and Mass Killing.* Oxford: Oxford University Press, 2002. Social-psychological account, readable and up-to-date.

Emmy E. Werner, *A Conspiracy of Decency: The Rescue of the Danish Jews.* Boulder, CO: Westview Press, 2002. The story of the famous rescue operation during the Second World War.

NOTES

1 James Waller, *Becoming Evil: How Ordinary People Commit Genocide and Mass Killing* (Oxford: Oxford University Press, 2002); see in particular ch. 3, "The 'Mad Nazi': Psychopathology, Personality, and Extraordinary Evil," pp. 55–93.
2 Greek Mythology Link, "Narcissus," http://homepage.mac.com/cparada/GML/Narcissus.html.
3 Anton Blok, "The Narcissism of Minor Differences," ch. 7 in Blok, *Honour and Violence* (Cambridge: Polity Press, 2001), p. 115.
4 Freud quoted in Blok, *Honour and Violence*, p. 117.
5 See Samuel Vaknin, *Malignant Self-love: Narcissism Revisited* (Skopje: Narcissus Publications, 2003).
6 "A narcissist openly reveals his megalomania, but craves admiration, praise, and flattery. He has little sense of humor, he cannot form significant relationships, and blows to his self-esteem can elicit violent anger. He has a paranoid distrust of others. He can appear self-confident and secure, but deep down feels shame, insecurity, and inferiority. . . . He may, at one moment, appear a charming, benign benefactor, and the next moment turn into a raging, aggressive attacker. . . . He has a distorted conscience. Depression is common." Neil J. Kressel, *Mass Hate: The Global Rise of Genocide and Terror* (New York: Plenum Press, 1996), p. 133.
7 Quoted in Barbara Ehrenreich, *Blood Rites: Origins and History of the Passions of War* (New York: Metropolitan Books, 1997), p. 210.
8 Simon Sebag Montefiore, *Stalin: The Court of the Red Tsar* (London: Phoenix, 2004), p. 617.
9 Vaknin, "Collective Narcissism," http://samvak.tripod.com/14.html; emphasis added, to stress that the "collective" character of such narcissism need not require unanimity or even a majority among the afflicted group. Precisely when ordinary grandiosity becomes pathological narcissism is difficult to discern, but as an American correspondent, Kathleen Morrow, points out, it seems to be tied to systemic factors. "An assumption of superiority is part of *every* national character. . . . If you listen long enough to any citizen of any nation, you will detect a trace of narcissistic unreality . . . part of the cultural mythology that holds the group together. (The French think they invented 'culture,' the Italians are sure they are the only people who really know how to 'enjoy life,' etc.) I tend to assume this almost universal tendency to national grandiosity is innocent enough – as long as the nation or group does not accumulate enough power to begin to try to impose its internal mythology on the rest of the world. . . . I suppose I'm arguing that US collective pathological narcissism is not a cultural or psychological problem as much as a systemic one. By systemic, I mean the global system, which at this point exhibits a number of power vacuums into which a too-powerful US can narcissistically rush." Morrow, personal communication, May 5, 2005.
10 For a pointed analysis of the collective narcissism of my other country of citizenship, see Clifford Krauss, "Was Canada Just Too Good to be True?," *New York Times*, May 25, 2005.
11 Cambodia under the Khmer Rouge (see Chapter 7) is another candidate, but I consider Khmer Rouge fanaticism to have been too shallowly rooted in society as a whole to merit inclusion.
12 Robert Jay Lifton, *Superpower Syndrome: America's Apocalyptic Confrontation with the World* (New York: Thunder's Mouth Press/Nation Books, 2003), p. 190.
13 For the full text, see "The National Security Strategy of the United States of America," http://www.whitehouse.gov/nsc/nss.html.
14 See Walter Pincus, "Pentagon Revises Nuclear Strike Plan: Strategy Includes Preemptive Use Against Banned Weapons," *Washington Post*, September 11, 2005, http://www.washingtonpost.com/wp-dyn/content/article/2005/09/10/AR2005091001053.html.

15 Quoted in Saul Friedländer, *Nazi Germany and the Jews, Volume 1: The Years of Persecution, 1933–1939* (New York: HarperCollins, 1997), p. 259.
16 Alexander Donat, *The Holocaust Kingdom* (Washington, DC: Holocaust Library, 1999), p. 197.
17 Michael Burleigh, *Ethics and Extermination: Reflections on Nazi Genocide* (Cambridge: Cambridge University Press, 1997), p. 191.
18 Patricia Marchak, *Reigns of Terror* (Montreal: McGill-Queen's University Press, 2003), p. 21.
19 Heizer quoted in Levon Marashlian, "Finishing the Genocide: Cleansing Turkey of Armenian Survivors, 1920–1923," in Richard G. Hovannisian, ed., *Remembrance and Denial: The Case of the Armenian Genocide* (Detroit: Wayne State University Press, 1999), p. 115. (Heizer's statement dates from July 1915.) The US consul in Mamouret-ul-Aziz, Leslie A. Davis, similarly reported that "The scenes of that week [of deportation] were heartrending. The [Armenian] people were preparing to leave their homes and to abandon their houses, their lands, their property of all kinds. They were selling their possessions for whatever they could get. The streets were full of Turkish women, as well as men, who were seeking bargains on this occasion, buying organs, sewing machines, furniture, rugs, and other articles of values for almost nothing. . . . The scene reminded me of vultures swooping down on their prey. It was a veritable Turkish holiday and all the Turks went out in their gala attire to feast and to make merry over the misfortunes of others." Davis quoted in Marchak, *Reigns of Terror*, p. 166.
20 Montefiore, *Stalin: The Court of the Red Tsar*, p. 265.
21 Gérard Prunier, *The Rwanda Crisis: History of a Genocide* (New York: Columbia University Press, 1997), p. 142.
22 Quoted in Jean Hatzfeld (trans. Linda Coverdale), *Machete Season: The Killers in Rwanda Speak* (New York: Farrar, Straus & Giroux, 2005), p. 87.
23 H.H. Gerth and C. Wright Mills, eds, *From Max Weber: Essays in Sociology* (New York: Oxford University Press, 1954), p. 180.
24 Burleigh, *Ethics and Extermination*, p. 164.
25 Montefiore, *Stalin*, p. 626.
26 "Everybody could hope for speedy advancement because every day somebody was plucked from their midst and had to be replaced. Of course, everybody was also a candidate for prison and death, but during the day they did not think about it, giving full rein to their fears only at night." Nadezhda Mandelstam, *Hope Against Hope* (New York: Modern Library, 1999), p. 282.
27 Prunier, *The Rwanda Crisis*, pp. 231–32.
28 Burke quoted in Linda Green, "Fear as a Way of Life," in Alexander Laban Hinton, ed., *Genocide: An Anthropological Reader* (Malden, MA: Blackwell), p. 307.
29 See J.S. Piven, *Death and Delusion: A Freudian Analysis of Mortal Terror* (Greenwich, CT: IAP Publishers, 2004).
30 Charny quoted in Leo Kuper, *The Prevention of Genocide* (New Haven, CT: Yale University Press, 1985), p. 196. In *The Denial of Death*, for me one of the twentieth century's most profound books, Ernest Becker traces both human pathologies and human civilization to the terror of death: "The idea of death, the fear of it, haunts the human animal like nothing else; it is a mainspring of human activity – activity designed largely to avoid the fatality of death, to overcome it by denying in some way that it is the final destiny for man." Becker, *The Denial of Death* (New York: The Free Press, 1973), p. ix. See also the discussion of psychological research on "mortality salience" and "terror management" in Kate Douglas, "Death Defying," *New Scientist*, August 28, 2004.
31 Ehrenreich, *Blood Rites*, p. 76.
32 On the psychology of "in-group–out-group differentiation," see Staub, *The Roots of Evil*, pp. 58–62.
33 Waller, *Becoming Evil*, p. 149.
34 Donald L. Horowitz, *The Deadly Ethnic Riot* (Berkeley, CA: University of California Press, 2001), p. 548.

35 Horowitz, *The Deadly Ethnic Riot*, p. 548.
36 René Lemarchand, "Disconnecting the Threads: Rwanda and the Holocaust Reconsidered," *Journal of Genocide Research*, 4: 4 (2002), p. 507.
37 Lemarchand, "Disconnecting the Threads," p. 513. A similar dynamic was evident in the Nazi SS, where not only was disobedience standardly punished by execution, but the loss of employment in the camps could mean a transfer to the mortal danger of the eastern front. Hence, according to Christopher Fettweis, "cowardice played an important role" in motivating SS members. "These men and women were well aware that to request a transfer might mean a trip to the Russian front, from which few people returned. The Jew-killing duties, while perhaps unpleasant, were relatively safe and provided a solid chance to survive the war. The Russian front must have provided quite an effective incentive to perform for those assigned to guard the trains, or to man the towers, or to work in the rear in the *Einsatzgruppen*." Fettweis, "War as Catalyst: Moving World War II to the Center of Holocaust Scholarship," *Journal of Genocide Research*, 5: 2 (2003), p. 229.
38 Raul Hilberg, *The Destruction of the European Jews* (3rd edn), Vol. 3 (New Haven, CT: Yale University Press, 2003), p. 1093. Mark Levene also points disparagingly to the fantastic "notion that worldwide Jewry, despite its dispersal, minority status and history of persecution, was actually spearheading an international, even cosmic conspiracy to emasculate and ultimately wipe out not only the German people but all western civilization." Levene, "Why Is the Twentieth Century the Century of Genocide?," *Journal of World History*, 11: 2 (2000), p. 323.
39 Omer Bartov, *Hitler's Army: Soldiers, Nazis, and War in the Third Reich* (New York: Oxford University Press, 1992), p. 126. Such propaganda had a duly fear-evoking effect on German fighting forces, who came to view their mission of occupation and genocide as a fundamentally defensive one, especially with regard to the Slavic enemy. One soldier wrote in August 1941: "Precisely now one recognizes perfectly what would have happened to our wives and children had these Russian hordes . . . succeeded in penetrating into our Fatherland. I have had the opportunity here to . . . observe these uncultivated, multi-raced men. Thank God they have been thwarted from plundering and pillaging our homeland." Cited in Bartov, *Hitler's Army*, p. 156.
40 A Hutu killer in the Rwandan genocide also recalled: "The perpetrators felt more comfortable insulting and hitting crawlers in rags rather than properly upright people. Because they seemed less like us in that position." Quoted in Hatzfeld, *Machete Season*, p. 132.
41 Wolfgang Sofsky, *The Order of Terror: The Concentration Camp* (Princeton, NJ: Princeton University Press, 1999), p. 267.
42 Horowitz, *The Deadly Ethnic Riot*, p. 393.
43 According to Terrence Des Pres, immersion in filth and excreta has much the same character, violating psychological taboos so deeply held that they are almost instinctive. "The shock of physical defilement causes spiritual concussion, and, simply to judge from the reports of those who have suffered it, subjection to filth seems often to cause greater anguish than hunger or fear of death. 'This aspect of our camp life,' says one survivor [of the Nazi camps, Reska Weiss], 'was the most dreadful and the most horrible ordeal to which we were subjected.' Another survivor [Leon Szalet] describes the plight of men forced to lie in their own excreta: they 'moaned and wept with discomfort and disgust. Their moral wretchedness was crushing.'" Des Pres, *The Survivor: An Anatomy of Life in the Death Camps* (Oxford: Oxford University Press, 1976), p. 66.
44 Evelin Lindner, "Gendercide and Humiliation in Honour and Human-rights Societies," in Adam Jones, ed., *Gendercide and Genocide* (Nashville, TN: Vanderbilt University Press, 2004), p. 40.
45 Retzinger and Scheff cited in Lindner, "Gendercide and Humiliation," p. 45.
46 Lifton, *Superpower Syndrome*, p. 103.
47 James Gilligan, "Shame, Guilt, and Violence," *Social Research*, 70: 4 (winter 2003), p. 1154.

48 Donald Horowitz likewise writes of "deadly ethnic riots" that "the reversal of invidious comparisons, the retrieval of imperiled respect, and the redistribution of honor are among the central purposive ideas embedded in the dramaturgy." Horowitz, *The Deadly Ethnic Riot*, p. 431.

49 Taner Akçam is strong on this: "Turkish nationalism arose as a reaction to the experience of constant humiliations. Turkish national sentiment constantly suffered from the effects of an inferiority complex. . . . Critical . . . was the fact that the Turks not only were continuously humiliated and loathed, but they were conscious of this humiliation. . . . A nation that was humiliated in this way in the past and is also conscious of that experience, will try to prove its own greatness and importance." Akçam, "The Genocide of the Armenians and the Silence of the Turks," in Levon Chorbajian and George Shirinian, eds, *Studies in Comparative Genocide* (London: Macmillan, 1999), p. 129. See also Akçam, *From Empire to Republic: Turkish Nationalism and the Armenian Genocide* (London: Zed Books, 2004), chs 2–3.

50 "Nazi doctors told me of indelible scenes, which they either witnessed as young children or were told about by their fathers, of German soldiers returning home defeated after World War I. These beaten men, many of them wounded, engendered feelings of pathos, loss, and embarrassment, all amidst national misery and threatened revolution. Such scenes, associated with strong feelings of humiliation, were seized upon by the Nazis to the point where one could say that Hitler rose to power on the promise of avenging them." Lifton, *Superpower Syndrome*, p. 111.

51 I have explored the link between "Humiliation and Masculine Crisis in Iraq," focusing on the invasion of 2003 and subsequent occupation and uprising, in an article of this name in *Al-Raida* (Beirut: Institute for Women's Studies in the Arab World), Vol. 21, July 2004. Available at http://adamjones.freeservers.com/iraq_crisis.htm.

52 See Jacques Semelin, "Toward a Vocabulary of Massacre and Genocide," *Journal of Genocide Research*, 5: 2 (2003), p. 207.

53 Quoted in Gilligan, "Shame, Guilt and Violence," p. 1162. Jessica Stern's interviews with Palestinian suicide bombers provide further evidence of humiliation as a motivating force. See Stern, *Terror in the Name of God: Why Religious Militants Kill* (New York: Ecco Press, 2003).

54 This is also evident, with generally more positive outcomes, in the history of movements for national autonomy or independence. Clearly, the educated and otherwise privileged are disproportionately represented among the leaderships of such movements.

55 James C. Scott, *Domination and the Arts of Resistance: Hidden Transcripts* (New Haven, CT: Yale University Press, 1990), p. 37.

56 Waller, *Becoming Evil*, p. 68.

57 Christopher Browning, *Ordinary Men: Reserve Police Battalion 101 and the Final Solution in Poland* (New York: Perennial, 1993), p. 184.

58 See Thomas Blass, *The Man Who Shocked the World: The Life and Legacy of Stanley Milgram* (New York: Basic Books, 2004).

59 Waller, *Becoming Evil*, pp. 103–4.

60 Stanley Milgram, *Obedience to Authority: An Experimental View* (New York: HarperPerennial, 1995), p. 33; emphasis added.

61 Milgram, *Obedience to Authority*, p. 40.

62 Milgram, *Obedience to Authority*, p. 34. "Subjects seemed able to resist the experimenter far better when they did not have to confront [the 'victim'] face to face" (p. 62).

63 One might expect a degree of trauma to have resulted to the subjects from learning their capacity to do harm, but according to Milgram, this was not the case. Nearly all subjects expressed gratitude for the insights that the experiments had provided them. The comment of one subject in a follow-up interview was: "I think people should think more deeply about themselves and their relation to their world and to other people." Milgram, *Obedience to Authority*, p. 196.

64 Milgram, *Obedience to Authority*, pp. 63, 161.

65 Browning, *Ordinary Men*, p. 172.

66 Milgram, *Obedience to Authority*, pp. 40, 62–63, 97, 118, 121.

67 See Waller, *Becoming Evil*, p. 106. For a recent evaluation of Milgram's work, see Thomas Blass, "Perpetrator Behavior as Destructive Obedience: An Evaluation of Stanley Milgram's Perspective, the Most Influential Social-psychological Approach to the Holocaust," ch. 4 in Leonard S. Newman and Ralph Erber, eds, *Understanding Genocide: The Social Psychology of the Holocaust* (Oxford: Oxford University Press, 2002), pp. 91–109.

68 Milgram, *Obedience to Authority*, pp. 5–6.

69 Milgram, *Obedience to Authority*, p. 155.

70 Milgram, *Obedience to Authority*, p. 48.

71 Milgram, *Obedience to Authority*, p. 51.

72 However, as Roy Baumeister notes, while "empathy may prevent cruelty in some cases . . . it can also serve it. The true sadist is not lacking in empathy – on the contrary, empathy helps the sadist to derive maximum pleasure and inflict the greatest pain." Baumeister, *Evil*, p. 247. For more on the psychology of torture and sadism, see Elaine Scarry, *The Body in Pain: The Making and Unmaking of the World* (New York: Oxford University Press, 1985), esp. ch. 1; and John Conroy, *Unspeakable Acts, Ordinary People: The Dynamics of Torture* (New York: Alfred A. Knopf, 2000).

73 Jonathan Glover, *Humanity: A Moral History of the Twentieth Century* (New Haven, CT: Yale University Press, 1999), p. 333. On Ridenhour's whistle-blowing, see Michael Bilton and Kevin Sim, *Four Hours in My Lai* (New York: Penguin, 1993), pp. 214–20.

74 Zygmunt Bauman, *Modernity and the Holocaust* (Ithaca, NY: Cornell University Press, 2000), p. 155.

75 Bauman, *Modernity and the Holocaust*, pp. 166–67.

76 Waller, *Becoming Evil*, pp. 222–23. Zimbardo's core results were published in two articles: Philip G. Zimbardo, "Pathology of Imprisonment," *Society*, 6 (1972), pp. 4–8; and Craig Haney, Curtis Banks, and Philip G. Zimbardo, "Interpersonal Dynamics in a Simulated Prison," *International Journal of Criminology and Penology*, 1 (1983), pp. 69–97.

77 Browning, *Ordinary Men*, p. 168.

78 Bauman, *Modernity and the Holocaust*, p. 167.

79 See, e.g., Patrick Jarreau, "America and Its Moral Superiority Complex," *Le Monde*, May 7, 2003.

80 Ryan Dilley, "Is It in Anyone to Abuse a Captive?," *BBC News Online*, May 5, 2004. http://news.bbc.co.uk/1/hi/magazine/3683115.stm.

81 Hilberg, *The Destruction of the European Jews*, Vol. 1, p. 318.

82 Hilberg, *The Destruction of the European Jews*, Vol. 2, pp. 589, 597–98.

83 Samuel P. Oliner and Pearl M. Oliner, *The Altruistic Personality: Rescuers of Jews in Nazi Europe* (New York: The Free Press, 1988), p. 20.

84 Henry R. Huttenbach, "In Memoriam: Per Anger, 1914–2002," *Journal of Genocide Research*, 5: 2 (2003), p. 191.

85 A concise and readable account of Wallenberg's efforts to save Hungarian Jews and his subsequent fate is John Bierman, *Righteous Gentile: The Story of Raoul Wallenberg, Missing Hero of the Holocaust* (rev. edn.) (London: Penguin, 1995).

86 John G. Heidenrich, *How to Prevent Genocide: A Guide for Policymakers, Scholars, and the Concerned Citizen* (Westport, CT: Praeger, 2001), p. 122.

87 Hannah Arendt, *Eichmann in Jerusalem: A Report on the Banality of Evil* (New York: The Viking Press, 1965), p. 130; emphasis added.

88 Survivor testimony quoted in Donald E. Miller and Lorna Touryan Miller, *Survivors: An Oral History of the Armenian Genocide* (Berkeley, CA: University of California Press, 1999), p. 13.

89 Oliner and Oliner, *The Altruistic Personality*, p. 155. The Oliners consider religious belief "at best . . . only weakly related to rescue" of Jews during the Second World War (p. 156).

90 Mike Collett-White, "'Rwanda's Schindler' Saved 1,268 Lives," *The Scotsman*, December

30, 2004. See also Jeevan Vasagar, "From Four-star Sanctuary to Star of Hollywood: The Hotel That Saved Hundreds from Genocide," *Guardian*, February 16, 2005, http://www.guardian.co.uk/rwanda/story/0,14451,1415516,00.html.

91 Oliner and Oliner, *The Altruistic Personality*, pp. 119, 134, 138, 143, 168–69, 197, 216–18.

92 Oliner and Oliner, *The Altruistic Personality*, pp. 159, 209.

93 Oliner and Oliner, *The Altruistic Personality*, p. 222. Such values and character traits may also be manifested collectively, as with the "conspiracy of decency" among Danes to preserve the country's Jewish population.

94 Oliner and Oliner, *The Altruistic Personality*, p. 86.

95 Oliner and Oliner, *The Altruistic Personality*, p. 257.

CHAPTER 11

The Sociology and Anthropology of Genocide

INTRODUCTION

The disciplines of sociology and anthropology are distinguished by the kinds of societies they study. Anthropologists have carried out work on mostly non-industrialized and "primitive" societies, while sociologists have focused on social patterns and processes within the industrialized "First World."[1] Anthropology also possesses a distinctive methodology: fieldwork. Nonetheless, the disciplines are linked by a common concern with societal and cultural processes, and it is appropriate to consider them together.

Sociology and anthropology also shared a reluctance, until relatively recently, to confront issues of genocide and state terror. "Many sociologists," stated Irving Louis Horowitz in the late 1980s, "exhibit a studied embarrassment about these issues, a feeling that intellectual issues posed in such a manner are melodramatic and unfit for scientific discourse."[2] Nancy Scheper-Hughes similarly described "the traditional role of the anthropologist as neutral, dispassionate, cool and rational, [an] objective observer of the human condition"; anthropologists traditionally maintained a "proud, even haughty distance from political engagement."[3]

Fortunately, Horowitz's evaluation is now obsolete, thanks to a host of sociologists who – perhaps more than any other group apart from historians – have made seminal contributions to genocide studies. They include Kurt Jonassohn, Pierre van den Berghe, Helen Fein, and Zygmunt Bauman. Anthropological inquiries were later in arriving, but recent years have seen the first anthologies on anthropology and genocide, as well as ground-breaking works by Alexander Laban Hinton, Nancy Scheper-Hughes, and Christopher Taylor, among others.[4]

In examining the contribution of sociological perspectives, this chapter focuses on three key themes: (1) the sociology of modernity, which has attracted considerable interest from genocide scholars in the wake of Zygmunt Bauman's *Modernity and the Holocaust*; (2) the sociology of "ethnicity" and ethnic conflict; and (3) the role of "middleman" or "market-dominant" minorities. It then addresses anthropological framings of genocide, focusing also on the work of forensic anthropologists.

SOCIOLOGICAL PERSPECTIVES

The sociology of modernity

Is genocide a modern phenomenon?[5] At first glance, the question seems banal. We have seen (Chapter 1) that the destruction of peoples on the basis of group identity extends back to mythic prehistory. At the same time, we know that in recent centuries, and especially during the past hundred years, the prevalence of genocide has taken a quantitative leap. The central issue is: Has that leap also been *qualitative*? Is there something about modernity that has become *definitional* to genocide?

In one of the most discussed works on the Jewish Holocaust, *Modernity and the Holocaust*, sociologist Zygmunt Bauman delivered a resounding "yes" to this question. "Modern civilization was not the Holocaust's *sufficient* condition; it was, however, most certainly its *necessary* condition. Without it, the Holocaust would be unthinkable."[6] His argument revolved around four core features of modernity: nationalism; "scientific" racism; technological complexity; and bureaucratic rationalization. Modern nationalism divided the world "fully and exhaustively . . . into national domains," leaving "no space . . . for internationalism" and designating "each scrap of the no-man's-land . . . [as] a standing invitation to aggression." In such a world, European Jews – with their international and cosmopolitan identity – could be construed as alien. They "defied the very truth on which all nations, old and new alike, rested their claims; the ascribed character of nationhood, heredity and naturalness of national entities. . . . *The world tightly packed with nations and nation-states abhorred the non-national void. Jews were in such a void: they were such a void.*"[7]

This existential unease towards the Jew was combined with scientific racism, which Bauman depicted as a modern phenomenon,[8] overlaying traditional intercommunal antipathies with a veneer of scientific rationality and medical pathology. This brought with it an impetus to total extermination of the racial Other: "The only adequate solution to problems posited by the racist world-view is a total and uncompromising isolation of the pathogenic and infectious race – the source of disease and contamination – through its complete spatial separation or physical destruction."[9]

How could such a totalizing project be implemented? For Bauman, the advent of modern technology and bureaucratic rationality was essential. The mass death that the Nazis developed and inflicted relied on products of the Industrial Revolution. Railway transport, gas chambers, Zyklon B cyanide crystals administered by men in gas masks – all were essentially modern inventions and had to be managed by a bureaucracy of death. The great German theorist of modern bureaucracy, Max Weber, emphasized "its peculiar, 'impersonal' character," which "mean[s] that the mechanism . . . is easily made to work for anybody who knows how to gain control over it." Weber also argued that "the bureaucratization of all [social] domination very strongly furthers the development of 'rational matter-of-factness' and the personality type of the professional expert," distinguished by his or her cool amorality and devotion to efficiency. Moreover, bureaucracy cultivates secrecy: "the concept of the 'official secret' is the specific invention of the bureaucracy."[10]

The processing of millions of "subhumans" for anonymous death was unthinkable in the absence of such a culture, according to Bauman:

> By its nature, this is a daunting task, unthinkable unless in conjunction with the availability of huge resources, means of their mobilization and planned distribution, skills of splitting the overall task into a great number of partial and specialized functions and skills to co-ordinate their performance. In short, the task is inconceivable without modern bureaucracy.[11]

Moreover, this "splitting [of] the overall task" into isolated and fragmented units of time, space, and work created a vital psychological distance between the victims and those participating in their annihilation. No individual – except, by reputation, the distant and semi-mythical *Führer* figure – exercised overall authority or bore overall responsibility. One did not commit mass murder per se. Rather, one operated a railroad switch, or dropped a few cyanide crystals into a shaft: "a cool, objective operation . . . mechanically mediated . . . a deed performed at a distance, one whose effects the perpetrator did not see," in Wolfgang Sofsky's words.[12] Much the same set of values, procedures, and behaviors characterized the nuclear mentality, with its potential for rationally administered omnicide (Chapter 2).[13]

Two main criticisms of this modernity-of-genocide thesis may be advanced. First, the supposed dividing line between historical and modern genocide may be more stylistic than substantive. The root-and-branch extermination of entire populations is entrenched deep in our history as a species. It is simply not the case that "the Holocaust left behind and put to shame all its alleged pre-modern equivalents, exposing them as primitive, wasteful and ineffective by comparison," as Bauman contended.[14]

The second criticism of the modernity-of-genocide thesis may be summarized in one word: Rwanda (see Chapter 9). There, around one million people were hunted, corraled, and exterminated in *twelve weeks* – a rate of killing exceeding by an order of magnitude that of the "modern" Nazi holocaust. Yet the genocide was carried out by men and women armed with little more than guns and agricultural implements.[15] It involved no appreciable role for scientific or technical experts. And *the killing was conducted face-to-face, intimately, and publicly*, with no resort to the physical and psychological distancing strategies and official secrecy supposedly necessary for "modern" mass slaughter.[16] One may argue that the Rwandan holocaust depended on a complex administrative apparatus; a racist ideology tinged with pseudo-science; and the industrial mass production of machetes, hoes, firearms, and grenades. But bureaucracy is an ancient phenomenon, as successive Chinese dynasties remind us, and one suspects that the ideology of hate developed by Hutu Power would have been just as functional without its vaguely modernist overtones.[17] Finally – with regard to the technology of death – guns, machetes, and explosives all pre-date the Industrial Revolution.

ETHNICITY AND ETHNIC CONFLICT

Loe, this is the payment you shall get, if you be one of them they terme, without.

Thomas Merton, 1637

Few concepts are as amorphous and yet important as ethnicity. On one hand, ethnic identifications seem so fluid and mutable as to lack almost any "objective" character. On the other hand, ethnicity is arguably the dominant ideological impetus to conflict and genocide worldwide.

Three historical phenomena account for the prominence of ethnicity in today's "global society." The first is nationalism, touched on in Chapter 2. As medieval Europe moved away from a quilt of overlapping sovereignties and towards the formation of modern states, it first fell under the sway of strong, centralizing monarchs. With the onset of the democratic age via the American and French revolutions, sovereignty was held increasingly to reside in "the people." But *which* people? How defined? The popular thrust gave rise in the nineteenth century to modern ethnic nationalism, as Western rulers and their populations sought an ideology that would unify the new realms. The result was what Benedict Anderson called "imagined communities": geographically disparate but mutually identified agglomerations defining themselves as "French," "German," "British," "Italian," and so on. The core idea was that the "imagined community" required a particular political form, the "nation-state," to achieve true realization.

On what basis were these communities imagined? It is worth pausing briefly to consider the bases or foundations of ethnicity, as they have been listed by a prominent scholar of the subject. Anthony Smith cited six foundations of ethnic identity: "1. a collective proper name, 2. a myth of common ancestry, 3. shared historical memories, 4. one or more differentiating elements of common culture, 5. an association with a specific 'homeland,' 6. a sense of solidarity for significant sectors of the population."[18]

While a refined concept of ethnicity is often considered to be a Western invention, this is open to challenge: the Han Chinese, for example, had a well-developed ethnic sensibility well before the West's rise to dominance.[19] Indeed, it could be argued that the concept is at least "latent" in all societies, independent of Western penetration and influence. Other social units – notably extended family, clan, and tribe – evince many of the same solidaristic bonds as ethnicity; they may be considered proto-ethnic groupings. Like ethnic groups, moreover, these identifications are meaningless without other collectivities defined against one's own. There are no in-groups without out-groups, with what Fredrik Barth has called "boundary maintenance mechanisms" serving to demarcate the two.[20]

When a dominant ethnic collectivity is established as the basis of a "nation-state," a quandary arises in dealing with the out-groups – "ethnic minorities" – that also find themselves within the boundaries of that state. Such minorities exist everywhere; even supposedly unified or organic nation-states (Japan is the most commonly cited example) have them. This often carries explosive consequences for intercommunal violence, including genocide, as we have had numerous opportunities to witness in these pages.

The second historical factor is the spread of imperialism and colonialism around the world (Chapter 2), which shaped the present-day configuration of nationalisms in important ways. Most obviously, it spurred the idea of ethnic nationalism (though some nationalisms, and a wide range of ethnic *identifications*, clearly existed independently of it). Despite the best efforts of colonizers to preserve those they subjugated from such dangerous influences, ethnic-nationalist ideologies were gradually absorbed and integrated into the anti-colonial movements that arose from the mid-nineteenth through mid-twentieth centuries. In addition, following the time-honored strategy of divide and rule, which aimed at *preventing* nationalism, the colonialists typically gathered a host of clans, tribes, and long-established "national" entities into a single territorial and administrative unit. A glance at the ethnic composition of countries such as Nigeria, Congo, and Indonesia suffices to remind us of the enormous diversity of peoples that comprised the deliberately *un*imaginable "communities" of colonialism.

The nationalist leaders who sprang to prominence in the colonized world in the 1920s and 1930s were thus confronted with the crushing challenge of either forging a genuine sense of national community among diverse peoples, or negotiating a peaceful and viable fragmentation of the colonial unit. For the most part, they chose to maintain the colonial boundaries. In some cases, this produced viable multiethnic states (Malaysia and Mauritius are often cited), but in many instances it did not. Sometimes the managed breakup of multiethnic entities led to massive violence (India, Palestine); in states where the leadership chose to preserve an artificial unity, time-bombs remained for the future (Nigeria, Indonesia, Yugoslavia). The ethnic violence associated with the collapse of the Soviet empire in 1991 is a recent example of this trend.

A final historical conjuncture, often overlooked, is *globalization.* Although globalizing trends can be traced back many centuries, they have reached a new stage of complex interconnectedness at the turn of the millennium. One advantage of ethnic identifications is that they offer a strong sense of psychological rootedness amidst change and upheaval. Amidst the rapid transformations associated with globalization, where is a stable sense of "we," and therefore of "me," to be found? The anthropologist Clifford Geertz has argued that:

> during the disorienting process of modernization . . . unintegrated citizens, looking for an anchor in a sea of changes, will grab hold of an increasingly anachronistic ethnic identity, which bursts onto the scene and then recedes as the process of structural differentiation moves toward a reintegrated society.[21]

One can question, though, whether such ethnic resurgence is a transitory phenomenon. As globalization proceeds alongside intense ethnic nationalism in many parts of the world, it may at least be argued that the "transition" is taking rather longer than many observers expected. Part of the misunderstanding may lie in the tendency to believe that ethnic identifications are not primordial but fictional – created and manipulated by self-interested elites to mobilize their followers. (This line of argument has been bolstered by recent "postmodern" orientations in the humanities and social sciences.)

There *is* an important sense in which ethnic identifications are "imagined" or "mythical."[22] As I will show below, they are also subject to endless manipulations by elite figures and violence specialists. Ethnic identifications are protean in the sense that all of the six "bases" that Anthony Smith identifies for ethnicity can be altered, though not always at will or completely. One can change one's territorial base and recast one's primary ethnic identification, as generations of immigrants to the ethnic "melting-pot" of the United States have done (while often maintaining a secondary attachment to the previous identification). Ancestral myths can be revised, reinterpreted, or abandoned. Historical memory, language, culinary taste, forms of artistic expression – all are highly mutable.

Over time, ethnic identifications often achieve intergenerational stability. They assume a practical force in individual and group psychology, societal structure, and political behavior that is impossible to ignore, least of all by those seeking to understand and confront genocide and other mass violence.[23] In *Becoming Evil*, James Waller presents evidence from psychology, sociology, and anthropology to show that these identifications originate deep in human social behavior: "Knowing who is kin, knowing who is in our social group, has a deep importance to species like ours." Moreover, "We have an evolved capacity to see our group as superior to all others and even to be reluctant to recognize members of other groups as deserving of equal respect." Members of a cannibal tribe in Irian Jaya, Indonesia, convey this pointedly: they define themselves as "the human beings," and all others as "the edible ones."[24]

Ethnic conflict and violence "specialists"

Some defining work on the sociology of mass violence has pointed to the role of individual and organizational actors in provoking and channeling violent outbreaks. Donald L. Horowitz, for example, stresses the importance of:

> organizations, often tied to ethnically based political parties, [that] reflect and reinforce interethnic hostility through propaganda, ritual, and force. They run the gamut from civilian to proto-military organizations, operating under varying degrees of secrecy and with varying degrees of coherence and military training. Their raison d'être is the alleged danger from the ethnic enemy.[25]

For his part, Paul R. Brass emphasizes the role of violence "specialists" operating within "institutionalized . . . systems" of violence generation:

> The kinds of violence that are committed in ethnic, communal, and racial "riots" are, I believe, undertaken mostly by "specialists," who are ready to be called out

> on such occasions, who profit from it, and whose activities profit others who may or may not be actually paying for the violence carried out. In fact, in many countries at different times in their histories, there have been regions or cities and towns which have developed what I call "institutionalized riot systems," in which known actors specialize in the conversion of incidents between members of different communities into ethnic riots. The activities of these specialists are usually required for a riot to spread from the initial incident of provocation.[26]

The significance of this category of actors to the fomenting and implementing of genocide should be recognized.[27] Note some of the "specialists" that Brass identifies: "criminal elements and members of youth gangs," "local militant group leaders," "politicians, businessmen, religious leaders," "college and university professors," "pamphleteers and journalists . . . deliberately spreading rumors and scurrilous propaganda," "hooligans" (ranging from Nazi thugs to modern soccer hoodlums), "communal political elites."[28] Add to this list the violence specialists cited by Charles Tilly in his study of *The Politics of Collective Violence*: "Pirates, privateers, paramilitaries, bandits, mercenaries, mafiosi, militias, posses, guerrilla forces, vigilante groups, company police, and bodyguards."[29] Beyond the essential (and universally acknowledged) role of state officials and security force commanders, what we have is a veritable who's-who of the leading *agents provocateurs* of genocide, its foot-soldiers, and its ideological defenders.

"MIDDLEMAN MINORITIES"

> The Greeks and Armenian merchants have been the leeches in this part of the world sucking the life blood out of the country for centuries.
>
> Admiral Mark L. Bristol, US High Commissioner to Turkey, 1922

Perhaps no collectivities are as vulnerable to hatred and large-scale killing as those "characterized as possessing an excess of enterprise, ambition, energy, arrogance, and achievement by those who believe themselves lacking such traits."[30] Such minorities are not necessarily immigrants or descendants of immigrants, but often they are, and this foreignness is a key factor in their targeting. Worldwide, reflecting both centuries-old patterns and more recent globalizing trends, populations have arrived or been introduced from outside the established society. Lacking a land-base, as well as the network of social relations that dominant groups can access, such groups normally settle in the cities or towns – often in neighborhoods or zones that quickly acquire a minority tinge. Even when they are brought in by a colonial power as indentured laborers (as with the Indians whom the British imported to Uganda, South Africa, Fiji, and elsewhere), there is a strong tendency for such groups to establish themselves in commercial trades.

Occupying an inherently vulnerable minority position, these sectors have historically been attractive to colonial powers as local allies. Such alliances allowed colonial powers to "divide and rule," with the aid of a minority that was (1) less anchored to the territory and dominant culture in question, and therefore less prone to push for autonomy or national independence; and (2) heavily dependent on colonial favor, and therefore more likely to be loyal to the colonizers. Colonial favor often translated into greater educational opportunities and positions in lower and middle sectors of the bureaucracy. However, even in the absence of such colonial backing, and in the face of strong opposition from the dominant society, such groups almost universally emphasize education as a means of moving beyond their marginal position and attaining prosperity. They typically display strong bonds of ethnic, cultural, and material solidarity among their members, and they may have the advantage of access to capital and trading relationships through remaining ties with their (or their ancestors') countries of origin.

A frequent result is that these minorities establish a high degree of prominence, sometimes even outright dominance, in key sectors of the national economy. Well-known examples include Jews, whom Amy Chua refers to as "the quintessential market-dominant minority,"[31] and the Chinese of Southeast Asia. East Indians achieved a similar position in many East African economies, while Lebanese traders came to dominate the vital diamond trade in West Africa. The Dutch, British, and Portuguese-descended Whites of Southern Africa may also be cited, along with the White "pigmentocrats" who enjoy elite status in heavily indigenous countries of Latin America. The potential for conflict, including for the violent or genocidal targeting of middleman minorities,[32] is apparent, though far from inevitable.[33] Through their common and preferential ties to colonial authorities, these minorities were easily depicted as agents of the alien dominator, opponents of national liberation and self-determination, and cancers in the body politic. Even today, their frequently extensive international ties and "cosmopolitan" outlook may grate on the majority's nationalist sentiments. Moreover, their previous relationship with a colonial power has often translated into a quest for alliances with authoritarian regimes in the post-colonial era. Elite Chinese businessmen in the Philippines and Indonesia, for example, were among the most enthusiastic and visible backers of the Marcos and Suharto dictatorships. When authoritarian rule collapsed, the mass hostility, resentment, and humiliation could be vented under democratic guise – a pattern that Chua has described well:

> In countries with a market-dominant minority and a poor "indigenous" majority, the forces of democratization and marketization directly collide. As markets enrich the market-dominant minority, democratization increases the political voice and power of the frustrated majority. The competition for votes fosters the emergence of demagogues who scapegoat the resented minority, demanding an end to humiliation, and insisting that the nation's wealth be reclaimed by its "true owners." Thus as America toasted the spread of global elections through the 1990s, vengeful ethnic slogans proliferated: "Zimbabwe for Zimbabweans," "Indonesia for Indonesians," "Uzbekistan for Uzbeks," "Kenya for Kenyans," "Ethiopia for Ethiopians," "Yids [Jews] out of Russia," "Hutu Power," "Serbia for Serbs," and so on. . . . As popular hatred of the rich "outsiders" mounts, the result is an ethnically charged political pressure cooker in which some form of backlash is almost unavoidable.

Among the strategies of backlash, the "most ferocious kind . . . is ethnic cleansing and other forms of majority-supported ethnic violence," up to and including genocide.[34] Rwanda in 1994 is the best example of democratization helping to spawn genocide against a prosperous minority. However, if we remove the democratic element from the equation, we can also add to the list the two other paradigmatic genocides of the twentieth century. The relative wealth, industriousness, and educational attainment of the Armenian minority, even under conditions of discrimination and repression in the Ottoman lands, made them an easy target for the fanatical nationalism of the Young Turks (Chapter 4). Similar hatred or at least distaste towards Jews in Germany and other European countries contributed to popular support for the Holocaust against them (Chapter 6). Note that all three of these genocides featured massive looting and plundering along with mass murder (see the discussion of genocide and greed in Chapter 10). Genocide offers an unprecedented opportunity to "redress" an economic imbalance by seizing the wealth and property of the victims, and to inflict on them the kind of humiliation that the dominant population may have experienced.

ANTHROPOLOGICAL PERSPECTIVES

I have long been jealous of anthropologists. Political scientists like myself are commanded to maintain a detached, "objective" view of their subject. Our research strategems are usually confined to the library and the office, with only occasional forays into the outside world. Anthropologists, by contrast, are allowed and encouraged to get their hands dirty. The defining method of anthropology – fieldwork – commands them to wade into the thick of their subject matter, and get to know the people they study. They may "emerge from the field exhausted," but they carry with them "a material of extraordinary richness and depth."[35] Reading anthropological case studies, one sees and hears the subjects, smells the air, even tastes the local food.

Anthropology "calls for an understanding of different societies as they appear *from the inside*,"[36] where anthropologists are seen as inevitable and integral participants in the cross-cultural encounter. They are expected to describe the impact of the experience on their own subjectivity. Assisting with the forensic excavation of mass graves in Guatemala, Victoria Sanford reported: "I'm not vomiting, I haven't fainted, what a beautiful valley, everything is greener than green, those are real bones, my god 200 people were massacred here, their relatives are watching."[37] It would be hard to describe such an experience as enjoyable. But it is certainly *revelatory*, both to author and reader, in a way that more detached analyses rarely are.

Anthropologists have produced some of the most profound and insightful treatises on genocide and genocidal societies. This is, however, a fairly recent development. As Alexander Laban Hinton writes in his edited volume, *Annihilating Difference: The Anthropology of Genocide*, the "shift in focus" derives from "a theoretical and ethnographic move away from studying small, relatively stable communities toward looking at those under siege, in flux, and victimized by state violence or insurgency movements."[38] It also reflects a recognition that anthropology was compromised, in the past, by its alliance with European imperialism.[39] Most nineteenth-century anthropologists took for granted European dominance over subject peoples. Their schema of classification tended to revolve around hierarchies of humanity: they sifted and categorized the peoples of the world in a way that bolstered the European claim to supremacy. Modern "scientific" racism was one result. Even the most liberal anthropologists of the pre-First World War period, such as Franz Boas, viewed the disappearance of many primitive civilizations as preordained; "salvage ethnography" was developed in an attempt to describe as much of these civilizations as possible before nature took its supposedly inevitable course.[40]

Perhaps neither before nor since have anthropologists played such a prominent role in state policy as during the Nazi era (Chapter 6). Gretchen Schafft noted that "German and, to a lesser extent, Austrian anthropologists were involved in the Holocaust as perpetrators, from its beginning to its conclusion . . . Never had their discipline been so well respected and received. Never had practitioners been so busy . . . while the price for not cooperating was 'internal exile,' joblessness, or incarceration."[41] Prominent anthropologists such as Eugen Fischer, Adolf Würth, and Sophie Ehrhardt flocked to lend a scientific gloss to the Nazis' preposterous racial theories about Jews, Roma, and Slavs; many of these "scholars" continued their work into the postwar period.[42]

However, contradictorily and simultaneously, anthropology was emerging as the most pluralistic and *least* ethnocentric of the social sciences. Under the influence of the discipline's leading figures – Franz Boas, the revolutionary ethnographer Bronislaw Malinowski, the Englishman A.R. Radcliffe-Brown, and the American Margaret Mead – a methodology was developed that encouraged nonjudgmental involvement in the lives and cultures of one's subjects. Hierarchies of "development" were undermined by anthropologists' nuanced study of "primitive" societies that proved to be extraordinarily complex and sophisticated. And the supposedly scientific basis for racial hierarchy was radically undermined by work such as that of Boas, who "researched the change in head shape across only one American generation," thereby "demonstrat[ing] to the world how race, language, and culture are causally unlinked."[43] Anthropologists played a remarkable and little-known role in drafting the Universal Declaration of Human Rights, cautioning the UN Commission devoted to this task against "ethnocentrism, the assumption of the superiority of one's own cultural values."[44] With the great wave of decolonization after the Second World War, it was anthropologists above all who went "into the field" to grapple with, and validate, the diversity of "Third World" societies.

Anthropology's guiding ideal of cultural relativism requires that the practitioner "suspend one's judgement and preconceptions as much as possible, in order to better understand another's worldview." In studying genocidal processes, the relativist approach emphasizes "local understandings and cultural dynamics that both structure and motivate genocide," and examines them in their broader cultural context. Rather than "simply dismissing *génocidaires* as 'irrational' and 'savage,'" the approach "demands that we understand them and their perspective regardless of what we think of perpetrators."[45]

Arguably, though, cultural relativism has its limits. At some point, if one is to confront atrocities, one must adopt a universalist stand (i.e., that atrocities are always criminal, and cannot be excused by culture). Nancy Scheper-Hughes, among others, has criticized cultural relativism as "moral relativism" that is "no longer appropriate to the world in which we live." If anthropology "is to be worth anything at all, it must be ethically grounded."[46] Alexander Hinton likewise suggests that relativism "played a key role in inhibiting anthropologists from studying genocide," together with other forms of "political violence in complex state societies."[47]

Partly because of relativist influences, and partly because of its preference for "studying small, relatively stable communities,"[48] anthropology's engagement with genocide came relatively late. Only in very recent years has a "school" begun to coalesce around these themes, developing a rich body of literature, particularly on terror and genocide in Latin America and Africa. Deploying fieldwork-based ethnography (literally, "writing about ethnic groups"), these researchers have amassed and analyzed a wealth of individual testimonies about the atrocities. In Victoria Sanford's estimation, this "is among the greatest contributions anthropology can make to understanding social problems – the presentation of testimonies, life histories, and ethnographies of violence."[49] Together with the reports of human rights organizations and truth commissions (see Chapter 15), these provide important evidence, for present and future generations, of the nature and scale of atrocity.

Anthropologists go further still, to analyze how memories of atrocities (see also Chapter 14) are interpreted within and across human cultures; how they are adopted as coping strategies in the aftermath of genocide;[50] and how they may become attached to familiar objects in the environment, irrupting at unexpected moments:

> [The] living memory of terror can reinvoke the physical and psychological pain of past acts of violence in unexpected moments. A tree, for example, is not just a tree. A river, not just a river. At a given moment, a tree is a reminder of the baby whose head was smashed against a tree by a soldier. The tree, and the memory of the baby it invokes, in turn reinvoke a chain of memories of terror, including witnessing the murder of a husband or brother who was tied to another tree and beaten to death – perhaps on the same day or perhaps years later.[51]

Culturally specific practices of terror are especially well suited to anthropological investigation. In his study of the Rwandan genocide, *Sacrifice as Terror*, Christopher Taylor showed how cultural dynamics, rituals, and symbolism may help to explain the particular course that the holocaust took. His analysis demonstrated – in Alexander Hinton's summary – that anthropological methods "explain why the violence was perpetrated in certain ways – for example, the severing of Achilles tendons, genital mutilation, breast oblation, the construction of roadblocks that served as execution sites, bodies being stuffed into latrines." The violence "was deeply symbolic," representing cultural beliefs about expulsion and excretion, obstruction and flow.[52] For example, Taylor pointed out the symbolism of the Nyabarongo River as a route by which murdered Tutsis were to be "removed from Rwanda and retransported to their presumed land of origin," thereby purifying the nation of its internal 'foreign' minority." In his interpretation,

> Rwanda's rivers became part of the genocide by acting as the body politic's organs of elimination, in a sense "excreting" its hated internal other. It is not much of a leap to infer that Tutsi were thought of as excrement by their persecutors. Other evidence of this is apparent in the fact that many Tutsi were stuffed into latrines after their deaths.[53]

An intimate familiarity with day-to-day cultural praxis allows anthropologists to draw connections between "exceptional" outbursts of atrocity, such as genocide, and more quotidian forms and structures of violence. The leading theorist in this regard is Nancy Scheper-Hughes, who in her classic study of a Brazilian village, *Death without Weeping*, explored the desensitization of women-as-mothers to the deaths of their infant children amidst pervasive scarcity.[54] This extended even to complicity in their offspring's deaths through the deliberate withholding of food and care, with the resulting mortality viewed as divinely ordained. Subsequently, Scheper-Hughes outlined a *genocidal continuum*, composed:

> of a multitude of "small wars and invisible genocides" conducted in the normative social spaces of public schools, clinics, emergency rooms, hospital wards, nursing homes, court rooms, prisons, detention centers, and public morgues. The continuum refers to the human capacity to reduce others to nonpersons, to monsters, or to things that give structure, meaning, and rationale to everyday practices of violence. It is essential that we recognize in our species (and in ourselves) *a genocidal capacity* and that we exercise a defensive hypervigilance, a hypersensitivity to the less dramatic, *permitted*, everyday acts of violence that make participation (under other conditions) in genocidal acts possible, perhaps more easy than we would like to know. I would include all expressions of social exclusion, dehumanization, depersonalization, pseudo-speciation, and reification that normalize atrocious behavior and violence toward others.[55]

She noted, for instance, that Brazilian "street children" experience attacks by police "that are genocidal in their social and political sentiments." The children "are often described as 'dirty vermin' so that unofficial policies of 'street cleaning,' 'trash removal,' 'fly swatting,' and 'pest removal' are invoked in garnering broad-based public support for their extermination." Through such practices and rhetoric, genocide becomes "socially incremental," something that is "experienced by perpetrators, collaborators, bystanders – and even by victims themselves – as expected, routine, even justified."[56] There seems a clear connection between such everyday rhetoric and the propaganda discourse of full-scale genocide, in which Native American children were referred to as "nits [who] make lice," Jews as "vermin," and Rwandan Tutsis as "cockroaches."

In closing this brief account of anthropological framings and insights, it is worth considering the role of *forensic anthropologists*. Bridging the natural and social sciences, they "have worked with health professionals, lawyers, photographers, and nongovernmental organizations to analyze physical remains and gather evidence with which to prosecute perpetrators."[57] Their core activities consist of the "search for, recovery, and preservation of physical evidence at the outdoor scene" of crimes and mass atrocities. They document how evidence relates to its "depositional environment," and use the data collected to reconstruct the events surrounding the deaths of the exhumed victims.[58]

In recent years, forensic anthropologists have become the most visible face of anthropology in genocide investigation and adjudication. Most notable is Clyde Snow (see Figure 11.1), a US forensic specialist who oversaw the exhumations at the Balkans massacre sites of Vukovar and Srebrenica. (These forensic excavations form the basis for an inevitably gruesome but illuminating book of photographs and text, *The Graves*; see "Further Study.") As Snow describes his task:

Figure 11.1 Forensic anthropologist Clyde Snow, inspecting a skull from the Anfal Campaign in northern Iraq (see Box 4a).

Source: Magnum Photos/ Susan Meiselas.

> When [societies] choose to pursue justice, we forensic anthropologists can put the tools of a rapidly developing science at the disposal of the survivors. We can determine a murder victim's age, sex and race from the size and shape of certain bones. We can extract DNA from some skeletons and match it with samples from the victims' relatives. Marks on the bones can reveal signs of old diseases and injuries reflected in the victims' medical histories, as well as more sinister evidence: bullet holes, cut marks from knives, or fracture patterns produced by blunt instruments. Taken together, such clues can tell us who victims were and how they died – clues crucial to bringing the killers to justice.[59]

Snow's first digs were conducted in Argentina during the 1980s, where he helped to train the Argentine Forensic Anthropology Team that exhumed victims of the "Dirty War" (see also Chapter 15). "Ample forensic evidence" underpinned the report of the Argentine truth commission, *Nunca Más* (Never Again), and the prosecutions of former *junta* leaders.[60] The team went on to conduct exhumations in El Salvador, at the site of the military massacre of some 700 civilians at El Mozote.[61] With assistance from the American Association for the Advancement of Science (AAAS), Snow subsequently trained members of the Guatemalan Forensic Anthropology Team.[62] The team's investigations were equally vital to the truth commission report that labeled the military regime's campaign against Mayan Indians in the Guatemalan highlands as genocidal (see Chapter 3), and assigned responsibility for more than 90 percent of the atrocities of the "civil war" to the government and the paramilitary forces it mobilized.[63]

Snow has conducted excavations at atrocity sites as geographically disparate as Ethiopia, Iraq, and the Philippines. His comment on the nature of his investigations summarizes the work of the conscientious anthropologists – and many others – who have informed our understanding of individual genocides: "You do the work in the daytime and cry at night."[64]

FURTHER STUDY

Zygmunt Bauman, *Modernity and the Holocaust.* Ithaca, NY: Cornell University Press, 2000. Influential sociological interpretation of the Jewish Holocaust.

Pierre L. van den Berghe, ed., *State Violence and Ethnicity.* Niwot, CO: University Press of Colorado, 1990. One of the best sociological works on genocide and state terror.

Paul R. Brass, ed., *Riots and Pogroms.* New York: New York University Press, 1996. Vigorous edited volume on the dynamics of ethnic violence.

Amy Chua, *World on Fire: How Exporting Free Market Democracy Breeds Ethnic Hatred and Global Instability.* New York: Anchor, 2004. Provocative overview of "market-dominant minorities."

Helen Fein, *Genocide: A Sociological Perspective.* London: Sage, 1993. Short, influential treatise.

H.H. Gerth and C. Wright Mills, eds, *From Max Weber: Essays in Sociology.* New

York: Oxford University Press, 1954. Writings of the great German theorist of authority, modernity, and bureaucracy.

Alexander Laban Hinton, ed., *Annihilating Difference: The Anthropology of Genocide.* Berkeley, CA: University of California Press, 2002. A ground-breaking anthology; see also *Genocide: An Anthropological Reader.*

Donald L. Horowitz, *The Deadly Ethnic Riot.* Berkeley, CA: University of California Press, 2001. Massive, eye-opening treatise on ethnic violence.

Irving Louis Horowitz, *Taking Lives: Genocide and State Power* (4th edn). New Brunswick, NJ: Transaction Publishers, 1997. Rambling sociological account.

Victoria Sanford, *Buried Secrets: Truth and Human Rights in Guatemala.* New York: Palgrave Macmillan, 2003. Sanford worked alongside the Guatemalan forensic anthropology team.

Gretchen E. Schafft, *From Racism to Genocide: Anthropology in the Third Reich.* Urbana, IL: University of Illinois Press, 2004. Explores anthropologists' eager complicity in Nazi social engineering.

James C. Scott, *Seeing Like A State: How Certain Schemes to Improve the Human Condition Have Failed.* New Haven, CT: Yale University Press, 1998. Fascinating study of "high-modernist" social planning, relevant to studies of state terror and totalitarian systems.

Jeffrey A. Sluka, ed., *Death Squad: The Anthropology of State Terror.* Philadelphia, PA: University of Pennsylvania Press, 2000. Another important anthology.

Anthony D. Smith, *National Identity.* London: Penguin, 1991. Fine primer on the ethnic and cultural roots of nationalism.

Wolfgang Sofsky, *The Order of Terror: The Concentration Camp,* trans. William Templer. Princeton, NJ: Princeton University Press, 1999. Profound, aphoristic study.

Eric Stover and Gilles Peress, *The Graves: Srebrenica and Vukovar.* Zurich: Scalo Publishers, 1998. Haunting images and text of forensic excavations in Bosnia and Croatia.

Christopher C. Taylor, *Sacrifice as Terror: The Rwandan Genocide of 1994.* Oxford: Berg, 1999. Valuable anthropological insights into the Rwandan holocaust.

NOTES

1 See Thomas Hylland Eriksen, *Small Places, Large Issues: An Introduction to Social and Cultural Anthropology* (London: Pluto Press, 2001), p. 29.

2 Horowitz quoted in Helen Fein, *Genocide: A Sociological Perspective* (London: Sage, 1993), p. 6.

3 Nancy Scheper-Hughes, "The Primacy of the Ethical: Propositions for a Militant Anthropology," *Current Anthropology,* 36: 3 (1995), pp. 410, 414.

4 See Alexander Laban Hinton, ed., *Annihilating Difference: The Anthropology of Genocide* (Berkeley, CA: University of California Press, 2002); Alexander Laban Hinton, ed., *Genocide: An Anthropological Reader* (London: Blackwell, 2002); Nancy Scheper-Hughes and Philippe Bourgois, eds, *Violence in War and Peace: An Anthology* (London: Blackwell, 2004); Jeffrey A. Sluka, ed., *Death Squad: The Anthropology of State Terror* (Philadelphia, PA: University of Pennsylvania Press, 1999).

5 "Modernity," as Hinton notes, "is notoriously difficult to define," but "can perhaps best

be described as a set of interrelated processes, some of which began to develop as early as the fifteenth century, characterizing the emergence of 'modern society.' Politically, modernity involves the rise of secular forms of government, symbolized by the French Revolution and culminating in the modern nation-state. Economically, modernity refers to capitalist expansion and its derivatives – monetarized exchange, the accumulation of capital, extensive private property, the search for new markets, commodification, and industrialization. Socially, modernity entails the replacement of 'traditional' loyalties (to lord, master, priest, king, patriarch, kin, and local community) with 'modern' ones (to secular authority, leader, 'humanity,' class, gender, race, and ethnicity). Culturally, modernity encompasses the movement from a predominantly religious to an emphatically secular and materialist worldview characterized by new ways of thinking about and understanding human behavior." Hinton, "The Dark Side of Modernity: Toward an Anthropology of Genocide," in Hinton, ed., Annihilating Difference pp. 7–8. For an ambitious anthology, see Stuart Hall *et al.*, eds, *Modernity: An Introduction to Modern Societies* (Cambridge, MA: Blackwell, 1996).

6 Zygmunt Bauman, *Modernity and the Holocaust* (Ithaca, NY: Cornell University Press, 2000), p. 13.

7 Bauman, *Modernity and the Holocaust,* pp. 53, 55; emphasis in original.

8 "As a conception of the world, and even more importantly as an effective instrument of political practice, racism is unthinkable without the advancement of modern science, modern technology and modern forms of state power. As such, racism is strictly a modern product. Modernity made racism possible." Bauman, *Modernity and the Holocaust,* p. 61.

9 Bauman, *Modernity and the Holocaust,* p. 76.

10 Max Weber, "Bureaucracy," in H.H. Gerth and C. Wright Mills, eds, *From Max Weber: Essays in Sociology* (New York: Oxford University Press, 1954), pp. 229, 233, 240. Lester R. Kurtz notes that bureaucracy evinces a tendency "to promote formal rather than substantive rationality, that is, the kind of thinking that emphasizes efficiency rather than moral or contextual considerations." Quoted in Robert Jay Lifton and Eric Markusen, *The Genocidal Mentality: Nazi Holocaust and Nuclear Threat* (New York: Basic Books, 1990), p. 180.

11 Bauman, *Modernity and the Holocaust,* p. 76.

12 Wolfgang Sofsky, *The Order of Terror: The Concentration Camp* (Princeton, NJ: Princeton University Press, 1999), p. 264. "Modern terror has no need of big criminals. For its purposes, the small-time tormentor suffices: the conscientious bookkeeper, the mediocre official, the zealous doctor, the young, slightly anxious female factory worker" (p. 278).

13 The classic study is Markusen and Kopf, *The Genocidal Mentality.*

14 Bauman, *Modernity and the Holocaust,* p. 89.

15 Michael Mann similarly notes that in the Nazi genocide against the Jews, "foreign collaborators, Romanian and Croatian fascists, used primitive techniques to almost as devastating effect" as high-tech gas chambers. Mann, *The Dark Side of Democracy: Explaining Ethnic Cleansing* (Cambridge: Cambridge University Press, 2005), p. 241.

16 "As for the supposedly desensitizing effects of bureaucratic distancing, the brutal face-to-face murder of the Tutsis by tens of thousands of ordinary Hutus, many of them poor farmers, utterly disproves that thesis." Marie Fleming, "Genocide and the Body Politic in the Time of Modernity," in Robert Gellately and Ben Kiernan, eds, *The Specter of Genocide: Mass Murder in Historical Perspective* (Cambridge: Cambridge University Press, 2003), p. 103.

17 For a contrary view, defining the core features of the Rwandan holocaust as "manifestations of the modern world," see Robert Melson, "Modern Genocide in Rwanda: Ideology, Revolution, War, and Mass Murder in an African State," ch. 15 in Gellately and Kiernan, eds, *The Specter of Genocide.*

18 Anthony D. Smith, *National Identity* (London: Penguin, 1991), p. 21.

19 I am grateful to Benjamin Madley for this insight.

20 Barth cited in Andrew Bell-Fialkoff, *Ethnic Cleansing* (New York: St. Martin's Griffin,

1999), p. 73. As Alexander Hinton notes, "It is one of the most vexing problems of our time that imagined sociopolitical identities are so often forged out of hatred toward contrasting others." Hinton, *Why Did They Kill? Cambodia in the Shadow of Genocide* (Berkeley, CA: University of California Press, 2005), p. 220. For a famous reading of the phenomenon, examining the constitutive impact of the "Orient" upon the "West," see Edward Said, *Orientalism* (New York: Vintage Books, 1979).

21 Geertz quoted in Ray Taras and Rajat Ganguly, *Understanding Ethnic Conflict: The International Dimension* (New York: Longman, 1998), p. 14.

22 See John R. Bowen, "The Myth of Global Ethnic Conflict," ch. 15 in Hinton, ed., *Genocide: An Anthropological Reader*, pp. 334–43.

23 Nancy Scheper-Hughes writes sardonically: "'Race,' 'ethnicity,' 'tribe,' 'culture,' and 'identity' were dutifully deconstructed and de-essentialized in Anthropology 101, where they were taught as historically invented and fictive concepts. Meanwhile . . . South African Xhosas and Zulus (manipulated by a government-orchestrated 'third force') daily slaughtered each other in and around worker hostels in the name of 'tribe,' 'ethnicity,' and 'culture.'" Scheper-Hughes, "The Primacy of the Ethical", p. 415.

24 James Waller, *Becoming Evil: How Ordinary People Commit Genocide and Mass Killing* (Oxford: Oxford University Press, 2002), pp. 153–54. He also points out (pp. 241–42) that in social–psychological experiments, "complete strangers arbitrarily assigned to groups, having no interaction or conflict with one another, and not competing against another group behaved as if those who shared their meaningless label were their dearest friends or closest relatives," and would rapidly come into conflict with those defined differently, but equally meaninglessly.

25 Donald L. Horowitz, *The Deadly Ethnic Riot* (Berkeley, CA: University of California Press, 2001), p. 243.

26 Paul R. Brass, "Introduction," in Brass, ed., *Riots and Pogroms* (Washington Square, NY: New York University Press, 1996), p. 12.

27 Horowitz makes explicit the link between ethnic rioting and genocide: "The deadly ethnic riot embodies physical destruction combined with degradation and the implicit threat of genocide. . . . The random, brutal killing of targets based merely on their ascriptive identity has . . . a proto-genocidal quality about it; it is an augury of extermination." Horowitz, *The Deadly Ethnic Riot*, pp. 432, 459.

28 Brass, "Introduction," pp. 12–13.

29 According to Charles Tilly, these actors "operate in a middle ground between (on one side) the full authorization of a national army and (on the other) the private employment of violence by parents, lovers, or feuding clans." Tilly, *The Politics of Collective Violence* (Cambridge: Cambridge University Press, 2003), p. 19.

30 Horowitz, *The Deadly Ethnic Riot*, p. 187. See also Walter P. Zenner, "Middleman Minorities and Genocide," in Isidor Wallimann and Michael N. Dobkowski, eds, *Genocide and the Modern Age: Etiology and Case Studies of Mass Death* (Westport, CT: Syracuse University Press, 2000), pp. 253–81. Ground-breaking genocide scholar Leo Kuper refers to these as "hostage groups"; that is, "hostages to the fortunes of the dominant group." Kuper, "The Genocidal State: An Overview," in Pierre L. van den Berghe, ed., *State Violence and Ethnicity* (Niwot, CO: University Press of Colorado, 1990), p. 44. See also the discussion in Kuper's *The Prevention of Genocide* (New Haven, CT: Yale University Press, 1985), p. 201.

31 Amy Chua, *World on Fire: How Exporting Free Market Democracy Breeds Ethnic Hatred and Global Instability* (New York: Anchor, 2004), p. 79.

32 Genocidal massacres may also be cited, such as the centuries of pogroms against European Jews, Indian uprisings against Whites in Upper Peru and Yucatán (Chapter 3), and the Hindu slaughter of Sikhs in India in 1984. Short of genocide or genocidal massacre, the strategy most commonly adopted against market-dominant minorities is mass expulsion. Idi Amin's banishing of Indians from Uganda in 1972 is an example; another is the "Boat People" expelled from Vietnam following the nationalist victory of 1975, aimed at "the elimination of ethnic Chinese and bourgeois Vietnamese from Vietnamese society."

Richard L. Rubinstein, *The Age of Triage: Fear and Hope in an Overcrowded World* (Boston, MA: Beacon Press, 1983), p. 176. This was also, of course, the dominant Nazi policy towards German Jews between 1933 and 1938 (Chapter 6).

33 Horowitz, for example, argues that "in comparative perspective," the targeting of "unusually prosperous or advantaged ethnic groups . . . is only a minor factor in target selection [for deadly ethnic rioting], operative under certain, specific conditions of riot leadership. Quite often, prosperous minorities are not targeted even during the most brutal riots." Horowitz, *The Deadly Ethnic Riot*, p. 5.

34 Chua, *World on Fire*, pp. 124–25.

35 Eriksen, *Small Places, Large Issues*, p. 27.

36 Eriksen, *Small Places, Large Issues*, p. 7.

37 Victoria Sanford, *Buried Secrets: Truth and Human Rights in Guatemala* (New York: Palgrave Macmillan, 2003), p. 31.

38 Alexander Laban Hinton, "The Dark Side of Modernity: Toward an Anthropology of Genocide," in Hinton, ed., *Annihilating Difference*, p. 2.

39 "[T]he work of anthropology, in its earliest instances of practice, composed a necessary first step that gave substance and justification to theories of 'natural' hierarchy that would eventually be employed to rationalize racism, colonialism, slavery, ethnic purifications and, ultimately, genocide projects." Wendy C. Hamblet, "The Crisis of Meanings: Could the Cure be the Cause of Genocide?," *Journal of Genocide Research*, 5: 2 (2003), p. 243.

40 See also the discussion of Patrick Brantlinger's *Dark Vanishings* in Chapter 3.

41 Gretchen E. Schafft, "Scientific Racism in Service of the Reich: German Anthropologists in the Nazi Era," in Hinton, ed., *Annihilating Difference*, pp. 117, 131. See also Schafft's full-length book, *From Racism to Genocide: Anthropology in the Third Reich* (Urbana, IL: University of Illinois Press, 2004).

42 See Sybil Milton, "Holocaust: The Gypsies," ch. 6 in Samuel Totten *et al.*, eds, *Century of Genocide: Eyewitness Accounts and Critical Views* (New York: Garland Publishing, 1997). According to the Web Hyperdictionary, "physical anthropology" is "the scientific study of the physical characteristics, variability, and evolution of the human organism." See http://searchbox.hyperdictionary.com/dictionary/physical+anthropology.

43 Paul A. Erickson and Liam D. Murphy, *A History of Anthropological Theory* (Toronto: Broadview Press, 2003), p. 76.

44 Geoffrey Robertson, *Crimes Against Humanity: The Struggle for Global Justice* (New York: The New Press, 2000), pp. 31–32. An anthropologist, W.G. Sumner, first used the term "ethnocentrism" in 1906, defining it as "the technical name for [a] view of things in which one's own group is the center of everything, and all others are scaled and rated with reference to it. . . . Each group nourishes its own pride and vanity, boasts itself superior, exalts its own divinities, and looks with contempt on outsiders." Quoted in Waller, *Becoming Evil*, p. 154.

45 Alexander Hinton, personal communication, July 24, 2005.

46 Scheper-Hughes, "The Primacy of the Ethical," p. 410.

47 Hinton, "The Dark Side of Modernity," in Hinton, ed., *Annihilating Difference*, p. 2.

48 Hinton, "The Dark Side of Modernity," p. 2.

49 Sanford, *Buried Secrets*, p. 210. In anthropological parlance, individual testimonies constitute the "emic" level of analysis, academic interpretations the "etic" level. See Eriksen, *Small Places, Large Issues*, p. 36.

50 See, e.g., Antonius Robben, "How Traumatized Societies Remember: The Aftermath of Argentina's Dirty War," *Cultural Critique*, 59 (winter 2005), pp. 120–64.

51 Sanford, *Buried Secrets*, p. 143.

52 Hinton, "The Dark Side of Modernity," p. 19. Hinton argues that symbolism "mediate[s] all our understandings of the world, including a world of genocide" (personal communication, July 24, 2005). See also Arjun Appadurai, "Dead Certainty: Ethnic Violence in the Era of Globalization," ch. 13 in Hinton, ed., *Genocide: An Anthropological Reader*, pp. 286–303.

53 Christopher C. Taylor, *Sacrifice as Terror: The Rwandan Genocide of 1994* (Oxford: Berg,

1999), p. 130. The phenomenon has its counterpart in other genocides; as early as 1940, the English novelist and essayist H.G. Wells pointed to "the victims smothered in latrines" in Nazi concentration camps, exemplifying "the cloacal side of Hitlerism." Quoted in Robertson, *Crimes Against Humanity*, p. 23. For another fascinating study of violent ritual and symbolism, see Antonius Robben, "State Terror in the Netherworld: Disappearance and Reburial in Argentina" (in Robben, ed., *Death, Mourning, and Burial: A Cross-Cultural Reader* [London: Blackwell 2005]), which explores the symbolic violation of "disappearance" in a culture that ascribes great significance to the physical corpse and rituals of burial.

54 Nancy Scheper-Hughes, *Death without Weeping: The Violence of Everyday Life in Brazil* (Berkeley, CA: University of California Press, 1993).

55 Nancy Scheper-Hughes, "Coming to Our Senses: Anthropology and Genocide," in Hinton, ed., *Annihilating Difference*, p. 369. See also Scheper-Hughes, "The Genocidal Continuum: Peace-time Crimes," ch. 2 in Jeannette Marie Mageo, ed., *Power and the Self* (Cambridge: Cambridge University Press, 2002), pp. 29–47.

56 Scheper-Hughes, "Coming to Our Senses," pp. 372–73.

57 Hinton, "The Dark Side of Modernity," p. 33.

58 Dennis C. Dirkmaat and J.M. Adovasion, "The Role of Archaeology in the Recovery and Interpretation of Human Remains from an Outdoor Forensic Setting"; cited at http://mai.mercyhurst.edu/Foren%20Anth/What%20is.htm.

59 Clyde Snow, "Murder Most Foul," *The Sciences* (May/June 1995), p. 16.

60 Snow, "Murder Most Foul," p. 20.

61 See Leigh Binford, *The El Mozote Massacre: Anthropology and Human Rights* (Tucson, AZ: University of Arizona Press, 1996); Mark Danner, *The Massacre at El Mozote: A Parable of the Cold War* (New York: Vintage, 1994).

62 "Originally a five-member group, the Guatemalan Forensic Anthropology Foundation now employs more than 60 people and has carried out more than 200 exhumations." Victoria Sanford, personal communication, June 15, 2005.

63 The activities of the Guatemalan forensic team are movingly described by Victoria Sanford in her book *Buried Secrets*, centering on exhumations in the Mayan village of Acul.

64 See the "Clyde Snow Information Page" at http://www.ajweberman.com/cs.htm.

CHAPTER 12

Political Science and International Relations

The core concern of political science is power: how it is distributed and used within states and societies. International relations (IR) examines its use and distribution among the state units that compose the international "system." Historically, IR's overriding concern is with peace and war, though in recent decades the discipline has grappled increasingly with the growth of international "regimes": norms, rules, and patterns of conduct that influence state behavior in a given issue area.

The relevance to genocide studies of all these lines of inquiry is considerable. We have already drawn upon the contributions of political scientists and IR theorists, notably in the analysis of "Imperialism, War, and Social Revolution" (Chapter 2). This chapter explores four further contributions of PoliSci and IR frameworks: empirical studies of genocide; the changing nature of war; the putative link between democracy and peace; and the role of ethical norms in constructing effective "prohibition regimes" worldwide.

EMPIRICAL INVESTIGATIONS

The most influential empirical investigators of state-directed mass killing are the US political scientists R.J. Rummel, Barbara Harff, and Ted Gurr, the latter two often working in tandem. Their studies have clarified considerably the scope and character of genocidal, "politicidal," and "democidal" murder in modern times. As with nearly all genocide scholars, their work is preventionist in orientation (see Chapter 6). They seek to determine the explanatory variables that can assist in identifying the

Figure 12.1 R.J. Rummel, political scientist and scholar of "democide."

Source: Courtesy R.J. Rummel.

genocide-prone societies of the present, and in isolating positive and constructive features that may inoculate societies against genocide and other crimes against humanity.

Rummel's book *Death by Government* (1997) coined the term "democide" to describe "government mass murder" – including but not limited to genocide as defined in the UN Convention. Examining the death-toll from twentieth-century democide, Rummel was the first to place it almost beyond the bounds of imaginability. According to his detailed study, somewhere in the range of *170 million* "men, women, and children have been shot, beaten, tortured, knifed, burned, starved, frozen, crushed, or worked to death; buried alive, drowned, hung, bombed, or killed in any other of the myriad ways governments have inflicted death on unarmed, helpless citizens and foreigners."[1] If combat casualties in war are added to the picture, "Power has killed over 203 million people in [the twentieth] century."[2]

Rummel identifies the "most lethal regimes," in terms of numbers of people exterminated, as the Soviet Union under Lenin and Stalin (Chapter 5), communist China (Box 3a), Germany under the Nazis (Chapter 6 and Box 6a), and Nationalist China (touched on briefly in Chapter 2). If the "megamurder" index is recalculated based upon a regime's time in power (i.e., as deaths per year), then Cambodia under the Khmer Rouge (Chapter 7), Turkey under Kemal Atatürk, and the Nazi puppet state in Croatia (1941–45) top the list.

Rummel discerned an underlying "Power Principle" in this human catastrophe, namely that "Power kills; absolute Power kills absolutely":

> The more power a government has, the more it can act arbitrarily according to the whims and desires of the elite, and the more it will make war on others and murder its foreign and domestic subjects. The more constrained the power of governments, the more power is diffused, checked, and balanced, the less it will aggress on others and commit democide.[3]

Accordingly, for Rummel, liberal democracies are the good guys. Only in situations of all-out international war, or when their democratic procedures are subverted by conniving elites, will they engage in democide on a significant scale. This argument ties in with the "democratic peace" thesis, and I will return to Rummel's work in addressing that thesis below. His significance, for the present, lies in his systematic and successful attempt to tabulate the gory toll of twentieth-century mass killing, and to tie this to the exercise of political power (or "Power") worldwide.

Barbara Harff and Ted Gurr have approached genocide and "politicide" – mass killing on the basis of imputed political affiliation – through the study of ethnic conflicts. In 1988, the authors compiled statistical data for genocides and politicides between 1945 and 1980, and published a ground-breaking analysis that sought to isolate where, and under what conditions, these phenomena are most likely to occur. Harff summarized their findings as follows:

> Revolutionary one-party states are the likeliest offenders. Genocides occur with alarming frequency during or shortly after the revolutionary takeovers. Especially dangerous are situations in which long-standing ethnic rivalries erupt and radicalized groups armed with a revolutionary ideology gain the upper hand. Communist ideologues tend to be most aggressive in their dealings with potential or past opposition groups. Interestingly enough, the length of democratic experience is inversely related to the occurrence of geno/politicides.[4]

The following year (1989), Gurr, working with James Scaritt, produced a valuable compendium of "minorities at risk," "distinguish[ing] ethnocultural minorities on the basis of present and past political discrimination, economic discrimination, their concentration regionally, numbers, and the minorities' political demands."[5] In recent years, Harff has conducted research at the US Naval Academy "in response to President Clinton's policy initiative on genocide early warning and prevention," utilizing statistical data of the State Failure Task Force.[6] Her important article for the *American Political Science Review* maintained a problematic distinction between genocides and politicides;[7] but her findings both buttressed and extended her earlier work with Gurr. "Empirically, all but one of the 37 genocides and politicides that began between 1955 and 1998 occurred during or immediately after political upheavals . . . 24 coincided with ethnic wars, 14 coincided with revolutionary wars, and 14 followed the occurrence of adverse regime changes."[8] She concluded that "the greater the magnitude of previous internal wars and regime crises, summed over the preceding 15 years, the more likely that a new state failure will lead to geno-/politicide." Among the key explanatory variables located by her study are:

- *Presence or absence of genocidal precedents:* "The risks of new [genocidal/politicidal] episodes were more than three times greater when state failures occurred in countries that had prior geno-/politicides."
- *Presence or absence of an exclusionary ideology:* "Countries in which the ruling elite adhered to an exclusionary ideology were two and a half times as likely to have state failures leading to geno-/politicide as those with no such ideology."
- *Extent of ethnic "capture" of the state:* "The risks of geno-/politicide were two and a half times more likely in countries where the political elite was based mainly or entirely on an ethnic minority."
- *Extent and depth of democratic institutions:* "Once in place, democratic institutions – even partial ones – reduce the likelihood of armed conflict and all but eliminate the risk that it will lead to geno-/politicide."
- *Degree of international "openness":* "The greater their interdependence with the global economy, the less likely that [national] elites will target minorities and political opponents for destruction."

Harff's research also turned up surprises. Ethnic and religious cleavages, in and of themselves, were strongly relevant only when combined with an ethnic minority's capture of the state apparatus. Poverty, which many commentators view as a virtual recipe for social conflict including genocide, could indeed "predispose societies to intense conflict," but these conflicts assumed genocidal or politicidal proportions only in tandem with features of the political system (a minority ethnicity in charge, the promulgation of an exclusionary ideology, and the like).

Harff concluded by arguing that "the risk assessments generated . . . signal possible genocides." Among the countries she placed at highest risk were Iraq, Afghanistan, Burma, Rwanda, Congo, and Somalia – a list with which few observers of current affairs would quibble. In keeping with preventionist discourse, she urged policy-makers to employ her and others' findings to make "timely and plausible assessments" and develop "anticipatory responses [that] should save more lives at less cost than belated responses after killings have begun."[9] Her variables are well worth bearing in mind for the evaluation of genocide prevention and intervention strategies that concludes this volume.

THE CHANGING FACE OF WAR

> *Kalash au bilash; kalash begib al kash.*
> (You're trash without a Kalashnikov [automatic rifle]; get some cash with a Kalashnikov.)
>
> Popular saying in Darfur, Sudan (see Box 9a)

Warfare has varied greatly over centuries and across human societies. Representatives of all of the disciplines explored in this section have provided a rich body of conflict case studies, and important exercises in comparative theory building.[10]

War in "primitive" societies ranges from the brutal and destructive (as with the Yanomami of Brazil and various New Guinean societies) to the largely demonstrative and symbolic (as among many native nations of North America).[11] The great empire builders of Central Asia laid waste to entire civilizations, but in Europe in the early modern period, war came to be waged by and against professional armies, with exemptions granted to civilians – in theory, and often in practice. Yet the two most destructive wars in history were centered precisely in civilized, modern Europe, where clashes of ideologies and national ambitions targeted principally the civilian population.

With the advent of the nuclear age, the potential destructive power of "total wars" became limitless. The superpowers stepped back from the brink, limiting their clashes to wars at the periphery of their respective spheres of influence. One IR scholar even wondered whether an "end to major war" was nigh.[12] That speculation may have been valid – and may still be valid – in the case of international wars pitting centralized states against each other, but a tectonic shift in the nature of war occurred during this period. Most wars were now *civil* wars, pitting armed groups (usually guerrillas) against other armed groups (usually state agents and paramilitaries) within the borders of a single country. Often, too, these conflicts demonstrated a strong ethnic element, although this tended to be downplayed in commentary and scholarship, which focused on the government–guerrilla dyad. Examples are the wars in Burma, Ethiopia, Kashmir (divided between India and Pakistan), and Guatemala; many others could be cited.

Some scholars of international relations declared that the end of the Cold War marked a break in the trajectory of modern war. In fact, the civil wars and "limited" imperial wars of the Cold War era arguably laid the foundations for war as it is waged around the world today. Conflicts in Central America (Guatemala, Nicaragua, El Salvador) and Africa (Angola and Mozambique) were incredibly destructive – the southern African conflicts alone killed well over a million people combined, and made refugees of millions more. Restraints on the targeting of civilians were either lax or non-existent. Terror strategies were widely employed, and by diverse actors: armies, paramilitary forces, freebooters, and mercenaries, with wide scope granted to criminal and profiteering elements. In Africa, the weapon of choice was the AK-47 automatic rifle – one of the rare Soviet products preferred over the capitalist competition.

The Cold War's demise magnified these trends, and added new ones. It is a truism that the withdrawal of the superpowers from extensive military engagement in the

Third World "lifted the lid" from simmering or dormant ethnic conflicts in many countries. Ethnically fueled wars have increased worldwide – although it may be debated whether this primarily reflects older tensions and conflicts, or "more immediate and remediable causes: political manipulation, belief traps and Hobbesian fear."[13]

Many states that had been propped up by one of the superpowers (or had played off the US and Soviet Union against each other) collapsed in the face of concerted popular resistance. This produced the great wave of democratization in East Asia, Latin America, and Eastern Europe at the end of the 1980s and into the 1990s, but it also led to "failed states," in which no central authority exerted effective control. Power and the means of violence devolved to decentralized networks of paramilitaries, warlords, freebooting soldiers or former soldiers, and brigands.

In such cases, these groups were often at odds or openly at war with one another – and usually with the civilian population as well. To shore up their power base, warlords and freebooters sought "rents" from the civilian population – in the form of mafia-style "protection money" or simple robbery – and from the natural resources on their territories, so that wars in Congo, Liberia, Sierra Leone, and Colombia, among many others, were sustained by the windfall profits to be made from

Figure 12.2 The new face of war: demobilized child soldiers in the Democratic Republic of Congo, 2002.
Source: Courtesy Dimitri Falk.

diamonds,[14] gold,[15] timber, oil, and drugs. These spoils were marketed internationally; the world had truly entered an age of *globalized* warfare, in which consumer decisions in the First World had a direct impact on the course and outcome of Third World conflicts.[16]

The implications of these trends for genocides of the present and future are profound:

- The fact that most "new wars" are civil wars means that norms of state sovereignty are less powerful inhibitors than with international wars. The latter may be muted or suppressed by collective security strategies deployed in recent decades. In any case, international wars are viewed as "threats to the system," and nearly always provoke an international outcry. No such effective "prohibition regime" exists in the case of civil conflicts (though one might be nascent). Contrast, for example, the response to Saddam Hussein's invasion of Kuwait with his much more severe depredations against Iraqi Kurds (see Box 4a).
- New wars feature a profusion of actors and agents, often making it difficult to determine who is doing what to whom. The most destructive war of recent times, in Congo (Box 9a), has killed perhaps four million people. But with a mosaic of local and outside forces, apportioning responsibility for genocide and other atrocities – and bringing effective pressure to bear on perpetrators – are tasks even more daunting than usual.
- To lend moral and political legitimacy to activities usually fueled by greed and power lust, new-war actors often play up ethnic and particularist identities. Campaigns of persecution against national and ethnic groups, including genocide, become a standard *modus operandi.* The wars of the 1990s in West and Central Africa and former Yugoslavia (Chapter 8) are prominent examples.
- The globalized arms trade and caches left over from Cold War struggles have flooded the territories in which new wars occur with cheap, light weaponry. In many countries, an AK-47 may be purchased for a few dollars. The loss of superpower sponsorship, and political–material competition among the various actors, spawn ever greater demands on the civilian population. Civilians may be murdered *en masse* if held to be in allegiance with one of the opposing groups, or insufficiently cooperative with extraction and taxation measures, or simply in the way of one or another side.
- The ambiguous, uncertain, and shifting control over territories and populations that characterizes these wars vastly increases the complexity of conflict suppression and humanitarian intervention. IR scholars speak of "complex humanitarian emergencies" in which war, genocide, social breakdown, starvation, refugee flows, and internally displaced populations all combine to produce a downward spiral of suffering and destruction. Aid agencies, journalists, and human rights monitors are all at greater risk in such circumstances, and may thus be more reluctant to enter the field and stay there. Without their expert witnessing and evaluations, events on the ground are further obscured, and considerable interventionist potential is squandered.
- If sufficient sources of "rent" can be extracted from the land and its population, these wars can become self-perpetuating and self-sustaining. The longer they drag

on, the likelier is massive mortality from hunger and disease – and the likelier that the only viable source of income and self-respect (for young men but also, increasingly, for young women) is to join a warring faction.

It is difficult to say whether the new wars are more likely to produce genocide, but at the very least, they contain a strong genocidal *potential*. And, all too frequently, a genocidal dynamic is central to the unfolding conflict.

DEMOCRACY, WAR, AND GENOCIDE/DEMOCIDE

> Societies are known by their victims.
>
> Richard Drinnon

Are democracies less likely to wage war and genocide against each other than are non-democracies? Are they less likely *in general* to wage war and genocide?

These issues have provoked arguably the most vigorous single debate in the international relations literature over the past three decades – the so-called "democratic peace debate." They have also given rise to one of the few proclaimed "laws," perhaps the *only* one, in this branch of the social sciences. Democracies, it is claimed, do not fight each other, or do so only rarely. Why might this be so? As IR scholar Errol Henderson summarizes:

> Theoretical explanations for the democratic peace emphasize either structural/institutional factors or cultural/normative factors in preventing war between democracies. The former posits that institutional constraints on the decision-making choices of democratic leaders make it difficult for them to use force in their foreign policies and act as a brake on conflict with other democracies. The latter assumes that democracies are less disposed to fight each other due to the impact of their shared norms that proscribe the use of violence between them.[17]

A "harder" version of the democratic peace hypothesis, advanced by R.J. Rummel, argues that democracies are far less likely than authoritarian states to commit democide, whether against their own populations or against others. Rummel concedes that democracies sometimes perpetrate democide, but "almost all of this . . . is foreign democide during war, and consists mainly of those enemy civilians killed in indiscriminate urban bombing." Acknowledging other examples, he claims that they are exceptions that prove the rule: "In each case the killing was carried out in a highly undemocratic fashion: in secret, behind a conscious cover of lies and deceit, and by agencies and power holders that had the wartime authority to operate autonomously. All were shielded by tight censorship of the press and control of journalists." In order for democratic states to become democidal, therefore, what makes them democratic has to be suspended, at least temporarily.[18]

There is much that is intuitively appealing about Rummel's formulations, and those of other proponents of the democratic peace hypothesis. First, it seems evident that genocides inflicted by democracies *against their own populations* are rare. One can think of exceptions – Sri Lanka in the 1980s is sometimes cited – but they do not come readily to mind. By contrast, this book overflows with examples of authoritarian, dictatorial, tyrannical, and totalitarian governments slaughtering their own populations (the USSR under Lenin and Stalin; China before and after the communist revolution; Cambodia under the Khmer Rouge; and so on). At a glance, too, the "law" that democracies do not fight each other seems empirically robust.

Things become more complicated, however, when we consider the history of colonizing liberal democracies; the nature of some of the indigenous societies they attacked; the secretive and anti-democratic character of violence by *both* democratic and authoritarian states; and the latter-day comportment of democracies, including the global superpower and non-Western democracies.

As we saw in Chapter 3, the strategy adopted towards indigenous peoples by Western colonial powers – in most cases, the most democratic states of their age – was frequently genocidal. Other, less democratic states were less likely to aggress internationally than the liberal democracies of the time (which were also, of course, the most technologically advanced countries, and hence best equipped to impose violence on others).[19]

The character of the indigenous societies that the colonialists confronted, moreover, was often no less democratic than the colonial states themselves – sometimes more so. As sociologist Michael Mann has noted:

> The "democratic peace" school have excluded groups like the [North American] Indian nations from their calculations on the somewhat dubious grounds that they did not have permanent differentiated states of the "modern" type. Though this is convenient for the self-congratulatory tone of much of their writings[,] it is illegitimate even by their own definitions. For Indian nations did develop permanent constitutional states through the mid-nineteenth century – for example, the Cherokee in 1827, the Choctaw, Chickasaw and Creeks in the period 1856–1867.[20]

Thus, when genocidal campaigns were waged against these nations, "liberal democracies were actually committing genocide against other democracies, repeatedly." In fact, Mann suggested, "If we counted up separately the cases where 'the people' of the United States, Canada and Australia committed mass murder on the individual Indian and aboriginal nations, we could probably tip Rummel's statistical scales over to the conclusion that democratic regimes were more likely to commit genocide than were authoritarian states."[21]

In examining *international* involvement in mass violence and atrocity, there is little doubt that the most consistently and aggressively violent country over the past half-century is also the world's leading liberal democracy. Whatever the brutality of the Soviets in Hungary (1956) or in Afghanistan (see Chapter 2), no power approaches the United States when it comes to instigation of, and complicity in, conflicts and atrocities worldwide. The majority of this violence, moreover, was not conducted through formal participation in formally declared wars, but took place "covertly."[22] As we saw, Rummel generalized about this theme, claiming that democratic democide represents a stark departure from democratic norms. But then, wonders Errol Henderson, should these agents of mass violence really be classed as democracies?[23]

Mann, for his part, pointed out that the enabling variables which Rummel cited for "democratic democide" – secrecy, censorship, lying, deceit – are also those which have typically enabled mass killing by *non*-democratic states. Authoritarian genocides similarly tend to be committed in wartime, and with attempts at secrecy. "Hitler committed almost all his murders during the war, and he did not dare make them public – indeed, nor did Stalin."[24]

Henderson, revisiting the data-set on democratic peace compiled by John Oneal and Bruce Russett (1997), pointed to sharp differences among Western liberal democracies, on one hand, and those he classified as "Hindu" democracies (India and Sri Lanka) and "Other" democracies (notably Israel), on the other. By retabulating Oneal and Russett's numbers, Henderson found that "Western democracies were significantly less likely to initiate interstate wars," but Hindu and other democracies "were significantly *more* likely to initiate them."[25]

On balance, and crucially including "extrastate" wars (wars against non-state entities, usually in a colonial and imperial context), "democratic states [are] in fact significantly *more likely* to become involved in – and to initiate – interstate wars and militarized international disputes," according to Henderson.[26] With regard to extrastate wars, "Western states – including the Western democracies – are more likely" to initiate and involve themselves in such conflicts. He concluded, provocatively and counter-intuitively, that "for all of its positive value as an egalitarian form of government, one of the key threats to peace for individual states is the presence of a democratic regime."[27]

What can we take away from these diverse arguments? First, even the skeptic Henderson acknowledges the "positive value" of democracy "as an egalitarian form of government." As Rummel argued, consolidated democratic regimes are much less likely to wage war and genocide against their own populations than are tyrannical states.

On the other hand, liberal democracy is no guarantee against domestic killing, as millions of indigenous peoples discovered. Nor, in a world where the greatest perpetrator of international violence is the liberal-democratic superpower, can democracy be seen as a cure-all.[28]

NORMS AND PROHIBITION REGIMES

International relations scholars have increasingly studied the role of norms and regimes in global affairs, notably (for our purposes) *humanitarian norms* and *prohibition regimes.* Regimes were defined by Stephen Krasner as "principles, norms, rules, and decision-making procedures around which actor expectations converge in a given issue-area." Norms are "specific prescriptions or proscriptions for action," while principles are "standards of behavior defined in terms of rights and obligations."[29]

Ethan Nadelmann has defined prohibition regimes as sets of "norms . . . which prohibit, both in international law and in the domestic criminal law of states, the involvement of state and nonstate actors in particular activities." Such regimes emerge:

> like municipal criminal laws . . . for a variety of reasons: to protect the interests of the state and other powerful members of society; to deter, suppress, and punish undesirable activities; to provide for order, security, and justice among members of a community; and to give force and symbolic representation to the moral values, beliefs, and prejudices of those who make the law.[30]

The key player in transforming norms into international regimes, especially prohibition regimes, is the *norm entrepreneur*, "an individual or organization that sets out to change the behaviour of others,"[31] and the *principled-issue networks* that norm entrepreneurs create. The history of the prohibition regime against genocide, weak and underdeveloped as it currently is, provides an excellent example of such entrepreneurship. Raphael Lemkin's decades-long campaign to develop a norm against genocide eventually generated a principled-issue network of scholars, government representatives, legal specialists, and human-rights activists; this network has grown exponentially, and exerted a real though limited influence on global politics.

Lemkin's campaign was described in general terms in Chapter 1. Here, I want to examine the nuts and bolts of his anti-genocide strategy, to demonstrate how successful norm entrepreneurship proceeds. (This discussion again draws heavily on Samantha Power's depiction of Lemkin's mission in *"A Problem from Hell"*).[32]

First, Lemkin perceived an important void in existing international law. While legislation and even military intervention were countenanced in cases of interstate violence, states had free rein to inflict violence on their own populations. To generate a norm and prohibition regime against such actions, a potent existing norm, and a defining regime of world affairs, had to be eroded. This was the norm of state sovereignty, and the international regime (the Westphalian state system) that it underpinned. As long as states forswore intervention in the "internal" affairs of other states, a principal cause of human suffering could not be confronted.

To define a new norm and sell it to the world, Lemkin invented a word that addressed the "crime without a name," as Winston Churchill had described Nazi atrocities in Eastern Europe. Lemkin struggled to find "a word that could not be used in other contexts (as 'barbarity' and 'vandalism' could) . . . one that would bring with it 'a color of freshness and novelty' while describing something 'as shortly and as poignantly as possible.'"[33] The term he finally settled on – genocide – proved to be one of the core *catalyzing ideas* of the twentieth century. With unprecedented speed, it led to the drafting of an international Convention against genocide, the foundation of a prohibition regime that today exhibits growing strength and complexity.

With his evocative term in hand, Lemkin physically planted himself at the heart of postwar international legislation and regime formation. In the surprisingly informal surroundings of United Nations headquarters, then housed in an abandoned war plant on Long Island, Lemkin obsessively lobbied delegates to the new organization, spending "endless hours haunting the drafty halls."[34] Few delegates escaped his (usually unwanted) attentions. From his one-room Manhattan apartment,

Lemkin fired off literally thousands of letters to government officials and politicians, religious and cultural figures, newspapers and their editors and assistant editors and reporters. In addition, "friends, friends of friends, and acquaintances of acquaintances" were drafted to the cause, providing background information and fresh contacts.

Throughout his campaign, Lemkin engaged in *norm grafting*. The task of the norm entrepreneur is greatly eased if s/he can point to previous, congruent norms that have achieved wide acceptance. If A, why not B? (If slavery is wrong, why not forced labor? If voting rights are extended to all adult males, why not to women?) Such grafting presumes a desire for moral and rhetorical consistency on the part of policymakers and publics.[35] Thus, Lemkin pointed to the huge gap in the evolving prohibition regime against war crimes and crimes against humanity. "If piracy was an international crime, he could not understand why genocide was not." In a similar vein, Lemkin wrote in the *New York Times*: "It seems *inconsistent* with our concepts of civilization that selling a drug to an individual is a matter of worldly concern [i.e., the basis for an international prohibition regime], while gassing millions of human beings might be a problem of internal concern."[36]

Norm entrepreneurs frequently exploit historical moments that provide a favorable environment for norm adoption and regime creation. These moments usually follow major upheavals that weaken preconceptions and undermine established frameworks. Lemkin's fortunate conjuncture was the "multilateral moment" (Power's phrase) immediately following the Second World War. In a few years, many of the international organizations, legal instruments, and regimes of today were first developed (often grafted onto previous institutions and regimes, as the UN grew out of the League of Nations). The revelation of the full horror of Nazi rule, especially the indelible reports and images from the death camps, undermined the legitimacy of state sovereignty as a shield against intervention and prosecution on humanitarian grounds.

Lemkin's greatest achievement was the UN Genocide Convention. "Just four years after Lemkin had introduced 'genocide' to the world, the General Assembly had unanimously passed a law banning it." Lemkin now turned his efforts (which by this point were undermining his health) to lobbying for ratification of the treaty, and the transformation of his norm into an effective prohibition regime. Using classic tactics of the norm entrepreneur, Lemkin crafted his messages and appeals carefully, individually, and with an eye for utilitarian impact. "He sent letters out in English, French, Spanish, Hebrew, Italian, and German. Long before computers or photocopiers" – two of the most powerful tools of the contemporary norm entrepreneur – "he handcrafted each letter to suit the appropriate individual, organization, or country. . . . He wrote to the leaders of the most influential political parties, the heads of the private women's or civic groups, and the editors of prominent newspapers." He also "attempted to mobilize American grassroots groups" and "enlisted a panoply of American civic organizations, churches, and synagogues."[37] With few material resources of his own, he "borrowed stationery from supportive community organizations, applied for grants to pay for postage, and sent thousands of letters to absolutely anybody whose moral heartstrings he felt he might tug or on whose connections he might prey to get the ear of a US senator."[38]

According to Power, Lemkin "varied his pitch," tailoring his message carefully and sometimes cynically to the object of his appeal. "If a country had experienced genocide in the past, he reminded its citizens of the human costs of allowing it. But if a country had *committed* genocide in the past, as Turkey had done [against the Armenians], Lemkin was willing to keep the country's atrocities out of the discussion, so as not to scare off a possible signatory" to the convention.[39] For similar reasons, Lemkin had avoided pushing for the inclusion of political groups in the UN definition of genocide. This, he feared, would provoke resistance among states fearful of having their political persecutions labeled as genocide. (In any case, Lemkin had never cared much about political groups. He did not consider them to be bearers of human culture in the same – archaic? – way that he viewed ethnonational groups.)

With his reluctance to include political groups, Lemkin contributed to some of the conceptual and legal confusion that has since surrounded the UN Convention.[40] On balance, though, it is hard to disagree with his own self-estimation (in pitching his story to publishers): that his life "shows how a private individual almost single handedly can succeed in imposing a moral law on the world and how he can stir world conscience to this end."[41]

IR theorists of norms and regimes describe a *tipping point* followed by a *norm cascade* in the diffusion of norms, analogous to the paradigm shifts in scientific knowledge studied by Thomas Kuhn.[42] One norm displaces another, decisively and definitively. At this point, norms become strongly entrenched in international regimes, including effective prohibition regimes.

With respect to the norm against genocide and crimes against humanity, we can observe that it has partially, not yet decisively, displaced the norm of state sovereignty. It appeared possible, in the immediate postwar period, that a tipping from sovereignty to cosmopolitanism and international governance could occur, but this idealistic vision faded rapidly with the onset of the Cold War. It does not seem a great deal closer to realization today, especially given the reluctance of the United States to participate in a range of key prohibition regimes, and its active undermining of others (such as the Torture Convention, the Geneva Conventions, and the International Criminal Court).

Thus, while the drive to suppress and prevent genocide has indeed spawned a norm and a prohibition regime, it is applied only weakly and inconsistently – compared, say, with norms against state-sponsored slavery, nuclear proliferation, assassination of foreign leaders, or piracy and hijacking.[43] The anti-genocide movement is best classed with a range of other norms and regimes that have made significant strides, but have yet to entrench themselves in international affairs: those against capital punishment, trafficking (in human beings, drugs, and ivory), and theft of intellectual property, to name a few.

In his seminal study of prohibition regimes, Ethan Nadelmann developed a five-stage model for their evolution. At first, "most societies regard the targeted activity as entirely legitimate"; indeed, "states are often the principal protagonists." Then, the activity is redefined as morally problematic or evil, "generally by international legal scholars, religious groups, and other moral entrepreneurs." Next, "regime proponents begin to agitate actively for the suppression and criminalization of the activity." If this stage is successful, "the activity becomes the subject of criminal laws and police actions throughout much of the world." In the fifth and final stage, "the incidence of the proscribed activity is greatly reduced, persisting only on a small scale and in obscure locations."[44] Using this model, we can position the anti-genocide regime – and the other comparatively weak regimes mentioned above – between Nadelmann's third stage, with "regime proponents . . . agitat[ing] actively for the suppression and criminalization of the activity," and stage four, in which the regime is "the subject of criminal laws and police actions throughout much of the world."

Most weaker prohibition regimes suffer from a number of debilities. They may be relatively recent (many were at Nadelmann's first stage of evolution just a few decades ago). Their core concepts or "catalyzing ideas" may be prone to ambiguities of definition and application. Enforcement mechanisms are underdeveloped, and often corrupt – suggesting a lack of political will, and attesting to the failure of activist mobilization to spur political actors to meaningful effort. All of these factors are evident in the case of the anti-genocide regime.

Prohibition regimes are also hampered where strong counter-incentives exist. It remains in the interest of vast numbers of ordinary people (or smaller numbers of powerful people) to undermine the regime and weaken its application. Just as the lure of illegal drugs for both consumers and vendors outweighs the ability of states to suppress these substances, so genocide holds an enduring appeal as a problem-solving strategy for states and other actors.[45]

According to Nadelmann, however, prohibition regimes are *more* likely to succeed when the targeted activity has a strong transnational dimension; when unilateral and bilateral means of enforcement are inadequate; when a norm "reflects not just self-interest but a broadly acknowledged moral obligation"; and when the activity is vulnerable "to global suppression efforts by states."[46] IR theorists Margaret Keck and Kathryn Sikkink point out additionally that prohibition regimes are boosted when "the causal chain [is] short," when "causes can be assigned to the deliberate 'intentional' actions of identifiable individuals," and when a universalistic "concern with bodily harm" underlies the prohibition effort.[47] In all these respects, the anti-genocide regime holds considerable potential. This may bode well for its future strengthening.

FURTHER STUDY

Susan Burgerman, *Moral Victories: How Activists Provoke Multilateral Action.* Ithaca, NY: Cornell University Press, 2001. Concise study with a Latin American focus.

Errol A. Henderson, *Democracy and War: The End of an Illusion?* Boulder, CO: Lynne Rienner, 2002. Myth-shattering analysis of democracies' involvement in international conflict.

Kalevi J. Holsti, *The State, War, and the State of War.* Cambridge: Cambridge University Press, 1996. Arguably the best introduction to global transformations in warfare.

Mary Kaldor, *New and Old Wars: Organized Violence in a Global Era.* Stanford, CA: Stanford University Press, 2001. Another core text of the new security studies.

Margaret E. Keck and Kathryn Sikkink, *Activists Beyond Borders: Advocacy Networks in International Politics*. Ithaca, NY, and London: Cornell University Press, 1998. The role of transnational nongovernmental networks in norm entrepreneurship and regime formation.

Stephen D. Krasner, ed., *International Regimes*. Ithaca, NY: Cornell University Press, 1983. Ground-breaking study.

R.J. Rummel, *Death by Government*. New Brunswick, NJ: Transaction Publishers, 1994. Comprehensive survey of government-directed mass killing, marred by cheerleading for liberal democracy.

Ward Thomas, *The Ethics of Destruction: Norms and Force in International Relations*. Ithaca, NY: Cornell University Press, 2001. Elegantly written study of normative constraints on war-making.

NOTES

1 R.J. Rummel, *Death by Government* (New Brunswick, NJ: Transaction Publishers, 1994). He considers this a fairly conservative estimate: "The dead could conceivably be nearly 360 million people." Rummel maintains an extensive website on democide at http://www.hawaii.edu/powerkills/welcome.html.

2 Rummel, *Death by Government*, p. 13. "If all these dead were laid out head to toe, assuming each to be an average of 5 feet tall, they would reach from Honolulu, Hawaii, across the vast Pacific and then the huge continental United States to Washington DC on the East Coast, *and then back again almost twenty times*" (emphasis in original).

3 Rummel, *Death by Government*, pp. 1–2.

4 Harff quoted in Helen Fein, *Genocide: A Sociological Perspective* (London: Sage, 1993), p. 40.

5 Fein, *Genocide*, p. 96. See Ted R. Gurr and James R. Scaritt, "Minorities at Risk: A Global Survey," *Human Rights Quarterly*, 11: 3 (1989), pp. 375–405; more recently, Ted Robert Gurr, *Peoples versus States: Minorities at Risk in the New Century* (Washington, DC: US Institute of Peace Press, 2000).

6 Barbara Harff, "No Lessons Learned from the Holocaust? Assessing Risks of Genocide and Political Mass Murder since 1955," *American Political Science Review*, 97: 1 (February 2003), p. 57. The State Failure Task Force "was established in 1994 in response to a request from senior US policymakers to design and carry out a data-driven study of the correlates of state failure, defined to include revolutionary and ethnic wars, adverse or disruptive regime transitions, and genocides and politicides."

7 For example, Harff writes ("No Lessons Learned . . . ?," p. 58): "In common usage the Kurds of Iraq are said to be victims of genocide. In fact many Iraqi Kurds serve in the Iraqi bureaucracy and military and some are members of the ruling Baath Party. The Kurds who were targeted for destruction in the *al Anfal* campaign of 1987 [see Box 4a] were the mainly rural supporters of the Kurdish Democratic Party and the Patriotic Union of Kurdistan. Thus, the event was a politicide." But if this distinction holds, then two of the three best-known genocides of the twentieth century – of Armenians and Rwandan Tutsis – should also probably be reclassified as "politicides." In the mass killing campaign of 1915–17 (Chapter 4), Turks defended their assault on Armenians as a reaction to the victims' supposed affiliation with rebel groups and the Russian enemy; not until much later (after the First World War) was the killing extended to Armenians outside the main "rebel" areas of Turkey or in neighboring countries. Likewise, Rwandan Tutsis were seen by the "Hutu Power" extremists as a fifth column for Tutsi rebels invading from Uganda; at no point in the 1994 genocide was there an attempt to extend

the killing to Tutsis residing outside Rwanda, in Uganda, Congo (then Zaire), and Burundi.

It is interesting to note that in her earlier writing (1987), Harff subsumed politicide under genocide: "My definition of genocide differs from the official definition . . . insofar as it broadens the scope of the victims and perpetrators. Thus, political opponents are included in my definition, though they lack the formal legal protection of the Convention on Genocide." Harff, "The Etiology of Genocide," in Michael N. Dobkowski and Isidor Wallimann, eds, *The Age of Genocide: Etiology and Case Studies of Mass Death* (Westport, CT: Greenwood Press, 1987), p. 44.

8 Harff, "No Lessons Learned . . . ?," p. 62.

9 Harff, "No Lessons Learned . . . ?," p. 72.

10 For an extensive interdisciplinary sampling, see my "Bibliography of War" at http://adamjones.freeservers.com/bibliography_of_war.htm.

11 According to David Kertzer, "in many parts of the world, warfare itself is highly ritualized, with a special permanent site for the hostilities, special bodily adornment, special songs and verbal insults, and rules about the actual conduct of combat. In many of these cases, as soon as an individual is seriously wounded, hostilities cease and a round of post-battle ritual begins." Kertzer quoted in Charles Tilly, *The Politics of Collective Violence* (Cambridge: Cambridge University Press, 2003), p. 86.

12 See John E. Mueller, *Retreat from Doomsday: The Obsolescence of Major War* (New York: Basic Books, 1989).

13 Jonathan Glover, *Humanity: A Moral History of the Twentieth Century* (New Haven, CT: Yale University Press, 1999), p. 141. For example, one of the most conflict-ridden countries in the world over the past three decades has been Somalia, yet this is "perhaps Africa's most homogeneous country from an ethnic point of view." Tilly, *The Politics of Collective Violence*, p. 72.

14 See Greg Campbell, *Blood Diamonds: Tracing the Deadly Path of the World's Most Precious Stones* (Boulder, CO: Westview Press, 2002).

15 See, e.g., Human Rights Watch, *The Curse of Gold*, June 2005, http://www.hrw.org/reports/2005/drc0505/.

16 This too has a precedent in the "limited" wars of the 1980s, when Nicaraguan *contra* rebels and the *mujahadeen* Islamists in Afghanistan trafficked drugs to finance weapons purchases, with the tacit approval and sometimes active complicity of the US government. See Peter Dale Scott and Jonathan Marshall, *Cocaine Politics: Drugs, Armies, and the CIA in Central America* (Berkeley, CA: University of California Press, 1991). For an overview of contemporary trends in historical context, see Peter Dale Scott, *Drugs, Oil, and War: The United States in Afghanistan, Colombia, and Indochina* (Lanham, MD: Rowman & Littlefield, 2003).

17 Errol A. Henderson, *Democracy and War: The End of an Illusion?* (Boulder, CO: Lynne Rienner, 2002), p. 4. See also Tarak Barkawi and Mark Laffey, *Democracy, Liberalism, and War: Rethinking the Democratic Peace Debate* (Boulder, CO: Lynne Rienner, 2001).

18 Rummel, *Death by Government*, pp. 14, 17. Among the other cases of "democratic democide" that Rummel cites in passing (pp. 14–16) are: "the large-scale massacres of Filipinos during the bloody US colonization of the Philippines at the beginning of [the twentieth] century, deaths in British concentration camps in South Africa during the Boar [*sic*] War, civilian deaths due to starvation during the British blockade of Germany in and after World War I, the rape and murder of helpless Chinese in and around Peking in 1900 [while crushing the Boxer Rebellion], the atrocities committed by Americans in Vietnam, the murder of helpless Algerians during the Algerian War by the French, and the unnatural deaths of German prisoners of war in French and US POW camps after World War II."

19 I do not mean to suggest that *only* democracies aggressed in this fashion – the counter-examples of Tsarist Russia and Imperial Japan may be cited – but rather that democracy seems to have provided no check to such aggression.

20 Michael Mann, "The Dark Side of Democracy: The Modern Tradition of Ethnic and Political Cleansing," *New Left Review*, 235 (May–June 1999), pp. 18–46.

21 Mann, "The Dark Side of Democracy," p. 26. On the same page, Mann argues that "deliberate genocidal bursts were more common among British than Spanish or Portuguese settlers. In both cases, we find that the stronger the democracy among the perpetrators, the greater the genocide."

22 I have prepared a table of "Key Instances of US Involvement in Mass Violence against Civilians since 1953" to buttress this claim: see http://www.genocidetext.net/us_violence.pdf. See also the bibliography of much of the "dissident" literature on US state violence supplied in Adam Jones, "Introduction: History and Complicity," in Jones, ed., *Genocide, War Crimes and the West: History and Complicity* (London: Zed Books, 2004), pp. 26–30.

23 See Henderson, *Democracy and War*, p. 82; emphasis added.

24 Mann, "The Dark Side of Democracy," p. 20.

25 Henderson, *Democracy and War*, p. 66; emphasis added.

26 Henderson, *Democracy and War*, p. 17.

27 Henderson, *Democracy and War*, p. 73; emphasis added.

28 It is also worth recalling the destruction inflicted by global capitalism under a liberal-democratic aegis, as noted in Chapter 1's discussion of structural violence.

29 Stephen Krasner, "Structural Causes and Regime Consequences: Regimes as Intervening Variables," *International Organization*, 36: 2 (1982), pp. 185–205.

30 Ethan Nadelmann, "Global Prohibition Regimes: The Evolution of Norms in International Society," *International Organization*, 44: 4 (1990), pp. 479–526.

31 Ann Florini, "The Evolution of International Norms," *International Studies Quarterly*, 40 (1996), p. 375.

32 Samantha Power, *"A Problem from Hell": America and the Age of Genocide* (New York: Basic Books, 2002). Power does not adopt the norm-entrepreneur framing, however; and I do not, of course, ascribe to Raphael Lemkin the vocabulary of norms, regimes, and so on.

33 Power, "*A Problem from Hell*," p. 42.

34 Power, "*A Problem from Hell*," p. 51.

35 The concept is similar to Keck and Sikkink's formulation of "moral leverage" as exercised by activist networks: "Material leverage comes from linking the issue of concern to money, trade, or prestige, as more powerful institutions or governments are pushed to apply pressure. Moral leverage pushes actors to change their practices by holding their behavior up to international scrutiny, or by holding governments or institutions accountable to previous commitments and principles they have endorsed." Margaret E. Keck and Kathryn Sikkink, *Activists Beyond Borders: Advocacy Networks in International Politics* (Ithaca, NY: Cornell University Press, 1998), p. 201.

36 Power, and Lemkin quoted in Power, "*A Problem from Hell*," p. 48; emphasis added. In similar fashion, activists seeking to memorialize certain genocides may also draw upon genocidal precedents. Thus, "proliferating Armenian discourses on [the genocide of] 1915 were coloured by connections with the Jewish Holocaust. This was entirely natural, given the proximity of the 'final solution,' the growing public awareness of it in the 1960s in the aftermath of the trial of Adolf Eichmann, and the fact that the Nazi campaigns of genocide had given decisive impetus to the establishment of the genocide convention." Donald Bloxham, *The Great Game of Genocide: Imperialism, Nationalism, and the Destruction of the Ottoman Armenians* (Oxford: Oxford University Press, 2005), p. 217.

37 Power, "*A Problem from Hell*," p. 72.

38 Power, "*A Problem from Hell*," p. 71.

39 Power, "*A Problem from Hell*," pp. 63–64.

40 Nor did Lemkin draw the line at behavior that many found boorish, if it would advance his cause. Power describes his "mix of flattery and moral prodding . . . [which] sometimes slipped into bluntly bullying his contacts and demanding that they acquire a conscience." *"A Problem from Hell,"* p. 71.

41 Lemkin quoted in Power, "*A Problem from Hell*," p. 77.
42 The term "norm cascade" was coined by Martha Finnemore and Kathryn Sikkink in "International Norm Dynamics and Political Change," *International Organization*, 52: 4 (autumn 1998), pp. 901–2. See also Thomas S. Kuhn, *The Structure of Scientific Revolutions* (Chicago, IL: University of Chicago Press, 1996).
43 "Piracy may be regarded as the very first 'crime against humanity,' its peculiarly barbaric quality derived from the taking of lives which were especially vulnerable while outside the protective realm of any nation." Geoffrey A. Robertson, *Crimes against Humanity: The Struggle for Global Justice* (New York: The New Press, 2000), p. 208. Accordingly, the international regime against piracy might be regarded as the first in history, with the possible exception of that against assassinating state leaders and diplomatic representatives.
44 Nadelmann, "Global Prohibition Regimes," pp. 484–86.
45 See Catherine Barnes, "The Functional Utility of Genocide: Towards a Framework for Understanding the Connection between Genocide and Regime Consolidation, Expansion and Maintenance," *Journal of Genocide Research*, 7: 3 (September 2005), pp. 309–30.
46 Nadelmann, "Global Prohibition Norms," p. 491.
47 Keck and Sikkink, *Activists Beyond Borders*, pp. 27, 53, 195.

CHAPTER 13

Gendering Genocide

> It is recommended that the definition [of genocide] should be extended to include a sexual group such as women, men, or homosexuals.
>
> Benjamin Whitaker, *Revised and Updated Report on the Question of the Prevention and Punishment of Genocide* (the UN Whitaker Report), 1985

The gender dimension of genocide and other crimes against humanity has only recently attracted sustained attention. Leading the way in the inquiry were feminist scholars, who paid particular attention to rape and sexual assault against women, and pressed for such crimes to be considered strategies of genocide. Other scholars and commentators have concentrated on the gender-selective killing of girl infants through female infanticide or denial of adequate nutrition and health care.

The term "gender" is one of the most contested in the social sciences. Not long ago, it was assumed that gender could be clearly distinguished from biological/physiological sex. Gender meant the way that societies and cultures ascribed particular "feminine" and "masculine" roles, expectations, and values to (biological) males versus females. This vocabulary still has its strong proponents.[1] In the past decade or so, however, the distinction between biological/physiological sex and cultural gender has begun to break down. Increasingly, scholars and activists argue that sex and gender overlap and are mutually constitutive. Such is the view of international relations scholar Joshua Goldstein, who views a strict gender–sex distinction as "construct[ing] a false dichotomy between biology and culture." Goldstein accordingly "use[s] 'gender' to cover masculine and feminine roles and bodies alike, in all their aspects, including the (biological and cultural) structures, dynamics, roles and scripts associated with each gender group."[2] His definition also guides discussion in this chapter. It allows us to explore the gendering of genocide both in its destructive impact on male and female bodies, and with regard to the cultural practices that influence physical experience.

Gender is not synonymous with women/femininity, despite its close association with feminist-influenced scholarship and policy-making. Some feminists have contended that gender *means* the oppression of women by men,[3] resulting in a certain tone-deafness to the particular ways in which men and masculinities are often the target of abuse and discrimination, up to and including genocidal atrocities. This chapter adopts a more inclusive view of gender. Indeed, it begins with one of the least-studied aspects of contemporary genocide: the gendercidal (gender-selective) killing of males.

GENDERCIDE VS. ROOT-AND-BRANCH GENOCIDE

The gendercidal targeting of a community's adult males, usually accompanied by slavery and/or concubinage for out-group women, has deep roots. In Homer's *Odyssey* (9: 39–61), the hero Odysseus describes his raid on Ismaros: "I pillaged the town and killed the men. The women and treasure . . . I divided as fairly as I could among all hands."[4] The Greek historian Thucydides (fifth century BCE) recorded a dialog between Athenian representatives and delegates from Melos, resisting Athenian control. In the military show-down that resulted, wrote Thucydides, "the Melians surrendered unconditionally to the Athenians"; the latter then "put to death all the men of military age whom they took, and sold the women and children as slaves."[5]

It is impossible to know how common this pattern of gender-selective slaughter of males was, compared with the root-and-branch extermination of every member of the opposing group – women, children, and the elderly along with adult men. (The term "root-and-branch" is also implicitly gendered: the root is the female that gives birth to the branch, the child. Thus, root-and-branch genocides are those that expand *beyond* adult males to remaining sectors of the targeted population.)[6]

In the modern era, gendercides against "battle-age" males have been more frequent than campaigns of root-and-branch annihilation. There is a brutal logic in this. Genocide usually occurs in the context of military conflict, or precipitates it. Males are everywhere those primarily designated to "serve" in the military. A deranged form of military thinking dictates that all men of battle age, whether combatant or non-combatant, are legitimate targets.[7]

In general, then, men are cast as "provocative targets," in Donald Horowitz's phrase:

> Experimental data indicate that provocative targets are more likely victims of aggression than are nonprovocative targets and that aggression may be regarded as less legitimate when the victim is weak or fails to retaliate. Men are attacked in riots and singled out for atrocities much more than women are, just as males are

> attacked more frequently than females are in experiments, and the skewing in both seems positively related to the strength of the target.[8]

As this suggests, there is also a logic to the physical preservation of women. They are deemed to pose no military threat, or a lesser one. They may have value as slaves and/or concubines. In addition, male-dominant society is overwhelmingly *patrilineal*, with descent traced through the father. The woman may be viewed as a "blank slate," able to adopt, or at least provide a conduit for, the ethnicity of a male impregnator; women may even be held to contribute nothing to the genetic mix per se. (This was a prominent theme as recently as the Rwandan genocide of 1994.)[9]

Reflecting such gendered assumptions and social structures, many cultures – perhaps most pervasively those of the Western world between the medieval era and the twentieth century – evolved norms of war that dictated protection for "civilians." This term also assumed gendered connotations, such that even today the phrase "women and children" seems synonymous with "civilian."[10] Of course, once women and children have been removed from the equation, only adult men remain, consigning this group to *non*-civilian status – though degrees of protection may be extended on the basis of (old) age or demonstrable non-combatant status (e.g., handicapped or injured men).

A key question with regard to gender and mass killing is, therefore: Will genocidal forces view the slaughter of "battle-age" males as a sufficient expression of the genocidal impulse? Or will they also target children, women, and the elderly? The resolution to the question usually unfolds sequentially: *once* the younger adult male population group has been targeted, will remaining population groups *then* be slaughtered? Obviously, removing the group most closely associated with military activity, and hence military resistance, makes targeting other group members easier, logistically speaking. It may be much *harder*, however, to motivate genocidal killers to do their work, given norms against targeting these "helpless" populations.

The twentieth and twenty-first centuries have witnessed both core types of genocide, as we have seen throughout this volume. Typical of gendercidal strategies was the war in Bosnia-Herzegovina, with its crowning mass slaughter at Srebrenica (Chapter 8). To the Bosnian case we can add literally dozens of others in which gender selectivity channeled, and significantly limited, the *strictly murderous* dimension of the genocide (which is the critical one, by my preferred definition). They include Bangladesh in 1971, Cambodia between 1975 and 1979, Kashmir/Punjab and Sri Lanka in the 1980s and 1990s, the genocidal massacres of Sikhs in New Delhi in 1984, Saddam Hussein's Anfal campaign against Iraqi Kurds in 1988, Kosovo and East Timor in 1999, and Chechnya, continuing today.[11]

In New Delhi, for example, where more than 5,000 Sikhs died in days of genocidal massacres, the gendered targeting of males was carried to almost surreal extremes:

> The nature of the attacks confirms that there was a deliberate plan to kill as many Sikh men as possible, hence nothing was left to chance. That also explains why in almost all cases, after hitting or stabbing, the victims were doused with kerosene or petrol and burnt, so as to leave no possibility of their surviving. Between October 31 and November 4, more than 2,500 men were murdered in different

> parts of Delhi, according to several careful unofficial estimates. There have been very few cases of women being killed except when they got trapped in houses which were set on fire. Almost all of the women interviewed described how men and young boys were special targets. They were dragged out of the houses, attacked with stones and rods, and set on fire. . . . When women tried to protect the men of their families, they were given a few blows and forcibly separated from the men. Even when they clung to the men, trying to save them, they were hardly ever attacked the way men were. I have not yet heard of a case of a woman being assaulted and then burnt to death by the mob.[12]

Delhi and, with it, Bangladesh, appear in Donald Horowitz's compendium of "deadly ethnic riots," which are closely linked to genocide (see also Chapters 11–12). Horowitz is emphatic about the gender dimension of such slaughters, and his comments may be used without qualification to describe genocide as well:

> While the violence proceeds, there is a strong, although not exclusive, concentration on male victims of a particular ethnic identity. The elderly are often left aside, and sometimes, though less frequently, so are children. Rapes certainly occur in ethnic riots, sometimes a great many rapes, but the killing and mutilation of men is much more common than is the murder or rape of women. Women are sometimes pushed aside or forced to watch the torture and death of their husbands and brothers. . . . Sometimes women are even treated courteously by their husbands' killers.[13]

It is important to point out that targeting "only" adult men is sufficient, under international law, to constitute genocide. This was confirmed in April 2004, when appeal judges of the International Criminal Tribunal for the Former Yugoslavia (ICTY) overturned a 2001 verdict against Bosnian Serb General Radislav Krstic, who had been found guilty "not of genocide but of aiding and abetting genocide" during the Srebrenica massacre. The appeals chamber determined that "by seeking to eliminate a part of the Bosnian Muslims" – those living in Srebrenica, and "the male Muslim" component of that group – genocide had indeed occurred under Krstic's supervision.[14] In its way, the verdict was as significant as that rendered earlier by the International Criminal Tribunal for Rwanda (ICTR) against Jean-Paul Akayesu. This established that the systematic rape of women could be considered genocidal when part of a broader campaign of group destruction (see the discussion of genocidal rape, below).

A very common result of gendercides against men is a glaring demographic disparity in the proportion of surviving women versus men. This is exemplified by cases such as northern Iraq, Cambodia, highlands Guatemala, and Rwanda – although one must be careful in evaluating the extent to which data truly reflect disproportionate male mortality, or alternatively an undercounting of males who may be in exile (as refugees or fighters), or in hiding to escape persecution and evade conscription.[15]

In the "root-and-branch" holocausts that the general public tends to view as the paradigm of genocide, a sequential progression is apparent along the lines described earlier. It is striking that all three of the "classic" genocides of the twentieth century – by the Turks against the Armenians; the Nazis against the Jews; and Hutus against Tutsis – followed roughly this pattern. The time separating the different stages was sometimes brief (in the Nazi case, only a few weeks), and the Rwandan case cannot be incorporated without serious qualification. Readers are invited to peruse the chapter-length treatments of these genocides through a "gendered" lens, to see how the progression from gendercidal to root-and-branch strategies occurred.

As noted in the Jewish Holocaust chapter, the shift from targeting "battle-age" non-combatant males, usually viewed as legitimate targets, to targeting children, women, and the elderly, may result in substantial emotional stress to killers. "While unarmed men seem fair game," wrote Leo Kuper, "the killing of women and children arouses general revulsion"[16] – though not in all situations, and not necessarily for long. Hence the escalation of Nazi killing of Jews, moving from adult males to other population groups;[17] hence, too, the development of distancing technologies such as gas vans and gas chambers, to reduce the trauma for murderers of women and children. One can also note the degeneration of more centralized control over genocidal killing in Rwanda. This appears to have been linked, in part, to concerns of ordinary Hutus that the murder spree was moving beyond acceptable targets.[18]

WOMEN AND GENOCIDE

The focus so far on the mass-murder component of genocide may have the undesirable effect of implying that women are exempted from the worst genocidal violence. Nothing could be further from the truth. First, root-and-branch genocides throughout history have killed tens or hundreds of millions of females. Many structural cases of genocide – such as mass famine, economic embargo, and so on – impact equally or more severely upon women and girls than upon men and boys.

Second, the micro-managed gender strategies employed, for example, at Srebrenica, are fairly rare, especially in the contemporary era of "degenerate war" (see chapters 2, 12). It is more common, as it was even in the Balkans genocides, for women to be exposed to direct abuses and atrocities. While these may be on average less deadly, they are no less "gendered." They range from verbal assault and humiliation, to physical attack and individual rape, to multiple and gang rape (often under conditions of protracted sexual servitude), to rape-murder on a large scale.

In December 1937, one of the most savage instances of genocidal rape inaugurated the so-called Rape of Nanjing. When Japanese forces seized the Chinese capital, up to a *quarter of a million* Chinese men were corraled and massacred, often after torture. Tens of thousands of women were also killed – usually after extended and excruciating gang rape. Kenzo Okamoto, a Japanese soldier, recalled: "We were hungry for women! Officers issued a rough rule: if you mess with a woman, kill her afterwards."[19] Another soldier stated: "Perhaps when we were raping [a female victim], we looked at her as a woman, but when we killed her, we just thought of her as something like a pig."[20] A Chinese eyewitness, Li Ke-hen, described "so many bodies on the street, victims of group rape and murder. They were all stripped naked, their breasts cut off, leaving a terrible dark brown hole; some of them were bayoneted in the abdomen, with their intestines spilling out alongside them; some had a roll of paper or a piece of wood stuffed in their vaginas." Almost no female was safe. Girls as young as 8, and elderly women, were raped and killed. Even those not murdered immediately were liable to be "turned loose in such a manhandled condition that they died a day or two later."[21]

The Japanese rape of women in the Asian-occupied territories featured in the indictment at the postwar Tokyo Tribunal – though the systematic conscription and sexual exploitation of Korean, Indonesian, and other women (the so-called "comfort women")[22] was not addressed. This may be because the victorious powers had overseen somewhat similar systems of female exploitation in their own spheres. Likewise, the mass rapes accompanying the Soviet conquest of eastern Germany in 1944–45 were not mentioned at the Nuremberg war crimes trials of 1945–46: the Soviets would never have permitted it.

Feminist author Susan Brownmiller's book *Against Our Will* (1975) marked the first systematic exploration of rape. It publicized the large-scale sexual violence against Bengali women during the Bangladesh genocide of 1971 (Box 8a), and the social rejection that raped women confronted in the aftermath. It was the Balkans wars of the 1990s, though, that exposed the issue of mass rape of women to international visibility (see the account of 16-year-old "E.," cited in Chapter 8). The term "genocidal rape" began to be widely employed to convey the centrality of sexual assault to the wider campaign of group destruction. Although rejected by some who argued that rape and genocide were distinct crimes, the concept gained further credibility with the horrific events in Rwanda in 1994. As the UN Special Rapporteur on Rwanda, René Degni-Ségui, pointed out, "rape was the rule and its absence the exception" during this genocide.[23] While estimates of women raped in the Balkans genocides ranged between 20,000 and 50,000, in Rwanda they were *ten times* higher – between 250,000 and 500,000. Moreover, as at Nanjing, rape was standardly accompanied by "extreme brutality" above and beyond the specifically sexual assault. "Rape accompanied by mutilation [was] reported to include: the pouring of boiling water onto the genital parts and into the vagina . . . the cutting off of breast(s) and the mutilation of other parts of the female body."[24] And rape was very often followed by death – sometimes (and still) years later, owing to the high proportion of Hutu rapists infected with the HIV virus (see Chapter 9, pp. 246, for one woman's story).

In part as a result of the scale and savagery of the Rwandan rapes, and reflecting years of feminist-inspired mobilization around the issue, in September 1998 the ICTR convicted Jean-Paul Akayesu for acts of genocide including sexual violence. As Human Rights Watch noted, this marked "the first conviction for genocide by an international court; the first time an international court has punished sexual violence in a civil war; and *the first time that rape was found to be an act of genocide [intended] to destroy a group.*"[25]

GENDERCIDAL INSTITUTIONS

An appreciation of female vulnerability to genocide is greatly increased if we expand our framing beyond politico–military genocides, to the realm of "gendercidal institutions." I refer here to patterned behavior, embedded in human societies, that exacts a death-toll sufficiently large in scale and systematic in character to be considered gendercidal.

For females, probably the most destructive such institution throughout history is female infanticide and neonaticide. The selective killing of newborn and infant girls reflects a culturally ingrained preference for male children. A nineteenth-century missionary in China, for example, "interviewed 40 women over age 50 who reported having borne 183 sons and 175 daughters, of whom 126 sons but only 53 daughters survived to age 10; by their account, the women had destroyed 78 of their daughters."[26] The Communist Revolution of 1949 made great strides in reducing discrimination against women and infant girls, but such millennia-old traditions are extremely difficult to root out. Today, numerous reports speak of large demographic disparities between males and females in parts of rural China, leading to widespread trafficking in women and adolescent girls as Chinese men seek to import wives from outside their regions.

The country where female infanticide and neonaticide are most widespread at present is India. For example, a study of Tamil Nadu state by the Community Service Guild of Madras found that "female infanticide is rampant" among Hindu families: "Of the 1,250 families covered by the study, 740 had only one girl child and 249 agreed directly that they had done away with the unwanted girl child. More than 213 of the families had more than one male child whereas half the respondents had only one daughter."[27] Among wealthier families in both India and China, however, infanticide is being replaced by sex-selective abortion, following *in utero* screening procedures that have spread even to isolated rural areas.

Among other gendercidal institutions targeting females, we can cite gendered deficiencies in nutrition and health care (reflecting the prioritizing of male family members for these resources); "honor" killings of women and girls, particularly in the Middle East, South Asia, and the Caucasus; and dowry killings and *sati* in India, the former referring to murders of young women whose families cannot provide sufficient dowry payments to the family of their designated spouse, while the latter institution consigns women to die on the funeral pyres of their husbands.

Gendercidal institutions have also targeted males throughout history, and exacted a vast death-toll. Military conscription is an outstanding example. Less widely known is *corvée* (forced) labor, which is both intimately related to and analytically distinct from military conscription. *Corvée* has overwhelmingly targeted adult men throughout history, killing in all likelihood hundreds of millions. There are grounds, in fact, for considering *corvée* to be the most destructive of all human institutions, even outpacing war. Ironically, forced labor remains legal today under the relevant international convention – but only when its targets are able-bodied adult males between the ages of 18 and 45.[28]

GENOCIDE AND VIOLENCE AGAINST HOMOSEXUALS

The phenomenon of discrimination and violence against homosexuals – especially gay men – is still pervasive. It is linked to the collective policing of gender, in which those who opt out of heterosexuality are seen as "asocial" threats. In the Nazi case (Box 6a), gay males were viewed as violating eugenic tenets. While the mentally handicapped were "useless eaters," gays were condemned as superfluous for their "failure" to help replenish the *Völk*.

Perhaps only in the Nazi case has violence against homosexual men attained a scale and systematic character that might be considered genocidal. Still, a glance around today's world shows the many ways that violence against gays exists along the genocidal continuum proposed by Nancy Scheper-Hughes (Chapter 11). For example, gay males – especially male prostitutes, the transgendered, and drag queens – are at extraordinary risk of vigilante-style killings in some Latin American societies. In Colombia between 1986 and 1990, "328 gay men were murdered in the city of Medellín alone."[29] More generally, Amnesty International reports, sampled by Stefanie Rixecker, demonstrate that a wide range of violence is "directed at queer individuals based upon their actual or perceived sexual preference":

> The types of abuses range from complaints of ill treatment while in police custody to rape, sexual abuse, sexual realignment surgery, extrajudicial executions and disappearances, and state-sanctioned execution. The murder of gays and lesbians due to their sexuality, or to associated behaviors and illnesses (e.g. HIV and AIDS), not only means that the individuals are targeted, but also – due to the relatively small numbers of gays and lesbians – becomes tantamount to genocide and now, more specifically, gendercide. Although a full complement of the gay community is not murdered in such acts, the relatively small statistical populations of gays and lesbians overall means that the annual toll of queer identities can be regarded as a genocidal act.[30]

A further connection may be drawn between the targeting of homosexuals and the specific strategies of torture, mutilation, and murder employed in most genocides. Both women and men are liable to be attacked in ways that violate and annihilate their normal sexual roles: women through genocidal rape, genital mutilation, ripping of fetuses from wombs; men by similar strategies of genital mutilation, sexual torture, *and genocidal rape.*[31] In cases of male-on-male rape, it is generally only the victim that is rendered "feminine" and imputedly homosexual. The male rapist preserves his safe heterosexual identification and, in perverse fashion, may even bolster it through sexual violation of another man.

ARE MEN MORE GENOCIDAL THAN WOMEN?

The most cursory examination of classical and contemporary genocides shows that the overwhelming majority of genocidal planners, killers, and rapists are men, just as men predominate as architects and wagers of war. There is also the lesser, but still striking, disproportion of men among murderers worldwide (especially mass and serial murderers). One wonders, in fact, whether for many people, a *sufficient* explanation of genocide (and war, and murder) would not be simply: "Boys will be boys." Likewise, when we focus on disproportionate male *victimization*, at least for genocide's most lethal strategies, patterns of intra-male competition and conquest seem significant. They are evident not only in most human societies, as anthropologists have shown, but among the higher primates that are humanity's closest relatives.[32]

Explanations for these tendencies and uniformities have spawned enduring, interdisciplinary, and so far inconclusive debates. There is no space to deal with these in detail here; I offer only a few observations.[33]

First, male dominance among killers' ranks is the result of global *patriarchy* – "rule by the fathers," that is, rule by men as heads of family units and by older and more powerful men within communities, rather than rule by men as an undifferentiated gender class. It is usually the patriarchs who decide to wage war and genocide. To this end, they must mobilize younger, subordinate males to inflict the actual violence. In addition, they, assisted by women as mothers and nurturers, must educate, train, and prepare younger generations of males to serve as soldiers, *génocidaires*, and cannon-fodder. This rite of passage qualifies them, if they survive, to join patriarchal ranks.

Men must thus be *shaped* and often *coerced* to perform violent tasks. The long, little-studied history of masculine resistance to military conscription, and the brutality of the "basic training" to which conscripts are generally exposed, suggest that a more peaceable disposition must be broken down and reconstructed for warlike or genocidal purposes.

A second question then presents itself: What happens when women are similarly *mobilized, forced, encouraged, allowed* to participate in genocide and other violence? Readers' minds might leap to the revelations from Abu Ghraib prison near Baghdad, where female guards were prominent as agents of abuse. The scholar of genocide, moreover, encounters the direct involvement of women at many points in history: torturing and executing prisoners-of-war (as was standard in Native American civilizations); joining men in attacking and pillaging refugee convoys (as Kurdish women did in the Armenian genocide); and actively involving themselves in "euthanasia" killings and concentration-camp atrocities under the Nazis (female camp guards "murdered as easily [as men]; their sadism was no less," notes James Waller).[34] This does not reckon with more diffuse and indirect forms of participation: providing moral and material support to male combatants and *génocidaires*; ostracizing males who seek to evade involvement in slaughter;[35] and providing political support, sometimes exceeding that of men, for violent and dictatorial leaders.[36]

There is, finally, a "Rwanda test" to apply to female participation in genocide. In the holocaust of 1994, Hutu women, uniquely in recorded history, were mobilized *en masse* as participants in genocide. "I had seen war before, but I had never seen a woman carrying a baby on her back kill another woman with a baby on her back," said a stunned officer with the United Nations Assistance Mission for Rwanda (UNAMIR).[37] Women also assumed leadership positions at national, regional, and local levels – as with Pauline Nyiramasuhuko, indicted by the International Criminal Tribunal for Rwanda (ICTR) for "personally direct[ing] squads of Hutu men to torture and butcher Tutsi men, and to rape and mutilate Tutsi women."[38] In light of this evidence, it may be that "the challenge for future research is to transcend our gendered expectations that women are basically innocent by nature, so that their acts of cruelty are viewed as deviant and abnormal, and approach their perpetration of extraordinary evil the same way we have men – as ordinary people influenced by dispositional, situational, and environmental factors."[39]

A NOTE ON GENDERED PROPAGANDA

A useful application of a gender perspective in genocide studies is to genocidal propaganda, so central in mobilizing populations to support and commit atrocities. This issue may be approached from various angles.

If men, overwhelmingly, must be mobilized to do the "dirty work" of genocidal killing, how are their gender sensibilities exploited? Perhaps the most common strategy is to accuse males who evince qualms about participation of being cowards – failed bearers of masculinity. A Rwandan official visiting a commune that was deemed "negligent" in its genocidal duties demanded to know "if there were no more men there, meaning men who could deal with 'security' problems."[40] Men who "shirked" their duties were denounced in terms little less venomous than those employed against Tutsis: "What are those sons of dogs fleeing from?"[41]

Men's designated role as "protectors" of women and children fuels potent propaganda strategies. Nazi troops dispatched to the fire-storm of the eastern front were exposed to speeches from their commanders, demanding to know "what would have happened had these Asiatic Mongol hordes succeeded to pour into . . . Germany, laying the country waste, plundering, murdering, raping?"[42] By implication, the German troops were justified in laying waste, plundering, murdering, and raping, as they did to an extent unseen since the days of the "Mongol hordes."

Women are generally cast in supporting roles in genocidal campaigns. Propaganda directed at them emphasizes their role as guardians of home and children. This has the added advantage of bolstering the self-image of males as protectors of (passive, defenseless) "womenandchildren."

A further important aspect of genocidal propaganda is the demonization of out-group men as a prelude to gender-selective round-ups and mass killing. The classic case is the construction of the "Eternal Jew" in Nazi propaganda, which paved the way for the Holocaust of 1941–45. This propaganda entrenched an image of the "wretched, disgusting, horrifying, flat-footed, hook-nosed dirty Jew"[43] – virtually always a *male* Jew. As Joan Ringelheim notes: "Legitimation for targeting Jewish men was plentiful in Nazi anti-Semitic and racist propaganda and, more to the point, in Nazi policy. The decision to kill every Jew did not seem to demand special justification to kill Jewish men. They were already identified as dangerous," thanks to years of grotesque imagery such as that depicted in Figure 13.1. "This was not so for Jewish women and children."[44] It comes as little surprise, then, that adult male Jews were the first to be rounded up and executed *en masse* on the eastern front, as a means of acclimatizing the killers to subsequent root-and-branch genocide.

In a similar vein, consider the language typically directed at population groups to mark them out for persecution or genocide: terms such as "monster," "beast/bestial," "devil/demon," "bandit," "criminal," "rapist," "terrorist," "swindler," "vagabond," "subhuman," "vermin," "exploiter". . . . Now, though the task be unpleasant, assign

Figure 13.1 Poster for the Nazi propaganda exhibition *Der Ewige Jude* (The Eternal Jew), 1937. The sinister-looking male Jew is shown as addicted to lucre (the coins in his outstretched hand), oppressive (the whip in the other), and allied with international communism (Germany with the hammer-and-sickle crooked under his arm). Depictions of out-group males as dangerous and malevolent are central to both genocidal propaganda and gendercidal massacre.

Source: Hoover Institution Archives Poster Collection.

Figure 13.2 "General Dallaire and his army have fallen into the trap of fatal women." Tutsi women, with badges/tattoos of support for the FPR (Rwandan rebel forces), are depicted seducing UN force commander Gen. Roméo Dallaire in this cartoon from the Hutu Power propaganda paper *Kangura* (February 1994). Genocidal propaganda against women often emphasizes their imputed sexual powers; in the Rwandan case, this paved the way for massive sexual violence against Tutsi women during the 1994 genocide.

Source: From Christopher Taylor, *Sacrifice as Terror: The Rwandan Genocide of 1994* (Oxford: Berg, 1994).

a human face to these caricatures. Is it a male or a female face that automatically leaps to mind?[45]

When women are targeted in genocidal and proto-genocidal propaganda, this tends to occur (1) on a lesser scale, (2) with a lesser variety of imagery, and (3) with a heavy concentration on the female's imputed sexual power (including her reproductive capacity) (Figure 13.2). Hence the regular use of terms such as "seducer," "prostitute," "whore," "baby factory." This emphasis on sexual power and capacity no doubt fuels the rampant sexual violence against women and girls, including extreme humiliation and savage mutilation, that is a standard feature of genocidal campaigns. Women, and men, may also be targeted for their supposed links to the supernatural ("witch" and, relatedly, "baby-killer").

The implicit gendering of much genocidal propaganda seems fundamental to marshaling support for gendercide and all-out genocide. As such, it would seem to have implications for strategies of genocide prevention. I return to this subject in the book's concluding chapter.

FURTHER STUDY

African Rights, *Rwanda: Not So Innocent: When Women Become Killers.* London: African Rights, 1995. Taboo-shattering account of women's participation in the 1994 genocide.

Gendercide Watch, www.gendercide.org. Educational website featuring two dozen detailed case studies of gendercide.

Michael P. Ghiglieri, *The Dark Side of Man: Tracing the Origins of Male Violence.* Cambridge, MA: Perseus Books, 2000. Argues that men are biologically programmed to wage war and commit genocide.

Joshua S. Goldstein, *War and Gender: How Gender Shapes the War System and Vice Versa.* Cambridge: Cambridge University Press, 2001. Wide-ranging inter-disciplinary overview.

Human Rights Watch, *Shattered Lives: Sexual Violence During the Rwanda Genocide and Its Aftermath.* New York: Human Rights Watch, 1996. Examines the targeting of women for rape in the Rwandan holocaust; available on the Web at http://hrw.org/reports/1996/Rwanda.htm.

Adam Jones, ed., *Gendercide and Genocide.* Nashville, TN: Vanderbilt University Press, 2004. The most wide-ranging book on gender-selective killing.

Claudia Koonz, *Mothers in the Fatherland: Women, the Family and Nazi Politics.* New York: Basic Books, 1987. Intensive inquiry into the diverse roles of German women under Nazism.

Rohit Lentin, ed., *Gender and Catastrophe.* London: Zed Books, 1997. Essays on the gendering of genocide, slavery, poverty, and famine, with an emphasis on women.

Lois Ann Lorentzen and Jennifer Turpin, eds, *The Women and War Reader.* New York: New York University Press, 1998. Solid anthology of writings on women's victimization and agency in wartime.

Caroline O.N. Moser and Fiona C. Clark, eds, *Victims, Perpetrators or Actors? Gender,*

Armed Conflict and Political Violence. London: Zed Books 2001. Groundbreaking edited collection.

Elenor Richter-Lyonette, ed., *In the Aftermath of Rape: Women's Rights, War Crimes, and Genocide.* Givrins: Coordination of Women's Advocacy, 1997. Examines genocidal rape, with emphasis on the Balkans and Rwandan cases.

Alexandra Stiglmayer, ed., *Mass Rape: The War against Women in Bosnia-Herzegovina.* Lincoln, NB: University of Nebraska Press, 1995. The standard source on sexual violence against women in the Balkans wars.

Klaus Theweleit, *Male Fantasies, Volume 1: Women, Floods, Bodies, History,* trans. Stephen Conway. Minneapolis, MN: University of Minnesota Press, 1987. Profound psychoanalytical study of fascism and masculinity.

Mary Anne Warren, *Gendercide: The Implications of Sex Selection.* Totowa, NJ: Rowman & Allanheld, 1985. Coined the term "gendercide," though with a focus on reproductive technologies.

NOTES

1 See, e.g., R. Charli Carpenter, "Beyond 'Gendercide': Operationalizing Gender in Comparative Genocide Studies," in Adam Jones, ed., *Gendercide and Genocide* (Nashville, TN: Vanderbilt University Press, 2004), pp. 230–56, esp. pp. 232–38.

2 Joshua Goldstein, *War and Gender* (Cambridge: Cambridge University Press, 2001), p. 2.

3 For instance, Mary E. Hawkesworth writes: "In principle, a gendered practice could privilege men or women. But the history of male dominance has resulted in systematic male power advantages across diverse social domains. Feminist usage of the adjective 'gendered' reflects this male power advantage. *Hence a gendered practice is synonymous with androcentric* [male-centered] *practice* in common feminist terminology." Hawkesworth, "Democratization: Reflections on Gendered Dislocations in the Public Sphere," in R.M. Kelly *et al.*, eds, *Gender, Globalization, and Democratization* (Lanham, MD: Rowman & Littlefield), p. 235, n. 2; emphasis added.

4 See the excerpts in Kurt A. Raaflaub, hand-out for Brown University Classics course (CL56), "War and Society in the Ancient World," http://www.brown.edu/Departments/Classics/CL56/CL56_HO1.html.

5 Thucydides, *The Peloponnesian War,* quoted in Frank Chalk and Kurt Jonassohn, *The History and Sociology of Genocide: Analyses and Case Studies* (New Haven, CT: Yale University Press, 1990), p. 73.

6 See Adam Jones, "Why Gendercide? Why Root-and-Branch? A Comparison of the Vendée Uprising of 1793–94 and the Bosnian War of the 1990s," *Journal of Genocide Research,* 8: 1 (2006), pp. 9–25.

7 A disturbing strand of just-war theory even justifies gender-selective extermination of males. The Enlightenment philosopher Vitoria stated: "Everyone able to bear arms should be considered dangerous . . . they may therefore be killed unless the opposite is clearly true." Michael Walzer wrote: "a soldier who, once he is engaged, simply fires at every male villager between the age of 15 and 50 . . . is probably justified in doing so." Vitoria quoted in R. Charli Carpenter, "'Women and Children First': Gender, Norms, and Humanitarian Evacuation in the Balkans 1991–95," *International Organization,* 57: 4 (fall 2003), p. 672; Walzer quoted in Carpenter, "Beyond 'Gendercide,'" p. 252, n. 13.

8 Donald L. Horowitz, *The Deadly Ethnic Riot* (Berkeley, CA: University of California Press, 2001), p. 148. Horowitz adds that "In experiments, males are also more selective

in their choice of targets; females distribute shocks more equally among targets. Perhaps selective targeting itself is a sex-skewed phenomenon"; that is, males are more likely to aggress against males selectively and disproportionately than are women (p. 148).

9 See Adam Jones, "Gender and Genocide in Rwanda," in Jones, ed., *Gendercide and Genocide*, p. 111.

10 See R. Charli Carpenter, "'Women, Children and Other Vulnerable Groups': Gender, Strategic Frames and the Protection of Civilians as a Transnational Issue," *International Studies Quarterly*, 49 (2005), pp. 295–334.

11 Most of these cases receive extended treatment on the Gendercide Watch site, http://www.gendercide.org. A question commonly asked is whether in such cases, men are being targeted "as a group" or "as such," rather than (for example) as combatants or potential combatants. The question is a valid one, in part because it is the case that *gender always combines with other variables* to produce genocidal outcomes. The most obvious are *ethnicity/nationality/race/religion/perceived political affiliation* (that is, there is no targeting of males as a global gender group, but rather of males belonging to one of these designated groups); *age* (with "battle-age" males more liable to be targeted than very young or very old ones); *community prominence* (the disproportionate representation of men among elites means that when "eliticides" occur, as in Burundi in 1972, the victims are overwhelmingly male); and *perceived military capacity* (given the prevailing cultural and practical identification of males with combatants). Often implicit in the question, however, is the notion that women and girls *are* victimized "as such" – primarily because they are female. In my view, this is untenable. When women are the victims of politico–military genocide, it is similarly on the basis of their ethnicity, perceived political affiliation, and so on (or because of their family relationship with men of these designated groups). The Nazis who killed Jewish women *en masse* did not kill German women – in fact, their slaughter of the Jews was often justified by the supposed need to protect German women. Even in the cases where a misogynistic worldview seems predominant, other variables are crucial. Female infanticide does not target females as a group, but rather those of a particular age, and usually of a particular (poorer) social class. The European witch-hunts of the medieval and early modern era, which resulted in a death-toll about 75 percent female, likewise did not designate all women as targets, but women perceived as a threat for their supposed liaisons with dark powers. *Age* and *marital status* were other important variables, with the majority of women designated as "witches" being older and more likely to be widows. Clearly, however, the gender variable is decisive in all these cases – as it is in the case of gendercidal killings of men. Finally, does the gendered hatred of women – misogyny – that factors in all these cases have a counterpart for male victims (misandry)? I contend that it does, and that it is evident, for example, in gendered propaganda. For further discussion, see Adam Jones, "Problems of Gendercide," in Jones, ed., *Gendercide and Genocide*, pp. 257–71.

12 Madhu Kishwar, "Delhi: Gangster Rule," in Patwant Singh and Harji Malik, eds, *Punjab: The Fatal Miscalculation* (New Delhi: Patwant Singh, 1985), pp. 171–78.

13 Horowitz, *The Deadly Ethnic Riot*, pp. 73, 123, n. 261.

14 Ian Traynor, "Hague Rules Srebrenica was Genocide," *Guardian*, April 20, 2004. http://www.guardian.co.uk/international/story/0,3604,1195429,00.html. See also the comments by Daniel Goldhagen concerning the Nazis' early gendercidal massacres of Jewish males on the Eastern front: "Even if . . . the initial order was to kill 'only' teenage and adult Jewish males – the order was still genocidal and clearly was understood by the perpetrators as such. . . . The killing of the adult males of a community is nothing less than the destruction of that community." Daniel J. Goldhagen, *Hitler's Willing Executioners: Ordinary Germans and the Holocaust* (New York: Vintage, 1997), p. 153.

15 See, e.g., the discussion of the Rwandan case in Jones, "Gender and Genocide in Rwanda," pp. 123–25; and of the Cambodian case in May Ebihara and Judy Ledgerwood, "Aftermaths of Genocide: Cambodian Villagers," in Alexander Laban Hinton, ed., *Annihilating Difference: The Anthropology of Genocide* (Berkeley, CA: University of California Press, 2002), pp. 275–80.

16 Leo Kuper, *Genocide: Its Political Use in the Twentieth Century* (London: Penguin, 1981), p. 46. Richard Rhodes also notes that "Men prepared to kill victims who are manifestly unthreatening – the elderly, unarmed women, small children, infants – behave differently from men prepared to kill victims such as men of military age who can be construed to be at least potentially dangerous." Rhodes, *Masters of Death: The SS-Einsatzgruppen and the Invention of the Holocaust* (New York: Alfred A. Knopf, 2002), p. 69. According to Rhodes (p. 167), the Nazis even "established mental hospitals and rest areas" to care for SS men "'who [had] broken down while executing women and children.'"

17 See the analysis of this escalation in Goldhagen, *Hitler's Willing Executioners*, pp. 149–51.

18 On this phenomenon, see Jones, ed., *Gendercide and Genocide*, pp. 24–25, 117–18.

19 James Yin and Shi Young, *The Rape of Nanking: An Undeniable History in Photographs* (Chicago, IL: Triumph, 1996), p. 188.

20 Iris Chang, *The Rape of Nanking: The Forgotten Holocaust of World War Two* (London: Penguin, 1998), pp. 49–50.

21 Historian David Bergamini, quoted in Yin and Young, *The Rape of Nanking*, p. 195.

22 Following the Japanese invasion of Manchuria in 1931, the Japanese army began to construct a network of hundreds of "comfort stations" across the occupied territories, "dup[ing] or forc[ing] Korean, Taiwanese, Chinese, Indonesian, Filipino, Japanese and Dutch women to work in them." Estimates of the number seized and exploited in this fashion range between 140,000 and 200,000. The "comfort women" experienced treatment that "was almost universally barbaric. They were forced to have sex with as many as 50 men a day, some were tied to beds with their legs open, and many were beaten by drunken soldiers." See Velisarios Kattoulas, "No Comfort for the Women," *Far Eastern Economic Review*, March 15, 2001. According to George Hicks, "The comfort system consisted of the legalised military rape of subject women on a scale – and over a period of time – previously unknown in history." Hicks, *The Comfort Women: Japan's Brutal Regime of Enforced Prostitution in the Second World War* (New York: W.W. Norton, 1994), pp. 16–17. Relatively few "comfort women" died as a direct result of Japanese mistreatment; most fatalities resulted from disease, or from Allied bombardments. Nonetheless, the death rate was high: about one in every six "comfort women" died during their period of servitude, according to Hicks. Those who survived faced continued shame and suffering upon their return home, and "for the most part kept silent about their experiences" until recent times, when they began to seek compensation for their suffering from the Japanese government (Hicks, *The Comfort Women*, pp. 164–65).

23 Quoted in Elenor Richter-Lyonette, "Women after the Genocide in Rwanda," in Richter-Lyonette, ed., *In the Aftermath of Rape: Women's Rights, War Crimes, and Genocide* (Givrins: Coordination of Women's Advocacy, 1997), p. 107.

24 Richter-Lyonette, "Women after the Genocide," p. 107.

25 "Human Rights Watch Applauds Rwanda Rape Verdict," Human Rights Watch press release, September 2, 1998, http://www.hrw.org/press98/sept/rrape902.htm; emphasis added. See also Teaching Human Rights Online, "Rape and Genocide in Rwanda: The ICTR's Akayesu Verdict," http://homepages.uc.edu/thro/rwanda/RwandaRapeCase2.htm.

26 Ansley J. Coale and Judith Banister, "Five Decades of Missing Females in China," *Demography*, 31: 3 (August 1994), p. 472.

27 Malavika Karlekar, "The Girl Child in India: Does She Have Any Rights?," *Canadian Woman Studies*, March 1995.

28 For detailed case studies of gendercidal institutions against females and males, see the Gendercide Watch website.

29 Amnesty International UK report, *Breaking the Silence*, cited in Stefanie Rixecker, "Genetic Engineering and Queer Biotechnology: The Eugenics of the Twenty-first Century?," in Jones, ed., *Gendercide and Genocide*, p. 188. See also media and human rights reportage on persecution and prosecutions of gay men in Egypt, e.g., Josh

Hammer, "One Man's Tale," *Newsweek*, February 16, 2002; "Egypt: Crackdown on Homosexual Men Continues," Human Rights Watch press release, 7 October 2003. http://hrw.org/press/2003/10/egypt100703.htm.

30 Rixecker, "Genetic Engineering and Queer Biotechnology," p. 188.

31 Men raped and sexually tortured in detention received no such attention. For discussion of the phenomenon, focusing on the Balkans case, see Augusta Del Zotto and Adam Jones, "Male-on-Male Sexual Violence in Wartime: Human Rights' Last Taboo?," paper presented to the Annual Convention of the International Studies Association (ISA), New Orleans, LA, March 23–27, 2002, available at http://adamjones.freeservers.com/ malerape.htm; and related observations in Adam Jones, "Straight as a Rule: Heteronormativity, Gendercide, and the Non-combatant Male," *Men and Masculinities*, forthcoming (2006).

32 For an argument along these lines, see Michael P. Ghiglieri, *The Dark Side of Man: Tracing the Origins of Male Violence* (Cambridge, MA: Perseus Books, 2000). Ghiglieri draws on studies of chimpanzee behavior, as well as psychological experiments, to support his assertion that "men are born ethnocentric and xenophobic by nature. Men bond along kin lines and/or via reciprocal altruisim to fight and kill other men genetically more distant from them in genocidal wars aimed at seizing or usurping what those other men possess, including the reproductive potential of their women" (p. 215).

33 The best and most readable overview of the debates, drawing on the hard-scientific as well as social-scientific literatures, is Goldstein, *War and Gender*, chs 3–4.

34 James Waller, *Becoming Evil: How Ordinary People Commit Genocide and Mass Killing* (Oxford: Oxford University Press, 2002), p. 300, n. 12.

35 "In Britain and America during [the] war, women organized a large-scale campaign to hand out white feathers to able-bodied men found on the streets, to shame the men for failing to serve in combat. . . . The white feather campaign was briefly resurrected in World War II, and the British government had to issue badges for men exempt on medical grounds." Goldstein, *War and Gender*, p. 272. "Many feminists, such as England's Isabella Pankurst, set the struggle for suffrage aside for an equally militant jingoism, and contented themselves with organizing women to support the war effort. 'The war is so horribly exciting but I cannot live on it,' one British suffragette wrote. 'It is like being drunk all day.'" Barbara Ehrenreich, *Blood Rites: Origins and History of the Passions of War* (New York: Metropolitan Books, 1997), p. 13.

36 It seems that at least as many women as men, perhaps more, supported Hitler and the Nazi regime; Tim Mason writes that "a variety of different sources convey the impression that in the later 1930s the Third Reich enjoyed a large measure of active and passive support among women, *a larger measure than it gained from among men*" (quoted in Robert Gellately, *Backing Hitler: Consent and Coercion in Nazi Germany* [Oxford: Oxford University Press, 2001], p. 16). Gellately explains this as follows: "Conservative, Catholic, and even liberal women by and large shared the point of view advocated by the Nazis, as to a 'naturally' determined sexual division of labour, and that it was important to reconstruct a 'community of the people' in which they would be involved primarily as wives and mothers, and 'not be forced to compete with men for scarce jobs and political influence'" (p. 10, citing Ute Frevert, *Women in German History*). Owing to gender-separated voting booths, we also know that more women than men voted in favor of perpetuating Augusto Pinochet's dictatorial rule in Chile in a 1989 plebiscite; "51% of women and 58% of men voted 'no'" to the dictator. (See the fine documentary, *In Women's Hands*, PBS/Annenberg Project, *Americas* series, 1993; statistic available at http://www.rit.edu/~cakgss/inwomenshands.html.) In both cases, one wonders whether the fact that it was overwhelmingly men who were targeted for harassment, detention, incarceration, torture, and murder by the regimes in question (the Jewish Holocaust apart) may have prompted a greater proportion of men to express opposition to those regimes when it was safe to do so. Finally, the recent prominence of women in the proto-genocidal Hindu-extremist movement in India has received increasing scholarly attention: see Parita Mukta's fascinating treatment, "Gender, Community and Nation," in Susie Jacobs *et al.*,

eds, *States of Conflict: Gender, Violence and Resistance* (London: Zed Books, 2000), pp. 163–78.

37 Quoted in Alison Des Forges, *Leave None to Tell the Story: Genocide in Rwanda* (New York: Human Rights Watch, 1999), p. 261. For numerous examples, see the groundbreaking African Rights report, *Rwanda: Not So Innocent: When Women Become Killers* (London: African Rights, 1995).

38 Kimberlee Acquaro and Peter Landesman, "Out of Madness, A Matriarchy," *Mother Jones*, January/February 2003. Available at http://www.motherjones.com/news/featurex/2003/01/ma_spc_01.html. The article is a good overview of women's position in Rwanda after the genocide, including the "unplanned – if not inadvertent – movement of female empowerment driven by national necessity." The trial of Nyiramasuhuko was ongoing at the time of writing (September 2005).

39 Waller, *Becoming Evil*, p. 301, n. 12.

40 Quoted in Des Forges, *Leave None to Tell the Story*, p. 459.

41 Quoted in African Rights, *Rwanda: Death, Despair and Defiance* (rev. edn) (London: African Rights, 1995), p. 82.

42 Commander of the Wehrmacht's II Corps to his troops, late December 1941; quoted in Omer Bartov, *Hitler's Army: Soldiers, Nazis, and War in the Third Reich* (New York: Oxford University Press, 1992), p. 132.

43 Saul Friedländer, *Nazi Germany and the Jews, Volume 1: The Years of Persecution, 1933–1939* (New York: HarperCollins, 1997), p. 124.

44 Joan Ringelheim, "Genocide and Gender: A Split Memory," in Ronit Lentin, ed., *Gender and Catastrophe* (London: Zed Books, 1997), p. 19. See also the heavily gendered depiction of the Jew in Adolf Hitler's *Mein Kampf* (Boston, MA: Houghton Mifflin, 1943), pp. 300–27.

45 See the discussion in Adam Jones, "Genocide and Humanitarian Intervention: Incorporating the Gender Variable," *Journal of Humanitarian Assistance*, February 2002, http://www.jha.ac/articles/a080.htm.

PART 4 THE FUTURE OF GENOCIDE

CHAPTER 14

Memory, Forgetting, and Denial

> Memory is life. It is always carried by groups of living people, and therefore it is in permanent evolution. It is subject to the dialectics of remembering and forgetting, unaware of its successive deformations, open to all kinds of use and manipulation. . . . Memory always belongs to our time and forms a lived bond with the eternal present.
>
> Pierre Nora

THE STRUGGLE OVER HISTORICAL MEMORY

"You speak about history," Soviet dictator Joseph Stalin told a gathering of his subordinates. "But one must sometimes correct history."[1] Never was that task pursued with more surreal dedication than under Stalin. Old photographs were doctored to eliminate Stalin's former Bolshevik colleagues, now labeled "saboteurs" and "enemies of the people" (see Chapter 5). The history of the Communist Party was rewritten to accord Stalin a central and heroic role. Inconvenient evidence was expunged, such as Lenin's warning shortly before his death that Stalin should be distrusted and marginalized. When the Nazi–Soviet pact was signed in August 1939, the erstwhile epitome of evil – the fascist German regime – became a friend and business partner. Less than two years later, Germany had launched the most destructive invasion of all time against the Soviet Union. Overnight, the Soviet people and official history had to shift again to accommodate total war against the former friend (and, before that, enemy).

As satirized by George Orwell in *Nineteen Eighty-Four*, Stalinism and other totalitarianisms have become classic cases of the manipulation of history and memory. Usually, however, things are not as clear-cut as dictatorial imposition. Rather, memory and history reflect an ongoing contestation and evolution, within both societies and individual hearts and minds.

To appreciate better the contested terrain that is human memory, consider the country where much of this book was written: Argentina. In 1976, against a backdrop of mounting social and economic chaos, a military regime under General Jorge Rafael Videla took power. A state of siege was declared. For the next seven years, Videla and his fellow generals presided over the most brutal of South America's modern military dictatorships. Between 10,000 and 30,000 people – suspected of involvement with leftist guerrillas, or of vaguer subversions – were "disappeared" by the authorities. Generally, they were tortured to death or executed; many of the bodies were dumped out of airplanes and into the Atlantic Ocean off the Argentine coast. Pregnant detainees were often allowed to give birth before being killed; the infants were then turned over to be adopted by military families.[2]

In 1982, following Argentina's defeat by Great Britain in the war over the Falkland Islands,[3] military rule began to crumble. In 1983, the state of siege was abrogated, and free elections were held. Raúl Alfonsín of the Radical Civic Union (UCR) was sworn in as president in December. That month also saw the creation of the National Commission on Disappeared People (CONADEP), which investigated the fate of those who vanished under the military regime. Its report was released in 1984 under the title *Nunca Más* (Never Again) – echoing the call of those who memorialize the Jewish Holocaust. The report "catalogued 8,960 unresolved 'disappearances,' but warned that the true figure might be higher. It also listed 340 clandestine abduction centres in Argentina, which it said were in use at the height of the repression."[4] In Argentina, the events are regularly referred to as "genocide," although this designation would be disputed by many genocide scholars.[5]

Of the state detention facilities, the most notorious was the Naval Mechanics School in the Palermo suburb of Buenos Aires (see Figure 14.1). Over time, the movement to memorialize the disappeared and compensate survivors began to push for the creation of a museum on the forty-two-acre property. In 2004, the government of Nelson Kirchner bowed to the pressure. It expropriated the site and declared it would house a "Museum of Memory," to educate current and future generations about the period of state terror.

But what memories, and whose, should be reflected? Was this form of memorialization even appropriate, with the atrocities still fresh in the national consciousness? An account by journalist Larry Rohter in the *New York Times* described "sharp differences" over these issues among human-rights activists.[6] The Mothers of the Plaza de Mayo had gathered throughout the military dictatorship in the central square of Buenos Aires, demanding information and the return of disappeared loved ones. Some members of the group argued that "museums mark the end of a story, and we haven't reached that point in Argentina yet," in the words of one leader, Hebe de Bonafini. "It's much too soon to be setting up a museum, because the historical events in question are too recent." Other organizations, however, strongly supported the project. One, called *Memoria Abierta* (Open Memory), set to work compiling an

Figure 14.1 The Naval Mechanics School in the Buenos Aires suburb of Palermo, Argentina, where hundreds of victims of the country's "Dirty War" (1976–83) were interned, tortured, and murdered by the military dictatorship. Today, as the banner hanging between the pillars proclaims, it is being turned into a "Memory Space" (*Espacio para la Memoria*). But for whose memory?

Source: Author's photo, 2005.

archive of over 4,000 photographs and a range of oral histories for deposit in the museum. According to Patricia Valdez, director of Memoria Abierta: "We do not want this museum for ourselves, but for Argentine society. It has to be a place that transcends the fluctuations of Argentine politics and lets the facts speak for themselves."

Even among those who generally supported the initiative, the appropriate range and limits of this "memory space" (*espacio para la memoria*) aroused controversy. In announcing the museum's creation on March 24, 2004, the anniversary of the 1976 *coup d'état*, President Kirchner "seemed to be suggesting that the focus will be on the military dictatorship that dominated the country from 1976 to 1983." Kirchner was leader of the Peronist Party, whose activists had been targeted in the so-called "Dirty War." But Peronism, too, stood accused of substantial atrocities during the 1970s. They included the formation of paramilitary organizations and death squads blamed for some 300 murders, as well as bombings and kidnappings. Limiting the museum's coverage to the 1976–83 period "would only distort historical realities," argued the Peronists' opponents.

Then there were the military leaders. Some had been tried and jailed after the return of democracy. After a series of "demonstration coups" by disgruntled military officers, in 1985 President Alfonsín declared a *punto final* (full stop) to the prosecutions. Those already jailed were pardoned by his Peronist successor, Carlos Menem, who declared he was acting in the interests of national unity and reconciliation.[7]

Predictably, some in the military rejected the museum initiative, opining (in the words of one senior officer) that it marked "not a closure or a healing of a wound, but the opening of another." Air force commander General Carlos Alberto Rhode claimed "there were errors and horrors by both camps" – the government and the small guerrilla movement that fought it during the years of *junta* rule. But some military personnel dissented, feeling the time had come to acknowledge past atrocities. Admiral Jorge Godoy, commander of the Argentine navy, pointedly described the Naval Mechanics School as "a symbol of barbarity and irrationality," the site of "aberrant acts, offensive to human dignity, ethics and law."

The debate over the Museum of Memory typifies what Elizabeth Jelin has called "'legitimacy' struggles over memory – who has what rights to determine what should be remembered and how":

> Such moments of contestation over commemorations and memorials are markers which provide clues to the processes of remembrance at the subjective and the symbolic levels, where the memories of different social actors are enacted and become "the present," making it easier to analyze the construction of collective, social and public memories.

But at these points, Jelin adds, "memories are multiple and at times in conflict."[8] In large part, this reflects one's positioning in the historical drama. Is one an older person, with direct memories of the events? Is one younger, seeking to uncover the secrets of one's elders, or alternatively to "let the past take care of the past" and move on? Is one a former collaborator with the repressive regime, anxious to justify the collaboration retrospectively, or to mitigate personal guilt through confession and public repentance? Is one a victim of the regime who feels that personal suffering constitutes "the basic determinant of legitimacy and the claim to truth"?[9] Or does suffering mean that one is unable to adopt an "objective" approach to the events?

The answers to these questions tell us something about how individual identities are constructed through selective memory (as all memory is). Cumulatively, they also say a great deal about how a society remembers, and *why* it remembers: that is, with what collective or public purpose.[10] To understand this more deeply, let us consider the German encounter with the history of massive Nazi atrocities against Jews and others – as well as the suffering and destruction inflicted on Germans by the Allies.

Germany and "the search for a usable past"

Germany's reckoning with its Nazi past may be divided into three principal stages. The first, extending from the war's end to about the mid-1960s, was one of willful amnesia, as Germans sought to put the war behind them. It has been argued that this act of politicized forgetting (see further below) was significant in allowing West Germans to build a prosperous and democratic state, while in Soviet-controlled East Germany, Nazi sins could be displaced onto "fascism," with the new communist entity heroicized accordingly. In West Germany, to the extent that victims were memorialized and commemorated, they were overwhelmingly *German* victims – such as the hundreds of thousands of German POWs who remained in Soviet camps, in many cases into the 1950s. The West German government under Konrad Adenauer did initiate substantial reparations payments to Jews in the form of financial transfers to Israel. This met with some public opposition. However, most Germans seem to have welcomed it as a means of bolstering their alliance with the West, rather than as an *entrée* to memorialization of Jewish suffering and German guilt.

The upheavals of the 1960s radically destabilized this historical narrative. Survivors and scholars of the genocide against the Jews explored the Holocaust systematically for the first time. German scholars asserted historical continuities between the Nazi and post-Nazi periods, including the role of large corporate enterprises that had managed the transition smoothly from fascism to democracy. Some younger Germans made pilgrimages to Israel to atone for the sins of their forebears. The *Schuldfrage* (guilt issue) had taken center stage, symbolized by Chancellor Willi Brandt's famous kneeling apology for Nazi crimes (the so-called *Kniefall*) on a July 1970 visit to Poland.[11] In academia, the ferment spilled over into the *Historikerstreit* (historians' debate) of the 1970s and 1980s, "a scholarly controversy over the place and significance of National Socialism and the Holocaust in the narrative of modern German history."[12] An older generation concerned with maintaining, for example, a distinction between Nazi and German army practice, was confronted by mostly younger scholars who challenged the assumptions and evasions of their seniors (see also Chapter 6).

This second stage saw the German and Nazi past problematized, rendered more complex and disturbing to ordinary Germans. It was prone to "irruptions of memory" of the kind described by Alexander Wilde. These are "public events that break in upon [the] national consciousness, unbidden and often suddenly, to evoke associations with symbols, figures, causes, ways of life which to an unusual degree are associated with a political past that is still present in the lived experience of a major part of the population."[13] One such irruption belonged to the realm of popular culture: the broadcast of the US television mini-series *Holocaust*, which offered Germans perhaps their first sustained depiction of the persecution of the Jews under Nazism. Another was the visit of US President Ronald Reagan to the Bitburg military cemetery, where German soldiers, including SS officers, were interred. The German soldiers were "victims of Nazism also," Reagan proclaimed. "They were victims, just as surely as the victims in the concentration camps."[14] His comments sparked a furor, among US military veterans as well as among Jewish intellectuals and activists. In

Germany, they provoked intense public discussion over whether Jewish and German victimization should be mentioned in the same breath.

A third, somewhat amorphous stage began in the 1990s, in the wake of the *Historikerstreit*, and carried over into the new millennium. It centered on the public debate over three controversial books. Daniel Jonah Goldhagen's *Hitler's Willing Executioners* accused "ordinary Germans" of perpetrating many of the genocidal atrocities of the Second World War. The book attracted a massive audience in Germany, especially among the younger generation. Günter Grass' *Im Krebsgang* (*Crabwalk*), meanwhile, described events at the end of the war, when the *Wilhelm Gustloff* cruise liner was torpedoed by a Soviet submarine, killing thousands of German civilian refugees. Lastly, Jörg Friedrich's *Brandstätten* (*Fire Sites*) provided grisly photographic evidence of the effects of Allied fire-bombing of German cities. (See Box 6a for more on Grass' and Friedrich's books.) Friedrich ably described the public's response to his book in terms that emphasized the emotional stress of repressing memories, and the catharsis of their expression:

> The bombing left an entire generation traumatised. But it was never discussed. There are Germans whose first recollections are of being hidden by their mothers. They remember cellars and burning human remains. It is only now that they are coming to terms with what happened. . . . [But] Germans in their seventies and eighties have not forgotten. Their memories are still vivid. People stand up in my public lectures and describe what befell their families. They have tears in their eyes and they can't breathe.[15]

Also significant was the late 1990s controversy over a traveling exhibition of photographs, organized by the Hamburg Institute for Social Research, that provided vivid and chilling evidence of German army participation in atrocities against Jews, Soviet prisoners-of-war, and others. The erstwhile distinction between Nazi "evil" and army "honor" was no longer tenable.[16]

Can a new, usable collective memory or public history be constructed out of these diverse strands and fragments? Robert Moeller, a leading scholar of the subject, appears to believe so. He favors narratives that "move beyond a language in which the categories of victim and perpetrator were mutually exclusive," seeking instead "to capture the complexities of individual lives and 'mass fates' by exploring how during the Third Reich it was possible both to suffer and to cause suffering in others."[17] But this project, it is fair to say, is only just beginning.

THE POLITICS OF FORGETTING

Forgetting – memory's intimate partner – may also be examined in its individual and collective dimensions. As Jörg Friedrich's comments above attest, individuals may seek to forget because it is painful to remember, or because they are convinced that no one will listen respectfully to their stories. Such was the case with many survivors of the Armenian and Jewish holocausts, who spent decades after the events seeking to consign them to the historical past and build new lives. Forgetting may represent a final stage of revision and reinterpretation, to cancel any dissonance with one's preferred self-image. A common strategy is to displace others' victimization onto oneself. Atrocities that one may have perpetrated, supported, or ignored are crowded out by memories of personal and collective victimization, whether experienced or imagined.

At a societal level, "memorycide" – Mirko Grmek's term – transfers to the collectivity the struggle within individual souls. Nations seek to glorify the past, forgetting its unsavory aspects. In the epilog to *Gulag*, her epic study of the Soviet concentration camps (Chapter 5), Anne Applebaum notes the unwillingness of post-Soviet Russians to come to terms with their twentieth-century history. The extent of popular complicity in repression is one reason: "Society is indifferent to the crimes of the past because so many people participated in them," according to Alexander Yakovlev, chair of a commission seeking to rehabilitate those unjustly convicted. In addition, adds Applebaum, "the dominance of former communists [in present-day governments] and the insufficient discussion of the past in the post-communist world is not coincidental." And forgetting may be useful for facilitating new bouts of repression:

> Acting in the name of the Soviet motherland, Stalin deported the Chechen nation to the wastes of Kazakhstan, where half of them died and the rest were meant to disappear, along with their language and culture [see Chapter 5]. Fifty years later, in a repeat performance, the Russian federation obliterated the Chechen capital, Grozny, and murdered tens of thousands of Chechen civilians in the course of two wars [see Box 5a]. If the Russian people and the Russian elite remembered – viscerally, emotionally remembered – what Stalin did to the Chechens, they could not have invaded Chechnya in the 1990s, not once and not twice. To do so was the moral equivalent of post-war Germany invading western Poland. Very few Russians saw it that way – which is itself evidence of how little they know about their own history.[18]

What is forgotten, there is no need to deny; but this is often not such a simple proposition. Irruptions of memory, struggles over historical interpretation, mean that inconvenient and dissonant evidence is always in danger of resurging to challenge societies' and individuals' most cherished perspectives. Where these challenges prove intolerable a new framework may be constructed – or a systematic campaign of denial mounted.

GENOCIDE DENIAL: MOTIVES AND STRATEGIES

Denial is viewed increasingly as a final stage of genocide, and an indispensable one from the viewpoint of the *génocidaires*. "The perpetrators of genocide dig up the mass graves, burn the bodies, try to cover up the evidence and intimidate the witnesses. They deny that they committed any crimes, and often blame what happened on the victims."[19] As Richard Hovannisian has written:

> Following the physical destruction of a people and their material culture, memory is all that is left and is targeted as the last victim. Complete annihilation of people requires the banishment of recollection and the suffocation of remembrance. Falsification, deception, and half-truths reduce what was to what may have been or perhaps what was not at all.[20]

The phenomenon of genocide denial is overwhelmingly associated with the Jewish Holocaust. Since this resurged in the public consciousness in the early 1960s, a diverse and interlinked network of Holocaust deniers has arisen. In Europe, a centuries-old tradition of anti-semitism (see Chapter 6) underlies their activities, which overlap with neo-Nazi violence against Jews and their property. In North America, the neo-Nazi element is also strong. In both "wings" of the denialist movement, however, academic figures – such as Arthur Butz in the US, David Irving in Great Britain, and Robert Faurisson in France – have also sought to provide a veneer of respectability for the enterprise.

We will consider specific denial strategies below, but before we do, it is important to stress that the Jewish Holocaust is not officially denied by any state or national elite (though denial is common intellectual currency in the Arab and Muslim world).[21] Thus, in the West at least, deniers of the Jewish catastrophe remain relatively marginal figures, with little access to the mainstream.

However, the broader phenomenon of genocide denial is far more deeply entrenched, often representing a societal consensus rather than a fringe position. Individual and collective narcissism (Chapter 10) play a pivotal role in buttressing denial; in many contexts, a denialist stance heads off cognitive dissonance between one's preferred view of self and country, and the grimmer reality. There is also usually an element of material self-interest. Denial can pay well, since it fortifies the status quo and serves powerful and prosperous constituencies, both political and corporate. Positive rewards are combined with sanctions. Failure to deny (that is, a determination to acknowledge) may result in the loss or denial of employment; decreased social standing; dismissal as a "kook" and a "radical"; and so on.

Among the most common discourses of genocide denial are the following:

"Hardly anybody died." Reports of atrocities and mass killings are depicted as exaggerated and self-serving. (The fact that some reports *are* distorted and self-interested lends credibility to this strategy.) Photographic and video evidence is dismissed as fake or staged. Gaps in physical evidence are exploited, particularly an absence of corpses. Where are the bodies of the Jews killed by the Nazis? (Incinerated, conveniently for the deniers.) Where are the bodies of the supposed thousands of Kosovars killed by Serbs in 1999? (Buried on military and police bases, or dumped in rivers and down mineshafts, as it turned out.) When the genocides lie far in the past, obfuscation is easier. Genocides of indigenous peoples are especially subject to this form of denial. In many cases, the groups in question suffered near-total extermination, leaving few descendants and advocates to press the case for truth.

"It was self-defense." Murdered civilians – especially adult males (Chapter 13) – are depicted as "rebels," "brigands," and "terrorists." The state and its allies are justified in eliminating them, though unfortunate "excesses" may occur. Deniers of the Armenian genocide, for example, play up the presence of armed elements and resistance among the Armenian population – even clearly defensive resistance. Likewise, deniers of Nazi genocide against Jews turn cartwheels to demonstrate "that *Weltjudentum* (world Jewry) had declared war on Germany in 1933, and the Nazis, as the ruling party of the nation, had simply reacted to the threat."[22] Jews were variously depicted as predatory capitalists, decadent cosmopolitans, and architects of global communism. The organizers of the third "classic" genocide of the twentieth century, in Rwanda, alleged that the assault on Tutsis was a legitimate response to armed invasion by Tutsi rebels based in Uganda, and the supposed machinations of a Tutsi "fifth column" in Rwanda itself.

A substrategy of this discourse is the claim that ***"the violence was mutual."*** Where genocides occur in a context of civil or international war, they can be depicted as part of generalized warfare, perhaps featuring atrocities on all sides. This strategy is standard among the deniers of genocides by Turks, Japanese,[23] Serbs, Hutus, and West Pakistanis – to name just a few. In Australia, Keith Windschuttle has used killings of whites by Aboriginals to denounce "The Myths of Frontier Massacres in Australian History."[24] (See also "*We* are the real victims," below.) Sometimes the deniers seem actually oblivious to the content of their claims, reflecting deeply embedded stereotypes and pervasive ignorance, rather than malicious intent. As I write these words, a CNN International reporter has just referred to the world standing by and "watch[ing] Hutus and Tutsis kill each other" during the Rwanda genocide of 1994.[25]

"The deaths weren't intentional." The difficulties of demonstrating and documenting genocidal intent are exploited to deny that genocide occurred. The utility of this strategy is enhanced where a longer causal chain underlies massive mortality. Thus, when diverse factors combine to cause death, or when supposedly "natural" elements such as disease and famine account for many or most deaths, this denialist discourse is especially appealing. It underpins most denials of indigenous genocides, for example (see Chapter 3). Deniers of the Armenian and Jewish holocausts also contend that most deaths occurred from privations and afflictions that were inevitable, if regrettable, in a wartime context – in any case, not genocidal.

"There was no central direction." Frequently, states and their agents establish a degree of deniability by employing freelance agents such as paramilitaries (as in Bosnia-Herzegovina and Darfur), criminal elements (e.g., the *chétés* in the Armenian genocide), or members of the targeted groups themselves (Jewish *kapos* in the Nazi death camps; Mayan peasants conscripted for genocide against Mayan populations of the Guatemalan highlands). State attempts to eliminate evidence may mean that documentation of central direction, as of genocidal intent, is scarce. Many deniers of the Jewish Holocaust emphasize the lack of a clear order from Hitler or his top associates to exterminate European Jews. Armenian genocide denial similarly centers on the supposed freelance status of those who carried out whatever atrocities are admitted to have occurred.

"There weren't that many people to begin with." Where demographic data provide support for claims of genocide, denialists will gravitate towards the lowest available figures for the targeted population, or invent new ones. The effect is to cast doubt on mortality statistics by downplaying the victims' demographic weight at the outbreak of genocide. This strategy is especially common in denials of genocide against indigenous peoples, as well as the Ottoman genocide against Armenians.

"It wasn't / isn't 'genocide,' because . . ." Here, the ambiguities of the UN Genocide Convention are exploited, and combined with the denial strategies already cited. Atrocious events do not qualify as "genocide" . . . because the victims were not members of one of the Convention's specified groups; because their deaths were unintended; because they were legitimate targets; because "only" specific sectors of the target group were killed; because "war is hell"; and so on.

"We would never do that." Collective pathological narcissism (see Chapter 10) occludes the acknowledgment, or even the conscious consideration, of genocide. When the state and its citizens consider themselves pure, peaceful, democratic, and law-abiding, responsibility for atrocity may be literally unthinkable. In Turkey, notes Taner Akçam, anyone "dar[ing] to speak about the Armenian Genocide . . . is aggressively attacked as a traitor, singled out for public condemnation and may even be put in prison."[26] In Australia, "the very mention of an Australian genocide is . . . appalling and galling and must be put aside," according to Colin Tatz. "A curious national belief is that simply being Australian, whether by birth or naturalisation, is sufficient inoculation against deviation from moral and righteous behaviour."[27] Comedian Rob Corddry parodied this mindset in the context of US abuses and atrocities at Abu Ghraib prison near Baghdad. "There's no question what took place in that prison was horrible," Corddry said on *The Daily Show with Jon Stewart*. "But the Arab world has to realize that the US shouldn't be judged on the actions of a . . . well, we shouldn't be judged on actions. It's our principles that matter, our inspiring, abstract notions. Remember: just because torturing prisoners is something we did, doesn't mean it's something we *would* do."[28]

"We are the real victims." For deniers, the best defense is often a strong offense. With its "Day of Fallen Diplomats," Turkey uses Armenian terrorist attacks against Turkish diplomatic staff to pre-empt attention to the Turkish genocide against Armenians. In the case of Germany and the Nazi holocaust, there is a point at which a victim mentality concentrating on German suffering leads to the horrors that Germans inflicted, on Jews and others, being downgraded or denied. In the Balkans, a discourse of genocide was first deployed by Serb intellectuals promoting a nationalist–xenophobic project; the only "genocide" admitted was that against Serbs, whether by Croatians in the Second World War (which indeed occurred), or in Kosovo at the hands of the Albanian majority (which was a paranoid fantasy). Notably, this stress on victimhood provided powerful fuel for unleashing the genocides in the first place; the discussion of humiliation in Chapter 10 is worth recalling here.[29]

DENIAL AND FREE SPEECH

What are the acceptable limits of denialist discourse in a free society? Should *all* denial be suppressed? Should it be permitted in the interest of preserving a liberal public sphere?

In recent years, many countries in the West have grappled with these questions. Varied approaches have been adopted, ranging from monitoring denialist discourse, to punitive measures including fines, imprisonment, and deportation. At the permissive end of the spectrum lies the United States. There, notorious deniers of the Jewish Holocaust, as well as neo-Nazi and Ku Klux Klan-style organizations, operate mostly unimpeded, albeit sometimes surveilled and infiltrated by government agents. A much harder line has been enforced in France and Canada. In France, Holocaust denier Robert Faurisson was stripped of his university teaching position and hauled before a court for denying that the Nazi gas chambers had existed. Eventually, in July 1981, the Paris Court of Appeals assessed "personal damages" against Faurisson, based on the likelihood "that his words would arouse in his very large audience feelings of contempt, of hatred and of violence towards the Jews in France."[30]

In Canada, Alberta teacher Jim Keegstra "for twelve years . . . indoctrinated his students with Jewish conspiracy explanations of history . . . biased statements principally about Jews, but also about Catholics, Blacks, and others."[31] His passage through the Canadian justice system was labyrinthine. In 1982, Keegstra was dismissed from his job and, in 1984, charged with promoting racial hatred. In 1985, he was convicted, and sentenced to five months in jail and a $5,000 fine. The decision was overturned by the Alberta Court of Appeal, however, citing Canada's Charter of Rights and Freedoms; but Canada's Supreme Court subsequently ruled (narrowly) that hate speech was *not* constitutionally protected. In 1992, Keegstra was retried in Alberta and convicted. Once again, the conviction was overturned on appeal, this time on procedural grounds. At the time of writing, it was possible the case would be heard a second time before the Supreme Court of Canada.[32]

Undoubtedly the most famous trial involving a genocide denier is the libel case brought in 2000 by David Irving, an amateur historian of some early repute who nonetheless cast doubt and aspersions on the genocide of the Jews. Deborah Lipstadt accused Irving of genocide denial in her book *Denying the Holocaust*, referring to him as a "discredited" scholar and "one of the most dangerous spokespersons for Holocaust denial."[33] She also pointed to his links with neo-fascist figures and movements. Irving exploited Britain's loose libel laws to file a suit for defamation. The resulting trial became a *cause célèbre*, with prominent historians taking the stand to outline Irving's evasions and obfuscations of the historical evidence, as well as the character of his personal associations. The final, 350-page judgment by Judge Charles Gray cited Irving for nineteen specific misrepresentations, and contended that they were deliberate distortions to advance a denialist agenda. Irving's suit was dismissed, leaving him with a two-million-pound bill for legal costs – though he was subject to no legal sanction per se.

The spectrum of policies towards deniers, from permissive to prosecutory, is mirrored by the debate among genocide scholars. Those who call for punitive measures against deniers stress the link between denial and genocide, including future genocides, as well as the personal suffering that denial inflicts on a genocide's survivors and their descendants. This argument is made eloquently by Roger Smith, Eric Markusen, and Robert Jay Lifton, who hold that:

> denial of genocide [is] an egregious offense that warrants being regarded as a form of contribution to genocidal violence. Denial contributes to genocide in at least two ways. First of all, genocide does not end with its last human victim; denial

> continues the process, but if denial points to the past and the present, it also has implications for the future. By absolving the perpetrators of past genocides from responsibility for their actions and by obscuring the reality of genocide as a widely practiced form of state policy in the modern world, denial may increase the risk of future outbreaks of genocidal killing.

They especially condemn the actions of some professional scholars in bolstering various denial projects:

> Where scholars deny genocide, in the face of decisive evidence that it has occurred, they contribute to a false consciousness that can have the most dire reverberations. Their message, in effect, is: murderers did not really murder; victims were not really killed; mass murder requires no confrontation, no reflection, but should be ignored, glossed over. In this way scholars lend their considerable authority to the acceptance of this ultimate human crime. More than that, they encourage – indeed invite – a repetition of that crime from virtually any source in the immediate or distant future. By closing their minds to truth such scholars contribute to the deadly psychohistorical dynamic in which unopposed genocide begets new genocides.[34]

The opposing view does not dispute the corruption of scholarship that genocide denial represents. However, it rejects the authority of the state to punish "speech crimes"; it stresses the arbitrariness that governs *which* genocide denials are prohibited; and it calls for proactive engagement and public denunciation in place of censorship and prosecution. A leading exponent of such views is the political scholar and commentator Noam Chomsky, whose most bitter controversy revolves around a defense of the right of Robert Faurisson to air his denialist views. In an essay titled "Some Elementary Comments on the Rights of Freedom of Expression," published (without his prior knowledge) as a Foreword to Faurisson's *Mémoire en défense*, Chomsky depicted calls to ban Faurisson from teaching, even to physically attack him, as in keeping with authoritarian tradition:

> Such attitudes are not uncommon. They are typical, for example, of American Communists and no doubt their counterparts elsewhere. Among people who have learned something from the 18th century (say, Voltaire) it is a truism, hardly deserving discussion, that the defense of the right of free expression is not restricted to ideas one approves of, and that it is precisely in the case of ideas found most offensive that these rights must be most vigorously defended. Advocacy of the right to express ideas that are generally approved is, quite obviously, a matter of no significance. . . . Even if Faurisson were to be a rabid anti-Semite and fanatic pro-Nazi . . . this would have no bearing whatsoever on the legitimacy of the defense of his civil rights. On the contrary, it would make it all the more imperative to defend them.[35]

Each of these perspectives brings important ideas to the table. To expand on Smith *et al.*'s reasoning: in most societies, some speech is subject to legal sanction – libelous, threatening, and obscene speech, for instance. It can reasonably be asked whether genocide denial does not do greater harm to society, and pose a greater threat, than personal libels or dirty words. Is not genocide denial a libel against an entire people? And is the threat it poses not extreme, given that denial may sow the seeds of future genocides?

The case is a powerful one, and yet I find myself generally in agreement with Chomsky. Free speech *only* has meaning at the margins. Banning marginal discourses undermines liberal freedoms. Moreover, only a handful of deniers – principally those assailing the Jewish and Armenian holocausts – have attracted controversy for their views. The president (François Mitterrand) of the same French state that prosecuted Robert Faurisson not only actively supported Rwanda's *génocidaires* – before, during, and after the 1994 catastrophe – but when asked later about the genocide, responded: "The genocide or the genocides? I don't know what one should say!" As Gérard Prunier notes, "this public accolade for the so-called 'theory of the double genocide' [i.e., by Tutsis against France's Hutu allies, as well as by Hutus against Tutsis] was an absolute shame."[36] It advanced a key thesis of genocide deniers: that the violence was mutual or defensive in nature. But Mitterrand's words were widely ignored; he was certainly in no danger of being arraigned before a tribunal. Likewise, the Canadian state that prosecuted Jim Keegstra was the same that shamefully "dodged implementation of the Genocide Convention" by "quietly redefining the crime in the country's domestic enforcement statute so as to omit any mention of policies and actions in which Canada was and is engaged," specifically its genocide against native peoples.[37] *Quis custodiet custodiens* – who will judge the judges?

One wonders, as well, whether the names and mendacious views of people such as Irving, Faurisson, and Keegstra would be remotely as prominent, if prosecutions and other measures had not been mounted against them.[38] (Indeed, it makes me queasy to print them here.) These individuals, and the initiatives they sponsor, are best confronted with a combination of monitoring, marginalization, and effective public refutation. Such refutation can be accomplished by visible and vocal denunciation, informed by conscientious reportage and scholarship, as well as through proactive campaigns in schools and the mass media.

While genocide denial in the public sphere may be destructive, for genocide scholars and students its consequences may actually be productive. Professional deniers have spurred scholarship in areas that otherwise might not have attracted it.[39] Moreover, not all "denial" is malevolent. Whether a genocide framework should be applied in a given case is often a matter of lively *and legitimate* debate. In recent decades, the character and content of mass killing campaigns in Bosnia and Kosovo, Darfur, Biafra (Nigeria), East Timor, Guatemala, and Vietnam have been intensively analyzed and hotly disputed. I believe this is to be encouraged, even though I find some of the views expressed to be disturbing and disheartening. Keeping denial of *all* genocides out of the realm of crime and punishment may be the price we pay for this vigorous exchange.[40]

FURTHER STUDY

Stanley Cohen, *States of Denial: Knowing about Atrocities and Suffering*. Cambridge: Polity Press, 2001. Acute insights into denial, and efforts to counter it, on both personal and societal levels.

Richard J. Evans, *Lying About Hitler: History, Holocaust, and the David Irving Trial*. New York: Basic Books, 2001. Briskly paced account of Irving's defamation suit, by a historian who served as a defense witness.

John R. Gillis, ed., *Commemorations: The Politics of National Identity*. Princeton, NJ: Princeton University Press, 1994. How collective memory shapes national identity.

Jeffrey Herf, *Divided Memory: The Nazi Past in the Two Germanies*. Cambridge, MA: Harvard University Press, 1997. Intricate rendering of Germany's "search for a usable past."

Richard G. Hovannisian, ed., *Remembrance and Denial: The Case of the Armenian Genocide*. Detroit, MI: Wayne State University Press, 1999. Seminal essays on Armenian genocide denial and its place in collective memory.

Deborah E. Lipstadt, *Denying the Holocaust: The Growing Assault on Truth and Memory*. New York: Plume, 1994. Survey of denial's exponents that prompted David Irving's failed legal action against Lipstadt.

David E. Lorey and William H. Beezley, eds, *Genocide, Collective Violence, and Popular Memory: The Politics of Remembrance in the Twentieth Century*. Wilmington, DE: Scholarly Resources, 2002. The best introduction to genocide and memory.

Peter Novick, *The Holocaust in American Life*. Boston, MA: Mariner Books, 2000. Fascinating exploration of how the Jewish Holocaust was remembered and deployed by American Jews and others.

George Orwell, *Nineteen Eighty-four*. London: Penguin, 1983. Dark satire of the manipulation of history and memory under totalitarianism.

Michael Shermer, *Denying History: Who Says the Holocaust Never Happened and Why Do They Say It?* (rev. edn). Berkeley, CA: University of California Press, 2000. Richly documented rebuttal of deniers of the Jewish Holocaust.

Jay Winter, *Sites of Memory, Sites of Mourning: The Great War in European Cultural History*. Cambridge: Canto, 1998. History, memory, and memorialization in post-First World War Europe.

NOTES

1 Simon Sebag Montefiore, *Stalin: The Court of the Red Tsar* (London: Phoenix, 2004), p. 142.

2 The two best English-language overviews are Martin Edwin Andersen, *Dossier Secreto: Argentina's Desaparecidos and the Myth of the "Dirty War"* (Boulder, CO: Westview Press, 1993), and Paul H. Lewis, *Guerrillas and Generals: The "Dirty War" in Argentina* (Westport, CT: Praeger Publishers, 2002). A concise summary from a genocide studies perspective is "The Disappearances: Mass Killing in Argentina," ch. 14 in Ervin Staub, *The Roots of Evil: The Origins of Genocide and Other Group Violence* (Cambridge:

Cambridge University Press, 1989), pp. 210–31. The kidnapping of infants was the subject of an Oscar-winning Argentine film, *The Official Story* (1985).

3 The Falkland Islands are known as Islas Malvinas to Argentines.

4 Amnesty International, "Argentina: The Military Juntas and Human Rights," in William L. Hewitt, ed., *Defining the Horrific: Readings on Genocide and Holocaust in the Twentieth Century* (Upper Saddle River, NJ: Pearson, 2004), p. 247.

5 In November 2003, together with a small group of other foreign scholars, I attended what was probably the first international conference on genocide in South America, held at the University of Buenos Aires. At a guess, 75 or 80 percent of the presentations dealt with the "genocide in Argentina" under military rule. Without exception, all the presenters took it as a given that the events in question had constituted genocide. This would be much more controversial among genocide scholars in the West, given the limited number of victims, and the fact that the violence was targeted against alleged members of a political group. In conversation with some of the Argentine scholars, though, it became clear to me that not only did they consider the term valid, but they regarded its application as *vital to memorializing the events and validating victims' suffering.*

6 Larry Rohter, "Debate Rises in Argentina on Museum of Abuses," *New York Times*, April 19, 2004. Unless otherwise specified, all quotes in this discussion of the Museum of Memory are drawn from Rohter's article.

7 However, *junta* leader General Videla was jailed in June 1997 for the kidnapping of children, which was held to lie beyond the boundaries of the *punto final.*

8 Elizabeth Jelin, "The Minefields of Memory," *NACLA Report on the Americas*, 32: 2 (September/October 1998), p. 25. Martha Minow writes: "Memorials can name those who were killed; they can depict those who resisted and those who rescued. They can accord honor and confer heroic status; they can express shame, remorse, warning, shock. Devoting public space to memories of atrocities means devoting time and energy to decisions about what kinds of memories, images, and messages to embrace, critique, and resist. . . . Vividly capturing and recasting memory, fights over monuments in the streets and in debates usefully disturb congealed memories and mark important junctions between the past and a newly invented present." Minow, *Between Vengeance and Forgiveness: Facing History after Genocide and Mass Violence* (Boston, MA: Beacon Press, 1998), pp. 138, 140.

9 Jelin, "The Minefields of Memory," pp. 26, 28.

10 For some nuanced and cautionary comments on public memory, see Jay Winter, "The Generation of Memory: Reflections on the 'Memory Boom' in Contemporary Historical Studies," *GHI Bulletin*, 27, http://www.ghi-dc.org/bulletin27F00/b27winter.html.

11 For text and a vivid photograph, see "Encyclopedia: Warschauer Kniefall," Nation Master.com, http://www.nationmaster.com/encyclopedia/Warschauer-Kniefall. "The event made Brandt widely unpopular in Germany, especially among conservatives and liberals but also many social democrats, and he was heavily criticized by the press for being unpatriotic. . . . Eventually, [however,] even many Germans came to see it as a courageous and honorable decision."

12 Robert G. Moeller, "War Stories: The Search for a Usable Past in the Federal Republic of Germany," in Lorey and Beezley, eds, *Genocide, Collective Violence, and Popular Memory*, pp. 206, 211.

13 Alexander Wilde, "Irruptions of Memory: Expressive Politics in Chile's Transition to Democracy," in Lorey and Beezley, eds, *Genocide, Collective Violence, and Popular Memory*, p. 4.

14 Quoted in Moeller, "War Stories," p. 210. On Bitburg, see also Jeffrey Herf, *Divided Memory: The Nazi Past in the Two Germanys* (Cambridge, MA: Harvard University Press, 1997), pp. 350–54.

15 Friedrich quoted in J.M. Coetzee, "Victims" (review of Günter Grass, *Crabwalk*), *New York Review of Books*, June 12, 2003.

16 See the companion volume for the exhibition: Hamburg Institute for Social Research,

The German Army and Genocide: Crimes Against War Prisoners, Jews, and Other Civilians in the East, 1939–1944 (New York: New Press, 1999).

17 Moeller, "War Stories," p. 216.

18 Anne Applebaum, *Gulag: A History* (London: Penguin, 2004), pp. 508–10.

19 Gregory H. Stanton, "Eight Stages of Genocide," http://www.genocidewatch.org/8stages.htm.

20 Richard G. Hovannisian, "Denial of the Armenian Genocide in Comparison with Holocaust Denial," in Hovannisian, ed., *Remembrance and Denial: The Case of the Armenian Genocide* (Detroit, MI: Wayne State University Press, 1999), p. 202.

21 For a summary, with many examples, see Anti-Defamation League, "Holocaust Denial in the Middle East: The Latest Anti-Israel Propaganda Theme," http://www.adl.org/holocaust/denial_ME/Holocaust_Denial_Mid_East_prt.pdf.

22 Michael Shermer and Alex Grobman, *Denying History: Who Says the Holocaust Never Happened and Why Do They Say It?* (Berkeley, CA: University of California Press, 2002), p. 40.

23 Japanese denial of its genocidal atrocities against the Chinese and other Asian peoples during the Second World War is one of the most notorious and best-studied cases. "Japan has always presented itself as the victim of the war and has consistently ignored and repressed any attempts to focus on its aggression and war crimes. . . . The Japanese government and society have conducted an intensive and successful repression of any information about the war in which Japan is not presented as a peace-loving nation or in which anything negative about its history is mentioned." Elazar Barkan, *The Guilt of Nations: Restitution and Negotiating Historical Injustices* (New York: W.W. Norton, 2000), pp. 50, 60. Japanese governments and education authorities have persistently depicted the Japanese invasion and occupation of its "Greater Asian Co-prosperity Sphere" as a defensive response to a campaign of US economic warfare and political isolation; downplayed the horrors of events such as the Nanjing Massacre of 1937–38 (see Chapter 2); and played up Japanese suffering at Allied hands, especially in the area-bombing raids and atomic attacks. For an overview, see Gavan McCormack, "Reflections on Modern Japanese History in the Context of the Concept of Genocide," ch. 16 in Robert Gellately and Ben Kiernan, eds, *The Specter of Genocide: Mass Murder in Historical Perspective* (Cambridge: Cambridge University Press, 2003), pp. 265–88.

24 For a summary and debunking, see Ben Kiernan, "Cover-up and Denial of Genocide: Australia, the USA, East Timor, and the Aborigines," *Critical Asian Studies*, 34: 2 (2002), pp. 180–82.

25 CNN International broadcast, December 31, 2004.

26 Taner Akçam, *From Empire to Republic: Turkish Nationalism and the Armenian Genocide* (London: Zed Books, 2004), p. 209.

27 Colin Tatz, *With Intent to Destroy: Reflecting on Genocide* (London: Verso, 2003), p. 137.

28 Corddry quoted in Alan Shapiro, "American Treatment of Iraqi and Afghan Prisoners: An Introduction," TeachableMoment.org, http://www.teachablemoment.org/high/prisoners.html.

29 A grimly ironic variation on this theme is the exceptionalist approach adopted by some victims of genocide or their descendants, claiming an "exclusivity of suffering" at the expense of other victim groups. Hence, for many years a tacit understanding prevailed among politically powerful sectors of Turkish and Israeli society to marginalize the Armenian genocide by proclaiming the uniqueness and incommensurability of the Jewish Holocaust. Thea Halo has contended, in turn, that too many scholars, activists, and scholar-activists have focused so intensively on Armenian suffering during and after the First World War that they have effectively denied comparable atrocities inflicted by the Ottomans upon other Christian populations of their realm, notably Assyrians and Pontic Greeks. Halo writes: "The expropriation of an evil so egregious and monumental, strips the other nameless victims of that same monumental evil, of their rightful place in history, as if they never existed, thereby assuring that their Genocide is complete." Halo,

"The Exclusivity of Suffering: When Tribal Concerns Take Precedence over Historical Accuracy," unpublished research paper, 2004.

30 Paris court judgment cited in Shermer and Grobman, *Denying History*, pp. 10–11.

31 David Bercuson and Douglas Wertheimer, quoted in Luke McNamara, "Criminalising Racial Hatred: Learning from the Canadian Experience," *Australian Journal of Human Rights*, 1: 1 (1994). Available online at http://www.austlii.edu.au/au/other/ahric/ajhr/V1N1/ajhr1113.html.

32 See McNamara, "Criminalising Racial Hatred." The case of Ernst Zündel, a German-born denier of the Jewish Holocaust, has also attracted polemics in recent years. Zündel became "a political hot potato to immigration officials in Canada and the United States." Moving from Canada to the US when the Canadian government denied his application for citizenship, Zündel was then deported back to Canada, and then on to Germany, where he sits in prison at the time of writing. See CBC News Online, "Indepth: Ernst Zundel," September 30, 2004, http://www.cbc.ca/news/background/zundel/; "Holocaust Denier Behind Bars in Germany," CTV.ca, March 2, 2005.

33 Richard J. Evans, *Lying About Hitler: History, Holocaust, and the David Irving Trial* (New York: Basic Books, 2001), p. 6. Evans was one of the historians who testified at the trial; his book provides an excellent overview of the proceedings.

34 Roger W. Smith, Eric Markusen, and Robert Jay Lifton, "Professional Ethics and the Denial of the Armenian Genocide," in Hovannisian, ed., *Remembrance and Denial*, pp. 287, 289.

35 Noam Chomsky, "Some Elementary Comments on the Rights of Freedom of Expression," http://www.zmag.org/chomsky/articles/8010-free-expression.html. Much controversy attached to Chomsky's comment in this essay that "As far as I can determine, he [Faurisson] is a relatively apolitical liberal of some sort."

36 Gérard Prunier, *The Rwanda Crisis: History of a Genocide* (New York: Columbia University Press, 1997), p. 339.

37 "Thus, the [UN] convention's prohibitions of policies causing serious bodily or mental harm to members of a target group and/or effecting the forcible transfer of their children were from the first moment expunged from Canada's 'legal understanding.' In 1985, the Canadian statute was further 'revised' to delete measures intended to prevent births within a target group from the list of proscribed policies and activities. . . . At least one Canadian court, moreover, has recently entered a decree making it a criminal offense for anyone to employ the term ['genocide'] in any other way." Ward Churchill, "Genocide by Any Other Name: North American Indian Residential Schools in Context," in Adam Jones, ed., *Genocide, War Crimes and the West: History and Complicity* (London: Zed Books, 2004), pp. 83–84.

38 After the David Irving decision, historian Andrew Roberts claimed the judgment against Irving was at best a partial victory, since "the free publicity that this trial has generated for him and his views has been worth far more than could ever have been bought for the amount of the costs." Quoted in Evans, *Lying About Hitler*, p. 235.

39 According to Colin Tatz, "for all the company they keep, and for all their outpourings, these deniers assist rather than hinder genocide and Holocaust research," in part by "prompt[ing] studies by men and women of eminence . . . who would otherwise not have written on genocide." Tatz, *With Intent to Destroy*, pp. 139–40.

40 For a discussion of responsible versus malicious denial of a genocide framework for Cambodia, see Ben Kiernan, "Bringing the Khmer Rouge to Justice," *Human Rights Review*, 1: 3 (April–June 2000), pp. 92–108.

CHAPTER 15

Justice, Truth, and Redress

What can justice mean when genocide is the issue?

Terrence Des Pres

The legal strictures against genocide constitute *jus cogens*: they are among the laws "accepted and recognized by the international community of States as a whole from which no derogation is permitted." Jus cogens is associated with the principle of *universal jurisdiction* (*quasi delicta juris gentium*), which "applies to a limited number of crimes for which any State, even absent a personal or territorial link with the offence, is entitled to try the offender."[1]

There is theory, however, and there is practice. After the UN Convention came into force in 1951, genocide was all but ignored in international law. On the international scene, the word was commonly deployed for propaganda purposes. For example, the resurgence of interest in the Jewish Holocaust, and the roughly contemporary rise of Israel to major-power status, made "genocide" an attractive verbal weapon for Palestinians and their Arab allies. National-level trials occasionally employed the term, as with Israel's prosecution of Adolf Eichmann in 1961, and Ethiopia's proceedings against members of the Dergue regime (see below). But overall, a conspiracy of silence prevailed in diplomatic quarters and at the United Nations. Diplomatic norms militated against such grave accusations, while states' bloody hands meant that there was always a danger that allegations could rebound on the accuser through the defense of *tu quoque*, "a plea that the adversary committed similar atrocities."[2]

Despite this passivity, the twentieth century *did* produce revolutionary new forms of international justice. Formal mechanisms ranged from the humanitarian law of the Hague Conventions (1899, 1907) and Geneva Conventions (1949); to war crimes tribunals at Nuremberg and for Yugoslavia, Rwanda, and Sierra Leone; and most recently to an International Criminal Court (ICC) with universal jurisdiction though, alas, not yet universal membership. These were accompanied by less formal institutions, such as the "truth commissions" mounted under both national and international aegis, and investigative bodies that may blow the whistle on genocide, whether past, present, or incipient. Such efforts also feature substantial public involvement, especially by religious and human rights NGOs, academics, and legal professionals – a phenomenon that can be traced back to the international campaigns against slavery and the Congo "rubber terror" in the nineteenth and early twentieth centuries.

This penultimate chapter explores the interrelation of justice, truth-seeking, and redress as they have evolved both nationally and internationally.

LEIPZIG, CONSTANTINOPLE, NUREMBERG, TOKYO

The move towards tribunals for war crimes and "crimes against humanity" reflected the growing institutionalization and codification of humanitarian instruments over the latter half of the nineteenth century. This was evident in the formative efforts of Henri Dunand and his International Committee of the Red Cross, founded in 1864. The Red Cross was a pioneering institution in addressing suffering that offends the human conscience. Leaders were also becoming more aware of "crimes against humanity," albeit selectively. Consider British politician William Gladstone's 1870 fulmination against Ottoman atrocities in the Balkans:

> Certain it is that a new law of nations is gradually taking hold of the mind, and coming to sway the practice, of the world; a law which recognises independence, which frowns upon aggression, which favours the pacific, not the bloody settlement of disputes, which aims at permanent and not temporary adjustments; above all, which recognises, as a *tribunal* of paramount authority, the general *judgment of civilised mankind*.[3]

Much the same speech could have been given for the drafting of the Rome Statute of the International Criminal Court (1998), suggesting that Gladstone was overly optimistic in his assessment. But his generation did witness epic advances in human freedom. The abolition of slavery in the United States (1861) and Brazil (1888) were high watermarks. They were accompanied by swelling campaigns against the Congo "rubber terror," pogroms against Russian Jews, and early Ottoman massacres of Armenians (1894–96, presaging the holocaust of 1915–16).

At century's end, Russian Tsar Nicholas convened an international conference on war prevention at the Hague in Holland. This led to two seminal conventions, in 1899 and 1907, that placed limits on "legitimate" methods of warfare, including bans on civilian bombardments and the use of poison gas. All sides abrogated the agreements only a few years later, during the First World War (1914–18). But the new framings shaped the postwar world – including the 1927 Protocol against chemical and biological warfare, which remains in force.

As part of the punitive peace imposed on Germany at Versailles, a few desultory trials of alleged war criminals took place before German courts at Leipzig. They ended in fiasco, with the Allies divided among themselves, and German opposition to the initiative effectively unchallenged. A similar dynamic prevailed in the trials that Allied occupiers imposed on Turkey, described in Chapter 4.

More high-profile, and successful, were the international tribunals at Nuremberg and Tokyo following the Second World War.[4] Trials were by no means foreordained as a strategy for handling German and Japanese war criminals. Intense debates took place within the Allied coalition during 1943–45. Both Winston Churchill and Joseph Stalin pushed for summary executions of top Nazi echelons.[5] Franklin Roosevelt considered the wholesale demilitarization, deindustrialization, and dismemberment of Germany (the so-called "Morgenthau Plan"). This was in harmony with much of public opinion in the Allied countries: few people viewed tribunals as the optimal way of dealing with enemy war crimes.

However, a legal process was finally settled upon in both the German and Japanese cases. This was, indisputably, a seminal advance in international jurisprudence. Nuremberg featured "the first official mention of genocide in an international legal setting," as all the German defendants were accused of "conduct[ing] deliberate and systematic genocide, viz., the extermination of racial and national groups, against the civilian populations of certain occupied territories."[6] Raphael Lemkin's tireless lobbying had paid dividends, though, as noted in Chapter 1, "genocide" formed no part of the Nuremberg verdicts. (Nor could it have, since it was not at the time enshrined in international law.)[7]

Both tribunals were flawed. Leaders were tried only for crimes committed in wartime. Nazi actions against the Jews prior to September 1, 1939, for example, were absent from the Nuremberg indictments. Nazi crimes against Jews, Roma, and other groups were downplayed, while charges of waging aggressive war were emphasized. Japanese atrocities against Chinese and other Asian civilians were similarly understressed, by contrast with allegations of the murderous abuse of Allied prisoners-of-war.

The long-established principle of *nullum crimen sine lege* – no crime without an accompanying law – was implemented in "an extremely loose and controversial" way at Nuremberg. Leaders were tried for crimes that had not formally existed at the time they were committed.[8] In addition, prosecutors at both the Nuremberg and Tokyo tribunals avoided charging Germans and Japanese with atrocities that the Allies had also inflicted. Thus, while indiscriminate bombardment of civilians was long established as a core war crime, it could not be prosecuted without providing the accused with a ready-made *tu quoque* defense. Even so, an Indian judge at Tokyo, Rahadbinod Pal, dissented from the majority verdict, labeling the trial a sham for its inattention to the Allies' own crimes.[9] In one case – that of unrestricted submarine warfare – the charges manifestly *did* overlap with Allied practice. Here, German Admiral Karl Dönitz's *tu quoque* defense was successful, leading to his acquittal, though he was convicted on "counts . . . [of] crimes against peace and war crimes – and sentenced to 10 years in prison."[10]

Figure 15.1 Judgment at Nuremberg, 1946: accused Nazi war criminals in the dock after the Second World War.
Source: United States Holocaust Memorial Museum.

For the Tokyo trials, the Allies did not prosecute Emperor Hirohito, the man who "had personally approved all his country's barbaric military ventures" before and during the Second World War, and allowed him to stay on the Japanese throne.[11] Nor was Hirohito the only accused war criminal allowed to evade justice. The US was particularly interested in military technology, including biological weapons. Thus, Japanese scientists associated with the Unit 731 biological experiments – which led, among other things, to the release of live plague bacilli over Chinese cities – were granted immunity from prosecution, in return for sharing their research and expertise with the Americans. In Europe, police and security forces were deemed vital to both sides in the emerging Cold War struggle, regardless of the role they had played in fascist persecutions. Soviet occupiers, for instance, incorporated Nazi-era personnel wholesale into the new Stasi security force of East Germany.

The tribunals were victor's justice, but they were also ground-breaking. Nuremberg established "two central precedents: that of individual criminal responsibility, and that of the universal jurisdiction over crimes against humanity."[12] Out of twenty-four indictments, two were dropped and three defendants acquitted; another seven were imprisoned and not executed. (In the Tokyo proceedings, seven defendants were sentenced to death, sixteen to life in prison, and two others to lighter terms.) There is also no discounting the bonanza that the tribunals represented for scholarship, and for the documentation of historical fact. Alan Bullock called Nuremberg, with its bounty of Nazi documents on public display, "an absolutely unqualified wonder . . . the greatest coup in history for historians."[13]

THE INTERNATIONAL CRIMINAL TRIBUNALS: YUGOSLAVIA AND RWANDA

It is one of history's ironies that the International Criminal Tribunal for the Former Yugoslavia (ICTY) was created to deflect accusations of Western complacency in the face of genocide.[14] In spring 1992, with war raging in Bosnia, voices were raised for the establishment of a UN-sponsored tribunal to try the perpetrators of atrocities. In May 1993, the Security Council created the ICTY at The Hague (hence, "the Hague tribunal"). For some time following, this was as far as the West was willing to go. The Balkan wars continued for another three years, with the worst single atrocity occurring near their end (the Srebrenica massacre of July 1995). The tribunal's creation did not prevent a recrudescence of conflict in Kosovo in 1998–99.

Following the Dayton Peace Accords of 1996, the ICTY process gradually began to gather steam. The unwillingness of occupying forces to seize indicted individuals, for fear of destabilizing the transition process, gave way to a more assertive attitude. The pace of arrests and prosecutions picked up substantially. With growing cooperation from Croatian authorities, more than half of the ICTY's indicted figures were in custody by 2001. The process climaxed with the extraordinary 2001 transfer of former Yugoslav President Slobodan Milosevic for prosecution by the tribunal.[15]

The ICTY won praise for impartiality. Its first conviction was issued against a Croatian (albeit one who served with Serb forces). The indictments of Croatian General Ante Gotovina and Kosovo Prime Minister Ranush Haradinaj (see Chapter 8) helped to balance the emphasis on Serb crimes against Bosnian Muslims, Croatians, and Kosovar Albanians. However, the ICTY was criticized for ruling out war crimes prosecutions of NATO leaders of the Kosovo war, accused of attacks on civilian targets and other breaches of international law.[16]

With the Hague tribunal in place, the UN could hardly avoid establishing a tribunal for the Rwanda genocide of 1994. The International Criminal Tribunal for Rwanda (ICTR) was housed at Arusha, Tanzania, where the abortive 1993 peace agreements had been signed (Chapter 9). The ICTR's gears ground painfully slowly, however. Understaffed and underfunded, it remains prone to allegations that it focuses exclusively on Hutu killers of Tutsis, with no consideration of Tutsi reprisal killings of Hutus.[17] Its operations also appear distorted by the more extensive genocide trials in Rwanda. These imposed the death penalty, while ICTR proceedings did not, leading to the paradox that *génocidaires* could escape execution at the ICTR, while their underlings could be (and were) sentenced to death by Rwandan judges.[18]

The international tribunals at the Hague and Arusha are extremely important to precedent-setting case law. In a few short years, the ICTY and ICTR together have contributed more to legal interpretations and applications of the Genocide Convention than all authorities in the preceding forty-five years. There follow some examples.

Jurisdictional issues

For decades, applications of international humanitarian law were muddled by the difficulty of determining which legal instruments could be imposed on sovereign states, and when – in peacetime, or solely in war? In civil wars, or only international ones? These matters are now largely resolved. In its "exhaustive analysis of customary and conventional international humanitarian law," the Hague tribunal concluded by decisively "severing . . . the category of crimes against humanity [including genocide] from any requirement of a connection to international wars, *or indeed to any state of conflict.*"[19] In the estimation of scholar Christopher Rudolph, this ICTY precedent "opened the door to international adjudication of internal conflicts."[20] It was seized upon by the Arusha tribunal in extending relevant international law to a "civil conflict" (the Rwanda genocide). The precedent has become a touchstone for advocates of universal jurisdiction in cases of genocide and other crimes against humanity.

The concept of a victim group

Many have criticized the UN Genocide Convention's exclusion of political and other potential victim groups. Moreover, the four core groups that the Convention *does* recognize – "national, ethnical, racial, and religious" – are notoriously difficult to define. Confronted with genocide in Rwanda, where populations sharing most of the usual ethnic markers – language, religion, a common history – descended into savage intercommunal killing, the ICTR chose to define an ethnic group as "one whose members share a common language and culture; or, a group which distinguishes itself as such (self identification); or, *a group identified as such by others, including perpetrators of the crimes (identification by others).*"[21] Identities may now be *imputed* to a collectivity, as well as avowed by one.

Gender and genocide

According to Steven Ratner and Jason Abrams, the ICTY's "indictments and jurisprudence have highlighted the role of sexual violence in the Balkan conflict and more clearly defined the status of such offenses in international criminal law."[22] For instance, in the Celibici case, the ICTY ruled that rape could constitute torture. The ICTR went further still. With the Akayesu decision of 1998, the Arusha tribunal, "in one of its significant innovations, defined rape as a form of genocide, in that it constitutes serious bodily or mental harm in accordance with article II(b) of the [UN] Convention."[23] Rape was also depicted as a form of "preventing births within the group," both physically and through inflicting psychological trauma on women.[24] From both perspectives, female rape victims are now viewed as victims in their own right, rather than a medium through which dishonor and dislocation may be visited upon a family or community. This new sensitivity reflects decades of successful feminist mobilization around the issue of rape, including ground-breaking analyses of rape in war and genocide.[25]

Neither the ICTY nor the ICTR has accompanied these advances with systematic attention to rape and sexual violence against males, especially in detention centers and prison camps. The ICTY tribunal reacted with unease to forays on the subject, while the ICTR has ignored it altogether.[26] However, the tribunals *did* make one essential contribution to legal understandings of gendercidal atrocities against men. In 2001, Bosnian Serb General Radislav Krstic became the first person to be convicted by the ICTY of aiding and abetting genocide. Krstic's lawyers had argued that because "only" adult males were killed at Srebrenica, the strategy was not genocidal against the community as a whole. In its 2004 verdict on Krstic's appeal, the court rejected these arguments, contending that selective killing of males constituted destruction of the Bosnian-Muslim population "in part," and this was sufficient to characterize the slaughter as genocide.[27]

NATIONAL TRIALS

Prosecution of genocide and other crimes at the national rather than international level carries certain advantages. Mechanisms for indictment, prosecution, and adjudication are already in place: this is a definitional feature of the modern state. Moreover, in countries where genocide and crimes against humanity have been committed, the matter is deeply personal:

> Where trials take place in the country where the offenses occurred, the entire process becomes more deeply connected with the society, providing it with the potential to create a strong psychological and deterrent effect on the population. This factor, combined with the greater access to evidence, witnesses, victims, and perpetrators, gives such tribunals a significant potential advantage over international tribunals.[28]

Unfortunately, perpetration of genocide on a national territory often correlates with underdeveloped and compromised legal institutions. Thus, the infrastructure for administering justice may be sorely inadequate. In Ethiopia, for instance, President Meles Zenawi's government charged more than 5,000 representatives of the brutal Dergue dictatorship with offenses that included crimes against humanity and genocide; but these "highly ambitious" prosecutions suffered from a "judicial system [that was] weak and lacking any tradition of independence."[29] Rwanda's formal post-genocide trials, as distinct from the *gacaca* experiment (see below), aroused strong international criticism for their selective and sometimes shambolic character.

National trials can also arouse national sentiment, to the detriment of the proceedings. This derailed the tribunals at Leipzig and Constantinople after the First World War. Even contemporary, advanced legal systems may be unduly swayed by such sentiment. Israel, for example, mishandled proceedings against John Demjanjuk, a US citizen extradited on charges of having served as a brutal guard ("Ivan the Terrible") at the Treblinka death camp. According to Geoffrey Robertson, some Israelis "wanted so badly to convict Demjanjuk that three experienced judges ignored exculpatory evidence and presided over an outrageously unfair show trial," sentencing the prisoner to death. Only when incontrovertible proof of mistaken identity was submitted at the appeal stage was Demjanjuk "grudgingly" cleared.[30]

In addition to Ethiopia's proceedings against the Dergue and Israel's against Demjanjuk, some major national trials for war crimes and crimes against humanity include:

- Proceedings against thousands of accused war criminals in Germany after World War Two, following on the Nuremberg tribunal but conducted by German courts. Result: minimal "denazification," with most former Nazi functionaries left unprosecuted.
- Israel's abduction and trial of leading Nazi bureaucrat Adolf Eichmann (1960–61). Result: Eichmann's conviction and execution (1962).[31]
- Argentina's prosecution and incarceration, in the mid-1980s, of leaders of the former military *junta* (see Chapter 14). Result: five leaders convicted and jailed, but pardoned several years later.
- Trials of accused *génocidaires* in Rwanda. Result: some trials and executions, general chaos, and the introduction of less formal *gacaca* proceedings (see below).
- A renewed round of trials in Germany in the 1990s, this time of former communist functionaries in the East German government. Result: a handful of convictions of low-level border guards; general impunity for higher-ups, sometimes on health grounds.

Domestic legislation on genocide is sometimes intriguing for its application of the UN Genocide Convention. Incorporation of the Convention into national law can be restrictive, based on self-serving "reservations," as with Canada's strategy to avoid mention or prosecution of genocide against native Canadians (see Chapter 14). But domestic framings can also be expansive and inclusive, perhaps charting a course for developments at the international level. This is especially notable in the case of designated victim groups for genocide. Bangladesh – with memories of the 1971 genocide still fresh (Box 8a) – added political groups to the Convention definition, as did Costa Rica in 1992 and Panama in 1993. Peru includes social groups, while Finland adds "a comparable group of people" to the Convention's core list of collectivities.[32] Another distinctive example is Cambodia, where, in light of the Khmer Rouge's strategies, genocide was defined in a Decree Law of July 1979 as including "planned massacres of groups of innocent people; expulsion of inhabitants of cities and villages in order to concentrate them and force them to do hard labour in conditions leading to their physical and mental destruction; wiping out religion;

[and] destroying political, cultural and social structures and family and social relations."[33]

The "mixed tribunals": Cambodia and Sierra Leone

The tribunals agreed for Cambodia and the West African nation of Sierra Leone provide an innovative "mixed" model that combines national and international representation. The trend-setter is Cambodia, where the model emerged after hard bargaining between the United Nations and the Cambodian government. The UN – supported by human rights NGOs in Cambodia and abroad – declared the country's post-genocide legal system incapable of administering justice fairly. Not only was the system ramshackle and underfunded, the argument ran, but it was vulnerable to intervention and control by the authoritarian Hun Sen government. Government representatives, by contrast, stressed the importance of homegrown justice. After tortuous twists and turns a compromise was reached, and a UN–Cambodia Agreement was signed in June 2003. According to Tom Fawthrop and Helen Jarvis, the mixed tribunal "is a carefully crafted structure designed to provide sufficient checks and balances. International jurists, lawyers and judges will occupy key roles as the co-prosecutor, co-investigating judge and two out of five trial court judges, and must be a party to conviction or exoneration of any accused."[34] The trials will be held in Cambodia, with a majority of Cambodian judges.

Although it took the Cambodian framework as its guide, the Special Court for Sierra Leone was first off the ground. It, too, includes both national and foreign justices, administering both domestic and international laws, with the national capital (Freetown) hosting the proceedings. Nine individuals from both government militias and RUF rebels stood trial for atrocities committed during a decade-long conflict that killed 50,000 civilians and became a byword for "new war" savagery (see Chapter 12).[35]

ANOTHER KIND OF JUSTICE: RWANDA'S *GACACA* EXPERIMENT

Among the glaring deficiencies of the ICTR in Arusha is that it will try just seventy cases before it closes in 2008. Meanwhile, well over 100,000 detainees languished for years, amidst squalid conditions, in Rwandan jails. Their incarceration was usually based on genuine suspicion of involvement in the genocide; some accusations, though, may have been concocted to settle personal scores or seize property. Clearly, the country's shattered legal system could never clear this backlog of tens of thousands of cases.

The solution eventually settled upon was *gacaca* (ga-CHA-cha). The word means "on the hilltop," a reference to the open-air justice meted out by "260,000 lay judges – old and young, men and women, Hutu and Tutsi," elected by popular vote in October 2001.[36] *Gacaca* tribunals are established at four levels, from cell through sector and district to province. The lowest-level tribunal handles Category 4 offenses, those against property only. Sector tribunals assess crimes involving injury, while district-level trials handle cases of killing but not the organization and direction of killing (Category 1 crimes). These fall outside the *gacaca* framework, and will be tried by government courts. Provincial tribunals serve as courts of final appeal for *gacaca* cases.[37]

At the trials, alleged victims and perpetrators are brought face to face, with witnesses speaking for each. The goal is *restorative* justice. Sentences emphasize redress through service to the community: "helping to build homes . . . maintaining green spaces, repairing schools and hospitals, and performing agricultural work." The advantage is that this "provides at least a taste of justice for the victims, in addition to rehabilitating offenders."[38]

Tutsi killers of Hutus during and after the genocide against Tutsis are not called to account by *gacaca.* Moreover, there is little in the way of Western-style judicial safeguards – no presumption of innocence, no defense lawyers, and "low standards of evidence," leaving "ample room for manipulation and corruption."[39] Despite these deficiencies, *gacaca* seems an inspired indigenous response to an enormous challenge – administering justice in a post-genocidal society with scant resources. In 2005, thousands of *gacaca* courts began to function, with the ambitious goal of trying 110,000 cases by 2008.

THE PINOCHET CASE

General Augusto Pinochet was first among equals in the military *junta* that overthrew the elected regime of Salvador Allende in Chile on September 11, 1973.[40] The coup was followed by a campaign against the Left, in which several thousand Chileans died. Many more were scarred physically and psychologically by torture, and tens of thousands forced into exile. Activists who fled one Southern Cone* country for refuge in another were hunted down and murdered in death-squad operations coordinated jointly by the region's dictators, Pinochet included.

In 1974, Pinochet appointed himself president. Repression, torture, and death-squad activity continued, albeit on a reduced scale. In 1989, confident that his free-market reforms and social conservatism would sway a majority of Chileans, Pinochet submitted to a plebiscite. A majority – though not a large one – rejected him. Pinochet duly left office in 1990, and a centrist government took power.

Pinochet lived on, wealthy and comfortable except for persistent back problems. In search of relief, he consulted physicians in London, where the former Conservative Prime Minister, Margaret Thatcher, was his regular visitor; she had staunchly backed Pinochet during her years in power. For its part, the Blair government dispatched Foreign Office staff to attend to the aging dictator's needs and concerns.

Press reports had alerted Spanish judge Baltasar Garzón to Pinochet's presence in Britain. In October 1998, Garzón procured a warrant for Pinochet's extradition. The former dictator, aware that legal proceedings were afoot, was preparing to flee

* The "Southern Cone" of South America consists of Argentina, Chile, Paraguay, and Uruguay.

when police detained him. He would remain under house arrest while the British considered Garzón's extradition request.

On March 24, 1999, the same day that NATO bombs began falling on Kosovo (Chapter 8), a panel of the House of Lords – the supreme British tribunal – voted 6-1 that norms of diplomatic immunity did not extend to Pinochet in his current situation.[41] British domestic opinion was divided over the detention and extradition request, however, with Lady Thatcher leading the chorus of protest. In the end, *realpolitik* ("reality politics") won out. In March 2000, a year-and-a-half after Pinochet's arrest, UK Home Secretary Jack Straw released him by government fiat, on "compassionate" grounds.[42]

This seemed an abortive conclusion to the drama. Nonetheless, the Pinochet case was recognized as a watershed in international humanitarian law. For the first time since the legally ambiguous Eichmann case,[43] a former leadership figure, accused of committing grave abuses in one state (but not of war crimes per se), was detained in another state for possible extradition to a third. Considerations of sovereign immunity were no longer determinant. As one of the British Law Lords wrote: "The trend was clear. War crimes had been replaced by crimes against humanity. The way in which a state treated its own citizens within its own borders had become a matter of legitimate concern to the international community."[44]

In a neat example of a political "feedback loop," international legal proceedings against Pinochet impacted upon the Chilean domestic agenda.[45] In closing his 2000 account of the Pinochet case, Geoffrey Robertson opined that Pinochet was "as likely to go to trial [in Chile] . . . as he is to heaven."[46] But in 2004, the Chilean Supreme Court suddenly declared Pinochet fit to stand trial, at age 89, for murders committed under his aegis. Shortly after the renewed legal process was announced, Pinochet entered hospital with a supposed "stroke." The Supreme Court was unimpressed. In the first days of January 2005, it reiterated that the process should go ahead, and placed the former dictator under house arrest.[47] In September 2005, Pinochet was formally stripped of his immunity from prosecution.[48] Impunity for Pinochet's colleagues and underlings had also evaporated, with "more than 300 retired officers, including 21 generals . . . in jail or facing charges."[49]

Where would it all end? In the wake of the Pinochet case (and Yugoslavia's surrender of Slobodan Milosevic to The Hague shortly thereafter), a certain nervousness attended the travel arrangements of despots and their henchmen worldwide.[50] Cuban President Fidel Castro allegedly "cancelled at least two trips out of Cuba, apparently fearing he could be arrested on US criminal charges." The former chief of Ethiopia's Dergue regime, Mengistu Haile Mariam, "faced an arrest threat in South Africa while receiving medical treatment there, causing him to return to safer exile in Zimbabwe."[51] Not even leaders of the self-proclaimed "world's greatest democracy" were safe. In late 2004, a Canadian group, Lawyers Against the War, sought unsuccessfully to have US President George W. Bush declared *persona non grata* prior to a state visit to Canada, on the basis of his alleged "grave crimes against humanity and war crimes" in Iraq.[52] In Germany soon afterwards, the Center for Constitutional Rights, based in New York, "filed a complaint . . . with the Federal German Prosecutor's Office against [US Defense Secretary Donald] Rumsfeld accusing him of war crimes and torture in connection with detainee abuses at Iraq's

Abu Ghraib prison."[53] As a result, Rumsfeld hedged on attending a conference in Germany in February 2005, until the German government guaranteed that he would not face arrest.[54]

THE INTERNATIONAL CRIMINAL COURT (ICC)

> Implicit within the logic of the term "crime against humanity" is the need for an international court.
>
> David Hirsh

The concept of a permanent international tribunal for war crimes and crimes against humanity is a venerable one. According to legal scholar William Schabas, Gustav Moynier of the Red Cross outlined an early plan in the 1870s.[55] But for most of the twentieth century, the one court with a claim to global jurisdiction – the International Court of Justice (ICJ) at the Hague, also known as the World Court – was limited mostly to territorial claims and resource disputes. When Nicaragua launched proceedings against the US in the 1980s for acts of material sabotage and support for *contra* rebels, the US at first argued that the ICJ lacked jurisdiction. When the ICJ begged to differ, the US withdrew from the proceedings and refused to abide by any judgment against it. The ICJ ruled in Nicaragua's favor, but was impotent to enforce its decision. "A court with teeth" in the humanitarian and human rights arena existed only in the Western European regional context: the European Court of Justice's decisions are binding upon all European Union members. However, the mounting impetus for a global prohibition regime against genocide, war crimes, and crimes against humanity led, in 1994, to the UN drafting a statute for a legal body along the lines of the Yugoslavia tribunal, but with global jurisdiction. A final version was drafted in Rome, with the "Rome Statute" passed on July 17, 1998. In April 2002, sixty-six countries – six more than required – voted to adopt the Statute, and it entered formally into force. By early 2005, 139 countries had signed the Statute, with ninety-seven "state parties" (those who had ratified it in national legislatures). Eighteen judges, including seven women, were appointed, and Luis Moreno Ocampo was selected as the first independent prosecutor. Notably, Moreno Ocampo first came to prominence through his prosecution of former *junta* leaders in Argentina.

The court is envisaged as an adjunct to legal proceedings at the national level. Only when national mechanisms prove incapable of handling a case can the ICC come into play. Individuals from states who are not signatories to the Rome Statute may still be tried, though only if referred to the Court by a signatory state. In general, ICC proceedings are to be activated only by a request from a member state, though some loopholes do exist. The independent prosecutor can initiate investigations on his or her own (*proprio motu*), while the UN Security Council may command the prosecutor to apply the court's jurisdiction even if s/he is reluctant to do so. A Pre-Trial Chamber will then issue warrants for the arrest of indicted individuals (it is individuals, not states or other entities, that are the focus of the ICC's operations).

Figure 15.2 Luis Moreno Ocampo, prosecutor of Argentine war criminals, appointed as the first prosecutor of the International Criminal Court (ICC).

Source: United Nations.

The Court's mandate extends to genocide, war crimes, crimes of "aggression," and crimes against humanity. The definition of "genocide" adopted by the ICC is identical to that of the UN Convention. Worth citing is the definition of "crimes against humanity" in the Rome Statute, since this category of crimes is more likely to feature in ICC deliberations than genocide per se.[56] This category also encompasses acts that overlap with the Genocide Convention,[57] and others that fall under some scholars' preferred definitions of genocide, including my own.[58] Crimes against humanity comprise:

> any of the following acts when committed as part of a widespread or systematic attack directed against any civilian population, with knowledge of the attack: (a) Murder; (b) Extermination; (c) Enslavement; (d) Deportation or forcible transfer of population; (e) Imprisonment or other severe deprivation of physical liberty in violation of fundamental rules of international law; (f) Torture; (g) Rape, sexual slavery, enforced prostitution, forced pregnancy, enforced sterilization, or any other form of sexual violence of comparable gravity; (h) Persecution against any identifiable group or collectivity on political, racial, national, ethnic, cultural, religious, gender . . . or other grounds that are universally recognized as impermissible under international law . . . (i) Enforced disappearance of persons; (j) The crime of apartheid; (k) Other inhumane acts of a similar character intentionally causing great suffering, or serious injury to body or to mental or physical health.

Despite the broad international consensus behind the ICC, many governments, including the US, have shied away from it. The Clinton government signed the Rome Statute in the knowledge that it was unlikely to be ratified by Congress.[59] The issue of universal jurisdiction, along with the semi-independent role of the prosecutor, were key sticking points. In May 2002, the Bush administration renounced the treaty, and declared that it would not tolerate the detention or trial of any US national by the ICC. Later the same year, Bush signed into law the "American Servicemembers Protection Act," authorizing the US president "to use all means . . . necessary to bring about the release of covered US persons and covered allied persons held captive by or on behalf of the [ICC]."[60] Wags referred to this as the "Invade the Hague Act," conjuring images of US troops descending on Dutch detention centers to free Americans accused of abuses and atrocities.

The ICC is "the body that may ultimately play the greatest role in interpreting the prohibition against genocide."[61] At the time of writing, though, "its power as part of the atrocities [prohibition] regime remains contested and indefinite."[62] Its broad mandate and intended permanence bode well, as does its popularity in most countries of the world. On the other hand, concessions made to placate US and other concerns (including an opt-out clause lasting fully seven years) evoked concern that the ICC might become just another toothless legal body.

INTERNATIONAL CITIZENS' TRIBUNALS

Often called "international people's tribunals," these bodies substitute accusations and public shaming for due process and enforcement. The formation of a citizens' tribunal implies that regular means of justice are inadequate – corrupt or compromised. "The people" – certain interested people – seize the initiative and stage a quasi-trial. This may publicize atrocities, raise public consciousness, or shatter taboos, for example about Western state involvement. (It is Western democracies that are usually both hosts and subjects of such proceedings.) Tribunals can place vital evidence on the public record, and point to gaps between legislation and its application, highlighting the immunity often extended to sovereign states and their representatives.

Citizens' tribunals receive a rare comparative analysis in a book by Arthur and Judith Klinghoffer.[63] The authors point out that, in many ways, the most remarkable and successful citizens' tribunal was the first. In February 1933, the month after Adolf Hitler came to power, the Reichstag Parliament building in Berlin was burned down. Three foreign and one German communist, along with the Dutchman Marinus van der Lubbe, were charged with the crime. The Nazis seized on the fire to declare a state of emergency, suspend the Weimar constitution, and begin their mass round-ups of communist suspects (Box 6a). Fearing that the German courts were too cowed to try the matter fairly, various public intellectuals, along with prominent socialists and communists, convened "The Commission of Inquiry into the Origins of the Reichstag Fire" in London in September 1933. Held a week before official proceedings were due to get underway in Germany, the tribunal pulled the rug out from the Nazis' planned show-trial. Placed in the hot seat by international media attention, a court in Leipzig convicted only van der Lubbe (he was subsequently executed). The four communists were acquitted. "The first international citizens' tribunal had taken on Nazi Germany, and had won," writes Arthur Klinghoffer. "Intellectuals had confronted a totalitarian state, and had successfully used public opinion as a weapon to further their cause."[64]

Four years later, supporters of exiled Russian communist Leon Trotsky organized a citizens' tribunal at his new (and final) home in Coyoacán, a Mexico City suburb. The intent of the Dewey Commission, chaired by the eponymous philosopher, was to denounce Soviet show-trials and accusations against Trotsky. The tribunal achieved some success in countering Stalinist propaganda, although its geographic remove from centers of Western public opinion limited its impact.

Much more visible was the International War Crimes Tribunal to judge US actions in the Vietnam War in 1967, known as the Russell Tribunal. Tribunal delegates voted unanimously that US actions did constitute genocide against the Vietnamese and other Indochinese peoples (for more on the US war against Vietnam, see Chapter 2). However, "this decision on genocide had little impact on the American public and was generally viewed by the press as verbal excess."[65]

Since the 1970s, tribunals have publicized the restitution claims of indigenous peoples; the Japanese "comfort women" issue; Western wars and sanctions against Iraq;[66] and the social damage associated with neoliberal economic measures imposed by the First World on the Third. As these examples suggest, "In essence, tribunals have become a weapon of the radical left in its battle with 'global capitalism'."[67]

It has been argued that "these tribunals do make some contribution to the pathetically limited possibilities of action for the punishment of genocide."[68] However, many observers consider them to be kangaroo courts: their "investigations sometimes seem perfunctory, and the verdict seems preordained," in Leo Kuper's words.[69] Richard Falk referred to the Russell Tribunal as "a juridical farce."[70] Law Professor Peter Burns likewise argues that "the desired conclusion[s]" of such tribunals are "inextricably woven into the accusations and process itself." He considers them to be "a form of overt morality play, relying upon polemic and theatre to achieve results that may be desirable ethically, but may or may not be desirable legally."[71]

TRUTH AND RECONCILIATION

Like *gacaca* in Rwanda, truth and reconciliation commissions are driven by a vision of restorative justice that "seeks repair of social connections and peace rather than retribution against the offenders." As such, these commissions have become the preferred option for societies (or their decision-makers) who wish to avoid arduous and possibly destabilizing criminal trials. For victims, such commissions provide a forum, perhaps the first they have had, for speaking of the horrors inflicted upon them or upon those whom they loved. Ideally, the result is *catharsis* – in this context, the mastering of one's pain through its articulation. "By confronting the past, the traumatized individuals can learn to distinguish past, present, and future. When the work of knowing and telling the story has come to an end, the trauma then belongs to the past; the survivor can face the work of building a future."[72] Validation may also lie in having one's testimony heard, corroborated, and integrated into a commission's published findings. A degree of moral order is restored to the world when one's suffering is taken seriously, and its perpetrators are viewed with obloquy. (Truth-telling may have a darker side, however, considered below.)

Some of the key questions for truth commissions are the following. *How long will the commission operate for?* The general trend is from a few months to a couple of years. *Who will fund it?* Significant resources may be available domestically, as in South Africa. In other cases foreign funding is crucial, and in a pair of instances the UN has played a formative role (El Salvador) or a prominent one (Guatemala). *Who will staff the commission?* The emphasis has been on prominent public figures from the country in question, widely seen as fair-minded and/or compassionate. *Will the commission examine alleged abuses by all sides in a given conflict, or one side only?* The strong tendency has been towards examining all sides' conduct, since this greatly bolsters the credibility of the commission's procedures and final report. *Will the commission have the power to dispense justice and grant amnesty?* Justice, no; and only South Africa's commission could grant amnesty to those who confessed before it.

In conducting its operations, *how will the commission elicit testimony?* Sessions may be held in public or behind closed doors. Anonymous testimony might be permitted, especially in the case of sexual crimes. *What standard of evidence will be required to draw publishable conclusions?* According to Hayner, the trend is towards "the 'balance of probabilities' standard for basic conclusions of fact. This . . . suggests that there is more evidence to support than to deny a conclusion, or that something is more likely to be true than not based on the evidence before the commission."[73] *Will the commission's report include prescriptions and recommendations?* In general, yes. Special attention is often paid to reforming the state security forces. Commissions may also provide critical documentation for subsequent criminal trials. *Will the commission name names?* More rarely.[74] There is a delicate balance to be struck between holding individuals accountable while risking (1) overturning the applecart of a delicate political transition, or (2) provoking threats and acts of violence against witnesses and commission staff. The UN-sponsored commission in El Salvador *did* name names, despite intense opposition from the Salvadoran government and military. The Guatemalan commission, by contrast, chose not to, though it left no doubt that state agents had committed the overwhelming majority of the atrocities (see Chapter 3).

Will truth commissions consider the roles of foreign actors? Generally not, though when such investigations *are* conducted, they may be revelatory. The 1992 report of the Chad truth commission, for example, produced a hard-hitting assessment of US aid to the goons of the Habré regime. The US also came under close scrutiny by the Guatemalan Commission for Historical Clarification. The commission obtained extensive documentation of the US role in overthrowing a democratic government in Guatemala (1954), then installing and sustaining the military dictators who eventually turned to full-scale genocide against Mayan Indians and domestic dissenters.

However, "most truth commissions have not investigated this international role at any depth; few have addressed the issue at all in their final report."[75] This reflects material and evidentiary constraints, as well as the complexity of some international involvements. (One balks at assessing the international dimension of the Congo conflict, for example, if a truth commission is ever struck with this mandate.) Sometimes the reluctance may derive from practical considerations. Many truth commissions, as noted, rely on international financial support – frequently from the United States.

Truth commissions resemble citizens' tribunals in compensating for a lack of "teeth" in their deliberations by creating ripples in the public sphere. In the commissions' case, this can produce a kind of quasi-legal sanction against offenders. Some of those named by commissions may avoid foreign travel, fearing arrest. At a more informal level, Hayner has vividly described the treatment accorded to leaders and high-profile agents of the former *junta* in Argentina. Many were never formally tried; some were jailed but released under an amnesty. Nevertheless, the revelation of their deeds, primarily through the Argentine truth commission and its *Nunca Más* report, carried lasting consequences for these individuals. "Whenever they venture into the streets or public places, [Generals] Videla, Massera, Camps, and several others have experienced spontaneous though nonviolent acts of repudiation: waiters refuse to serve them, other patrons leave the place or sit far away from them, some actually defy their bodyguards and confront them with the opinion that most Argentines have of them."[76]

A question remains: Is the truth always desirable? In personal terms, truth-telling about atrocity is often deeply traumatizing for the teller. Yael Fischman and Jaime Ross describe the "recurring themes" of torture survivors in therapy:

> fear of destroying others, such as relatives and therapists, by relating the trauma; fear of loss of control over feelings of rage, violence, and anxiety; shame and rage over the vulnerability and helplessness evoked by torture; rage and grief at the sudden and arbitrary disruption of individual, social, and political projects, and at the violation of rights; guilt and shame over surviving and being unable to save others; guilt over bringing distress on self and family and over not protecting them . . . fear and rage at the unpredictability of and lack of control over events; grief over the loss of significant others, through both death and exile; and loss of aspects of the self, such as trust and innocence.[77]

Outside the formal therapeutic environment, though, almost no mechanism to elicit truth-telling – be it a truth commission, a human rights investigator, or a journalist – provides meaningful follow-up to traumatized survivors. Truth-divulging may also be "dangerous and destabilizing" on a national level, according to Hayner, "disrupt[ing] fragile relationships in local communities recently returned to peace."[78] She cites Mozambique, where "people across the political spectrum, including victims, academics, government officials and others . . . said, 'No, we do not want to reenter into this morass of conflict, hatred, and pain. We want to focus on the future. . . . We prefer silence over confrontation, over renewed pain. While we cannot forget, we would like to pretend that we can.'"[79]

These attitudes were not ostrich-like. Rather, they signaled a process of peace and reconciliation that had come about "remarkably quickly" in Mozambique, many observers describing it "with a sense of wonder." From the day a peace agreement was signed ending one of Africa's most brutal twentieth-century wars, "the former warring enemies have lived in peace virtually without incident." Rituals of purification and reconciliation were performed at the village level, beyond the reach of state initiatives.[80] "We were all thinking about how to increase peace and reconciliation," said one Mozambican official, "but when we came to the grassroots, they were reconciling already. Our ideas were only confusing and stirring up trouble."[81]

THE CHALLENGE OF REDRESS

- *Switzerland, March 1995.* In a declaration that the London *Times* described as "visionary," the government announced the creation of a $5 billion humanitarian fund "to be dispensed to [Jewish] Holocaust victims who lost their money in Swiss banks and, further, to amend historical injustice worldwide." The announcement came after decades of stonewalling by banks about accounts deposited by European Jews who were later killed in the Holocaust. The banking system had been "geared to plunder and profit from unclaimed accounts," using the money "to facilitate Swiss business deals with Eastern Europe." Only after a sustained campaign by the World Jewish Congress, headed by Canadian businessman Edgar Bronfman, were the banks persuaded that redress was in order. This took the form of direct payments to thousands of descendants of Jewish depositors, as well as a wider aid initiative aimed at bolstering human rights and preventing future holocausts. By December 1997, forty-one countries were participating in a conference aimed at "making amends for participation in, or profit from, Nazi plunder."[82]
- *Durban, South Africa, September 2002.* The UN-sponsored World Conference against Racism issued a final declaration calling for redress for the damage inflicted on African peoples by the scourge of slavery, together with other "historical injustices [that] have undeniably contributed to poverty, underdevelopment, marginalisation, social exclusion, [and] economic disparities." Proposed "in a spirit of solidarity" were measures including "debt relief, "promotion of foreign direct investment," "market access," "infrastructure development," "human

resource development," and "education, training and cultural development."[83] In the same year, the Apartheid Debt and Reparations Campaign in the US launched a lawsuit in New York targeting "banks and other companies in six Western countries, seeking redress for 'aiding and abetting a crime against humanity.'"[84] The city of Liverpool in the United Kingdom issued "an unreserved apology for the city's involvement in the slave trade," recognizing its "untold misery" and its destructive impact on "Black people in Liverpool today."[85]

- ***Scotland/New Zealand, January 2005.*** The Perth Museum announced the return to New Zealand of two tattooed Maori heads – *toi moko* – taken as curiosities by a Scottish ship's surgeon in 1822. The decision followed a formal request for repatriation issued by the Te Papa National Museum in Wellington.[86] Te Papa planned to store the heads, and more than fifty others, in a special section for *wahi tapu* artifacts. These were defined as "sites and places sacred to Maori people in the traditional, religious, ritual or mythological sense."[87] The events exemplified a growing trend for human remains seized in colonial times to be treated with respect, as opposed to derision or clinical disregard. Frequently, where remains are held in foreign collections as relics or cultural curiosities, they are repatriated, often with an accompanying burial ceremony.

These three vignettes bear upon the central issue of redress for past atrocities and abuses. The *Concise Oxford Dictionary* defines redress as to "set right, remedy, make up for, get rid of, rectify . . . [a] distress, wrong, damage, grievance, [or] abuse." Colin Tatz, summarizing the arguments of Mari Matsuda, cites "five prerequisites for a meritorious claim for redress: a 'human injustice' must have been committed; it must be well-documented; the victims must be identifiable as a distinct group; the current members of the group must continue to suffer harm; and such harm must be causally connected to the past injustice."[88]

Forms of redress are numerous, and sometimes amorphous. Penalties imposed by official tribunals, such as the ICTR and ICTY, certainly qualify, as do the decisions of less formal processes (such as *gacaca* in Rwanda). The healing that ideally accompanies truth commissions and formal acts of reconciliation may also constitute redress. Compensation is a regular feature: it can take the form of monetary payments (as in the Swiss case), territorial agreements, restitution of property or cultural objects (like the Maori heads), profits from exploitation of natural resources, and affirmative action policies in public and private sector employment (such as in South Africa after 1994).

A critical role may be played by formal *apologies*. Martha Minow emphasizes "the communal nature of the process of apologizing," which "requires communication between a wrongdoer and a victim. . . . The methods for offering and accepting an apology both reflect and help to constitute a moral community."[89] Memorable apologies include:

- German Chancellor Willi Brandt's *Kniefall* (kneeling apology) at a Polish war memorial in 1970.
- Queen Elizabeth's 1995 *mea culpa* to New Zealand Maoris for British violation of the Waitingi Treaty of 1840: "The Crown expresses its profound regret

and apologizes unreservedly for the loss of lives because of hostilities arising from this invasion and at the devastation of property and social life which resulted."[90]

- The annual "Sorry Day," instituted by white Australians after the publication of *Bringing Them Home*, the report of the Aboriginal and Torres Strait Islander Commission (Chapter 3). This popular form of apology contrasted sharply with the government's reaction to the report, which expressed only "regret" for past treatment of Aborigines.[91]
- President Bill Clinton's 1998 apology at Kigali airport for Western inaction during the genocide in Rwanda.[92]
- The 2004 apology by Heidemarie Wieczorek-Zeul, Germany's development aid minister, to Namibian Hereros for "atrocities . . . [that] would have been termed genocide" (Chapter 3).

The danger is that apology may provide a cheap substitute for genuine redress. Does it not "merely whitewash the injustice?" wonders Elazar Barkan.[93] However, apologies may also be the *entrée* to significant material compensation and institutional transformation. A US congressional apology to Japanese Americans for their internment during the Second World War came as part of a Civil Liberties Act, under which the US government paid out 80,000 claims worth $1.6 billion, in addition to opening a Japanese American National Museum in Los Angeles. Queen Elizabeth's declaration to the Maoris was accompanied by a substantial land settlement and the granting of extensive fishing rights to Maoris. Profits from these sources "within a few years . . . became a significant source of Maori income."[94] In Canada, a Royal Commission on Aboriginal Peoples acknowledged in 1996 that "great wrongs have been done" to Native Indians. This half-apology was followed by the allotting of hundreds of millions of dollars "to community-based healing initiatives for victims" of the residential school system (see Chapter 3); the designation of Indians as "first nations" (as in the US); and the creation in April 1999 of a new territory, Nunavut, for northern Inuit peoples, with a concomitant share of profits from the land's abundant natural resources.[95]

By contrast, a failure or refusal to apologize signifies a continuing intransigence towards material and institutional forms of redress. Notorious *non*-apologies of recent times include Turkey's for the genocide against Armenians; nations of the Americas for the crimes of Atlantic slavery; and Central European countries for the mass expulsion of ethnic Germans at the end of the Second World War and after.[96] Nonetheless, the apologetic trend prevails, suggesting a strengthing of the humanitarian regime first forged in the mid-nineteenth century.

FURTHER STUDY

Hannah Arendt, *Eichmann in Jerusalem: A Report on the Banality of Evil.* New York: The Viking Press, 1965. Arendt's controversial account of the trial in Israel of Adolf Eichmann, the ultimate bureaucratic killer.

Elazar Barkan, *The Guilt of Nations: Restitution and Negotiating Historical Injustices.*

New York: W.W. Norton, 2001. Wide-ranging overview of contemporary forms of redress.

Roy Gutman and David Rieff, *Crimes of War: What the Public Should Know*. New York: W.W. Norton, 1999. Richly (sometimes disturbingly) illustrated encyclopedia.

Priscilla B. Hayner, *Unspeakable Truths: Confronting State Terror and Atrocity*. New York: Routledge, 2001. Energetic insider account of truth commissions.

David Hirsh, *Law against Genocide: Cosmopolitan Trials*. London: Glasshouse Press, 2003. Moderately helpful study, focusing on four recent trials related to genocide and crimes against humanity.

Martha Minow, *Between Vengeance and Forgiveness: Facing History after Genocide and Mass Violence*. Boston, MA: Beacon Press, 1998. A good introduction to truth and redress.

Nunca Más: The Report of the Argentine National Commission on the Disappeared. New York: Farrar Straus Giroux, 1986; Spanish edition online at http://www.nuncamas.org/index.htm. The ground-breaking investigation of crimes by the Argentine military *junta* (1976–83).

Steven R. Ratner and Jason S. Abrams, *Accountability for Human Rights Atrocities in International Law: Beyond the Nuremberg Legacy* (2nd edn). Oxford: Oxford University Press, 2001. Best read alongside Schabas (see below), with a useful Cambodia case study.

W. Michael Reisman and Chris T. Antoniou, eds, *The Laws of War: A Comprehensive Collection of Primary Documents on International Laws Governing Armed Conflict*. New York: Vintage, 1994. Core texts with commentary.

Geoffrey Robertson, *Crimes against Humanity: The Struggle for Global Justice*. New York: The New Press, 2000. Thin on genocide, but elegantly written and bracingly opinionated.

William A. Schabas, *Genocide in International Law: The Crime of Crimes*. Cambridge: Cambridge University Press, 2000. Dry, and prohibitively expensive, but an indispensable reference work.

Sarah B. Sewall and Carl Kaysen, eds, *The United States and the International Criminal Court: National Security and International Law*. Lanham, MD: Rowman & Littlefield, 2000. Essays analyzing the ICC initiative in historical context.

NOTES

1 William A. Schabas, *Genocide in International Law: The Crime of Crimes* (Cambridge: Cambridge University Press, 2000), p. 354. Some examples of crimes that command universal jurisdiction are "hijacking and other threats to air travel, piracy, attacks upon diplomats, [threats to] nuclear safety, terrorism, *apartheid* and torture."

2 Schabas, *Genocide in International Law*, p. 341.

3 Gladstone quoted in Gary Jonathan Bass, *Stay the Hand of Vengeance: The Politics of War Crimes Tribunals* (Princeton, NJ: Princeton University Press, 2000), p. 33; emphasis added.

4 The official names of the tribunals were the International Military Tribunal (Nuremberg, created in August 1945) and the International Military Tribunal for the Far East (Tokyo,

created in January 1946). For more on the tribunals, see Joseph E. Persico, *Nuremberg: Infamy on Trial* (London: Penguin, 1995), and Arnold C. Brackman, *The Other Nuremberg: The Untold Story of the Tokyo War Crimes Trials* (New York: William Morrow, 1987).

5 See Richard Overy, "Making Justice at Nuremberg, 1945–1946," http://www.bbc.co.uk/history/war/wwtwo/war_crimes_trials_01.shtml.

6 Samantha Power, *"A Problem from Hell": America and the Age of Genocide* (New York: Basic Books, 2002), p. 50 (quoting the Nuremberg indictments). Although their trials received far less public attention than did those of the top Nazi leaders, Nuremberg also tried members of the *Einsatzgruppen* killing squads who rampaged through Polish and Soviet territories in 1941–42. These defendants "had been *directly* involved in the supervision and implementation of mass murder, war crimes, and genocide. Of the twenty-four accused, twenty-one were sentenced. Among those, two commanders, ten leaders, and two officers were sentenced to death." James Waller, *Becoming Evil: How Ordinary People Commit Genocide and Mass Killing* (Oxford: Oxford University Press, 2002), p. 92.

7 "Genocide was mentioned at Nuremberg, but was not included in the charges against the defendants and was not an operative legal concept." Arthur Jay Klinghoffer and Judith Klinghoffer, *International Citizens' Tribunals: Mobilizing Public Opinion to Advance Human Rights* (New York: Palgrave, 2002), p. 195 (n. 5).

8 Steven R. Ratner and Jason S. Abrams, *Accountability for Human Rights Atrocities in International Law: Beyond the Nuremberg Legacy* (2nd edn) (Oxford: Oxford University Press, 2001), p. 22. Martha Minow points out that "no prior law made it clear that individuals could be charged with the crime of waging aggressive war; the same held true for crimes against humanity, including murder, extermination, enslavement, and persecution on the basis of views or identities." Minow, *Between Vengeance and Forgiveness: Facing History after Genocide and Mass Violence* (Boston, MA: Beacon Press, 1998), p. 33.

9 Geoffrey Robertson, *Crimes against Humanity: The Struggle for Global Justice* (New York: The New Press, 2000), p. 224.

10 David Hirsh, *Law against Genocide: Cosmopolitan Trials* (London: Glasshouse Press, 2003), p. 42.

11 Robertson, *Crimes against Humanity*, p. 222.

12 Hirsh, *Law against Genocide*, p. xvi.

13 Bullock quoted in Richard J. Goldstone and Gary Jonathan Bass, "Lessons from the International Criminal Tribunals," in Sarah B. Sewall and Carl Kaysen, eds, *The United States and the International Criminal Court: National Security and International Law* (Lanham, MD: Rowman & Littlefield, 2000), p. 54.

14 Bass writes that the ICTY "was an act of tokenism by the world community, which was largely unwilling to intervene in ex-Yugoslavia but did not mind creating an institution that would give the *appearance* of moral concern." Bass, *Stay the Hand of Vengeance*, p. 214.

15 By one recent count, the ICTY had issued eighty public indictments, with a number of others kept under seal. Forty-nine indicted people were in detention at The Hague, with another thirty-one at large. Eleven convictions had been issued and fifteen cases were on appeal. Anne E. Mahle, "The Ad Hoc Criminal Tribunals for the Former Yugoslavia and Rwanda," http://www.pbs.org/wnet/justice/world_issues_hag.html.

16 For a nuanced examination, see David Bruce MacDonald, "The Fire in 1999? The United States, NATO and the Bombing of Yugoslavia," ch. 16 in Adam Jones, ed., *Genocide, War Crimes and the West: History and Complicity* (London: Zed Books, 2004), pp. 276–98.

17 Rory Carroll, "Genocide Tribunal 'Ignoring Tutsi Crimes,'" *Guardian*, January 13, 2005. "A former prosecutor, Carla del Ponte, promised to charge members of the RPF [the Tutsi-led Rwandan Patriotic Front] but before doing so she was removed from her post by a unanimous vote in the UN security council in August 2003. Her successor, Hassan Bubacar Jallow, showed no such zeal."

18 See Minow, *Between Vengeance and Forgiveness*, p. 41. As of April 2004, the ICTR had completed nine cases (including appeal stages) with twelve cases being tried or pending appeal. Ten defendants were "sentenced to life imprisonment, three were acquitted, while the rest received different jail terms ranging from 10 to 35 years. Out of the 12 cases pending appeal, two of them have been acquitted at the trial stage." Twenty-three defendants were in custody awaiting trial. Fondation Hirondelle, "ICTR/Genocide/ Commemoration – Basic Facts on the ICTR," http://www.hirondelle.org/hirondelle.nsf/0/d5df8df93c71b8aac1256e69004c22ce?OpenDocument.
19 Robertson, *Crimes against Humanity*, p. 296; emphasis added.
20 Christopher Rudolph, "Constructing an Atrocities Regime: The Politics of War Crimes Tribunals," *International Organization*, 55: 3 (Summer 2001), p. 667.
21 Yusuf Aksar, "The 'Victimized Group' Concept in the Genocide Convention and the Development of International Humanitarian Law through the Practice of Ad Hoc Tribunals," *Journal of Genocide Research*, 5: 2 (2003), p. 217; emphasis added.
22 Ratner and Abrams, *Accountability for Human Rights Atrocities*, p. 201.
23 Schabas, *Genocide in International Law*, p. 384.
24 Schabas, *Genocide in International Law*, p. 174.
25 See, e.g., Susan Brownmiller, *Against Our Will: Men, Women, and Rape* (New York: Bantam, 1975); Alexandra Stiglmayer, ed., *Mass Rape: The War against Women in Bosnia-Herzegovina* (Lincoln, NB: University of Nebraska Press, 1994).
26 See Augusta Del Zotto and Adam Jones, "Male-on-male Sexual Violence in Wartime: Human Rights' Last Taboo?," paper presented to the Annual Convention of the International Studies Association (ISA), New Orleans, LA, March 23–27, 2002. Available at http://adamjones.freeservers.com/malerape.htm.
27 Judge Meron stated: "By seeking to eliminate a part of the Bosnian Muslims, the Bosnian Serb forces committed genocide. They targeted for extinction the 40,000 Bosnian Muslims living in Srebrenica, a group which was emblematic of the Bosnian Muslims in general. They stripped all the male Muslim prisoners, military and civilian, elderly and young, of their personal belongings and identification, and deliberately and methodically killed them solely on the basis of their identity." Ian Traynor, "Hague Rules Srebrenica Was Genocide," *Guardian*, April 20, 2004, http://www.guardian.co.uk/print/0,3858,4905287-103645,00.html.
28 Ratner and Abrams, *Accountability for Human Rights Atrocities*, p. 182.
29 Ratner and Abrams, *Accountability for Human Rights Atrocities*, p. 175.
30 Robertson, *Crimes against Humanity*, p. 240.
31 "Eichmann managed to escape [Germany] and flee to Argentina. Eventually abducted by Israeli intelligence agents in Argentina, he was brought to Israel to stand trial. He was charged with fifteen counts of crimes against the Jewish people and against humanity, and of war crimes. Eichmann's trial opened on April 11, 1961, and ended on August 14 of the same year. He was found guilty and sentenced to death (Israel allows the death penalty only for crimes of genocide). An appeal of his death sentence was rejected in May 1962. Eichmann was hanged in the Ramla prison on the night of May 31, 1962. His body was cremated and his ashes spread over the sea, outside the territorial waters of Israel." Waller, *Becoming Evil*, p. 95.
32 Schabas, *Genocide in International Law*, p. 351 (n. 28).
33 Cited in Tom Fawthrop and Helen Jarvis, *Getting Away with Genocide? Elusive Justice and the Khmer Rouge Tribunal* (London: Pluto Press, 2004), p. 223.
34 Fawthrop and Jarvis, *Getting Away with Genocide?*, p. 240.
35 See "Q & A: Sierra Leone's War Crimes Tribunal," *BBC Online*, March 10, 2004, http://news.bbc.co.uk/2/hi/africa/3547345.stm; also the Special Court's website at http://www.sc-sl.org.
36 Lyn S. Graybill, "Ten Years After, Rwanda Tries Reconciliation," *Current History*, May 2004, p. 204.
37 George Packer, "Justice on a Hill," in Mills and Brunner, eds, *The New Killing Fields: Massacre and the Politics of Intervention* (New York: Basic Books, 2002), pp. 133–34.

38 Graybill, "Ten Years After," pp. 203, 205.
39 Packer, "Justice on a Hill," p. 135.
40 Allende died in the coup, apparently by his own hand as military forces invaded the Moneda presidential palace.
41 A technical consideration dictated, however, that Pinochet could be extradited only for crimes committed after Britain's incorporation of extraterritorial torture as a crime under domestic law. Thus, only offenses from the final two years of Pinochet's rule – not the most repressive – could be extraditable.
42 A good investigation of the events, with many key documents, is Diana Woodhouse, *The Pinochet Case: A Legal and Constitutional Analysis* (Oxford: Hart Publishing, 2000).
43 "Ambiguous," because Eichmann's arrest by Israeli agents was technically a violation of Argentine sovereignty (and was protested as such); furthermore, Eichmann was dispatched clandestinely to Israel to stand trial, rather than being formally extradited.
44 Lord Millet quoted in Robertson, *Crimes against Humanity*, p. 395.
45 Ernesto Verdeja also refers to the Pinochet detention as "an example of how international events can redefine domestic political contours," and this was well before the Chilean Supreme Court's declaration that Pinochet was fit to stand trial. Verdeja, "Institutional Responses to Genocide and Mass Atrocity," in Jones, ed., *Genocide, War Crimes and the West*, p. 339.
46 Robertson, *Crimes against Humanity*, p. 400.
47 They were, of course, sometimes put on trial for other things, such as corruption (as with Arnoldo Alemán of Nicaragua and Carlos Andrés Pérez of Venezuela).
48 "Court Paves Way for Pinochet Trial," Associated Press dispatch on CNN.com, September 14, 2005, http://edition.cnn.com/2005/WORLD/americas/09/14/chile.pinochet.ap.
49 "Writing the Next Chapter in a Latin American Success Story," *The Economist*, April 2, 2005.
50 See Marc Weller, "On the Hazards of Foreign Travel for Dictators and Other International Criminals," *International Affairs*, 75: 3 (1999), pp. 599–617.
51 John G. Heidenrich, *How to Prevent Genocide: A Guide for Policymakers, Scholars, and the Concerned Citizen* (Westport, CT: Praeger, 2001), p. 67.
52 "Lawyers Attempt to Have President Bush Declared Persona Non Grata in Canada," Information Clearing House, November 19, 2004, http://207.44.245.159/article7349.htm.
53 See Charles Aldinger, "Rumsfeld Debating Whether to Avoid Germany," Reuters dispatch, February 4, 2005.
54 See "Germany Rejects Rumsfeld War Crimes Probe," *Jurist*, February 10, 2005, http://jurist.law.pitt.edu/paperchase/2005/02/germany-rejects-rumsfeld-war-crimes.php.
55 Schabas, *Genocide in International Law*, pp. 368–69.
56 As Fawthrop and Jarvis note in the Cambodian context, "whereas proving genocide can be very problematic because of the legal complexities relating to the definition of the crime, conviction for crimes against humanity is far more likely." Fawthrop and Jarvis, *Getting Away with Genocide?*, p. 173.
57 For example, it is hard to see how "inhumane acts of a similar character intentionally causing great suffering, or serious injury to body or to mental or physical health" (ICC Statute) differ appreciably from the Genocide Convention's injunction against "causing serious bodily or mental harm to members of the group."
58 Note especially the much wider range of "identifiable group[s] or collectivit[ies]" whose persecution constitutes crimes against humanity under the ICC Statute.
59 For a summary of the US position on the Genocide Convention, see Samantha Power, "The United States and Genocide Law: A History of Ambivalence," ch. 10 in Sewall and Kaysen, eds, *The United States and the International Criminal Court*, pp. 165–75.
60 For the complete text of the bill, see http://www.theorator.com/bills107/s857.html.
61 Alexander K.A. Greenawalt, "Rethinking Genocidal Intent: The Case for a Knowledge-based Interpretation," *Columbia Law Review*, 99 (1999), p. 2269.

62 Rudolph, "Constructing an Atrocities Regime," p. 678.
63 Klinghoffer and Klinghoffer, *International Citizens' Tribunals.*
64 Arthur Jay Klinghoffer, "International Citizens' Tribunals on Human Rights," in Jones, ed., *Genocide, War Crimes and the West*, pp. 350–51.
65 Klinghoffer and Klinghoffer, *International Citizens' Tribunals*, p. 156.
66 See, e.g., the "Criminal Complaint" filed by former US Attorney General to the International Court [People's Tribunal] on Crimes Against Humanity Committed by UN Security Council on Iraq, held in Spain in November 1996: Jones, ed., *Genocide, War Crimes and the West*, pp. 270–73; and, most recently, "Declaration of the Jury of Conscience – World Tribunal on Iraq," Istanbul, June 23–27, 2005, http://www.wagingpeace.org/articles/2005/06/27_jury-of-conscience-declaration.htm.
67 Klinghoffer and Klinghoffer, *International Citizens' Tribunals*, p. 10.
68 Leo Kuper, *The Prevention of Genocide* (New Haven, CT: Yale University Press, 1985), p. 193.
69 Ibid.
70 Falk quoted in Klinghoffer and Klinghoffer, *International Citizens' Tribunals*, p. 134.
71 Professor Peter Burns of the University of British Columbia, personal communication, May 12, 2005.
72 Minow, *Between Vengeance and Forgiveness*, pp. 60, 67.
73 Priscilla B. Hayner, *Unspeakable Truths: Confronting State Terror and Atrocity* (New York: Routledge, 2001), p. 232.
74 "While most commissions have had the power to name perpetrators, however, only a few have done so: El Salvador, Chad, the second commission of the African National Congress, and the South African Truth and Reconciliation Commission." Hayner, *Unspeakable Truths* pp. 107–8.
75 Hayner, *Unspeakable Truths*, p. 75.
76 Hayner, *Unspeakable Truths*, p. 111.
77 Fischman and Ross, article on "Group Treatment of Exiled Survivors of Torture," in the *American Journal of Orthopsychiatry*; quoted in Victoria Sanford, *Buried Secrets: Truth and Human Rights in Guatemala* (New York: Palgrave Macmillan, 2003), p. 241.
78 Hayner, *Unspeakable Truths*, p. 185.
79 Ibid.
80 See also Carolyn Nordstrom, "Terror Warfare and the Medicine of Peace," in Catherine Besteman, ed., *Violence: A Reader* (New York: Palgrave Macmillan, 2002), pp. 273–96.
81 Hayner, *Unspeakable Truths*, pp. 190–91. For a similar report from Uganda, see Marc Lacey, "Atrocity Victims in Uganda Choose to Forgive," *New York Times*, April 18, 2005. "Remarkably, a number of those who have been hacked by the rebels [of the Lord's Resistance Army], who have seen their children carried off by them or who have endured years of suffering in their midst say traditional justice must be the linchpin in ending the war. Their main rationale: the line between victim and killer is too blurred."
82 Elazar Barkan, *The Guilt of Nations: Restitution and Negotiating Historical Injustices* (New York: W.W. Norton, 2000), pp. xv, 92, 95. For an overview of the campaign to win restitution payments from Swiss banks, see Raul Hilberg, *The Destruction of the European Jews* (3rd edn), Vol. 3 (New Haven, CT: Yale University Press, 2003), pp. 1274–82.
83 See Document 4, "The World Conference against Racism: Declarations on the Transatlantic Slave Trade," in Jones, ed., *Genocide, War Crimes and the West*, pp. 377–78.
84 Francis Njubi Nesbitt, "Coming to Terms with the Past: The Case for a Truth and Reparations Commission on Slavery, Segregation and Colonialism," in Jones, ed., *Genocide, War Crimes and the West*, p. 374.
85 "Pressure Mounts on Britain to Remember Its Slave Trade Past," *OneWorldUK*, August 26, 2002.
86 "Maori Heads to be Returned to New Zealand," *The New Zealand Herald*, January 13, 2005.
87 Definition from New Zealand Historic Places Trust, http://www.historic.org.nz/Register/wahi_tapu.html.

88 Colin Tatz, *With Intent to Destroy: Reflecting on Genocide* (London: Verso, 2003), p. 105.
89 Minow, *Between Vengeance and Forgiveness*, p. 114.
90 Queen Elizabeth quoted in Elazar Barkan, *The Guilt of Nations: Restitution and Negotiating Historical Injustices* (New York: W.W. Norton, 2001), p. 264.
91 "A 'Sorry Day' in Australia," *BBC Online*, May 26, 1998, http://news.bbc.co.uk/1/hi/world/asia-pacific/100476.stm.
92 Clinton's apology ran as follows: "It may seem strange to you here, especially the many of you who lost members of your family, but all over the world there were people like me sitting in offices, day after day after day, who did not fully appreciate the depth and the speed with which you were being engulfed by this unimaginable terror. The international community, together with nations in Africa, must bear its share of responsibility for this tragedy as well. We did not act quickly enough after the killing began. We should not have allowed the refugee camps to become safe haven for the killers. We did not immediately call these crimes by their rightful name: genocide. We cannot change the past. But we can and must do everything in our power to help you build a future without fear and full of hope." Cited in *PBS Online News Hour*, http://www.pbs.org/newshour/bb/africa/jan-june98/rwanda_3-25a.html.
93 Barkan, *The Guilt of Nations*, p. 323.
94 Barkan, *The Guilt of Nations*, pp. 30, 273.
95 Tatz, *With Intent to Destroy*, p. 167.
96 A small step was taken by the Czech government in August 2005, apologizing to ethnic-German expellees who were "active opponents of Nazism." See "Czechs Apologize for Mistreating German Anti-Nazis in WWII," Reuters dispatch in *Haaretz.com*, August 30, 2005.

CHAPTER 16

Strategies of Intervention and Prevention

"'Never Again,'" wrote human rights scholar Thomas Cushman, ". . . embodies in crystalline form the preventative discourse" that dominates comparative genocide studies:

> through empirical and scientific observation of operationally defined cases of genocide, one can isolate the variables and causal mechanisms at work and predict future genocides. Armed with such predictions, one can take specific practical steps to intervene and stop genocides from occurring. The key to success is the development of political mechanisms or structures, which will heed the scientific understanding and possess the political will, which means basically the ability and the physical force necessary to intervene to stop genocide.[1]

Cushman viewed such optimism skeptically. He rejected the notion that all genocides can be prevented or suppressed, but he recognized that some can be, and he argued for strategies sensitive to historical context and key actors' practical limitations. With such cautions in mind, this chapter tries to avoid easy answers and past solutions. But it recognizes, and indeed typifies, the concern of the vast majority of genocide scholars not just with understanding genocides of the past, but with confronting present genocides and preventing them in the future.

Why should genocide be prevented? In a moral sense, the answer may seem self-evident: to preserve people and collectivities at risk of destruction. But what if moral considerations are excluded, and rational self-interest is stressed? This would at least have the advantage of appealing to a broader range of potential supporters for the project.

In his thoughtful book *How to Prevent Genocide*, John Heidenrich addressed this question head-on. He pointed out that genocides typically generate refugee flows that can overwhelm neighboring countries and destabilize regions. Today, up to twenty-seven million people may also be "internally displaced" worldwide as a result of genocide. "Such global multitudes of homeless and often stateless people have repeatedly drained the resources of the world's emergency aid services." He added that "every major genocidal crisis also shakes the international order. No one in 1994 expected that, within two years, mass killings in tiny Rwanda would plunge the enormity of Zaire/Congo into a civil war drawing in countries from almost half of Africa – but that is what happened."[2]

It is thus in the self-interest of humanity – both morally and practically – to oppose this crime against humanity. What are the most reliable warning signs and facilitating conditions of genocide? What ideas have been proposed for genocide intervention and prevention? What might we add to the mix? And what is the role of central actors, from the international community and organizations, to the concerned and potentially genocidal individual?

WARNING SIGNS

What are the most reliable indicators that genocide might be in the offing? Although there is no "general 'essence' of genocide . . . across time and space," some traits, phenomena, and enabling conditions may serve as red flags.[3] In outlining them here, I touch on some possible intervention strategies, but postpone a more substantial engagement with this theme until later in the chapter.

- ***A history of genocide and intercommunal conflict.*** As political scientist Barbara Harff reminded us, "perpetrators of genocide often are repeat offenders, because elites and security forces may become habituated to mass killing as a strategic response to challenges to state security."[4] Genocide is thus frequently dependent on pre-existing patterns of state behavior and state–society relations. Psychologist Ervin Staub pointed in similar fashion to "ideologies of antagonism" among communal groups, "the outcome of a long history of hostility and mutual violence."[5]
- ***Severe economic crisis.*** Few factors seem so operative in genocidal violence as economic upheaval and catastrophe. When the material basis of people's lives is thrown into question, they are depressingly prone to seek scapegoats among minorities (or majorities); to heed an extremist political message; and to be lured by opportunities to loot and pillage. Economic crisis may undermine the legitimacy and administrative capacity of state authorities, who may be more likely to lash out genocidally as a means of maintaining power. Such crises also encourage the rise of rebellious, revolutionary, and secessionist movements. These movements may fuel the ruling authorities' paranoia, and sometimes contain a genocidal impetus of their own.
- ***Mobilization along lines of communal cleavage.*** It is natural for people of a particular religion, language, or history – the usual markers of "ethnic" identity

– to associate with others who share those traits. Social and political mobilization along these lines is not inherently bad and violence-provoking. Indeed, if successfully managed, it may *head off* outbreaks of violence. No one anticipates a genocidal outbreak in Belgium or Switzerland, for example – two countries whose political systems are largely structured along communal lines.

Nonetheless, a healthy and nongenocidal society will, in place of or in addition to such mobilizations, include a range of "cross-cutting" forums, movements, and socialization mechanisms that encourage people to move beyond limited identifications to a more cosmopolitan vision. Such relations can help offset us-and-them thinking, as Ervin Staub wrote: "To evolve an appreciation of alikeness and a feeling of connectedness, members of subgroups of society must live together, work together, play together; their children must go to school together. Members of different nations must also work and play together. . . . To reduce prejudice requires positive contact."[6]

National and, in particular, federal governments have a central responsibility to ensure that communal identities are successfully managed, and that constituencies are represented fairly in the halls of political and economic power. Political scientist Kal Holsti argues that "the most important [variable] is inclusiveness":

> There must be a deliberate policy by governments not to exclude specific groups from participating in the political system. If you look at Rwanda, Burundi, or Liberia and other places, the one thing they have in common is that one group – whether a minority or a majority – systematically excludes other groups from political participation, from government largesse, and from government programs. In some cases excluded groups were thrown out of the country; in other cases they were killed in genocides or politicides; in yet other cases they were simply denied the vote or in other ways discriminated against. In the countries that have succeeded, there is an attempt to be politically inclusive. . . . There is no single formula, but the common characteristic . . . is an inclusive political system and political parties that transcend ethnic and language groups and that focus instead on policy differences.[7]

- ***Hate propaganda.*** A standard feature of genocidal mobilization is hate propaganda, including in mass media, public political speech, personal websites, and graffiti. The proliferation of media organs and other institutions devoted to hate speech is usually identifiable, though an increase in frequency and/or intensity of annihilationist rhetoric may be harder to measure. To the extent that it can be gauged, it may identify future *génocidaires* – and their targets. Hate speech underpins "exclusionary ideologies . . . that define target groups as expendable."[8]

  How can one confront hate propaganda? Pluralistic societies encounter some of the same vexing questions as in the case of genocide denial (Chapter 14), notably: is it legitimate to suppress dissident speech? Whereas denialism can be confronted with logical and empirical refutation, and includes a grey area of legitimate discussion and debate, hate propaganda directly incites violence. But repressing it may only spur the hatred that underlies it, and give publicity to the propagandists. Constructive countermeasures – support for pluralistic media projects and political initiatives; effective use of education systems – are generally preferable.[9] However, while this argument may be comfortably advanced in democratic living rooms, it has different implications in societies where history and current indicators warn of genocide. Suppressing ethnic hate propaganda in Rwanda, for instance, may run counter to cherished liberal principles; but I, for one, would not object to it.

- ***Unjust discriminatory legislation and related measures.*** Some discriminatory legislation may actually help suppress a potential genocide. For example, an affirmative action policy (*Bumiputra*, or "sons of the soil") was instituted in Malaysia after ethnic rioting between Malays and ethnic Chinese. It proved acceptable to both groups, advancing Malays in areas where they were under-represented, while preserving the rights of the Chinese minority and stanching violence against it. In general, though, discrimination embodied in law (and in deliberately unequal systems of "justice") serves to marginalize and isolate a designated group – perhaps as a prelude to genocide.

  Another kind of discriminatory legislation deserves attention: that aimed at restricting possession of firearms. My liberal sympathies incline me towards effective gun control as a measure of a civilized society. However, the argument advanced by Jay Simkin *et al.*, members of the odd-sounding group Jews for the Preservation of Firearm Ownership (www.jpfo.org), rings true. They contend that most instances of mass killing have been preceded by systematic campaigns to seize arms from intended genocidal targets.[10] A reasonable middle ground may lie in promoting the restriction of firearm ownership in plural societies, while recognizing that campaigns to suppress private gun ownership in illiberal and repressive societies *may* aim to deny a minority the means to resist genocide.

- ***Severe and systematic state repression.*** Repression and outright state terror are especially trenchant indicators that a genocidal campaign may be brewing. Regardless of whether genocide ensues, such abuses must be denounced and suppressed. The imposition of emergency measures; restrictions on civil liberties; the banning or harassing of opposition parties and organizations; arbitrary detentions and large-scale round-ups of civilians; the advent or increased use of torture as state policy; substantial flows of refugees and internally displaced persons (IDPs) – should all arouse deep concern, and may well presage a genocidal outbreak.

  These acts are predominantly inflicted in authoritarian and underdeveloped societies, but citizens of democratic countries should acknowledge that they are not immune to creeping societal repression. They should be alert to violations of democracy and human rights at home and abroad, exploiting liberal democracy's broad freedoms in doing so.

  The groups most likely to be targeted for repression include ethnic, racial, and religious minorities; "middleman" groups, especially those occupying an envied place in the economy (see Chapter 11); political dissidents and accused "enemies of the people," especially those involved in nationalist and secessionist movements or class rebellions; and finally, groups labeled as "outcasts," "asocials," and "rootless and shiftless," or depicted as outside the universe of obligation (Chapter 1).

My own contribution to early-warning mechanisms revolves around the vulnerability of adult males, notably men of "battle age" (roughly 15–55). As I argued in Chapter 13, there are grounds for claiming that this group, usually described as the least vulnerable, is in fact *most* vulnerable to genocide and the repression that routinely precedes it – if by "most vulnerable" we mean most *liable* to be targeted for mass killing and other violent atrocities.[11] The United Nations and other international organizations, governmental and nongovernmental, require a paradigm shift in their thinking on gender, violence, and humanitarian intervention – one that allows specific (not exclusive) attention to be paid to adult men and male adolescents. How, for example, might greater sensitivity to the vulnerability of "battle-age" males at Srebrenica have assisted in heading off the gendercide of July 1995?[12]

HUMANITARIAN INTERVENTION

> When people's lives are at risk from persecution, there is a strong moral obligation to do what is reasonably possible to help. It is not enough to seal up the windows against the smell.
>
> Jonathan Glover

The 1990s inaugurated a new age of humanitarian intervention. With the end of the Cold War, the way lay open for hard-nosed *realpolitik* to be set aside in favor of efforts to help suffering and persecuted peoples. The United Nations would finally come into its own as the arbiter and peace-builder that Franklin Roosevelt originally envisaged. Regional actors would step up to address nearby trouble spots.

At the same time, the collapse of the Soviet empire and of superpower rivalries had allegedly "lifted the lid off" a host of simmering conflicts, mostly ethno-national in nature. One prominent observer warned of a "coming anarchy" of state collapse and untrammeled violence.[13] In many parts of the world – Africa, former Soviet Central Asia, the Caucasus, the Balkans – anarchy indeed arrived.

During this period, "humanitarian intervention" came to be associated with a military response to atrocities, separating warring factions, supervising negotiations, and brokering political settlements. The four key cases of, and debates over, humanitarian intervention in the 1990s – Iraqi Kurdistan (1991); Bosnia-Herzegovina (1992–95); and Kosovo and East Timor (both 1999) – all featured such interventions. However, might such military interventions instead represent *failures*, in the same way that successful fire-fighting can attest to inadequate fire prevention? In this discussion, I first address *non*-military intervention strategies. Military solutions should be a last resort, although mounted resolutely and with all dispatch when necessary.

The authors of a Canadian-sponsored report, *The Responsibility to Protect*, propose a useful range of non-military strategies. These "may come in the form of development assistance and other efforts to help address the root cause of potential conflict; or efforts to provide support for local initiatives to advance good governance, human rights, or the rule of law; or good offices missions, mediation efforts and other efforts to promote dialogue or reconciliation."[14] Lending political support – whether good offices, formal mediation, or simply rhetorical support – to governments that act respectfully towards their citizens is one of the most constructive interventionist measures.[15]

Conversely, *withholding* aid may be a potent intervention strategy. Obviously, it is essential that military and "security" aid are not provided to forces of repression. However, the history of recent decades suggests that such forces are often favored aid recipients. France, for instance, armed and trained the Rwandan *génocidaires* even when their murderous intentions were plain, and continued to support them after they had slaughtered up to a million of their fellow citizens. As pointed out in Chapter 12, the United States is without twentieth-century equal in supporting forces of atrocity and genocide beyond its borders.

With regard to economic intervention, it is worth abiding by medicine's Hippocratic oath: First, do no harm. Interventionist economic policies such as "austerity" measures and "structural adjustment" programs may increase social stress in a way that contributes directly or indirectly to genocide. Rwanda and, arguably, Yugoslavia in the 1980s and 1990s provide examples. Cheerleading for wholesale economic "globalization" should thus be rejected. As international legal theorist Richard Falk has written, "Economic globalisation . . . weakens the overall capacity and will of governments to address human wrongs either within their own society or elsewhere. . . . It seems appropriate to link economic globalisation with a high threshold of tolerance for human wrongs, at least for now."[16] Moreover, if structural and institutional violence can themselves constitute genocide, then structural adjustment measures and the like may be not only a *cause* of genocide, but a *form* of it.

Sanctions

Economic and political sanctions lie at an intermediate point between "soft" intervention strategies and military intervention. As *The Responsibility to Protect* summarized such measures, they may include "arms embargoes," "ending military cooperation and training programmes," "financial sanctions," "restrictions on income-generating activities such as oil, diamonds . . . logging and drugs," "restrictions on access to petroleum products," "aviation bans," "restrictions on diplomatic representation," "restrictions on travel," and "suspension of membership or expulsion from international or regional bodies."[17] To this list might be added the application of judicial sanctions, such as indictments for war crimes and genocide.

The difficulty with sanctions lies in targeting them to impede a repressive or genocidal leadership, without inflicting generalized human suffering. In two twentieth-century cases, human destruction caused by malevolent and/or misdirected sanctions could be considered genocidal. The economic blockade imposed on Germany during *and after* the First World War killed up to three-quarters of a million people.[18] The sanctions imposed on the Iraqi population in peacetime provide a second case (see Chapter 1).

In part as a result of the Iraqi catastrophe, "blanket economic sanctions in particular have been increasingly discredited in recent years," because they impose "greatly disproportionate . . . hardships" on civilians.[19] Appropriately targeted measures, however, may repress would-be *génocidaires*. These actions can include freezing of bank accounts; travel bans; and (more controversially) sporting, cultural, and academic boycotts.

The United Nations

The UN has an abysmal record in confronting and forestalling genocide. According to Leo Kuper and others, this reflects the organization's foundation on Westphalian norms of state sovereignty (Chapter 12), and the desire of most member states to avoid shining a spotlight on their own atrocities, past or present.

There is and always has been another side to the UN, however, typified by the extraordinarily effective specialized agencies (UNICEF, the World Food Program, and so on), and by the UN's contribution to peacekeeping and peace-building around the world. Since the late 1980s, the UN has increasingly stressed peace-*building*, described by UN Secretary-General Kofi Annan as:

> the creation or strengthening of national institutions, monitoring elections, promoting human rights, providing for reintegration and rehabilitation programmes, as well as creating conditions for resumed development. Peacebuilding does not replace ongoing humanitarian and development activities in countries emerging from crises. Rather, it aims to build on, add to, or reorient such activities in ways that are designed to reduce the risk of a resumption of conflict and contribute to creating conditions most conducive to reconciliation, reconstruction and recovery.[20]

These measures are vital to making "Never Again" a reality. Peace-building has been implemented most visibly in three Central American countries (El Salvador, Nicaragua, and Guatemala) after their civil wars. In coordination with non-governmental organizations, both indigenous and foreign, the UN oversaw the demobilization and reintegration of fighting forces; constructed new societal institutions virtually from scratch; organized and supervised elections; monitored violations of human rights; and assisted the work of truth-and-reconciliation commissions, among other duties. On balance, this must be counted as a major UN success, providing a wealth of knowledge and practice for future genocide prevention and conflict resolution.

Overall, significant evidence supports the conclusion of *The Responsibility to Protect* that the UN "is unquestionably the principal institution for building, consolidating and using the authority of the international community."[21] As John Heidenrich noted, "by signing the UN Charter, every member has obligated itself to adhere to the most basic norms of civilized conduct, which means that only through outright hypocrisy can a government commit a crime as grievous as genocide." Moreover, "only the United Nations has the Security Council, the only international body with the global legal right to compel countries to adhere to international humanitarian treaties and customs, by force if necessary."[22]

WHEN IS MILITARY INTERVENTION JUSTIFIED?

Kenneth Roth, executive director of Human Rights Watch, sets a useful standard for military intervention. "Given the death, destruction, and disorder that are often inherent in war and its aftermath," he writes, "humanitarian intervention" – by which he means *military* intervention – "should be reserved as an option only in situations of ongoing or imminent mass slaughter. Only the direst cases of large-scale slaughter can justify war's deliberate taking of life." Thus, Roth argues,

> military action must be the last reasonable option. Second, the intervention must be primarily guided by a humanitarian purpose. Third, it should be conducted to maximize respect for international human rights law. Fourth, it must be reasonably likely to do more good than harm. Finally, it should ideally, *though not necessarily*, be endorsed by the UN Security Council or another body with significant multilateral authority.[23]

In the wake of the Kosovo intervention, carried out without UN Security Council authorization, an Independent International Commission was formed under the stewardship of South African Judge Richard Goldstone (who also spent two years as head of the ICTY tribunal at the Hague). One commission member, political scientist Mary Kaldor, summarized the commission's conclusion "that the Kosovo intervention was illegal, because there was no Security Council resolution, *but legitimate* because it resolved a humanitarian crisis and had widespread support within the international community and civil society." The "illegal but legitimate" verdict was an elegant one, but attested to "very dangerous" gaps and imprecisions in international law and interventionist policies.[24]

Many commentators, however, have criticized military interventions as currently framed, because they tend to accord *carte blanche* to powerful states (themselves at no risk of military intervention) to dictate to the world's weaker states. In the view of US Law Professor Stephen Holmes, this may extend to mounting invasions on supposedly "humanitarian" grounds. For all the lofty rhetoric that accompanies them, Holmes argued, military interventions are usually selective, self-interested, and counterproductive.[25] A veritable cottage industry of texts sprang up following the 1999 Kosovo intervention, depicting it as malignant imperialism rather than an altruistic venture.[26] The broader point – that "humanitarian" intervention often masks imperial ambition – is cogent. Intervention discourse may legitimately be analyzed for ulterior motives, although their existence is inevitable and should not rule out intervention altogether.

Consider, for example, the place of regional actors in the intervention equation. Such actors have played *the* key role in virtually all successful interventions against genocide over the past three-and-a-half decades ("success" being measured by a halt to the killing). In 1971, India, the regional hegemon of South Asia, intervened to stop the genocide against Bengalis in East Pakistan (see Box 8a). In 1979, Tanzania overthrew the Idi Amin government in Uganda, ending his depredations (though installing a new regime under Milton Obote that proved little better). Also in 1979,

Vietnam invaded Cambodia and pushed the Khmer Rouge regime to the margins. NATO's 1999 intervention in Kosovo brought an end to Serb genocide in the province, and allowed 800,000 ethnic Albanian refugees to return. Later that same year, Australia played the leading role in ending Indonesia's genocidal occupation of East Timor; at the dawn of the new millennium, Nigeria headed the interventions in Sierra Leone and Liberia staged by ECOWAS (the Economic Community of West African States).

In none of these interventions, with the possible exception of Australia in East Timor, did moral and humanitarian considerations act as primary catalysts. Ulterior motives were always present.[27] However, in a world of states that is still run on classical notions of sovereignty and *realpolitik*, one arguably takes what one can get. Ulterior motives may even be welcome for the added spur they provide to needed interventions.

The advantages of intervention by regional actors are several. Geographical contiguity minimizes logistical difficulties, although this may be offset by a lack of resources (apart from the Australian case, all the interventions cited above were carried out by poor developing nations). With contiguity often comes a degree of ethnocultural similarity, making it less likely that interventions will be seen as foreign or imperial. Regional powers may also have a vested interest in guarding against the spill-over of genocide, something that more distant actors might not share.

At the same time, however, vested interests operate, and may undermine the intervention. The conflict in Congo – Africa's first "world war" (Box 9a) – fed the expansionist aspirations and pillaging ambitions of a host of African nations. Logistical difficulties are likely to prevail where regional actors are underdeveloped, with limited resources. In such cases, material assistance from the developed world is critical. Political scientist Alan Kuperman has argued that "only the US military has a large, long-haul cargo air fleet," without which "rapid reaction to most parts of the world is impossible."[28] Journalist Michael Hirsh goes so far as to argue that the "most important future role for the UN" might be that of "a legitimizer for local forces" to intervene, with assistance and logistical backing from the developed countries who supply most of the UN's budget.[29]

A standing "peace army"?

In a contribution to his edited *Encyclopedia of Genocide*, Israel Charny proposed the creation of an International Peace Army as a "standing machinery . . . for responding to eruptions of genocide, at any time or place in the world." Such a force:

> would move automatically into action any time that authenticated reports are received of the mass killing of any group of unarmed civilians, such as the ethnic cleansing of a village or a region. The basic mandate of the *International Peace Army* would be to take action in the same way that we are accustomed today in democratic countries to call on the police at the first evidence of murder or even possible murderous assault.[30]

The Peace Army would be pluralistic in composition (with "nationals from a very wide range of countries"). Charny divided the Peace Army into three units: one military, another medical and humanitarian, and a third designed "for the Rebuilding of Safe and Tolerant Communities." In a nod to the growing scope and complexity of UN peacekeeping and peace-building operations from the late 1980s, this final component would bring "skilled administrators and technicians for reestablishing the basic structure of community life." It would also aim to "mobilize indigenous leaders of the peoples involved in the conflict – religious leaders, political leaders, popular folk heroes including media celebrities, sports stars, beloved popular singers, leaders in education, and so on of the indigenous culture – who will agree to speak to the building of a new era of tolerance and reconciliation."[31]

A Peace Army may seem utopian, but contemporary developments make it less so. For one thing, Charny's imagined force would be an "affiliated police arm" of the United Nations.[32] In the new millennium, the UN has taken steps to establish a standing army that, with the input of humanitarian organizations, could fulfill many of the functions Charny envisaged. The plan calls for twelve nations – Canada and Denmark have already signed on – to contribute to a 6,000-strong force on standby for a call from the Secretary-General and the Security Council. A different, possibly complementary, Dutch proposal calls for a "fire brigade" of 2,500 to 5,000 soldiers as "a permanent, rapidly deployable brigade" to intervene in genocidal outbreaks. Five thousand troops is roughly the force that Major-General Roméo Dallaire pleaded for when the Rwandan genocide was underway. "If I had had such a force available to me while I was the UNAMIR Force Commander sometime in mid-April, we could have saved the lives of hundreds of thousands of people," Dallaire asserted.[33]

The European Union, which after the UN represents the world's leading force for democracy, peace, and humanitarianism,[34] has considered creating an "EU Rapid Reaction Force" (ERRF), capable of deploying up to 60,000 soldiers within sixty days and maintaining them in the field for up to one year. The EU has also floated the idea of "battle groups" consisting of elite battalions of 1,500 soldiers, able to deploy within fifteen days and stay in the field for a month. Not to be left out, by 2010 the African Union also seeks to develop an African Standby Force consisting of "regionally-based standby brigades, numbering between 3,500 and 5,000 troops," deployable within two weeks.[35] All these initiatives are guided by a perception that the hidebound, bureaucratic process of deploying peacemaking and peacekeeping operations gives *génocidaires* and war criminals too great a head start. For the UN and the Europeans alike, there is the added attraction of developing a military force that does not rely on the US for funding and logistics.

Finally, there is the possibility of an "international legion of volunteers," as Heidenrich has discussed. Such corps have played an important role in some conflicts, from the Spanish Civil War to the French Foreign Legion's varied postings. Some proposals even envisage the use of mercenaries in this role, arguing that the unsavory reputation attached to these forces is outdated.[36]

IDEOLOGIES AND INDIVIDUALS

Who am I and of what am I capable?

James Waller

Our analysis now shifts from the national and international–political sphere to the more intimate level of human beings' minds and hearts. What difference can individual witnessing make to genocide? How do ideologies, whether religious or secular, spur us to genocide perpetration – and prevention? And how can we confront and mitigate our own potential to inflict or support genocidal acts?

The role of the honest witness

Witnessing and transmitting are central to genocide prevention and intervention. The key is *honest, accurate* witnessing, combined with the capacity to communicate what one has witnessed. The "relentless keepers of the truth," as Russian intellectual Nadezhda Mandelstam called them, are genocide's most powerful opponents, and "the best proof that good, not evil, will prevail in the end."[37] Conversely, those who fail to witness honestly – who turn away, distort, and deny – are reliable allies of the *génocidaires.*

A fascinating contrast in honest versus dishonest witnessing is provided by the terror-famine in Ukraine (1932–33). At the height of the famine, with millions dying throughout the countryside, British socialists Sidney and Beatrice Webb traveled to the USSR. They kept well away from the starving rural areas, and subsequently wrote "a glowing account" of their visit (*Soviet Communism – A New Civilisation,* published in 1935). The *New York Times*' Moscow correspondent, Walter Duranty, also avoided all mention of the famine and the state's genocidal manipulation of it. Duranty's reports influenced the Roosevelt administration's decision to recognize the Soviet government – in 1933, as famine, collectivization of the countryside, and the crushing of peasant resistance all reached their zenith.[38]

The witnessing of British journalist Malcolm Muggeridge was radically different. Arriving in the Soviet Union in 1933, Muggeridge took the simple expedient of buying a train ticket to journey through the heartland of Ukraine and the North Caucasus. *En route,* he witnessed some of the horrific scenes of famine described in Chapter 5. "*Whatever else I may do or think in the future, I must never pretend that I haven't seen this,*" Muggeridge wrote in his diary.[39] He returned to publish an account of "millions of starving peasants, their bodies often swollen from lack of food," struggling with "soldier members of the GPU [secret police] carrying out the instructions of the dictatorship of the proletariat." The Stalinist forces, Muggeridge wrote, "had gone over the country like a swarm of locusts and taken away everything edible . . . [and] had reduced some of the most fertile land in the world to a melancholy desert."[40]

Like Muggeridge, the diplomats, missionaries, and some German soldiers who witnessed the Armenian genocide were central to catalyzing international protest, and some small intervention in the Armenian plight. Their writings and photographs are essential to our current understanding of the genocide, and serve as a bulwark against the efforts of those who deny it (see chapters 4, 14). By contrast, the withdrawal of nearly all media and most foreign observers from Rwanda in the early stages of the 1994 genocide meant that only the most fragmentary imagery and testimony of that holocaust reached the outside world. Even in an age of globalized mass communication, the Rwandan *génocidaires* inflicted their horrors with only rare outside witnesses, and no outside intervention.

Often, honest witnessing must be carried out at great risk of capture, torture, and death. At such times it inspires real awe. A dramatic example is Jan Karski, a Polish diplomat in his late twenties, who sought to bring the truth of the Jewish Holocaust to the outside world. Operating throughout Nazi-occupied Poland, Karski "disguised himself as a Jew, donning an armband with the Star of David, and smuggled himself through a tunnel into the Warsaw ghetto. Posing as a Ukrainian militiaman, he also infiltrated Belzec, a Nazi death camp near the border between Poland and Ukraine." One marvels at the danger and spectacular deception hinted at in this passage. At the end of 1942, Karski escaped to London "carrying hundreds of documents on miniature microfilm contained in the shaft of a key." He immediately sought a meeting with representatives of the Jewish community. Passing on Karski's reports to the World Jewish Congress in New York, Ignacy Schwartzbart, a prominent London Jew, urged his audience to "*BELIEVE THE UNBELIEVABLE.*"[41] Even many Jews, however, found the information too unbelievable to be credited. This serves as a painful reminder that no link need exist between honest witnessing and genocide prevention. A host of unpredictable factors – above all, public attention and political will – must come into play if information is to translate into action.[42]

In the contemporary age, the witnessing of human rights organizations and activists is indispensable. Global NGOs such as Human Rights Watch, Amnesty International, the Red Cross, and Doctors Without Borders, as well as legions of national and regional projects, provide the most extensive, detailed, and informed analyses of rights violations and human suffering. One activist describes their core approach as "*promoting change by reporting facts.*"[43]

Other activist initiatives preserve past traumas, including genocide, in historical memory – another form of witnessing. One example is the Russian Memorial Society. "Memorial was founded by a group of young historians, some of whom had been collecting oral histories of [Gulag] camp survivors for many years," writes Anne Applebaum. "Later, Memorial would also lead the battle to identify the corpses buried in mass graves outside Moscow and Leningrad, and to build monuments and memorials to the Stalinist era." By the end of the 1990s, Memorial had established itself as "the most important centre for the study of Soviet history, as well as for the defence of human rights, in the Russian federation." Its publications were "known to Soviet scholars around the world for their accuracy, their fidelity to facts, and their careful, judicious archives."[44]

Ideologies, religious and secular

> The imagination and the spiritual strength of Shakespeare's evildoers stopped short at a dozen corpses. Because they had no *ideology*.
>
> Alexander Solzhenitsyn, *The Gulag Archipelago*

The role of religious belief in genocide prevention and intervention may be viewed from two perspectives. On one hand, religious believers throughout history have derived from their faith an abiding love and respect for humanity. In a practical sense, this has led them to cross lines of religion, ethnicity, and social class to help genocide's victims. In colonial Spanish America, Bartolomé de las Casas denounced atrocities against the Indians with a passion that still cuts through cant nearly five centuries later (though Las Casas supported the importation of African slaves to reduce the burden on indigenous peoples). Catholics in Poland during the Second World War regularly sheltered Jews (see Chapter 10). One such rescuer, Irene Gut Opdyke, was a devout believer who wrote in her memoirs: "Courage is a whisper from above: when you listen with your heart, you will know what to do and how and when."[45] Post-genocide Rwanda witnessed a surge of converts to Islam, since the country's Muslim minority, by contrast with its Catholic Church, had saved Tutsis rather than standing by as they were massacred – or joining in. Surely, the humane and cosmopolitan vision guiding much religious belief and practice is to be acknowledged and admired.

The case of Rwanda's Catholic Church, however, reminds us that religious believers often play a negligent or even murderous role in genocide.[46] "The very worst things that men have ever done," said British politician William Gladstone, "have been done when they were performing acts of violence in the name of religion."[47] In the opinion of the great sociologist Barrington Moore, Jr. – summarized by his student Charles Tilly – monotheistic religions, in particular, foster "gross intolerance, hence readiness to kill outsiders, because of their sharply drawn distinctions between the worthy and the unworthy, the pure and the impure."[48] But polytheism provides no barrier to fanaticism, as Muslim and Sikh survivors of Hindu nationalist violence can attest.

The distinguishing element here is not religious belief per se, but *extremism and exclusivism* through a religious lens. There are few more important tasks of genocide prevention than confronting religious extremists and fundamentalists, at home and abroad – not with persecution or bombs, which would only fuel their martyr complex, but wherever possible with a pluralistic, humanistic education system, and a cosmopolitan[49] counter-discourse (including by religious moderates) in the public sphere.

Secular ideologies are also Janus-faced in relation to genocide. Democratic and pluralistic ideologies are primarily responsible for our concern about genocide and human rights violations. The very idea of "human rights" is a product of the secular Enlightenment in Europe, though it resonates with many religious and philosophical traditions worldwide. These ideologies have underpinned enormous positive changes in human civilization. State-sponsored slavery is no more.[50] The most blatant forms of colonialism have mostly been expunged from the Earth. Major wars and genocides across a range of previously conflictive "dyads" are now unlikely or unthinkable

(France and Germany is the most commonly cited pairing). Institutions whose gratuitous cruelty has something in common with the sadism of genocide – such as drawing-and-quartering or breaking on a wheel[51] – are also historical relics.

Secular-humanist ideologies have given rise to the idea of global civil society and "world citizenship," vital to transcending the differences of culture, class, and religion that can fuel genocides. A world citizen holds that:

> Everyone is an individual endowed with certain rights and subject to certain obligations; everyone is capable of voluntaristic action seeking rational solutions to social problems; everyone has the right and obligation to participate in the grand human project; everyone is, therefore, a citizen of the world polity. World citizenship is the institutional endowment of authority and agency on individuals. It infuses each individual with the authority to pursue particularistic interests, preferably in organizations, while also authorizing individuals to promote collective goods defined in largely standardized ways.[52]

But secular ideologies have also *underpinned* most genocides of the last two centuries. One thinks of the genocidal expansionists into an economically "unexploited" North America; the Young Turk modernizers of the Ottoman Empire, and their counterparts in Stalinist Russia; the Nazis with their fanatical racism and nationalism; and the Khmer Rouge communists in Cambodia. The genocidal consequences of much secular ideology were eloquently conveyed by a repentant Communist Party activist, speaking about the imposition of famine and collectivization on the Soviet countryside:

> With the rest of my generation I firmly believed that the ends justified the means. Our great goal was the universal triumph of Communism, and for the sake of that goal everything was permissible – to lie, to steal, to destroy hundreds of thousands and even millions of people, all those who were hindering our work or could hinder it, everyone who stood in the way. And to hesitate or doubt about all this was to give in to "intellectual squeamishness" and "stupid liberalism," the attribute of people who "could not see the forest for the trees." . . . I was convinced that I was accomplishing the great and necessary transformation of the countryside; that in the days to come the people who lived there would be better off for it; that their distress and suffering were a result of their own ignorance or the machinations of the class enemy; that those who sent me – and I myself – knew better than the peasants how they should live, what they should sow and when they should plow.[53]

A mirror image of such thinking in the capitalist West depicts those who stand in the way of "modernization" and "development" as backward and disposable, while the millions of casualties inflicted by colonial famines or contemporary "structural adjustment" policies are justified by the noble ends of market liberalism.

There is a critical individual dimension – in both senses of the word "critical" – to religious and secular ideologies alike. Each person must monitor, as objectively as possible, the tendency to hatred and exclusivism that is present in us all. The temptation always exists to believe *we* are superior and right – whether we bolster this with religious belief, a secular stance, or a mix of the two. Actually, we *might* be "superior" and in the right! I do believe some epistemologies (strategies of knowing), moral frameworks, and social options are superior to others, or I would not be writing this book. But we must guard against hubris. As Ruby Plenty Chiefs reminds us: "Great evil has been done on earth by people who think they have all the answers."[54]

How can you as an individual monitor your beliefs, and reduce (forgive me) your genocidal potential?

- ***Educate yourself broadly and deeply.*** If your beliefs are congruent with reality and a viable moral framework, they should not collapse in the face of divergent or opposed views. Expose yourself to these viewpoints, by consulting a wide range of media – that is now easier than ever. Learn from contrary-minded others. Surprisingly often, you will find that those who think differently become more familiar to you, even real friends. This should make you less likely to support their marginalization or extermination.
- ***Travel if you can.*** This is also easier than ever, even outside the privileged West. My own most intensive learning has come from traveling as much of the world as time and money have allowed. Talk to people in those distant lands, like-minded and otherwise. You are bound to discover strong bonds of commonality; once you have visited a place and interacted with its inhabitants, you are less likely to want to return to kill them, or to support anyone with that agenda. If you *can't* travel, or won't, then at least read voraciously (history, current affairs, travel accounts, and guides); watch the History Channel and Discovery Channel; surf the Net for relevant perspectives and insights. As always, seek to balance your receptivity with critical thinking and a healthy dose of skepticism.
- ***"Keep [y]our consciences soft and vulnerable."*** "Only then," write Donald and Laura Miller, "will we rise up to challenge the suffering that surrounds us. Denial of evil is a defense mechanism that a just world simply cannot afford."[55] Be open to the distress of others, and to discrimination against them. As the Argentine revolutionary Ché Guevara wrote in a 1966 letter to his children: "Above all, be capable always of feeling to your very depths any injustice committed against anyone in any part of the world."[56]

  There is denial of evil and there is saturation by evil. It is easy, in the face of genocide's massive violence, to allow it and similar tragedies to slide into abstraction. Aid agencies speak of "compassion fatigue." Allen Feldman pointed to a "cultural anesthesia" born of "generalities of bodies – dead, wounded, starving, diseased, and homeless . . . pressed against the television screen as mass articles."[57] Soviet dictator Joseph Stalin famously commented, "One death is a tragedy; a million deaths is a statistic."[58]

  The solution lies in empathy and learning. I recall sitting in a restaurant in Colombia in 1994, watching fragmentary images on TV of dozens of bodies floating down a river somewhere far away. These are today among the indelible images of the Rwandan holocaust. My thought at the time? "Oh jeez, more tribal violence in Africa." Only after plowing through a few thousand pages of testimony and reportage on the genocide, material that stunned and changed me, did I feel I had expiated the shame of that first ignorant, cavalier reaction.

- ***Question authority.*** I do not say "Reject authority." Much authority is *authoritative* rather than *authoritarian.* It derives its legitimacy from a power to persuade through reason and moral appeal. On the other hand, the great majority of genocides are carried out under authoritarian rule of one kind or another, and formally democratic societies are far from immune to these temptations – especially in times of proclaimed emergency. Many if not most of the readers of this book will be called upon, at some point in their lives, to decide whether to support a call to large-scale collective violence. Is that call warranted, or is it a summons to atrocity? All authority rests on conformity, and conforming may be immoral or inhuman. When this is the case, move beyond questioning to active opposition.
- ***Support worthy causes.*** You know a few already. Some of those devoted specifically to genocide prevention may be found on the webpage for this book (http://www.genocidetext.net). Consider supporting by *participating*, not just by contributing money. Participation brings you into contact and solidarity with other human beings. This is essential to building a global movement against genocide.

  Proponents of worthy causes may sometimes use violence to achieve their goals – typically, to bring an end to violence (including structural violence) by an oppressor. These actions may not be pretty, but neither, unfortunately, are they obsolete. Violent resistance to the planners and perpetrators of genocide, *while it is underway*, is an incontestable right. Likewise, all peoples have the right to resist aggressive war waged against them, if their resistance does not descend into mass atrocity.

  Beyond this, I offer only tentative comments about whether to support a given movement that practices violence. I have strongly backed movements that used violence to defend civilian populations, for positive social revolution, and for national independence (the Sandinistas in Nicaragua; the FMLN guerrillas in El Salvador; South Africa's ANC; Fretilin in East Timor). I have also supported state-led military interventions that suppressed genocide – Vietnam in Cambodia, or NATO in Kosovo (though in the latter case, I criticized the military strategy, based on high-altitude bombing, as cowardly and ineffective).

  As Alan Kuperman has pointed out, however, violent resistance and military intervention may provide just the "provocation" that would-be *génocidaires* are seeking to implement their final solution. Thus, violence should be employed only and truly *in extremis*, as a defensive response to manifestly intolerable treatment. It is a cliché to say that non-violent means should be tried first, second, and third. It becomes less of a cliché when we appreciate the enormous power of non-violent resistance, which has toppled dictatorships around the world.[59]

CONCLUSION

This book has tried to provide an introduction to the concept and practice of genocide. We have considered both genocide's roots in antiquity and its manifestations in modern and contemporary periods. The intimate relationships between genocide, war, imperialism, and social revolution have been explored, together with diverse social science perspectives on the phenomenon. We have examined how legal institutions and mechanisms evolved to confront genocide; how genocides worked their way into collective memory; and the role that gender plays.

One might express optimism or pessimism about the chances of establishing an effective anti-genocide regime. But a mood changes nothing.[60]

Anything in the human order that can be understood can be confronted. In the case of a blight as pernicious and enduring as genocide, we are morally obliged to do so. Actions taken today carry special significance, with so many human and planetary issues demanding attention. To stage an effective confrontation, we need to perceive the linkages between genocide and other pressing challenges. Hence, in part, my preference for a broad and inclusive genocide framework, rather than a conceptually restrictive or narrowly legalistic one. Meaningful "peace" cannot exist alongside massive inequalities in wealth, health, and education. And it will do us little good to suppress genocide and establish amity among peoples, if the Earth itself finally rebels against the species that has done it so much ecocidal damage.

The odds of overcoming these multifarious challenges are impossible to estimate, but I believe we have an obligation to face them squarely. I hope I have persuaded you, if you needed persuading, that the struggle against genocide deserves a prominent place on the human agenda. May I welcome you to the struggle?

FURTHER STUDY

John G. Heidenrich, *How to Prevent Genocide: A Guide for Policymakers, Scholars, and the Concerned Citizen.* Westport, CT: Praeger, 2001. Emphasizes military intervention.

Leo Kuper, *The Prevention of Genocide.* New Haven, CT: Yale University Press, 1985. Kuper's second and final book on genocide focuses on UN performance and preventive strategies.

PreventGenocide.org. http://www.preventgenocide.org. Indispensable resources and prevention strategies.

Neal Riemer, ed., *Protection Against Genocide: Mission Impossible?* Westport, CT: Praeger, 2000. Short, readable volume on genocide prevention.

Nicholas Wheeler, *Saving Strangers: Humanitarian Intervention in International Society.* Oxford: Oxford University Press, 2000. Now the standard text on humanitarian intervention.

NOTES

1 Thomas Cushman, "Is Genocide Preventable? Some Theoretical Considerations," *Journal of Genocide Research*, 5: 4 (2003), pp. 528, 531.

2 John G. Heidenrich, *How to Prevent Genocide: A Guide for Policymakers, Scholars, and the Concerned Citizen* (Westport, CT: Praeger, 2001), p. 18.

3 Cushman, "Is Genocide Preventable?," p. 525.

4 Barbara Harff, "No Lessons Learned from the Holocaust? Assessing Risks of Genocide and Political Mass Murder since 1955," *American Political Science Review*, 97: 1 (February 2003), p. 62.

5 Ervin Staub, "The Psychology of Bystanders, Perpetrators, and Heroic Helpers," in Leonard S. Newman and Ralph Erber, eds, *Understanding Genocide: The Social Psychology of the Holocaust* (Oxford: Oxford University Press, 2002), p. 30.

6 Ervin Staub, *The Roots of Evil: The Origins of Genocide and Other Group Violence* (Cambridge: Cambridge University Press, 1989), p. 274.

7 Interview with Kal Holsti, Vancouver, BC, January 2001.

8 Ted Robert Gurr and Barbara Harff, *Ethnic Conflict in World Politics* (Boulder, CO: Westview Press, 1994), p. 80.

9 For a constructive discussion of "the creation and evolution of caring, connection, and nonaggression," emphasizing education and socialization, see ch. 14 in Staub, *The Roots of Evil*, pp. 274–84.

10 For an overview of the empirical evidence, see David Kopel, review of Jay Simkin *et al.*, *Lethal Laws* (Milwaukee: Jews for the Preservation of Firearm Ownership, 1994), in *New York Law School Journal of International and Comparative Law*, 15 (1995), pp. 355–98, available at http://www.lethallaws.com/kopel.htm.

11 R. Charli Carpenter has deepened and problematized this framing of "vulnerability" in important respects, emphasizing physical capacity as well as liability to violent victimization. See Carpenter, "Women and Children First: Gender Norms and Humanitarian Evacuation in the Balkans, 1991–1995," *International Organization*, 57: 4 (Fall 2003), pp. 661–94.

12 See Adam Jones, "Genocide and Humanitarian Intervention: Incorporating the Gender Variable," *Journal of Humanitarian Assistance*, February 2002, http://www.jha.ac/articles/a080.htm.

13 See Robert D. Kaplan, *The Coming Anarchy: Shattering the Dreams of the Post Cold War* (New York: Random House, 2000).

14 International Commission on Intervention and State Sovereignty (hereafter, ICISS), *The Responsibility to Protect* (Ottawa, ON: International Development Research Centre, 2001), p. 19.

15 The European Union and the Organization of American States, two of the most vigorous intergovernmental organizations, adopted charters or constitutional provisions requiring that their members adhere to democratic standards and procedures. Both also have judicial mechanisms with enforcement powers, though these are much more entrenched in the EU than in the OAS. The EU, of course, is also a huge *economic* bloc, membership in which brings tangible material benefits. It is intriguing to observe how the lure of entry to the bloc has acted to dampen or divert conflict in two countries riven in the recent past by intercommunal conflict (the Croatian case was cited in Chapter 8). From the 1970s to the 1990s, the policy adopted by Turkey towards its large Kurdish minority in the southeast of the country was very close to genocidal: tens of thousands killed, hundreds of thousands uprooted, intensive suppression of Kurdish language and media, and so on. Now, with negotiations for EU membership a real possibility, Turkey has adopted more progressive – or at least less vicious – policies towards the Kurds. There seems no reason, apart from lack of political will, why Russian membership in the EU, or Chinese membership in the World Trade Organization, could not be made contingent on similar policies towards Chechnya or Tibet.

16 Richard Falk, "The Challenge of Genocide and Genocidal Politics in an Era of Globalisation," in Tim Dunne and Nicholas J. Wheeler, eds, *Human Rights in Global Politics* (Cambridge: Cambridge University Press, 1999), p. 191.
17 ICISS, *The Responsibility to Protect*, pp. 30–31.
18 "After the Armistice [of November 1918], the blockade was extended to the Baltic ports and continued until the Allies were satisfied with German compliance with their demands. The journalist Walter Duranty visited Lübeck in 1919 and found people living on potatoes and black bread. They had no meat, butter, milk or eggs. A doctor told him that 90 per cent of the children were anaemic or below weight, and that more than half of them had rickets or tuberculosis. . . . The senior German delegate at Versailles, Graf Ulrich von Brockdorff-Rantzau, expressed some of the [German] resentment: 'The hundreds of thousands of noncombatants who have perished since November 11 because of the blockade were destroyed coolly and deliberately, after our opponents had won a certain and assured victory. Think of that, when you speak of guilt and atonement.'" Jonathan Glover, *Humanity: A Moral History of the Twentieth Century* (New Haven, CT: Yale University Press, 1999), pp. 65–66.
19 ICISS, *The Responsibility to Protect*, p. 29.
20 Annan quoted in ICISS, *The Responsibility to Protect*, p. 40.
21 ICISS, *The Responsibility to Protect*, p. 48.
22 Heidenrich, *How to Prevent Genocide*, p. 61.
23 Kenneth Roth, "Setting the Standard: Justifying Humanitarian Intervention," *Harvard International Review* (spring 2004), p. 59; emphasis added. For a similar (and earlier) framing, see Nicholas Wheeler, *Saving Strangers: Humanitarian Intervention in International Society* (Oxford: Oxford University Press, 2000), pp. 33–34. Wheeler's book is the best argument for a "solidarist" approach to intervention in what he calls "supreme humanitarian emergencies," defined as "extraordinary situations where civilians in another state are in imminent danger of losing their life or facing appalling hardship, and where indigenous forces cannot be relied upon to end these violations of human rights" (p. 50).
24 Mary Kaldor in "Humanitarian Intervention: A Forum," *The Nation*, July 14, 2003, p. 13. "The commission went on to argue that a gap between legality and legitimacy is very dangerous and needs to be removed by specifying conditions for humanitarian intervention." This was the challenge taken up, not entirely successfully in my view, by the ICISS.
25 Stephen Holmes, "Looking Away," *London Review of Books*, November 14, 2002.
26 See Michael Parenti, *To Kill a Nation: The Attack on Yugoslavia* (London: Verso, 2000); Noam Chomsky, *The New Military Humanism: Lessons from Kosovo* (Monroe, ME: Common Courage Press, 1999); Philip Hammond and Edward S. Herman, eds, *Degraded Capability: The Media and the Kosovo Crisis* (London: Pluto Press, 2000); and Diana Johnstone, *Fools' Crusade: Yugoslavia, NATO, and Western Delusions* (New York: Monthly Review Press, 2003).
27 India relished the opportunity to deal a blow to its erstwhile rival Pakistan by severing its eastern wing. It was also confronted by an unmanageable flood of refugees from the genocide, as was Tanzania in the Ugandan case. (The regime that replaced Amin in Uganda, that of Milton Obote, was also no less murderous than its predecessor.) Vietnam had deep political rivalries with the Khmer Rouge, close ties to the Vietnamese minority in Cambodia, and desires to establish itself as the regional hegemon. Member countries of NATO were profoundly concerned by the security implications of hundreds of thousands of Kosovar refugees destabilizing neighboring countries in a corner of Europe that had already spawned one world war. Only in the East Timor case, I have argued (Box 7a), was moral suasion – brought to bear by morally imbued protests domestically and abroad – truly decisive in persuading Australia to lead the intervention, when considerations of *realpolitik* dictated otherwise. However, to the extent that it became politically untenable for the Australian government to act otherwise, we may also argue that practical considerations outweighed humanitarian ones.

28 Alan J. Kuperman, "Humanitarian Hazard: Revisiting Doctrines of Intervention," *Harvard International Review* (spring 2004), p. 67.
29 Michael Hirsh, "Calling All Regio-Cops: Peacekeeping's Hybrid Future," *Foreign Affairs* (November–December 2000), p. 5.
30 Israel W. Charny, "An International Peace Army: A Proposal for the Long-range Future," in Charny, ed., *The Encyclopedia of Genocide* (Santa Barbara, CA: ABC-CLIO, 1999), p. 650.
31 Charny, "An International Peace Army," pp. 650–52.
32 Charny, "An International Peace Army," p. 650.
33 Dallaire quoted in Heidenrich, *How to Prevent Genocide*, pp. 200–1. Heidenrich's ch. 12, "The Evolution of an Idea," explores the various proposals for a UN standing force.
34 An *Economist* reviewer notes, for example, "the stunning success of the EU in democratising and liberalising its near neighbours, by the simple expedient of holding out the carrot of membership." "An Optimist's View," *The Economist*, February 26, 2005.
35 See Tim Pippard and Veronica Lie, "Enhancing the Rapid Reaction Capability of the United Nations: Exploring the Options," United Nations Association-UK, July 2004, http://www.una-uk.org/UNandC/rapidreaction.html.
36 See, e.g., the analysis of a British government Green Paper on the subject in "Peace-keeping 'Role' for Mercenaries," *BBC Online*, February 13, 2002, http://news.bbc.co.uk/1/hi/uk_politics/1817495.stm.
37 Nadezhda Mandelstam, *Hope Against Hope* (New York: Modern Library, 1999), p. 383.
38 Ian Hunter, "A Tale of Truth and Two Journalists," in William L. Hewitt, ed., *Defining the Horrific: Readings on Genocide and Holocaust in the Twentieth Century* (Upper Saddle River, NJ: Pearson Education, 2004), p. 134.
39 Muggeridge quoted in Hunter, "A Tale of Truth," p. 135; emphasis added.
40 Muggeridge quoted in Robert Conquest, *The Harvest of Sorrow: Collectivization and the Terror-Famine* (New York: Oxford University Press, 1986), p. 260.
41 Samantha Power, *"A Problem from Hell": America and the Age of Genocide* (New York: Basic Books, 2002), p. 32.
42 Staub, *The Roots of Evil*, p. 282.
43 Quoted in Margaret E. Keck and Kathryn Sikkink, *Activists Beyond Borders: Advocacy Networks in International Politics* (Ithaca, NY: Cornell University Press, 1998), p. 19; emphasis added. For an overview of the history and activities of Amnesty International, see Jonathan Power, *Like Water on Stone: The Story of Amnesty International* (London: Penguin, 2002).
44 Anne Applebaum, *Gulag: A History* (London: Penguin, 2003), p. 497. The contribution of artists, writers, and other shapers of cultural form also provides a potent form of witnessing, albeit usually at some remove from events. It would be hard to overstate the importance of films such as *Schindler's List* and *The Killing Fields* in conscientizing mass publics to the Jewish and Cambodian genocides, respectively. "Norm entrepreneurs" (ch. 12) frequently use books – both non-fiction and fiction – to confront genocide and other crimes against humanity. Sometimes these can become true "culture carriers." Harriet Beecher Stowe's *Uncle Tom's Cabin* alerted millions of nineteenth-century readers to slavery's depredations; in contemporary times, Jonathan Schell's *The Fate of the Earth* strongly inspired the anti-nuclear movement. Finally, though they are always vulnerable to charges of grandstanding, celebrities have brought important visibility to genocide's victims or potential victims – as with Richard Gere and Tibet, or Sting with the rainforest Indians of Brazil.
45 Irene Gut Opdyke with Jennifer Armstrong, *In My Hands: Memories of a Holocaust Rescuer* (New York: Anchor Books, 2001).
46 The controversy over the Catholic Church's actions during the Jewish Holocaust may be revisited in this context (see Chapter 6).
47 Quoted in Peter Balakian, *The Burning Tigris: The Armenian Genocide and America's Response* (New York: HarperCollins, 2003), p. 121.

48 Charles Tilly, *The Politics of Collective Violence* (Cambridge: Cambridge University Press, 2003), p. 8; see also Barrington Moore, *Moral Persecution in History* (Princeton, NJ: Princeton University Press, 2000).

49 The term "cosmopolitan" was first deployed in the modern era by Immanuel Kant in a classic essay, *Perpetual Peace* (1795). Mary Kaldor "use[s] the term . . . to refer both to a positive political vision, embracing tolerance, multiculturalism, civility and democracy, and to a more legalistic respect for certain overriding universal principles which should guide political communities at various levels, including the global level." Kaldor, *New and Old Wars: Organized Violence in a Global Era* (Stanford, CA: Stanford University Press, 2001), p. 116. See also the discussion of "the re-emergence of cosmopolitanism" in David Hirsh, *Law against Genocide: Cosmopolitan Trials* (London: Glasshouse Press, 2003), pp. 13–17; and S. Vertovec and R. Cohen, eds, *Conceiving Cosmopolitanism* (Oxford: Oxford University Press, 2002).

50 Ethan Nadelmann claims that "no other international prohibition regime so powerfully confirms the potential of humanitarian and similar moral concerns to shape global norms as does the regime against slavery and the slave trade." Nadelmann, "Global Prohibition Regimes: The Evolution of Norms in International Society," *International Organization*, 44: 4 (fall 1990), available at http://www.criminology.fsu.edu/transcrime/articles/GlobalProhibitionRegimes.htm.

51 For a grisly description of the kinds of public execution common in "civilized" Europe as recently as the eighteenth century, see the opening pages of Michel Foucault's *Discipline and Punish: The Birth of the Prison* (New York: Vintage, 1979) – but not before lunch.

52 John Boli and George M. Thomas, "INGOs and the Organization of World Culture," in Boli and Thomas, eds, *Constructing World Culture: International Nongovernmental Organizations since 1875* (Stanford, CA: Stanford University Press, 1999), pp. 39–40.

53 Testimony quoted in Conquest, *The Harvest of Sorrow*, p. 233. Nadezhda Mandelstam wrote of "this craving for an all-embracing idea which would explain everything in the world and bring about universal harmony at one go." Under Stalinism, "Life was deviating from the blueprints, but the blueprints had been declared sacrosanct and it was forbidden to compare them with what was actually coming into being." Mandelstam, *Hope Against Hope*, pp. 115, 163.

54 Ruby Plenty Chiefs quoted in Martha Minow, *Between Vengeance and Forgiveness: Facing History after Genocide and Mass Violence* (Boston, MA: Beacon Press, 1998), p. 8.

55 Donald E. Miller and Lorna Touryan Miller, *Survivors: An Oral History of the Armenian Genocide* (Berkeley, CA: University of California Press, 1999), p. 5.

56 Guevara letter reproduced in the Museo Ernesto Che Guevara, Alta Gracia, Argentina; my translation.

57 Feldman quoted in Liisa H. Malkki, "Speechless Emissaries: Refugees, Humanitarianism, and Dehistoricization," in Alexander Laban Hinton, ed., *Genocide: An Anthropological Reader* (Malden, MA: Blackwell, 2002), p. 353.

58 Stalin quoted in David Remnick, *Resurrection: The Struggle for a New Russia* (New York: Vintage, 1998), p. 288.

59 The lives and writings of twentieth-century figures such as Mahatma Gandhi, Martin Luther King, the Dalai Lama, and Aung San Suu Kyi provide important insights and inspiration, as does Jonathan Schell's recent study, *The Unconquerable World: Power, Nonviolence, and the Will of the People* (New York: Metropolitan Books, 2003). See also Peter Ackerman and Jack DuVall, *A Force More Powerful: A Century of Nonviolent Conflict* (New York: Palgrave, 2000).

60 As Noam Chomsky put it: "There is no measure of how optimistic you ought to be. In fact, as far as optimism is concerned, you basically have two [options]. You can say, 'Nothing is going to work, and so I am not going to do anything.' You can therefore guarantee that the worst possible outcomes will come about. Or, you can take the other position. You can say: 'Look, maybe something will work. Therefore, I will engage myself in trying to make it work and maybe there is a chance that things can get better.' That is

your choice. Nobody can tell how right it is to be optimistic. Nothing can be predicted in human affairs . . . nothing." "An Interactive Session with Noam Chomsky," Asian College of Journalism, Chennai, India, http://www.greenmac.com/World_Events/aninterac.html.

INDEX